T0360453

DRIVERS OF COMPETITIVENESS

DRIVERS OF COMPETITIVENESS

Diego Comin
Dartmouth College, USA

 **World Scientific**

NEW JERSEY · LONDON · SINGAPORE · BEIJING · SHANGHAI · HONG KONG · TAIPEI · CHENNAI · TOKYO

Published by

World Scientific Publishing Co. Pte. Ltd.

5 Toh Tuck Link, Singapore 596224

USA office: 27 Warren Street, Suite 401-402, Hackensack, NJ 07601

UK office: 57 Shelton Street, Covent Garden, London WC2H 9HE

Library of Congress Cataloging-in-Publication Data
Names: Comin, Diego.
Title: Drivers of competitiveness / Diego Comin.
Description: New Jersey : World Scientific, 2015.
Identifiers: LCCN 2015030238| ISBN 9789814704724 (hc : alk. paper) |
    ISBN 9789814704731 (pbk : alk. paper)
Subjects: LCSH: Technological innovations--Economic aspects. | Diffusion of innovations |
    Organizational change. | Competition.
Classification: LCC HC79.T4 .C656 2015 | DDC 338.6/048--dc23
LC record available at http://lccn.loc.gov/2015030238

British Library Cataloguing-in-Publication Data
A catalogue record for this book is available from the British Library.

In-house Editors: Dr. Sree Meenakshi Sajani/Li Hongyan

Typeset by Stallion Press
Email: enquiries@stallionpress.com

Printed in Singapore

To Marco and Enzo

Contents

Acknowledgments

This book is the result of seven years of field research. During this time, I have traveled around the world, met hundreds of managers, entrepreneurs, government officials and taxi drivers (yep, I do learn a lot from taxi drivers too); I have also conducted academic research that has provided rigorous foundations for the analysis of competitiveness; I have engaged in long conversations with colleagues and friends that have challenged, complemented and shaped my own views; and I have tested the cases with hundreds of MBA students and executive whom I have taught at the Harvard Business School (HBS).

Clearly, both the learning process and the production of the cases contained in this book have been possible only because I have benefited from the input and help of many people who I am profoundly grateful. First, I have learnt a lot from all my former colleagues at the Harvard Business School. Starting with Julio Rotemberg, who recruited me in 2007, and ending with my friend and mentor Dick Vietor. I am especially indebted to my co-authors (both colleagues and students) for offering me the possibility to work hand-in-hand to bring the world to the classroom through our cases studies. Finally, I am grateful to Dick Vietor, Laura Alfaro, Gunnar Trumbull and Rafael di Tella for allowing me to include four of their cases in the book.

My assistant Chris Grosse has helped me get the permissions to include the quotations in all of my cases, and has expedited the process to obtain the permissions from HBS Publishing to reproduce the cases. I also thank HBS Publishing for its collaboration.

Much of what I know about competitiveness I learnt in the field, both through the trips to write cases and through immersion experiences (IXP) which I designed and lead. Both of these activities were possible by the support of HBS, and in particular, Nitin Nohria who openly recognized the value that my IXPs for the school. In addition to the institutional support from HBS, the success of the IXPs required the collaboration of local partners and the hard work of HBS students that took part in them. I am grateful also to the numerous partners we have studied and worked with in Malaysia and Peru. I am equally grateful to the students that found ways to improve the competitiveness of the partners whether they were companies, sectors or countries. Some of the cases in this book germinated from their innovative visions.

I would like also to take advantage of this opportunity to acknowledge those that have supported financially the research that provides a foundation for this book. This includes the National Science Foundation, the Institute of New Economic Thinking, HBS, and Dartmouth College.

At a more personal level, this book would not have been possible without the help, understanding and love of my family. My wife has not only understood but also nourished my passion for learning. My children, Marco and Enzo have added a new dimension to my live, one that makes it full. I dedicate this book to them.

Introduction

Productivity and competitiveness have become hot topics among managers and policy-makers.[a] The truth is that they have always been, but the global financial crisis has brought their popularity to new heights. As the global downturn impacted one economy after another, companies and countries have writhed to keep their necks above water. When demand is low, there are only two ways out. To become more efficient by increasing productivity, or to become more competitive by attracting somebody else's demand.

Competitiveness used to be the turf of strategy courses where one would learn about the Five Forces and different ways to achieve product differentiation. Not anymore. As the crisis has painfully shown, macroeconomic variables and other aggregate factors are key to design and evaluate companies' strategies. Furthermore, there are important similarities in how countries and companies cope with aggregate factors. Take for example the rise of China after joining WTO in 2001. It opened new opportunities for the most attractive exports from a country such as Malaysia that now could be sold in China, but also supposed challenges for the least attractive Malaysian exports that now had to compete with Chinese companies. Isn't that the same as what China's accession to the WTO has supposed for GE? Can GE learn something from Malaysia's response, and Malaysia from GE's?

I think so. In contrast to the strategy view of competitiveness, the macroeconomic approach stresses factors that affect symmetrically the companies in a country. As a result, analyzing how X affects a company or the aggregate of all companies (i.e. the country) is kind of similar.[b]

---

[a] See for example, Obama Urges U.S. Competitiveness Ahead of Speech *New York Times*, January, 22, 2011; China Isn't Losing Its Manufacturing Competitiveness After All *Wall Street Journal*, September 7, 2011.

[b] One corollary of this argument is that macroeconomic factors affect many (potentially all) companies in the country. Therefore their implications for welfare are orders of magnitude larger than those of factors that just impact one company (or that have opposite effects in multiple companies).

Of course, the fact that X can potentially affect us all, does not mean that *ex-post* it has the same impact. Some companies see the tsunami coming and get ready for it while others are caught by surprise. The cover picture of the book exemplifies this message. The 2013 America's Cup was disputed by two teams, the Oracle and Team New Zealand. The Oracle had a technologically superior boat. Indeed, it was so superior that all the experts anticipated an easy win. However, Team New Zealand came out with a superior strategy to deal with a contextual challenge that both teams needed to confront — to navigate upwind in the third leg of each race. The Kiwis' strategy was to navigate upwind by zigzagging on a 52 degree angle instead of using the conventional angle of 45 degrees. The Oracle team used a narrower angle of 42 degrees. Team New Zealand had to cover a longer distance but the wider angles allow it to foil. That is, to navigate at fast speeds by having the hull above water. The superior strategy to handle a contextual factor permitted Team New Zealand to reach, what it seemed, and unsurmountable advantage over Oracle. The take away from this example is that knowledge about the context and about how to best respond to it is the best source of competitive advantage. That is the *raison d'être* for this book.

Through a series of case studies, this book develops an original framework to understand the drivers of productivity and competitiveness for companies and countries.[c] The cases have been used at the Harvard Business School (HBS) to teach the first year required course, Business, Government and the International Economy (BGIE) and the second year elective Drivers of Competitiveness (DOC). I have also used some of the cases in executive programs (at HBS and elsewhere) and to teach advanced undergraduate courses at Dartmouth College.

Several features make the cases included in the book uniquely suited to study the drivers of productivity and competitiveness. First, some of the cases are focused on individual companies and organizations, some on sectors and other on countries. By studying all these different aggregation levels, it becomes quite clear that the issues and framework of analysis are scalable. Second, the cases cover the full spectrum of countries, from very poor to very rich. This permits the reader to understand what factors are more relevant for competitiveness at each level of development. Third, an overwhelming majority of the cases are brand new. Therefore, the issues covered are set in the backdrop of the global financial crisis. The reader can obtain a unique perspective on the crisis, and how it impacted differently companies and governments in different countries.

A conceptual framework emerges from the analysis of the cases. The framework has several interlinked levels. The first level defines productivity and competitiveness. There is wide consensus on the measurement of productivity.

---

[c]Other existing frameworks to think about some of these issues include Porter's competitive advantage of nations framework (Porter, 1990) and the Growth Diagnostics framework (Hausman, Klinger and Wagner, 2008).

For example, one measure is total factor productivity, which is defined as a residual in output after taking into account the usage of factors of production such as capital and labor.[d] However, there is much less agreement about the right measures of competitiveness. For example, according to the World Economic Forum, "Competitiveness is defined as the set of institutions, policies and factors that determine the level of productivity of a country."[e]

This definition highlights the importance of productivity for a country's competitiveness but ignores the role of wages or exchange rates. A broader approach followed in this book consists of using unit labor costs as a measure of a country's competitiveness. Unit labor costs are defined as the ratio of nominal wages per hour (in U.S. dollars) to real value added per hour and are interpreted as the cost of producing one unit of output. Countries with high unit labor costs are less competitive than countries with lower unit labor costs. Similarly, as countries experience increasing unit labor costs, their competitiveness declines.

Note that the differences between productivity and competitiveness (as measured by unit labor costs) are stark. The U.S. is clearly more productive than China, but surely it is less competitive. Also, unlike productivity, competitiveness is a relative concept: a country's ability to capture international markets or to attract foreign direct investment depends on its unit labor costs *vis-à-vis* the relevant competitors.[f]

In a second level, the framework defines the mechanisms that drive productivity growth. These are processes such as investment, or technological improvement that make companies more productive. These mechanisms are not fundamental forces. They are just the channels by which the fundamental forces affect productivity (see **Exhibit 1**).

In a third level, we find the fundamental drivers of productivity. These are factors such as policies, institutions or the know-how accumulated in the company's or country's history. These factors affect mechanisms such as capital accumulation and technology upgrade through adoption or innovation and, hence, drive the productivity of the companies in a country. In addition to affecting competitiveness (i.e. unit labor costs) by their effect on productivity, the fundamental drivers may also influence wages. For example, labor market institutions such as unions or the wage bargaining process play a key role in the dynamics of wages.

---

[d]For more on TFP, see Comin (2008).

[e]Schwab (2011), The Global Competitiveness Report 2011–2012 *World Economic Forum.*

[f]This book's emphasis on both productivity (and its drivers) and on factors that affect a country's performance in international markets is very consistent with Porter and Rivkin (2012) who argue that a location is competitive if the companies that operate there "are able to compete in the global economy while supporting high and rising living standards for the average [citizen]." In the terminology used in this book and in the economics profession, the first condition refers to a country's competitiveness while the second refers to its productivity.

Exhibit 1.   Schematic Description of Framework

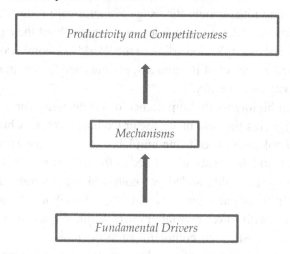

The framework that emerges from this book presents three main contributions over the literature. First, it articulates new insights based both on the cases and academic research on how various fundamental factors affect the adoption and diffusion of new technologies and their effects on the productivity of companies and countries at different levels of development. Second, the framework emphasizes the effects on future productivity of current competitiveness and technology adoption/development efforts. These dynamic considerations provide a rationale for the wide-spread government' concerns on competitiveness. Third, by recognizing the static and dynamics consequences of technology on productivity and competitiveness, the framework develops new managerial implications and provides guidance for more effective government policies.

Since this is a casebook, the introduction is the only vehicle for the author to directly communicate with the reader. Therefore, I have beefed it up a bit with respect to regular textbooks. The rest of this introduction is divided as follows. I have presented the book outline followed by the description of the conceptual framework that integrates the cases and concluded the introduction by anticipating some high level managerial implications that shall become much more concrete for the reader as he analyzes the cases.

Book Outline

The cases that compose the book are organized around three broad themes: (i) globalization/openness, (ii) institutions and markets and (iii) innovation and technology. The rationale for these themes will become clear shortly when I discuss the analytical framework that emerges from the book. But, previewing the argument below, these themes capture what in my view are the key fundamental drivers of productivity and competitiveness.

The theme "Globalization/openness" captures the factors that govern how a company interacts with other companies in/from other countries. This includes the accessibility to foreign markets to sell products, to import inputs, and to organize more efficiently the supply chain. It also includes the arrival of competitors from foreign markets or the change in the terms of trade that may induce domestic factors to be reallocated in the economy. The cases covered in the first part also explore how capital markets' integration affects the competitive landscape of companies and what risks it may entail. The module also studies the impact of foreign direct investment in the development of economies and how local companies may take advantage of the inflow of foreign capital and know-how. Finally, the first part also analyzes how governments have reacted to the challenges and opportunities brought by globalization. For example, some cases present situations where governments decide to raise barriers to international capital flows (Malaysia and China), others where countries decide to give up such barriers (e.g. EU members) and others where in addition they give up their monetary policy by joining a currency union (e.g. EU members in the euro).

The sequence of cases in the first part consists on: (i) Singapore, (ii) Malaysia (A), (iii) Malaysia (B), (iv) China and (v) four central European countries (Hungary, Czech Republic, Slovakia and Poland). In these cases, the international themes are the central topics of discussion. In the other two parts of the book, there are several cases where international themes are also very significant. These include the cases of Spain, ABB and the U.S. current account.

The second module of the book is centered around the theme of institutions and markets. According to the Merriam-Webster dictionary, an institution is "a custom, practice, or law that is accepted and used by many people". These explicit and implicit rules may impact directly the actions and strategies followed by companies. But institutions also impact companies indirectly by shaping the markets where they operate. For example, inadequate institutions may reduce the ability of markets to assign efficiently factors of production reducing the ability of their companies to compete globally.

Of course, there are many institutions and the intention of the module is not to cover them all but to highlight some of the most significant effects they have on companies. For example, the cases of South Africa and Egypt highlight the importance of political institutions for competitiveness and study how political transitions take place. The cases on Spain and South Africa investigate different aspects of labor markets and their consequences on productivity and competition. The Spain case studies the role of wage bargaining institutions and of dual labor markets which emerge from simultaneous presence of contracts with high and low firing costs.

In South Africa the emphasis is on the role of unions. The cases on family groups in Peru and the South Africa study the consequences of barriers to entry. Finally, the Spain case also studies the consequences of a wide range of banking regulations.

The institutions module is covered by five cases: (i) South Africa (A), (ii) South Africa (B), (iii) Egypt, (iv) Peru family groups and (v) Spain. This selection ensures the coverage on institutions in both developing and developed economies. In addition to the cases in this module, there are other cases in the book where institutional aspects are important. For example, in Inkaterra, China, ABB and Palm oil in Malaysia.

The third theme of the book deals with how countries and companies develop and adopt new technologies (broadly understood) which raise both their productivity and competitiveness. As I argue in the presentation of the analytical framework, technology is not a fundamental factor. It is the result of the decisions of companies and innovators that develop and adopt them. These decisions are impacted by a wide range of factors. Some of them are covered in the previous parts of the book (international openness and institutions). Others drivers of technology are factor endowments (e.g. human and physical capital) and the know-how developed by companies by acquiring familiarity with previous technologies.

The nine cases in the module cover a wide range of perspectives on the broad issue of technology and innovation. The Inkaterra case deals with innovation in services (eco-tourism). The ABB case is about a company's decision to innovate in China and the answers to two central concerns it faces: what products to develop there and how to deal with the risk of imitation. Several cases in the module deal with the relevance of technological know-how in an activity to innovate. The case on indigenous innovations is a counter-example. It investigates how some Chinese companies have become world class in a sector where they had no tradition, renewable energies. The case on the College of Engineering and Technology (CoET) discusses the complexities of commercializing innovations. The case on palm oil, studies the steps necessary to create a new market, and how technology development and marketing are complementary. The two Fraunhofer cases provide a unique opportunity to explore the German innovation system both from a positive and from a normative perspective. The last two cases of the module stand out from the rest. The Great Moderation is really about the drivers of macroeconomic stability in the U.S. Some of the contending hypotheses rely heavily on technological factors as sources of the moderation. The book ends with the case on the U.S. current account deficit. This case is a great contrast with both the Fraunhofer and the China unbalanced cases.

As it is clear from this list, the cases in the third module cover all possible economic contexts from very poor to very rich. This variation invites to diving into what innovation means at different stages of development and in particular to differentiate between innovation and technology adoption or adaptation.

Another strength of the sequence of cases in the module is that they emphasize the many externalities and market frictions that are present when it comes to innovation. Traditionally, these externalities have been an invitation to government intervention. However, I think it is worthwhile making two important remarks. First, the type of government interventions explored in the literature on optimal R&D has been almost universally limited to R&D subsidies (and equivalent policies). The module clearly advocates for broader interventions where the government not only "pays the bill" but also is directly involved in conducting R&D. Second, good managers could attain competitive advantage by finding ways to internalize the externalities that plague innovation and to overcome some of the market frictions. This angle is under-explored in the academic literature and I would invite participants in the discussions of the cases to think seriously about this idea.

An Integrative Framework

The conceptual insights of the cases and academic research that constitute the foundations for this book can be organized around an original integrative framework on the sources of productivity and competitiveness. A schematic description of the framework is presented in **Exhibit 2**. A natural way to measure.

The rest of the section elaborates the framework and maps each of its components to specific cases from the module.

Exhibit 2.   The Framework

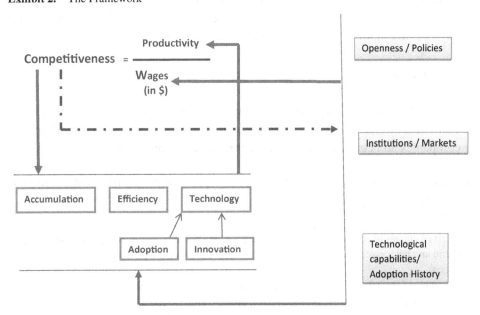

Definitions

A company is more competitive than another when it can produce a given product or service at a lower cost or a superior product at a comparable cost. This definition of competitiveness is based on the concept of unit costs of production. That is the cost faced by a company to produce one unit of a given product or service. One simple approach to measuring unit costs is the so-called unit labor costs.[g] Formally, unit labor costs are computed as the wage rate per hour divided by the real value added per hour. To make unit labor costs comparable across countries, wages are expressed in US dollars. Differences in quality across products and services enter in this definition through the value added per hour component. Products of higher quality have associated a higher value added because buyers are willing to pay more for them or because they want to buy more units.[h] Note that unit labor costs can be defined for companies as well as for countries. Therefore, unit labor costs allow us to evaluate the competitiveness at both the micro and the macro level.

There are two important observations about competitiveness worth highlighting. First, while a country's productivity is an absolute variable, its competitiveness (or lack thereof) is defined relative to other countries. Because of this relative nature of competitiveness, the ascent (or fall) of other countries (e.g. China versus Malaysia) has an impact on a country's competitiveness. Second, when evaluating the competitiveness of two companies, we need to make sure that we are not comparing apples and oranges. The unit labor costs of a country are informative relative to the countries that operate in a similar region of the product space. That is why, one way countries try to regain competitiveness is by attempting to produce more sophisticated products (i.e. moving up in the value chain). This is, for example, what Malaysia is attempting with the New Economic Model.

Mechanisms

Productivity is a central dimension of competitiveness as well as a variable of independent interest because it determines the well-being of nations. The productivity of companies and countries can increase through three mechanisms:

(1) The accumulation of factors of production. That is, through investment in human and physical capital.[i]

---

[g]For certain classes of production functions which are very commonly used in macroeconomics, unit costs and unit labor costs are equivalent. This is for example the case with Cobb–Douglas production functions.

[h]An example of the latter would be tickets for a good movie.

[i]Solow (1956).

(2) The reallocation of factors to more efficient uses. This occurs when companies find better ways to use their capital and labor, or when market frictions are smoothed out resulting in a more efficient allocation of capital and labor across companies.[j] For example, affirmative action programs like those described in the Malaysia and South Africa cases have been identified as frictions that prevent an efficient allocation of resources in the economy. Relaxations of these programs (such as the NEM) should allow more skilled workers to access jobs where their skills are most productive. This should lead to productivity improvements for the overall economy.

(3) Improvements in the technology used in production. A technology is just a way to produce something. This definition comprises both embodied technologies (e.g. machines, software) and disembodied technologies (e.g. managerial techniques and process innovations). Improvements in technology may come either from the development of new technologies (i.e. innovation) or from the adoption of technologies that already exist.

The relative importance of these productivity growth mechanisms depends both on the horizon we consider and on the level of development of the country. In the short term, productivity growth is more likely to come from capital accumulation or increased efficiency. Technology improvements, both through adoption and innovation, take time before they are materialized and have significant effects on output. Therefore technology adoption is not a significant driver of short-term improvements in productivity.[k] In the long term, however, factor accumulation and reallocation play a limited role in productivity growth. Diminishing returns to investment in human and physical capital imply that growth in the long term cannot be purely based on factor accumulation. Similarly, there is a limit to the productivity gains associated with improving the allocation of resources in the economy. Once the efficient allocation is achieved, there is no room for additional productivity gains from reallocating existing resources. These observations are most evident in the Singapore and China cases.

The relevance of the different mechanisms evolves as countries develop (see **Exhibit 3**). Market frictions are more significant in developing than in developed economies (e.g. South Africa, China especially during the 1980s and 1990s). Therefore there is more room for productivity growth through improved resource reallocation in developing countries. Human and physical capital shortages are also more prevalent in developing countries. Hence, fostering factor accumulation is likely to be more conducive to growth in developing countries than in developed

---

[j] Hsieh and Klenow (2009).
[k] See Reinhardt (1994).

Exhibit 3. Normative Predictions on Sources of Productivity Growth by Income Level

	Accumulation	Efficiency	Technology Adoption	Innovation
Developed Economies			X	X
Developing Economies	X	X	X	

economies.[1] Firms in developing countries upgrade their technologies almost exclusively by adopting technologies invented elsewhere. That is the case both because other companies have previously confronted the technological problems that companies in developing economies confront and because they typically do not have the capabilities to develop brand new technologies. For most companies in developed economies adoption is also the main channel of technology improvement. However, some companies in a few rich countries such as the U.S., Germany or Japan are more likely to confront new technological problems that require innovating (see the Fraunhofer case).

Fundamental Forces

The mechanisms that lead to productivity improvements are not primitives of the economy. They are just channels through which factors that may be more fundamental affect productivity and competitiveness. What are those fundamental forces? For concreteness, I focus on three types of fundamental characteristics (see **Exhibit 2**):

(1) **Openness and policies**. It has been discussed above how several dimensions of openness affect the mechanisms that drive productivity. Other policies that may trigger the mechanisms in the framework are policies that affect human capital accumulation (such as schooling subsidies or subsidies to on the job training programs) and policies that foster innovation (e.g. R&D subsidies) and technology adoption (e.g. subsidies to technology licenses).

(2) **Markets and institutions**. The previous section elaborated on how labor market institutions affect productivity. Financial regulations and financial institutions also affect productivity. Well-working financial markets tend to allocate capital to where the private return is highest. However, private and social returns may not coincide because of the presence of externalities. In those occasions, well-working financial markets may have a negative effect on productivity because

---

[1]Another argument for the higher relevance of accumulation in developing than in developed economies is that improved allocation of resources tends to increase the marginal product of capital. As a result, when countries and companies find ways to reallocate their factors of production they tend to create new opportunities to increase their capital.

they reallocate capital to projects with lower social return despite their high private return. In the case of Spain, for example, the highest private return was in the construction sector which surely is not the activity that conduces to highest productivity in the long term. Conversely, the Fraunhofer case illustrates a type of activities (i.e. applied R&D) where public involvement helps improve the allocation of capital.

Another role played by financial markets is to pool risks and, in this way, providing insurance to entrepreneurs. Recent evidence shows that this role of financial markets is important for the adoption of new technologies in their early stage of diffusion but not in countries that start adopting technologies with long lags.[m]

(3) **Historical endowment**. Factor endowments affect capital accumulation and technology upgrading. Because of diminishing returns, abundance of capital (physical or human) reduces the scope for productivity growth from accumulation. Technology upgrading, both through innovation and technology adoption, is very human capital-intensive.[n] Therefore, an abundance of human capital facilitates productivity improvements from the upgrade of technology. Often technological knowledge is not just embodied in the people but in organizations and in groups of firms located in a given geographic area which collectively can accumulate the expertise needed to develop and adopt new technologies. Research about the nature of this collective technological knowledge has shown that it is hard to accumulate, it is sticky geographically, and it is very persistent in history.[o]

In addition to affecting the mechanisms that drive productivity, the fundamental aspects of the economy have an independent effect on the other component of unit labor costs, wages. This is most clear for labor market institutions. Strong unions may obtain wage increases larger than the actual increases in productivity leading to higher unit labor costs. This is what was observed in the cases of Spain and South Africa. In the Germany case, on the other hand, unions accepted lower wage increases than productivity growth increasing the competitiveness of German manufacturing companies.

Factor endowments and migration policy also crucially affect wage dynamics. In the China and Malaysia cases it was observed how wages increase less than productivity growth because the presence of a large surplus of labor. In China, the surplus of labor comes from the rural areas and in Malaysia it comes from other countries in South East Asia. The NEM implemented in Malaysia intends to curve

---

[m] See Comin and Nanda (2014).
[n] See Comin and Hobijn (2004).
[o] Comin, Easterly and Gong (2010) and Comin, Dmitriev and Rossi-Hansberg (2012).

migration. The rationale for this policy is that by raising the wage of unskilled workers, companies will be more inclined to shift their activities to those that rely more on skilled labor and on technology. In this way, the government intends that the measure leads to an increase in productivity and, ultimately, to a reduction in unit labor costs. Whether policies that intend to raise wages ultimately lead to increases in productivity and competitiveness remains to be seen.

Feedback: From Competitiveness to Future Productivity

The analysis presented thus far raises an important question. If productivity is the only driver of living standards, then why is there so much concern among business and political leaders on competitiveness? The answer this framework provides to this question is that current competitiveness matters for future productivity. This feedback from competitiveness to future productivity occurs because persistent changes in the competitiveness of an economy can affect its fundamental characteristics. The cases in the book highlight at least five different feedback channels.

(1) *Learning by exporting*. Competitive manufacturing firms export to foreign markets. There is increasing evidence that firms become more productive by exporting.[p] This is in part the case because, by interacting with competitors and suppliers in foreign markets, exporting firms improve their technological knowledge.[q] As discussed in the China case, these forces have allowed Chinese companies to become more productive and produce ever more sophisticated products over time.

(2) *Learning from FDI*. Competitive economies are attractive locations for multinationals to shift their productive activities. As shown in the cases of China and Singapore, FDI brings technological expertize. Large and persistent flows of technological knowledge can affect the historical endowment of technological knowledge.

Concerns about current competitiveness may lead governments to implement new policies that will affect future productivity. The module highlights at least three different policy responses which I describe next.

(3) *Protectionism*. Economies that experience a reduction in their competitiveness tend to lose manufacturing jobs. Often, lost jobs generated larger value added per worker than jobs newly created in the service sector. As a result, displaced workers experience a reduction in their income. In response to this decline in wages (actual or foreseen) interest groups tend to lobby for protectionists

---

[p]See Blalock and Gertler (2004), Salomon and Shaver (2005), Fernandes and Isgut (2008) and Boermans (2010).
[q]Exporters also learn about foreign consumer's value.

measures which, if implemented, would make the economy less open. The political pressures for protectionism are highlighted in the U.S. current account case.

(4) *Increased market efficiency.* A different response to a loss in competitiveness is to reform the economy in order to make it more competitive. In the Spain and South Africa cases, the reforms involve the labor market. In Malaysia, instead, part of the NEM intends to reduce employment quotas for "bumiputera" and to liberalize certain sectors that are highly regulated.

(5) *Transfer of technological knowledge.* Given the importance of technological knowledge for adoption and productivity, governments are often inclined to facilitate the accumulation of such knowledge to allow their companies to move up in the value chain. These objectives are the rationale for policies and public organizations discussed in this module such as the ETP (Economic Transformation Program)/NEM in Malaysia, the new growth model (NGM) in South Africa, and Fraunhofer in Germany.

Managerial Implications

Needless to say that a measure of the interest of a book like this is how much it can help managers formulate better strategies. In that respect, I am glad to report that the discussions of the cases in the book have been rich in managerial implications. Without going into much detail, to not give them away in the introduction, here are a few high level topics where the book can impact managers.

First, an important decision growing companies need to face at some point is where to locate plants/offices to expand internationally. Answering this question involves resolving a number of tradeoffs. Should a company be closer to suppliers or to buyers? Should it prioritize cost of production or potential productivity gains? Should it be close to competitors or far from them? Is the imitation of the company's technology by indigenous firms a concern? Studying the drivers of competitiveness through the lenses of the cases in the book can be of great help for managers to strike the right balance when expanding internationally.

Second, the international economy has become the wild West. Economies are more integrated than even before as it is clear from the Central Europe, and Malaysia cases. China's exchange rate policy as well as the transformation of the Chinese economy are having seismic effects on the competitiveness of companies in other countries. By studying these and other key issues, the book cautions managers about the importance of adjusting their international strategies to the new reality in world markets.

Third, the fundamental drivers of productivity emphasized in the cases create challenges and opportunities for firms. Managers should be aware of them and find ways to minimize the former and take advantage of the latter. For example, the Spain case suggests that managers can reduce the negative productivity effects of dual labor markets by using permanent contracts as an incentive device for workers on temporary contracts, and by inducing workers to engage in on-the-job training programs.

Fourth, several cases (e.g. Fraunhofer, China, Singapore) stress the importance of knowledge flows for the current and future productivity of the firm. Managerial decisions affect the amount of knowledge created and assimilated by the company. Managers should be aware that engaging in current innovation and technology adoption increases not only the company's current productivity but also their technological knowledge which may reduce the costs of future technological upgrades. The assimilation of technological knowledge may also be affected through training programs, seminars and interactions with other departments familiar with complementary technologies. Finally, private companies should be aware that the tendency to have a narrow research focus prevents them from exploiting inter-disciplinary innovation opportunities. Exploitation of such opportunities may be possible by cooperating with other companies or with government organizations that have the relevant expertise.

Fifth, credit is the grease for economies and companies to work. However, various cases (e.g. U.S., Spain, family groups) illustrate how the credit allocation rules followed by banks may impact negatively in the medium term performance of the economy and on the competitiveness of companies. Bank managers should be aware of these consequences and weight them against the short-term profits they have accrued before the economic collapse.

Bibliography

[1] Acemoglu, D., S. Johnson and J. Robinson (2001). The Colonial Origins of Comparative Development: An Empirical Investigation, *The American Economic Review*, Vol. 91, No. 5, pp. 1369–1401.

[2] Aghion, P., P. Antras and D. Comin (2012). National Innovation Systems, Harvard *mimeo*.

[3] Aghion, P., D. Comin, P. Howitt and I. Tecu (2009). When Does Domestic Savings Matter for Growth? HBS wp. 09-080.

[4] Aghion, P. and P. Howitt (1992). A Model of Growth through Creative Destruction, *Econometrica*, Vol. 60, No. 2, pp. 323–351.

[5] Author, D., D. Dorn, and G. Hanson (2011). The China Syndrome: Local Labor Market Effects of Import Competition in the United States, MIT *mimeo*.

[6] Bentolila, S. and J.J. Dolado (1994). Labour Flexibility and Wages: Lessons from Spain, *Economic Policy*, Vol. 18, pp. 53–99.

[7] Blalock, G. and P. Gertler (2004). Learning from Exporting Revisited in a Less Developed Setting, Haas School of Business *mimeo*.

[8] Blanchard, O. and A. Landier (2001). The Perverse Effect of Partial Labor Market Reform: Fixed Duration Contracts in France, *NBER Working Paper 8219.*

[9] Blomstrom, M. and A. Kokko (1998). Multinational Corporations and Spillovers *Journal of Economic Surveys*, Vol. 12, pp. 247–277.

[10] Boermans, M. (2010). Learning-by-Exporting and Destination Effects: Evidence from African SMEs, HU University *mimeo.*

[11] Brown, C., C. Gilroy and A. Kohen, (1983). Time-Series Evidence of the Effect of the Minimum Wage on Youth Employment and Unemployment, *The Journal of Human Resources*, Vol. 18, pp. 3–31.

[12] Calmors, J. (1993). Centralisation of Wage Bargaining and Macroeconomic Performance: A Survey, *OECD Economic Studies*, No. 21, pp. 161–191.

[13] Caselli, F. and J. Coleman (2001). Cross-Country Technology Diffusion: The Case of Computers, *The American Economic Review*, Vol. 91, No. 2, pp. 328–335.

[14] Comin, D. (2004). R&D: A Small Contribution to Productivity Growth, *Journal of Economic Growth*. December 2004, Vol. 9, No. 4, pp. 391–421.

[15] Comin, D. (2008). Total Factor Productivity, *The New Palgrave Dictionary of Economics*. 2nd edn. Edited by Steven Durlauf and Lawrence Blume. Palgrave Macmillan.

[16] Comin, D., M. Dmitriev and E. Rossi-Hansberg (2012). Spatial Diffusion of Technology, *mimeo.*

[17] Comin, D., W. Easterly and E. Gong (2010). Was the Wealth of Nations Determined in 1000 B.C.?, *American Economic Journal Macroeconomics*, Vol. 2, No. 3, pp. 65–97.

[18] Comin, D. and B. Hobijn (2004). Cross-country Technological Adoption: Making the Theories Face the Facts, *Journal of Monetary Economics*, Vol. 51, pp. 39–83.

[19] Comin, D. and B. Hobijn (2007). Implementing Technology, NBER wp. 12886.

[20] Comin, D. and B. Hobijn (2009). Harvard Business School Working Paper, No. 10-035.

[21] Comin, D. and B. Hobijn (2010). An Exploration of Technology Diffusion, *The American Economic Review*, Vol. 100, No. 5, pp. 2031–2059.

[22] Comin, D. and B. Hobijn (2011). Technology Diffusion and Postwar Growth, *NBER Macroeconomics Annual*, Vol. 25, pp. 209–259.

[23] Comin, D., B. Hobijn and E. Rovito (2008). Technology Usage Lags, *Journal of Economic Growth*, Vol. 13, No. 4, pp. 237–256.

[24] Comin, D. and M. Mestieri (2011). The Intensive Margin of Technology Adoption, In *Handbook of Economic Growth*, edited by Philippe Aghion and Steven Durlauf. Elsevier, forthcoming.

[25] Comin, D. and R. Nanda (2012). Financial Development and Technology Diffusion, HBS *mimeo.*

[26] Diamond, P. (1982). Aggregate Demand Management in Search Equilibrium, *Journal of Political Economy*, Vol. 90, No. 5, pp. 881–894.

[27] Driffill, J. (2006). The Centralization of Wage Bargaining Revisited: What Have We Learnt?, *Journal of Common Market Studies*, Vol. 44, No. 4, pp. 731–756.

[28] Fedderke, J. and W. Simbanegavi (2008). South African Manufacturing, Industry Structure and its Implications for Competition Policy, University of Cape Town wp. No. 111.

29 Fernandes, A. and A. Isgut (2008). Learning-by-Exporting Effects: Are They for Real? World Bank *mimeo*.

30 Freeman, C. (1987). Japan: A new national innovation system?, in Dosi, G., C. Freeman, R. R. Nelson, G. Silverberg and L. Soete (eds.) *Technology and Economy Theory*, London: Pinter.

31 Gene Grossman and Elhanan Helpman (1991). Quality Ladders in the Theory of Economic Growth, *Review of Economic Studies*, Vol. 58, No. 1, pp. 43–61.

32 Hall, R. and C. Jones (1999). Why Do Some Countries Produce So Much More Output Per Workers Than Others? *The Quarterly Journal of Economics*, Vol. 114, No. 1, pp. 83–116.

33 Hausman, R., B. Klinger and R. Wagner (2008). Doing Growth Diagnostics in Practice: A Mindbook, CID wp No. 177.

34 Hsieh, C. and P. Klenow (2009). Misallocation and manufacturing TFP in China and India, *The Quarterly Journal of Economics*, Vol. 124, No. 4, pp. 1403–1448.

35 Izquierdo, M., E. Moral and A. Urtasun (2003). The Collective Bargaining System in Spain: An analysis with individual agreement data, *Documento Ocasional*, No. 0302, Bank of Spain.

36 Jones, C. and J. Williams (2000). Too Much of a Good Thing? The Economics of Investment in R&D, *Journal of Economic Growth*, Vol. 5, No. 1, pp. 65–85.

37 Klenow, P. and A. Rodriguez-Clare (1998). The Neoclassical revival of Growth economics: Has it Gone Too Far?" *NBER Macroeconomics Annual 1997*, Bernanke, B. and J. Rotemberg eds., Cambridge, MA: MIT Press, pp. 73–102.

38 Lagos, R. (2006). A Model of TFP, *Review of Economic Studies*, Vol. 73, No. 4, pp. 983–1007.

39 Mincer, J. (1976). Unemployment Effects of Minimum Wages, *Journal of Political Economy*, Vol. 84, No. 4, Part 2, pp. S87–S104.

40 Mortensen, D. and C. Pissarides (1994). Job Creation and Job Destruction in the Theory of Unemployment, *Review of Economic Studies*, Vol. 61, No. 3, pp. 397–415.

41 Porter, M. (1990). The Competitive Advantage of Nations, *Harvard Business Review*, Vol. 68, No. 2, pp. 73–93.

42 Porter, M. and J. Rivkin (2012). The Looming Challenge to U.S. Competitiveness, *Harvard Business Review*, Vol. 90, No. 3, pp. 54–62.

43 Reinhardt, Forest L. "Accounting for Productivity Growth TN." Harvard Business School Teaching Note 795-038, October 1994.

44 Romer, P. (1990). Endogenous Technological Change, *Journal of Political Economy*, Vol. 98, No. 5, Part 2, pp. S71–S102.

45 Salomon, R. and M. Shaver (2005). Learning by Exporting: New Insights from Examining Firm Innovation *Journal of Economics & Management Strategy*, Vol. 14, No. 2, pp. 431–460.

46 Solow, R. (1956). A Contribution to the Theory of Economic Growth, *Quarterly Journal of Economics*, Vol. 70, No. 1, pp. 65–94.

I
Globalization

Introduction to Globalization

Globalization is intimately related to competitiveness. At one very basic level, without some degree of openness countries cannot compete in international markets. Note that, in the limit where countries are in complete autarky, the mere notion of competitiveness becomes void. Over the last 40 years, economies have become more open and interdependent. International capital flows have exploded, successive rounds negotiations of the GATT[a] have brought down tariffs, trade flows have exploded, companies have taken advantage of the new opportunities by offshoring greater portions of the production processes. All these developments have had asymmetric effects for companies and citizens in all countries. While some have fared well, others have been negatively impacted by globalization.

The centrality of globalization for competitiveness (and to a lesser extent for productivity) makes it the natural starting point of the journey. And there is probably no better way to start than with one of the countries that has benefitted the most from the international economy, even before the last globalization wave: Singapore. The development experience of Singapore is one of the miraculous stories in economics that deserves special study. Its size and the detailed planning from the government invite companies to draw lessons from Singapore's experience on how to take advantage of globalization. In particular, it is still a mystery how Singapore managed to assimilate the technologies of foreign companies that engaged in FDI and to move up to sectors where that knowledge was valuable to attain higher productivity.

The cases of China and Malaysia provide complementary views on central aspects of the relationship between globalization and competitiveness. Malaysia is a small open economy, while China is a big (relatively) closed economy. For a year or so, Malaysia imposed capital controls towards the end of the Asian crisis. These experiences enable discussions on the tensions that come with capital flows and whether it is possible/desirable to open the current account while closing the capital account. The two cases also illustrate nicely how opening up to trade shapes the specialization patterns in the economy, and the consequences this may have for competitiveness and long-run productivity. Finally, both cases and heavy on economic policy and in particular on how governments and companies have tried to reign the forces of trade and how successful they have been.[b]

---

[a]GATT stands for General Agreement on Tariffs and Trade.

[b]The Malaysia cases can be taught in one session or in two separate sessions. If they are taught in two sessions, a natural division is to focus first on the events and effects of the Asian crisis and on the appropriateness of the government responses. The second session could deal with the drivers of the slowdown in investment and productivity growth as well as on the appropriateness for business of the NEM and the ETP. A one session discussion would ideally combine these issues by focusing generally on the tensions that come with capital flows and on the consequences of globalization for business.

An extreme case of international integration is that of a currency union. The case on central Europe dives into how the economies of various central European counties were affected by the global financial crisis and invites students to discuss whether companies and citizens may or may not be better off in a currency union while the global economy is tanking.

Case Synopses and Assignment Questions

Singapore's 'Mid-life Crisis'?

Since its expulsion from Malaysia in 1965, Singapore had transformed itself from a third world island nation into a vibrant city-state with one of the highest levels of GDP per capita in the world. However, sluggish demand among Singapore's major trade partners began testing the nation's export-driven growth model. It was also becoming clear that the Singaporean government could no longer focus single-mindedly on economic growth. Was Singapore facing a mid-life crisis? If so, how could the government revive optimism in the nation's future?

Assignment Questions (AQ):

1. How did Singapore achieve extremely high economic growth rates after 1965?
2. How has productivity growth been attained, and how can it be sustained?
3. What is your evaluation of Lee Hsien Loong's new strategy? Will it work?

China "Unbalanced" 711-010

In 2010, Wen Jiabao looked back at the financial crisis with some satisfaction. Using aggressive fiscal and monetary policy, China had weathered the crisis successfully, growing 8.7% annually in 2010. Most of the unemployed workers had returned to work, often demonstrating for higher wages or better working conditions. Wen, however, was really focused on his new development strategy-shifting away from export-led growth to ease domestic and international pressures. But many institutional challenges seemed to hamper domestic demand, and Wen was particularly concerned with pressures from America, on China's policies for trade, exchange rates, energy and investment.

AQ:

1. How has China grown so fast for so long?
2. Has China's growth been good for Mexican companies?
3. Should the Communist party liberalize financial markets in China? What aspects (if any), when and at what speed?
4. And the exchange rate?

5. How would that affect American companies?
6. Will China be the number 1?

Malaysia, People First? 710-033

On March 30, 2010, Prime Minister Najib Razak presented his new economic model (NEM) for Malaysia. With the goal of raising per capita income to over $15,000 by 2020 from the current level of $6,634, the plan included measures to improve human capital, reduce migration and privatize inefficient government linked corporations (GLCs). However, the most controversial part of the NEM was the dismantling of the new economic policy (NEP), an affirmative action program for native Malays that had alleviated racial tensions and reduced inter-racial income inequality over the previous 40 years though, some argued, at the cost of fostering corruption.

Malaysia (B): The Economic Transformation Program

This case presents the Economic Transformation Program (ETP) designed by the Malaysian government meant to revamp productivity growth after a decade of slow down. It also presents the procedures and outcome of the ETP. Follow up to Malaysia: People First? Very transparent view of policy making in Malaysia.

AQ:

On the First decade:

1. Did capital controls helped Malaysian companies? And foreign companies? In the short or in the Medium term?
2. Is the market disciplining Malaysia in 1997?
3. Why did Mahathir not impose capital controls in 1997? Why did he impose them on September 1st 1998?
4. If it was feasible, should Greece impose capital controls within the euro?

On the Second decade:

1. Is china a good or a bad influence for Malaysian companies?
2. What about for Malaysian people?
3. Is the ETP likely to work? What aspects? Why?
4. How would you solve the competitiveness problems of Malaysian companies?

Central Europe after the Crash: Between Europe and the Euro

This case reviews the financial crisis in central Europe in late 2008, and summarizes how four central European countries-Poland, the Czech Republic, Hungary and Slovakia-have coped with the economic downturn.

AQ:

1. Are there significant differences in the impact that the global financial crisis has had in the four central European countries studied in the case? Why is that?
2. Would Hungarian companies prefer they were in the euro? What about Polish companies?
3. If you were the CEO of an American multinational, in which of these countries would you be more likely to invest?

Singapore's "Midlife Crisis"?

Richard H. K. Vietor* and Hilary White*

In two years' time, Singapore will be 50 years old. We have progressed far as a country but we seem to be trapped in a mid-life crisis.[1]

— Goh Chok Tong, Emeritus Senior Minister of Singapore
Served as Prime Minister, 1990–2004

We have to decide whether we are changing direction or not, and I believe we are at an inflection point . . . still hoping to go up but not so fast.[2]

— Lee Hsien Loong, Prime Minister of Singapore

Since its expulsion from Malaysia in 1965, Singapore had transformed itself from a third world island nation into a vibrant city-state with one of the highest levels of GDP per capita in the world. In 50 years, Singapore's per capita GDP had grown from US$427 to US$52,052 in 2012.[3]

However, sluggish demand among Singapore's major trade partners began testing the nation's export-driven growth model. While GDP growth hit an impressive 14.8% in 2010, it had dropped to only 1.3% in 2012.[4] An Economic Strategies Committee (ESC), established in 2009 by Prime Minister Lee Hsien Loong, sought to redefine Singapore's growth strategy in order to negotiate the challenges and opportunities of the coming decade. Moving forward, Singapore would boost the skills of its

*Reprinted with permission of Harvard Business School Publishing.

This case was prepared by Professor Richard H. K. Vietor and Research Associate Hilary White. Singapore's "Midlife Crisis"? 714-039 labor force, increase productivity, and become a hub for cross-border activities in Asia.

It was also becoming clear that the Singaporean government could no longer focus single-mindedly on economic growth. Singapore faced several demographic concerns, including an aging population and low fertility rate. How could the nation provide for the health and retirement needs of its aging population? Moreover, foreigners now accounted for over a third of Singapore's population. The country's growing dependency on foreign labor was taxing public infrastructure and pushing up housing costs. Competition had increased for housing, access to education, and a variety of consumer durables, while income inequality was deepening.

Worried about the future of their country, Singapore's two former prime ministers had voiced concerns. Goh Chok Tong warned that Singapore was in danger of entering a "mid-life crisis," while the nation's founding father Lee Kuan Yew asked, "Will Singapore be around in 100 years? I am not so sure . . . . I am absolutely sure that if Singapore gets a dumb government, we are done for."[5] Commenting on Goh's characterization, the chairman of the Economic Development Board (EDB), Leo Yip, stated, "There is no crisis. We are in a transition. We are in a different phase, socially, economically, politically. I certainly don't see any loss of optimism, any loss of hope."[6] Much pressure lay on the shoulders of current Prime Minister Lee Hsien Loong as he wondered how Singapore could balance its growth strategy with the nation's mounting list of social concerns. Was Singapore facing a midlife crisis? If so, how could the government revive optimism in the nation's future?

Background

Singapore was a small island city-state located between the tip of Malaysia and the islands of Indonesia (see **Exhibit 1** for a map). Singapore comprised one main island measuring 49 by 25 kilometers and more than 30 smaller surrounding islands.[7]

In 2013, the country had a population of 5,312,400, over 28% of which were non-residents. The majority of Singapore's resident population was ethnically Chinese (74.2%). The second- and third-largest ethnicities were Malay (13.3%) and Indian (9.2%). The foreign population was dominated by Indonesians and Malaysians. Given the nation's diverse cultural makeup, Singapore had four official languages: English, Tamil, Mandarin, and Malay.

Founding of Modern Singapore

In 1819, Sir Stamford Raffles arrived on the island of Singapura during his search for a potential port to support British trade routes in Southeast Asia. Due to its

Exhibit 1. Map of Singapore

Source: Courtesy of the University of Texas Libraries, the University of Texas at Austin.

natural harbor and strategic location between the southernmost tip of continental Asia and the top of the Malay Peninsula, one of the two gateways between the Indian Ocean and China Sea, Singapore was a logical location for a port city. At the time of Raffles' arrival, Singapore was indirectly ruled by the Johor sultanate under Dutch influence, and the island had a population of only 150. However, Raffles' purchase of Singapore from the Johor sultanate sparked Dutch opposition to the British occupation. The disagreement was finally settled under the Anglo–Dutch Treaty of 1824, in which ownership of Singapore was transferred to the British East Trading Company in exchange for a monetary payment. Later named the capital of the Straits Settlements, which also included the Penang and Malacca colonies, Singapore developed from a fishing village into a thriving port for the Malayan region.

It was not until the 1870s that Singapore emerged as a major center for trade between the East and West. In 1869, the Suez Canal was opened, offering a more direct voyage between Europe and Asia. Additionally, the advent of steam transport drew more trading ships through the Straits of Malacca, earning Singapore the nickname "Gate of the East."[8] Between 1871 and 1902, Singapore's total average annual trade increased sixfold.[9] Attracted by the island's prosperity, Singapore developed a sizable immigrant population from China, India, Malaysia and Europe.

Singapore's prosperous growth was interrupted in December 1941 when the Japanese invaded during World War II. By February, the British had surrendered Singapore to the Japanese, who occupied the island for the next three-and-a-half years. Following the war, control over the island was returned to the British, who dismantled the Straits Settlement and declared Singapore an independent crown colony.

Yet Singaporeans questioned the ability of the British colonial power to effectively protect their state, and the merchant class petitioned the British government for increased representation. In 1953, the governor appointed Sir George Rendel to conduct a comprehensive review of the Singaporean constitution. Following the report's recommendation for limited self-rule, 25 of the 32 seats of the legislative assembly were popularly elected, while a cabinet was chosen from among assembly members. The British retained control over Singapore's defense, security, and foreign affairs. Following a series of popular protests, a delegation was soon sent to London to argue for full self-rule. The British conceded, and all seats of the legislative assembly became open during the 1959 election. The People's Action Party (PAP) won 43 of the 51 seats, and a 35-year-old member of the delegation to London, Lee Kuan Yew, was chosen prime minister.

In 1963, in an effort to gain some economies of scale and scope, Singapore joined with Malaysia and parts of Borneo to form the Federation of Malaysia. Soon, however, relations between Singapore and the Malay central government deteriorated. Singapore was required to pay a large percentage of its budget to the Malay government, and as Malay–Chinese riots broke out across the island, Malaysia voted to expel Singapore from the federation. Singapore became an independent nation on August 9, 1965. "For me," Prime Minister Lee tearfully reflected, "it is a moment of anguish. All my life, my whole adult life, I have believed in the merger and unity of the two territories."[10]

Singapore under Lee Kuan Yew

Upon inheriting the now independent nation, Lee Kuan Yew faced a formidable challenge. With minimal natural resources of its own and a population of 2 million people, Singapore had a GDP per capita of only US$516.[11] Lee recalled, "We had faced tremendous odds with an improbable chance of survival. Singapore was not a natural country but man-made, a trading post the British had developed as a nodal point in their worldwide maritime empire. We inherited this island without its hinterland, a heart without a body."[12]

As Great Britain eliminated its naval presence, Singapore worked to strengthen its defense system. Moreover, the break with Malaysia had left Singapore vulnerable to extremist political groups. In response, the cabinet approved the creation of the Ministry of Interior and Defense, which was charged with developing a police and military force.

The prime minister's next challenge was to address basic social needs. British withdrawal left Singapore plagued by high unemployment, measuring 14% in 1959, and a housing shortage.[13] In 1960, the government formed the Housing Development Board (HDB) to quickly build subsidized public housing. By 1965, over 54,000 flats had been completed.[14] The HDB became the primary avenue for achieving home-ownership in Singapore. In 2013, 82% of Singaporeans lived in HDB housing.[15]

The Singaporean government maintained a strong involvement in economic policy, developing forward-looking strategies for long-term growth. After a failed attempt at import substitution from 1959 to 1965, the government switched to export-oriented industrialization. First, the government realized that hostilities among its neighbors and regional poverty necessitated Singapore to look for trade partners outside the region. The government sought to attract multinational corporations (MNCs) to invest in manufacturing in Singapore for exporting products back to the developed world.[16] Second, Lee held a vision of creating a "First World Oasis in a Third World Region" by establishing first-rate infrastructure in health care, education, housing, and transportation. On Singapore's ambitious economic goals, Lee reflected, "I concluded an island city-state in Southeast Asia could not be ordinary if it was to survive."[17]

Government Structure

Singapore had a parliamentary democracy modeled after the Westminster system. Based on geography and population, Singapore was divided into 27 electoral constituencies, including 15 Group Representation Constituencies (GRCs) and 12 Single Member Constituencies (SMCs). In a system unique to Singapore, within the GRCs, political parties nominated three to six candidates, one of whom had to belong to a racial minority, and electors voted for their preferred team of individuals to serve as their member of parliament (MP).[18] In the SMCs, electors voted for a single individual to be their MP. Additionally, the constitution allowed for up to nine non-constituency MPs to be appointed from members of the opposition party, in order to ensure a minimum opposition representation. The president also held the ability to appoint up to nine nominated MPs for half-terms, in order to bring non-partisan views into the legislature.[19]

The constitutional head of state was the popularly elected president, although the position was primarily ceremonial. The president appointed the nation's prime minister, choosing the MP with the majority of the parliament's support. With consultation from the prime minister, the president appointed the cabinet from the elected MPs. Under the prime minister, the cabinet comprised 14 to 16 ministers responsible for administering affairs of the state.

Lateral job switching was a common practice of the Singaporean government. Members of the civil service switched jobs and agencies every few years, and it was possible for a bureaucrat to move from working in defense to labor and education. Lateral job switching provided a holistic view of government. As Prime Minister Lee commented, "It's a tremendous advantage because if you come in cold like David Cameron or Barack Obama, it takes a long time to come up to speed."[20]

Nanny State

> *If Singapore is a nanny state, then I am proud to have fostered one.*[21]
> — Lee Kuan Yew, Prime Minister, 1959–1990

Since the 1959 elections, the PAP developed an efficient system of government control over the economy and welfare of its citizens. Nicknamed the "nanny state," the Singaporean government provided world-class services for its citizens, including public housing and a leading public education system. To ensure a "clean and green" Singapore, the nation instituted an infamous ban on chewing gum, imposed heavy fines for littering, and established an annual tree-planting day. Tough measures were taken to limit traffic congestion. In addition to heavy taxation, certificates of entitlement (COEs) were required to own and operate a vehicle. A limited number of COEs were available for public bidding, with permit prices reaching over 75,000 Singapore dollars (S$) for small cars in 2013.[22]

Singapore also enjoyed one of the lowest crime rates in the world, largely due to the nation's reliance on strict penalties. Judicial caning still remained a common form of punishment for men under the age of 50, even for non-violent crimes such as vandalism. Singapore's media were also heavily censored. The circulation of publications considered to be "engaging in the domestic politics of Singapore" could be prohibited; Reporters Without Borders ranked Singapore 135 out of 179 nations on its Press Freedom Index.[23]

While the nanny state provided a high quality of life for its citizens, not all were content with the PAP's style of governance. Critics complained that the PAP used government-funded benefits to ensure a steady foundation of public support and thus had minimal political opposition. In the early 1990s, for example, the PAP directed renovation priorities to districts that had voted in favor of the party. "I think [Singaporeans] know," commented the then deputy prime minister, "that the way they vote will influence their own personal well-being — their town, their neighborhood, their property values."[24] The PAP's one-party rule, while firm, did foster the rapid development of Singapore's economic and social institutions.

Yet by 2011, the PAP's long-standing control showed signs of weakening. In the May general election, the PAP won 81 of 87 parliamentary seats and only 60.1% of the popular vote, the smallest margin since the country achieved independence.[25] Some pointed to the nation's rising income inequality, growing housing costs, influx of foreigners, and the limited presence of the opposition party in government as possible causes of the PAP's poor performance in the elections.

Recognizing ministerial salaries as a possible source of contention, the prime minister appointed a committee to review the remuneration of the nation's leaders. Singaporean government officials were among the highest paid in the world. The high salaries were set "so that people of the right caliber are not deterred from stepping forward to lead the country."[26] Under the committee's recommendations, salaries were benchmarked against the private sector, so that a new minister would receive compensation equal to 60% of the median income earned by Singapore's 1,000 highest-paid citizens. The salary was linked to fixed and variable components, which fluctuated according to both individual and national performance.[27] Consequently, the prime minister's salary was reduced 36% to S$2.2 million (US$1.7 million), while newly appointed ministers earned S$1.1 million in 2012.[28]

Moreover, the generous compensation was believed to discourage corruption. Businessman Koh Boon Hwee commented, "I don't think Singaporeans begrudge what we pay our leaders — it's all they make. It's all transparent. Elsewhere in the world, politicians find other ways to make their money."[29] Singapore was well recognized for its honesty and transparency; the 2012 Transparency International Corruption Perceptions Index ranked Singapore 5 out of 172 nations.[30]

Economic Growth

Since independence, the Singaporean government exercised firm control over the nation's economic growth (see **Exhibit 2** for economic indicators). The government focused on six main policies: investment in government-owned corporations, promoting foreign direct investment (FDI), free trade, a pro-business environment, a tight monetary policy, and high savings. Guiding the nation's economic growth strategy was the Economic Development Board (EDB). Set up in 1961, the EDB was formed by the Ministry of Trade and Industry (MTI) to act as "the spearhead for industrialization by direct participation in industry."[31] Initially, the EDB targeted four industries: ship repair and containers, metal engineering, chemicals, and electrical equipment.[32]

Exhibit 2.   General Economic Indicators

	1980	1985	1990	1995	2000	2005	2006	2007	2008	2009	2010	2011	2012	2013
GDP (current prices, S$ billions)	25.8	40.6	70.4	123.4	162.6	208.8	231.4	271.2	272.0	279.9	322.4	344.7	358.5	372.8
As percentage of GDP														
Private Consumption	51.1%	45.4%	45.4%	41.4%	41.9%	40.1%	38.6%	35.6%	38.5%	37.5%	35.5%	36.0%	37.1%	37.1%
Government Consumption	9.7%	13.5%	9.5%	8.4%	10.9%	10.5%	10.3%	9.5%	10.5%	10.3%	10.2%	9.7%	9.4%	10.2%
Gross Fixed Capital	39.5%	40.6%	31.1%	32.6%	30.3%	21.1%	21.7%	24.5%	28.3%	29.3%	26.1%	25.5%	26.9%	25.9%
Stock Building	5.5%	0.3%	3.9%	0.7%	2.9%	−1.2%	−0.7%	−1.4%	2.1%	−1.6%	1.7%	1.8%	3.5%	3.1%
Exports of Goods and Services	201.6%	150.9%	177.4%	183.0%	192.3%	229.7%	233.3%	214.7%	230.3%	191.9%	199.3%	200.2%	195.1%	190.5%
Imports of Goods and Services	208.6%	150.7%	167.4%	166.3%	179.5%	200.3%	203.6%	183.9%	209.4%	168.4%	172.8%	173.8%	172.6%	167.5%
Statistical Discrepancy	1.2%	0.0%	0.0%	0.3%	1.11%	0.0%	0.3%	1.0%	−0.3%	1.0%	0.0%	0.6%	0.7%	0.6%
Real GDP Growth	na	−0.7	10.1	7.3	9.0	7.4	8.6	9.0	1.7	−0.8	14.8	5.2	1.3	4.1
Real GDP per capita (current prices, US$)	4,990	6,749	12,745	24,702	23,414	29,401	33,089	38,762	39,385	37,880	45,637	51,235	52,052	54,776
GDP per capita (US$ at PPP)	na	9,030	14,300	21,030	26,430	35,400	38,410	41,230	40,560	39,360	44,900	47,150	47,440	50,420
Population (millions)	2.4	2.7	3.0	3.5	4.0	4.3	4.4	4.6	4.8	5.0	5.1	5.2	5.3	5.4
Unemployment (%)	na	na	na	1.7	2.6	3.1	2.7	2.1	2.3	3.0	2.2	2.0	1.9	1.9

Source: Created by case writer using data from the Economist Intelligence Unit, March 2014. National income account data for 2007–2013 is from Singapore Department of Statistics, February 2015.

Government-Owned Companies

To jump-start economic growth, the Singaporean government took a proactive role by creating several government-led corporations (GLCs) and statutory boards to provide the infrastructure necessary to attract foreign investment and provide for the basic needs of Singapore's people. To complement the initiatives of the EDB, the Jurong Township Corporation (JTC) was created to guide the construction of industrial estates, while the Development Bank of Singapore took over industrial financing from the EDB. The Public Utilities Board addressed electricity and water needs, while the HDB oversaw public housing. Soon, the government held stakes in a wide variety of firms all across the economy, including a bird park, an airline, a shoemaker, several utilities and a shipping company.[33]

MTI established Temasek Holdings in 1974 to manage these investments on a commercial basis.[34] By 2013, after significant privatizations, Temasek held more than S$215 billion in assets, yielding a shareholder return since inception of 16%.[35] Despite being government-owned, Temasek claimed it was an independent, commercially run firm (although its CEO, Ho Ching, was the prime minister's wife). Temasek executives did not sit on the boards of its held companies. Like privately owned firms, Singapore's GLCs were focused on market performance, rather than wider government-dictated social initiatives.[36]

Foreign Direct Investment and Pro-Business Environment

With a low capital base in the 1960s, the Singaporean government looked to FDI as a central component of its growth strategy. Singapore's encouragement of FDI was unique in a period when many developing nations were suspicious of foreign involvement in the economy. Despite its colonial past, Singapore warmly welcomed FDI. As Lee Kuan Yew described, Singapore "had no xenophobic hangover from colonialism."[37] Through MNCs, Singapore could benefit by gaining employment opportunities, technology transfers, and managerial expertise. EDB Chairman Leo Yip explained, "It's what the leading companies in the world can offer us. Global companies from the U.S., Europe, and Japan, they bring the leading-edge technology, production chains, and business practices into Singapore. They bring expertise. Why should we stop harnessing that?"[38]

Since Singapore lacked cheap land, natural resources, and even labor to attract MNCs, the government pledged to create an efficient business environment by investing in basic infrastructure, creating an educated labor force, and providing tax incentives for foreign firms. Internationally, Singapore gained a positive reputation for its pro-business environment. In 2013, the World Bank named Singapore the top country for doing business, earning high rankings for its ease of starting a business, access to credit, protecting investors and dealing with construction permits.[39]

Moreover, Singapore was ranked second out of 144 countries on the World Economic Forum's Global Competitiveness Rankings.[40] Foreign direct investment into Singapore amounted to US$70.8 billion, or US$56.6 billion (see **Exhibit 3** for balance of payments and **Exhibits 4a** and **4b** for foreign investment into Singapore by origin and by destination).[41]

Infrastructure: In 1965, the majority of Singapore's economy focused on low-end commerce, with most of the nation's fledgling industries small in scale and concentrated on domestic consumption.[42] The government's first step was to attract labor-intensive manufacturing by investing heavily in industrial sites. The first major project of government-owned JTC was to convert the Jurong swampland into an industrial estate for manufacturing firms, complete with already-built factories. Later, in 1991, the JTC began to construct Jurong Island, an S$7 billion land-reclamation project on seven small islands for the energy and petrochemical industries. Private companies invested an additional S$42 billion in capital equipment. By the mid-2000s, the JTC launched One-North, a 200-hectare "live-work-play-learn" environment, designed to create synergies across Singapore's leading industries, including media, biomedical sciences, and infocomm technologies.

Efficiency: Early on, Singapore developed a reputation as a quick-start environment for manufacturers. In 1968, Texas Instruments decided to locate a semiconductor assembly plant in Singapore, and the EDB ensured that production was able to start within 50 days of the decision.[43] Other foreign firms, including National Semiconductor and Hewlett-Packard, soon followed. Two years later, General Electric had established six new facilities, becoming Singapore's largest employer by the end of the decade.[44] One EDB official described the streamlined system: "You could just walk into the EDB office, discuss your project, and lease a factory site or standard building on the spot."[45]

As the economy grew increasingly diversified, the government maintained its efficient bureaucracy. In 2012, a new company could incorporate online in less than 24 hours.[46] The World Bank ranked Singapore third of 189 countries for the ease of starting a new business.[47]

Tax incentives: The EDB also aimed to create a tax-friendly environment for manufacturing firms. In 1967, the government instituted the Economic Expansion Incentives Act (EEIA) to encourage "pioneer industries" and exports by providing tax relief. In the latest version of the EEIA, pioneer certificates were awarded to new firms and activities investing in Singapore, providing exemptions from corporate taxes for up to 15 years.[48]

Tax incentives were valuable tools of the EDB for restructuring the economy away from labor-intensive manufacturing and toward services and high-value

Exhibit 3.   Balance of Payments (S$ billions)

	2006	2007	2008	2009	2010	2011	2012	2013
Current Account Balance	**57.33**	**69.85**	**40.80**	**48.70**	**84.57**	**82.16**	**64.28**	**68.07**
Trade Balance	80.34	87.07	60.56	71.72	90.01	91.40	76.13	84.93
Exports of goods	446.32	470.84	501.62	419.69	505.88	546.10	544.59	546.64
Imports of goods	365.97	383.77	441.05	347.97	415.87	454.71	468.46	461.71
Net Services	−11.52	−4.07	−2.19	−2.50	3.15	0.87	0.48	0.39
Export of services	93.67	111.31	126.34	118.70	137.29	146.10	148.81	161.90
Import of services	105.19	115.38	128.54	121.20	134.14	145.23	148.32	161.50
Net Primary Income	−8.33	−8.53	−12.29	−14.71	−1.53	−2.75	−3.92	−8.71
Net Secondary Income	−3.15	−4.61	−5.27	−5.81	−7.05	−7.36	−8.41	−8.55
Capital and Financial Account	**−28.53**	**−36.95**	**−22.99**	**−35.74**	**−30.51**	**−55.60**	**−35.59**	**−48.84**
Financial Account	**−28.53**	**−36.95**	**−22.99**	**−35.74**	**−30.51**	**−55.60**	**−35.59**	**−48.84**
Net Direct Investment	28.70	15.18	7.62	1.29	38.56	37.32	41.95	46.14
Assets	−29.61	−55.61	−9.64	−34.98	−34.55	−33.02	−28.84	−33.86
Liabilities	58.31	70.79	17.26	36.27	73.12	70.34	70.80	80.00
Net Portfolio Investment	−25.72	−71.51	16.38	−60.69	−53.12	−16.09	−61.45	−56.10
Assets	−44.37	−99.35	37.10	−62.41	−55.37	−9.94	−64.02	−63.24
Liabilities	18.65	27.84	−20.72	1.72	2.24	−6.14	2.58	7.13
Financial Derivatives	−9.56	−0.83	2.82	−20.49	−2.51	−14.95	−19.96	−3.78
Other Investments	−21.95	20.20	−49.81	44.15	−13.44	−61.89	3.87	−35.10
Net Errors and Omissions	**−1.81**	**−3.60**	**0.72**	**3.49**	**3.41**	**−5.07**	**3.91**	**3.50**
Overall Balance	**27.00**	**29.30**	**18.53**	**16.46**	**57.48**	**21.49**	**32.61**	**22.73**
Change in Official Reserves	**−27.00**	**−29.30**	**−18.53**	**−16.46**	**−57.48**	**−21.49**	**−32.61**	**−22.73**

Source: Singapore Department of Statistics, March 2014. Data for 2013 are from Economic Survey of Singapore, 2013.
Note: The capital account is consolidated under the financial account. An increase in reserve assets is indicated by a minus (−) sign. Statistics for 2013 are preliminary.

Exhibit 4a.   Cumulative Foreign Investment into Singapore by Origin (stock at year-end; % of total)

	2008	2009	2010	2011	2012
United States	10.4%	10.2%	10.7%	11.7%	14.7%
Netherlands	12.0%	10.7%	9.7%	9.8%	8.7%
Japan	9.8%	8.8%	8.6%	7.9%	7.9%
British Virgin Islands	7.6%	6.9%	8.0%	7.9%	7.8%
United Kingdom	9.3%	8.6%	7.9%	8.3%	6.6%
Cayman Islands	5.8%	6.3%	7.1%	7.0%	6.2%
Switzerland	4.6%	4.7%	4.3%	4.3%	4.3%
Bermuda	4.5%	4.2%	4.0%	2.9%	4.1%
Hong Kong	2.3%	3.2%	3.0%	3.4%	3.8%
Malaysia	2.5%	2.8%	2.3%	2.8%	3.6%
Others	31.2%	33.6%	34.4%	34.0%	32.2%
ASEAN	3.7%	4.1%	3.7%	3.9%	4.9%
Asia	23.5%	25.4%	24.4%	24.1%	24.5%
EU	30.1%	29.1%	28.1%	29.0%	25.9%
Total Direct Investment (S$ billions)	**509.6**	**574.9**	**626.6**	**673.8**	**732.1**

Source: Created by case writer using data from the Singapore Department of Statistics, March 2014.

Exhibit 4b.   Cumulative Foreign Investment Abroad by Destination (stock at year-end; % of total)

	2008	2009	2010	2011	2012
China	17.4%	16.7%	16.9%	19.1%	19.8%
United Kingdom	6.4%	8.7%	9.2%	8.3%	9.5%
Hong Kong	6.4%	6.3%	5.8%	8.6%	8.4%
Australia	5.8%	6.2%	7.8%	7.9%	8.2%
Indonesia	7.1%	7.6%	7.3%	7.8%	8.0%
Malaysia	7.8%	7.1%	6.9%	6.9%	7.0%
British Virgin Islands	9.9%	9.5%	8.4%	7.3%	6.9%
Thailand	6.1%	5.5%	4.7%	4.4%	4.1%
Mauritius	3.6%	4.5%	5.5%	4.1%	3.7%
Cayman Islands	3.0%	2.6%	2.3%	2.3%	2.4%
Others	26.4%	25.3%	25.3%	23.2%	22.0%
ASEAN	24.0%	23.1%	22.2%	22.1%	21.7%
Asia	56.4%	54.6%	53.5%	57.9%	56.8%
EU	9.7%	11.8%	12.8%	12.2%	13.1%
Total Direct Investment (S$ billions)	**312.4**	**372.3**	**429.4**	**446.8**	**459.7**

Source: Created by case writer using data from the Singapore Department of Statistics, March 2014.

manufacturing. In 1983, pioneer status was extended to include service firms. In the mid-1980s, the government began granting reduced corporate tax rates for firms with headquarters located in Singapore. As of 2013, a variety of corporate incentives targeted land intensification and productivity; research and development, particularly in new technologies; fixed capital expenditures on equipment used abroad; and marketing of products internationally.[49] The corporate tax rate was 17%.[50]

An educated labor force: Since independence, Singapore's leaders had invested heavily in education. The education minister, Heng Swee Keat, reflected,

> From day one, the founding generation of leaders has been very focused on education for two simple reasons. First, Singapore is a small place with zero resources. Second, when we became independent, we were a very fragmented society; we were multiracial, multicultural, and multireligious. Education has always been seen as critical to the country's sense of cohesion, identity as an independent nation, and to the success of Singapore, as an economy and as a society.[51]

While MNCs brought technical expertise to the island, the government realized that increased manpower training was necessary to develop the skills required for export-oriented manufacturing. Goh Keng Swee, then the minister of finance, explained in his 1970 budget speech, "When foreign corporations bring their expertise, what we experience as a developing nation is a brain-drain in reverse.... [I]n the long term the scientific know-how and technological processes which we now borrow from abroad must in course of time develop on an indigenous base at our institutions."[52] Throughout the 1970s, the government focused on upgrading technical skills. A technical education department was added to the Ministry of Education to train secondary students as skilled workers for the shipbuilding, metalworking, chemical and precision engineering industries. By 1976, nearly a fifth of the secondary student population had received technical training.[53]

Moreover, the government worked to create a globally competitive workforce. Singapore was committed to forming a bilingual population, proficient in an indigenous language, such as Chinese, Tamil, or Malay, and English. Since 1960, all primary schools had been required to teach a second language, and the policy was extended to secondary schools six years later.[54] The bilingual requirement positioned Singapore as a "meeting point" for conducting business between the East and West. In the early 1970s, the government began sending young Singaporeans abroad to work in apprenticeship programs with firms such as Tata in India and Philips in the Netherlands as part of an overseas training program.[55] Between 1979 and 1982, the Singaporean government also formed institutes of technology in partnership with Japan, Germany, and France.[56]

By the 1980s, the government recognized that Singapore's competitiveness in labor-intensive manufacturing was eroding due to labor shortages, and the economy needed a transition toward more technology- and capital-intensive industries. Consequently, the EDB launched a "second industrial revolution," aimed at moving

Singapore's manufacturing up the value chain. The minister of the MTI commented in 1981, "The prime objective of the plan is to develop Singapore into a modern industrial economy based on science technology, skills and knowledge."[57] Parliament created the Skills Development Fund to upgrade the skill base of the labor force. The fund, based on a cost-sharing principle, encouraged employers to invest in further training of their employees through government-provided financial incentives. The government also accelerated the movement away from low-cost industries by raising wages and increasing the education level of the labor force. In 2012, nearly 50% of Singapore residents aged 25 to 34 were university graduates (see **Exhibit 5** for educational attainment figures).[58]

Over-dependency on MNCs?: While MNCs served as a critical element of the nation's development strategy, some worried about Singapore's capacity to create its own domestic firms. Businessman Koh Boon Hwee commented, "I worry about the fact that Singapore has not been able, besides the original creation of companies such as Singtel and Singapore Airlines, to create domestic enterprises. I do not believe you can create a sense of nationhood without firms, which are also indigenous. If all we become is a hotel for foreign businesses, we are dead in the long run."[59] Deputy Prime Minister Tharman Shanmugaratnam also commented on entrepreneurial culture:

> We started in an accidental way, with a small market where import substitution couldn't work. It was an existential crisis, which meant we had to solve problems and create jobs quickly. That shaped the strategy of bringing in the MNCs. Government too invested in areas like steel, as local entrepreneurs were not keen to commit significant capital for uncertain rewards at the time. The success of those early decades left a legacy, in our corporate structure as well as the attitudes of the young. It's not permanent, but there is a real legacy of people preferring to work for the MNCs if they can.[60]

Consequently, there was growing pressure for Singapore to produce its own globally competitive firms. 99% of Singaporean businesses were small and medium-sized

Exhibit 5.   Educational Attainment (% of population aged 25 years and older)

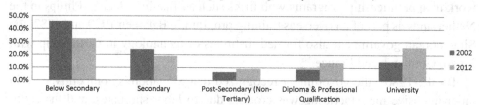

Source: Teo Zhiwei, "Educational Profile of Singapore Resident Non-Students, 2002–2012," *Statistics Singapore Newsletter*, Singapore Department of Statistics, March 2013, p. 3.

enterprises (SMEs) with either annual sales turnover of less than S$100 million or employment under 200 workers. The Standards, Productivity and Innovation Board (SPRING) targeted the competitiveness of SMEs at home, while International Enterprise Singapore (IE Singapore) helped domestic businesses grow into international companies. Tan Kai Hoe, SPRING's CEO, explained how his organization supported SMEs: "We are clear that we only incentivize things that will be useful for the whole environment. For those who want to grow, we want to support them. We want to upgrade their capabilities; we don't want to subsidize them."[61] SPRING Chairman Philip Yeo added, "If all they are doing to grow is focusing on the domestic market and eating each other's lunch, it isn't feasible to use public funding."[62]

Trade

Once Singapore focused on exports, the government removed nearly all of the existing tariffs and invested in port infrastructure (see **Exhibit 6** for GDP by sector).[63] By 1975, Singapore operated the third-busiest container port in the world.[64] In 1983, the government created the Trade Development Board (later renamed IE Singapore), the central agency for directing Singapore's external economy.

As the nation established manufacturing and services as "twin pillars of the economy" in the 1980s and gradually transitioned into complex, high-value manufacturing over the next three decades, trade volume eventually amounted to more than two times its GDP (see **Exhibit 7** for Singapore's trade volume). As a result of

Exhibit 6. GDP by Sector

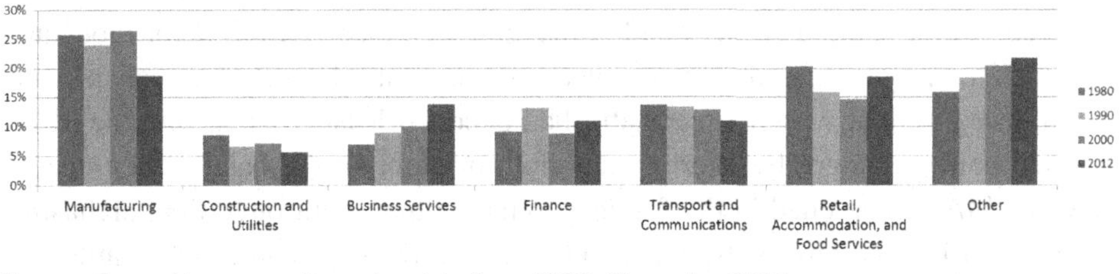

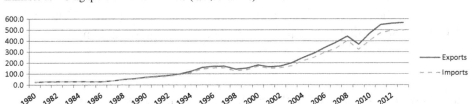

Source: Created by case writer using data from CEIC, November 2013.

Exhibit 7. Singapore's Trade Volume (US$ billions)

Source: Created by case writer using data from the Economist Intelligence Unit, March 2014.

Singapore's large volume of trade in goods and services, the economy was very sensitive to changes in global demand, particularly among its major trading partners — China, United States, Europe and Hong Kong (see **Exhibit 8** for trade percentages with major partners).

In order to further promote its international trade, Singapore established a network of free trade agreements (FTAs) with its main trade partners, including the United States, China, and India. Singapore was also a member of the ASEAN Free Trade Area, which aimed to attract greater FDI to the region. In 2013, Singapore hoped to ratify a free trade agreement with the European Union, the country's largest trade partner. The EU–Singapore FTA was scheduled to go into effect in 2015.

Monetary Policy

Formed in 1971, the Monetary Authority of Singapore (MAS) served as the nation's central bank, with the mandate to "regulate all elements of monetary, banking and financial aspects of Singapore." The MAS was later granted regulatory power over the insurance and securities industries, as well. To complement the MAS's conservative monetary policy, the government created its private sovereign wealth fund, the GIC, in 1984 to seek long-term returns on Singapore's rapidly accumulating foreign reserves. Unlike the portfolios held by the MAS and Temasek, the GIC did not publicly disclose its assets.

Singapore's central bank had several unique characteristics. Ravi Menon, the managing director of the MAS, explained, "We don't have statutory independence, but we have operational autonomy."[65] Additionally, rather than regulating the monetary system through changes to the interest rate, the MAS had an exchange rate–centered policy, using a basket-band-crawl approach (see **Exhibit 9** for monetary policy). The Singaporean dollar was measured against a basket of currencies and was allowed to float within a preestablished band. At least twice a year, the MAS effected policy changes by altering the width or slope of the band. When necessary, the MAS intervened in the foreign exchange market through the purchasing or selling of U.S. dollars on the spot and forward foreign exchange (FX) markets.[66] Menon commented, "Unlike major advanced economies, we don't have the option [to control the interest rate]. You can't control the interest rate and the exchange rate at the same time when you have free capital flows. It has been since 1981 that this has been the case.... We are a price taker on the interest rate."[67] This policy worked to control inflation due to the huge volume of exports and imports.

Savings

The Central Provident Fund (CPF) acted as the primary vehicle for Singapore's social security system. Self-reliance was a key principle of the CPF system, and

Exhibit 8.   External Trade: Major Partners and Commodity Exports

	2006	2007	2008	2009	2010	2011	2012	2013
Imports by Origin (%)								
EU	11%	12%	12%	14%	12%	13%	13%	12%
China	11%	12%	11%	11%	11%	10%	10%	12%
Malaysia	13%	13%	12%	12%	12%	11%	11%	11%
United States	13%	12%	12%	12%	11%	11%	10%	10%
Taiwan	6%	6%	5%	5%	6%	6%	7%	8%
South Korea	4%	5%	6%	6%	6%	6%	7%	6%
Japan	8%	8%	8%	8%	8%	7%	6%	5%
Indonesia	6%	6%	6%	6%	5%	5%	5%	5%
United Arab Emirates	2%	2%	2%	2%	2%	3%	4%	4%
Saudi Arabia	4%	3%	5%	3%	4%	5%	5%	3%
Other	21%	20%	22%	23%	23%	23%	23%	22%
Total (S$, billion)	**378.9**	**396.0**	**450.9**	**356.3**	**423.2**	**459.7**	**474.6**	**466.8**
Exports by Destination (%)								
Malaysia	13%	13%	12%	11%	12%	12%	12%	12%
China	10%	10%	9%	10%	10%	10%	11%	12%
Hong Kong	10%	10%	10%	12%	12%	11%	11%	11%
Indonesia	9%	10%	11%	10%	9%	10%	11%	10%
EU	11%	11%	10%	10%	10%	9%	9%	8%
United States	10%	9%	7%	7%	6%	5%	5%	6%
Japan	5%	5%	5%	5%	5%	4%	4%	4%
South Korea	3%	4%	4%	5%	4%	4%	4%	4%
Australia	4%	4%	4%	4%	4%	4%	4%	4%
Taiwan	3%	3%	3%	3%	4%	4%	4%	4%
Other	21%	23%	25%	25%	24%	25%	25%	26%
Total (S$, billion)	**431.6**	**450.6**	**476.8**	**391.1**	**478.8**	**514.7**	**510.3**	**513.4**
Exports by Commodity (%)								
Oil	16%	18%	24%	20%	22%	27%	26%	24%
Non-oil	84%	82%	76%	80%	78%	73%	74%	76%
Food, Beverage and Tobacco	1%	2%	2%	2%	2%	2%	2%	2%
Crude Materials	1%	1%	1%	1%	1%	1%	1%	1%
Chemicals and Chemical Products	11%	12%	10%	12%	12%	13%	13%	12%
Manufactured Goods	4%	5%	5%	4%	4%	4%	4%	4%
Machinery and Transport	58%	55%	51%	52%	51%	46%	45%	46%
Miscellaneous Manufactured Articles	7%	7%	6%	7%	7%	7%	8%	9%
Other	18%	19%	26%	22%	24%	28%	27%	26%
Re-exports	**47%**	**48%**	**48%**	**49%**	**48%**	**45%**	**44%**	**47%**
Total (S$, billion)	**431.6**	**450.6**	**476.8**	**391.1**	**478.8**	**514.7**	**510.3**	**513.4**

Source: Created by casewriter using data from the Singapore Yearbook of Statistics, 2013. Data for 2013 are from Economic Survey of Singapore, 2013.

Exhibit 9. Monetary Policy

	1980	1985	1990	1995	2000	2005	2006	2007	2008	2009	2010	2011	2012	2013
Exchange Rate (S$ per US$, average)	2.1	2.2	1.8	1.4	1.7	1.7	1.6	1.5	1.4	1.5	1.4	1.3	1.2	1.3
Consumer Price Index (2005 = 100)	65.5	76.7	81.6	92.6	96.8	100.0	101.0	103.1	109.9	110.6	113.7	119.6	125.1	128.1
Consumer Price Index (% change)	na	0.5	3.5	1.7	1.3	0.5	1.0	2.1	6.6	0.6	2.8	5.2	4.6	2.4
Deposit Rate	9.4	5.0	4.7	3.5	1.7	0.4	0.6	0.5	0.4	0.3	0.2	0.2	0.1	0.1
Lending Rate	11.7	8.1	7.4	6.4	5.8	5.3	5.3	5.3	5.4	5.4	5.4	5.4	5.4	5.4
M2 (billions, S$)	16.1	28.1	61.8	102.0	170.9	219.8	262.4	297.6	333.4	371.2	403.1	443.4	475.4	495.9
M2 Growth	na	3.8	20.0	8.5	−2.1	6.2	19.4	13.4	12.0	11.3	8.6	10.0	7.2	4.3

Source: Created by case writer using data from the Economist Intelligence Unit, March 2014.

the program operated on a fully funded basis. Through the CPF, the government collected and invested workers' savings to be paid back with interest upon retirement. Not until age 55 could members withdraw savings in excess of the minimum sum, that is, the income needed for a basic standard of living during retirement (S$148,000 as of July 2013).[68] Upon reaching the CPF drawdown age, members could opt to receive their monthly payouts from their retirement accounts. In 2013, the drawdown age was 63 but was set to increase to 65 by 2018, due to the rising life expectancies of Singaporeans. Extraordinarily high contribution rates for employers and employees varied according to national macroeconomic objectives and age of the employee (see **Exhibit 10a** for rates of contribution).

The CPF was originally created in 1955 as a retirement savings scheme, although it had since been expanded to include health care, homeownership and asset enhancement. The CPF was divided into four accounts: (1) an ordinary account for housing, insurance, investment, and education; (2) a special account for old age and retirement-related financial products; (3) Medisave for medical insurance and hospitalization fees; and (4) a retirement account, which was created on the member's 55th birthday by transferring savings from the other three accounts. Each of the accounts received a different percentage of the monthly contributions (see **Exhibit 10b** for CPF contribution rates by age group).

In 1968, the government introduced the Public Housing Scheme, which allowed CPF contributors to use their CPF savings to buy an HDB flat. In 1981, the Residential Properties Scheme expanded the CPF home-buying program to include private properties. Three years later, CPF was expanded to include health-care savings. Medisave was designed as a savings mechanism to pay for personal and dependents' health-care expenses, including Medishield insurance premiums. In January 2013, the Medisave minimum sum was raised to S$38,500, in order to keep pace with health-care inflation.[69] The government also opened a CPF Medisave account for each child born and contributed S$3,000. While the ordinary account had a guaranteed rate of interest of 2.5% and the remaining accounts accrued 4%, CPF members

Exhibit 10a. Historical Rates of Contribution to the Central Provident Fund, 1955–2013 (% of gross wages)

	1955	1970	1975	1980	1985	1990	1995	2000	2013
By Employer	5	8	15	20.5	25	16.5	20	12	15.5
By Employee	5	8	15	18	25	23	20	20	20
Total	10	16	30	38.5	50	39.5	40	32	35.5

Source: CPF, 2001 and 2012 Annual Reports.
Note: After 1988, rates varied according to worker age. The rates for 55 and under are shown.

Exhibit 10b.   Central Provident Fund Contribution Rates and Breakdown, 2013

Age Group	Contribution Rate (% of wage)			Credited into (% of wage)		
	By Employer	By Employee	Total	Ordinary Account	Special Account	Medisave Account
35 years and below	16	20	36	23	6	7
35–45 years	16	20	36	21	7	8
45–50 years	16	20	36	19	8	9
50–55 years	14	18.5	32.5	13.5	9.5	9.5
55–60 years	10.5	13	23.5	12	2	9.5
60–65 years	7	7.5	14.5	3.5	1.5	9.5
Above 65 years	6.5	5	11.5	1	1	9.5

Source: CPF, 2012 Annual Report.

Exhibit 10c.   CPF Account Balances and Annual Contributions, 2008–2013

	2008	2009	2010	2011	2012	As of September 2013
Total Number of CPF Members (millions)	3.23	3.29	3.34	3.38	3.42	3.48
Total Number of Active CPF Members (millions)	1.61	1.64	1.7	1.74	1.79	1.83
Total Number of Active Employers	108,279	114,837	118,940	123,263	128,373	133,454
In S$ millions						
Total Members' Balance	151,307.1	166,804.0	185,888.0	207,545.5	230,157.7	248,110.2
Ordinary Account Balance	65,341.1	70,593.8	77,939.5	85,084.8	91,862.0	97,142.8
Special Account Balance	30,547.3	35,389.2	40,392.7	46,533.7	53,191.9	58,775.4
Medisave Account Balance	42,928.2	46,238.0	50,671.2	55,329.3	60,024.4	64,221.2
Retirement Account Balance and Others	12,490.5	14,583.0	16,884.6	20,597.7	25,079.3	27,970.7
Total Contributions	20,294.0	20,125.0	21,993.0	24,628.0	26,048.0	—
Net Withdrawals	10,966.0	10,719.0	9,617.0	10,437.0	11,727.0	—

Source: Central Provident Fund Board, "CPF Statistics," November 20, 2013, http://mycpf.cpf.gov.sg/
CPF/About-Us/CPF-Stats/CPF_Stats.htm, accessed December 9, 2013.

could choose to invest their savings in low-risk assets under the asset enhancement benefit.

The CPF became increasingly important as Singapore's low fertility rate and aging population pushed up the nation's old age dependency ratio. In 2013, there were eight economically active individuals supporting one elderly Singaporean.

Exhibit 11. Distribution of Population by Age

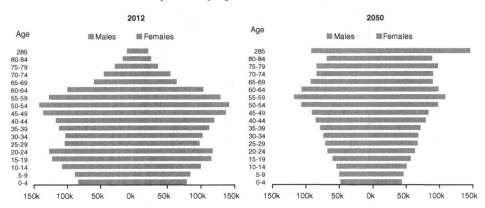

Source: National Population and Talent Division, "A Sustainable Population for a Dynamic Singapore," Population White Paper, January 2013, p. 12.

By 2030, this number was expected to drop to 3.5 (see **Exhibit 11** for population distribution by age).[70] The mandatory participation in the CPF appeared a viable solution for minimizing the demographic problem. By 2011, however, only 45% of CPF members had saved the recommended amount for retirement.[71]

CPF savings were invested in special fully guaranteed government bonds, called Special Singapore Government Securities (SSGS). SSGS earned a coupon rate, which was pegged to the CPF member-interest rate. In December 2011, SSGS stock amounted to S$216 billion, over 60% of the government's gross debt.[72] Insurance funds were invested separately in a range of assets.[73] According to the Singaporean constitution, the government could not spend money raised from such borrowing. Therefore, proceeds were grouped with the rest of the government reserves, which were then invested by the MAS, the Government Investment Corporation (GIC), or Temasek.[74] Singapore had one of the high national savings rates in the world (see **Exhibits 12a** and **12b** for savings and investment details).

Transitioning to a Knowledge-Based Economy

Beginning in the mid-1980s, the Singaporean government recognized that it could no longer compete on cost alone in the increasingly competitive global marketplace. First, the government strengthened regional partnerships to overcome market constraints and thus created the Singapore-Johor-Riau Growth Triangle to capitalize on the economic links between Singapore, Indonesia and Malaysia. Yip explained, "What these two neighbors offer in terms of supply side factors — ample land, manpower, energy — complements what we don't have. We have other strengths. It makes sense for us to join forces with them." In turn, Singapore provided access

Exhibit 12a.   Savings and Investment (as a percentage of GDP)

	2006	2007	2008	2009	2010	2011	2012	2013
GDP	**231,407.2**	**268,062.2**	**269,658.1**	**274,655.3**	**315,921.2**	**334,092.7**	**345,560.5**	**370,064.5**
Savings:								
Consumption (government and private)	48.9%	46.6%	50.4%	49.4%	47.7%	48.5%	48.9%	48.7%
Statistical Discrepancy	−0.3%	−0.2%	1.4%	−0.4%	−1.4%	−1.7%	−1.9%	−2.0%
Gross Domestic Savings	50.8%	53.2%	51.0%	50.2%	50.9%	49.8%	49.2%	49.3%
Net Income and Current Transfers from Abroad	−5.0%	−4.9%	−6.5%	−7.5%	−2.7%	−3.0%	−3.6%	−4.7%
Gross National Savings	**45.9%**	**48.3%**	**44.5%**	**42.7%**	**48.2%**	**46.8%**	**45.6%**	**44.6%**
Investment:								
Net Borrowing and Current Transfers from Abroad	−24.8%	−26.1%	−15.1%	−17.7%	−26.8%	−24.6%	−18.6%	−18.4%
Gross Capital Formation	**21.1%**	**22.2%**	**29.3%**	**25.0%**	**21.4%**	**22.2%**	**27.0%**	**26.2%**

Source: Created by casewriter using data from Singapore Department of Statistics, November 2013. Figures for 2013 are from Economic Survey of Singapore, 2013.

Note: Figures for 2013 are preliminary.

Exhibit 12b. Savings and Investment Contributions (% of GDP)

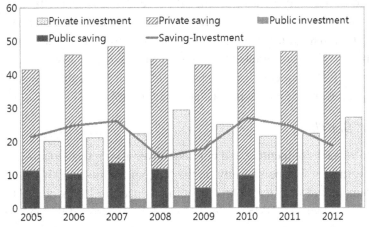

Source: International Monetary Fund, "Singapore — Staff Report for the 2013 Article IV Consultation," IMF Country Report No. 13/328, November 2013, p. 30.

to its infrastructure, capital and growing technology base. Yip continued, "For example, we work with the Indonesian islands of Batam, Bintan and Karimun to enhance the business environment. We do some training for officials. We also look at opportunities MNCs might have and bring those investments into these three islands. Because of our relationship with these companies, we beg[a]n those conversations, and we ask[ed] them, would you consider setting up a production plant in Batam?"[75]

Second, the EDB aimed to transition Singapore into a "total business center."[76] Chemicals; electronics and precision engineering; logistics and transportation services; infocomms; and media were already strong industries in Singapore. To support these clusters, the EDB promoted comple-mentary services, including product redesign, process automation and associated business services, like regional coordination, procurement, administration and management. The government aimed to diversify the economy by promoting services, along with manufacturing, as twin pillars of the economy. The goal was also to create Singapore as a location where MNCs could locate their regional operational headquarters. On the new strategy, the EDB's then assistant managing director, Chua Taik Him, commented:

> We know that what we have been doing well is our cash cow. We don't intend to throw that away, but we are aware that competition is increasing, and we need to be ready for it. We want to encourage innovation and entrepreneurship through the economy. We'll do this by investing in our human capital, technology, and infrastructure. This will be done by Singapore, not just EDB. We have a *national* mindset.[77]

The government also targeted the nation's technology base. In 1991, the National Science and Technology Board (renamed the Agency for Science, Technology, and Research, or A*STAR, in 2001) launched the national technology plan, which committed S$2 billion toward research and development over five years. Under the plan, investments went toward grants to encourage private-sector R&D investment, the recruitment of R&D personnel, and greater funding for research centers.[78] A second five-year plan, worth S$4 billion, was launched in 1996.

The Next "Big Thing"

In order to remain competitive and continue diversifying the economy, the Singaporean government was persistently on the lookout for the next "big thing." While the government had invested in biotechnology since the 1980s, the EDB targeted the biomedical sciences (BMS) industry, which encompassed the pharmaceutical, medical technology, biotechnology and health-care services sectors, as its next key cluster alongside chemicals, engineering and electronics. Setting aside S$1 billion, the government aimed to create a "one-stop" center for biomedical firms. To meet the research and manufacturing needs of the BMS companies, the JTC constructed an 18-acre industrial park, known as "Biopolis," in the One-North development for established and newly started biomedical companies. The chairman of A*STAR, Lim Chuan Poh, explained, "Singapore differentiates itself by being an international research hub in Asia with a rich mix of local and international talent."[79] To encourage aspiring scientists, A*STAR launched a series of scholarships for Singaporean undergraduates and graduates. The EDB, meanwhile, worked to attract MNCs, including Novartis, GlaxoSmithKline and Pfizer.

Since 2000, the output of the BMS sector increased fivefold to S$29.4 billion in 2012, surpassing electronics as the biggest contributor to manufacturing in terms of value added.[80] On the nation's progress, Lim commented, "Biopolis was conceived as part of a bold vision to establish the BMS as a key pillar of Singapore's economy. That vision has become a reality. Today, Biopolis is a thriving eco-system of public research institutions and corporate labs and a vibrant community of local and international biomedical scientists carrying out world-class R&D."[81]

Navigating a New Global Landscape

Following the global financial crisis, Singapore's strong exports led the country's swift recovery, achieving GDP growth of nearly 15% in 2010. However, emerging Asia's robust return to growth was not matched elsewhere, and global demand began to wane. Recognizing that the new global environment altered the effectiveness of Singapore's export-led strategy, the prime minister established the economic strategies committee (ESC) with the goal of "develop[ing] strategies for Singapore to

Exhibit 13. Economic Strategy Committee's Recommended Key Strategies

Source: Economic Strategies Committee, "Report of the ESC: High-skilled People, Innovative Economy, Distinctive Global City," February 1, 2010.

maximize our opportunities in a new world environment, by building our capabilities and making the best use of our resources, with the aim of achieving sustained and inclusive growth."[82] In 2010, the ESC released its recommendations for the next stage of Singapore's development. The new strategy centered on three broad priorities for Singapore's future: "high-skilled people, innovative economy, distinctive global city" (see **Exhibit 13** for the committee's recommended strategies).

Targeting Productivity

For four decades, the Singaporean government had regulated productivity, first under the National Productivity Board (1972), which eventually evolved into SPRING. SPRING's founding mission was "to raise productivity so as to enhance Singapore's competitiveness and economic growth for a better quality of life for our people."[83] SPRING's mission had since focused on helping Singapore's SMEs grow into globally competitive firms and on building trust in the country's products and services.

To coordinate the national effort to raise productivity, the government formed the new Economic Strategies Committee. First on the committee's agenda was addressing productivity. Dependent on large inflows of foreign workers to meet labor demands, the government had to rethink the use of labor force growth as a driver of the economy. Singapore attracted highly skilled international workers to complement its small domestic population in developing high-value manufacturing and services industries. Additionally, as the nation's domestic population became increasingly educated, there was a shortage of individuals willing to fill low-skill positions in construction, tourism and the marine sector; therefore, Singapore turned to lower-cost labor sourced from its Asian neighbors. Since 2000, an estimated 5% of GDP growth per year was driven by increases in labor.[84] Labor input's share of GDP had consistently risen since the 1980s, while total factor productivity had declined (see **Exhibit 14** for employment and productivity figures, and **Exhibits 15a** and **15b** for contributions to GDP growth and a comparison of productivity).

Foreign workers had come to represent nearly a third of the workforce, one of the highest ratios in the world. The influx of foreigners was causing friction among Singaporeans, who blamed these non-residents for taxing the public transportation system and exacerbating the country's space limitations. As the number of highly compensated international workers grew, so did housing costs. The growth in foreign workers was also expanding wage distribution. As Singapore sought highly skilled and educated professionals, often from abroad, the nation had to offer competitive wages comparable with other advanced economies, driving the upper band of wage distribution ever higher. The number of individuals with more than US$1 million in "investable assets" was forecast to double from 2010 to 2015, reaching 133,000 individuals.[85] On the opposite end of the wage scale, the availability of low-skilled workers in Asia pulled down wages.

Singapore also struggled with an aging population. From 2011 to 2030, the median age of Singapore's population would rise from 39 years to 47 years.[86] With a low fertility rate, there were fewer young citizens to replace retiring Singaporeans, causing a drop in the nation's domestic workforce. Moreover, evidence suggested that there existed a negative correlation between a nation's median age and total factor productivity.[87]

In response, the ESC set the ambitious goal of productivity growth of 2% to 3% per annum from 2010 to 2020. In tackling the nation's long-standing productivity and demographic problems, the government proposed three strategies. First, the government determined that it needed to reduce the nation's reliance on foreign workers via a set of foreign-worker levies, which would gradually be increased from July 2010 to July 2012. The goal of the pricing mechanism was to stabilize the foreign share of the workforce at around one-third of the population. The levy was designed to be flexible, in order to maintain Singapore's pro-business environment and be responsive to economic fluctuations. By restricting labor access, the government hoped that companies, particularly SMEs, would invest more in productivity improvements and the skills of their employees. Former EDB Managing Director Swan Gin Beh explained, "SMEs have had the ability to bring in lower-cost workers from outside of Singapore instead of biting the bullet and investing in productivity measures."[88]

Exhibit 14. Employment and Productivity

	2002	2003	2004	2005	2006	2007	2008	2009	2010	2011	2012	2013
Labor Force (thousands)	2,320.6	2,312.3	2,341.9	na	2,594.1	2,750.5	2,939.9	3,030.0	3,135.9	3,237.1	3,361.8	3,443.7
Resident Labor Force (thousands)	1,667.9	1,706.4	1,733.4	na	1,880.8	1,918.1	1,928.3	1,985.7	2,047.3	2,080.1	2,119.6	2,138.8
Unemployment Rate	3.6	4.0	3.4	3.1	2.7	2.1	2.3	3.0	2.2	2.0	1.9	1.9
Median Monthly Income (including CPF), S$	2,380.0	2,410.0	2,326.0	na	2,449.0	2,543.0	2,897.0	2,927.0	3,000.0	3,249.0	3,480.0	3,705.0
Real Wage Index (2005 = 100)	94.1	95.3	97.1	100.0	102.2	106.3	105.1	101.7	104.5	105.2	102.9	104.9
Real Wage Growth (%)	1.2	1.2	1.9	3.0	2.2	4.0	−1.1	−3.2	2.7	0.7	−2.2	2.0
Nominal Wage Growth (%)	0.8	1.7	3.6	3.4	3.2	6.2	5.4	−2.7	5.6	6.0	2.3	4.4
Labor Productivity Growth (%)	5.6	5.5	7.0	4.0	0.8	2.2	−4.6	−2.9	10.3	2.5	−2.0	1.5
Unit Labor Cost Growth (%)	−3.7	−3.4	−3.8	1.4	2.0	6.1	4.2	0.8	−2.6	3.5	4.1	NA
Total Factor Productivity Growth (%)	5.2	4.0	7.0	4.5	2.6	3.1	−4.8	−4.0	10.3	3.8	−0.7	2.7

Source: Created by casewriter using data from the Economist Intelligence Unit, March 2014. Labor force, income, and unit labor cost data are from the Ministry of Manpower, "Singapore Yearbook of Manpower Statistics, 2013," June 2013.

Exhibit 15a. Contributions to GDP Growth (percentages; decade averages)

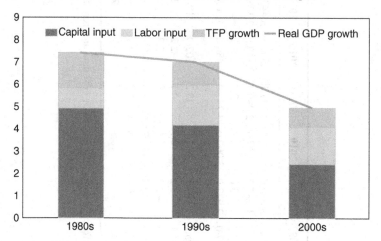

Source: International Monetary Fund, "Singapore 2012 Article IV Consultation," IMF Country Report No. 12/248, August 2012.

Exhibit 15b. International Comparison of Sectoral Productivity

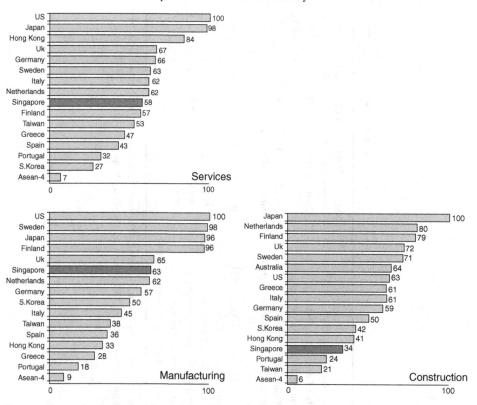

Source: Economic Strategies Committee, "Report of the ESC: High-skilled People, Innovative Economy, Distinctive Global City," February 1, 2010.

The levy amount varied according to the qualification of the worker and the existing share of employed foreigners in that sector. By applying a sectoral approach, the government could remain flexible in attracting talent in the sciences, engineering, design and finance. Per-worker levies varied between S$250 and S$750 per month.[89] However, employers were not required to pay CPF contributions for their foreign workers, causing some critics to argue that hiring foreigner workers was still more profitable than hiring domestically. Additionally, the levies risked undermining the pro-business environment for international investors that Singapore had been refining for the past 50 years. A letter from nine foreign business groups, including the U.S. Chamber of Commerce, explained,

> Singapore's openness to foreign labor has enabled it to attract, retain and absorb the best of foreign talent, providing it with a clear competitive advantage over its neighbors . . . . [Although] Singapore continues to attract significant foreign investment, we nevertheless fear current implementation of revised labor policy risks negatively impacting Singapore's economy and reputation as an open economy.[90]

Between Singapore's aging population and reduction in foreign laborers, the country would experience a significant reduction in labor force growth, which the government hoped to counterbalance by increasing both labor productivity and the labor participation rate. Yip explained, "A big part of our challenge is on the supply side domestically — the manpower situation. [It means] a transition from where we were. It means an adjustment that is not going to be so straightforward for companies. How do they make the transition? And us as an economy? If it is not smoothly done, we lose competitiveness, and we lose companies. It is a decade-long restructuring."[91] In April 2010, the National Productivity and Continuing Education Council (NPCEC) was established to coordinate the national-level push to improve productivity through business restructuring and retraining the workforce. Emphasizing the importance of national coordination, Tan Kai Hoe commented, "You have to make sure the companies and the skill sets of the people are all moving together in tandem to shift the economy."[92]

Singapore's productivity had lagged behind that of other developed nations in many sectors, and the NPCEC targeted individual industries for improvement. Chaired by the deputy prime minister, the council selected 16 priority sectors, including construction, electronics, precision engineering, accountancy, and logistics, for which specific steps to increase productivity were outlined in sectoral "road maps." For example, for the construction industry, the government pledged S$250 million in incentives to develop civil engineering capabilities, adopting new technologies and upgrading workers' skills.[93] Each sector also had a target goal; within construction, the council aimed to improve productivity by 20% over the course of the decade.

Additionally, the NPCEC's sectoral approach was complemented by three horizontal strategies, such as encouraging the adoption of infocomm technologies, an S$100 million fund to encourage productivity improvements through higher wages and more training for low-income workers, and greater educational opportunities for SMEs.

On the employee-level, the NPCEC was also in charge of expanding the national continuing education and training (CET) program in order to supply Singaporeans with the skills needed for employment in new growth industries. The program set the goal that 50% of the resident workforce would hold at least a diploma qualification by 2020, in comparison to 36% in 2007.[94] Through the creation of two new CET centers specializing in aerospace engineering, precision engineering, logistics, social services and process manufacturing and through the expansion of existing centers, the NPCEC aimed to train 240,000 individuals per year by 2015, up from 80,000 in 2010.[95]

Singapore also aimed to increase its resident labor force participation rate, despite having a low unemployment rate of around 2%. The female participation rate among those ages 25 to 64 was 69.9% in 2011, while male participation measured 92.1%, one of the highest in the world.[96] First, the government adopted new initiatives to encourage later retirements. In 2011, the government introduced the Special Employment Credit, designed to encourage employees to hire Singaporeans over the age of 50. The credit amounted to 8% of an employee's monthly wages. While the minimum retirement age was maintained at 62, the Retirement and Re-employment Act, instituted in January 2012, required employers to offer reemployment contracts to employees until the age of 65.[97] The government also continued to promote flexible schedules through its Work-life Works! Fund, which provided a onetime grant to employers for adopting work-life strategies in the workplace, such as enhanced leave and flexible hours and the Flexi-works! Scheme, which provided financial incentives for companies to hire part-time workers.

Innovative Economy

The government also aimed to derive greater commercial value from its R&D efforts. Singapore pledged to raise its R&D expenditure to 3.5% of GDP by 2015.[98] From 2011 to 2015, the government committed S$16 billion in order to turn Singapore into a leading R&D hub.[99] However, the majority of R&D spending came from the private sector (see **Exhibit 16** for details on R&D expenditure). As part of the plan, the government pledged S$735 million in scholarships and fellowships to attract new talent, introduced greater competition-based funding in order to spur innovation, prioritized projects with a multidisciplinary approach, offered greater support for commercialization efforts, and encouraged more public–private collaborations.

Exhibit 16. Research and Development Expenditure: Gross, Business and Public (% GDP)

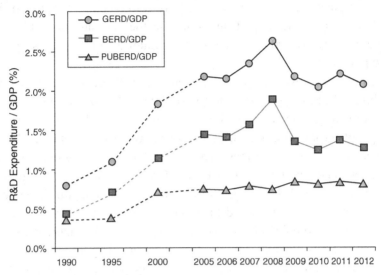

Source: Agency for Science, Technology and Research, "National Survey of Research and Development in Singapore, 2012," December 2013.

There existed much interagency collaboration to improve commercial innovation. The EDB's chairman explained, "We go see a company, and they say we want to build a business control tower, but we also want to build innovation capability. After that we will bring along our A*STAR colleagues because A*STAR has built up the capabilities of innovation in the Singapore economy, and we want the company to have access to that. Then it becomes a joint conversation between the EDB, A*STAR and the company."[100] SPRING's chairman, Philip Yeo, elaborated, "If you are a company looking for science expertize, you can loan out an A*STAR scientist, and SPRING will help pay."[101]

Singapore as a Global-Asia Hub

The ESC's growth strategy also aimed to strengthen Singapore's role as a regional and global hub. Yip explained, "We are a hub for global companies in Asia and, in turn, also a location for Asian companies to go global. It's global companies coming here, building a strategic base for Asia and beyond. It's all part of Singapore's Global-Asia positioning."[102] In addition to attracting international investors through its high-value manufacturing, Singapore aimed to grow complementary services, such as R&D, IP management and headquarter-related activities. Beh explained: "It's not just about the clustering of industries, but also about the clustering of skills. For example, this enabled us to extend into marketing and branding activities." Singapore aimed to attract MNCs looking to expand into Asia by developing its

Asian market research intelligence and training capable "Asia-ready" managers. Moreover, Singapore's reputation for integrity differentiated the nation from its Asian neighbors and encouraged investment in the new nutrition and consumer products cluster. Beh clarified, "The trust premium is very high, and people are willing to pay for it."[103]

Furthermore, the government sought to encourage Singaporean firms looking to expand abroad. IE Singapore aimed to foster globally competitive firms through its "global company partnership." IE Singapore sought to understand a firm's existing strategy, plan for overseas growth, and then draw upon its network of 35 global offices to provide recommendations on how to best move into international markets. The agency also helped with manpower development, market access support, and access to financing. In 2012, the government introduced trade financing and political risk insurance, which provided financing to mitigate the performance impact on investments due to political uncertainties. In 2011, IE Singapore supported 336 international projects, the majority of which were in emerging markets.[104] IE Singapore's CEO commented, "It is critical for Singaporean companies to look at internationalization as a long-term competitive strategy. It is not a question of whether we should venture into these markets, but how quickly and effectively we do so."[105]

Singapore also aimed to become a global-Asia financial hub. In 2012, financial services accounted for 12% of GDP.[106] While operating as a regional financial center, many speculated whether Singapore would surpass Switzerland as the world's leading wealth management center. In 2012, assets under management in Singapore reached S$1.63 trillion (US$1.29 trillion).[107] Switzerland, by contrast, held US$2.9 trillion. Since the 2008 financial crisis, Asia's growth rate remained robust in relation to the rest of the world, and private wealth followed a similar trend; BCG estimated that private wealth in Asia grew 12.9% from 2012 to 2013, as compared with 6% in North America, Europe, and Japan.[108] Consequently, 70% of the assets held in Singapore originated from Asia.

Singapore aimed to grow its tourism industry. In 2010, the country opened its first two casinos, Sentosa and Marina Bay Sands. Within two years, the country's receipts from tourism had doubled to S$18 billion.[109] Moreover, the ESC recommended that Singapore develop its "cultural tourism sector," including the rejuvenation of the Civic District as an arts and cultural center.

Negotiating Land and Energy Constraints

As Singapore's population continued to grow, the government had to carefully consider how to use the island's limited resources. The ESC recommended accelerating the shift toward more land-efficient activities through continued master planning of industrial parks. The government also explored the possibility of using subterranean spaces to expand the nation's footprint.

In 2013, the government released its new draft master plan, which laid out Singapore's urban development strategy for the next 10 to 15 years. Singapore ranked as having the highest quality of life in Asia, and the master plan provisioned for more public housing and evenly distributed recreational green space. The master plan also provided for expansion of the public transportation system; by 2030, over 80% of Singaporeans would live within a 10-minute walk from the rapid transit system.[110] The plan would also help decentralize economic activity across the island.

As a small city-state, Singapore was disadvantaged by its lack of any of its own natural resources, and remained dependent on energy imports. Moreover, Singapore was expected to experience growth in competition over energy within Asia during the coming years. ASEAN as a whole was a net importer of energy, and Southeast Asia's energy demand was forecast to grow 80% over the next 25 years.[111] As a result, energy security was a growing concern. More than 80% of Singapore's electricity was generated from natural gas, piped in from Indonesia and Malaysia via four separate pipelines. In 2006, the government introduced its plan to build the country's first liquefied natural gas (LNG) terminal on Jurong Island to reduce reliance on piped imports. In May 2013, the LNG terminal was completed, initially capable of processing 3.5 million tons per year. This capacity was expected to increase to 6 million tons per year by the end of 2013.[112] The new terminal also opened up opportunities for LNG-related businesses, including increased trade and bunkering, that is, the provision of fuel to ships. Singapore was already the largest bunkering port in the world.

Addressing Social Concerns

We must now make a strategic shift in our approach to nation-building.[113]

— Lee Hsien Loong, National Day Rally Speech

In August 2013, Prime Minister Lee opened his National Day Rally speech arguing that Singapore was at a turning point. With a growing number of social pressures facing Singaporeans, the prime minister contended that the government would have to reconceptualize how it supported the individual. Announcing significant alterations to the nation's health-care, housing and education systems, the prime minister stressed that Singapore had to remain self-reliant, and that these changes could not come at the cost of passing debt on to future generations (see **Exhibit 17** for an overview of public finance figures).

First, the government pledged to maintain Singapore as a "fair and a just society," despite the nation's growing wealth inequality and rising house prices. Since 1990,

Exhibit 17.   Public Finance (S$ billions)

	FY2005	FY2006	FY2007	FY2008	FY2009	FY2010	FY2011	FY2012	FY2013	FY2014 (Budgeted)
Operating Revenue	**28.2**	**31.3**	**40.4**	**41.1**	**39.5**	**46.1**	**51.1**	**54.3**	**57.1**	**59.5**
Tax Revenue, of which:	25.7	28.8	36.6	37.7	36.6	41.8	46.1	48.8	51.2	53.2
Income tax	11.7	13.2	14.9	17.1	16.8	18.1	20.2	21.9	22.0	23.5
Assets taxes	1.9	2.1	2.6	2.9	2.0	2.8	3.9	3.7	4.1	4.4
Taxes on motor vehicles	1.4	1.7	2.2	1.8	1.9	1.9	1.9	1.9	1.6	1.4
Other tax revenue	10.7	11.8	16.9	15.8	16.0	19.1	20.0	21.3	23.4	24.0
Other Operating	2.5	2.5	3.7	3.4	2.9	4.2	5.0	5.5	5.9	6.3
Total Expenditures	**28.6**	**29.9**	**33.0**	**38.1**	**41.9**	**45.3**	**46.6**	**47.3**	**52.3**	**56.7**
Social Development	11.7	12.7	14.3	15.9	18.1	20.1	21.7	21.6	23.4	27.0
Education	6.1	7.0	7.5	8.2	8.7	9.9	10.7	10.3	11.0	11.5
Health	1.8	1.9	2.2	2.7	3.6	3.7	3.9	4.5	5.5	7.1
Security	11.8	12.4	13.2	14.0	14.4	14.6	14.8	14.3	17.7	17.2
Economic Development	3.7	3.8	4.3	6.9	8.0	9.2	8.6	9.5	9.5	10.0
Government	1.4	1.1	1.2	1.2	1.3	1.4	1.5	1.9	1.7	2.4
Primary Surplus	-0.5	1.4	7.4	3.0	-2.3	0.7	4.5	7.0	4.8	2.8
Special Transfers	0.8	3.6	2.1	7.1	5.5	7.1	8.4	8.9	8.8	12.1
Net Investment Income	2.8	2.1	2.4	4.3	7.0	7.4	7.9	7.9	7.9	8.1
Overall Budget Surplus	**1.5**	**-0.1**	**7.7**	**0.2**	**-0.8**	**1.0**	**4.0**	**5.8**	**3.9**	**-1.2**

Source: Yearbook of Statistics Singapore, 2013. FY2012 and FY2013 figures are from the Economic Survey of Singapore, 2013. FY2014 figures are from Ministry of Finance, March 2014.

Note: Figures for FY2013 are preliminary. Expenditure figures include both development and operating expenditures. Special transfers refer to discretionary transfers made by the government; these include one-off direct transfers to businesses and households, as well as top-ups to endowments and trust funds.

Exhibit 18.   Gini Index, Before and After Government Transfers and Taxes

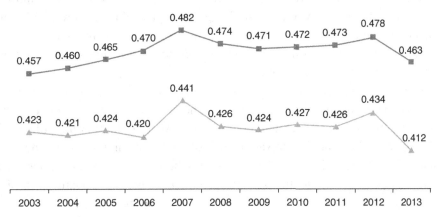

■ Based on Household Income from Work Per Household Member
(Including Employer CPF Contributions)

▲ Based on Household Income from Work Per Household Member
(Including Employer CPF Contributions) After Accounting for Goverment
Transfers and Taxes*

Source: Singapore Department of Statistics, "Key Household Income Trends, 2013," February 2014.

Singapore's Gini coefficient had risen, and it remained one of the highest in Asia (see **Exhibit 18** for the Gini index from 2003 to 2013).[114] Moreover, BCG found that Singapore had the highest concentration of millionaires in the world.[115] Housing prices were also on the rise. Between 2009 and 2012, private home prices grew 55%, and Singaporeans were struggling to keep pace with the price growth.[116] Over this same period, housing debt grew 18% per annum, and total outstanding home loans amounted to 46% of GDP.[117]

The government pledged that housing had and would continue to be an essential element of sharing the nation's success. The prime minister maintained, "Home ownership is still a fundamental principle for Singapore."[118] In 2011, the HDB unlinked new flat prices from the resale market to keep prices affordable for first-time buyers. While prices on the resale market increased 12.5% since the unlinking, new flat prices remained stable.[119] To ensure adequate supply, over 72,000 flats were constructed in the 2012–2013 financial year, up 30% from the previous year.[120] Additionally, the government increased the Special CPF Housing Grant and the Step-Up Housing Grant to help low- and middle-income households afford three- and four-room flats.

Second, the prime minister pledged to strengthen social safety nets by promising universal health care. The existing catastrophic health insurance scheme, Medishield, was converted into Medishield Life. Under the new plan, coverage would continue for life, rather than stopping at age 90, and it would cover all

Singaporeans.[121] While benefits were also set to increase, premiums would also rise. Group president of the GIC, Lim Siong Guan, praised the government's commitment to health-care issues: "Often, Singapore's approach tends to be purely rational. This time, and I believe it was quite deliberate, it addressed the emotions. Health care for the aging is an emotional issue."[122]

Lastly, the government reaffirmed its commitment to a mobile, meritocratic society by preserving open access to education. The government pledged to contribute between S$200 and S$240 per annum to the Edusave account of every child aged 7 to 16, which could be applied toward educational enrichment programs. The prime minister also vowed to keep admissions to top schools open, providing greater bursary schemes to low-income students and encouraging admissions boards to consider wide-ranging qualities, such as character, leadership and resilience.[123]

Conclusion

While the prime minister's speech was well received, many worried whether the government would be able to strike a balance between enhancing social safety nets and maintaining the culture of self-reliance, which had been critical to national economic success. Menon explained, "I am concerned about how this new social compact will evolve. Our challenge is about creating one that is compassionate yet does not lead down a slippery slope towards unsustainability. The risk is that more will be demanded by the middle class even as the government extends help to the poor. The government is very judicious and careful how it does this, but in a democracy, you can't control this entirely."[124] Others wondered whether the government's actions would create a culture of dependency among future Singaporeans. Koh stated, "I worry about the new generation who has never seen Singapore as a colony, whose expectations of government are rising dramatically."[125] Without the guidance of the pioneer generation, would Singapore maintain its legacy of economic drive? Lim summarized, "What I worry about is whether young Singaporeans understand that inheritance is not something to be squandered but something we keep working on to keep up its value. People recognize that Singapore in its early years was man-made. The future success of Singapore must continue to be a human creation."[126]

As Singapore's 50th anniversary approached, Prime Minister Lee wondered whether his predecessor was correct. Had Singapore Inc., after a half-century of impressive growth, reached its midlife crisis?

Endnotes

[1] Goh Chok Tong, "Averting a mid-life crisis," *Today*, August 12, 2013, http://www.todayonline.com/singapore/averting-mid-life-crisis, accessed December 9, 2013.

[2] Interview with Lee Hsien Loong, Prime Minister of Singapore.

[3] Professor Vietor is immensely grateful to Daren Tang (AMP 185) for helping to arrange interviews and facilitating his research trip to Singapore. He would like to give an additional thanks to Abel Ang (AMP 183) for his assistance while in Singapore.

[4] World Bank Development Indicators database, accessed December 9, 2013.

[5] Lee Kuan Yew, "Lee Kuan Yew on fate of Singapore in 100 years' time," *Strait Times*, August 11, 2013, http://www.straitstimes.com/breaking-news/singapore/story/lee-kuan-yew-fate-singapore-100-years-time-20130811, accessed December 9, 2013.

[6] Interview with Leo Yip, Chairman of the Economic Development Board.

[7] Department of Statistics Singapore, "Yearbook of Statistics Singapore 2013," August 2013, http://www.singstat.gov.sg/publications/publications_and_papers/reference/yearbook_2013/yos2013.pdf.

[8] W. G. Huff, *The Economic Growth of Singapore: Trade and Development in the Twentieth Century* (Cambridge, UK: Cambridge University Press, 1997), p. 8.

[9] *Ibid*, p. 11.

[10] "Singapore is Out," *Straits Times*, August 10, 1965.

[11] World Bank Development Indicators database, accessed December 9, 2013.

[12] Lee Kuan Yew, *From Third World to First: The Singapore Story, 1963–2000* (New York: Harper Collins, 2003), p. 3.

[13] Chan Chin Bock, *Heart Work: Stories of How EDB Steered the Singapore Economy from 1961 into the 21st Century* (Singapore: Singapore Economic Development Board, 2002), p. 15.

[14] Housing Development Board, "HDB History," February 3, 2012, http://www.hdb.gov.sg/fi10/fi10320p. nsf/w/AboutUsHDBHistory?OpenDocument, accessed December 9, 2013.

[15] *Ibid.*

[16] Lee, *From Third World to First*, p. 58.

[17] *Ibid.*, p. 7.

[18] Elections Department of Singapore, "Types of Electoral Divisions," October 3, 2013, http://www.eld.gov.sg/elections_type_electoral.html, accessed December 9, 2013.

[19] Parliament of Singapore, "Members of Parliament," December 5, 2013, http://www.parliament.gov.sg/members-parliament, accessed December 9, 2013.

[20] Interview with Lee Hsien Loong, Prime Minister of Singapore.

[21] Lee, *From Third World to First*.

[22] Christopher Tan, "COE prices mixed in latest exercise; aggressive promos keep small car market up," *Strait Times*, November 20, 2013, http://www.straitstimes.com/breaking-news/singapore/story/coe-prices-end-mixed-latest-bidding-exercise-20131120, accessed December 5, 2013.

[23] Reporters Without Borders, "Press Freedom Index 2011/2012," January 25, 2012.

[24] Sumiko Tan, "PM: Your vote will have immediate impact on your life," *Straits Times*, December 24, 1996.

[25] Shamim Adam and Weiyi Lim, "Singapore's Lee Retains Power with Smallest Margin Since 1965," Bloomberg, May 7, 2011, http://www.bloomberg.com/news/2011-05-07/singapore-s-people-s-action-party-keeps-parliamentary-majority-state-says.html, accessed December 7, 2013.

26 Prime Minister's Office, "Salaries for a Capable and Committed Government," December 30, 2011, http://www.psd.gov.sg/content/dam/psd_web/white_paper/White %20Paper%20-%20Salaries%20for%20a%20Capable%20and%20Committed%20 Govt.pdf/jcr%3acontent/renditions/original.res/White%20Paper%20-%20Salaries %20for%20a%20Capable%20and%20Committed%20Govt.pdf.

27 *Ibid.*

28 Shamim Adam, "Singapore May Cut Lee's Pay to $1.7 million as Minister Salaries Reduced," Bloomberg, January 4, 2012, http://www.bloomberg.com/news/2012-01-04/singapore-to-cut-ministers-pay-on-panelrecom   mendations-after-2011-polls.html, accessed December 9, 2013.

29 Interview with Koh Boon Hwee, Chairman of Far East Orchard.

30 Transparency International, Corruption Perceptions Index 2012, http://www.transpa rency. org/country#SGP, accessed December 9, 2013.

31 Quoted from Huff, *The Economic Growth of Singapore*, p. 309.

32 Lee, *From Third World to First*, p. 59.

33 Temasek, "Portfolio at Inception," *Temasek Review 2013*, http://www.temasekreview. com.sg/#portfolio-temasekPortfolioAtInception, accessed December 9, 2013.

34 Temasek, "Portfolio Value Since Inception," *Temasek Review 2013*, http://www.tema sekreview.com.sg/#portfolio-portfolioValueSinceInception,   accessed   December   9, 2013.

35 Temasek, "Overview from Our Chairman," *Temasek Review 2013*, http://www.tema sekreview.com.sg/ #overview-fromOurChairman, accessed December 9, 2013.

36 Carlos D. Ramirez and Ling Hui Tan, "Singapore, Inc. Versus the Private Sector: Are Government-Linked Companies Different?" International Monetary Authority, Working Paper WP 03/156, July 2003.

37 Huff, *The Economic Growth of Singapore*, p. 36.

38 Interview with Leo Yip, Chairman of the EDB.

39 World Bank, "Ease of Doing Business in Singapore 2013," http://www.doingbusiness. org/data/exploreeconomies/singapore/, accessed December 9, 2013.

40 Kris Schwab, "The Global Competitiveness Report 2013–2014," World Economic Forum, 2013.

41 Balance of Payments, Singapore Yearbook of Statistics, 2013.

42 Economic Development Board, "Our History," September 15, 2012, http://www. edb.gov.sg/content/edb/en/why-singapore/about-singapore/our-history/1960s.html, accessed December 15, 2013.

43 Lee, *From Third World to First*, p. 61.

44 *Ibid.*, p. 62.

45 Tan Sek Toh, in Bock, *Heart Work*, p. 38.

46 World Bank, "Ease of Doing Business in Singapore 2013," http://www.doingbusiness. org/data/ exploreeconomies/singapore/, accessed December 9, 2013.

47 *Ibid.*

48 J. F. Ermisch and W. G. Huff (1999), "Hypergrowth in an East Asian NIC: Public Policy and Capital Accumulation in Singapore," *World Development*, Vol. 27, no. 1, p. 26.

[49] Economic Development Board, "Incentives for Businesses," November 15, 2013, http://www.edb.gov.sg/content//en/why-singapore/ready-to-invest/incentives-for-busin esses.html, accessed December 9, 2013.

[50] World Bank, "Ease of Doing Business in Singapore 2013."

[51] Interview with Heng Swee Keat, Minister of Education.

[52] Goh Chor Boon and S. Gopinathan, "The Development of Education in Singapore Since 1965," World Bank, June 2006, p. 22.

[53] *Ibid.*, p. 18.

[54] *Ibid.*, p. 8.

[55] UNCTAD, "World Investment Report 2005: Transnational Corporations and the Internationalization of R&D," United Nations, 2005, p. 205.

[56] *Ibid.*, p. 205.

[57] Quoted from Richard H.K. Vietor and Emily J. Thompson, "Singapore, Inc.," HBS No. 703-040 (Boston: Harvard Business School Publishing, 2008).

[58] Teo Zhiwei, "Educational Profile of Singapore Resident Non-Students, 2002–2012," *Singapore Department of Statistics Newsletter*, March 2013.

[59] Interview with Koh Boon Hwee, Chairman of Far East Orchard.

[60] Interview with Tharman Shanmugaratnam, Deputy Prime Minister and Minister of Finance.

[61] Interview with Tan Kai Hoe, Chief Executive Officer of SPRING Singapore.

[62] Interview with Philip Yeo, Chairman of SPRING Singapore.

[63] Huff, *The Economic Growth of Singapore*, p. 35.

[64] Quoted from Vietor and Thompson, "Singapore, Inc."

[65] Interview with Ravi Menon, Managing Director of the Monetary Authority of Singapore (MAS).

[66] Monetary Authority of Singapore, "Monetary Policy Operations in Singapore," March 2013.

[67] Interview with Ravi Menon, Managing Director of the Monetary Authority of Singapore (MAS).

[68] Ministry of Manpower, "Central Provident Fund," September 25, 2013, http://www.mom.gov.sg/ employment-practices/employment-rights-conditions/cpf/Pages/default.aspx, accessed December 9, 2013.

[69] "Medisave Minimum Sum," *CPF Trends*, February 2013, http://mycpf.cpf.gov.sg/NR/rdonlyres/ 47052D5F-31BF-4D2F-8CDA-CC15E91824D0/0/CPFTrends_Medisave MinimumSum2012.pdf

[70] Central Provident Fund, "Overview," January 22, 2013, http://mycpf.cpf.gov.sg/ CPF/About-Us/Intro, accessed December 9, 2013.

[71] Ministry of Finance, "Growing Incomes and Strengthening Social Security," 2012, http://app.mof.gov.sg/data/cmsresource/SPOR/2012/SPOR%202012%20Chapter% 202.pdf.

[72] Ministry of Finance, "Singapore Government Borrowings: An Overview," July 2012, http://app.mof. gov.sg/data/cmsresource/SGB.pdf.

73 OECD, "About the Central Provident Fund," 2012, http://www.oecd.org/finance/private-pensions/46260911.pdf.

74 GIC, "GIC and the Reserves of Singapore," http://www.gic.com.sg/en/faqs/search/ 201-gic-and-the-reserves-of-singapore#47, accessed December 9, 2013.

75 Interview with Leo Yip, Chairman of the EDB.

76 Economic Committee, "The Singapore Economy: New Directions," Ministry of Trade and Industry Singapore, February 1986, http://www.mti.gov.sg/ResearchRoom/Documents/app.mti.gov.sg/data/pages/885/doc/econ.pdf, p. 7.

77 Quoted from Vietor and Thompson, "Singapore, Inc."

78 Sachin Chaturvedi (2005), "Evolving a National System of Biotechnology Innovation: Some Evidence from Singapore," Science, Technology & Society, Vol. 10, no. 1, pp. 105–127.

79 Interview with Lim Chuan Poh, Chairman of A*STAR.

80 Agency for Science, Technology and Research, "Singapore's Biopolis: A Success Story," media release, October 16, 2013, http://www.a-star.edu.sg/Portals/0/media/Press%20Release/Media%20Release_Gala%20 Dinner_16Oct.pdf; also, Ministry of Trade and Industry, "Economic Survey of Singapore, 2012," February 2013, http://www.mti.gov.sg/ResearchRoom/SiteAssets/Pages/Economic-Survey-of-Singapore-2012/FullReport_AES2012.pdf.

81 Agency for Science, Technology and Research, "Singapore's Biopolis: A Success Story."

82 Economic Strategies Committee, "Report of the Economic Strategies Committee: High-skilled People, Innovative Economy, Distinctive Global City," February 1, 2010.

83 Ministry of Trade and Industry Singapore, "About MTI: SPRING Singapore (Standards, Productivity and Innovation Board)," September 1, 2008, http://www.mti.gov.sg/AboutMTI/Pages/SPRING%20Singapore%20 (Standards,%20Productivity%20and%20Innovation%20Board).aspx, accessed February 3, 2014.

84 Ibid.

85 Jeremy Grant, "Singapore PM promises 'strategic shift' to protect city state's success," Financial Times, August 18, 2013, http://www.ft.com/intl/cms/s/0/94e0e446-0822-11e3-badc-00144feabdc0.html, accessed December 9, 2013.

86 Ministry of Trade and Industry, "Occasional Paper on Population and Economy," September 25, 2012.

87 Ibid.

88 Interview with Swan Gin Beh, Permanent Secretary of the Ministry of Law, former Managing Director of the EDB.

89 Ministry of Manpower, "Levies & Quotas for Hiring Foreign Workers," October 9, 2013, http://www.mom.gov.sg/foreign-manpower/foreign-worker-levies/Pages/ levies-quotas-for-hiring-foreign-workers.aspx, accessed December 9, 2013.

90 Neil Gough, "Singapore to Give Citizens Priority for Job Openings," New York Times, September 23, 2013.

91 Interview with Leo Yip, Chairman of the EDB.

92 Interview with Tan Kai Hoe, Chief Executive Officer of SPRING Singapore.

93 Ministry of Finance, "Raising Productivity: Skills, Innovation, and Economic Restructuring," Singapore Budget 2010, February 24, 2010, http://www.mof.gov.sg/budget_2010/key_initiatives/raising_productivity. html, accessed December 9, 2013.

94 Ministry of Manpower, "Continuing Education & Training," October 10, 2012, http://www.mom.gov.sg/skills-training-and-development/adult-and-continuing-education/cet-masterplan/Pages/default.aspx, accessed December 9, 2013.

95 Economic Strategies Committee, "Report of the Economic Strategies Committee: High-skilled People, Innovative Economy, Distinctive Global City," February 1, 2010.

96 Ministry of Trade and Industry, "Occasional Paper on Population and Economy," September 25, 2012.

97 Ministry of Manpower, "Retirement and Re-employment Act," June 20, 2013, http://www.mom.gov.sg/employment-practices/employment-rights-conditions/retirement/Pages/ retirement. aspx, accessed December 9, 2013.

98 Economic Strategies Committee, "Report of the Economic Strategies Committee: High-skilled People, Innovative Economy, Distinctive Global City."

99 National Research Foundation, "Overview," September 27, 2013, http://www.nrf.gov.sg/research/r-d-ecosystem, accessed December 9, 2013.

100 Interview with Leo Yip, Chairman of the EDB.

101 Interview with Philip Yeo, Chairman of SPRING Singapore.

102 Interview with Leo Yip, Chairman of the EDB.

103 Interview with Swan Gin Beh, Permanent Secretary of the Ministry of Law, former Managing Director of the EDB.

104 Jonathan Kwok, "Singapore firms still growing strongly abroad," *Straits Times*, reprinted by SPRING Singapore, February 21, 2012, http://www.spring.gov.sg/NewsEvents/ITN/Pages/Singapore-firms-still-growing-strongly-abroad-20120221.aspx#.UqY4VvRDvXo, accessed December 9, 2013.

105 *Ibid.*

106 "Singapore Growth Surprises on Surge in Financial Services," Reuters, May 22, 2013, http://www.cnbc. com/id/100759827, accessed December 9, 2013.

107 Ravi Menon, "MAS Annual Report 2012/2013," press conference, July 23, 2013, http://www.mas.gov.sg/News-and-Publications/Speeches-and-Monetary-Policy-Statements/2013/MAS-Annual-Report-2012-13-Press-Conference.aspx, accessed December 9, 2013.

108 Jeremy Grant, "Singapore loosens Switzerland's grip on wealth management," *Financial Times*, July 23, 2013, http://www.ft.com/intl/cms/s/2/048c3630-f39f-11e2-942f-00144feabdc0.html#axzz2jJ8CJvoI, accessed December 9, 2013.

109 "Casino Fever in Asia," editorial, *New York Times*, January 23, 2014.

110 Urban Redevelopment Authority, "Draft Masterplan 2013," November 20, 2013, http://www.ura.gov.sg/ MS/DMP2013/introduction/master-plan-2013.aspx, accessed December 9, 2013.

111 S. Iswaran, "Speech during the Committee of Supply Debate Under Head V," speech, March 11, 2013.

112 Singapore LNG Corporation, "Our Business Model," http://www.slng.com.sg/ business-our-business-model.html, accessed December 9, 2013.

113 Lee Hsien Loong, "National Day Rally 2013," speech, ITE Headquarters and College Central, August 18, 2013.

114 International Monetary Fund, "Singapore — Staff Report for the 2013 Article IV Consultation," IMF Country Report No. 13/328, November 2013, p. 7.

115 Boston Consulting Group, "BCG: Wealth Managers Need Wake-up Call to Lift Profits amid Tough Markets," press release, May 21, 2012, http://www.bcg.com/media/PressReleaseDetails.aspx?id=tcm:12-106884, accessed December 10, 2013.

116 International Monetary Fund, "Singapore — Staff Report for the 2013 Article IV Consultation," IMF Country Report No. 13/328, November 2013, p. 7.

117 "Singapore's Banks: Perils of a gilded age," *The Economist*, August 3, 2013.

118 Lee, "National Day Rally 2013," speech.

119 Rachel Chang, "Budget 2013: New HDB Flats to Become Cheaper," *Straits Times*, March 9, 2013, http://www.straitstimes.com/the-big-story/budget-2013/story/budget-2013-new-hdb-flats-become-cheaper-20130309, accessed December 10, 2013.

120 Olivia Siong, "HDB Builds More Flats, Records Higher Net Deficit," Channel NewsAsia, October 16, 2013, http://www.channelnewsasia.com/news/singapore/hdb-builds-more-flats/849480.html, accessed December 10, 2013.

121 Lee, "National Day Rally 2013,"speech.

122 Interview with Lim Siong Guan, Group President of the GIC (investment manager for Singapore's foreign reserves).

123 *Ibid.*

124 Interview with Ravi Menon, Managing Director of the Monetary Authority of Singapore (MAS).

125 Interview with Koh Boon Hwee, Chairman of Far East Orchard.

126 Interview with Lim Siong Guan, Group President of the GIC (investment manager for Singapore's foreign reserves).

China "Unbalanced"

Diego Comin* and Richard H. K. Vietor*

*We urgently need to transform the pattern of economic development,"
pronounced Premier Wen Jiabao in March 2010. "We will work hard to
put economic development on the track of endogenous growth, driven by
innovation.*

— Premier Wen Jiabao, March 2010[1]

Since the early 2000s, the success of China's export-led growth strategy had been alienating major trade partners especially Europe and the United States. By 2005, China's trade surplus had reached $134 billion, of which $114 billion was with the United States alone. Foreign-invested firms accounted for more than half of this amount.[2] In the U.S., organized labor and various pundits and politicians increasingly blamed China for the loss of as many as 3.5 million manufacturing jobs.[3] U.S. Senator Chuck Schumer (D-NY) became a leading voice calling for punitive tariffs if China did not allow its currency, the yuan, to appreciate.[4] When China did allow the yuan to appreciate beginning in May 2005, the yuan grew by almost 21% over the next three years, from 8.3 to 6.8 yuan per dollar. However, in October 2008, China once again froze the exchange rate. By then, China's trade surplus with the United States had grown to $258 billion, while its overall current account surplus reached $426 billion.

---

*Reprinted with permission of Harvard Business School Publishing.
China "Unbalanced" 711-010.
This case was prepared by Professors Diego Comin and Richard H. K. Vietor with assistance from Juliana Seminerio.

Although political complaints about China's export-led growth model achieved limited traction, the global financial crisis brought the problem to light. In the fourth quarter of 2008, China's exports shrank for the first time since 1978. In the first quarter of 2009 they dropped by 25%. Chinese savings stood at 51%, with consumption at 36%. As thousands of processing and assembly plants were forced to close, laying off as many as 20 million workers, it now became absolutely clear to China's leadership that the growth model was flawed — excessive savings and export-investment, with little domestic consumption, worsening income distribution between East and West, inadequate health care and non-existent pensions leveraging off of low-wage exports to rich countries. "High-speed growth," observed a high-ranking Chinese official, "based on very high-speed consumption of resources natural and labor — with a cost to the environment has created a situation of export dependency . . . [T]his is not sustainable. We need to change our model to get sustained growth in the future."[5]

A $586 billion spending package designed to stimulate domestic consumption and investment provided a start but only a start. After growing at 9.4% annually for more than three decades and with a population of more than 1.3 billion, China had become the second-largest economy in the world (adjusted for purchasing power parity) and increasingly served as a model of successful autocratic capitalism for other developing countries (see **Exhibit 3a**).[6] Changing both its macro economy and its microeconomic institutions would be a huge undertaking. Premier Wen Jiabao proposed a number of initiatives, but their possible implementation speed was uncertain.

Meanwhile, 8,000 miles away, in May 2010, Senator Schumer and seven co-sponsors introduced new legislation to impose sanctions on "currency manipulators."[7]

"To Get Rich Is Glorious"

The strategy of export-led growth had begun in 1978, when Deng Xiaoping acceded to power. At the time, China was a poor, unsuccessful communist state, having suffered under 10 years of Mao Zedong's cultural revolution. With a closed economy, inefficient collective agriculture and money-losing state-owned enterprises, China's population of just under 1 billion had an income of $353 per capita, an entire nation in poverty.

After Mao's death, the pragmatic Deng Xiaoping began a series of reforms aimed at growing China's economy while retaining political power in Beijing. Some worked; some failed. To curb population growth, Deng inaugurated a one-child policy, enforced with fines, sterilization and occasionally forced abortions. Population growth fell from more than 2% to less than 1% over the next 19 years. To aid the disastrous agricultural collectives, Deng spread the household responsibility system, in which farmers could use their surplus capacity to produce fruit, meat and vegetables to be sold on the black market. Over the next six years, market incentives more than doubled agricultural output, making China self-sufficient for at least the next 10 years.

Town and village enterprises (TVEs) socialist organizations owned by local or provincial authorities sprang up everywhere, financed by the farmers' surplus earnings. These firms produced labor-intensive products such as shirts, pants, Christmas ornaments, sneakers, radios, picture tubes and eventually automobiles for export through Hong Kong to markets in the West. TVEs grew 30% annually, eventually employing 140 million people in 22 million firms.

Special economic zones (SEZs), perhaps Deng's most famous innovation, were organized in Guangdong (near Hong Kong) and Fujian (opposite Taiwan). With cheap labor, adequate power and no taxes, these zones began attracting foreign direct investment. In the early 1980s, most of this came from expatriate Chinese living in Hong Kong. Eventually, however, Taiwanese, Europeans, Americans and finally Japanese began investing bringing in a total of $250 billion by the time of Deng's death and more than $900 billion by 2010. More than 500,000 foreign-invested enterprises produced 54% of China's exports.

Fixing state-owned enterprises (SOEs) proved less successful. During Deng's administration, some SOEs tried adopting a "management responsibility system," modeled after the system in agriculture. However, managers could not lay off excess workers and a black market for industrial goods did not exist. Thus, it remained for Jiang Zemin, who replaced Deng, to undertake privatization. Between 1997 and 2007, the share of SOEs and collectively owned enterprises in employment in domestic companies declined from 81% to 46%.[8]

Deng gradually decontrolled most prices, began negotiating with the WTO and, in 1994, undertook both tax and currency reforms. Beijing's share of rural and property taxes had been declining for more than a decade. In 1994, the government enacted personal income taxes, corporate income taxes and a value-added tax — a significant portion of which went to the central government.

During this time, China had maintained two separate currencies, the domestic yuan (the renminbi), which was fixed and gradually devaluing from 1.8 to 5.74 and the foreign exchange certificate (10/dollar), which foreign investors bought on a swap market. By 1994, however, maintenance of this dual system had become impossible. On January 1, 1994, the government unified the two currencies and set the exchange rate at 8.7 yuan/dollar. The following November, the yuan appreciated to 8.3, where it remained fixed until May 2005.

Between 1978 and 1997, this strategy proved to be fantastically successful. Nominal GDP growth averaged about 18%, with inflation fluctuating between 3% and

24%. The real economy grew in excess of 9% annually. Merchandise trade, which ran a deficit as late as 1980, reached a surplus of $20 billion by 1997, while the current account, in deficit as late as 1993, reached a surplus of $7 billion. Foreign exchange reserves reached $149 billion.

Entry into the World Trade Organization

China had failed to gain WTO membership under Deng Xiaoping and had continued to seek "most favored nation" status from the United States throughout the late 1990s. During this period, China lowered its tariffs considerably and began large-scale privatization of SOEs and TVEs. However, the annual review process, which invariably exposed human rights issues, was a source of humiliation for the Chinese government and hard-line officials inside China were as much a problem as demanding U.S. negotiators. Officials anticipated that WTO membership would undo much of the institutional apparatus of socialism. Despite these concerns, China finally gained WTO membership in December 2001.

The terms that China agreed to could be roughly classified into three realms: Reforms facilitating foreign enterprise, reforms promoting free trade and systemic reforms aimed at improving the transparency and predictability of China's laws. While the deadlines for most reforms occurred between 2001 and 2006, a few requirements would be implemented more gradually, through 2015. China was required to report its implementation to the WTO annually and would be evaluated by other WTO members in a process called the Transitional Review Mechanism every year for eight years, with a final report in the tenth year.

In setting tariff levels, China was forced to agree to some stricter concessions than other developing countries. Agricultural subsidies, for example, were limited to 8.5% of production costs, rather than the usual 10%. Furthermore, China was subject to several punitive safeguards. WTO member countries were allowed to impose quotas for up to 12 years in response to a rapid surge in Chinese imports. Specific safeguards were allowed (and rapidly implemented) on textiles. To protect against dumping, for 15 years WTO members were allowed to estimate the production cost of Chinese goods based on input costs in other, non-market countries.[9]

Reforms Facilitating Foreign Enterprise in China

For foreign-invested firms that sold goods in China, the most significant restrictions were those limiting distribution — wholesaling, retailing and franchising. For service firms, geographic location and scope were limited. China promised to phase in full trading and distribution rights for foreign-owned firms and joint ventures. Telecommunications and insurance were opened immediately and banks more gradually. By 2006, foreign firms were generally satisfied with this opening, although banks were still constrained in branching and retail operations. Competition in the state-owned sector, however, remained circumscribed, as China put its largest, strategic firms into a state-owned Assets Supervision and Administration Commission and continued to favor them with subsidies and industrial policies (see **Exhibit 4b**).

Reforms Facilitating Free Trade

China did lower tariffs significantly, from an average of 31% in 1997 to less than 14% by 2005. Tariffs remained significant in apparel and automobiles and a tariff-rate quota system in agriculture continued to plague foreign food exporters. China agreed to stop subsidizing exports and to cap subsidies on domestic industries. National treatment also committed China to treating imported goods comparably with domestic goods when making regulatory judgments, levying fees and assessing complaints.

Implementation of these provisions was frustratingly slow. Although the government issued the new rules, they were often not enforced until foreign firms litigated or complained to the WTO. China was, understandably, loath to abandon programs to aid its "pillar industries," such as steel, petrochemicals, cement, machinery and automobiles.

Systemic Reforms

The third broad category of reforms to which China agreed was systemic: Changes to the country's legal framework that were designed to remedy some of the main obstacles to foreign enterprise and trade. Transparency, a fundamental principle of the WTO, was almost non-existent. Foreign firms had difficulty learning of new rules and remained too susceptible to capricious practices that customs officials used to block imports.

Protection of intellectual property rights was a similarly difficult condition of Chinese law. Chinese theft of foreign intellectual property was epidemic before WTO accession, with many firms losing proprietary technologies to their competitors through employee defection, misappropriation, and copying of sensitive documents. Although China had committed to tighten its legal protection of patents, trademarks, trade secrets and copyrights, the enforcement of rules at local levels and in dozens of cities was spotty at best. In 2010, despite complaints about intellectual property protection from the American Chamber of Commerce in China,[10] one could easily find copies of CDs for a couple of bucks, software for $20 and counterfeit Gucci bags or Rolex watches for under $25.[11]

Capital Controls

By 2001, the IMF recorded that China had controls in 11 out of 13 different types of capital accounts transactions. These included transactions related to capital market securities, money market instruments, commercial and financial credits, direct investment and the liquidation of direct investment, real estate transactions and personal capital movements among others.[12] Traditionally, China had encouraged FDI inflows and tightly regulated FDI outflows, portfolio flows and most external debts.[13]

Prior to 2003, foreign investors could not invest in local bonds and could only purchase local B-shares denominated in foreign currency. The qualified foreign institutional investor (QFII) scheme launched in 2003 intended to boost the domestic stock markets. As of 2007, the investments of the 52 QFII investors represented 3% of China's stock market capitalization.[14]

On 2004, the Chinese government started to loosen a number of restrictions on outward direct investment while it strengthened some controls on inward direct investment.[15] As of June 2006, the government had scrapped foreign exchange quotas for outward FDI, improved access to offshore guarantees issued by Chinese Banks, allowed all profits to be reinvested abroad and simplified the approval and annual reviews process.[16]

Between 2001 and 2005, remittances inflows increased threefold while outflows remained nearly stagnant. The Chinese government required in late 2004 banks to report conversions into renminbi in excess of $10,000.

Until April 2006, non-bank Chinese residents were prohibited from directly investing in securities overseas while Chinese banks could invest their foreign exchange in fixed income assets. With the qualified domestic institutional investors (QDII) scheme, Chinese individuals and companies could invest in overseas securities. In particular, this program allowed Chinese companies and individuals to convert renminbi deposits into dollars and invest in fixed income products and stocks. These transactions were conducted through authorized financial institutions and were subject to quotas. Further, the QDII scheme also allowed Chinese insurers to convert renminbi into dollars and invest abroad in bond and money market assets subject to prudential regulations.[17]

On August 2007, the State Administration of Foreign Exchange launched a *trial effort* that allowed Chinese citizens to open accounts at the Tianjin branch of the bank of China and then exchange yuan for Hong Kong dollars with the purpose of buying shares in the Hong Kong stock exchange. In principle, there was no limit in the amount of stocks they could buy.

Consequences of WTO Accession

Fuelled by exports that grew by 27% annually, China's economy took off after 2001. Real GDP growth accelerated from the 8%–9% level to 10%–11% annually (see **Exhibit 3a**). Products entering U.S. and European markets were, initially, labor-intensive, low-value-added goods — toys, textiles and garments, footwear and furniture. After 2004, however, these goods included more value-added content — electronics (including cell phones and electrical machinery), power generation equipment and auto parts (see **Exhibit 5a**). The mix of products that China exported resembled the mix in much richer countries.[18]

Imports, of course, also grew rapidly, but only by 24% annually as China acquired raw materials and intermediate goods from its South Asia neighbors to assemble and re-export. Thus, China's trade surplus grew to $360 billion by 2010, a gap of 8% of GDP. The gap, however, was asymmetrical. China ran a deficit with several Asian countries, but large surpluses with Europe, Japan and especially the United States. In 2008, the China–U.S. bilateral balance was $258 billion, dropping only slightly to $232 billion in 2009 (see **Exhibit 4a**). Between 2000 and 2009, the U.S. had lost an estimated 5.5 million jobs in manufacturing alone.[19]

Foreign direct investment also exploded (see **Exhibit 1**). While thousands of companies from East Asia and the West had already invested there, the flow accelerated with the prospect of growth inside of China. By 2008, China reported $148 billion in annual direct investment, a net of $95 billion. Over the whole period, investment inflows amounted to 3.5% of China's GDP.

As a consequence of its huge surplus on the current account, the massive direct investment inflows and limited capital outflows, China's reserves of foreign exchange grew rapidly. By 2004, the annual increase in reserves had exceeded $200 billion — most of which was invested in U.S. treasury bills or other financial assets. By 2010, China's foreign exchange reserves were thought to exceed $2.8 trillion, of which perhaps 66% were dollar-denominated (see **Exhibit 5b**). In 2007, the government established the China Investment Corporation, funded with $200 billion to invest in foreign equities.

Productivity

The evolution of GDP and labor productivity in China outpaced every other country in the world. Between 1997 and 2010, GDP had grown at an average annual rate of 9.5%, while labor productivity grew at 8.5%. Underlying this, total factor productivity (TFP) appeared to have grown by 4.7% per year, a rate significantly higher

Exhibit 1. Balance of Payments

(Billions US$$)	1995	1996	1997	1998	1999	2000	2001	2002
Current Account	**1.6**	**7.2**	**37.0**	**31.5**	**21.1**	**20.5**	**17.4**	**35.4**
Goods exports	128.1	151.1	182.7	183.5	194.7	249.1	266.1	325.7
Goods imports	−110.1	−131.5	−136.4	−136.9	−158.7	−214.7	−232.1	−281.5
Trade balance	18.1	19.5	46.2	46.6	36.0	34.5	34.0	44.2
Services credit	19.1	20.6	24.6	23.9	26.2	30.4	33.3	39.7
Services debit	−25.2	−22.6	−28.0	−26.7	−31.6	−36.0	−39.3	−46.5
Balance on goods & services	12.0	17.6	42.8	43.8	30.6	28.9	28.1	37.4
Income credit	5.2	7.3	5.7	5.6	8.3	12.5	9.4	8.3
Income debit	−17.0	−19.8	−16.7	−22.2	−22.8	−27.2	−28.6	−23.3
Balance on gds., serv. & inc.	0.2	5.1	31.8	27.2	16.2	14.2	8.9	22.4
Current transfers credit	1.8	2.4	5.5	4.7	5.4	6.9	9.1	13.8
Current transfers debit	−0.4	−0.2	−0.3	−0.4	−0.4	−0.5	−0.6	−0.8
Capital Account	**0.0**	**0.0**	**0.0**	**0.0**	**0.0**	**0.0**	**−0.1**	**0.0**
Financial Account	**38.7**	**40.0**	**21.0**	**−6.3**	**5.2**	**2.0**	**34.8**	**32.3**
Outward direct investment	−2.0	−2.1	−2.6	−2.6	−1.8	−0.9	−6.9	−2.5
Inward direct investment	35.8	40.2	44.2	43.8	38.8	38.4	44.2	49.3
Portfolio Investment Assets	0.1	−0.6	−0.9	−3.8	−10.5	−11.3	−20.7	−12.1
Equity securities	0.0	0.0	0.0	0.0	0.0	0.0	0.0	0.0
Debt securities	0.1	−0.6	−0.9	−3.8	−10.5	−11.3	−20.7	−12.1
Portfolio investment liabilities	0.7	2.4	7.8	0.1	−0.7	7.3	1.2	1.8
Equity securities	0.0	0.0	5.7	0.8	0.6	6.9	0.8	2.2
Debt securities	0.7	2.4	2.2	−0.7	−1.3	0.4	0.4	−0.5
Other investment assets	−1.1	−1.1	−39.6	−35.0	−24.4	−43.9	20.8	−3.1
Of which banks	0.0	0.0	−12.6	2.8	6.1	−21.4	16.8	−10.3
Other investment liabilities	5.1	1.3	12.0	−8.6	3.9	12.3	−3.9	−1.0
Of which banks	−4.0	−6.0	7.0	−3.2	−5.0	−8.3	−1.3	−1.7
Net errors and omissions	**−17.8**	**−15.5**	**−22.1**	**−18.9**	**−17.6**	**−11.7**	**−4.7**	**7.5**
Change in reserves	**−22.5**	**−31.7**	**−35.9**	**−6.2**	**−8.7**	**−10.7**	**−47.4**	**−75.2**
Memorandum item								
Current account as % of GDP	0.21%	0.81%	3.75%	3.01%	1.92%	1.72%	1.32%	2.43%

(Continued)

Exhibit 1. (*Continued*)

(Billions US$$)	2003	2004	2005	2006	2007	2008	2009	2010
Current Account	**45.9**	**68.7**	**134.1**	**232.7**	**354.0**	**412.4**	**261.1**	**305.4**
Goods exports	438.3	593.4	762.5	969.7	1,220.0	1,434.6	1,203.8	1,581.4
Goods imports	−393.6	−534.4	−628.3	−751.9	−904.6	−1,073.9	−954.3	−1,327.2
Trade balance	44.7	59	134.2	217.7	315.4	360.7	249.5	254.2
Services credit	46.7	62.4	74.4	92.0	122.2	147.1	129.5	171.2
Services debit	−55.3	−72.1	−83.8	−100.8	−130.1	−158.9	−158.9	−193.3
Balance on goods & services	36.1	49.3	124.8	208.9	307.5	348.9	220.1	232.1
Income credit	16.1	20.5	39.0	54.6	83.0	101.6	108.6	144.6
Income debit	−23.9	−24.1	−55.1	−60.0	−75.2	−83.9	−101.3	−114.2
Balance on gds., serv. & inc.	28.2	45.8	108.7	203.5	315.3	366.6	227.4	262.4
Current transfers credit	18.5	24.3	27.7	31.6	42.6	52.6	42.6	49.5
Current transfers debit	−0.8	−1.4	−2.3	−2.4	−4.0	−6.8	−8.9	−6.6
Capital Account	**0.0**	**−0.1**	**4.1**	**4.0**	**3.1**	**3.1**	**4.0**	**4.6**
Financial Account	**52.8**	**110.7**	**96.9**	**48.6**	**92.0**	**43.3**	**176.9**	**221.4**
Outward direct investment	0.2	−1.8	−11.3	−21.2	−17.0	−53.5	−43.9	−60.2
Inward direct investment	47.1	54.9	117.2	124.1	160.1	175.1	114.2	185.1
Portfolio Investment Assets	3.0	6.5	−26.2	−110.4	−2.3	32.7	9.9	−7.6
Equity securities	0.0	0.0	0.0	−1.5	−15.2	−1.1	−33.8	−8.4
Debt securities	3.0	6.5	−26.2	−109.0	12.9	33.9	43.7	0.8
Portfolio investment liabilities	8.4	13.2	21.2	42.9	21.0	9.9	28.8	31.7
Equity securities	7.7	10.9	20.3	42.9	18.5	8.7	28.2	31.4
Debt securities	0.7	2.3	0.9	0.0	2.5	1.2	0.6	0.3
Other investment assets	−17.9	2.0	−48.9	−31.9	−151.5	−106.1	9.4	−116.3
Of which banks	−15.7	3.0	−23.7	3.0	−23.4	−49.4	22.1	−24.0
Other investment liabilities	12.0	35.9	44.9	45.1	81.8	−15.0	58.5	188.7
Of which banks	10.3	13.4	9.2	25.3	6.9	−13.6	3.1	91.5
Net errors and omissions	**38.9**	**10.5**	**15.8**	**−0.7**	**11.5**	**20.9**	**−41.4**	**−59.8**
Change in reserves	**−137.5**	**−189.8**	**−251.0**	**−284.7**	**−460.7**	**−479.6**	**−400.5**	**−471.7**
Memorandum item								
Current account as % of GDP	2.78%	3.53%	5.87%	8.35%	10.13%	9.10%	5.17%	5.15%

Sources: IMF eLibrary, Balance of Payments Statistics (BOP), accessed Oct. 26, 2011. GDP from EIU CountryData, accessed Oct. 26, 2010.

Exhibit 2.   Exchange Rate

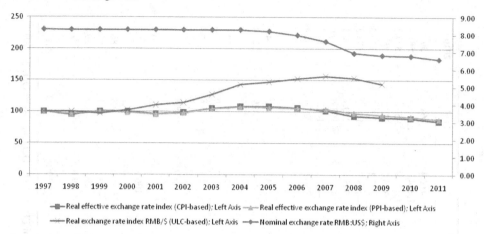

-■- Real effective exchange rate index (CPI-based): Left Axis   -▲- Real effective exchange rate index (PPI-based): Left Axis
-×- Real exchange rate index RMB/$ (ULC-based): Left Axis   -◆- Nominal exchange rate RMB:US$: Right Axis

Source: Compiled by author with data from the Economist Intelligence Unit, accessed July 16, 2010, with additional data from Niall Ferguson and Moritz Schularick, "The End of Chimerica," Harvard Business School Working Paper No. 10-037, 2009.

Note: An increase in the exchange rate indicates a depreciation of the RMB. Effective exchange rates are based on a weighted basket of currencies, where the weights are given by trade shares. CPI stands for consumer price index; PPI stands for producer's price index; ULC stands for unit labor costs. ULCs computed for manufacturing.

than the high rates observed in the East Asian miracle economies (i.e. South Korea, Taiwan, Singapore and Hong Kong; see **Exhibits 3a, 6a** and **6b**).[20]

The roots of Chinese productivity growth can be traced to several factors. The migration from rural to urban regions and the reduction in the market share of SOEs entailed a massive reallocation of capital and labor to more productive uses (see **Exhibits 6c** and **6d**). It should be noted, however, that coastal TFP growth between 1996 and 2004 was 4.57%, while inland regions grew TFP at "only" 1.7%.[21] Foreign direct investment brought better technologies and more sophisticated managed practices and also opened new and larger markets. A related channel that yielded new technologies was importing equipment goods that embodied productivity. Massive investments in infrastructure, moreover, reduced communications and transportation costs and made electric energy available at greater scale and lower cost. The access to international markets also created opportunities that spurred Chinese entrepreneurs to start new businesses, invest in modern equipment and produce at a more productive scale.

As the Communist Party became more willing to embrace the principles of capitalism and implement its WTO commitments, distortions that had impeded the smooth functioning of markets were removed. Some authors used the dispersion of productivity across firms as a sign of such distortions. In 1998, this dispersion was

Exhibit 3a. Growth Productivity and Wages

	1997	2000	2001	2002	2003	2004	2005	2006	2007	2008	2009	2010**	2011**
GDP (% real change pa)	9.3	8.4	8.3	9.1	10.0	10.1	10.4	11.7	13.0	9.6	8.6	9.9	8.3
Labor productivity growth (%)*	7.9	7.4	6.9	8.0	9.0	9.0	9.5	10.8	12.2	8.9	7.8	9.2	7.5
Total factor productivity growth (%)*	4.1	3.9	3.6	4.5	5.0	5.2	5.6	6.7	8.4	5.1	4.0	5.5	4.1
Labor productivity growth manufacturing (%)	8.0	15.6	14.1	23.8	24.9	15.2	19.8	16.4	18.9	11.0	na	na	na
Average real manufacturing wages (% change pa)	2.4	11.9	11.0	13.3	12.5	8.4	10.6	12.3	11.5	5.0	na	na	na
Unit manufacturing labor costs in RMB (% change pa)	−2.8	−3.4	−2.4	−11.3	−11.3	−2.9	−7.5	−2.4	−2.6	0.0	na	na	na

Source: Compiled with data from the Economic Intelligence Unit, accessed December 15, 2009, with additional data from Niall Ferguson and Moritz Schularick, "The End of Chimerica," Harvard Business School Working Paper No. 10-037, 2009.

Note: *Estimate **Forecast

Exhibit 3b. GDP Components

	1997	2000	2001	2002	2003	2004	2005	2006	2007	2008	2009	2010**	2011**
Nominal GDP (trillion Yuan)	8.2	9.9	10.9	12.0	13.6	16.0	18.9	22.2	26.3	30.7	33.5	38.1	42.7
Private consumption (% of GDP)	45	46	45	44	42	40	38	36	36	35	35	36	36
Government consumption (% of GDP)	14	16	16	16	15	14	14	14	13	13	13	14	14
Gross fixed investment (% of GDP)	32	34	35	36	39	41	41	41	40	41	45	47	48
Stockbuilding (% of GDP)	5	1	2	2	2	3	2	2	2	2	1	1	1
Exports of G&S (% of GDP)	21	23	23	25	29	34	36	38	39	36	28	28	27
Imports of G&S (% of GDP)	17	21	21	23	27	31	31	31	30	28	23	25	25

Source: Compiled with data from the Economic Intelligence Unit, accessed December 15, 2009.

Note: *Estimate **Forecast

Exhibit 4a. U.S. Trade Balance with China (inverted scales)

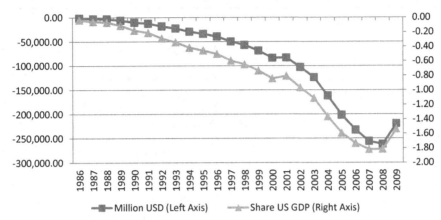

Source: Compiled with data from the Economist Intelligence Unit, accessed July 20, 2010.

Exhibit 4b. SOEs under the Supervision of the State-owned Assets Supervision Administration Commission

- Three oil companies
- Two power grid and five major power generation companies
- Four largest steel companies
- Chalco (aluminum company)
- First Automotive and Dongfeng Motor
- Five electrical machinery companies
- Three major airlines
- Four large telecom companies
- One of each from coal, construction, metals and food trading companies
- Three Gorges Project Corporation
- State Development Investment Corporation
- 11 military investment companies

Source: Compiled by case writer with data from the State-owned Assets Supervision and Administration Commission of the State Council, http://www.sasac.gov.cn, accessed July 2010.

approximately 20% higher than in the U.S. By 2005, the gap had been reduced to 12%.[22]

Energy and Raw Materials — The "Going Out" Strategy

With more than 1.3 billion people and a GDP growth rate exceeding 9% annually, China was short of raw materials — food, iron ore, alumina, copper, coal, natural gas

Exhibit 5a.   China Top Exports and Imports in 2008 (billion USD)

Exports		Imports	
Category	**Volume**	**Category**	**Volume**
Electrical machinery and equipment	342	Electrical machinery and equipment	266.5
Power generation equipment	268.6	Mineral fuel and oil	169.1
Apparel	113	Power generation equipment	138.9
Iron and steel	101.8	Ores, slag and ash	86.4
Optics and medical equipment	43.4	Optics and medical equipment	77.7
Furniture	42.8	Plastics and articles thereof	48.9
Inorganic and organic chemicals	42.4	Inorganic and organic chemicals	48.5
Vehicles, excluding railway	39.3	Iron and steel	35.1
Toys and games	32.7	Vehicles, excluding railway	26.9
Mineral fuel and oil	31.6	Copper and articles thereof	26.1

Source: U.S.–China Business Council, 2010 Annual Report.

Exhibit 5b.   China's Foreign Exchange Reserves in USD-Denominated Assets (billion USD)

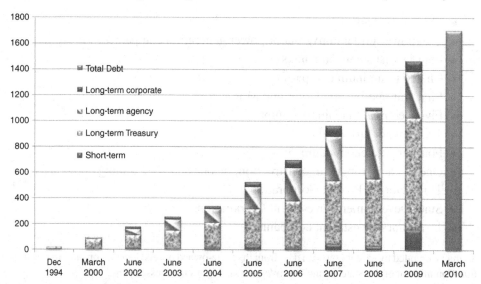

Source: Compiled with data from Economist Intelligence Unit Country Reports, various years, http://countryanalysis.eiu.com/country_reports, accessed July 2010; and U.S. Department of the Treasury, "Report on Foreign Holdings of U.S. Securities at end-June 2009," TG-677, April 30, 2010, http://www.treas.gov/press/releases/tg677.htm, accessed July 21, 2010.

Note: USD assets are approximately 70% of total foreign exchange.

Exhibit 6a. Sectoral GDP Growth, 1980–2005

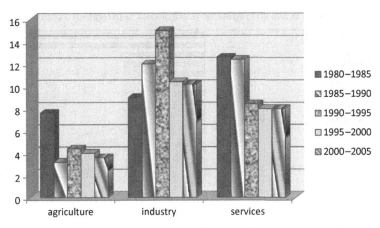

Source: Compiled with data from *OECD Economic Surveys: China.*

Exhibit 6b. Factors Contributing to Output Growth, 1988–2008

	1988–1993	**1993–1998**	**1998–2003**	**2003–2008**
GDP Growth	9	10.2	8.7	10.8
Capital Contribution	4.4	5.4	4.7	6
Labor Contribution	0.7	0.5	0.5	0.4
TFP Growth	3.6	4	3.2	4.1
of which: Sectoral Shifts	1.6	1.3	−0.1	2.7

Source: Compiled with data from *OECD Economic Surveys: China.*

Note: Capital contribution is the growth of capital stock time's share of capital in GDP. Labor contribution is the growth in labor force times share of labor in GDP. TFP growth is approximately equal to the growth in real GDP minus contributions of capital and labor. Sectoral shifts measure the gain in productivity due to different levels of productivity.

and petroleum. The export-led growth strategy, plus the growth needed for domestic consumption, had fuelled massive demand for all sorts of raw materials. Despite the success of Deng's agricultural policies, the growth of caloric appetites (with domestic incomes) had incurred significant demand for imported beef, chicken, soybeans and wheat. The construction of national infrastructure necessitated extraordinary amounts of iron ore, alumina, copper and metallurgical coal. And above all, China's commitment to the automobile, with a goal of producing 20 million annually, required a great deal of petroleum, despite limited domestic reserves. In May 2010, China was consuming 9.2 million barrels of petroleum products daily, yet producing only 3.9 million — and the difference, already 5.3 million barrels daily, had to be imported.[23] The International Energy Association (IEA) projected that

Exhibit 6c.   Extent of Inter-Province Migration Flows by Province (in 2009)

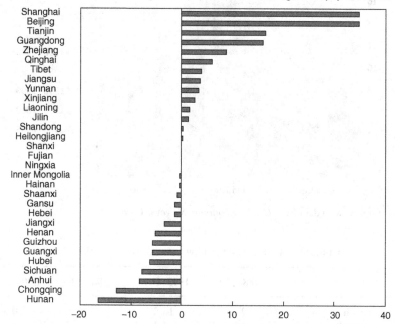

Source: *OECD Economic Surveys: China*, volume 2010/6 (February 2010): 142.

Exhibit 6d.   Sources of the Rural–Urban Income Differential

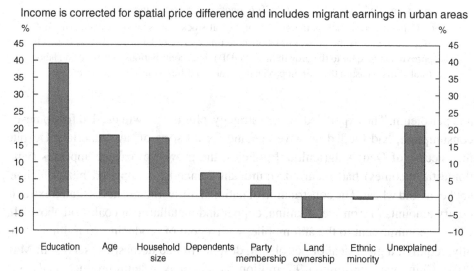

Source: *OECD Economic Surveys: China*, volume 2010/6 (February 2010): 146.

Exhibit 7a. Estimated Shares by Country of China's Overseas Equity Oil Production, Q1 2010

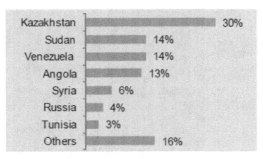

Source: International Energy Agency, Oil Market Report website, June 10, 2010, 21.

Exhibit 7b. 2009 China Crude Imports by Region

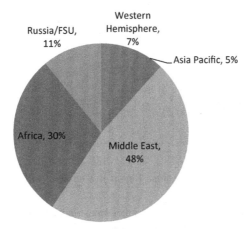

Source: Created by author with data from International Energy Agency, Oil Market Report website, June 10, 2010, 21.

by 2030, China would be importing more than 12 million barrels a day, or three-fourths of the oil it would need.[24] To a lesser extent, the same was true for natural gas, which would be used for gas turbines as a replacement for China's abundant but more polluting coal.

Sometime after the Asian crisis, about a decade earlier, the Chinese government adopted a "going out" strategy (see **Exhibits 7a** and **7b**). The three national oil companies CNPC, Sinopec and CNOOC began ramping up their upstream investment activities overseas, displacing Western firms in places like Angola and investing in countries like Sudan, where Western firms could not go. In the 15 months prior to April 2010 alone, these companies spent $29 billion to acquire oil and gas assets outside of China. CNPC and Sinopec were involved with eight countries in 11 loan-for-oil deals worth $77 billion. Further, these companies entered contracts to invest at least $18 billion in future exploration and development in Iraq, Iran, Venezuela

Exhibit 7c.   Map of China

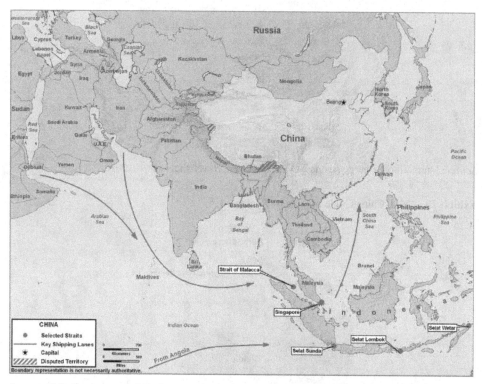

Source: U.S. Department of Defense, Annual Report to Congress: Military Power of the People's Republic of China, 2009.

Note: "China's Critical Sea Lanes. Like many other industrialized East Asian Countries, China is heavily dependent upon critical sea lanes for its energy imports. Over 80% of China's crude oil imports transit the Strait of Malacca."

and Angola. In the first four months of 2010, these three Chinese oil companies spent $10.9 billion to purchase Syncrude, a Canadian tar sands company; Arrow Energy, an Australian coal bed methane company; and 50% of Bridas, an Argentinean oil company.[42]

This "going out" strategy was driven by a sense of geopolitical insecurity. The Chinese government realized it would be a huge net importer of fuels and other minerals for the indefinite future and it worried about access to those minerals and fuels, not only in a competitive squeeze (where prices went up sharply and supplies became constrained), but also in a security situation. The Chinese, whose navy remained weak, fully realized that the United States controlled critical sea lanes. Indeed, over 80% of China's oil supply transited the Strait of Malacca (see **Exhibit 7c**).

This resource-acquisition strategy seemed to fit well with Chinese foreign policy. For the past several years, according to Thomas Lum, "China ha[d] bolstered its diplomatic presence and garnered international goodwill through its financing of infrastructure and natural resource development projects, assistance in the carrying out of such projects and large investments in many developing countries." This policy was "driven primarily by Beijing's desire to secure and transport natural resources ... and secondarily for diplomatic reasons."[26]

As a result of these investments, China became a top trading partner to Africa and Southeast Asia, and by late 2010 was second after the United States as a market for Latin American commodities. While the Chinese government did not report aid accurately (including gifts, loans, and government-sponsored investments), a study by the NYU Wagner School put China's aid amount at $25 billion for 2007.[27] In Africa, for example, nearly 70% of China's infrastructure financing was concentrated in Angola, Nigeria, Ethiopia and Sudan, all of which had oil fields.[28] Additionally, China pledged $16 billion in aid, loans and investment for Latin America, with another $8.2 billion for Brazil.[29]

Chinese Military Build-up

As an increasingly affluent great power, China had for some time been investing in its military. Not surprisingly, China's reported expenditures were far lower than all outside estimates. In 2008, for example, China reported defense expenditures of $60 billion, while observers estimated the total to be between $105 and $140 billion. Additionally, although Beijing publicly asserted that China's military modernization was "purely defensive in nature," China had for several years invested in projecting its power abroad. In 2010, the People's Liberation Army had an estimated troop strength of about 1,250,000. China's naval forces included 75 principal ships (though the navy had no aircraft carriers), mostly supplied by Russia and more than 60 submarines. Its air wing included more than 500 tactical aircraft and an inventory of about 1,000 short-range ballistic missiles. Moreover, China's armaments industry was developing air- and ground-launched cruise missiles, a dozen variants of anti-ship cruise missiles and a nuclear force of seven types of intercontinental ballistic missiles with ranges of 1,700 to 7,000 kilometers.[30]

Financial Crisis

The global recession that struck in the autumn of 2008 began in the U.S. sub-prime mortgage market and rapidly spread to markets worldwide. As consumers in developed economies stopped consuming, China and other exporting nations felt

the impact immediately in trade, foreign direct investment and even some contagion from defaulting loans. In the fourth quarter, the value of Chinese exports and
imports reversed, with growth rates plummeting from 25% to negative 1.65%. As
this decline worsened during the Chinese Spring Festival in January and February
2009, thousands of plants closed and as many as 15% of China's 130 million migrant
workers lost their jobs and returned to their rural homes.

The centralized communist government reacted quickly. In September 2008, the
Bank of China cut key interest rates for the first time since 2002 (see **Exhibit 8a**),
then cut them further over the next few months. In October, it halted the appreciation of the currency at 6.8 yuan/dollar. To support exports, the Ministry of Finance
and the State Administration of Taxation increased the export-tax rebate on labor-
intensive goods. Then, on November 9, the government announced a 4 trillion yuan
($586 billion) stimulus package to be spent by the end of 2010 (see **Exhibits 8b
and c**). This package targeted key areas such as housing, rural infrastructure, transportation, health and education, the environment, innovation, low-income housing and disaster rebuilding. (In May 2008, the Sichuan earthquake had injured or
killed hundreds of thousands and destroyed infrastructure in 51 counties, resulting
in an estimated loss of 252 billion yuan.) Along with the spending, the government implemented a series of tax cuts to improve producer competitiveness and
enacted reforms of social security and health care. The cost for these additional
measures was about 850 billion yuan over the next two years. The huge government banks, moreover, opened their loan windows and financed bond issues
through SOEs.

Not only was this stimulus package significantly larger (as a percent of GDP) than
those of the U.S. or Europe, but it was implemented much more quickly. Because
local provinces had already submitted projects to the National Development and
Reform Commission (central-government laws did not require extensive procedural
safeguards) and because government-owned banks began lending immediately, the
stimulus took effect much faster than elsewhere — in four months or even less. As
Premier Wen summarized in 2010,

> We vigorously expanded consumer spending . . . The central government
> provided 45 billion yuan in subsidies for rural residents to purchase home
> appliances and motor vehicles . . . We halved the purchase tax on small-
> displacement automobiles. We reduced or exempted taxes on buying and
> selling homes . . . Throughout the year, 13.64 million motor vehicles were
> sold . . . [and] commodity housing sales amounted to 937 million square
> meters.
>
> We promoted rapid growth in investment. We guided and stimulated
> non-government investment by means of well-leveraged government
> investment. In 2009, the central government's public investment was

Exhibit 8a. Fiscal Balance and Domestic Credit

	1997	2000	2001	2002	2003	2004	2005	2006	2007	2008	2009	2010	2011
Budget balance (% of GDP)	−0.71	−2.52	−2.31	−2.62	−2.15	−1.30	−1.21	−0.75	0.59	−0.41	−2.21	−2.60	−2.40
Budget revenue (% of GDP)	10.59	13.57	15.04	15.71	15.92	16.47	16.77	17.49	19.51	19.99	20.42	20.00	19.90
Budget expenditure (% of GDP)	11.31	16.09	17.35	18.32	18.07	17.77	17.98	18.24	18.92	20.40	22.63	22.60	22.30
Public debt (% of GDP)*	7.44	27.58	27.35	27.10	26.80	25.10	23.00	20.80	17.30	15.60	16.90	17.90	18.60
Stock of domestic credit (% of GDP)	97.41	120.24	123.77	143.44	151.24	140.02	131.63	130.27	129.10	123.63	147.87	158.11	159.58

Source: Compiled with data from the Economic Intelligence Unit, accessed December 15, 2009.
Note: *Estimate

Exhibit 8b. Interest Rates and Inflation

	1997	2000	2001	2002	2003	2004	2005	2006	2007	2008	2009	2010*	2011**
Consumer prices (% change pa; av)	2.79	0.34	0.69	−0.72	1.05	3.93	1.72	1.75	4.78	5.98	−0.73	3.10	3.30
Lending interest rate (%)	8.64	5.85	5.85	5.31	5.31	5.58	5.58	6.12	7.47	5.31	5.31	5.60	6.20
Deposit interest rate (%)	5.67	2.25	2.25	1.98	1.98	2.25	2.25	2.52	4.14	2.25	2.25	2.60	3.20
Stockmarket index	1,258	2,192	1,713	1,419	1,569	1,330	1,230	2,701	5,521	1,925	3,437		

Source: Compiled with data from the Economic Intelligence Unit, accessed December 15, 2009.
Note: *Estimate **Forecast

Exhibit 8c.   Fiscal stimulus plan

bn yuan until 2010		bn yuan per year	
Total expenditure in investment	4000	**Total current expenditure and tax cuts**	850
Railways, roads, airports and	1500	**(financed by the government)**	
electricity generation		Subsidies for durable goods in rural	40
Low-cost housing	400	households	
Rural development and infrastructure	370	Program "Cars in rural areas"	5
Innovation	370	Agricultural subsidies	123
Environment	210	Subsidies to agricultural machinery	14
Hospital and schools	150	Interest rate subsidies for technological	20
Reconstruction of 2008 earthquake	1000	improvement	
		Worker training	42
Financed by:		Tax breaks to small cars	30
Central government	1180	Social security programs	293
Local governments (bonds and loans)	600	Health system reform (annual over three	283
SOEs (loans)	2220	years)	

Source: OECD, China in the 2010s Rebalancing Growth and Strengthening Social Safety Nets.

924.3 billion yuan, 503.8 billion yuan more than in the previous year's budget. . . .

We further strengthened the work related to agriculture, rural areas and farmers. The central government used 725.3 billion yuan to support agriculture. . . .

We intensified industrial restructuring. We formulated and implemented a plan for restructuring and invigorating ten key industries (automobile, iron and steel, shipbuilding, petrochemical, textile, nonferrous metal, equipment manufacturing, electronic information industries and light industry).[31]

Economic growth slowed initially, but almost exclusively in exports. The economy quickly regained vigor and, in 2009, real GDP grew by 8.7% (see **Exhibits 3a** and **b**).

The Harmonious Society

Although the market reforms undertaken since 1978 had spurred private enterprise and rapid growth, they had distributed the benefits unevenly and significantly eroded social safety nets. State-owned enterprises had offered cradle-to-grave care, part of a system based on *danwei*, or work units, that provided health, education, pensions and other benefits.[32] But the dismantling of the public sector in China and the growth of private firms had undermined the provision of this "iron rice bowl." SOEs no longer

Exhibit 9. China's Income Inequality

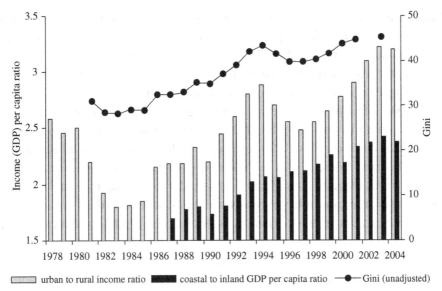

Legend: urban to rural income ratio ▪▪▪ coastal to inland GDP per capita ratio ─●─ Gini (unadjusted)

Source: Huang and Luo (2008), cited in X. Luo and N. Zhu, "Rising Income Inequality in China: A Race to the Top," World Bank Policy Research Working Paper 4700, 2008, 3.

ran their own health-care clinics; public hospitals increasingly operated like private hospitals; meager pensions were non-transferrable, or lost entirely.

The eight-fold increase in per capita income achieved between 1980 and 2010 had been inequitably allocated. One reason was that the unemployment rate had doubled, including among migrant workers, reaching 10% in 2009. Most of the economic development, moreover, had occurred in the coastal regions, where export-led growth and foreign direct investment had transformed the economy. While the nominal GDP per capita had reached $4,909 by 2010 and several hundred million Chinese peasants had escaped abject poverty, the GINI index — a measure of inequality — had jumped from 0.32 to 0.48 by 2005 (see **Exhibit 9**). 10% of the population earned 45% of the national income, or 11.8 times as much per capita as the poorest 10%.[33] Worse still, the income gap was largely geographic — coastal communities were rich, with dozens of billionaires, while rural areas in the west were still quite poor. These differences, along with the government's sometimes arbitrary decisions, precipitated more than 50,000 local disturbances annually.

As early as October 2003, in the Communist Party's Third Plenum, legislators unveiled proposed amendments to the state constitution aimed at rebalancing income distribution between urban and rural, east and west. In October 2005, the Fifth Plenum approved the 11th Five-Year Economic Program, which aimed at building a *harmonious society* and these efforts intensified after the financial crisis.

The Hukou System

While some of the problem was merely geographic — exporters preferred the coast — much of the difficulty pertained to China's outdated system for controlling population movement, the *hukou system*. This system was established in the 1950s to keep rural people active in farming to maximize food production. The *hukou* was a permit that categorized people by location and as agricultural or non-agricultural. In the 1990s, a few provinces began abolishing annual quotas for changing *hukou* from agricultural to non-agricultural. In smaller towns, the barriers to obtaining a local *hukou* were eased in 1998 for people with a stable source of income and adequate housing. Most of this relaxation occurred in inland and western areas. Some provinces required a non-local *hukou* holder to surrender all land-use rights in the village of origin. In larger towns and cities, it remained all but impossible for a migrant to obtain a local *hukou*. Special skills, capital, or education were required.[34]

With 10 million migrant workers moving to the cities each year, the *hukou* system remained a huge obstacle. Without local *hukou* registration, temporary migrants were "systematically denied access to better-remunerated, safer jobs with a certain degree of job security."[35] Moreover, health care, housing, pensions and children's education were all tied to the *hukou*. In March 2010, 11 Chinese newspapers "defied party strictures and teamed together to publish an extraordinary joint editorial. It called on . . . the National People's Congress . . . to scrap the *hukou* system as soon as possible. 'We hope,' it said, 'that a bad policy we have suffered for decades will end with our generation.'"[36]

Health Care

Health care was an unfortunate victim of China's economic reform. Affordability and access, once part of the "iron rice bowl," were now gone for hundreds of millions of Chinese. As late as 2008, few Chinese families had adequate health insurance. Most health facilities were publicly owned, yet relied on revenue-generating activities to survive. Thus, while technically "public," they behaved as "private, for-profit" entities. The government, which wanted these facilities to survive, set prices for high-tech diagnostic services above cost and allowed a 15% profit margin on drugs. Winnie Yip and William Hsiao commented on the consequences of the new system, saying, "Thus, providers over-prescribe drugs and tests and hospitals race to introduce high-tech services and expensive imported drugs."[37]

These distortions yielded perverse outcomes. For example, 75% of patients suffering from a common cold were prescribed antibiotics. China's health care costs rose 16% annually for two decades — 7% faster than GDP. The biggest problems, therefore, were health-care impoverishment and severe inequities across regions.

Between 1993 and 2003, urban income grew from 1,942 to 3,462 yuan, while inpatient expenditure per admission grew from 1,598 to 7,098 yuan.[38] One survey suggested that a third of households reduced consumption or were impoverished by health-related expenditures.[39]

In April 2009, the government unveiled its plan for health care reform:

> It will spend an additional 850 billion RMB ($125 billion) over the next three years, to invest in five specific areas: (1) expand insurance coverage with a target of achieving universal coverage by 2011... (2) increase government spending on public health services, especially in low-income regions ... (3) establish primary-care facilities — community health centers in urban areas and township health centers in rural areas ... (4) reform the pharmaceutical market ... and (5) pilot test public hospital reforms.[40]

Pensions

One reason why Chinese citizens saved so much and consumed so little, was the insecurity they sensed with regard to the future. The collapse of the "iron rice bowl" left many with valueless pensions, or none at all. Moreover, the introduction of the one-child policy, combined with rapid economic growth, led the fertility rate to plunge to less than 1.5%. Thus, an elderly (65+) population of 90 million in 2010 was predicted to rise to more than 230 million by 2030.[41] Building new social security systems was therefore a priority of the Hu Jintao/Wen Jaibao government.

As with health care, rural–urban differences and migration made provision of pensions much more difficult. Rural elderly in China worked much longer (10 years on average) than urban workers, who generally retired between 60 and 65 years of age. The main source of income for rural elderly was either continuing employment or family support. For urban workers, by contrast, the main source of income was pensions paid by the government.

In 2005, the government undertook significant pension reform for urban workers. The new system had three parts: (1) a flat-rate pension related to the local average wage, (2) a component that related the individual's pension to his or her lifetime average earnings and (3) a revaluation of the second component based on the interest on one-year bank deposits. This system, however, was essentially a guideline, implemented differently in 1,000 different counties. Contribution rates, moreover, differed widely across municipalities and provinces.

Rural pensions, which covered some 12 million people in 2008 and paid out an average of $6 per retiree per month, underwent major reform in June 2009. The new, voluntary program would be introduced gradually over the next 12 years, with the objective of providing a pension equivalent to 25% of average per-capita rural household income on a flat-rate, non-contributory system. An additional 10%

could be added on a contributory basis.[42] Support for migrants, who were mostly self-employed, added more complications. In 2008, only 17% of migrant workers (about 130 million) had pension coverage.

Employment and Unemployment

The financial crisis, unsurprisingly, made finding work more difficult in China — not just for unskilled migrant workers, but for college graduates as well. Even before the crisis, about 12% of China's six million college graduates were unemployed. In February 2009, the government began urging graduates to work in rural areas or smaller enterprises; as village officials, rural teachers, or doctors; or as commu- nity social workers. The civil service, meanwhile, had become intensely competi- tive, with only 13,500 jobs for more than 800,000 applicants.[43] By 2010, the press was reporting squalid "ant" enclaves of unemployed college students being formed around major cities, inhabited by perhaps three million jobless or underemployed students.[44]

While unemployment remained a continuing concern of the government, worker demands and sharply rising wages were also problems. As late as 2006, compensation for manufacturing workers was only $0.81 per hour — about 2.7% of comparable costs in the U.S.[45] Poor working conditions and low wages led to an increasing number of suicides and labor outages, reported in 2009 and 2010. At Foxconn International, a 400,000-worker operation in Shenzhen owned by Hon Hai Precision Industry of Taipei, 10 workers committed suicide in the first five months of 2010. At Omron Corp., a Japanese factory in southern China, workers staged a walkout in mid-July, demanding monthly salaries be raised from 1,300 yuan to 1,800 yuan ($265). Other companies like Yum Brands, Honda, and Toyota had begun raising wages from 20% to 25%.[46] In late 2010, average wages for migrant workers was closer to 2,000 yuan/month ($293), although minimum wages in some areas were still as low as 630 yuan ($93).[47] Once the Chinese economy recov- ered in late 2009, labor shortages for skilled workers had become a widespread problem.[48]

Banking, Housing and the Yuan

Banking

China's banking sector was not significantly affected by the financial crisis. It had not traded extensively in derivatives and the state's control over the banking system prevented a credit crunch. China's banking system was dominated by four big, state-owned banks with collective assets of over 33 trillion yuan in 2009. There were also some smaller, commercial banks that remained profitable and had lower non-performing loan ratios than the big four. Finally, there were 140 city commercial banks in 2009 with strong ties to their local government.

Years of government-directed lending had led state-owned banks to accumulate large amounts of non-performing loans. The People's Bank of China (PBOC) estimated non-performing loans to be between 21.4% and 26.1% of the total lending of China's four big banks in 2002. In 1999, four asset management companies were established to transfer the non-performing assets from the banks. These companies repackaged the non-performing loans into viable assets and sold them off to investors.

The central government allowed banks to raise capital through bonds or stock issues. By July 2010, the four largest banks were listed companies traded at the stock exchange and their collective market capitalization was approximately $650 billion. All four banks were among the top 10 banks worldwide according to market capitalization. Industrial and Commerce Bank and China Construction Bank occupied the top two spots. Additionally, PBOC's decision to decontrol interest rates had accompanied the reform of the banking system.

However, the system was still relatively closed. Some foreign banks had minority stakes in Chinese firms, but foreign-owned operations on the mainland had a market share of less than 1% of profits, while Chinese banks made less than 4% of their profits abroad. As of 2010, the PBOC still set most interest rates, including most lending interest rates and interest rates on checking and savings accounts.

China, like many other economies, had used an expansionary fiscal and monetary policy to counter the recession. But unlike most countries, the central government had financed only about a quarter of the stimulus package. Loans granted by state-owned banks financed most of the rest (see **Exhibit 8b**). As a result, credit increased rapidly despite the recessionary environment. Some 9.95 trillion yuan in lending was granted in 2009, with another 7.5 trillion yuan in credit being issued during 2010. In response, the money supply increased by 30%.

Housing Bubble

Such an extraordinary expansion of the money supply, however, did not lead to a commensurate increase in inflation. Many feared that the excess liquidity had been directed towards asset purchases and that this could eventually overheat the economy.

Between December 2008 and December 2009, housing prices in China increased by 8%, while land prices for residential or commercial buildings increased by 16%. These trends masked significant regional heterogeneity. In Shenzhen, for example, housing prices had increased by 19%, while in Tangshan they declined by 2%. The prospect of such capital gains fueled a boom in residential investment, which grew by

16% in 2009.[49] Many saw these developments as a housing bubble that resembled those of Western nations such as the U.S. or Spain. According to Ken Rogoff, a Harvard economist and former chief economist at the International Monetary Fund (IMF), "You're starting to see [a] collapse in property and it's going to hit the banking system."[50]

However, some authorities were less concerned about the potential effects of the bubble on the economy. Mortgages were a rarity. In the words of Jin Liqun, chairman of the supervisory board of the China Investment Corporation and former vice-minister of finance, "it is too burdensome to ask for a mortgage. When somebody wants to buy a house, she just saves and asks for money from the family until she can pay it in full." As a result, a collapse in real estate prices would have reduced the wealth of the housing owners, but would not have adversely affected the banks' balance sheets.[51]

Finally, even if a significant share of the loans had been written off, the system could absorb the hit. The regulator was very effective and had managed to induce banks to raise capital by about an eighth in 2010. And, above all, China had its extraordinarily high savings rate. With piles of excess deposits, banks did not rely on volatile debt markets for funding. This allowed banks to face any future bad-debt problems with optimism, using their high lending profits to replenish capital. As a backstop, China's government, with little debt and large foreign reserves, had deep pockets.

Real Exchange Rate

A question on everyone's mind was exactly how much the yuan was undervalued. According to Eswar Prasad, an economist at Cornell University and the former head of the China desk at the IMF, "every estimate of the appropriate level of the currency is fraught with uncertainty."[52]

Studies to determine the degree of undervaluation of a currency were based on the real exchange rate. The real exchange rate was a measure of the value of a country's goods against those of another country, a group of countries, or the rest of the world, at the prevailing nominal exchange rate.[53] The estimates for the undervaluation of the yuan differed widely, ranging from zero to 50% depending on the countries taken as benchmark and the price deflators used (see **Exhibit 2**).[54]

Contention also arose over the consequences of China's exchange rate policy on growth. A study found that an appreciation of the yuan by, for example, 10% would shave about 0.86% off China's annual growth rate.[55] Some economists challenged the magnitude, robustness and nature of these effects, arguing that they may have reflected the beneficial effects on growth of other policies that incidentally led to an undervalued yuan.[56]

Wen Jiabao's Plans for 2010

In his March 2010 speech on China's strategy, Premier Wen Jiabao expressed satisfaction about China's recovery from the financial crisis. Always a realist, though, Wen highlighted the many entrenched problems still affecting China's economic development:

> There is insufficient internal impetus driving economic growth; our independent innovation capability is not strong; there is still considerable excess production capacity in some industries and it is becoming more difficult to restructure them. . . . [T]he foundation for keeping agricultural production and farmers' incomes growing steadily is weak; latent risk in the banking and public finance sectors are increasing; and major problems in the areas of healthcare, education, housing, income distribution and public administration urgently require solutions."[57]

After setting a growth target of 8% for GDP in 2010, Wen outlined the government's focus. In addition to better macro-economic control, the government needed to continue to promote "restructuring," encourage domestic demand and invest in domestic infrastructure. He also called for greater balance between regions, further development of the service sector, rural and institutional reform and above all, the "promotion of social harmony."[58]

However, "social harmony" did not seem to extend to some large European and American companies. Throughout the early summer of 2010, more and more CEOs from companies such as Siemens, BASF, Google and GE complained about protectionism and unfair trade and investment restrictions. Jurgen Hambrecht, chief executive of BASF, complained about the forced transfer of business and technology know-how to Chinese firms in exchange for market access. Frustrated by the regulatory environment, Jeff Immelt of GE remarked, "I am not sure that in the end they want any of us to win, or any of us to be successful."[59]

On June 18, 2010, the People's Bank of China decided to allow the exchange rate of the yuan to appreciate gradually under tight bands. By July 4, it had moved to 6.78% — up 0.04 yuan/dollar from its previous fixed rate. In New York, this gave Chuck Schumer pause. The U.S. unemployment rate was still 9.5% and Schumer did not think that .04 represented much of a change . . . but it was a change.[60]

Endnotes

[1] Wen Jiabao, "Report on the Work of the Government," Xinhua News Agency, March 5, 2010, p. 13.

[2] "Trade Policy Review, Report by China," World Trade Organization, April 26, 2010, p. 17.

3 "Employment, Hours, and Earnings from the Current Employment Statistics Survey (National)," U.S. Bureau of Labor Statistics, http://www.bls.gov/ces/home.htm# analytical. Statistics are seasonally adjusted and are measured as of July of each year.

4 David Lawder, "Senators say China suppresses IMF yuan criticism," Reuters, May 18, 2010, http://www.reuters.com/article/idUSTRE64H4TI20100518, accessed January 5, 2011.

5 Interview with the authors, March 15, 2010.

6 Stefan Halper, *The Beijing Consensus: How China's Authoritarian Model Will Dominate the Twenty-First Century* (New York: Basic Books, 2010).

7 "Schumer, joined by bipartisan group of senators, calls for China to stop suppressing IMF report that could be smoking gun on China's currency manipulation," Office of Senator Charles Schumer press release, May 18, 2010.

8 Zheng Song, Kjetil Storesletten, and Fabrizio Zilibotti, "Growing Like China," (paper, November 2009), http://homepage.fudan.edu.cn/~zsong/Michael_files/Research/glc_091125.pdf, accessed January 5, 2011.

9 World Trade Organization, http://www.wto.org/english/news_e/pres01_e/pr243_e.htm; and the *China Business Review* 30, no. 5 (September/October 2003).

10 *2009 White Paper: American Business in China*, American Chamber of Commerce in the People's Republic of China, p. 15.

11 Visit by the author, March 2010.

12 Xiao, F. and D. Kimball (2006), "Effectiveness and Efects of China's Capital Controls," http://www.apeaweb.org/confer/sea06/papers/kimball-xiao.pdf

13 Guonan, M. and R. McCauley (2007), "Are China's Capital Controls still Binding?" BIS. http://www.defi-univ.org/IMG/pdf/Ma-McCauley.pdf

14 Foreign ownership in the stock market in Korea was 40%, in Taiwan, 7%, in India, 6%. Guonan, M. and R. McCauley (2007) *op. cit.*

15 For example, it imposed a quota on offshore borrowing by foreign banks operating in China. Ouyang, A., R. Rajan and T. Willet (2007), "China as a Reserve Sink: The Evidence from Offset and Sterilization Coefficients", Hong Kong Monetary Authority WP No. 10/2007.

16 Guonan, M. and R. McCauley (2007) *op. cit.*

17 Guonan, M. and R. McCauley (2007) *op. cit.*

18 Dani Rodrik (2006), "What's So Special about China's Exports?" China & World Economy, Institute of World Economics and Politics, Chinese Academy of Social Sciences, Vol. 14, no. 5, pp. 1–19.

19 U.S. Bureau of Labor Statistics, "Employment, Hours, and Earnings."

20 There is a debate about the growth rates of TFP both in China and in the East Asian miracle economies. Estimates for China based on official data imply an average annual TFP growth rate between 1980 and 2009 of 4.6%. The estimates from Hsieh on the average growth rate across the four Asian miracle economies (i.e., South Korea, Taiwan, Singapore, and Hong Kong) between 1960–1995 are of 2.5% per year.

21 Chih-Hai Yang (February 2009), "Technological sources and regional productivity growth in China," *China Economic Journal*, Vol. 2, no. 1, pp. 73–92.

[22] Chang-Tai Hsieh and Pete Klenow (November 2009), "Misallocation and Manufacturing TFP in China and India," *Quarterly Journal of Economics*, Vol. 124, pp. 1403–1448.

[23] International Energy Agency, Oil Market Report website, June 10, 2010, 12, 22.

[24] *World Energy Outlook 2008*, International Energy Agency.

[25] *Ibid.*, 21.

[26] Thomas Lum *et al.* (2009), "China's Foreign Aid Activities in Africa, Latin America, and Southeast Asia," Congressional Research Service, February 25, p. 2.

[27] *Understanding Chinese Foreign Aid: A Look at China's Development Assistance to Africa, Southeast Asia and Latin America*, NYU Wagner School, April 25, 2008.

[28] *OECD and Africa*, OECD, March 2008.

[29] *Understanding Chinese Foreign Aid*, NYU Wagner School.

[30] "Military Power of the People's Republic of China: A Report to Congress Pursuant to the National Defense Authorization Act," U.S. Department of Defense, 2009.

[31] Wen Jiabao, "Report on the Work of the Government," March 2010, pp. 1–3.

[32] David Bray, *Social Space and Governance in Urban China: the Danwei System from Origins to Reform* (Stanford: Stanford University Press, 2005).

[33] "Income Gap Widens in First Quarter," *China Daily*, June 19, 2005, http://www.chinadaily.com.cn/english/doc/2005-06/19/content_452636.htm.

[34] *OECD Economic Surveys: China*, volume 2010/6 (February 2010): pp. 164–165; Wing Chan and Will Buckingham (2008), "Is China Abolishing the *Hukou* System?" *China Quarterly*, Vol. 195, pp. 582–606.

[35] Huafeng Zhang (2010), "The *Hukou* system's constraints on migrant workers' job mobility in Chinese cities," *China Economic Review* 21, pp. 51–64.

[36] "Briefing — Migration in China," *The Economist*, May 8, 2010, 25.

[37] Winnie Yip and William Hsiao (2009), "China's health care reform: A tentative assessment," *China Economic Review*, Vol. 20, p. 614.

[38] *Ibid.*

[39] S. Hu *et al.* (2008), "Reform of How Health Care is Paid for in China: Challenges and Opportunities," *Lancet*, Vol. 372, pp. 1846–1853.

[40] Winnie Yip and William Hsiao (2009), "China's health care reform," *China Economic Review*, Vol. 20, p. 613.

[41] B. O'Neill and S. Scherbov (2010), "Interpreting UN Urbanization Projections Using a Multi-state Model," cited in *OECD Economic Surveys: China*, p. 184.

[42] *Ibid.*, pp. 189–193.

[43] "China rolls out fresh policies to help college graduates find jobs," *China View*, February 15, 2009, http://news.xinhuanet.com/english/2009-02/15/content_10824372.htm.

[44] "China's Ant Tribe: Millions of Unemployed College Grads," *Wandering China*, Feburary 8, 2010, http://wanderingchina.wordpress.com/2010/02/08/chinas-ant-tribe-millions-of-unemployed-college-grads.

[45] *Monthly Labour Review*, U.S. Bureau of Labour Statistics, April 2009, quoted by Stephen Roach in *The Economist*, July 18, 2010.

[46] Ting-I Tsai and Owen Fletcher, "Higher Wages in China Ripple," *Wall Street Journal*, July 22, 2010, b-2.

[47] Malcolm Moore, "How much higher can factory wages go?" *China Economic Review*, March 11, 2010; and Uking Sun, "No cheap labor? China increases minimum wages," *China Daily*, July 2, 2010.

[48] *China Country Report*, Economist Intelligence Unit, July 2010, p. 14.

[49] It had risen by 21% in 2008. China Monthly Economic Indicators, OECD, January 2010.

[50] Susan Li and Jacob Greber, "China Property Market Beginning Collapse that May Hit Banks, Rogoff Says," July 6, 2010, via Bloomberg, accessed January 5, 2011.

[51] Despite that, Chinese authorities intensified a crackdown on property speculation after announcing that the economy had expanded at an 11.9 percent annual pace in the first quarter, the most since 2007. Measures included raising minimum mortgage rates and down payment ratios for some home purchases. State media reported some discussion of a trial property tax.

[52] Vikas Bajaj, "Coming Visit May Signal Easing by China on Currency," *New York Times*, April 1, 2010.

[53] Luis A.V. Catao, "Why Real Exchange Rates?" *Finance & Development*, September 2007, p. 46, http://www.imf.org/EXTERNAL/PUBS/FT/FANDD/2007/09/pdf/basics. pdf, accessed July 12, 2010.

[54] Jeffery Frankel (2009), "New Estimation of China's Exchange Rate Regime," *NBER Working Paper No. 14700*; and Vikas Bajaj, "Coming Visit May Signal Easing by China on Currency," *New York Times*, April 1, 2010.

[55] Dani Rodrik (2008), "The Real Exchange Rate and Economic Growth," *Brookings Papers on Economic Activity*, Fall 2008, pp. 365–439.

[56] Michael Woodford (2009), "Is an Undervalued Currency the Key to Economic Growth?" Columbia University, *Discussion Paper 0809-13*.

[57] Wen Jiabao, "Report on the Work of the Government," p. 9.

[58] *Ibid.*, pp. 10–29.

[59] Quoted in Daniel Drezner, "The Death of the China Lobby," *Foreign Policy*, July 23, 2010, http://drezner.foreignpolicy.com / posts / 2010 / 07 / 20 / the_death_of_the_china_ lobby.

[60] David Lawder, "Senators say China suppresses IMF yuan criticism," Reuters, May 18, 2010, http://www.reuters.com/article/idUSTRE64H4TI20100518, accessed January 5, 2011.

Malaysia: People First?

Diego Comin* and John Abraham*

Today I ask you to join me in this task of renewing Malaysia. I urge you to rise to the challenge of building a One Malaysia. People First. Performance Now.

— Prime Minister Najib, April 3, 2009

We're so plugged into the World economy. . . .

— Prime Minister Najib, September 29, 2009

On March 30, 2010, Prime Minister Najib Razak presented his new economic model (NEM) for Malaysia.[1] With the goal of raising per capita income to over $15,000 by 2020 from the current level of $6,634, the plan included measures to improve human capital, reduce migration, and privatize inefficient government-linked corporations (GLCs). However, the most controversial part of the NEM was the dismantling of the new economic policy (NEP), an affirmative action program for native Malays that had alleviated racial tensions and reduced inter-racial income inequality over the previous 40 years though, some argued, at the cost of fostering corruption.

Few would have guessed that less than a year after taking office on April 3, 2009, Najib would be presenting the most radical program since the NEP was introduced in 1971 by his father, Abdul Razak, Malaysia's second prime minister. But the situation inherited by Najib could hardly have been worse. The economy was in the midst of

*Reprinted with permission of Harvard Business School Publishing.
Malaysia People First 710-033.
This case was prepared by Professor Diego Comin and John Abraham (Harvard University 2010).

a deep recession, the first since the Asian crisis in 1998. Growth had never recovered the pace it had achieved before the Asia crisis, and investment had plunged from 45% of GDP to 19%.

The political situation was almost as delicate as the economic. The ruling political coalition, the Barisan Nasional (BN), united three of the largest political parties — the United Malays National Organization (UMNO), the Malaysian Chinese Association (MCA), and the Malaysian Indian Congress (MIC). In the March 2008 elections the opposition coalition, formed by the People's Justice Party (PKR), the Democratic Action Party (DAP), and the Islamic Party of Malaysia (PAS) was a close contender. For the first time since the country gained independence from Britain in 1957, the BN had not won two-thirds of the seats required to pass constitutional amendments.

But despite the strength of the PKR opposition, Najib could anticipate an even stronger opposition from his own party, UNMO. The NEP had been its flagship program over the last 40 years and an unquestionable pillar of Malaysian development strategy. Would UMNO and the ethnic Malays be ready to give it up? Would the NEM suffice to achieve Najib's goal by 2020?

Profile

The Federation of Malaysia, a Southeast Asian country with a tropical climate, is divided into two main regions: peninsular Malaysia, extending southward from China and Thailand, and East Malaysia, across the China Sea from the mainland on the island of Borneo (see **Exhibit 1a**). As of 2009, Malaysia reported a population of 28.3 million people,[2] and Kuala Lumpur, the capital and largest city, registered nearly 2 million residents. The country comprised many regional ethnic and religious groups, although Islam was the official state religion and Malaysian the official language. As of 2004, the three largest ethnic groups were the native Malays (*bumiputera*) 50.4%, Chinese 23.7%, and Indians 7.1%, although there were a significant number of legal and illegal immigrants from neighboring countries (see **Exhibit 1b**).[3]

In 2009, Malaysia's per capita income based on purchasing power parity was $14,700, as compared with $4,000 for Indonesia, $8,100 for Thailand, and $27,700 for Korea.[4] Rich in biodiversity and natural resources, Malaysia owed its early development to rubber, tin, and palm oil. In 2007, agriculture contributed 10% to its GDP, industry 48%, and services 42%.[5] Malaysia was open to trade, with exports at 87.3% of GDP and imports at 64.5% of GDP in 2009.[6] China accounted for 12.9% of Malaysia's trade, Singapore 12.7%, the United States 11.1%, Japan 11%, Thailand 5.6%, Korea 4.2% and Hong Kong 4.0%.[7] Its major exports were electronics and electrical machinery, chemical and petrochemical products and commodities.[8]

Exhibit 1a.   Map of Malaysia

Source: Central Intelligence Agency, www.cia.gov/cia/publications/factbook/geos/my.html, accessed March 2010.

Exhibit 1b.   Population by Ethnic Group and Legal Status

	Bumiputera			Non-*Bumiputera*				
Year	Malay (%)[a]	Other (%)[a]	Total (%)[a]	Chinese (%)[a]	Indian (%)[a]	Other (%)[a]	Total Citizens (in millions)	Total People (in millions)
1947			49.3	38.3	10.9	1.5	4.9	
1957			49.8	37.2	11.1	2.0	6.3	
1970			53.1	35.4	10.6	0.8	8.8	
1980			55.3	33.8	10.2	0.7	11.4	
1999			62.5	26.6	7.5	3.5	21.1	
2000	53.4	11.7	65.1	26.0	7.7	1.2	21.9	23.3
2004[b]	50.4			23.7	7.1			25.6

Sources: Adapted from Donald Snodgrass, Inequality and Economic Development in Malaysia (Kuala Lumpur: Oxford University Press, 1980); K.S. Jomo, A Question of Class (New York: Monthly Review Press, 1988); Economist Intelligence Unit (EIU), EIU Country Profile 2000 Malaysia Brunei (2000); and Institute of Strategic and International Studies (Malaysia), www.jaring.my/isis/merc/populati.htm.; 2000: From Malaysia Census, Department of Statistics. CIA Fact book for 2004.

Notes: May not add up to 100% due to rounding.

[a]% of total citizens, [b]except for 2004; Total people includes non-citizens.

Malaysia was served by a network of 94,500 kilometers of primary and secondary roads, 70,970 kilometers of which were paved. These included 580 kilometers of superior quality expressways connecting Kuala Lumpur with Singapore, the nation-state at the southern tip of peninsular Malaysia, and with major seaports and other destinations. However, the road transportation system was still underdeveloped in East Malaysia.

Background: Colonial Rule and Independence

Britain established colonial rule in what is now Malaysia when the East India Company landed its ships there in 1786. Rubber plantations and tin mines fueled British mercantilist trade with Malaysia, and to better exploit these resources, Chinese and Indian immigration was encouraged. The colonial administration attempted to respect Malay "ownership" by preserving Malay interests in "education, public affairs and the economy."[9]

When Malaysia gained independence in 1957, it enjoyed substantial opportunities for growth. The colonial system had bequeathed it good infrastructure, a robust primary export sector, an efficient administrative framework and a common law tradition.[10] However, racial tensions stood in the way of national unification. The colonial system had never promoted racial integration.[11] Native Malays, supported by the British administration, saw themselves as the rightful "owners," but generations of Chinese and Indian immigrants were interwoven in a patchwork culture.[12] The *bumiputera* majority held political power but had not prospered economically, while the Chinese and Indian groups enjoyed economic success but lacked political clout (see **Exhibits 2a** through **2c**).[13] Ultimately, the groups agreed to ensure *bumiputera* political control in exchange for citizenship and language rights, and ethnically defined political groups united behind the Barisan Nasional (BN) to establish a ruling party. Although the three groups struck a peaceful balance, the society and the political system remained racially divided.

Exhibit 2a.   Income Distribution by Ethnicity (1970), (as a percentage of total households, in Malaysian ringgit)

Income Range (per month)	Malay	Chinese	Indian	Other
RM 1–100	22.9	2.6	1.3	0.2
RM 100–199	19.1	7.8	4.4	0.1
RM 200–399	10.4	11.9	3.5	0.1
RM 400–699	3.0	5.3	1.2	0.1
RM 700 and above	1.3	3.7	0.8	0.3
Total	56.7	31.3	11.2	0.8

Source: Created by casewriter using data from Government of Malaysia, Mid-Term Review of Second Malaysia Plan (Kuala Lumpur, 1973).

Note: Data is for Peninsular Malaysia only.

Exhibit 2b.   Incidence of Poverty in Peninsular Malaysia

(In percentages)	1970	1980	1990	1995	2000[a]	2007[a]
Households below poverty line	49.4	33.8	15.0	9.1	5.5	3.6

Sources: Adapted from Government of Malaysia, Third Malaysia Plan (Kuala Lumpur, 1976); Government of Malaysia, *Sixth Malaysia Plan* (Kuala Lumpur, 1991); Government of Malaysia, *Seventh Malaysia Plan* (Kuala Lumpur, 1996); and Government of Malaysia, *Eighth Malaysia Plan* (Kuala Lumpur, 2001), and New Economic Model for Malaysia Part I. NEAC, 2010.

Note: The poverty line income is, according to official definitions, the monthly income necessary to cover minimum nutritional requirements and essential non-food expenses.

[a] Figures for 2000 and 2004 refer to all of Malaysia, which comprises Peninsula Malaysia, Sabah and Sarawak.

Exhibit 2c.   Ownership Distribution by Ethnicity (share capital[a] of limited companies)

(In percentages)	1970	1975	1980	1985	1990	1995	2000	2004
Bumiputera	2.4	9.2	12.5	19.1	19.3	20.6	18.9	18.9
Individuals & Institutions	1.6	3.6	5.8	11.7	14.2	18.6	17.2	17.2
Trust Agencies	0.8	5.6	6.7	7.4	5.1	2.0	1.7	1.7
Non-*Bumiputera*[b]	28.3	37.5	44.5	47.7	46.8	43.4	41.3	40.6
Chinese	27.2	—	—	45.3	45.5	40.9	38.9	39
Indians	1.0	—	—	1.2	1.0	1.5	1.5	1.2
Others	—	—	—	1.3	0.3	1.0	0.9	0.4
Nominee companies	6.0	—	—	7.2	8.5	8.3	8.5	8.0
Foreigners	63.4	53.3	43.0	26.0	25.4	27.7	31.3	32.5
Total (RM million)[c]	5,329	15,084	32,420	77,964	108,377	179,792	332,418	529,769

Sources: Government of Malaysia, *Second Malaysia Plan* (Kuala Lumpur, 1971); Government of Malaysia, *Third Malaysia Plan* (Kuala Lumpur, 1976); Government of Malaysia, Mid-term Review of *Fourth Malaysia Plan* (Kuala Lumpur, 1983); Government of Malaysia, *Seventh Malaysia Plan* (Kuala Lumpur, 1996); Government of Malaysia, *Eighth Malaysia Plan* (Kuala Lumpur, 2001); and Government of Malaysia, *Ninth Malaysia Plan* (Kuala Lumpur, 2006).

Notes: [a] At par value.
[b] Data for 1975 and 1980 includes shares held by nominee companies.
[c] Excludes shares held by federal, state and local governments.

Exhibit 2d.   Income Inequality

	1970	1987	1997	2007
Gini Coefficient	0.513	0.456	0.459	0.441

Source: Created by case writer using data from New Economic Model for Malaysia Part I. NEAC, 2010.

Development Strategies

In Malaysia's colonial era, the economy was dominated by the primary sector. Half of GNP was accounted for by agriculture, forestry, and fishing, as well as two valuable but volatile commodities: tin and rubber.[14] As rubber and tin prices surged and sank in the 1950s and 1960s, the overall economy expanded and contracted with them. To free itself from erratic commodity prices set in international markets, the new Malaysian state focused on diversifying the economy.[15] To this end, the government devoted nearly half of its development spending on building a modern transport, power and communications infrastructure from 1956 to 1970.

Import Substitution

In its early years as a nation, the country adopted an import substitution industrialization (ISI) strategy, promoting domestic production to substitute for manufactured imports. By providing infrastructure, credit facilities and fiscal incentives, this strategy encouraged capital investments by mainly foreign manufacturing companies seeking to increase their market share.[16] The 1958 Pioneer Industries Ordinance granted tax relief on profits for "pioneer firms" over time periods depending on the size of the investment.[17] Intended to help new industries while they were just becoming established, the fiscal incentives were in principle temporary, though in practice they could be extended by various means. In addition, producers were granted tariff protection that tended to last even longer. These incentives led to higher investment rates. However, they tended to favor large, capital-intensive, usually foreign companies. The domestic capital participating in the ISI initiatives in the 1960s was rather small, mainly involving ethnic Chinese in food-processing, plastic and wood-based industries.[18]

Most foreign companies enjoying the benefits of import substitution merely established subsidiaries for assembling, finishing and packaging goods. Since the materials and technology were typically imported from the parent company, they were poorly linked to the rest of the national economy; modern technologies did not diffuse widely to domestic producers.[19] Overall, the 1960s saw moderate increases in wages for capital-intensive industries, but unemployment remained high and domestic demand meager.[20] Nevertheless, real GDP growth accelerated from 2.6% during the 1950s to 6% during the 1960s.[21]

By the late 1960s, the growth model seemed increasingly inadequate. Growth had been geographically imbalanced, centered on peninsular Malaysia and had exacerbated ethnic tensions. The share of business owned by *bumiputera* was only 2.4%, while Chinese and foreign ownership shares amounted to 27.2% and 63.4% respectively (see **Exhibit 2c**). Non-*bumiputera* groups felt that the government was limiting their economic opportunities, while the *bumiputera* were not convinced their interests were being adequately protected.[22] In May 1969, ethnic hostilities exploded in riots that shook the nation and left hundreds dead.

The extreme social distress and hostility led to much soul searching for Malaysian leaders. Mohammed Mahathir, a founding member of UMNO and eventually prime minister, postulated that the origins of the intense conflict lay in economic "imbalance" — Malay disappointment and resentment at the Chinese wealth — and many political leaders shared his view (see **Exhibits 1b** and **2c**). This conclusion led them to shift development goals from pure growth to "balanced growth" in accordance with social objectives.[23] In 1971, Abdul Razak, second prime minister of Malaysia, embodied these development goals in the New Economic Policy (NEP). This reinvention of the nation's socio-economic paradigm sought to achieve "national unity" by both ending poverty and restructuring society to eliminate the identification of race with economic status.[24] The plan called for a dramatic change in equity ownership: foreign ownership, standing at about 60%, was to be reduced to no more than 30% by 1990, while *bumiputera* ownership should rise from 2.4% to no less than 30%. Additional rules guided lending practices, interest rates, and bank licensing.

Export Orientation

Beginning in the early 1970s, the government implemented a host of policies to realize these objectives. Given the limited successes of ISI, the government turned to export-oriented industrialization (EOI). In 1971 the Free Trade Zone Act set up special low-tariff zones to encourage companies to manufacture for export.[25] Price discrimination, quotas, fiscal incentives, administrative support, and government-linked corporations (GLCs) were deployed to promote economic activity and "balance" the economy. The quotas and subsidies protected infant corporations from international competition while they got started but also insulated established private firms and GLCs alike and crystallized inefficiencies. Labor quotas mandated that *bumiputera* be appointed to high level positions in GLCs, a provision hoped to foster entrepreneurship.

The formation of free trade zones and tax incentives succeeded in expanding the manufacturing sector at an average annual rate of 22.9% and dramatically increasing exports.[26] Electronics and textile manufacturers began popping up around the country, setting up labor-intensive operations that both absorbed surplus labor and increased productivity. Western firms including Intel, National Semiconductor, and 3M invested heavily in Malaysia.[27] Despite a sharp contraction due to the 1973 oil crisis, overall growth for the decade clocked in at over 7% per year.

Heavy Industry and Liberalization

On July 16, 1980, Mahathir became Malaysia's fourth prime minister after Hussein Onn stepped down due to health reasons. Mahathir was the nation's first prime minister that came from a modest social background and, after 22 years in office, he would become one of the most significant figures in Malaysia's history.

Around the time Mahathir took office, Malaysia's growth strategies ran into problems. Its export-oriented growth was constrained by trade and transport barriers, industrialized economies' growing preference for importing raw materials rather than manufactured goods, and a prolonged global slowdown.[28] The public expenditure programs and GLCs, for their part, produced "bloated bureaucracy, inferior services, economic inefficiency, high costs, low productivity, and limited innovation."[29] Part of the problem was lack of expertise among government-appointed *bumiputera* managers. State-sponsored businesses were expected to pursue social and redistributive objectives, according to the NEP, and political motivations outweighed efforts to improve efficiency and maximize profits.[30] As well, major state enterprises often suffered from poor oversight and scarce audits.

In a move away from export-oriented policies, the government now attempted to diversify the industrial sector by promoting heavy industrialization through import substitution — cement, petrochemicals, iron, steel, paper, and machinery production, as well as the "national car," the Proton Saga. The hope was to stimulate backward linkages, as Korea and Japan had done. Under the umbrella "Look East" policy, Dr. Mahathir organized the Heavy Industrialization Corporation of Malaysia (HICOM) as a holding company for joint ventures with foreign firms, despite resistance from his cabinet and widespread criticism.[31] However, the new heavy industrialization effort forced the government to undertake massive investment and privatize many GLCs.[32] Facing pressures to deregulate from the West and international economic organizations, the government put companies under *bumiputera* control, despite the shortage of competent and experienced *bumiputera* managers.[33]

Commodity prices plunged in the mid-1980s and Malaysia's terms of trade deteriorated, instigating a current account deficit, along with the widening budget deficit and a growth slowdown. Facing a downturn in 1985, the government sought to consolidate and liberalize the banking sector, and it provided incentives for FDI inflows. Relaxing restrictions on foreign equity holdings made Malaysia more attractive to foreign investors.[34] For example, in 1985 new guidelines were announced which allowed highly export-oriented companies to be wholly foreign-owned.[35] By the end of the decade, banks were free to set deposit and lending rates within some bands dictated by Bank Negara. Improvements in external conditions yielded growth of more than 9% for 1988–1990 and for the first time, in 1989 manufacturing overtook agriculture in its share of GDP. Real GDP averaged a respectable 6.0% growth over the decade.

In the 1991 Sixth Malaysia plan, Prime Minister Mahathir introduced his Vision 2020. The vision called for the nation to achieve a self-sufficient industrial, Malaysian-centric economy by 2020. In order to achieve that vision, Mahathir predicted that the nation required an annual real GDP growth of 7% over the 30-year period. In line with this goal, real GDP grew at an annual average of 9.6% from 1991 to 1996 and inter-racial redistribution accelerated (see **Exhibit 2c**).

Malaysia was viewed internationally as a hotbed of growth (see **Exhibits 3a and 4**).[36] The share of FDI in total investment reached a record high of 23% in 1992, a result of government location incentives, and tax allowances and deductions.[37] Capital poured into electronics and other export-oriented sectors. Real estate also gained traction, and the tallest building in the world, the Petronas Tower, was erected. The slow but continual liberalization of the banking sector advanced, finally allowing banks to borrow abroad and lend foreign exchange to both non-residents and residents, though the loans to residents needed approval. Portfolio inflows and outflows were largely unrestricted, and only foreign corporations borrowing domestically were subject to ceilings. Despite temporary capital controls implemented in 1993 over concerns about the ringgit's strength, regulation in Malaysia was opening the door to international synergies.

Some observers pointed to vulnerabilities within what seemed to be a sturdy economy. Pegging the ringgit to a basket of currencies encouraged "domestic financial institutions to accumulate large amounts of short-term foreign currency denominated loans."[38] In addition, these policies may have caused the exchange rate to appreciate and discouraged export growth, instigating current account deficits. Others were concerned about the massive inflows of portfolio investments (see **Exhibit 4**), lending portfolios heavily exposed to the property sector's exuberance, and the dramatic acceleration of bank lending (see **Exhibit 3c**).[39] However, the government's close involvement with the banking industry was seen as a signal to foreign investors that it would not let domestic financial institutions fail.[40] Regardless, none of these factors were thought to cause a serious imbalance, and few predicted a contraction, let alone the massive financial turmoil that would ravage the country.

The Asian Crisis

In late 1997, Malaysia's decade of exuberant growth came to a sudden halt. Already in March 1996, the Thai government had been forced to purchase $4 billion in real

Exhibit 3a.   Output, Productivity and Costs

	1996	1997	1998	1999	2000	2004	2005	2006	2007	2008	2009[a]	2010[b]
GDP per head ($ at PPP)	7,875	8,395	7,682	8,079	9,018	10,854	11,531	12,362	13,238	13,860	13,530	13,950
GDP (% real change pa)	10.0	7.3	−7.4	6.1	8.9	6.8	5.3	5.8	6.2	4.6	−1.7	3.5
Labor productivity growth (%)	7.3	3.5	−8.5	3.1	3.8	5.3	5.0	3.1	3.6	3.4	−1.8	2.5
Total factor productivity growth (%)	4.1	0.9	−9.7	3.0	3.9	4.5	3.7	2.6	2.9	2.3	−3.1	1.7
Average real wages (% change pa)	4.8	4.5	−4.7	−0.6	0.4	2.5	1.9	0.4	1.9	−0.9	−0.3	−1.0
Unit labor costs (% change pa in US$)	0.5	−7.3	−21.4	2.2	−1.7	−0.2	1.3	5.1	8.8	5.3	−7.6	2.7
Labor costs per hour (US$)	2.7	2.6	1.9	2.0	2.1	2.3	2.4	2.6	2.8	3.1	2.9	3.0
Labor force (millions)	8.5	8.7	8.9	9.2	9.6	10.4	10.4	10.7	10.9	11.1	11.2	11.3
Unemployment rate	2.5	2.5	3.2	3.4	3.1	3.6	3.6	3.3	3.2	3.3	3.8	3.7

Source: Created by casewriter using data from Economist Intelligence Unit, www.eiu.com, accessed October 3, 2010.

Note: [a]Estimates.
[b]Forecasts.

Exhibit 3b.　GDP and Components

	1996	1997	1998	1999	2000	2004	2005	2006	2007	2008	2009[a]	2010[b]
Private consumption (% of GDP)	46.0	45.3	41.6	41.6	43.8	44.0	44.8	45.0	45.8	45.2	45.7	45.6
Government consumption (% of GDP)	11.1	10.8	9.8	11.0	10.2	12.6	12.3	11.9	12.2	12.5	13.5	13.4
Gross fixed investment (% of GDP)	42.5	43.1	26.8	21.9	25.3	21.0	20.5	20.8	21.7	19.6	18.7	20.4
Stock building (% of GDP)	−1.0	−0.1	−0.2	0.5	1.6	2.1	−0.5	−0.3	0.0	−0.5	−0.7	0.2
Exports of G&S (% of GDP)	91.6	93.3	115.7	121.3	119.8	115.4	117.5	116.5	110.5	103.6	87.3	92.3
Imports of G&S (% of GDP)	90.2	92.4	93.7	96.3	100.6	95.0	94.6	93.9	90.2	80.5	64.5	72.0
Domestic demand (% of GDP)	98.6	99.1	78.0	74.9	80.8	79.6	77.2	77.4	79.7	76.9	77.2	79.6
Gross national savings (% of GDP)	38.0	37.2	40.1	37.5	33.8	31.9	35.4	37.7	37.4	37.7	35.2	32.3

Source: Created by casewriter using data from Economist Intelligence Unit, www.eiu.com, accessed October 3, 2010.

Note: [a] Estimates.

[b] Forecasts.

Exhibit 3c.   Credit and Financial Indicators

	1994	1995	1996	1997	1998	1999	2000	2006	2007	2008	2009	2010[b]
Nominal GDP[a]	196	223	254	282	283	301	356	574	640	739	730	742
Stock of domestic credit[a]	219	282	361	460	459	451	493	684	728	853	927	985
Loans extended by banking system (% growth)												
Manufacturing	—	—	14.8	18.5	2.0	0.6	3.3	6.0	12.3	6.5	−4.0	—
Property	—	—	26.8	34.0	6.9	2.3	5.6	0.7	11.0	12.6	11.4	—
Lending interest rate (%)	—	—	10.1	11.5	9.7	7.8	7.5	6.6	6.3	5.9	5.0	5.1
Deposit interest rate (%)	—	—	7.2	9.1	5.8	3.3	3.5	3.2	3.2	3.0	2.1	2.5
Money market interest rate (%)	—	—	6.9	7.8	9.4	4.1	3.2	3.6	3.6	3.6	2.2	2.5
Long-term bond yield (%)	—	—	6.8	7.0	7.7	6.5	5.9	4.3	3.7	4.1	4.1	4.3
Consumer prices (% change pa; av)	3.5	3.5	3.5	2.6	5.3	2.8	1.6	3.6	2.0	5.4	0.5	1.5
Stockmarket index	971	995	1,238	594	586	812	680	1,096	1,445	877	1,273	—

Source: Economist Intelligence Unit, www.eiu.com, accessed October 3, 2010.

Note: [a]bn RM.

[b]Forecasts.

Exhibit 3d. Government Finance

	1996	1997	1998	1999	2000	2004	2005	2006	2007	2008	2009[a]	2010[b]
Budget balance (% of GDP)	0.7	2.4	-1.8	-3.2	-5.5	-4.1	-3.6	-3.3	-3.2	-4.8	-7.6	-5.8
Budget revenue (% of GDP)	23.0	23.3	20.0	19.5	17.4	21.0	20.3	21.5	21.9	21.6	21.6	20.2
Budget expenditure (% of GDP)	22.3	21.0	21.8	22.7	22.9	25.1	23.9	24.8	25.1	26.5	29.2	26.0
Debt interest payments (% of GDP)	2.7	2.3	2.4	2.6	2.5	2.3	2.2	2.2	2.0	1.7	1.9	2.3
Primary balance (% of GDP)	3.4	4.6	0.7	-0.5	-3.0	-1.8	-1.4	-1.2	-1.2	-3.1	-5.7	-3.5
Public debt (% of GDP)	35.3	31.9	36.4	37.3	35.2	45.7	43.8	42.2	41.7	41.5	48.7	53.1

Source: Created by case writer using data from Economist Intelligence Unit, www.eiu.com, accessed October 3, 2010.

Note: [a]Estimates.
[b]Forecasts.

Exhibit 4. Balance of Payments (US$ millions)

	1996	1997	1998	1999	2000	2005	2006	2007	2008	2009
Goods exports	76,985	77,538	71,883	84,052	98,429	141,808	160,916	176,433	199,733	157,632
Goods imports	−73,137	−74,029	−54,378	−61,404	−77,602	−108,653	−123,474	−139,243	−148,472	−119,339
Trade balance	3,848	3,509	17,505	22,648	20,827	33,156	37,441	37,190	51,261	36,472
Service balance	−2,437	−2,570	−1,610	−2,816	−2,807	−2,380	−1,970	690	51	382
Income balance	−4,690	−5,366	−3,904	−5,497	−7,608	−6,318	−4,712	−4,055	−7,137	−3,229
Transfers balance	−1,182	−1,509	−2,462	−1,728	−1,924	−4,477	−4,560	−4,582	−5,262	−4,539
Current account	−4,461	−5,936	9,529	12,607	8,488	19,980	26,200	29,243	38,914	30,907
Capital account	—	—	—	—	—	—	−72	−28	187	—
Direct investment net	5,078	5,137	2,163	2,473	1,762	994	53	−2,687	−7,827	−2,505
Portfolio Investment assets	n.a.	n.a.	n.a.	−133	−387	−715	−2,121	−3,940	−2,878	−1,061
Portfolio investment liabilities	−268	−248	283	−892	−2,145	−2,985	5,557	9,320	−21,083	−5,524
Other investment assets	4,134	−4,604	−5,269	−7,936	−5,565	−4,877	−8,562	−17,376	3,826	—
Other investment liabilities	533	1,912	272	—	—	−2,164	−6,769	3,707	−5,352	—
Financial account	9,477	2,197	−2,551	−6,619	−6,276	−9,806	−11,812	−11,024	−33,974	—
Net errors and omissions	−2,503	−136	3,040	−1,276	−3,221	−6,555	−7,451	−5,047	−8,578	—

(*Continued*)

Exhibit 4. *(Continued)*

	1996	1997	1998	1999	2000	2005	2006	2007	2008	2009
Change in reserve assets	−2,513	3,875	−10,018	−4,712	1,009	−3,620	−6,864	−13,144	3,450	—
Current account balance (% of GDP)	−4.4	−5.9	13.1	16.0	9.1	14.5	16.7	15.7	17.6	16.2
Total external debt (% of GDP)	39.3	47.1	58.7	52.9	44.7	37.7	36.1	28.9	24.5	25.4
Short-term debt (% of total)	11.0	14.9	11.7	7.6	4.9	9.6	8.5	8.2	6.9	6.1
Foreign reserves, end of year ($bn)[a]	27	21	26	31	28	70	82	101	91	95
Nominal exchange rate (Malaysian ringgit per US$)	2.5	2.8	3.9	3.8	3.8	3.8	3.5	3.3	3.3	3.5
Real effective exchange rate (base year = 1997)[b]	105.1	100.0	79.8	80.5	81.6	74.6	76.9	82.5	84.2	81.5

Sources: Adapted from IMF, International Financial Statistics (CD-ROM, 2000); Bank Negara Malaysia, Monthly Statistical Bulletin (www.bnm.gov.my).

Note: [a]Includes adjustments to the total value of assets to reflect currency and other gains and losses incurred, real and unrealized, in the period.
[b]An increase in the real effective exchange rate index represents a real appreciation.

estate developers' debt. In January 1997, the collapse of several major Korean and Thai firms warned of danger. A Korean chaebol, Hanbo Steel, led the way, crumbling under the weight of a $6 billion debt, and soon two others, Sammi Steer and Kia Motors, were dragged down. In February, a Thai finance company, Somprasong, missed its payment due on a foreign debt, sending shivers among investors who worried Thai banks were overexposed to a souring real estate market. Almost immediately, lending ceased and property prices plummeted.[41] Over the next five months, the Thai government injected nearly $8 billion into distressed firms. The Bank of Thailand made a commitment to defend the currency, spending $28 billion in exchange reserves and instituting feeble, loophole-ridden capital controls in May. But massive capital flight put intense downward pressure on the region's currencies. On July 2, the Thai government was forced to float the baht.

Shortly after the devaluation of the Thai baht, a modest tremble in the region's other currencies became a forceful tumble, as capital was siphoned out. Just 10 days after the Thai devaluation, the Philippines experienced a panicked outflow and abandoned their peg. By August, Malaysian and Indonesian defense efforts were overwhelmed, forcing both to adopt a floating regime. Shortly afterwards, speculators abandoned the Taiwanese dollar and ravaged the Hong Kong Stock Exchange, which lost nearly a quarter of its value in four days. By mid-November, the crisis eroded the Korean won, forcing the government to float. International speculators trounced governments' efforts to buy back their sickly currencies by pulling $60 billion out of the region in the second half of 1997 and another $55 billion in 1998.

By November of 1997 it became clear that the region's trouble was not a temporary setback but a financial meltdown. Real economic growth plummeted, and it seemed the era of the "Asian Miracles" had come to a close (see **Exhibit 5**). Indonesia, Korea, the Philippines, and Thailand turned to the International Monetary Fund (IMF) for assistance and agreed to the Fund's "structural adjustment" programs. The provisions of the austerity packages were designed to address three broad areas — macroeconomic stabilization, financial sector reform, and structural reform. They were intended to "restore market confidence in the crisis countries and stem the outflow of capital."[42] Governments were forced to reign in fiscal deficits and increase interest rates. The IMF mandated that countries shut down insolvent financial instructions and recapitalize weak ones, increase financial oversight, and open borders to foreign financial firms. Additionally, the IMF required trade liberalization, more market competition, and privatization of state owned enterprises.[43] In exchange for their compliance, the Asian countries received unprecedented assistance packages from the IMF. It provided standby loans, disbursed over three years, for a total of $17.2 billion to Thailand, $40 billion to Indonesia, $57 billion to Korea, and $1 billion to the Philippines. Despite the stringent reform conditions and inflow

Exhibit 5. Comparative Economic Indicators

	1994	1995	1996	1997	1998	1999
Korea						
GDP growth (%)	8.3	8.9	6.8	5.0	−5.8	10.9
Investment rates (% of GDP)	36.5	37.2	37.9	34.2	20.9	—
Government fiscal balances (% of GDP)	0.3	0.3	0.1	−1.3	−3.8	−4.6
Current account (% of GDP)	−1.0	−1.7	−4.4	−1.7	12.6	6.0
Foreign reserves (in months of imports)	2.6	2.5	2.3	1.4	5.1	5.8
Nominal exchange rate (to the US dollar)	803.4	771.3	804.5	951.3	1,401.4	1,188.8
Real exchange rate (100=1997)	90.0	90.6	91.1	81.8	56.2	60.6
Stock market index	1,027.4	882.9	651.2	376.3	562.5	1,028.1
External debt (% of GDP)	18.0	17.5	22.3	28.7	43.4	31.9
Short term debt (% of total)	43.7	54.3	57.5	39.3	20.2	26.8
Bank lending to private sector (growth rate, %)	20.1	15.4	20.0	22.0	—	—
Inflation rate (CPI, %)	7.7	7.1	3.9	3.1	5.3	−2.0
Singapore						
GDP growth (%)	11.2	8.4	7.5	8.0	1.5	5.4
Investment rates (% of GDP)	33.5	34.5	37.0	38.7	33.5	—
Government fiscal balances (% of GDP)	16.3	14.6	10.6	11.7	—	—
Current account (% of GDP)	16.4	17.3	15.9	15.8	20.9	25.0
Foreign reserves (in months of imports)	5.9	5.7	6.0	5.5	7.3	7.0
Nominal exchange rate (to the US dollar)	1.5	1.4	1.4	1.5	1.7	1.7
Real exchange rate (100=1997)	98.4	100.0	103.5	105.7	101.8	95.4
Stock market index	533.6	555.4	536.1	425.9	382.5	668.8
External debt (% of GDP)	10.8	9.8	10.7	—	—	—
Short term debt (% of total)	13.3	14.6	19.8	—	—	—
Bank lending to private sector (growth rate, %)	15.3	20.3	15.8	12.7	—	—
Inflation rate (CPI, %)	3.1	2.6	1.2	1.4	−1.5	−1.3
Indonesia						
GDP growth (%)	7.5	8.2	7.8	4.7	−13.2	0.8
Investment rates (% of GDP)	30.1	31.9	30.7	31.8	14.0	—
Government fiscal balances (% of GDP)	0.9	2.2	1.2	−0.7	−2.4	—
Current account (% of GDP)	−1.6	−3.2	−3.4	−2.3	4.2	4.1
Foreign reserves (in months of imports)	3.2	2.9	3.5	3.0	5.3	6.1

(Continued)

Exhibit 5.   (*Continued*)

	1994	1995	1996	1997	1998	1999
Nominal exchange rate (to the US dollar)	2,160.8	2,248.6	2,342.3	2,909.4	10,013.6	7,855.2
Real exchange rate (100=1997)	111.3	107.6	111.4	100.0	48.7	72.4
Stock market index	469.6	513.8	637.4	401.7	398.0	676.9
Foreign debt (% of GDP)	61.0	61.5	56.7	63.1	152.7	105.3
Short term debt (% of total)	18.0	20.9	25.0	24.1	13.3	13.3
Bank lending to private sector (growth rate, %)	23.0	22.6	21.5	46.4	—	—
Inflation rate (CPI, %)	7.8	9.9	8.7	12.6	73.1	15.2
Thailand						
GDP growth (%)	8.9	8.8	5.5	−1.3	−9.4	4.2
Investment rates (% of GDP)	40.3	41.6	41.7	30.1	25.3	—
Government fiscal balances (% of GDP)	1.9	2.9	2.4	−0.9	−3.5	−2.7
Current account (% of GDP)	−5.6	−8.1	−8.1	−2.0	12.8	10.0
Foreign reserves (in months of imports)	5.4	5.0	5.1	4.1	6.4	6.7
Nominal exchange rate (to the US dollar)	25.1	24.9	25.3	31.4	41.4	37.8
Real exchange rate (100=1997)	109.8	108.0	113.5	100.0	86.3	91.5
Stock market index	1,360.1	1,280.8	831.6	372.7	355.8	481.9
External debt (% of GDP)	45.4	49.4	50.0	62.9	77.4	77.5
Short term debt (% of total)	44.5	49.5	41.4	37.2	27.3	24.3
Bank lending to private sector (growth rate, %)	30.3	23.8	14.6	19.8	—	—
Inflation rate (CPI, %)	5.1	6.0	4.0	3.0	8.7	−4.3

Sources: Adapted from World Bank, World Development Indicators (CD-ROM, 2000 and 2001); EIU data, www.eiu.com; Bloomberg, World Equity Indices; IMF, International Financial Statistics (CD-ROM, 2000).

of aid, the economic pain did not subside anytime soon. Not until the second half of 1998 did the economies show positive growth.

Amid the painful economic contraction, rising poverty rates, and increasing inequality, political unrest was churning. In Indonesia, opposition to Suharto, the ruler of 30 years, began to intensify, with calls for fundamental political reform. Eleven days after a violent uprising during which four students were killed, on May 21, 1998, Suharto stepped down. In Thailand, too, economic crisis precipitated political change. Long-discussed constitutional reform measures were finally promulgated on October 11, 1997, establishing a bicameral legislature and a 200-member senate.

Exhibit 6. Exchange Rate per US dollar (1997–1999)

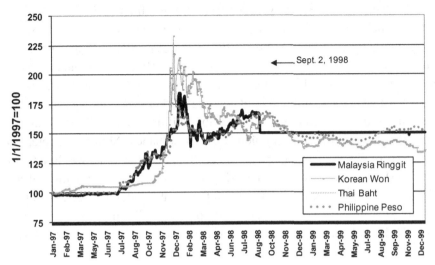

Source: Created by case writer using data from Bank Negara Malaysia (www.bnm.gov.my).

Crisis in Malaysia

After the Thai devaluation, the specter of regional crisis suddenly became a reality in Malaysia. The country watched as funds were violently sucked out of domestic institutions and asset prices sank (see **Exhibits 3c** and **4**). Feeble efforts to maintain foreign exchange reserves were quickly swamped (see **Exhibit 6**). On July 14, 1997, the central bank, Bank Negara Malaysia (BNM) stopped defending the currency and helplessly watched as the ringgit depreciated from RM 2.5 against the U.S. dollar to a record low of RM 4.88.[44] As the currency lost value, asset prices sank, and pressure on the banking sector mounted, further spreading panic among investors. The amounts non-performing loans accelerated skyward, and the economy contracted 5% by mid-1998. International investors interpreted this collapse as a manifestation that the market was exerting "good discipline on the management of the country."[45] Mahathir challenged this view: "The idea that the market will discipline governments is sheer nonsense."[46] Despite the difficulties, Malaysia did not turn to the IMF for help, unlike its neighbors.

In August and September of 1997, officials were conjuring methods to curb outflows. BNM imposed limits on forward currency transactions by non-residents, and Prime Minister Mahathir established a fund to buy stock sold by Malaysians at a premium, while stock sold by foreigners would sell for market value. Despite their preliminary antidotes, the financial sector collapse marched on, for what seemed to Mahathir no intrinsic reason. At the annual meeting of the World Bank and IMF in Hong Kong on September 20, 1997, the frustrated prime minister condemned currency traders as "unnecessary, unproductive, and immoral."[47]

Meanwhile, Anwar Ibrahim, deputy prime minister and finance minister, was gaining international favor for his "orthodox" perspective and his prescriptions deemed "virtual IMF" policies.[48] On December 3, 1997, he announced a reform package that included an 18% public spending cut, limitations on banks' exposure to the real estate market, and new bank lending guidelines.[49] But the prime minister was not pleased. While Indonesia, Korea, the Philippines, and Thailand all turned to the IMF for assistance and implemented its demands, Mahathir wrote, "What the Minister of Finance, together with the central bank, had done was to implement a virtual IMF [package] without the IMF loans; namely, a combination of a tight monetary and fiscal policies, raising the interest rate to defend the exchange rate, attempting to strengthen the banking system through the more stringent prudential standards, and cutting down public expenditure to improve the current account balance."[50]

Facing continued decline and growing frustrated, Mahathir grew wary of Anwar's virtual IMF policies, and called upon Nor Mohamed Yakcop, the former head of foreign exchange trading at BNM, as an advisor. The prime minister also established the National Economic Action Council (NEAC) in January 1998 to manage the financial crisis. The new group issued a comprehensive National Economic Recovery Plan (NERP) on July 23, 1998; its goal was to stabilize ringgit depreciation and restore market confidence through more than 580 detailed recommendations.[51] Meanwhile Yakcop and Mahathir sought policies that would more directly control the outflow of capital and the continued depreciation of the ringgit. On September 1, 1998, Bank Negara imposed new regulations, which included: a requirement that all offshore ringgit holdings be repatriated within a month; a prohibition of ringgit lending to non-residents; a 12-month waiting period for non-residents to convert ringgit proceeds from the sale of Malaysian securities held in external accounts; and restrictions on residents' investment abroad without prior approval from Bank Negara. To prevent further currency fluctuations, the ringgit was pegged at RM 3.8 to the U.S. dollar (see **Exhibit 6**).

On September 2, 1998, the day after the capital control announcement, Mahathir fired Anwar. On September 20, Anwar was arrested and accused of sodomy. When he appeared in court on September 29 with a swollen eye and bruises, he complained of having been beaten "severely" while in police custody. Anwar was subsequently convicted of obstruction of justice and sodomy and sentenced to six years in jail.[52]

Meanwhile, BNM was working to restructure the banking sector. In June and August of 1998, *Danaharta* and *Danamodal* were set up as vehicles to carve non-performing loans off banks' balance sheets and recapitalize failing institutions. As a complement, the Corporate Debt Restructuring Committee (CDRC) was established to facilitate "faster and more effective debt resolution" between creditors and borrowers.[53]

Malaysia's decision to stem capital outflows via capital controls was an unorthodox policy decision and took the international community by surprise. Generally, the outcry was negative as the move was seen as an affront to conventional economic policy. In a letter responding to Dr. Mahathir's capital control announcement, Paul Krugman wrote "I was as surprised as anyone when you announced sweeping currency controls . . . and I'm worried your approach may be tending toward draconian."[54] Krugman summarized the international community's concern that the measures would be extremely distortionary and be used as a new alternative not a method of reform.[55] The domestic response was mixed but firms were pleased to see more stability in the system. Whether due to policy or subsiding nervousness, performance in the banking and corporate sector was well on its way to recovery by 2000. Bank lending was remobilized and the real lending rate bounced back to healthy levels.[56] Dr. Zeti, Bank Negara governor, had no doubt about the appropriateness of the policies taken during the crisis: "Our strategy was the right one. Without outside strategic assistance, the country rebounded without the pains of massive corporate shutdowns, high unemployment and costs to the tax payers."

Recovery

By the first quarter of 1999 contractions abated, and GDP growth resumed, culminating in 6% growth for the entire year followed by an 8.9% growth rate in 2000.[57] Total factor productivity rose from −9.7% growth in 1998 to 3.9% in 2000. Macroeconomic fundamentals also quickly regained strength: CPI growth retreated from its 5.2% maximum in 1998 to 1.5% in 2000 and unemployment remained steady throughout the period.[58] Lending interest rates slowly returned to normalcy, averaging 6.3% from 2001–2008, down from the 1997 high of 11.5% (see **Exhibits 3a** and **3c**).

Financial Reform

Despite the quick rebound of economic fundamentals, the crisis was a wakeup call for developing economies of the challenges they faced as new players in the global economy. In Malaysia, both the five-year plans and the broader Vision 2020 had heavily bet on openness to the world economy to achieve its development and distributional goals. However, regardless of whether the Asian crisis was driven by fundamental vulnerabilities or by capricious investor sentiment, it had shown how defenseless developing economies were against international capital flows. The comprehension of this reality triggered a wave of financial reforms that intended to reduce the vulnerability of the financial system and, by extension, of the whole economy.

In July 1999, BNM announced a bank consolidation program with the objective of increasing the efficiency of the banking sector.[59] The fragmented and "over-banked" system funneled credit to highly volatile sectors (e.g. property and consumption credit), aligned with politically affiliated corporations, and provided little disclosure of financial undertakings.[60]

In May 2000, Dr. Zeti,[61] was appointed as the seventh governor of BNM. She had been deputy governor since 1995 responsible for economics, reserve management, foreign and money market operations, and exchange controls. She thus became the first female BNM governor and one of the few female central bankers around the world.

To reduce exposure to future contagion, along with other officials, she set out to fortify Malaysia's battered reserves and deepen the reform the financial system. By March 2008, BNM had accumulated $120 billion in reserves, up from the low of $10.2 billion in January 1999 (see **Exhibit 4**).[62] This reserve position was sufficient to finance 9.5 months of imports and was equivalent to 7.1 times the short-term external debt.

The 2001–2010 Financial Sector Masterplan (FSMP) sought to correct the industry's lack of international competitiveness, poor regulation, and inadequate supervision, as well as fragmentation of the banking sector. The 58 domestic financial institutions that existed in 1999 were consolidated to just 20 institutions by 2005 (see **Exhibit 7**). This consolidation, together with improved banking technology, supported productivity growth in the sector of 5.8% per year between 1993 and 2004.

A variety of measures were implemented to strengthen the financial sector and improve transparency. The FSMP heightened BNM scrutiny, mandating comprehensive reviews of each bank's financial position every six months. In an effort to ensure that financial conglomerates did not undertake excessive risk while still allowing

Exhibit 7. Number of Financial Institutions and Asset Distribution

	No. of Institutions					Total Assets (%)	
	1980	1990	1997	1999	2005	1997	2005
Commercial Banks:							
Domestic	21	22	22	21	10	57	73.6
Foreign	17	16	13	13	12	16.7	19.2
Finance Companies	47	45	39	25		20	0
Merchant Banks	12	12	12	12	10	6.3	7.2

Source: Created by case writer using data from Bank Negara Malaysia.

innovation, forward-looking stress tests were required. The Credit Bureau carried out additional reviews to buttress risk management and provide further assurance that strategic investments were sound. Malaysian financial firms were required to conform to international accounting standards. The Perbadanan Insurance Deposit Malaysia (PIDM), a national deposit insurance system, was established on September 1, 2005, to prevent bank runs. At the same time, financial institutions, historically ridden with government involvement, were more directly exposed to market discipline. A consumer education program, *BankingInfo*, was launched in 2003 to improve financial literacy.[63] The Credit Counseling and Debt Management (CCDM) agency, a consumer watchdog office, was set up in 2006 to further educate consumers and help them manage money.

Dr. Zeti also focused on developing the Malaysian bond market.[64] Her intent was to channel domestic savings to productive domestic investment and to establish Malaysia as a center for debt security origination. Diversifying the financial landscape, Dr. Zeti argued, would give "access to more innovative and sophisticated financing solutions . . . to meet the growing economy's diverse funding requirements."[65] Continuing efforts that began as far back as 1986, national mortgage corporations, rating agencies, and depository and settlement systems were set up to support the development of the new market. Regulations were loosened to attract investment from non-residents.[66] Electronic systems such as the *Fully Automated System for Tendering* were set up to quicken and standardize tendering practices. The *Bond Information and Dissemination System* was established to ensure liquidity and the price discovery process in the debt securities market by reinforcing timely information flow.[67] By 2009, Malaysia's bond market was the largest of the ASEAN region and accounted for 58% of corporate financing.[68]

Back to Normal?

Despite the Malaysian economy's strong rebound in 1999, its performance during the 2000s decade revealed that something had change. Between 2001 and 2008, GDP grew at an average annual rate of 3.7%, 2.6% points lower than the pre-crisis average during the 1990s (see **Exhibit 8a**). Though total factor productivity growth remained roughly constant, averaging around 3.2% per year in both periods, labor productivity growth dropped sharply, from 5.7% to 2.4% (see **Exhibits 8a** and **8e**). Domestic savings rose from 39% of GDP to 43%, and the return on companies listed in the Kuala Lumpur Stock Exchange rose from 11.1% in 1997 to 15.8% in 2007 (see **Exhibits 8b** and **8c**). But domestic investment collapsed from 39% to 22% (see **Exhibit 8b**), and FDI inflows as a share of GDP declined from an average of 6.5% in 1990–1997 to 3% in 2001–2008. FDI outflows increased gradually to reach almost 7% of GDP by 2008 (see **Exhibit 8d**).

Exhibit 8a. Performance before and After Asian Crisis

Variable	Period	Malaysia	China	Hong Kong	India	Indonesia	Korea (Rep.)	Philippines	Singapore	Thailand	Vietnam
Real GDP per capita	1990–1997	6.3	9.7	3.1	3.3	5.6	6.0	0.8	5.1	5.5	6.2
(Growth rate)	2001–2008	3.7	9.3	4.5	6.2	4.0	4.0	3.3	3.5	4.1	6.1
GDP per person employed	1992–1997	5.7	10.5	3.4	3.6	4.7	4.7	0.5	6.1	5.3	6.5
(Growth rate)	2001–2008	2.4	9.0	2.9	5.6	3.7	3.3	1.9	2.5	3.7	5.1
Gross domestic savings	1990–1997	38.8	41.8	32.4	22.6	32.0	36.2	16.2	47.8	35.4	14.2
(% of GDP)	2001–2008	42.6	46.2	31.5	29.0	29.9	31.8	13.8	46.3	32.2	29.0
Gross fixed capital formation	1990–1997	39.3	32.5	28.7	22.7	27.7	37.0	22.7	35.5	39.6	25.7
(% of GDP)	2001–2008	22.1	39.5	21.9	28.3	22.0	28.9	15.9	24.2	26.2	32.9

Source: Created by case writer using data from World Development indicators, World Bank, accessed March 28, 2010.

Exhibit 8b.   Investment and Savings-Investment Gap

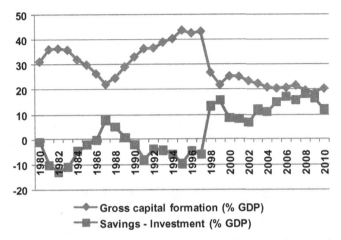

Source: Created by case writer using data from Economist Intelligence Unit, www.eiu.com, accessed October 3, 2010.

Exhibit 8c.   Return on Equity for the Companies listed in the KL Stock Exchange

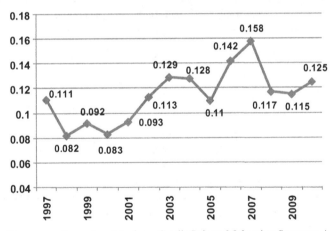

Source: Created by case writer using data from Credit Suisse: Malaysian Strategy: A Curate's egg.

Note: 2009 and 2010 are estimates.

The collapse in investment caught everyone by surprise. In interviews in September 2009, government officials and business leaders inevitably mentioned the drop in investment.[69] The question in everybody's mind: "Why has investment fallen?" Several hypotheses competed to explain this puzzle.

Scars from the Asian crisis: Some international investors saw the decline in growth and investment as scars from the financial crisis. Enmeshed in the tangle of that crisis, Malaysia missed out on the dot com boom and the capital deepening of

Exhibit 8d.   Inward and Outward FDI (%GDP)

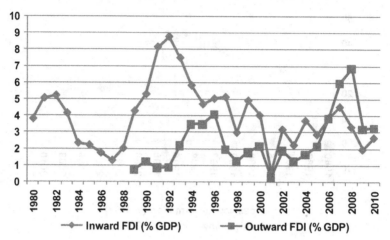

Source: Created by case writer using data from Economist Intelligence Unit, www.eiu.com, accessed October 3, 2010.

Exhibit 8e.   Evolution of Productivity Growth by Sector

	1980–1990	1990–1997	1997–2000	2000–2008
Agriculture	6.2	7.7	2.7	2.4
Mining	13.0	5.2	1.7	2.0
Manufacturing	5.2	7.3	6.3	2.9
Construction	0.7	6.4	−4.7	1.0
Utilities	9.9	8.9	−0.2	3.5
Transport	5.1	8.6	4.9	3.3
Trade	1.7	10.7	1.5	2.8
Finance	3.5	6.5	2.6	3.7
Other Services	−0.5	3.6	0.6	1.4

Source: Created by case writer using data from Malaysia Productivity Corporation.

Note: Labor productivity is defined as Value added per employee.

computerization brought with it.[70] According to Stephen Hagger, managing director of Credit Suisse in Malaysia: "The Asian crisis was partly economic and partly political. Those on the wrong side of the political fence either lost assets or came close to it. This resulted in a long-term lack of confidence. Economically it was also painful. Because of the way that Malaysia dealt with the crisis it was death by a thousand cuts. As such, the country did not enjoy the sharp rebound of other countries. This further hit confidence. Finally, Malaysians became wary of debt, especially debt denominated in foreign currencies." (See **Exhibit 4.**)

GLCs: For most Malays, the culprit was somewhere else. According to Amir-sham A. Aziz, head of the National Economic Advisory Council (NEAC), "GLCs [did] not compete on an equal footing with private companies." For example, he mentioned the case of Air Asia, a low-cost Malaysian carrier owned by a former Warner Music executive that was denied a permit to fly to Sydney because of a debt with the publicly owned Kuala Lumpur airport.[71]

The strong presence of government linked corporations (GLCs) in the economy could be crowding out private investment. Sharing this view, Prime Minister Najib stated that "in the interest of a more optimal and balanced co-existence between GLCs and non-GLCs, GLCs needed to divest non-core and non-competitive assets."[72] Azman Mokhtar, managing director of the sovereign wealth fund Kazanah, interpreted this statement as applying to both individual GLCs and to Kazanah. Between 2004 and 2009, Kazanah made divestments totaling RM 12 billion.

Another reason for the negative impact of GLCs in the economy had to do with their management practices. Dr. Mahathir noted that "companies and services owned and managed by [the] government have been less successful or have run at a loss because the government's management methods differ greatly from those of the private sector."[73] With their sights firmly fixed on achieving Vision 2020 goals, in January 2005 the government launched the Putrajaya Committee on GLC High Performance, a 10-year effort to improve the performance of GLCs to be at least comparable to that of private domestic firms and to transform several to be regionally or globally competitive.[74] The March 2009 Mid-Term Review of this program noted marked improvement in the composition and effectiveness of GLCs boards, the regulatory environment, capital management practices, and leadership development (see **Exhibit 9a**).[75] These changes did not go unnoticed by foreign investors who noted that the combination of better business boards, more strongly enforced regulations, and a generational change resulted in better run GLCs.[76]

Exhibit 9a.   Quality of Institutions Indicators

	1996	1998	2008
Ease of doing business index (world ranking)	—	—	21
Cost of business start-up procedures (% of GNI per capita)	—	25.9[a]	14.7
Rule of Law (% countries with worse index)	77	65	65
Regulatory quality (% countries with worse index)	74	69	60
Government effectiveness (% countries with worse index)	80	69	84
Stability and absence of violence (% countries with worse index)	71	51	50
Voice and accountability (% countries with worse index)	38	44	32
Control of corruption (% countries with worse index)	74	73	63

Source: Created by case writer using data from World Bank.

Note: [a] 2003.

Exhibit 9b.   Malaysia's Higher Education Stocks Lag behind Its Level of Development

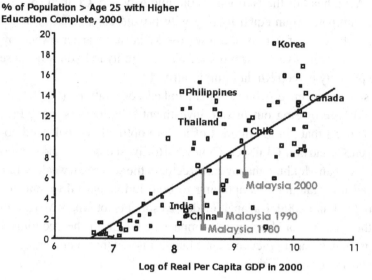

Source: Malaysia Firm Competitiveness, Investment climate and Growth, World Bank report No. 26841-MA, June 30, 2005.

Exhibit 9c.   Share of Medium and High Technology Products in Directly Threatened Exports

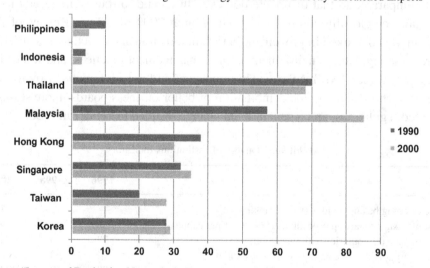

Source: "Integrated Production Networks in East Asia," Lall, "Integrated Production Networks in East Asia," World Bank (2003).

Shortage of skills: The shortage of skills proved to be a significant drag on the Malaysian economy.[77] A study showed that over 40% of manufacturing firms surveyed identified skills shortage as a "severe" or "very severe" problem.[78] One manifestation of this problem was the time it took to fill vacancies for skilled workers. On average, in manufacturing, it took almost 12 weeks to fill vacancies of professionals and almost 9 weeks to fill vacancies of technicians. Another survey conducted on Japanese companies in Asia reported that 38% had difficulties recruiting local engineers in Malaysia, while only 28% had similar difficulties in Singapore.[79]

The skills shortage resulted partly from an insufficient supply of college graduates (see **Exhibit 9b**). Although the fraction of Malaysians with tertiary education had tripled since 1990, it still was below the level of similar-income countries. A second factor contributing to the shortage of skills was the brain–drain. Many workers with higher education found it profitable to leave Malaysia in search for higher wages abroad. College graduates in Malaysia made 22% more than non-college graduates, compared with 60% more in the OECD. Finally, a third contributor to the shortage of skills was the mismatch between the qualifications of the graduates and those required by the manufacturing companies. This mismatch was so pervasive that, despite the need for college-educated workers in industry, one in four unemployed workers had a college education.

Firms coped with the shortage of skills in part by providing significant training to workers. Nevertheless, two recent studies estimated that the skills shortage cost Malaysian firms between 11% and 15% in sales.[80]

External environment: In addition to these internal factors, the external environment faced by Malaysian companies had changed after the Asian crisis. During the 1990s and early 2000s, poorer countries such as China, India and Vietnam had experienced very high growth rates and narrowed their productivity gap with Malaysia. Their improved productivity, together with lower wages, attracted significant FDI flows, and these countries became active exporters in niches traditionally dominated by Malaysia (see **Exhibit 9c**). According to Dr. Zeti: "The pattern of trade has changed."

The Global Financial Crisis

The global recession in 2008–2009 began in the U.S. subprime mortgage market and spread to the worldwide economy. Malaysia was hit hard by the global downturn, as its economy contracted for the first time in 10 years. Between the last quarter of 2007 and the first quarter of 2009, GDP declined 7.8%. Towards the end of 2009, it started to grow again leaving the yearend GDP decline at 1.7%.

A significant contributor to this decline was the reduction of inventories, which alone accounted for a 2.5% drop in GDP (see **Exhibit 10a**). Overall investment

Exhibit 10a.   Contribution to Real GDP Growth of Each GDP Component

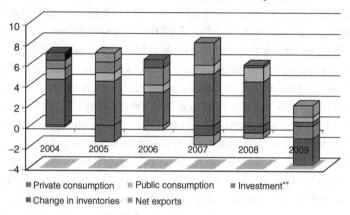

Source: BNM and authors' calculations.

Note: ** Includes both private and public investment.

Exhibit 10b.   Consumer Sentiment and Employment during the Global Financial Crisis

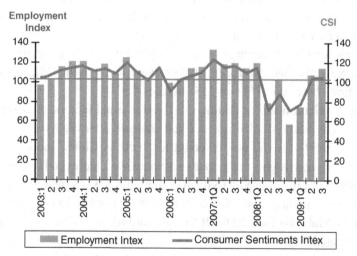

Source: Malaysian Institute of Economic Research.

contributed an additional 1.2%. However, private and public investment moved in opposite directions. While real private investment declined by 21.8%, public investment increased by 12.9%.[81] Real exports declined by 12%, and imports fell by 13.1%.

Amidst the spreading malaise, FDI inflows declined precipitously. Between 2007 and 2008 they fell 13%, and in 2009 they were estimated to decline by another 60%. Productivity also worsened. Total factor productivity declined by 3.1% between 2008 and 2009. A measure of productivity in durable manufacturing — the inverse of the relative price of investment[82] — declined by 11.6% between the third quarter of 2008 and the third quarter of 2009.

Despite the significant economic trouble, employment remained relatively resilient. Recorded unemployment increased slightly to 3.8%, though officials statistics did not record unemployment of illegal immigrants who were more likely to suffer the adjustment. Consumer confidence held up (see **Exhibit 10b**).

According to the IMF, "Malaysia's financial sector [. . .] faced the crisis from a position of strength and [. . .] coped well."[83] It had ample foreign exchanges reserves [\$91 billion]; the balance sheets of banks, corporations and households were in good shape; trade had become more diversified than in the past; and internal demand had gained importance as a driver of growth prior to the crisis.

Policymakers responded promptly to the crisis. In July 2008, BNM started to loosen monetary policy in anticipation of the slowdown, despite incipient inflationary pressures.[84] The measure was initially criticized by the IMF.[85] Further interest rate cuts followed in fall 2008, until the policy rate reached 2%. Reserve requirements were also cut to reduce the cost of financial intermediation. Liquidity support in the interbank market kept the overnight rate close to the policy rate, ensuring that rate cuts were passed along to borrowers. During 2009, credit growth decelerated, but remained high — approximately 10% — and well above nominal GDP growth.

In early November 2008, a first fiscal stimulus package of about 1% of GDP was announced. It comprised public works, education programs, some pro-business initiatives, as well as a reduction in employees' contributions to the pension fund.[86] In March 2009, a second stabilization package that amounted to approximately 9% of GDP was announced. It would be implemented over two years. Approximately 40% of the total corresponded to loan guarantees. It also included infrastructure projects, worker training programs, the recruitment of public sector employees and exemptions for interest on housing loans and income tax deductions for laid-off workers.

Najibnomics

On April 2, 2009, Abdullah Badawi, fifth prime minister of Malaysia, resigned following increasing opposition within his party (UMNO). Badawi's position had deteriorated after he lost the super-majority in the March 2008 elections and after the detentions of a blogger, a member of parliament, and a reporter under the Internal Security Act, which allowed for indefinite detention without trial.

On April 3, 2009, Najib Razak, the deputy prime minister, was sworn in as prime minister. In his inaugural speech, Najib announced as his first actions the removal of bans on two newspapers run by opposition parties, Suara Keadilan and

Harakahdaily, and the release of 13 people held under the Internal Security Act. He pledged to conduct a comprehensive review of this much-criticized law. He also emphasized his commitment to tackling poverty, restructuring Malaysian society, expanding access to quality education for all, and promoting renewed "passion for public service."

Some of these goals were part of a broader initiative proposed by Najib on September 16, 2008, under the name "1Malaysia." 1Malaysia called on the cabinet, government agencies, and civil servants to more strongly emphasize ethnic harmony, national unity, and efficient governance.

In the past, the NEP had attempted to achieve ethnic harmony through affirmative action programs that targeted capital ownership, employment and education quotas, as well as implementing a system of subsidies on basic commodities. However, these programs were quite costly and introduced inefficiencies in the economy.[87] The subsidies, for example, were universal and even benefited wealthy Malays and foreign citizens who crossed the border from Thailand or Singapore to buy cheap oil in Malaysia.

Malaysia had what Dr. Nungsari Ahmad, the executive director of research at Khazanah, called a "huge fiscal problem." The tax base was small. Only one million out of 11 million workers paid income taxes. As a result, only 30% of government revenues came from income taxes, 30% from corporate taxes and the remaining 40% from other sources, mainly oil and gas. The non-oil government deficit was expected to widen to 15% of GDP in 2009. Despite the fact that the debt-to-GDP ratio had already surpassed 50%, the budget deficit was projected to remain large over the medium term.

In addition, Malaysia faced the risk of losing its traditional comparative advantage as an electronics producer and manufacturing assembly center to China and Vietnam, while not being competitive in higher value added activities with countries such as Singapore, Korea or Taiwan. It faced the risk of what Harvard Business School Professor Dick Vietor called being "stuck in the middle."[88]

Despite the severity of the 2009 recession, Najib's cabinet was more concerned about these medium-term threats to Malaysia's prosperity than about the short-term downturn. According to Nor Mohamed Yakcop, former minister of finance and current minister of the Economic Planning Unit, "Malaysia should shift to high quality economic growth model which is based on technology, innovation, productivity and creativity. It has to take into account the elements of more competitive global business environment and identification of various new opportunities abroad".[89]

Najib's New Economic Model (NEM) attempted to facilitate this fundamental transformation by making the economy more market-friendly while ensuring ethnic harmony. Najib intended to attain these seemingly incompatible goals with a radical change in the policies that had underlain the NEP. He would first eliminate subsidies on basic commodities except for low income families. He thought a more direct way to ensure ethnic harmony was to increase the incomes of poor households.

Between 1999 and 2009, the labor force had increased from 9.2 to 11.2 million people. A large majority of this increase was fueled by the arrival of foreign workers, as their share in the labor forced climbed from 4.5% to 18%. Approximately 30% of the non-Malaysian workers were illegal, and a large majority was unskilled. The expansion of labor supply kept real wages relatively flat despite the gains in productivity. The Gini coefficient had been deteriorating from 0.446 in 1990 to 0.462 in 2004, the third worst in Asia.

Najib believed that restricting the inflow of foreign workers would lift wages of unskilled Malay workers. But with this measure, he also wanted to send a signal to Malay companies. The world was changing quickly and they needed to be ready to change with it or risk being left behind. They could no longer build their advantage on cheap labor. Malaysian companies needed to move up the value chain so that they could continue to compete in the global market but not at the expense of the workers' income.

According to Mr. Amirsham, "Malaysia needs to build on the sectors where we have a comparative advantage and move upstream in search of higher value-added activities. For example, we can use our expertise in palm oil to become the most efficient bio-fuel producer in the world and a leading player in biodegradable plastics." Dr. Zeti considered that banking could also become a strategic sector: "Nothing really stops Malaysia from being the world's centre in Islamic finance." Other high value-added activities in the list included logistics, tourism, healthcare, petroleum, and petrochemicals.[90]

The transition, however, required addressing fundamental problems. First, Malaysia needed to solve the shortage of skilled workers. The government was devoting 23% of its operating expenditure and 18% of development expenditure to education. Much of this effort was channeled to the creation of new universities. The creation of new niches required innovation and knowledge creation. However, Malaysia's investment in R&D, at 0.64% of GDP, was similar to the level other developing countries such as Thailand or South Africa and far from that of developed economies such as Singapore, Korea, or Hong Kong. Finally, Malaysia needed entrepreneurs who would capitalize on these growth opportunities. Malaysian society was not very entrepreneurial.[91] To correct that, Saifuddin Bin Abdullah, deputy minister of higher education, was planning on introducing a mandatory entrepreneurship course. The government was also considering facilitating the job of entrepreneurs by reforming the bankruptcy law to introduce a form of Chapter 11 since the current law "only gave entrepreneurs one chance to fail."[92]

Foreign multinationals could also play an important role in transforming the Malaysian economy. To attract and maintain foreign investment, Najib undertook a series of pro-market reforms. These included allowing foreign investors to hold majority stakes in most enterprises excluding "strategic" industries such as banking, telecommunications, and energy, easing insurance regulation, and lowering the minimum quota for Malay ownership in publicly traded companies from 30% to 12.5%. He also liberalized 27 minor sub-sectors, exempting them from the minimum required *bumiputera* equity of 30%.[93] In late 2009, the government debated the pace at which the liberalization process should be extended to other sectors. The NEAC supported fast implementation to reduce uncertainty and avoid a slowdown in investment. To buy out the resistance of the local elites, Najib created a RM 500 million fund that would finance new *bumiputera* companies.

The Way Forward

We know what to do; we know what we should do economically; we know what needs to be changed. However, we are caught in a comfort zone. The biggest problem is political. We need to take the short term pain to get to the long term benefit. And get the whole country behind that.

— Nor Mohamed Yakcop[94]

As time and again in Malaysia history, race was intertwined with politics and the economy. The recession had been Najib's best argument to sell his NEM to the population. As the recession eased, *bumiputera* opposition to the plan started to grow. Indeed, it grew even within the ranks of Najib's own party, UMNO. Some party members were siding with Perkasa, a new Malay-rights group led by Ibrahim Ali, a former UMNO Member of Parliament. Mr. Ibrahim argued that *bumiputera* were not ready to compete on a level field with other races.[95]

Unfortunately, racial and religious tensions went often hand-in-hand. On January 8, 2010, three churches in Malaysia were firebombed as religious tension escalated over a court decision that allowed a Catholic publication to use the word "Allah" for God. Catholics claimed this was a long-standing practice given that, in Malay, there was no other word to refer to God.

Even if religious tensions and political opposition to the NEM eased, the success of the new model required private companies to conquer high-value-added niches. Some, such as Dr. Nungsari, understood the challenges involved: "We are a good meeting place. We have always been a bunch of traders. That's what we are good at." The weak economy and uncertainty about the global economy made the challenge faced by the private sector even more daunting. However, at this point, the NEM seemed to be only one way to achieve Vision 2020. Could Malaysia finally be one? Would companies leave their comfort zone and do their part?

Appendix: Islamic Banking

Since the late 1970s, Islamic banking has provided Muslim countries with a regional alternative to Western-style banking. Islamic law prohibits the use of *riba* (usury), which is interpreted to proscribe all forms of interest. Debate between modernists and fundamentalists surrounds the use of interest on "productive investment" as opposed to "predetermined returns on capital." But the more common and influential interpretation bans the use of interest entirely.[96] Shari'a principles emphasize employing resources with productive (not exploitative) intentions.[97] The Association of Islamic Banking Institutions Malaysia states that economic resources should be used to eradicate "all forms of inequality, injustice, exploitation, oppression, and wrongdoing whereby a person either deprives others of their rights or does not fulfill his obligations towards them."[98] To do so, Islamic financiers contend that banking should be asset/equity based and personalized to provide commitment and monitoring devices.

While the Shari'a interdiction of interest has been in effect to greater and lesser degrees for centuries, some of the roots of interest-free banking are relatively recent and not clearly Islamic in origin.[99] In the early 1960s, the Egyptian countryside developed cooperative-savings banks, drawing on German experience with local savings institutions.[100] The cooperatives served as savings centers for small farmers, who could eventually draw lines of credit. In order to provide for the operational costs of the bank and support 'social services,' funds of *zakat* (voluntary payments) revenues were pooled and set aside.[101] The Egyptian government buttressed the small institutions through official sanction and tax exemptions. This formula for "partnership" was intended to stand in contrast to the typical lender–borrower relationship and served as the basis for the broader institutionalization of Islamic banking.[102] Amidst a boom of petrodollars and savings, the Dubai Islamic Bank opened its doors in 1975 as the first private commercial Islamic banking organization.[103] Over the next several decades, Islamic financial institutions, with various sets of regulatory qualifications (e.g. Islamic banks versus investment companies), sprang up throughout the Muslim world.

In Malaysia, the legal basis for the establishment of Islamic banks was the Islamic Banking Act (IBA), which came into effect on April 7, 1983. The IBA provides BNM with powers to supervise and regulate Islamic banks, similar to the case of other licensed banks. The Government Investment Act 1983 was also enacted at the same time to empower the Government of Malaysia to issue Government Investment Issue (GII), which are government securities issued based on Shari'a principles. The first Islamic bank established in the country was Bank Islam Malaysia Berhad (BIMB), which commenced operations on July 1, 1983.

Today, all major domestic and foreign banks in Malaysia have an Islamic finance affiliated bank. By 2007, Malaysia's Islamic banking assets reached $65.6 billion with an average annual growth rate of 18–20%.[104] To ensure financial tools are Sharia compliant, all Islamic banks employ to internal Sharia Committees. Further, to provide uniformity of the often ambiguous religious laws across the country, the Sharia Advisory Council of BNM guides acceptable practice within Malaysia.

To understand the differences between conventional and Islamic banking, it is worthwhile to consider the examples of profit sharing, essentially deposit returns and a bond issue. In a conventional banking system, a bank attracts deposits by providing interest on its liabilities. The pool of total deposits is available to the bank for investment, subject only to regulatory guidelines such as capital requirements. Profit emerges from the difference between the rate of return on its investment and the interest paid out to depositors. Islamic banking achieves the same result under a different name. Mudharabah, or profit sharing, involves a capital provider (depositor), bank and an entrepreneur or other investment opportunity. The capital provider through the bank provides funds for investment projects and the returns of the project are split between the depositor and bank at a pre-specified profit sharing ratio. All losses are borne by the capital provider.

Islamic bond issues employ a more complicated diversion in the flow of funds avoid interest payments. Conventionally, the debt issuer and two banks (a primary and secondary) execute the deal, each with its own legal council. Debt purchasers buy bonds directly and receive interest payments from the borrowing company. To execute the same transaction in a Sharia conforming framework, the following steps are necessary: The 'debt issuer' must set up a Special Purpose Vehicle (SPV) to intermediate the transaction, to which the company will sell assets for the amount of financing it would like to raise. The SPV then owns a portion of the company's assets and will lease them back with a pre-specified maturity date (exactly analogous to a bond maturity). The lease payments will then be passed on to the *sukuk* (Islamic bond) holders, in payment for the amount of the original amount given to the company via the SPV.

Endnotes

[1] "Malaysia Outlines New growth Strategy" Liz Gooch, *New York Times*, March 30, 2010.

[2] Department of Statistics Malaysia, visited March 29, 2010: http://www.statistics.gov.my/portal/index.php?option=com_content&view=article&id=50%3Apopulation&catid=38%3Akaystats&Itemid=11&lang=en.

[3] In addition to native Malays, some other native people were also considered *bumiputera*. Percentages of ethnic groups are from the CIA World Factbook, https://www. cia.gov/library/publications/the-world-factbook/geos/my.html, accessed March 29, 2010:

Information on immigrants are from the Department of Statistics Malaysia: International Migration in Malaysia, http://www.unescap.org/STAT/meet/egm2006/ses.4_Malaysia.pdf, accessed March 20, 2010. Much of the evolution in the ethnic composition of the population was due to interethnic differences in fertility rates.

4 CIA Factbook, visited March 21, 2010.

5 The World Bank Group: World Development Indicators.

6 Economic Intelligence Unit.

7 Calculated from Bank Negara Malaysia: Direction of External Trade.

8 Bank Negara Malaysia: 2009 Annual Report.

9 Edmund Terence Gomez and K. S. Jomo, *Malaysia's Political Economy: Politics, Patronage, and Profits*, 2nd edn. (Cambridge: Cambridge University Press, 1999).

10 On the good infrastructure: Raja Nazrin, *Essays on Economic Growth in Malaysia in the Twentieth Century* (Cambridge: Harvard University, 2000), p. 170. On the robust primary export sector: Prema-Chandra Athukorala, *Crisis and Recovery in Malaysia: The Role of Capital Controls* (U.K.: Edward Elgar Publishing, Inc., 2001), p. 8. On the efficient administrative framework: Rawi Abdelal, Laura Alfaro, *Malaysia: Capital and Control*, Harvard Business School Case 9-702-040 (2003). On the common law tradition: Anita Doraisami, *The Legal and Financial Determinants of Malaysian Corporate Performance*. Malaysian Journals of Economic Studies, Vol. 40, Nos. 1 & 2, June–December 2003. p. 126.

11 Edmund Terence Gomez and K. S. Jomo, *Malaysia's Political Economy: Politics, Patronage, and Profits*, 2nd edn. (Cambridge: Cambridge University Press, 1999), p. 10.

12 Abdelal and Alfaro, *Malaysia: Capital and Control*.

13 Malcolm Cook, *Banking Reform in Southeast Asia: The Region's Decisive Decade*. (New York: Routledge, 2008) p. 71; Athukorala, *Crisis and Recovery in Malaysia* p. 8; Asan Ali Golam Hassan, *Growth, Structural Change and Regional Inequality in Malaysia*. (Aldershot: Ashgate Publishing 2004).

14 Datuk Dr. Zainal Aznam Yusof, The Malaysian Economic Model: A Case of Heterodoxy, in *Readings on Development: Malaysia 2057: Uncommon Voices, Common Aspirations*. Eds. Nungsari Ahmad Radhi and Suryani Senja Alias, Khazanah Nasional Kuala Lumpur, p. 198.

15 Datuk Dr. Zainal Aznam Yusof, The Malaysian Economic Model: A Case of Heterodoxy, in *Readings on Development: Malaysia 2057: Uncommon Voices, Common Aspirations*, Eds. Nungsari Ahmad Radhi and Suryani Senja Alias, Khazanah Nasional Kuala Lumpur, p 198.

16 Junid Saham, *British Industrial Investment in Malaysia, 1963–1971*, (Kuala Lumpur: Oxford University Press, 1980).

17 These were mainly new import substituting manufacturing firms.

18 Gomez and Jomo, *Malaysia's Political Economy*, p. 17.

19 Ranald Taylor, *Technical Progress and Economic Growth: An Empirical Case Study of Malaysia*, (U.K.: Edward Elgar, 2007), p. 101.

20 Taylor, *Technical Progress and Economic Growth: An Empirical Case Study of Malaysia* (U.K.: Edward Elgar, 2007), p. 101; Gomez and Jomo, *Malaysia's Political Economy*, (Cambridge: Cambridge University Press, 1999), p. 16.

21 Raja Nazrin, *Essays on Economic Growth in Malaysia in the Twentieth Century* (Cambridge: Harvard Univerisity, 2000), p. 170.

22 On non-*bumiputera* beliefs that the government was limiting their opportunities: Cook, *Banking Reform in Southeast Asia: The region's decisive decade*, p. 71. On *bumiputera* concerns about their interests not being protected: Authukorala, *Crisis and Recovery in Malaysia: The Role of Capital Controls*, p. 9.

23 Authukorala, *Crisis and Recovery in Malaysia: The Role of Capital Controls*, p. 9. Taylor, *Technical Progress and Economic Growth: An Empirical Case Study of Malaysia*, p. 72.

24 On the goal of national Unity: Dr. Mahathir bin Mohamad, *The Way Forward*, p. 8. On the goals of ending poverty and restructuring society to end identification of race with economic status: *Second Malaysia Plan Document 1971*.

25 Gomez and Jomo, *Malaysia's Political Economy*, p. 18.

26 On the role of free-trade zones: James B. Ang, *Financial Development and Economic Growth in Malaysia*, (New York: Routledge, 2009), p. 43.

27 Jomo and Gomez. *Malaysia's Political Economy: Politics, Patronage, and Profits*, p. 18.; Abdelal and Alfaro, *Malaysia: Capital and Control*.

28 On industrialized economies preference for important raw materials: Renuka Mahadevan, *Sustainable Growth and Economic Development: A Case Study of Malaysia*, (U.K.: Edward Elgar Publishing, 2007), p. 8.

29 Gomez and Jomo, *Malaysia's Political Economy*, p. 76.

30 On the NEP requirement to pursue social and redistributive objectives: *Mid-Term Review of the Ninth Malaysia Plan, 2006–2010*, p. 62, accessed January 4, 2010.

31 Gomez and Jomo, *Malaysia's Political Economy*, p. 78.

32 On the need to promote massive investment spending: Ang, Financial Development and Economic Growth in Malaysia, p. 41; Cook, Banking Reform in Southeast Asia, p. 70; Mahadevan, Sustainable Growth and Economic Development, p. 8.

33 Gomez and Jomo, *Malaysia's Political Economy*, p. 76.

34 J. V. Jesudasan, *Ethnicity and the Economy: The State, Chinese Business, and Multinationals in Malaysia*, (Singapore: Oxford University Press, 1989), pp. 410–412.

35 C. Edwards, *The Role of Foreign Direct Investment in Malaysian Development Experience: Changes and Challenges*, (Kuala Lumpur: National Institute of Public Administration, 1994).

36 FDI flows were almost completely free, with only a few sectoral limitations; Abdelal and Alfaro, *Malaysia: Capital and Control*.

37 On FDI as a share of investment: Ang, *Financial Development and Economic Growth in Malaysia*.

38 Cook, *Banking Reform in Southeast Asia*.

39 Cook, *Banking Reform in Southeast Asia*; Ang, *Financial Development and Economic Growth in Malaysia*; Authukorala, *Crisis and Recovery in Malaysia: The Role of Capital Controls*; Gomez and Jomo, *Malaysia's Political Economy*.

40 Thomas Oatley, *International Political Economy: Interest and Institutions in the Global Economy*, 3rd edn. (Pearson Longman, 2008), p. 339.

41 Abdelal and Alfaro, *Malaysia: Capital and Control*.

42 Oatley, *International Political Economy*, p. 341.

43 Oatley, *International Political Economy*, p. 341.

44 Gomez and Jomo, *Malaysia's Political Economy: Politics, Patronage, and Profits*, p. 188.

45 Victor C.S. Liew, Executive Vice President, Treasury, Overseas Union Bank, Singapore. Abdelal and Alfaro, *"Malaysia: Capital and Control," HBS No. 702-040* (Boston: Harvard Business School Publishing, 2002), p. 14.

46 Dr. Mahathir Mohamad, fourth Prime Minister of Malaysia, Kuala Lumpur. Abdelal and Alfaro interview, October 8, 2001: Rawi E. Abdelal and Laura Alfaro, *" Malaysia: Capital and Control," HBS No. 702-040* (Boston: Harvard Business School Publishing, 2002), p. 14.

47 Quoted in John Ridding and James Kynge, "Complacency Gives Way to Contagion," *Financial Times*, January 13, 1998.

48 Raphael Pura (1997), "Malaysia's Finance Chief Gains in Stature: Anwar Emerges from Economic Crisis as Voice of Reason," *Wall Street Journal*, September 22.

49 Samuel Bassey Okposin and Cheng Ming Yu (2001), Economic Crisis in Malaysia: Causes Implications, & Policy Prescriptions. *Journal of Economics and Management* 9, Vol. 2, p. 121.

50 Mahathir (2004), *The Malaysian Currency Crisis: How and Why It Happened*. Pelanduk Publications, Kuala Lumpur, p. 26.

51 Okposin and Yu, *Economic Crisis in Malaysia*, p. 123.

52 In 2004, the Federal Court reversed the second conviction and he was released. In July 2008, he was arrested over allegations he sodomized a male aide. On August 26, 2008, Anwar won the Permatang Pauh election returning to the Parliament as leader of the Malaysian opposition.

53 Abdul Ghani Zamani (2006), Re-engineering the Malaysian Financial System to Promote Sustainable Growth, *BIS paper no. 28*.

54 Paul Krugman (1998), "An Open Letter to Prime Minister Mahathir," September 28, 1998, reprinted in *Fortune*, Vol. 138, no. 6, pp. 35–36.

55 Krugman later changed his position in the debate against capital controls and argued that they were a useful way to prevent self-fulfilling prophecies.

56 Authukorala, *Crisis and Recovery in Malaysia: The Role of Capital Controls*, (Edward Elgar Publishing, 2001), p. 100–03.

57 Figures from Economist Intelligence Unit data. Accessed March 22, 2010.

58 Figures from Economist Intelligence Unit data. Accessed March 22, 2010.

59 Announcement of Bank Negara Malaysia, 1999.

60 Alias Radam, A. H. Baharom, A.M. Dayang-Affizzah, and Farhana Ismail (2008). Effect of Mergers on Efficiency and Productivity: Some evidence for banks in Malaysia. IUP Journal of Bank Management, vol. 8, no. 1.

61 Dr Zeti is the daughter and the only child of the country's famous academician, Professor Diraja Tun Ungku Aziz. Her grandfather, the late Datuk Jaafar Mohamed was the first Chief Minister of Johor, while UMNO founder the late Datuk Onn Jaafar was her granduncle.

62　Bank Negara Malaysia, http://www.bnm.gov.my/ index.php?ch=8&pg=14& ac=1606. Accessed November 4, 2009.

63　Abdul Ghani Zamani, (2006). Reengineering the Malaysian Financial System to promote Sustainable Growth, *BIS paper No. 28*.

64　All these accomplishments did not go unnoticed. In 2003, Euromoney named Dr Zeti as Central Bank Governor of the Year for her role in the reform of the exchange rate, the capital markets, and the banking industry. According to Steve Hagger: "Dr. Zeti is an understated hero."

65　Dr. Zeti speech 18 August 2009. http://www.bis.org/review/r090827d.pdf, Accessed January 4, 2010.

66　Dr. Zeti speech 18 August 2009. http://www.bis.org/review/r090827d.pdf, Accessed December 28, 2009.

67　Zamani, *ibid*.

68　Zamani, *ibid*.

69　Virtually all the persons interviewed to prepare this case expressed their perplexity with respect to the collapse of domestic investment. This includes: Stephen Hagger (Managing Director of Credit Suisse Malaysia), Dr. NungSari Ahmad (Executive Director, Research and Investment Strategy, Kazanah Nasional), Najib Tun Razak (Prime Minister and Minister of Finance I), Amirsham Abdul Aziz (Head of National Economic Advisory Council, NEAC), Nor Mohamed Bin Yakcop (Minister of the Economic Planning Unit, EPU), Azman Mokhtar (Managing Director of Kazanah Nasional), Mohamed Sidek (Chief Secretary to the Government of Malaysia), Dr. Wan Abdul Aziz (Secretary General of Treasury), Mr. Lee Heng Guie (Chief Economist of CIMB).

70　Authors interview with Steve Hagger, Kuala Lumpur, September 29, 2009.

71　Authors interview with Amirsham Abdul Aziz, Putrajaya, September 29, 2009.

72　Mokhtar, Azman. "Graduating to a Higher Class: Catalysing a New Domestic Economy." p. 289. In Nungsari Ahmad and Suryani Senja eds. *Readings on Development: Malaysia 2057*. Khazanah Nasional, 2009.

73　Gomez and Jomo, *Malaysia's Political Economy*, p. 80.

74　GLC Transformation Programme: Mid-Term Progress Review. March 2009.

75　GLC Transformation Programme: Mid-Term Progress Review. March 2009.

76　Authors interview with Steve Hagger, Kuala Lumpur, September 29, 2009.

77　Authors interview with Deputy Minister of Higher education, in Putrajaya, Accessed September 28, 2009.

78　"Addressing Skills Gap: Malaysian case study" presentation by K. Yogeesvaran, 21 November 2005.

79　"Comparative survey of labor environment in ASEAN, China, India" October 2006, Japan External Trade Organization (JETRO) Overseas Research Department.

80　Albert G. Zeufack, "Skill shortages and mismatch in Malaysia and Thailand: Evidence from linked employer-employee data". Presented at the National Economic Outlook Conference, December 2nd, 2009. Yogeesvaran, ibid.

81　Bank Negara Malaysia, http://www.bnm.gov.my/view.php?dbIndex=0&website_id=1 &id=770, Accessed March, 29, 2010:

82 This is regarded as a good proxy for the productivity of the durable manufacturing sector when prices reflect marginal costs of production which, typically, move inversely to productivity.

83 IMF Public Information Notice (PIN) No. 09/106, August 14, 2009.

84 Authors interview with Dr. Zeti. Bank Negara Governor, Kuala Lumpur, September 28, 2009.

85 It affected negatively the grade assigned by the *Global Finance* magazine to central bankers around the world. After 2 years of being awarded an A, in 2008 she was given "only" B+. However, in 2009, Dr. Zeti's vision was acknowledged again with an A.

86 Specifically, the contribution rate was reduced by 3 percentage points for the next two years. It was estimated that this measure would raise disposable income by 1% of GDP per year.

87 The annual cost of subsidies was estimated to be RM 26bn.

88 Richard Vietor, Conference in Terenagganu, Malaysia on July 18th, 2008, titled "Stuck in the Middle."

89 Authors interview with Nor Mohamed Yakcop, Putrajaya, Accessed September 29, 2009.

90 Mokhtar, Azman. "Graduating to a Higher Class: Catalysing a New Domestic Economy." pp. 291–292. In Nungsari Ahmad and Suryani Senja eds. *Readings on development: Malaysia 2057*. Khazanah Nasional, 2009.

91 2% of the college graduates became self-employed.

92 Authors interview with Amirsham Abdul Aziz, Putrajaya, Accessed September 29, 2009.

93 Malaysia in major liberalization drive, *Financial Times*, http://www.ft.com/cms/s/0/9daad488-6538-11de-8e34-00144feabdc0.html?nclick_check=1, June 30, 2009. Accessed December 27, 2009.

94 Authors interview with Nor Mohamed Yakcop, Putrajaya, Accessed September 29, 2009.

95 "Out with the new." *The Economist*, 3-11-2010. Accessed March 29, 2010.

96 Nazih N. Ayubi, *Political Islam: Religion and Politics in the Arab World*, (London: Routledge, 1991), p. 181.

97 International Association of Islamic Banks, http://www. saudinf.com/, Accessed March 30, 2010,

98 Association of Islamic Banking Institutions Malaysia, http://aibim.com/content/view/17/34/, Accessed on April 1, 2010.

99 Subhi Y. Labib, (1969). Capitalism in Medieval Islam, *The Journal of Economic History*, Vol. 29, No. 1, pp. 79–96.

100 Ayubi, *Political Islam*, p. 180.

101 Ayubi, *Political Islam*, p. 180.

102 Association of Islamic Banking Institutions Malaysia, http://aibim.com/content/view/17/34/, Accessed April 1, 2010.

103 Ayubi, *Political Islam*, p. 180.

104 Bank Negara Malaysia: Annual banking Statistics 2007.

Malaysia: The Economic Transformation Program (B)

Diego Comin* and Ku Kok Peng*

I must execute or be executed.

— Najib Razak, Prime Minister of Malaysia, 23 March 2010[a]

On October 25, 2010, Prime Minister Najib Razak launched the Economic Transformation Program (ETP), which was built on the New Economic Model that aims to make Malaysia a high-income nation by 2020 in an inclusive and sustainable manner.

The ETP's 10-year targets were clearly defined: to generate US$444 billion in investments in order to generate a Gross National Income (GNI) of US$523 billion and create 3.3 million incremental jobs, in the end-point year of 2020. The 2020 GNI translates into a GNI per capita of US$15,000 to make Malaysia a high-income economy, as defined by the World Bank.[b]

*Reprinted with permission of Harvard Business School Publishing.

This case was prepared by Professor Diego Comin and independent researcher Ku Kok Peng

Malaysia: The Economic Transformation Program 713-008

[a] Speech to Credit Suisse Asian Investment Conference, Hong Kong, 2010.

[b] "Economic Transformation Programme: A Roadmap for Malaysia," PEMANDU (Performance Management and Delivery Unit), Prime Minister's Department, Malaysian Government, October 26, 2010, http://etp.pemandu.gov.my/upload/etp_handbook_chapter_1-4_economic_model.pdf, pp. 75, 111, accessed September 2012.

Business as Usual is Not Good Enough

Najib realized that to achieve high-income nation status, the business as usual approach was no longer sufficient. Bold and radical changes coupled with rapid decision-making and execution was desperately needed.

He enlisted the help of a man with a great deal of experience in the corporate world, Idris Jala, for the task. Idris was sworn in as Minister in the Prime Minister's Department and Chief Executive Officer of Performance Management and Delivery Unit (PEMANDU) on September 1, 2009. He initially worked on the Government Transformation Program, tackling pressing social issues: crime, corruption, education, poverty, basic infrastructure in rural areas, urban public transport and cost of living.

Idris, who rescued Malaysia Airlines from bankruptcy by turning around the national carrier from a nine-month record loss of US$400 million to a record profit of US$260 million in less than two years, was then asked to spearhead the ETP.[c]

Staying Focused

Idris' radical transformation approach was unprecedented. He invited more than 1,000 private sector businessmen and professionals, top civil servants and non-governmental organization activists into a mammoth 1,000-person workshop with the purpose of determining 12 National Key Economic Areas (NKEAs).

This was a two-step process. First, the compounded annual growth rate (CAGR) for each sector was determined by taking the simple average of: (1) Malaysia's CAGR between 2000 and 2009, (2) the global mean CAGR between 2010 and 2020, and (3) the global best practice CAGR factored against the probability of success in Malaysia by 2020. The CAGR for each sector was then applied to its income in 2009 to determine the projected income in 2020.

Combined, these NKEAs — Oil, Gas & Energy, Financial Services, Palm Oil & Rubber, Agriculture, Communications Content & Infrastructure, Business Services, Electrical & Electronics, Wholesale & Retail, Healthcare, Education, and Tourism — were expected to contribute 73% of Malaysia's GNI in 2020, indicating the magnitude of their importance.[d,e]

---

[c]Malaysia Airlines, "Five Star Value Carrier: Business Transformation Plan (BTP 2)," January 2008, http://docsfiles.com/pdf_five_star_value_carrier_business_transformation_plan_btp_2.html, accessed September 2012.

[d]Greater Kuala Lumpur was not included to avoid double-counting.

[e]PEMANDU (Performance Management and Delivery Unit), Prime Minister's Department, Malaysian Government, "Economic Transformation Programme: A Roadmap for Malaysia,"

This collaboration between the public and private sectors was then taken to the next stage: the labs. Involving over 500 participants from almost 300 organizations (350 persons from 200 companies and 150 persons from 60 public institutions), these labs, which lasted nine weeks, were hothouses for the purpose of determining the baseline environment and case for change, problem-solving and prescribing strategic shifts.

Furthermore, the lab participants had to refine the details of specific projects that will attract investment, create incremental jobs (especially those with higher pay), and generate a positive GNI. They were also asked to identify private sector project champions as well as the required facilitation and policy support of the government and challenged to promote private investment over public investment.

The Pengerang Independent Deepwater Oil Storage Terminal was one of many examples. As part of a plan to develop a Malaysia–Singapore regional oil storage mechanism, a refining and trading hub similar to that of Amsterdam–Rotterdam–Antwerp, a five million cubic meter oil storage facility was proposed by the Johor state government, Vopak, and Dialog as a public–private partnership initiative. The investment of US$1.4 billion, 90% funded by the two private entities, was expected to generate over US$500 million in GNI and create 800 new jobs by 2020.[f] The federal government provided fiscal incentives, while the state government facilitated various approval processes.

Projects such as the above were also subjected to over 600 syndication meetings with stakeholders from the private sector, government, and non-governmental organizations to ensure that the ideas were truly robust and market-driven.

Playing the Game of the Impossible

The projects that were implementable in the foreseeable future, became known as Entry Point Projects. In all, 131 were identified, supplemented by 60 Business Opportunities with ready frameworks to be converted into EPPs in the future.[g]

To illustrate, Tourism NKEA has 12 EPPs, ranging from establishing three new premium outlets, creating global biodiversity hubs, and developing an eco-nature

October 26, 2010, http://etp.pemandu.gov.my/upload/etp_handbook_chapter_1-4_economic_model.pdf, pp. 85, 94, accessed September 2012.

[f]PEMANDU press release, "ETP in overdrive with 19 developments worth RM67 billion," January 11, 2011, http://www.pmo.gov.my/?menu=news&page=1729&news_id=5819&news_cat=4, accessed September 2012.

[g]Executive Summary, "Economic Transformation Programme: A Roadmap for Malaysia," PEMANDU, Prime Minister's Department, Malaysian Government, Putrajaya, Malaysia, October 26, 2010, http://etp.pemandu.gov.my/upload/etp_executive_summary_booklet.pdf, pp. 6, 16, accessed September 2012.

integrated resort, to targeting more international events, establishing Malaysia as a leading business tourism destination and improving rates, mix and quality of hotels. Development of food and beverage outlets, local transportation and tour operations were Business Opportunities identified for the future.

When consolidated, the 131 EPPs were expected to attract a cumulative investment of US$444 billion, create 3.3 million incremental jobs over 10 years and generate US$523 in GNI in the end-point year of 2020, raising GNI per capita from US$6,700 in 2009 to US$15,000 in 2020.[h] ETP calls for the investment to be drawn from the private sector, government-linked companies and the government in a 60:32:8 ratio, with a domestic-foreign investment split 73:27, averaged over 10 years. If successful, this breakdown will propel private investment growth to 12.8% between 2011 and 2015.

For Idris, it is crucial for Malaysia to be anchored on the correct goals. He asserted, "to transform the Malaysian economy, our 'true north' is extremely clear: investment, jobs, and GNI. These targets have to be stretched to get people to think out of the box and come out with real, but creative solutions. That is the essence of the game of the impossible."[i]

'Delivery' is Not Optional after Becoming 'Pregnant'

To make the government accountable for its execution, extensive public engagements were held with the larger business community and the public-at-large after the workshop and labs had ended. Open days were held to showcase the output, attracting more than 13,000 people. The 605-page ETP roadmap itself was an exercise to further make the government 'pregnant' with the promise to deliver the actions prescribed; hence there is no option but to 'deliver' on these promises. Lead ministers for the NKEAs were identified, key performance indicators were set for each minister and monthly steering committee meetings chaired by lead ministers with all relevant NKEA stakeholders were held under the close monitoring of PEMANDU. This culminated in two bi-annual 'report card' discussions with Prime Minister Najib on the progress of the NKEAs under the charge of the lead ministers. With explicitly detailed action items, there is no room to hide behind opaque and imprecise statements.

---

[h]PEMANDU, Prime Minister's Department, Malaysian Government, "Economic Transformation Programme: A Roadmap for Malaysia," October 26, 2010, http://etp.pemandu.gov.my/upload/etp_handbook_chapter_1-4_economic_model.pdf, pp. 59, 75, accessed September 2012.
[i]Idris Jala, interview with case writer.

Exhibit 1.

Methodology on the selection of NKEAs

Formula

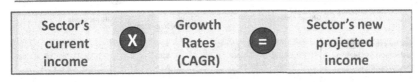

| Sector's current income | X | Growth Rates (CAGR) | = | Sector's new projected income |

Step 1

1. Take all sectors individual contribution GNI per capita

2. Rank them by order of contribution

Step 2

3. Establish Malaysia's historical growth per sector

4. Establish international benchmarks (historical & projections / forecasts)

5. Determine Malaysia's projection based on (3) & (4) above

Step 3

6. Rank all sectors by order of contribution

7. Select the sectors that contribute (~50% of the GNI per capita)

Formula to determine growth rate (CAGR)

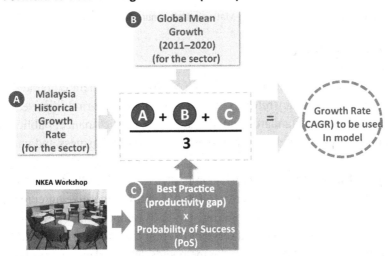

A Malaysia Historical Growth Rate (for the sector)

B Global Mean Growth (2011–2020) (for the sector)

NKEA Workshop

C Best Practice (productivity gap) x Probability of Success (PoS)

$$\frac{A + B + C}{3} = \text{Growth Rate (CAGR) to be used in model}$$

Source: Pemandu, Idris Jala Presentation to Malaysia IXP, January 2012.

Exhibit 2.

Projecting 2020 GNI Contribution

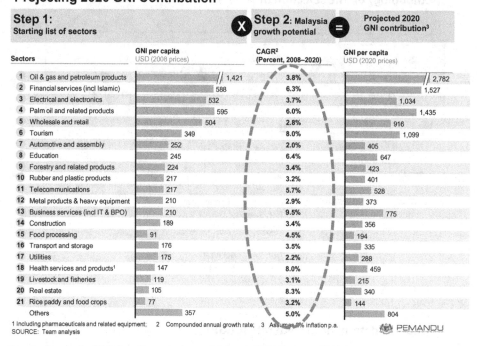

Sectors	GNI per capita USD (2008 prices)	CAGR[2] (Percent, 2008–2020)	GNI per capita USD (2020 prices)
1 Oil & gas and petroleum products	1,421	3.8%	2,782
2 Financial services (incl Islamic)	588	6.3%	1,527
3 Electrical and electronics	532	3.7%	1,034
4 Palm oil and related products	595	6.0%	1,435
5 Wholesale and retail	504	2.8%	916
6 Tourism	349	8.0%	1,099
7 Automotive and assembly	252	2.0%	405
8 Education	245	6.4%	647
9 Forestry and related products	224	3.4%	423
10 Rubber and plastic products	217	3.2%	401
11 Telecommunications	217	5.7%	528
12 Metal products & heavy equipment	210	2.9%	373
13 Business services (incl IT & BPO)	210	9.5%	775
14 Construction	189	3.4%	356
15 Food processing	91	4.5%	194
16 Transport and storage	176	3.5%	335
17 Utilities	175	2.2%	288
18 Health services and products[1]	147	8.0%	459
19 Livestock and fisheries	119	3.1%	215
20 Real estate	105	8.3%	340
21 Rice paddy and food crops	77	3.2%	144
Others	357	5.0%	804

1 Including pharmaceuticals and related equipment;   2 Compounded annual growth rate;   3 Assumes 2% inflation p.a.
SOURCE: Team analysis   PEMANDU

Source: Pemandu, Idris Jala Presentation to Malaysia IXP, January 2012.

Becoming Competitive

To facilitate the accomplishment of the NKEAs, the government embarked on six cross-sector clusters of policy reforms known as Strategic Reform Initiatives (SRIs). They cover competition, standards and liberalization, public finance, public service delivery, human capital development, government's role in business and narrowing disparities.

The key goal was to make Malaysia competitive globally. Efforts such as establishing and enforcing competition laws to remove anti-competitive agreements and abuse of dominant positions, accelerating standards adoption and development in order to enable Malaysian goods and services to compete internationally and liberalizing key services sub-sectors to raise competencies, are good examples of how this goal was approached. Others include reducing the tax gap to strengthen Malaysia's fiscal position, up-skilling and re-skilling programs and setting minimum wage to spur productivity, divesting government-controlled companies to reduce crowding-out the private sector, and implementing a market-friendly targeted affirmative program to promote Bumiputera competitiveness that is needs-based and transparent and has an exit strategy.

Execution, Execution, Execution

The first year's results of the ETP were far ahead of the ETP's original targets. A committed investment of US$59.7 billion was secured, leading to a GNI and incremental jobs forecast of US$43.2 billion and 313,741, respectively.

In reviewing the progress from 2011, Idris said that 2012 will not be a year in which Malaysia introduces new programs, but rather one in which the country must follow through on existing programs and execute, execute, execute.[j]

---

[j]Idris Jala, interview with case writer.

Central Europe After the Crash:
Between Europe and the Euro

Diego Comin*, Dante Roscini* and Elisa Farri*

This note briefly reviews the financial crisis in central Europe in late 2008 and summarizes how four central European countries — Poland, the Czech Republic, Hungary and Slovakia — have coped with the economic downturn. (See **Exhibit 1** for the main economic indicators of these countries.)

From Prosperity to Crisis

Until the autumn of 2008, the countries of central Europe had enjoyed a decade of unprecedented prosperity, with some seeing annual growth rates of nearly 10% a year. Poland, the Czech Republic, Hungary and Slovakia experienced the highest growth rates in the region. (See **Exhibit 2** for real GDP growth rates in central Europe from 1999 to 2009.)

As central European countries reoriented their economies westward and joined the European Union (EU), they also embraced capitalism. Their policy-makers adopted the institutions and practices of their West European neighbors, and in many cases privatized and deregulated their economies much more fully than in the West. Productivity increased dramatically. For such countries, joining the EU also meant integration with European and world markets. In Hungary, Slovakia and the

Exhibit 1.   Main Economic Indicators, 2008

Indicators	Poland	Slovakia*	Czech iRepublic	Hungary
Population (million)	38.1	5.5	10.2	9.9
GDP per head (US$ at PPP)	17,510	21,830	25,630	19,720
Real GDP growth (%)	4.9	6.4	3.0	0.6
GDP per head (US$ at PPP)	17.5[†]	21.7[†]	25.7[†]	19.8[†]
Inflation (annual % change)[‡]	4.2	3.9	6.3	6.0
Current-account balance (US$ billion)	−28.5	−6.4	−6.6	−12.9
Trade balance	−24.4	−1.1	6.4	175.0
General government gross debt (% of GDP)	47.1	28.7	26.7[†]	67.7[†]
External debt stock (US$ million)	211.2[†]	na	80.7[†]	164.4[†]
Exchange rate: Home country currency to US$	2.4	1.4	19.3	172.1
Lending interest rate (%)	na	5.7[†]	6.3	10.2
Consumer price index (%)	4.2	4.4	6.3	6.1
Foreign reserves (€ billion)[§]	52.2	12.6	24.2	17.4
Currency risk rating	BB	NA	BBB	B
Sovereign risk rating	BB	NA	BBB	B
Banking sector risk rating	BB	NA	BBB	B
Political risk rating	BBB	NA	A	A
Economic structure risk rating	BB	NA	BBB	B

Source: The Economist Intelligence Unit, www.eiu.com, accessed September 2009. (Where relevant, numbers have been changed from European to American format.)
Notes: *Slovakia was admitted to the Eurozone in January 2009.
[†]Economist Intelligence Unit estimates.
[‡]Source: European Central Bank, Annual Report, www.ecb.eu.
[§]End-period.

Czech Republic, exports accounted for 80% to 90% of GDP over the previous two years. (See **Exhibit 3** for data on exports and imports of goods and services as a percentage of GDP from 1999 to 2009; and **Exhibit 4** for the main trading partners of these countries in 2008.)

In the summer of 2007, the burst of the housing bubble destabilized the U.S. financial sector. By mid-2008, the crisis hit the developing and the transition countries[1] and central Europe witnessed the worst output collapse since the recession that followed the end of communism.

Vulnerable Economies

In March 2009, the IMF published the results of its survey on the implications of the global financial downturn for low-income countries. It drew up a "watch list" of 26 vulnerable countries, some of which were in central Europe.

Exhibit 2. Real GDP Growth Rates, 1999–2009

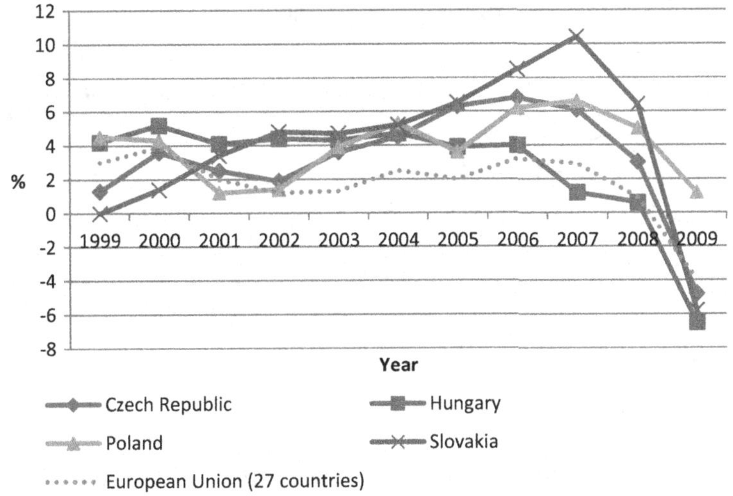

Source: Compiled by case writers from http://epp.eurostat.ec.europa.eu, accessed January 2010.

Vulnerability to crisis in central Europe had deep roots. In 1989, the fall of communism led to a thorough transformation from a centrally planned economy to one based on a free market. In an effort to de-monopolize the power of the state and free up the economy, central European governments introduced substantial reforms to deal with the structural distortions that they had inherited from past regimes.

The four pillars of these countries' transition programs included the liberalization of prices, trade activities, exchange rates and capital flows. There were downsides to the transition, however. The removal of price controls and quantity allocations, together with weak monetary and fiscal controls, contributed to extremely high levels of inflation, or even hyperinflation. In the early 1990s, more than half of the transition countries experienced at least one year with annual inflation rates above 1,000%.[2] The introduction of fixed or crawling exchange rates proved effective in guiding the disinflation programs.[a] The illusory safety of anchored exchange rates attracted large inflows of speculative lending from Western banks. (See **Exhibit 5** for data on total foreign debt from 1993 to 2008, and **Exhibit 6** for the exposure of West European banks to the crisis in central Europe.) The growth of short-term borrowing accompanied higher incomes, faster growth rates and greater openness to trade.

In the late 1990s, inflation persistence initially resulted in a real appreciation of exchange rates, and then in a sharp decline in the competitiveness of exports.

---

[a] See also "*Classification of exchange rate arrangements and monetary policy frameworks*," IMF, June 30, 2004, http://www.imf.org/external/np/mfd/er/2004/eng/0604.htm, accessed September 2009.

Exhibit 3.   Exports as a % of GDP, 1999–2009

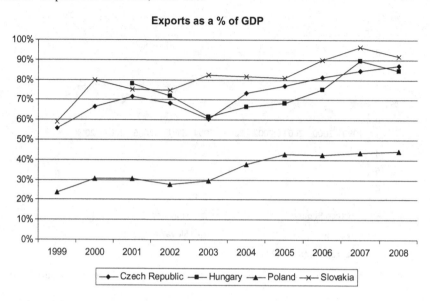

Imports as a % of GDP, 1999–2009

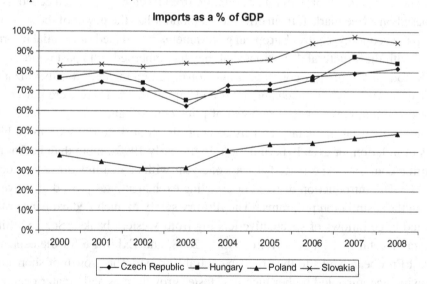

Source: Compiled by casewriters from http://epp.eurostat.ec.europa.eu, accessed September 2009.

Exhibit 4.   Trading Partners, Destination of Exports and Origin of Imports, 2008

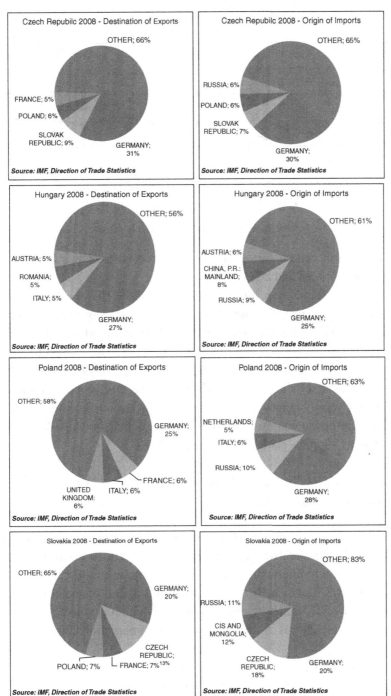

Source: Compiled by case writers from www.imf.org, accessed September 2009.

Exhibit 5.   Total Foreign Debt as a Share of GDP, 1993–2008

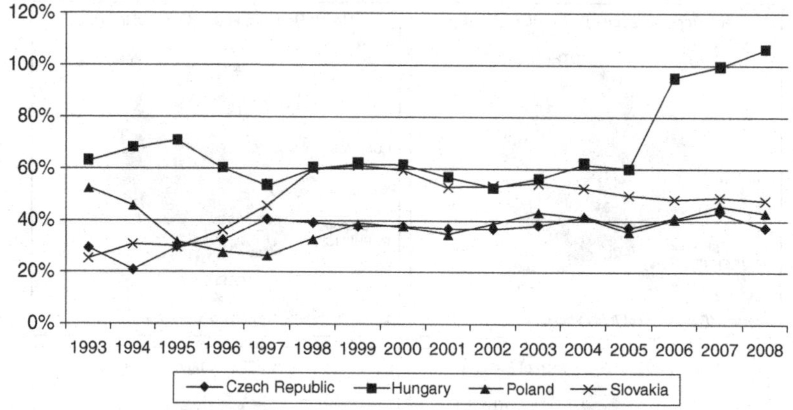

Source: Compiled by case writers from www.eiu.com, accessed September 2009.

As a result, several central European countries moved toward inflation-targeting strategies between 1998 and 2001.[b]

In May 2004, eight Soviet bloc countries joined the EU: the Czech Republic, Estonia, Hungary, Latvia, Lithuania, Poland, Slovakia and Slovenia. For these countries, admission to the EU created expectations that their productivity levels would converge further with those of other member countries. These expectations led to increased capital inflows, consumption, and imports. (See **Exhibit 7a** for the foreign-currency-denominated debt of households in four central European countries from 2005 to 2008.) The dynamics of this convergence created short-term imbalances in the central European countries: current-account deficits increased, and inflation surged as money supplies started to increase in 2006.

The Financial Crisis in Central Europe: A Strange Way to Celebrate an Anniversary

On the 20th anniversary of the fall of communism, central Europe found itself deeply affected by the worldwide economic turmoil, despite its recently acquired EU membership and large international reserves built up during the previous decade. In September 2008, Lehman Brothers went bankrupt and financial markets froze throughout the world. Suddenly, central Europe, which had entered the crisis with macroeconomic imbalances, found itself with little international finance.

---

[b]Inflation targeting is a framework for monetary policy characterized by the public announcement of official quantitative targets, or target ranges, for the inflation rate over a defined time horizon and by explicit acknowledgment that low, stable inflation is monetary policy's primary long-term goal. (Ben S. Bernanke *et al.*, "*Inflation targeting: lessons from the international experience*" (Princeton University Press, 1999).)

Exhibit 6. Exposure of Western Banks to Crisis in Central Europe (data as of year-end 2008)

Reference Country	Top Foreign Banks	Market Share (as % of total banking assets in reference country)	Exposure (as % of total assets)	Total Assets Invested in Reference Country (in € billions)	Total Assets (in € billions)	Domicile
Hungary	Raiffeisen	7.5%	13.5%	9.4	69.6	Austria
	OTP	20.4%	66.8%	25.6	38.3	Hungary
	Unicredit	7.2%	0.8%	9.0	1,071.6	Italy
	KBC	4.9%	1.8%	6.1	340.1	Belgium
	ING	8.2%	0.7%	10.3	1,395.5	Netherlands
	Erste	1.4%	0.8%	1.7	208.7	Austria
	Intesa	8.7%	1.7%	10.9	637.0	Italy
	Citi	2.0%	0.2%	2.5	1,543.5	US
Poland	Raiffeisen	2.7%	10.1%	7.0	69.6	Austria
	Commerzbank	7.4%	3.3%	19.3	593.8	Germany
	Eurobank	1.6%	5.1%	4.0	79.3	Greece
	KBC	14.1%	10.9%	37.0	340.1	Belgium
	ING	3.4%	0.6%	9.0	1,395.5	Netherlands
	Erste	4.8%	6.0%	12.5	208.7	Austria
	Citi	3.9%	0.7%	10.1	1,543.5	US
Czech Republic	Raiffeisen	4.5%	10.0%	6.9	69.6	Austria
	Commerzbank	2.4%	0.6%	3.6	593.8	Germany
	Unicredit	23.7%	3.4%	36.5	1,071.6	Italy
	KBC	7.1%	3.2%	11.0	340.1	Belgium
	ING	24.3%	2.7%	37.4	1,395.5	Netherlands
	SocGen	16.1%	2.3%	24.8	1,067.1	France
	Citi	0.6%	0.1%	0.9	1,543.5	US

Source: *Emerging Europe Banking — What's next*? Morgan Stanley, February 2009. (Where relevant, numbers have been changed from European to American format.)

Note: Market share is calculated by taking bank's assets over the period and dividing it by the total assets of the market in the reference country over the same period. As of end of 2008, total banking assets amounted to €126 billion in Hungary, €262 billion in Poland and €154 billion in the Czech Republic. (*Source*: The Economist Intelligence Unit, www.eiu.org.)

(1) Unicredit (Italy) holds a 59.3% stake. (2) Commerzbank (Germany) holds a 70% stake. (3) ING (Netherlands) holds a 75% stake. (4) Allied Irish Banks (Ireland) holds a 70.5% stake. (5) Banco Comercial Portugues (Portugal) holds a 65.5% stake. (6) Citigroup (US) holds a 75% stake. (7) KBC (Belgium) holds an 80% stake. (8) Subsidiary of Raiffeisen Zentralbank Osterreich (Austria). (9) Rabobank (Holland) holds a 59.4% stake. (10) Subsidiary of General Electric's (US) financial arm. (11) The Czech Republic National Bank only posts rankings of banks based on basic capital.

Exhibit 7a.   Foreign-Currency-Denominated Debt of Households in Central Europe, 2005–2008

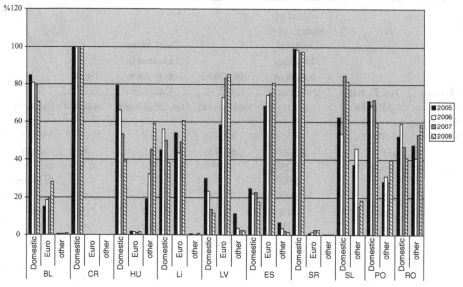

Source: R. Barrel *et al.*, "Household debt and foreign currency borrowing in new member states of the EU," http://www.euroframe.org/fileadmin/user_upload/euroframe/docs/2009/EUROF09_Barrell_Fic_etal.pdf, accessed October 2009.

Note: BL = Bulgaria, CR = Czech Republic, HU = Hungary, LI = Lithuania, LV = Latvia, ES = Estonia, SR = Slovakia, SL = Slovania, PO = Poland, RO = Romania.

Exhibit 7b.   Foreign-Currency-Denominated Debt of Firms in Central Europe, 2005–2008

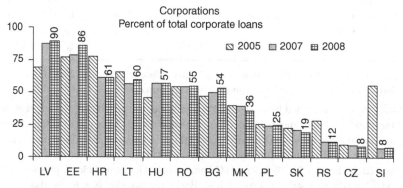

Source: http://www.cnb.cz/m2export/sites/www.cnb.cz/en/public/media_service/conferences/spee-ches/ download/tuma_090324_nature_of_the_crisis.pdf, accessed September 2009.

Note: LV = Latvia, EE = Estonia, HR = Croatia, LT = Lithuania, HU = Hungary, RO = Romania, BG = Bulgaria, MK = Macedonia, PL = Poland, SK = Slovakia, RS = Serbia, CR = Czech Republic, SI = Slovenia.

The first-round effects in central Europe were primarily driven by three factors: the collapse of commodity prices, the fall in exports and the drying-up of capital inflows. On the output side, there was widespread and sharp contraction in the first quarter of 2009, due largely to a rapid decline in domestic demand.

The second-round effects were caused by a slowdown in the European banking sector. Financial integration, in the form of large debt flows, foreign direct investments (FDI) and the increasing presence of foreign banks, had all played an integral role in the development model of transition countries in central Europe. For example, before the financial crisis, Hungary and Poland had experienced a decade of rapid expansion of bank credit to the private sector.

Troubles in the banking sector originated mainly from high volumes of non-performing loans[c] denominated in foreign currencies. Because of falling exchange rates, most central European investors found themselves in too much debt and many declared insolvency. (See **Exhibit 8** for data on currency exchange rates from August 2007 to August 2009.) The strong presence of Western European banks in the region, which held 50% to 80% market share depending on the country, was a particular

Exhibit 8.   Currency Exchange Rates, August 2007–August 2009

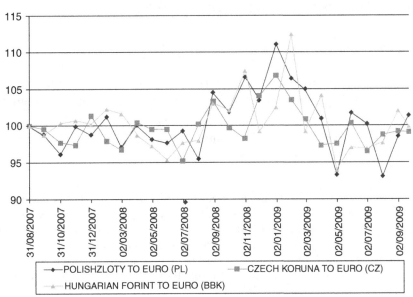

Source: Compiled by case writers from Thomson-Reuters data stream, accessed September 2009.

Note: An inflation targeting regime was introduced in 1998 in Czech Republic, in 2000 in Poland and in 2001 in Hungary. A free-floating regime was introduced in 2000 in Poland and in 2008 in Hungary. Indices were rebased to 100 on August 31, 2007. Monthly end-of-period data.

---

[c]Non-performing loans include those that have been in default, or close to being in default, for at least three months.

concern. "Most of the banks in this region are from the Eurozone[d] and will have to undergo further recapitalization," declared Gillian Edgeworth, an economist with Deutsche Bank in London.[3] According to some analysts, if central European banks received further infusions of capital from Western governments, which were straining to pay for stimulus packages, this might put additional pressure on the Euro as well.

Because many central European countries shared foreign parent banks, one of the key threats was the danger of contagion. Difficulties in some countries could negatively affect neighboring countries because of the loss of depositor confidence, which could result in a run on the banks, collapsing currencies, or the withdrawal of foreign banks from the area. Of the different types of private capital flows, short-term loans were the most likely to be withdrawn during difficult times. Therefore, even a relatively healthy economy and banking system like that of the Czech Republic, which had a reasonable loan-to-deposit ratio and scarce foreign exchange-denominated lending to households, could be highly vulnerable.

Yet not all central European countries were struggling for the same reasons. In fact, countries with large pre-crisis credit booms and high levels of private external debt suffered the largest output declines. (See **Exhibit 9** for data on stock price indices from December 31, 2007, to August 31, 2009.)

Bailing Out Central Europe

Central European countries can be classified according to the type of lending institutions on which they rely. EU member states are supported by direct funding from the European Union.[e] In contrast, non-EU member states depend on multilateral support from international lending institutions such as the IMF and the European Bank for Reconstruction and Development (EBRD).

---

[d]The Eurozone is composed of EU member states that have adopted the euro as the single currency, in accordance with the Treaty and in which a single monetary policy is conducted under the jurisdiction of the Governing Council of the European Central Bank (ECB). In 2000, the Euro area comprised Austria, Belgium, Finland, France, Germany, Ireland, Italy, Luxembourg, the Netherlands, Portugal and Spain. Greece became a member of the Euro area on January 1, 2001. Slovenia became a member of the Euro area on January 1, 2007. (The OECD Glossary of Statistical Terms, at http://stats.oecd.org/glossary/detail.asp?ID=862.)

[e]Funding comes in the form of loans that have to be repaid in five years. Aid packages are designed to ease countries' external financing constraints when they cannot access the international capital markets at reasonable interest rates. The EU, with its first-class creditor status, borrows at favorable AAA interest rates on world markets. Then, the raised funds are passed on to the member states in need, which benefit from the EU's better credit rating. If a member state fails to pay back its loans, the EU has to step in as guarantor. (European Commission, Economic and Financial Affairs, "*EU steps in with emergency financing for three member states*," July 14, 2009, http://ec.europa.eu/economy_finance/een/014/article_8884_en.htm, accessed September 2009.)

Exhibit 9. Stock Price Indices, December 31, 2007–August 31, 2009

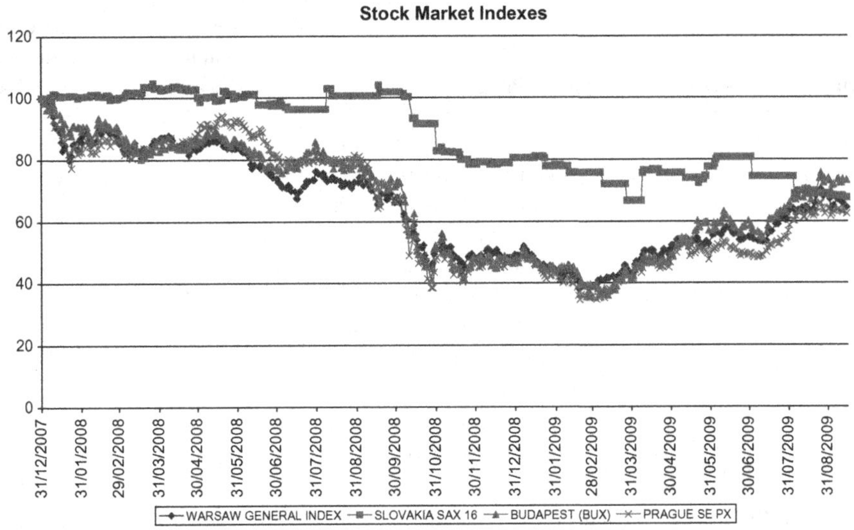

Stock Market Indexes

Source: Compiled by case writers from Thomson-Reuters data stream, accessed September 2009.

Note: Indices rebased to 100 on December 31, 2007, end of period data.

Despite their membership in the EU, however, central European countries had to resort to international rescue packages. In October 2008, Hungary was among the first EU member states to obtain financial support from the IMF. (See **Exhibit 10** for a summary of international rescue packages for Hungary and Poland.) Support from national authorities, international organizations, and regional banking groups was unprecedented in size, scope, and speed.[4]

Yet initially, the help given by the EU faltered for two reasons. First, the EU lacked the financial resources and ad hoc procedures to face the magnitude of the crisis. Second, due to strong internal debates, EU governments could not agree on how far to go in propping up non-Eurozone members. Germany, for example, declared that it would only help bail out countries that belonged to the Eurozone.[f]

After initial hesitation, the European Commission approved and co-financed several IMF-led programs in the region. Technically known as balance-of-payments (BoP) assistance, EU funding amounted to about €15 billion, and was granted to Hungary, Latvia and Romania in 2008. As economic conditions kept worsening in early 2009, the EU raised its overall ceiling of funding from €25 billion to €50 billion. The aid from the EU, however, did not come without strings. Beneficiary countries had to commit themselves to repaying debts, reforming their taxation

---

[f]Bruno Waterfield, "*Return of the East–West divides: European Union in chaos as global recession deepens*," March 15, 2009, www.telegraph.co.uk, accessed September 2009.

Exhibit 10.   Lending to Hungary and Poland

Country	Lending Institution	Type of Program	Lending Amount (US$ billion)	Lending Amount (€ billion)
Hungary	IMF	Stand-by Arrangement (This program is designed to help countries address short-term balance of payments problems.)	$15.7	€12.5
	European Union	Medium-term financial assistance (The Council of Ministers approved the "medium-term financial assistance program" on November 4, 2008.)	$8.0	€6.5
	World Bank		$1.3	€1.0
Poland	IMF	Flexible Credit Line (This program is for countries with very strong fundamentals, policies and track records of policy implementation and is particularly useful for crisis prevention.)	$20.6	€16.4

Source: The International Monetary Fund, www.imf.org, accessed September 2009.

systems, reducing overall spending, and increasing their administrative capacity so as to better absorb transfers of aid from the EU.[5]

Since 2004, there has been an ongoing debate about whether the EU should give central European countries a shortcut to join the Eurozone, and thus access to the safety and stability net offered by the EU. Still, the ripple effects of devaluation could destabilize foreign-owned banks in the region.

The Different Policy Responses

After a decade of pro-cyclical economic policies, central European governments had to cut spending and reduce public services in late 2008. These measures were part of the stabilization programs initiated by the governments to minimize the effects of the slowdown and lay the groundwork for economic recovery. Major actions by the central European governments included changes in the following areas:

1. Social and structural policies such as raising labor-market participation, implementing social safety nets, and rolling back the second-pillar pension schemes to reduce the number of early retirees.

2. Financial policies such as bank recapitalization and nationalization, restoring market confidence, and strengthening home/host country coordination.
3. Fiscal policies to restore the balance of payments, especially in those countries with euro-adoption ambitions, such as Poland.
4. Limited monetary policies to respond to fixed exchange rates and heavy foreign currency-denominated lending. (See **Exhibit 11** for data on monetary policy strategies of six non-Eurozone EU member states.)

Exhibit 11. Monetary Policy Strategies of Six Non-Eurozone EU Member States, as of End of 2008

Country	Regime	Monetary Policy Strategy	Currency	Features
Bulgaria	Currency Board	Exchange rate target	Bulgarian Lev	Exchange rate target: Peg to the euro at BGN 1.95 euro within the framework of a currency board arrangement.
Czech Republic	Floating exchange rate	Inflation target	Czech Koruna	Inflation target: 3% ±1 percentage point until end-2009. From 2010, 2% ±1 percentage point. Managed floating exchange rate.
Hungary	Floating exchange rate	Inflation target	Hungarian Forint	Inflation target: 3% ±1 percentage point, a medium-term target since 2007. Free-floating exchange rate.
Poland	Floating exchange rate	Inflation target	Polish Zloty	Inflation target: 2.5% ±1 percentage point (12-month increase in the CPI). Free-floating exchange rate.
Romania	Floating exchange rate	Inflation target	Romanian Leu	Inflation target: 3.8% and 3.5% ±1 percentage point for end-2008 and end-2009, respectively. Managed floating exchange rate.
Slovakia	EMU (adopted the euro as of January 2009)	Inflation target	Slovak Koruna	Inflation target was set at below 2% for end-2008.

Source: Compiled by case writers from European System of Central Banks (ESCB), http://www.ecb.int/stats, accessed September 2009.

The Case of Poland

After a period of steady expansion driven by the investment boom and the rapid growth of credit that followed its accession to the EU, Poland entered the crisis with relatively limited internal and external imbalances.[6] Nonetheless, Poland's GDP growth declined significantly, from 5.1% in 2008 to 1.4% in 2009.[7]

By mid-2008, due to the recession in Poland's principal export markets in particular, Western Europe and the U.S., Poland's exports had decreased by 30% in the first quarter of 2009. Poland's imports had declined even more, reducing its current account deficit and making net trade an inadequate explanation.

The slowdown in growth could be traced to investment. Between 2008 and 2009, investment in Poland declined by 1%. One culprit was a tightening in the supply of credit. However, despite evidence that credit tightened for both corporate and individual borrowers, the spread between borrowing and lending rates declined, and the credit-to-GDP ratio grew through 2008 and remained flat during 2009. (See **Exhibit 12** for data on the evolution of the spreads between borrowing and lending rates from 2005 to 2009; and the annual growth rate of stock of domestic credit, from 2007Q1 to 2009Q1.)

The Polish banking system weathered the crisis well. Poland experienced a shorter credit expansion than other countries in central Europe. NPLs (non-performing loans) were not very high (5%) but started to increase in 2009, especially in the non-financial corporate sector. Nevertheless, the banking sector remained well capitalized, with a capital adequacy ratio (CAR) of 11.7% by May 2009. Further, it was expected to remain relatively strong. Among the eight largest banks[8] in Poland, only one did not pass a "stress test" that involved simulating an increase in its NPLs to 15%.

In November 2008, the NBP, Poland's central bank, cut rates by 250 basis points to 3.5%, and lowered its reserve requirement by 50 basis points to 3%. To safeguard financial stability, Polish authorities undertook tight counter-cyclical policy measures, such as tax cuts, limited employment subsidies, and mortgage support for the unemployed. These policies were likely to be transitory, because if the recession persisted, they would push the debt-to-GDP ratio above the 55% threshold mandated by the constitution. In April 2009, Prime Minister Donald Tusk announced that Poland was interested in a one-year precautionary arrangement under the IMF's Flexible Credit Line in the amount of $20.5 billion.[9]

According to the IMF and the EU, Poland was the only economy in the EU to grow in 2009.[10]

Exhibit 12. Evolution of the Spreads between Borrowing and Lending Rates from January 2005–June 2009; and Annual Growth Rate in Stock of Domestic Credit from 2007 to the First Quarter of 2009

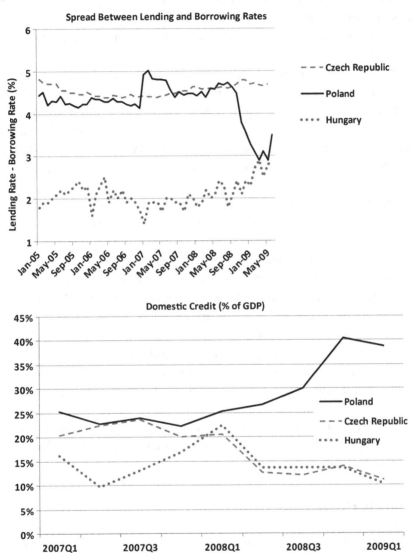

Source: Compiled by case writers from at www.eiu.com data, accessed on September 2009.

Note: Domestic credit as a % of GDP is computed as domestic credit divided by GDP in local currency unit (LCU).

A Two-Speed Europe

The eastward growth of the European Union has not only influenced politics in the countries that joined but also altered the dynamics within the EU.[g] In particular, it has raised important questions about the impact of EU membership on new member states and vice versa.

One dynamic that has become apparent in the enlarged EU is tension between the old and new Europe. For example, among the new member states, those that are poorer, more peripheral and newer as nation states have shown a stronger preference for the Anglo-American model of social policy, as opposed to the traditional European model based on social cohesion and solidarity. Further, "social dumping," which refers to differences between wages in the old and new member states, has provoked strong criticism inside the EU.

In fact, the financial crisis is playing a key role in deepening the so-called east-west division in Europe. European economies are rebounding at different speeds, complicating the European Central Bank's efforts to put the EU region back on stable footing. In addition, the growing sense of a two-speed Europe, along the lines of the iron curtain that once separated communist from capitalist states, has been exacerbated by the pressures of classic "beggar thy neighbor" actions aimed to protect individual countries' own industries and jobs.

Meanwhile, some analysts believe the crisis could be a valid opportunity to accelerate the process of structural reform in central European countries.[11] Still, at a time when strong leadership and public trust are needed more than ever, some experts fear that the crisis could jeopardize democracy across the region. Signs of social unrest are increasing, and public discontent is expected to worsen as governments cut spending to reduce deficits. In March 2009, the Czech government lost a parliamentary no-confidence vote, just a few days after Hungary's prime minister resigned amid battles over spending cuts.

Transition in Crisis?

The crisis has highlighted some flaws in the development models that transitional countries have pursued. In the last decade, growth came from strong exports of goods and services as well as huge inflows of capital. The net effect was beneficial, but the disadvantage was reflected in a heavy dependence on demand from West Europe. According to a 2009 report by the EBRD, central Europe needs more foreign capital

---

[g]On May 1, 2004, 10 members of the former Eastern bloc and Yugoslavia joined the EU: Cyprus, the Czech Republic, Estonia, Hungary, Latvia, Lithuania, Malta, Poland, the Slovak Republic and Slovenia. In 2007, two new countries joined the EU: Romania and Bulgaria.

to escape the current downturn. In addition, ex-communist economies need to (a) improve their legal systems to re-gain the confidence of foreign investors worried about contracts and property rights, (b) restructure their social safety nets, and (c) invite more market competition by lowering informal barriers to entry that were linked to the old networks of the communist era.

However, the main decision for central European governments trying to address these problems is whether to extend their transition agendas, or to replace them.

Endnotes

1   Stefan Wagstyl, "EBRD cautions on currency debt," *Financial Times*, November 2, 2009, via Factiva, Accessed November 4, 2009.

2   Paul Wachtel and Iikka Korhonen, "Observations on disinflation in transition economies," Bank of Finland, 2004, http://www.bof.fi/NR/rdonlyres/26F2C777-642E-4415-AA70-07861E5EE3B7/0/dp0504.pdf, Accessed September 2009.

3   Nelson D. Schwartz, "As It Falters, Eastern Europe Raises Risks," *New York Times*, February 23, 2009, http://www.nytimes.com/2009/02/24/business/worldbusiness/24-euro.html?_r=1, via Factiva, Accessed September 2009.

4   "Down in the dumps," *The Economist*, Accessed November 5, 2009.

5   European Commission, Economic and Financial Affairs, "EU steps in with emergency financing for three member states," *European Economy News*, Issue 14, July 14, 2009, http://ec.europa.eu/economy_finance/een/014/article_8884_en.htm, Accessed September 2009.

6   The International Monetary Fund (IMF), "Republic of Poland: 2009 Article IV Consultation," August 21, 2009, IMF website, http://www.imf.org/external/pubs/cat/longres.cfm?sk=23212.0.

7   Economic Intelligence Unit.

8   These banks accounted for 54% of total banking-sector assets.

9   The FCL was an instrument established in early 2009 that was available to fund member countries deemed to have very strong fundamentals, policies and track records of policy implementation.

10   "Down in the dumps," *The Economist*, Accessed November 5, 2009.

11   Nouriel Roubini, "Eastern European Tinderbox: How Explosive Could It Get?" *RGE Monitor*, February 25, 2009, http://www.advisorperspectives.com/commentaries/rge_022509.html.

II
Institutions

Introduction

Both the actual and the optimal strategies for firms depend on the institutional rules that constrain them as well as on the functioning of markets where they operate. Studying these interactions between strategy and institutions/markets is a central piece of any positive or normative discussion on competitiveness. In this module, I invite the discussion leaders to deeply explore these considerations through a sequence of cases that cover a wide range of institutions in contexts that represent an ample range of development stages.

The institutions covered in this module govern the political system (e.g. democracy versus autocracy), the labor markets (unions strength, bargaining process, firing costs in contracts, . . .), credit markets, default procedures, banking regulations and product market regulations. The cases in the module show that, though the issues vary with the level of development, the importance of institutions for the evolution of productivity and competitiveness does not diminish as countries develop.

Institutions are persistent,[a] but not static. This invites the discussions to gravitate not only over how institutions impact companies' performance but on why institutions evolve the way they do. On this issue, the contrast between the South Africa and the Egypt cases is particularly striking. In both countries there have been historical tensions towards democratization. Most observers predicted a violent transition for South Africa, while in Egypt a peaceful transition seemed more likely. Since 1994, the franchise has been extended quite peacefully to the black population in South Africa and they have not used their new political rights to expropriate the white minority. In Egypt, a violent uprising in 2011 led transitorily to democratic elections which were followed two years later by the arrest of president-elect Morsi and to an eventual return to a military rule. Similarly, the emergence of large family groups in Peru, or the evolution of the labor and financial markets in Spain are manifestations of the underlying institutions in the country. Why do institutions evolve the way they do and what can business learn from these patterns?

Synopses and Assignment Questions

South Africa (A): Stuck in the Middle

Fifteen years after ending apartheid, formal unemployment in South Africa was still at 24%. While the country had grown at 4 to 5% annually during the 2000s, the

---

[a]Though probably less so than what one would imagine. The polity Index, a widely used measure of political institutions (e.g. how democratic a country is), has an autocorrelation of about 0.3 after 50 years. The persistence of income and technology after 50 years, for example, is close to 1.

financial crisis set it back by 1 million more unemployed. Moreover, it seemed as if the nation were stuck between low wage and fully developed competitors. The government of Jacob Zuma has just adopted a "New Growth Path," hoping to create several million jobs over the next few years. Both the Finance Minister and the head of the Central Bank support the initiative, but worry how they can sustain fiscal discipline and control inflation, in light of these stimulative policies. Organized labor, meanwhile, has little sympathy for any sort of sacrifice.

South Africa (B): Getting Unstuck?

AQ:

1. Why has unemployment stayed so high in South Africa?
2. Has BEE been a good thing or not, on net?
3. Is South Africa "stuck in the middle?"
4. Does the New Growth Path make sense? Will it work?

Egypt: Turbulence and Transition?

The case uses the political history of Egypt over the last 50 years to explore (i) political transitions and (ii) how political institutions may impact the competitiveness of companies. In particular, the current political instability in Egypt invites to study the factors that make political transitions a source of social and economic turbulence as well as the ways in which companies (domestic and multinationals) may cope with that.

AQ:

1. How would you characterize Egypt's economic situation before 2010?
2. Were political institutions good for Egyptian companies between independence and 2010?
3. Why has there been a political transition? Why has it been so violent?
4. Are there business opportunities in the transition?

Peru: Family Groups and Competitiveness

The predominance of Family Groups is an important feature of many economies, especially in developing countries. This case focuses on Peru and studies the prevalence of the four most significant family groups in the various sectors of economic activity. The case explores the histories of these groups to facilitate a discussion on the origins of Family Groups. It also documents the current economic environment in Peru and other peers to enable the reader to form an opinion on the impact that Family Groups have on productivity and competitiveness.

AQ:

1. Are Family groups a problem or a solution?
2. Why do they arise?
3. Do they facilitate or prevent FDI inflows?
4. Should they be regulated? If so, how?

Spain: Can the House Resist the Storm?

On September 16, 2008, President Rodriguez Zapatero recognized the severity of Spain's macroeconomic situation and clearly pointed to the culprit in front of the Spanish Congress: "Let nobody doubt it; there is already a wide consensus about the origin of the crisis: [It is] in the U.S. and its subprime mortgages." During the last eight years, Spain had gone through a phenomenal expansion that has had many important ingredients: immigration, housing boom, banking and financial market regulation, current account deficit, and productivity growth. This case analyzes how they interacted during the period 2000–2007 and what drove the Spanish recession in 2008.

AQ:

1. Why has unemployment increased so much in Spain since 2008?
2. Why did the party end up so bad? Are banks victims or culprits?
3. Would leaving the Euro be the solution to Spain's problems?
4. What are the lessons of the Spanish crisis for companies?

South Africa (A): Stuck in the Middle?

Richard H. K. Vietor* and Diego Comin*

In mid-February 2011, Pravin Gordhan, finance minister of South Africa, agonized over the final draft of the budget for 2011–2012. The document had been developed over the past two months to implement his country's new strategy for economic development, titled the "New Growth Path."

After several years of above-average growth and declining unemployment, South Africa had hit a wall in 2008 when the global financial crisis struck. As economic growth turned sharply negative, employment fell by more than a million jobs (7% of the workforce), driving unemployment up to 25% and leaving half of all young people (ages 18–25) unemployed. Only 41% of the working-age population had jobs.[1] Yet wages continued to rise faster than inflation; in 2010 they rose nearly twice as fast! With productivity lagging, unit labor costs were rising annually by 6.8%.[2] (See **Exhibits 1a** and **2c.**)

These problems had plagued South Africa since the end of apartheid, in 1994. To deal with them, Nelson Mandela had adopted a strategy of GEAR — Growth, Employment and Redistribution. Thabo Mbeki had proposed ASGISA — Accelerated and Shared Growth Initiative of South Africa. And recently, Gordhan's colleague Ebrahim Patel, minister of economic development, had proposed the New Growth Path — a plan that had President Jacob Zuma's blessing.

As Minister Gordhan reviewed the draft, several issues crossed his mind. Perhaps foremost was revenue growth. While South Africa's tax base had expanded from

---

*Reprinted with permission of Harvard Business School Publishing.
This case was prepared by Professor Richard H. K. Vietor and Diego Comin.
South Africa(A): Stuck in the middle? 711-084.

Copyright © 2011–2013 President and Fellows of Harvard College; all rights reserved.

Exhibit 1a. Nominal GDP and Composition

	1994	2000	2005	2006	2007	2008	2009	2010	2011[a]
Nominal GDP (in billions of rand)	482.1	922.1	1,571.1	1,767.4	2,016.2	2,274.1	2,396.0	2,636.5	2,866.8
Growth in GDP deflator	9.59	8.81	5.45	6.53	8.06	8.90	7.16	7.10	4.80
Real GDP Growth	3.18	4.07	5.14	5.45	5.42	3.51	−1.70	2.74	3.64
Real GDP per capita (in thousands of 2005 rand)	26.4	28.9	33.1	34.6	36.2	37.2	36.4	37.3	38.8
Expenditure Approach									
Private consumption (% of GDP)	62.3	63.4	63.1	63.2	62.7	61.5	60.8	61.3	63.9
Government consumption (% of GDP)	20.0	18.1	19.5	19.7	18.9	18.9	21.1	21.4	22.1
Gross fixed investment (% of GDP)	15.2	14.9	16.8	18.3	20.2	23.1	22.2	19.7	19.3
Stockbuilding (% of GDP)	1.7	0.8	1.2	1.4	1.1	−0.5	−2.6	−0.2	0.3
Exports of G&S (% of GDP)	22.1	27.9	27.4	30.0	31.5	35.6	27.4	26.2	27.0
Imports of G&S (% of GDP)	19.9	24.9	27.9	32.5	34.2	38.6	28.3	29.0	33.1
Gross National Savings (% of GDP)	16.8	15.6	14.5	14.4	14.2	15.3	15.6	15.7	14.0
Value Added Approach									
Agriculture (% of GDP)	4.6	3.3	2.7	2.9	3.0	3.1	2.9	3.0	3.0
Industry (% of GDP)	35.0	31.8	31.2	31.2	31.2	32.3	31.1	31.1	31.8
Services (% of GDP)	60.4	65.0	66.2	60.0	65.7	64.6	66.0	66.0	65.2

Source: Compiled by case writer with Economist Intelligence Unit data, http://www.eiu.com; accessed March 12, 2011.
Note: [a]Denotes forecasts.

Exhibit 1b.   Production and Value of Production Indices of Mineral Extraction

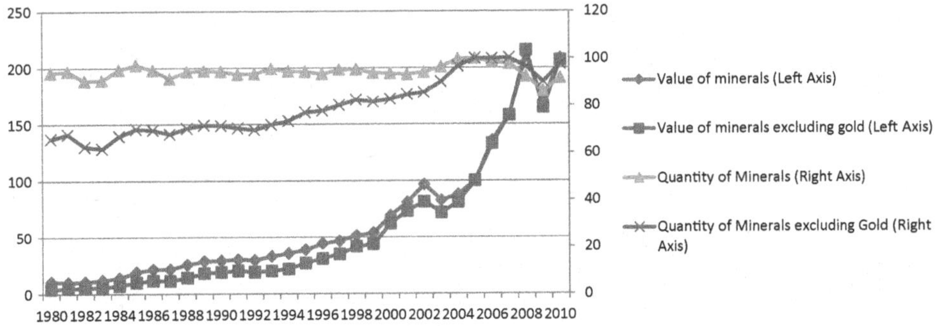

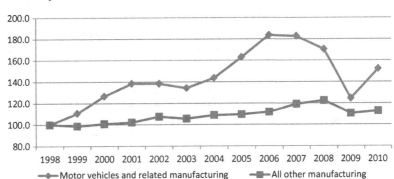

Source: Created by case writer with data from Statistics South Africa, accessed February 28, 2011.

Exhibit 1c.   Output Indices in Motor Vehicles and Other Manufacturing Sectors

Source: Created by case writer with data from Statistics South Africa, accessed February 28, 2011.

3 million to 10 million people, Gordhan nonetheless questioned how quickly the economy could grow over the next three years (4.3% was the projection for 2012). On the expenditure side, he wondered if increasing spending 8.7% annually made sense, in terms of a projected fiscal deficit of −5.3% of GDP, headline inflation of 4.9%, and a current account deficit projected at −4.2% of GDP.[3] And finally, he wondered if the microeconomic targets of his proposed spending — health, education, infrastructure, and social protection — were correctly balanced, affordable, and achievable?

With a GDP per capita of $7,000 ($10,500 adjusted for purchasing power parity), South Africa seemed "stuck in the middle" between low-wage competitors like China and India, and high-income exporters like Japan, Germany, and the U.S. To use an analogy from corporate strategy, this implied that South Africa, like a handful of other developing countries, needed a focused or differentiated strategy to develop successfully. Minister Gordhan agreed: "The next few years are the time to lift South Africa to a new growth trajectory." And the New Growth Path was the vehicle, which was considered "a unique mix between the first world and the third world."[4]

Exhibit 2a.   Non-Agricultural Formal Employment and Real GDP, 1967–2002

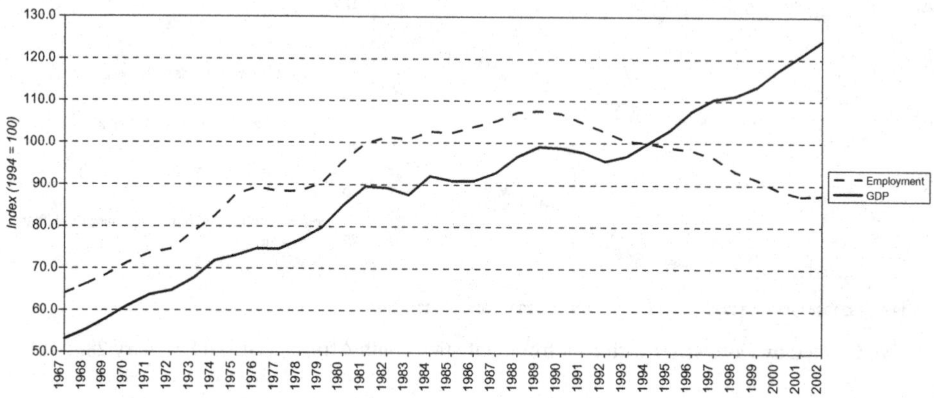

Source: Haroon Bhorat and Natasha Mayet, "Labour Demand Trends and the Determinants of Unemployment in South Africa," May 2010, p. 45.

Note: The employment indices published in the SARB Quarterly Bulletins are based on Statistics SA data from two sets of surveys: the Manpower Surveys and the Surveys of Employment and Earnings (from 1998 onward).

Exhibit 2b.   Composition of Employment

Sector	2001	2009[a]
Formal (%)	62.7	70.4
Informal (%)	16.4	15.5
Agriculture (%)	9.2	5.1
Private households (%)	10.5	9
Total	11.181 million	12.907 million

Source: Compiled by casewriter with data from 2001 Labor Force Surveys, 2009 Statistics South Africa.
Note: [a]2009 data is through third quarter.

Exhibit 2c.   Average Annual Growth Rate of Output, Productivity and Wages

	1996–2001	2001–2006	2006–2011
Real GDP growth (%)	2.80	3.84	3.17
Labor productivity growth (%)	5.8	3.4	1.6
Total factor productivity growth (%)		2.5	0.1
Average real wages (% change p.a.)	0.2	0.3	2.4
Average nominal wages (% change p.a.)	10.6	7.1	10.4
Average nominal wages in $ (% change p.a.)	−9.2	17.9	7.0
Unit labor costs (% change p.a.)	−15.0	14.5	5.4

Source: Compiled by case writer with data from EIU and case writers' calculations.
Note: Unit labor costs are nominal wages in $ divided by real labor productivity.

Exhibit 2d. Compensation to Employees (% GDP)

Source: Created by case writer with data from the Reserve Bank of South Africa.

Exhibit 2e. Cummulative Labor Productivity Growth 1990–2008

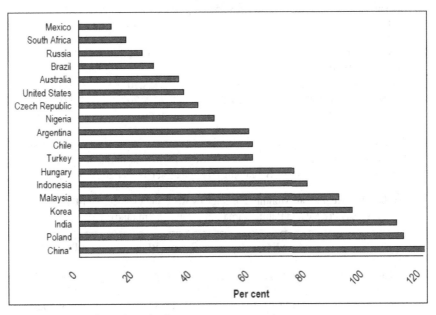

Source: International Labour Organisation.

Exhibit 2f.   Nominal Unit Labor Costs: Percentage Change over Previous Four Quarters

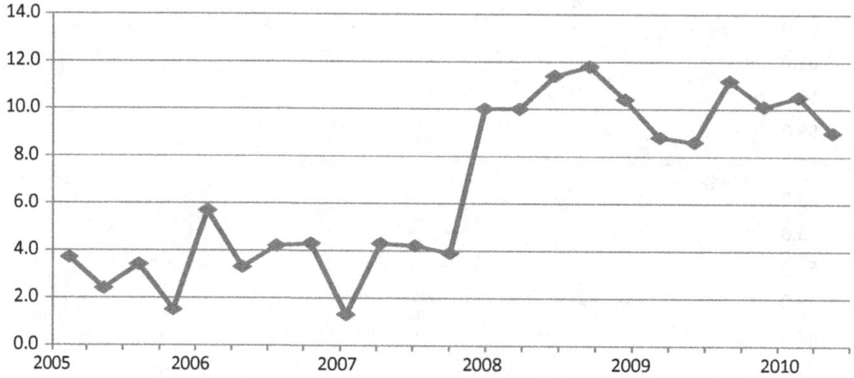

Source: Gill Marcus, governor of South African Reserve Bank, address to National Union of Metal Workers South Africa, Eskom National Shop Steward Council, February 2011.

Exhibit 2g.   Real Mean Monthly Earnings by Occupation: Non-Bargaining Council versus Private and Public Bargaining Councils (in rand)

	Non-BC	Private BC	Public BC
Managers	9578.95	3444.90	
Professionals	6553.86	3484.41	5382.01
Clerks	3273.02	3010.72	4103.71
Service Workers	1597.00	1904.62	3799.76
Skilled Agr Workers	2750.13		2120.43
Craft & Trade Workers	2219.72	2458.70	2412.40
Operators & Assemblers	2121.28	2218.76	3189.78
Elementary Workers	1149.60	1968.76	2091.25
Total	3271.79	2286.87	4257.43

Source: Haroon Bhorat *et al.*, "Analysing Wage Formation in the South African Labour Market: The Role of Bargaining Councils," September 2007, pp. 33, 35.

Exhibit 2h.   Real Mean Monthly Earnings by Race and Gender: Non-Bargaining Council versus Private and Public Bargaining Councils (in rand)

	Non BC	Private BC	Public BC
African	2158.82	1738.45	3829.55
Coloured	2794.53	2510.62	4017.41
Asian	3427.78	3382.69	4582.80
White	6961.31	4481.74	6220.84
Male	3398.64	2560.05	4296.07
Female	3038.92	1521.38	4220.95
Total	3271.79	2286.87	4257.43

Source: Haroon Bhorat *et al.*, "Analysing Wage Formation in the South African Labour Market: The Role of Bargaining Councils," September 2007, pp. 33, 35.

A Fractured Rainbow

South Africa, nearly as large as Western Europe minus Spain, was home to 49 million people. It was divided into two main regions: a relatively arid inland plateau, and coastal plains on three sides. Because of different climatic zones — winter rainfall in the southwest and summer rainfall in the east — early pastoral people of the west (KhoiSan) rarely interacted with iron-age cultivators (Bantu) who occupied the east.[5]

But European settlers, representing the Dutch East India Company, arrived in 1652, establishing a fort at Table Bay (Cape Town). Over the next century and a half, Dutch colonial settlers spread north, extending control over indigenous laborers, indenturing women, and enforcing travel passes for the "bastard hottentots." Their language evolved into Afrikaans. The British, meanwhile, had captured Cape Town from the Dutch and established a crown colony in 1806. By then, emigration to the north and west caused pressures between the Xhosa and competing tribes, resulting in inter-tribal wars in which Zulus, headed by Shaka, dominated.[6]

Britain curtailed the slave trade and in 1828, outlawed slave ownership. When the Cape Colony's governor followed suit (Ordinance 50), the policy was opposed by both British settlers and Afrikaners, who continued their discriminatory practices.[7] In 1865, census data reported that South Africa's population consisted of 180,000 Europeans (British and Afrikaners), 200,000 Hottentots and others collectively called "coloured," 100,000 blacks (Black Africans who dominated eastern populations), and a few thousand Asians — mostly of Indian extraction.

The face of South Africa changed forever when alluvial diamonds were discovered in 1867, at the confluence of the Vaal and Harts Rivers. For the next 20 years, diamond mining boomed until businessman Cecil Rhodes acquired control of the Kimberly mines, renamed DeBeers Consolidated Mines. About this same time, gold was discovered 30 miles from Pretoria, at what is today Johannesburg.[8] Together, these discoveries inspired a huge immigration into the country. Eventually the discovery of platinum, chrome, manganese, nickel, iron, and coal made South Africa the world's premier producer of rare minerals.

An influx of Europeans eventually led to the Boer War (1899–1902), in which the British engaged in a scorched-earth policy, leaving thousands of Afrikaners to die in concentration camps. The Peace of Vereeniging led to Britain's formal establishment of "a self-governing community, supported by well-treated and justly-governed black labor..."[9] But black Africans were disenfranchised, and "pass laws" restricting travel were tightened. On May 31, 1910, South Africa became a "self-governing dominion" of the British Empire.

Segregation and Apartheid

The era of formal segregation in South Africa — 1910–1948 — was a period dominated by racist assumptions in Africa, much of Asia, and the U.S. In South Africa, where whites dominated the economy, race determined one's class. White mineworkers, for example, earned 10 times as much as black mineworkers for the same job. By the early 1990s, the top 10% of the population earned 67 times that of the bottom 20%.[10]

With the influx of black Africans into cities during World War II, the worries of Afrikaners about race relations deepened. The word "apartheid" was coined to mean "apartness." When the National Party won the election in 1948, the prime minister appointed Hendrik Verwoerd to the senate, and then the minister of native affairs. Between 1948 and 1964, the latter half of which Verwoerd was prime minister, apartheid was implemented in its most brutal form.

Four ideas, according to historian Leonard Thompson, were at the heart of apartheid:

> First, the population of South Africa comprised four "racial groups" — white, Coloured, Indian and African — each with its own inherent culture. Second, Whites, as the civilized race, were entitled to have absolute control over the state. Third, white interests should prevail over black interests; the state was not obliged to provide equal facilities for the subordinate races. Fourth, the white racial group formed a single nation with Afrikaans and the English-speaking components, while Africans belonged to several [eventually 10, geographically] distinct nations.[11]

During the next three decades, the National Party, led by JBM Hertzog and Verwoerd, ruled a racist and increasingly ruthless state. These ideas were written into law: the Prohibition of Mixed Marriages Act, the Immorality Act, and the Population Registration Act. Pass laws were strengthened, and Africans were removed from farms to homelands and from urban neighborhoods to satellite townships. They were fenced, guarded, and impoverished. Their education was constrained. "If the native in South Africa today," testified Verwoerd in 1953, is being taught to expect that he will live his adult life under a policy of equal rights, he is making a big mistake."[12] "Whites Only" notices appeared everywhere — taxis, buses, elevators, hearses, restaurants, church halls, cinemas, schools and universities.

Black Resistance

Under the combined weight of poverty, forced resettlement and repression, the structure of the black community broke down. In townships, like Soweto, millions lived eight-to-twenty in shacks often thrown together with scrap lumber and corrugated metal and a single water tap would be shared by 25,000. Uneducated children stole to survive and eventually acquired guns.

Opposition to apartheid swelled. The African National Congress, formed in 1912, became the spear of resistance. Headed by lawyers, clergy and journalists, the ANC developed a platform against segregation — *Africans' Claims in South Africa.* Among the activists were Oliver Tambo, Walter Sisulu and Nelson Mandela (who later became president of the Republic of South Africa). In 1955, 3,000 delegates assembled to adopt the Freedom Charter:

> We the People of South Africa declare for our country and the world to know that South Africa belongs to all who live in it, black and white, and that no government can justly claim authority unless it is based on the will of all the people.[13]

As protests escalated into violence, the ANC leadership was arrested and imprisoned on Robben Island. The police bore down; in the township of Sharpeville, they killed 69 protesters, half of whom were women and children. In 1976, crackdowns led to the killing of 575 people in Soweto. Steve Biko, head of the South African Students Organization, was beaten to death by police in 1977.[14]

Finally, international pressure began to mount on the South African government. The UN Security Council imposed an arms embargo in 1977 and foreign investors began to pull out. In 1985, the U.S. Congress passed the Comprehensive Anti-Apartheid Act (over President Reagan's veto), imposing a wide-ranging boycott on commerce with South Africa. Finally, in 1989, F.W. de KIerk succeeded President Botha after the latter's stroke. In 1990, de Klerk lifted bans on the ANC, suspended capital punishment and freed political prisoners. And on February 9, after being incarcerated for 27 years on Robben Island, Nelson Mandela was released to a tumultuous public welcome.

The New South Africa

In the 1994 election, the African National Congress won 252 seats (the National Party got 82 and the Inkatha Freedom Party, dominated by Zulus, got 43). Nelson Mandela was elected president, with Thabo Mbeki as deputy president (de Klerk was also a deputy president, but he soon resigned). A new constitution, approved in December 1996, established a unitary state with a strong federal government — two houses of parliament governing nine provinces. The executive branch chose a cabinet of 27 ministers, and a Bill of Rights provided for 11 official languages and a commission on human rights.

South Africa's infrastructure, designed for two different races, was bifurcated. For the white population, there were modern highways, 21,000 kilometers of railways, five million telephone connections, modern radio and television, and Eskom — a state electric company that provided 40,000 megawatts of power at a mere 2.3 cents per kilowatt-hour. SASOL, the state petrochemical company, used liquefaction technology to convert coal to liquid fuel. Universities, a first-world healthcare system and a weapons sector were globally competitive.

At the same time, most black homes lacked electricity. Access to water was rare and indoor plumbing was almost non-existent. The black population seldom owned cars, had scarce access to telephones, and was totally lacking adequate housing. Most blacks had no schools; and for those who did have schools, the teachers lacked qualifications. Approximately five million people (over four years old) had no education whatsoever, and an estimated 37% of the population was illiterate (see **Exhibit 5a**). Thousands of new schools, millions of books and 100,000 trained teachers would be needed.

South Africa's income distribution was among the most skewed on earth — 0.64 on the GINI index (see **Exhibit 9d**). While the top 10% of the population enjoyed a per capita income of $12,810, the bottom 30% received an average of a mere $334.[15] This inequitable distribution, compounded by widespread poverty and a history of armed conflict, gave rise to endemic crime. The most serious problems were murder, rape, motor vehicle theft and robbery. More than two million serious crimes were reported in 1996 — about one for every 21 citizens (see **Exhibit 9a**). With law enforcement underfunded and understaffed, private security services proliferated. Affluent homes in the Johannesburg suburbs were walled and barb-wired, with electronic gates and guard dogs.[16]

A final, devastating social problem was HIV/AIDS (see **Exhibit 9b**). The massive movement of people throughout southern Africa had aggravated the country's exposure to AIDS. By 1995, an estimated 1.8 million people, 90% of whom were African, were infected. The highest infection rate was for females in their teens or early 20s. Figures showed a doubling rate of 15 months — by the spring of 1997, an estimated 2.5 million people were HIV positive and that number would more than double again by 2004. Poverty, congestion, cultural prejudices and lack of education all contributed to the epidemic.[17] An impossibly huge task lay ahead.

Private sector: South Africa's large, private enterprises were comparable to those in OECD economies, albeit relatively labor-intensive and higher-cost. The mining industry accounted for about 9% of South Africa's GDP but nearly 50% of its foreign exchange earnings. It employed 600,000 (see **Exhibit 1b**). Metals refining, manufacturing, information technology, weapons and financial services were well developed, employing several million more. Agriculture and forestry had also been successful — South Africa was one of only a few net agricultural exporters. And tourism held a huge potential (see **Exhibit 4c**).

Yet because of the years of international isolation, South Africa's business structure was highly concentrated.[18] Interlocking conglomerates were dominated by a few financial institutions — Old Mutual, Sanlam, SBIC, and ABSA — which each controlled more than R100 billion in assets. More than 70 other groups controlled between R4 and R50 billion each. Several large multinationals, such as Shell, Daimler-Benz and Volkswagen, were also active in South Africa.

"Unbundling" and "black empowerment" were structural phenomena that had proceeded hand-in-hand since 1994. "Unbundling" referred to the restructuring of business ownership by selling off diverse operating units of large conglomerates. To ameliorate racial oppression, "black empowerment" encouraged the rise of black managers to senior executive positions and, more specifically, the emergence of black-owned or black-controlled conglomerates. Through the use of pension funds from black unions, leveraged buyouts gave rise to 18 black-controlled firms listed on the Johannesburg Stock Exchange. A new black business leadership, headed by Cyril Ramaphosa, Saki Macozoma, Patrice Motsepe and Bridgette Radebe in mining; Andile Ngcaba in communications; Mzi Khumalo at JCI; Reuel Khoza (Eskom); and a dozen others, emerged — serving on dozens of boards, owning significant equity stakes in financial firms and maintaining close ties with the ANC and the government.[19]

Labor: South Africa had a decades-old tradition of labor organizations. In 1996, some 200 unions represented about 3.5 million workers. These were organized into several federations, the largest of which were COSATU (the Congress of South African Trade Unions), with 1.6 million members, and FEDUSA (the Federation of Unions of South Africa), with 600,000 (see **Exhibit 3c**). Sometimes unions could be a source of justice, but other times, they were a source of self-interest, commented one member of the ANC's National Executive Committee. Perhaps, when it came to recent increases in wages, excessive self-interest was being displayed.[20]

GEAR: Growth, Employment and Redistribution (GEAR) was a macroeconomic strategy overseen by Trevor Manuel, the new minister of finance, and adopted by the government in 1996. It followed several previous strategies, including the ANC's Reconstruction and Development Program (1994), which had not made any significant progress. GEAR was designed to deliver real GDP growth of 6% in four years, creating 400,000 jobs annually. This was more than double the existing job-growth trajectory and was necessary to cut structural unemployment that had surpassed 37% (see **Exhibits 3a** and **3b**).[21]

GEAR had seven parts: (1) an acceleration of fiscal reform with a deepening of the tax base and a reduction of the deficit to 3% of GDP; (2) a gradual relaxation of exchange controls and a reduction of inflation through high interest rates; (3) trade and industrial policy reforms, including a reduction in tariffs and tax incentives to stimulate investment; (4) public-sector asset restructuring, with public–private

Exhibit 3a.   Unemployment Rates Official versus Broad Definition

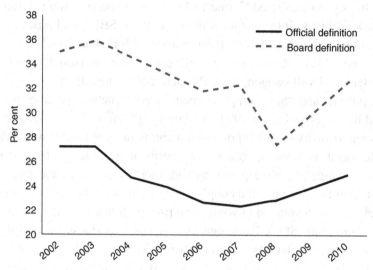

Source: Statistics South Africa.

Note: Broad definition includes not-employed persons of working age who want a job but may not be actively looking for one.

Exhibit 3b.   Unemployment Rates (Narrow Definition), by Race, 1995–2009

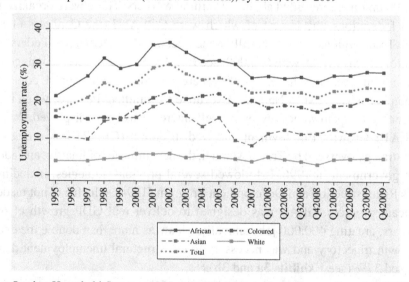

Source: October Household Surveys, 1995 and 1997; Labour Force Survey, Setember 2000–2007; Quarterly Labour Force Survey, Quarter 1–4, 2008, and Quarter 1–3, 2009 (Statistics South Africa, in Haroon Bhorat and Natasha Mayet, "Labour Demand Trends and the Determinants of Unemployment in South Africa," May 2010, 16).

Exhibit 3c.   South African Union Density, 2000–2007

	Public Sector	**Private Sector**	**Total**
1995	0.4	0.3	0.3
	(927)	(1,815)	(2,742)
2000	0.5	0.2	0.2
	(1,093)	(1,708)	(2,800)
2001	0.6	0.2	0.3
	(1,095)	(1,803)	(2,898)
2002	0.5	0.2	0.3
	(1,103)	(1,692)	(2,795)
2003	0.5	0.2	0.3
	(1,117)	(1,744)	(2,871)
2004	0.5	0.2	0.2
	(1,079)	(1,654)	(2,735)
2005	0.5	0.2	0.3
	(1,149)	(1,965)	(3,115)
2006	0.5	0.2	0.2
	(1,116)	(1,853)	(2,969)
2007	0.5	0.2	0.3
	(1,333)	(2,102)	(3,435)

Source: October Household Survey, 1995, and Labour Force Survey, September 2000–2007, in Haroon Bhorat and Natasha Mayet, "Labour Demand Trends and the Determinants of Unemployment in South Africa," May 2010, 53.

Notes: 1. Public Sector Union Membership based on employed union members within Community, Social and Personal Services sector.
2. Number of Union members in '000, in parentheses.

partnerships in transportation and telecommunications; (5) an expansion of public infrastructure investment; (6) a structured flexibility within the collective bargaining system to support a two-tiered wage system; (7) and a social agreement to facilitate wage and price moderation, accelerate investment, and enhance public-service delivery.[22]

Under Presidents Nelson Mandela and then Thabo Mbeki after 2000, the South African economy performed reasonably well. That is, the real GDP grew at 3%–5% annually, with inflation easing from 9% to 4% by 2005. Budget deficits shrunk from 4.3% to 0.6% of GDP, while public debt eased to 36%. Interest rates dropped (from 17% to 10%; see **Exhibit 7a**), and investment recovered to 17% of GDP. Trade in goods and services was nearly balanced, while the exchange rate actually strengthened after 2002, back to 6.4 rand/1 dollar in 2005 (see **Exhibit 4b**). Only the current account suffered, dropping from a surplus of R7 billion in 2002 to a deficit of R64 billion by 2005 (see **Exhibit 4a**).

Exhibit 4a.   Balance of Payments 2006–2010 ($US billion)

	2006	2007	2008	2009	2010[a]
Current-account balance	−13.7	−20.0	−20.1	−11.3	−14.2
Trade balance	−4.2	−5.2	−4.4	0.5	1.0
Goods: exports fob	65.8	76.4	86.1	66.5	85.3
Goods: imports fob	−70.0	−81.6	−90.6	−66.0	−84.3
Services: balance	−2.0	−2.7	−4.2	−2.8	−4.3
Services: credit	12.2	13.8	12.8	12.0	14.3
Services: debit	−14.2	−16.5	−17.0	−14.8	−18.5
Income: balance	−5.2	−9.8	−9.1	−6.4	−7.5
Income: credit	6.1	6.9	5.9	4.0	7.4
Income: debit	−11.2	−16.7	−15.1	−10.4	−15.0
Current transfers: balance	−2.4	−2.4	−2.3	−2.7	−3.4
Current transfers: credit	0.9	1.1	1.4	1.2	1.6
Current transfers: debit	−3.3	−3.5	−3.7	−3.9	−5.0
Capital Account Balance	0.0	0.0	0.0	0.0	0.0
Financial Account Balance	15.3	20.7	11.8	16.3	18.9
Net direct investment flows	−6.1	2.8	11.8	4.0	1.6
Inward direct investment	−0.2	5.7	9.6	5.4	2.0
Outward direct investment	−5.9	−3.0	2.1	−1.3	−0.4
Net portfolio investment flows	18.1	5.6	−13.6	11.9	16.3
Inward portfolio investment	21.9	13.7	−7.6	13.4	19.1
Outward portfolio investment	−2.2	−3.4	−6.7	−1.7	−2.7
Other capital flows (net)	1.8	7.7	14.3	0.6	1.0
Errors and omission	2.1	5.0	10.5	−0.8	0.0
Change in international reserves	−3.7	−5.7	−2.2	−4.2	na
International reserves	25.6	31.3	33.5	37.7	na
Current Account (% GDP)	−5.3	−7	−7.1	−4.1	−3.4

Source: Compiled by casewriter with data from the Federal Reserve Bank of South Africa and the IMF.

Note: [a]Includes data for the first three quarters of 2010, seasonally adjusted and annualized.

Yet it was unemployment that remained the biggest problem. While the unemployment rate did fall to a low of 22% in 2007, the broad definition (which included informal workers) remained between 28% and 34% (see **Exhibit 3b**).[23] The problem was partly historic. Under apartheid, pass laws had kept people pinned down in rural areas, without much education. Thus, the unemployed usually resided far from potential jobs, and search costs were very high.[24] This in part accounted for the unusually low participation rate of 46%.

Exhibit 4b. Exports and Imports

Exports as a % of total exports of goods[a]		Imports as a % of total imports of goods[b]	
Germany	6.6	Germany	19.6
Japan	6.1	Japan	5.5
UK	7.9	UK	8.4
US	8.9	US	12.8
Principal exports as a % of total exports of goods		**Principal imports as a % of total imports of goods**[b]	
Platinum	13.0	Petrochemicals	13.6
Gold	12.0	Equipment components for cars	5.0
Coal	7.0	Motor cars & other components	3.3
Cars & other components	3.0	Petroleum oils & other	3.7

Source: Compiled by casewriter with data from the Federal Reserve Bank of South Africa and the IMF.

Note: [a]On a free-on-board (FOB) basis.
[b]On a cost, insurance, and freight (CIF) basis.

Exhibit 4c. International Tourism to South Africa

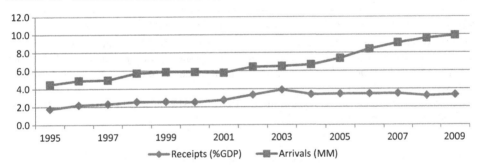

Source: Compiled by casewriter with data from World Development Indicators, accessed March 12, 2011.

Mbeki

After the imprisonment of Nelson Mandela in 1964, the young activist Thabo Mbeki left South Africa to live in exile in England. While there, he participated in the first-year economics degree program at the University of London from 1961–1962 and earned a Master of Economics degree from the University of Sussex in 1966. After receiving military training in the Soviet Union, he worked for the ANC in London, Botswana, Zambia and Nigeria, eventually joining the National Executive Committee. After returning to South Africa, Mbeki was elected deputy president in 1994. He acceded to the presidency in 1999 and was re-elected in 2004. But shortly

Exhibit 5a.   Education in South Africa Compared with the Region

	South Africa	Middle Income	Sub-Saharan Africa	SA Ranking
Literacy rate, adult total (% of people ages 15 and above) 2008	89.0	82.7	62.6	62/114
Primary completion rate, total (% of relevant age group) 2007	85.8	93.1	61.3	99/139
Secondary School Enrollment (% net)	71.9	na	na	67/114
Public spending on education, total (% of GDP)	5.3	na	na	26/92

Source: Compiled by casewriter with data from The World Bank, 2006.

Exhibit 5b.   R&D Expenditures and High-Tech Exports

	South Africa	Middle Income	Sub-Saharan Africa	SA Ranking
R&D expenditure[a] (% of GDP)	1.0	1.0	na	32/74
High-tech exports[b] (% of manufactured exports)	5.2	16.5	3.4	66/119

Source: Compiled by casewriter with data from The World Bank, 2006.

Notes: [a]Expenditures for R&D are current and capital expenditures (both public and private) on creative work undertaken systematically to increase knowledge, including knowledge of humanity, culture, and society, and the use of knowledge for new applications. R&D covers basic research, applied research, and experimental development.

[b]High-technology exports are products with high R&D intensity, such as in aerospace, computers, pharmaceuticals, scientific instruments, and electrical machinery.

Exhibit 6.   Government Budget

	2006	2007	2008	2009	2010
Budget revenue (% of GDP)	25.55	28.11	27.62	26.50	29.00
Budget expenditure (% of GDP)	25.02	26.93	28.22	32.30	34.30
Primary balance (% of GDP)	2.44	2.98	1.13	−4.10	−3.50
Budget balance (% of GDP)	0.53	1.18	−0.61	−5.80	−5.30
Public debt (% of GDP)	31.37	26.72	24.97	29.80	32.60

Source: Compiled by casewriter with data from Economist Intelligence Unit, accessed March 15, 2011.

before the end of his term in 2008, he was recalled by the ANC's National Executive Committee and replaced by Kgalema Motlanthe, followed by Jacob Zuma, whom Mbeki had tried assiduously to have convicted on corruption (for an arms deal with the United Kingdom).

Source: ©2005–2011 Zapiro (all rights reserved). Printed with permission from www.zapiro.com. For more Zapiro cartoons, visit www.zapiro.com.

Exhibit 7a. Interest Rates

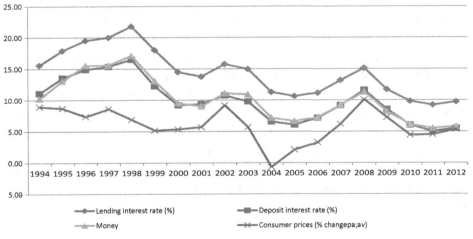

Source: Created by casewriter with data from International Monetary Fund and the World Economic Outlook Database, accessed April 2010.

Note: 2011 and 2012 data are forecasts.

Exhibit 7b.   Exchange Rate

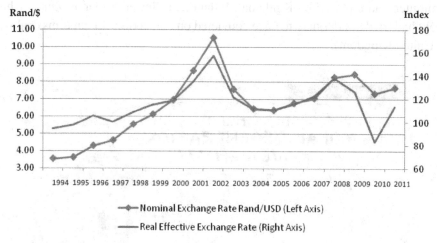

Source: Created by case writer from Economist Intelligence Unit data, World Development Indicators, accessed March 1, 2011.

Note: An increase in the exchange rate implies a depreciation of the rand. A real effective exchange rate is based on CPI deflators.

Despite relatively healthy macroeconomic performance, Thabo Mbeki's presidency had not been without controversy. Microeconomic performance lagged, the president's treatment of AIDS was a disaster, his "quiet diplomacy" with regard to the "Global Political Agreement" (Robert Mugabe of Zimbabwe) failed and his Black Economic Empowerment (BEE) program yielded mixed results.

Failure to invest adequately in public infrastructure, failure to privatize the floundering public-sector enterprises and failure to improve the nation's educational outcomes were stand-outs among various microeconomic problems during his presidency. As part of the government's efforts to reduce deficits, it had invested far too little in public infrastructure — roads, rails, ports and power system.

For example, Eskom, as previously mentioned, was a huge coal-fired state utility, generating surplus electricity (40%) at a very low cost. Indeed, when its spare capacity could not be sold, it extended transmission lines and power sales north to Zimbabwe, Zambia and beyond. Some of its smaller plants were moth-balled. Yet for more than 10 years, as the South African economy grew, Eskom's spare capacity diminished, investments in modern distribution infrastructure were ignored, and no new power plants were built. By 2005, the municipality of Johannesburg suffered frequent power failures, which only worsened during the next few years. In January 2008, the crisis resulted in nationwide blackouts that culminated in a complete shut-down of the mines.[25]

Exhibit 8. Ease of Doing Business Indicators: South Africa, 2010

	Middle Income Countries	Sub-Saharan Africa (all income levels)	South Africa	SA Ranking
Ease of Doing Business				32/183
Total corporate tax rate (% of profit)	42.6	70.6	30.0	38/182
Time required to start a business (days)	40.2	47.3	22.0	66/144
Logistics Performance Index[a]	2.7	2.4	3.5	27/154
Difficulty of hiring	31.8	na	44.0	na
Rigidity of hours	40.1	na	40.0	na
Difficulty of firing	33.2	na	40.0	na
Non-wage labor costs	16.7	na	2.4	na
Firing costs			24.0	na
Rigidity of employment index (0 = less rigid to 100 = more rigid)[b]	26.9	35.4	35.0	120/183

Source: Compiled by case writer with data from The World Bank.

[a]Logistics performance index: Overall (1 = low to 5 = high)

[b]The rigidity of employment index measures the regulation of employment, specifically the hiring and firing of workers and the rigidity of working hours. This index is the average of three sub-indexes: a difficulty of hiring index, a rigidity of hours index, and a difficulty of firing index. The index ranges from 0 to 100, with higher values indicating more rigid regulations.

Note: A higher ranking corresponds to a better performance. The Logistics Performance Index overall score reflects perceptions of a country's logistics based on efficiency of customs clearance process, quality of trade- and transport-related infrastructure, ease of arranging competitively priced shipments, quality of logistics services, ability to track and trace consignments, and frequency with which shipments reach the consignee within the scheduled time. The index ranges from 1 to 5, with a higher score representing better performance. Data are from Logistics Performance Index surveys conducted by the World Bank in partnership with academic and international institutions and private companies and individuals engaged in international logistics. The 2009 surveys covered more than 5,000 country assessments by nearly 1,000 international freight forwarders. Respondents evaluated eight markets on six core dimensions on a scale of 1 (worst) to 5 (best). The markets are chosen based on the most important export and import markets of the respondent's country, random selection, and, for landlocked countries, neighboring countries that connect them with international markets. Scores for the six areas were averaged across all respondents and aggregated to a single score using principal components analysis. Details of the survey methodology and index construction methodology are in J-F Arvis *et al.*, *Connecting to Compete 2010: Trade Logistics in the Global Economy* (2010).

Transnet, the state transportation holding company, had similar problems. With 100,000 employees, Transnet ran the ports, the rails and South African Airways. Saki Macozoma, an anti-apartheid activist and subsequent recipient of BEE equity in Standard Bank, worked to correct the problems at Transnet. He restructured the pensions and the balance sheet and completed the incorporation of South African Airways. In 2003, Maria Ramos — the hard-charging director general of the National

Exhibit 9a.   Homicide Rates per 100,000 People

	South Africa	Middle Income Countries	Sub-Saharan Countries	SA Ranking
Source:				
World Health Organization	39.5	6.7	17.2	192/196
National Sources	69	9.2	na	130/130

Source: Compiled by case writer with data from World Development Indicators.

Exhibit 9b.   Prevalence of HIV/AIDS in the Population

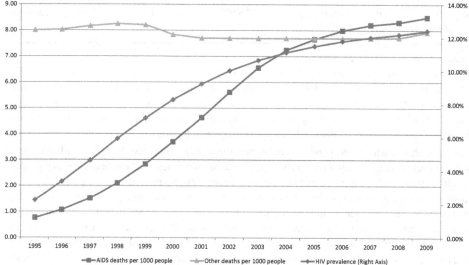

Source: Created by case writer using data from World Development Indicators, accessed March 10, 2011.

Treasury — took over at Transnet. The organization was a huge, mismanaged bureaucracy.[26] Ramos continued to deal with issues of fraud and corruption while working toward organizational restructuring, new investment and transformation of the BEE program.

While still deputy president, Thabo Mbeki had begun denying that AIDS was caused by HIV (human immunodeficiency virus). Rather, Mbeki and his minister of health, Manto Tshabalala-Msimang, attributed AIDS to poverty. Initially, they promoted Virodene, a quack 'cure' for AIDS, consisting of a toxic industrial solvent. When AZT became available, Mbeki rejected it as toxic. He apparently felt that AIDS was a form of Western racism — an alleged "African disease." At the AIDS

Exhibit 9c. Evolution of Poverty

	1995	2005
	R322 a month poverty line	
African	63.04%	56.34%
Colored	39.00%	34.19%
Asian	4.71%	8.43%
White	0.53%	0.38%
Total	**52.54%**	**47.99%**
	R174 a month poverty line	
African	38.18%	27.15%
Colored	14.62%	12.30%
Asian	0.82%	1.60%
White	0.23%	0.01%
Total	**30.92%**	**22.68%**

Source: Compiled by casewriter with data from Haroon Bhorat and Carlene van der Westhuizen, "Economic Growth, Poverty and Inequality in South Africa: The First Decade of Democracy."

Notes: Poverty lines are in 2000 prices. All changes between 1995 and 2005 are statistically significant at the 95% level.

Exhibit 9d. Evolution of Gini Coefficient

	1995	2005
African	0.56	0.61
Colored	0.49	0.59
Asian	0.46	0.56
White	0.44	.0.51
Total	**0.64**	**0.72**

Source: Compiled by casewriter with data from H. Bhorat and T. Hacobs, "Income and Non-Income Inequality in Post-Apartheid South Africa: What Are the Drivers and Possible Policy Interventions," DPRU Working Paper 09/138.

2000 Conference in Durban, Mbeki again claimed that AIDS was just a disease of poverty, so poverty was the real problem. For three more years, Mbeki and much of the ANC persisted in this view, preventing the distribution of antiretroviral drugs that could have relieved the country's 6.5 million cases of AIDS by 2004 (see **Exhibit 9a**).[27]

To South Africa's north, Zimbabwe was falling apart. Under the dictatorial and inept hands of Robert Mugabe, this once agriculturally rich country was unraveling. Corruption, property seizures, rigged elections and violent attacks

Table 1. Codes for Broad-Based Black Economic Empowerment (2007)

Element	Weighting	Compliance Targets
Ownership	20 points	25%+1
Management Control	10 points	(40–50%)
Employment Equity	15 points	(43–80%)
Skills Development	15 points	3% of payroll
Preferential Procurement	20 points	70%
Enterprise Development	15 points	3% (NPAT)
Socio-Economic Development	5 points	1% (NPAT)

Source: South Africa Department of Trade and Industry, "The BEE Codes of Good Practice," http://www.dti.gov.za/bee/beecodes.htm, accessed August 23, 2007.

on political opponents had brought Zimbabwe's economy to a halt. Inflation ran rampant and the currency collapsed. Seeing Mugabe as a revolutionary brother, Mbeki refused to lean on him, instead opting for "quiet diplomacy." He repeatedly claimed that Zimbabwe's elections were free and fair and that Mugabe supported human rights.

Perhaps Mbeki's preeminent accomplishment was black economic empowerment. In January 2004, the Broad-Based Black Economic Empowerment Act of 2003 took effect, after Mbeki had tired of affirmative action's slow pace. The Act required each industry sector to adopt a charter for broad-based empowerment of "formally disadvantaged people" (Blacks, Colored, Asians and Women). The Black Economic Empowerment Advisory Council was created to approve codes of conduct for firms and government entities (and to force industries without a plan to adopt one).[28]

Eventually, in 2007, this law was codified. The generic requirements entailed integration across seven areas. Points were assigned to specific targets, and all enterprises were expected to progress. (Small and medium enterprises (SMEs) had a slightly different set of codes.)

Volkswagen provided an example of BEE implementation. By 2010, it had earned 7.01 points in the area of management control, with four members of top management coming from formerly disadvantaged groups. Volkswagen did much better with skills development, since it operated a training school for automotive workers.[29] At Anglo American plc, even more progress had been made. Some 26% of ownership and 46% of management was in the hands of disadvantaged South Africans.[30] Both firms had made substantial progress in the areas of preferential procurement and enterprise development.

There was, however, a downside to BEE. In his book on South Africa, R.W. Johnson describes at depressing length the hundreds of corrupt BEE deals that, over the decade of the 2000s, created a new black elite. Prominent ANC members, ex-cabinet ministers, friends of Mbeki and friends of the ANC extracted hundreds of billions of rand from the equity of South Africa's private sector, producing a few billionaires and several hundred millionaires. Cheryl Carolus, the former secretary general of the ANC, was typical. Her consortia acquired a R3.8 billion piece of DeBeer's equity. When criticized in the press, she merely shrugged: "I can't be held responsible for all the problems of the world."[31]

South Africa's Labor Market

Strong unions were sometimes been blamed for South Africa's high unemployment and its lack of international competitiveness. According to one expert:

> Wage formation in the South African labor market is effectively managed, governed and operationalized through two key avenues. These are firstly through institutionalized bargaining between employer and employee representatives and secondly through government-mandated wage minima set for very specific sectors under particular conditions. In the former case, this bargaining takes place through either a formal bargaining council (usually sectorally representative) or more informal bargaining fora. The state only involves itself in sectors which tend to be unorganized . . . and those which may be deemed to contain a disproportionate share of low paid, vulnerable workers. In both environments, the relevant legislation governing these decisions includes the Labor Relations Act of 1995 and the Basic Conditions of Employment Act of 1997.[32]

Before 1995, unions bargained within the existing framework of industrial councils. Very little bargaining took place at the plant or firm level, outside the system of industrial (renamed "bargaining") councils. These were voluntary organizations made up of representatives of unions and employer associations. While a union's power might be diluted by removing its bargaining activities from the shop floor, by joining with other unions in a larger bargaining council, it expanded its power over employers. The issues on which the councils negotiated "generally included wages, social welfare benefit funds and conditions of employment such as working hours."[33]

Bargaining councils remained the focus of the 1995 Labor Relations Act. While participation was voluntary, the Act provided inducements for unions and employers to participate. The most important was the ability to have a council's agreement extended to all employers and employees in that sector. Section 32 of the Act provided that the bargaining council could ask the minister of labor to extend a collective agreement to non-parties who fall within the council's jurisdiction. And

Part D explicitly provided for the establishment of bargaining councils in the public service.[34] While the number of councils declined from 104 in 1983 to 48 in 2004, the number of employees covered by them doubled, from 1.2 to 2.7 million (see **Exhibits 2g** and **2h**).[35]

The Basic Conditions of Employment Act of 1997 "regulate[d] working time and hours of work (including overtime), different categories of leave, particulars of employment and remuneration, termination of employment, prohibition of employment of children and forced labor."[36]

The real issue the Acts tried to address, explained one black African leader, "was the existence of poverty and the history of exploitation. Understanding the relationship between productivity and costs is not on the minds of labor or politicians…the link between wages and productivity is lost in the thicket of history."[37]

Financial Crisis, Jacob Zuma, and the World Cup

No sooner had Jacob Zuma acceded to the presidency of South Africa, replacing Thabo Mbeki in a bitter, intra-ANC rivalry, than the global financial crisis struck hard at South Africa's exports. After slowing in 2008, real export growth fell 19% in 2009; consumption and investment followed suit. By the time of Zuma's election in April, manufacturing had fallen 15% and mining 13%. Employment dropped sharply, eventually by one million workers (see **Exhibits 3a and 3b**).

The new Zuma government maintained spending, despite a sharp drop in revenues, driving the fiscal balance down from a surplus of 1.2% to a deficit of 5.3% of GDP by 2010 (see **Exhibit 6a**). Pravin Gordhan, the new finance minister, used spending on infrastructure (preparing for the World Cup in 2010) and social welfare as an effective stimulus package. The central bank, meanwhile, dropped interest rate sharply, from 12% to 7% by the end of 2009 (see **Exhibit 7a**).

After three quarters of negative growth, the South African economy snapped back and began growing again by 2.7% in 2010. Roads, rails, hotels, and football stadiums were refurbished, or built, and the World Cup proved to be a huge success in the winter of 2010 — with tourism rising 14.1% for the year. The real effective exchange rate of the rand increased 8.9% between December 2009 and September 2010. Only job creation lagged, with unemployment returning (in the formal sector) to 25% (see **Exhibit 3a**).

Organized labor did not help the country's financial crisis. The year 2010 proved to be a year of extraordinary strike action, approaching 15 million working days — five times the normal level. In the first half of 2010, manufacturing and mine strikes had resulted in one-year or two-year settlements for 10% annual wage increases.[38] Then, just after the World Cup, nurses, teachers and other civil-servants struck and refused, along with COSATU, to accept the government's offer of a 7.5%

increase in wages (plus R800 in a monthly housing allowance). These unions cited recent wage settlements for rail and port operators (11% at Transnet) and electric power (9% at Eskom). But the 7.5% would add R6.5 billion to the R23.5 billion already budgeted for increases in the public-sector wage bill.[39] Despite the government's efforts to be firm, President Zuma's dependence on COSATU had weakened his resolve.

The New Growth Path

On November 23, 2010, Minister Ebrahim Patel released the framework for the New Economic Growth Path:

> This document reflects Government's commitment to prioritizing employment creation in all economic policies. It lays out strategies to enable South Africa to grow in a more equitable and inclusive manner in the future, fulfilling the promise of our democracy. The centerpiece of the new growth path is a massive investment in infrastructure and people through skills development, together with smart government and better coordination with the private sector and organized labor so that we can achieve our national goals.[40]

The report first laid out weaknesses in the South African economy. In addition to unemployment and inequality, it cited high carbon emissions, commodity-based revenue dependence, a persistent balance-of-trade deficit funded with short-term capital inflows, and economic concentration. The plan's goals were (1) to create 5 million jobs, (2) to grow the economy, (3) to lower income inequality, and (4) improve the environment. In the short run, the plan would accelerate employment through direct employment schemes and targeted subsidies. Over the medium term, it would support labor-absorbing activities (in agriculture, light manufacturing, and services). And in the longer term, the plan would increasingly support knowledge- and capital-intensive sectors (see **Appendix A**).[41]

The job drivers identified by the plan were as follows: (1) public investment in infrastructure to create employment directly; (2) targeting more labor-absorbing activities — the agricultural and mining value chains, manufacturing and services; (3) taking advantage of new opportunities in the knowledge and green economies; (4) leveraging social capital in the social economy; and (5) fostering rural development.[42]

The plan went on to identify specific job targets, sector by sector, by 2020. Thus, for example, infrastructure would create 250,000 jobs, agriculture and agro-processing 500,000, the green economy 660,000, and so forth.

The New Growth Path laid out a few macroeconomic provisions, including a looser monetary policy and, gradually, a more restrictive fiscal policy. The monetary policy stance would "continue to target low and stable inflation but will do more to support a more competitive exchange rate and reduced investment costs through lower real interest rates."[43] Gill Marcus, governor of the Reserve Bank, was OK with the plan's implication. She stated:

> ...the implementation of micro-economic policies as outlined in the New Growth Path, as well as the cohesion and sequencing of policy, was critical. Should the policies as set out be implemented, then there could be easier monetary policy and lower interest rates. [The inflation target, which is set by government, is a band of between 3% and 6%.] The inflation outlook has been revised, rising to the upper limit of the band in the forecast period to end 2012 — but this could be affected by the oil price rises which pose a real risk to inflation.[44]

For the microeconomy, the plan offered 10 programs:

1. Active industrial policy, including targeted education and training and greater support for R&D.
2. Rural development.
3. A competition policy, with investigations in areas of strategic importance and careful evaluation of mergers.
4. Improvements in education and skills training.
5. Promotion of small and medium enterprise, and the reduction of red tape.
6. Broad-based Black Economic Empowerment — a "much stronger focus on the broad-based elements of the BEE regulations."
7. Labor policies "to find ways to raise multi-factor productivity . . . ." Government will pursue "a national Productivity Accord supplemented by sector and workplace productivity agreements."
8. A technology policy, including enhanced R&D.
9. Developmental trade policies, including targeted export promotion and maximizing relations with China, India, and Brazil.
10. Policies for African development, to support regional growth and infrastructural development.[45]

Finally, the New Growth Path reminded citizens that not all of these steps could be secured by government action. Social partners — business and labor — also needed to commit to a broad development pact on wages, prices, and executive bonuses. In particular, the plan called for "moderate wage settlements for workers earning between R3,000 and R20,000 per month, possibly to inflation plus a modest real increase, with inflation-level increases for those earning over R20,000 a month . . . ."[46]

Interestingly, the New Growth Path, generally dismissed by business as an impossible dream, was supported by the ANC and the SACP (South African Communist Party), but not supported by COSATU. COSATU promptly prepared a 131-page analysis, generally complaining that it was another neo-liberal program, like ASGISA and GEAR earlier, that did not fundamentally correct the apartheid wage gap nor restructure class-power relationships between owners and management.[47] This seemed to be what was meant by Lesetja Kganyago, director general of the National Treasury, who blamed concentrated business and organized labor, in part: "Insiders (people working) too often raised the bar against outsiders — the unemployed."[48] Gill Marcus, governor of the Reserve Bank, seemed to appreciate the plan: "It really matters because something is on the table that will help create a cohesive policy framework that we can all work towards."[49]

How Far to Go?

Finance Minister Pravin Gordhan thought hard about his budget draft — how much to spend, and on what? How much to tax, and from where? In his State of the Nation address two weeks earlier, the President had made his vision for the future abundantly clear: "We want to have a country where millions more South Africans have decent employment opportunities, which has a modern infrastructure and vibrant economy and where the quality of life is high."[50] And the left, generally, wanted the government to spend, to reduce unemployment. Perhaps, admitted one ANC leader, the left had too much faith in Keynes.[51] Gordhan's budget needed to fund the priority programs of the New Growth Path. The only question was, by how much?

Gordhan knew that "change processes are decades-long processes." And he knew that "government could not do it on its own."[52] In fact, he thought about quoting a budget tip he received from one Mandisa Motha-Ngumla:

> Government must teach its people to fish; not be suppliers of fish. The latter is not sustainable; the government pond will never be able to supply more fish in 20 years than it is doing now to the ever growing masses of people of this country. Let's work to reduce dependency and give back dignity that was eroded by our past.[53]

As Gordhan considered these words, he pondered how best to "get unstuck."

Appendix A. 2010/11–2012/13 Industrial Policy Action Plan, February 2010

Sector	Share of Manufacturing Employment	Share of Manufacturing Value Added	Constraints	Actions Planned
Metal fabrication, capital equipment and transport equipment	24%	4.3%	• Lack of long-term procurement planning • Government and state enterprises demand unrealistically short delivery times • Lumpy, ad hoc procurement • Lack of competitive financing • Inadequate capital investment • Out-of-date production capabilities • Increasing global cost competition	• Identification of fleet programs and products to make investments in associated supply chains viable, promoting local manufacturing • Competitive financing program for suppliers into public capex programs • Benchmarking and matchmaking program • National tooling initiative • National foundry technology network
"Green" and energy-saving industries	700 Workers	R 220 MM per year	• High initial cost of solar water heating • Insufficient installers to ramp up to targets set by Department of Energy • Poor quality products • Testing bottlenecks	• Rollout of national solar water heating program and manufacturing and installation capacity • Demonstrate viability of concentrated solar thermal as a major renewable energy generation source • Development of an industrial energy efficiency program • Strengthen water efficiency standards • Development of sector strategies for other green industries

(Continued)

(*Continued*)

Sector	Share of Manufacturing Employment	Share of Manufacturing Value Added	Constraints	Actions Planned
Agro-processing	15.7%	2.3%	• Trade policies such as subsidies, tariffs and sanitary and phyto-sanitary standards • Slow growth in developed countries • Underinvestment in new plant and machinery • Regulatory barriers	• Establishment of a National Food Control Agency • Development of the aquaculture sector to supplement dwindling wild fish stock • Development of marine aquaculture zones • Establish aquaculture hatcheries • Development of the organic food sector • Development of high-value agriculture niche markets • Development of a small-scale milling industry • Competitiveness enhancement in the fruit and vegetable canning industry
Automotives, components and medium and heavy commercial vehicles	10%	1.6%	• Economies of scale are not internationally optimal • Relatively small number of automotive components dominating exports • Local content has stagnated • Gaps in manufacturing competitiveness levels of automotive component suppliers	• Automotive Production and Development Program • Identification of opportunities to broaden and deepen automotive component manufacturing • Competitiveness improvement of automotive component manufacturers • Enterprise reference architecture portal for SME suppliers

(*Continued*)

(Continued)

Sector	Share of Manufacturing Employment	Share of Manufacturing Value Added	Constraints	Actions Planned
				• Mentorship of SME component manufacturers • Medium and heavy commercial vehicle development action plan • Commercialization of South Africa's electric car
Downstream minerals beneficiation		<10% of gross revenue of all minerals in South Africa	• Monopolistic pricing of raw materials • Producers "locked in" to long-term supply targets of basic commodities • Security and cost of energy supply • Limited R&D skills • Trade barriers • Lack of infrastructure linking locations of mining operations and manufacturing centers	• Setting minimum beneficiation levels for key commodity chains • Gold loan scheme to promote jewelry production
Plastics, pharmaceuticals and chemicals	2.8% + 0.7% + 6.9% = 10.4%	0.6% + 3.2% = 3.8%	• Plastics: Import parity pricing of polymers and other key inputs • Pharmaceuticals: Downward pressure on prices, lack of key skills in drugs and pharmaceuticals, Small size of South African market	• Polypropylene beneficiation • Domestic production of ARV APIs • Domestic production of vaccines • Domestic production of biological medicines • Investigation of opportunities for downstream beneficiation of fluorspar

(Continued)

(Continued)

Sector	Share of Manufacturing Employment	Share of Manufacturing Value Added	Constraints	Actions Planned
			• Chemicals: land availability for new investments, time delays in Environmental Impact Assessment approvals, lengthy time to resolve land claims	• Investigate costs / benefits of proposed new liquid fuels projects
Clothing, textiles, footwear and leather	9.7%	0.8%	• Current strength and volatility • Ongoing surge of global imports • Illegal imports, inadequate policing of 'country of origin' labeling legislation • Lack of skilled personnel • Outdated capital equipment and technology • Historical deficit in innovation, R&D	• Clothing and textiles production incentive and competitiveness program • Program to clamp down on illegal imports • Program to upgrade skills in the sector • Audit of textiles capabilities • Innovation and technology • Promotion of domestic manufacturing and sustainable black ownership
Biofuels	na	na	• Variety of complex regulatory barriers in the sector • Recent reduction of commercial viability of some investments within the sector	• Production of biodiesel • Accelerated development in the biofuels sector
Forestry, timber, paper & pulp and furniture	10.3%	1.7%	• Expensive water licenses • Lack of necessary skills and relevant technology and grow trees optimally • Reluctance to invest in forestry business	• Integrated approach to fast-tracking issuing of water licenses • Skills transfer and technology upgrading program for small-scale saw millers

(Continued)

(Continued)

Sector	Share of Manufacturing Employment	Share of Manufacturing Value Added	Constraints	Actions Planned
			• Much of the suitable land for afforestation has land claims that need to be resolved • Insufficient supply of raw materials to meet demand • Influx of cheap exports takes demand away from local products • Competitiveness in skills and quality	• Furniture clusters to benefit from economies of scale and shared information • Furniture center of competence • Establishment of charcoal manufacturing enterprises • Biomass sub-sector development
Cultural industries: Crafts, film and music	2.9%	0.01%	• Lack of coordination, information dissemination and a common vision • Lack of data and up-to-date market intelligence • Weak skills in manufacturing enterprise • High and uncompetitive product prices • Lack of R&D and common marketing strategy • High transportation costs	• Establishment of craft hubs to facilitate access to local and global markets • Development of the Mzansi Collection Concept Store, a market access program targeting rural enterprises • Development of a music industry strategy
Tourism	438,509 direct jobs, 603,201 indirect jobs	R 194.5 bn: contribution to GDP	• Difficulty of individual tourism enterprises to access foreign markets • High cost of air travel to South Africa	• Niche tourism development • Tourism export development and promotion • Airline pricing structure investigation

(Continued)

(Continued)

Sector	Share of Manufacturing Employment	Share of Manufacturing Value Added	Constraints	Actions Planned
Business Process Services	Potential to create 100,000 new jobs	Potential to contribute up to R 1 bn to GDP	• High cost of telecommunication • Lack of availability of necessary skills	• Rollout of BPS incentive program to overcome high costs of telecommunications • Skills development and training for the BPS sector
Advanced manufacturing: nuclear, nuclear component and equipment manufacturing	N/A	N/A	• Nuclear: requires construction of one new nuclear reactor every 18–24 months for successful localization, meeting nuclear quality accreditation and regulatory standards, requires access to global supply chains, funding and skills development, requires various investments and government leadership • Advanced materials sector: Lack of innovative engineers, inadequate commercialization • Aerospace and Defense: loss of critical skills, rapid technology changes, lack of funding and investment • Digital TV and STB: lack of capacity for small scale firms	• Nuclear build program to ensure participation in global nuclear value chains • Conformity assessment framework for the South African nuclear industry • Skills development support • Development of Centurion Aerospace Village as a sustainable supplier base • Materials for the aerospace industry • Manufacturing of STBs and Digital TVs

Source: 2010/11–2012/13 Industrial Policy Action Plan, February 2010, South Africa Ministry of Economic Development.

Endnotes

[1] National Treasury, Republic of South Africa, *Budget Review 2011*, February 23, 2011, 4.

[2] South Africa Reserve Bank, *Quarterly Bulletin*, December 2010, 18.

[3] National Treasury, *Budget Review 2011*, 9, 10, 19, 23.

[4] Pravin Gordhan, Minister of Finance South Africa, interview with co-author, February 28, 2011.

[5] Merton Dagut, ed., *"South Africa: The New Beginning"*, (London: Euromoney Publications, 1991), 16, pp. 40–41.

[6] Leonard Thompson, *"A History of South Africa"*, (New Haven: Yale University Press, 1995), chapter 2.

[7] *Ibid.*, pp. 50–56.

[8] William Worger, *"South Africa's City of Diamonds: Mine Workers and Monopoly Capitalism in Kimberly, 1867–1895"*, (New Haven: Yale University Press, 1987).

[9] Governor Alfred Milner, quoted in L. Thompson, *A History of South Africa*, 144.

[10] South African Foundation, *"Growth for All: An Economic Strategy for South Africa"* (Johannesburg, February 1996), 2.

[11] L. Thompson, *History of South Africa*, 190.

[12] Quoted in "Fatima Meer", *Higher than Hope* (New York: Harper & Rowe, 1988), 67.

[13] Quoted in *House of Assembly Debates*, February 3, 1969, 90.

[14] Donald Woods, *Biko: The Revised Edition* (New York: Henry Holt, 1987).

[15] Haroon Bhorat et al., "Income and Non-Income Inequality in Post-Apartheid South Africa: What are the Drivers and Possible Policy Interventions?" *DPRU Working Paper 09/138*, August 2009, pp. 8, 62.

[16] Criminal Information Management Center, *1996 Report on Crime* (http://196.33.208.55/miovs.html); South African Institute of Race Relations, *Fast Facts*, April 1997, 2.

[17] South Africa Department of Health, *Health Trends in South Africa 1994* (April 1995).

[18] Manufacturing concentration levels in South Africa were generally higher than manufacturing in OECD countries of comparable or larger size. Concentration had increased from 1976 through 1996, in the course of Apartheid conglomeration, but then, with unbundling, become somewhat less concentrated by 2001. See Table 5, "C5 Concentration Index for South African Manufacturing Industry," in Johannes Fedderke and Witness Simbanegavi, "South African Manufacturing Industry Structure and its Implications for Competition Policy," *Working Paper No. 111, December 15, 2008*, 33, http://www.econrsa.org/papers/w_papers/wp111.pdf.

[19] R.W. Johnson, *South Africa's Brave New World: The Beloved Country Since the End of Apartheid* (New York: The Overlook Press, 2009).

[20] Member of the ANC National Executive Committee, interview with a co-author, March 2, 2011.

[21] Mike Brown, "The GEAR Economy," Societe Generale Frankel Pollak, May 1997.

22 South Africa Department of Finance, *Growth, Employment and Redistribution: A Macroeconomic Strategy*, June 14, 1996, 2–5.

23 National Treasury, *Budget Review 2011*, 4.

24 Bobby Godsell, Chairman of Business Leaders South Africa, interview with a co-author, March 1, 2011.

25 R.W. Johnson, *South Africa's Brave New World*, pp. 473–481.

26 R.W. Johnson, *South Africa's Brave New World*, p. 491.

27 R.W. Johnson, *South Africa's Brave New World*, pp. 178–211.

28 Republic of South Africa, Law 25899, vol. 463, January 9, 2004.

29 Volkswagen South Africa, "Proud History," http://www.vw.co.za/en/volkswagen_group southafrica/about/history_and_milestones.html, accessed March 2011.

30 Anglo American plc company brochure, "Transformation and Empowerment: Making a Meaningful Difference," 2010, http://www.angloamerican.co.za/~/media/Files/A/ Anglo-American-South-Africa/ Attachments/media/Anglo-American-Transformation-and-Empowerment-2011.pdf; Anglo American in South Africa, interviews with co-author, March 2, 2011.

31 Cheryl Carolus, quoted in R.W. Johnson, *South Africa's Brave New World*, p. 418.

32 Haroon Bhorat and Natasha Mayet, "Labour Demand Trends and the Determinants of Unemployment in South Africa," May 2010, pp. 51–52.

33 Haroon Bhorat *et al.*, "Analysing Wage Formation in the South African Labour Market: The Role of Bargaining Councils," September 2007, 3.

34 *Ibid.*, 11.

35 Shane Godfrey, Jan Theron and Margareet Visser (2007), "The State of Collective Bargaining in South Africa," (Cape Town: Development Policy Research Unit, 2007) pp. 26–28.

36 Bhorat *et al.*, "Analysing Wage Formation," p. 11.

37 Black African leader, interview with co-author, March 4, 2011.

38 Reserve Bank of South Africa, *Quarterly Bulletin*, December 2010, 16.

39 Economist Intelligence Unit, *South Africa*, September 2010.

40 South African Government Information, "The New Growth Path: the Framework," November 23, 2010. http://www.info.gov.za/speech/DynamicAction?pageid=461& sid=14787&tid=24857.

41 "The New Growth Path: The Framework," 6.

42 *Ibid.*, pp. 9–10.

43 *Ibid.*, p. 16.

44 Gill Marcus, governor of the South African Reserve Bank, interview with co-author, March 4, 2011.

45 "The New Growth Path: The Framework," pp. 17–25.

46 "The New Growth Path: The Framework," p. 26.

47 COSATU, "A Growth Path Towards Full Employment," February 2011.

[48] Lesetja Kganyago, Director General of the Ministry of Finance, interview with co-author, February 28, 2011.

[49] Gill Marcus, interview with co-author.

[50] President Jacob Zuma, State of the National Address, quoted in Pravin Gordhan, "Budget Speech 2011," February 23, 2011, p. 1.

[51] Member of the ANC's National Executive Committee, interview with co-author.

[52] Pravin Gordhan, interview with co-author.

[53] "The New Growth Path: The Framework," p. 41.

South Africa (B): Getting Unstuck?

Richard H. K. Vietor* and Diego Comin*

On February 23, 2011, Finance Minister Pravin Gordhan presented the South African budget for fiscal year 2011/2012. It was, as the exhibits suggest, an aggressive budget, designed to kick off the "New Growth Path" that the government had articulated three months earlier. Expenditures were forecast to rise by R82 billion; revenue by R69 billion. If the economic forecasts below were born out, this fiscal plan would yield a deficit of R155 billion, or 5.3% of the GDP. If the economy were to grow 4.2%, this would only increase the debt by 1.1%. With a gradually improving economy, this deficit was expected to shrink gradually, over the next two years, back to 3.8% of GDP. Spending would concentrate on education, housing and community amenities, social protection, environmental protection, and defense. Debt service was expected to rise by 16% annually, to R104 billion.

Minister Gordhan justified this aggressive strategy as necessary to deal with unemployment and to start on the New Growth Path:

> All of this, and more, we must do within a sound fiscal framework. We must also recognize that we are taking steps, this year and next, on a long-term growth path, a decades-long transformation and expansion of our social and economic possibilities.[1]

---

*Reprinted with permission of Harvard Business School Publishing.

This case was prepared by Professors Richard H.K. Vietor and Diego Comin.

South Africa (B): Getting Unstuck? 711-085.

Macroeconomic Outlook in the 2011 Budget

Real Growth (% per annum)	2010 Estimate	2011	2012 Forecast	2013 Forecast
Household consumption	4.6	4.2	4.3	4.5
Capital formation	3.6	3.9	5.5	6.8
Exports	5.3	6.0	6.4	7.3
Imports	10.4	8.5	7.0	7.4
Gross domestic product	**2.7**	**3.4**	**4.1**	**4.4**
Consumer price inflation (CPI)	4.3	4.9	5.2	5.5
Current account balance (%/GDP)	3.2	4.2	4.9	5.0

Source: National Treasury, Republic of South Africa, *Budget Review 2011*, February 2011, p. 9.

Consolidated Government Fiscal Framework (in millions of rand)

	Revised Estimate	Medium-Term Estimates		
	2010/2011	2011/2012	2012/2013	2013/2014
Revenue	**755.0**	**824.5**	**908.7**	**1017.2**
% of GDP	*28.3%*	*28.3%*	*28.4%*	*28.8%*
Expenditures	**897.4**	**979.3**	**1061.2**	**1151.8**
% of GDP	*33.6%*	*33.6%*	*33.2%*	*32.6%*
Budget balance	**−142.6**	**−154.8**	**−152.9**	**−134.6**
% of GDP	*−5.3%*	*−5.3%*	*−4.8%*	*−3.8%*
Gross Domestic Product	*2666.9*	*2914.9*	*3201.3*	*3,536.8*

Source: National Treasury of South Africa, *Budget Review 2011*, February 2011, p. 5.

"With jobs comes dignity," concluded Minister Gordhan. "With dignity comes participation. And from participation emerges prosperity for all."[2]

Consolidated Government Expenditures in Billions of Rand, 2010/2011

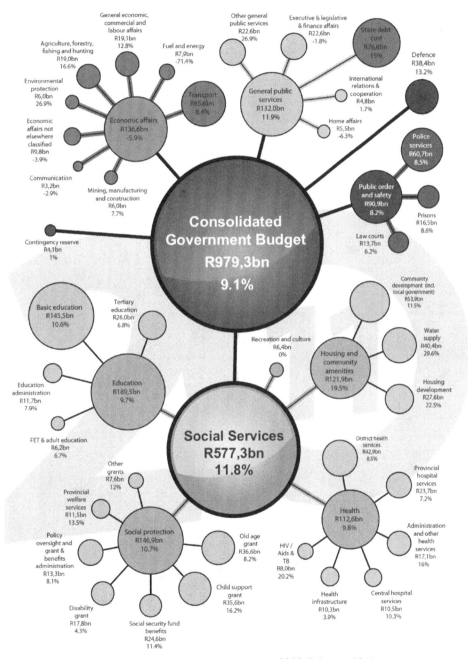

Source: National Treasury of South Africa, *Budget Review 2011*, February 2011.

Endnotes

[1] Pravin Gordhan, "Budget Speech 2011," February 23, 2011, p. 3.

[2] *Ibid.*, p. 42.

Egypt: Turbulence, and Transition?

Diego Comin*, Mohamed Heikal* and Adam Said*

Power tends to corrupt; absolute power corrupts absolutely.

— Lord Acton

Politicians are people who, when they see light at the end of the tunnel, go out and buy some more tunnel.

— Sir John Quinton

On November 27th of 2011, Mohamed Said sat poised in front of his TV depicting chaotic scenes of protest in Egypt, his native country, taking place only one day before the first truly democratic parliamentary elections in the nation's recent history.

An Egyptian expatriate, Said had often wondered when would be the right time to leverage his experience and expand his commodity trading business to Egypt. The country was clearly in dire need of basic commodities, supply management, and key infrastructure investment; skills his firm had built its reputation on. While he was under no illusion that such a task would be quite risky at present times, the entrepreneurial spirit within Mohamed saw through the current polarization among the Egyptian society and recognized a long-term economic opportunity at play. His father had left the country, along with hundreds of his countrymen, under the

*Reprinted with permission of Harvard Business School Publishing.
This case was prepared by Professor Diego Comin and Mohamed Heikal and Adam Said (MBAs 2012).
Egypt: Turbulence and Transition 713-014

nationalistic Nasser rule. The words his mother shared as he boarded the boat to the United States still resonated strongly today: "Never come back!" The repeated failures of governments since then, albeit with their numerous and varied policy shifts, seemed to give reason to her advice.

As he pondered about his path forward, he had to look back at the 60 years since the start of the Egyptian republic system. History has it that since the 1952 overthrowing of the Monarchy, a procession of civilian-clad military presidents have ruled the country with absolute power and virtually no checks and balances. Was this revolution different? Was the economic situation to improve? More importantly, would labor productivity ever recover from decades of poor policy?

The Monarch, the British Rule and the Birth of the Modern Egyptian Military Institution

Egypt was under British rule since 1882, although technically still part of the weakened Ottoman Empire up until the end of the First World War, and was ruled by King Farouk of the Muhammad Ali dynasty since 1936. He abdicated his throne in 1952 following the military *coup d'état* led by the Free Officers Movement.

In the few years preceding the revolution, Egypt faced a number of challenges both internally and externally.

British Influence

In 1922 the United Kingdom unilaterally declared Egyptian independence while retaining control of the Suez Canal, Sudan (which was a part of Egypt under British rule) and all external borders. On the ground however, British influence continued to dominate Egypt's political life at the cost of the King's personal status in front of his own people and military. On February the 4th 1942, following a ministerial crisis and clashes in opinions between the King and British ambassador Sir Miles Lampson on which party should lead the formation of the next government, British tanks and troops surrounded Abdeen Palace. Sir Lampson decided to force the Monarch's hand by insisting that he abdicate or agree to his choice for prime minister.

1948 Arab-Israeli War

In 1948, Egypt, Jordan, Syria, Saudi Arabia and Iraq went to war against the newly established Israeli state. Leaders of the Arab countries, including King Farouk, were hoping to use this opportunity to leverage on Arab public sentiment and increase legitimacy of their rule post World War II, reality on the ground was starkly different. Less than a year later, Egypt signed an Armistice agreement with Israel. The political ramifications of the 1948 war loss were tremendous. The population lost the little confidence and trust they had in their King who was willing to send Egyptians to the frontline underequipped to simply advance a political goal. In the aftermath of Egypt's defeat, a young officer, Colonel Gamal Abdel Nasser, founded the Free Officers Movement with the sole purpose of unseating the Egyptian monarchy, reclaiming full Egyptian sovereignty from the United Kingdom and vying to end wide-spread corruption.

The 1952 Egyptian "Revolution"

The 1952 Egyptian revolution traces its early beginnings to the 25th of January, a date now more synonymous with the 2011 start of the Egyptian peoples' revolt against Mubarak. On that day, British occupation troops killed 50 policemen in the city of Ismailia in a one-sided battle after their refusal to hand-over suspected militants who had just carried out an attack against British interests in the nearby city of Suez. The following day, a series of mass riots erupted across the country in protest to the muted reaction by the government and King Farouk. In down-town Cairo, amidst an unexplained absence of security forces and fire brigades, protesters and rioters turned their anger against foreign owned establishments by burning and looting some 750 buildings. Cairo descended into chaos with the King, the British and the Egyptian Prime minister blaming each other for the security failings.

On Wednesday the 23rd of July, a group of young officers operating under the name of the Free Officers Movement carried out a military coup by taking control of key military and police command and communication centers. At 7:30 a.m, Egyptians woke up to the voice of Anwar El Sadat, one of its future presidents, on public radio announcing the first communiqué of the Free Officers Movement.

> "Egypt has passed through a critical period in her recent history charac-
> terized by bribery, mischief, and the absence of governmental stability.
> All of these were factors that had a large influence on the army. Those
> who accepted bribes and were thus influenced caused our defeat in the
> Palestine War. As for the period following the war, the mischief-making
> elements have been assisting one another, and traitors have been com-
> manding the army. They appointed a commander who is either ignorant
> or corrupt. Egypt has reached the point, therefore, of having no army to
> defend it. Accordingly, we have undertaken to clean ourselves up and
> have appointed to command us men from within the army whom we trust
> in their ability, their character, and their patriotism. It is certain that all
> Egypt will meet this news with enthusiasm and will welcome it. As for
> those whose arrest we saw fit from among men formerly associated with
> the army, we will not deal harshly with them, but will release them at the
> appropriate time. I assure the Egyptian people that the entire army today

> has become capable of operating in the national interest and under the rule of the constitution apart from any interests of its own... May God grant us success."

Immediately after the announcement, jubilant crowds descended the streets of Egypt's main cities chanting for the army and heralding its establishment as the people's savior from corruption, foreign occupation and a flamboyant Monarch.

King Farouk abdicated power shortly after the coup and the country's fate was entrusted in the hands of the Revolutionary Command Council ("RCC") composed of the nine senior members of the Free Officers Movement along with Mohamed Naguib, a senior Egyptian general who, for the following two years would nominally assume the role of president and prime minister.

The Nasser Era

Political and Constitutional Reform

Following the success of their ascent to power, the RCC abrogated the 1923 constitution. It drafted an interim constitutional charter legitimizing their temporary hold of power and abolished all political parties, who were condemned by the new leadership as traitors and collaborators with the British rule and the ex-King. The Muslim Brotherhood, a nascent religious movement at the time, was also deemed a threat to the fragile Egyptian democracy and outlawed. A three year transitional rule was declared after which the RCC promised Egypt would undergo free elections, for the very first time in history, to select its leadership.

Halfway into the three year transitional rule and following major disagreements and in-fighting over leadership of the RCC, Gamal Abdul Nasser successfully completed his rise to fame, first becoming RCC chairman, prime minister and then Egypt's second President. Over the next 16 years, Nasser would actively stifle opposition to tighten his grip on absolute power. He enforced a one party state system, the wide use of secret police cells, and phone-line tapping of anyone of economic or political significance in the country.

In January 1954, the charismatic Nasser announced plans for drafting a new permanent constitution to lay the foundation of the first Egyptian republic and declared the "success of the revolution" in attaining its goals. The new constitution gave Egyptian women the right to vote for the first time and paved the way for the formation of a national assembly. Many, however, were critical of the vast powers given by the constitution to the country's president including the right to unilaterally appoint and dissolve the cabinet and its individual ministers. Though many constitutions followed over the next six decades, the distribution of power would remain fairly constant.

Economic Model Adopted for Development

Egypt underwent major policy shifts edging it closer towards a socialist system. The first economic reform enacted under the RCC's rule was that of agrarian land reform. Previously, less than 6% of Egypt's population owned more than 65% of the land in Egypt, while at the very top less than 0.5% of Egyptians owned more than one-third of all fertile land.[1] The new laws limited personal ownership of more than 210 acres, redistributed what was deemed as excess ownership to local farmers, established a system of cooperatives for produce trading and agrarian education and set price caps to the rental rate charged by landlords. The reform had mixed results on agricultural productivity. While proponents point to an increase of cultivable land by a third during Nasser's rule, opponents argue it permanently stifled economies of scale and investment in innovation.

Egypt pursued a state centric industrialism model, undertook huge infrastructure projects and adopted consecutive five-year plans with the aim of doubling the gross domestic product in a decade. The Egyptian state invested in high priority industries such as steel manufacturing, cotton ginning and the Aswan Dam, which produced around 50% of Egypt's electricity needs at the height of its productivity.[2] To finance the Aswan Dam project, Nasser nationalized the Suez Canal, which was jointly owned by British and French governments. These nations quickly retaliated by invading the Suez Canal in 1956 while the Israeli army swept through the Sinai Peninsula. The UK, France and Israel were forced to withdraw less than a month later after intense political pressure by the US and the Soviet Union.

The industrial transformation underwent by Egypt was phenomenal: Egypt's real GDP grew at an average rate of 9% per annum for almost a decade and the share of manufacturing to Egypt's GDP rose from around 14% in the late 1940s to 35% by the early 1970s.[3] Critics, however, point to the high import tariffs in place at the time distorting the results and to the inefficiency present in state-owned production facilities up to the present day.

Demographic Composition

In the early 1960s Egypt's population stood at 28M people with a high growth rate of 2.6%.[4] This rate was comparable to most nations in Africa. The main driver of this trend was the high fertility rate.

Egypt, at the time, was known to be a cosmopolitan country with a significant immigrant population. The burgeoning trade economy based in Alexandria attracted international workers from Greece, Italy, Turkey and other developed nations. The English dominance ensured a cohesive culture. While native Egyptian Muslims represented by far the largest ethnic group, it seemed to embrace and accept this internationalization with no significant ethnic conflict.

Coptic Christians, a native church of Egypt with its own pope in Alexandria, had significant representation across the country both in numbers and culturally with around a 10% representation in the population.

The interventionist rule and nationalization efforts of Nasser had a significant impact on the nation's demographic composition. Firstly, many of the Egyptian elite fled the country as they had seen their assets seized and often were at risk of detention. While little historical data is available, it also appeared clear that the opportunity for immigrants had been dramatically lowered. The ethnic diversity across the nation subsequently decreased, as the economic center of the nation shifted away from Alexandria.

Conflicts and Wars

From 1952 to 1970, Egypt was involved in four large-scale military conflicts. On the 5th of June in 1967, Israel attacked Egypt and Syria and managed to invade both the Sinai Peninsula and the Golan Heights in less than six days.

The loss of a significant part of Egyptian land led Nasser to publicly apologize for the defeat and offer his immediate resignation from the presidency. The next day, massive support protests gripped the nation and Nasser withdrew his resignation. The defeat took its toll on Nasser in terms of political clout as well as personal health. President Gamal Abdul Nasser died of cardiac arrest in early 1970. Hundreds of thousands of Egyptians poured into the streets publicly mourning his death on the following day.

The King of War and Peace

The death of Nasser presented the RCC with its toughest crisis. Though the temptations of power were great, none of the senior members were willing to assume the burden of responsibility at such a critical stage. The burden to fill the presidential seat of a defeated country fell to Anwar El Sadat, also a member of the Free Officers Movement. Observers at the time were puzzled by the choice of a virtually unknown political player.

1973 War

After six years of intense preparation, on the 6th of October 1973, Egyptian military forces launched an attack in an attempt to reclaim the Sinai Peninsula. The surprise attack destroyed Israeli defenses positioned on the Suez Canal and allowed Egyptian tanks and troops to advance 12 miles into the Peninsula. The ensuing victory reinstated Egyptian pride in the military institution and catapulted Sadat to new heights of political stardom on the domestic stage. President Sadat seized the moment to steer Egypt into a new direction both politically and economically.

1977 Peace Negotiations with Israel and Foreign Policy Shifts

On 9th of November 1977, Egyptian President Anwar El Sadat stunned the world by declaring his willingness and intention to go to Jerusalem and speak before the Knesset in a televised address to the parliament. While the ground breaking speech eventually led to the peace accords of 1979 between Egypt and Israel, it also led to a deterioration of relationships with neighboring Arab countries who felt betrayed by President Sadat's unilateral course of action. The Arab league suspended Egypt's membership in 1979 and moved its headquarters from Cairo to Tunis. Egypt, once considered the Pan-Arab heart and soul under Nasser, was swiftly changing lanes under Sadat.

Political Reforms

One year into office, Sadat proclaimed the start of the "corrective revolution", purging government and military establishments of Nasser regime supporters ("Nasserists") in a bid to establish and strengthen his own rule. Sadat also ordered the release of Islamic leaders jailed during the Nasser era. Allegations that Sadat actively endorsed and financially supported Islamic movements in a bid to counter the effect of youth socialist movements were widespread.[5]

Though President Sadat formally re-instated a multi-party electoral system in 1977, little political change actually took place. As a result, while new parties emerged, they did little to offer any real political differentiation and never posed a real threat to Sadat's National Democratic Party (NDP).

Economic Policy Shift

The Egyptian economy had been devastated by the six years of war. The Suez Canal, an important stream of foreign currency inflow, had been closed for most of the conflict. Sadat used his immense post-war popularity to push through vast economic reforms that ended the socialistic controls of Nasser. The most important aspect of which was the Infitah or "open door policy." Under the Infitah, the government quickly loosened controls over the economy and encouraged private domestic and international capital flows. While the reforms created a wealthy and successful upper class and a small middle class, they had little effect upon the average Egyptian, who faced crippling inflation and began to grow dissatisfied with Sadat's rule. In 1977, massive spontaneous riots (the "Bread Riots") involving hundreds of thousands of Egyptians erupted when the state announced that it was retiring subsidies on basic food materials. The riots ended with the deployment of the army in Cairo and the re-institution of price controls.[6]

Over the next four years, in the absence of government budget surpluses and adequate local savings, Egypt adopted a development strategy for which continuous flows of imported capital, and commodities were indispensable. External financing contributed as much as 80% of public investment. To balance the state budget and pay for food imports, the Sadat regime became increasingly dependent on foreign aid. Egypt imported some 60% of its food, at an annual cost of $4.4 billion by 1981. Nearly half of all foreign exchange earnings went to pay for these necessities. The country's total foreign debt, under $3 billion in 1973, had ballooned to $16 billion by 1979.[7]

The Pharaohs' Lonely Demise

The final years of the Sadat rule came to be known as the darkest years of his rule. Allegations of corruptive practices by Sadat's family during the Infitah plagued the move to a free market system. Inflationary pressures had eaten away his public support from rural Egyptians, who were the cornerstone support of the 1952 revolution. Islamic movements were infuriated with his unequivocal support to the US and peace with Israel. Amid public discontent, a deteriorating relationship, and growing fear over personal security, Sadat cracked down hard on all forms of political opposition. In February of 1981 and in a desperate throw of the dice, Sadat ordered sweeping waves of arrests on not only opposition figures but also noted men and women in the business elite, legal system, journalism, universities, former ministers, and even the Egyptian Coptic Pope.

On October 6th, 1981, while overseeing a military parade commemorating the 1973 war victory, Sadat was assassinated by an Islamist cell within his own military. It was carried out by a group with clear religious motivation who sought to eliminate the leader but not to overthrow the regime itself. Most striking was the ensuing silence of the population — unusual among a people not accustomed to hiding their feelings in critical moments for their nation.

The Mubarak Era

Conservatism and Caution: Maintain the Status Quo

Mohamed Hosny Mubarak, Sadat's vice president and head of the air force during the 1973 war, was sworn in office the next day. Upon taking office, the President released all political detainees of Sadat's last years vowing for reconciliation and a period of national consensus building. Mubarak also committed to step down after two terms in office and reinstate a healthy Egyptian economy and political system. The fragile economic *status quo*, though unsustainable, was little changed over the course of the first decade of Mubarak rule. Politically, the new president vowed to uphold the peace treaty signed with Israel, aligned himself as a close ally of the United States and the Western World, and successfully restored Arab relations with Egypt.

Emergency Law and Political Rights

During three decades in power, Mubarak maintained the necessity of the emergency law, which extended police powers, suspended constitutional rights, and legalized censorship of the media to counter Islamic terrorist attacks. The law, however, was soon to be more widely used to curtail opposition meetings, break-up protests, and jail political activists indefinitely without charges.

In 2005, and after continuous international pressure to allow for more political freedom, President Mubarak, for the first time in Egypt's history, allowed for a multi-candidate ballot in presidential elections. The proposed amendments fell well short of democratic expectations and were seen by many political commentators as just a change of "façade", as it enforced virtually impossible conditions for fielding opposition and independent presidential candidates.

Economic Liberation and the Onslaught of Technocrat Governments

Starting in 1991, Mubarak pushed for a gradual and slow shift in economic policies to a free market, export and FDI driven economy. Mubarak entrusted the implementation of these policies to a succession of non-military technocrat cabinets; a shift from the long held norms of quasi-military cabinets over the last decades. Simplification of tariff and tax structures, privatization of state-owned enterprises, and active encouragement of the local private sector were the main staples of Mubarak's economic diet. New laws governing investment, capital market, and foreign ownership of companies were passed in a slow and gradual process. Egypt witnessed a strong economic recovery over the 2001–2010 period with real growth averaging 5%, FDI increasing to unprecedented levels, and non-oil exports soaring to unparalleled heights. Nonetheless, the new economic policies were criticized for inflationary pressures and local currency devaluation shocks following the abolishment of the fixed exchange rate system in 2001 (See **Exhibit 2** for Macro Data). More importantly, to this date, not a single government was able to significantly decrease public subsidies on bread and fuel to the Egyptian population, with subsidies and social grants representing an exceptional 36% of the government's total expenditure in 2010.[8]

Military's Expanding Role in Business

With Mubarak famously proclaiming throughout his tenure that wars were a matter of the past, surpluses in the military budget spiraled from the annual inflow of around $1.2 billion in US military financial aid committed during the peace accords. Many political observers referred to an implicit agreement between Mubarak and his army generals; whereby the military institution would keep and reinvest their surpluses in economic activities in return for their gradual withdrawal from the political scene and their support for technocrat governments to lead the way forward. As a result, the military significantly expanded its presence in business through the reconditioning of war factories and the establishment of new business projects. While no data exists about the military budget, it is widely known that the military operates companies that produced and sold everything from household white goods and bottled water to laptops and televisions. "It's a business conglomerate, like General Electric," said Robert Springborg, professor of national security affairs at the Naval Postgraduate School in Monterey.[9]

Demographic Composition

In the late 1980s the population had risen above 50 million people. Although the growth rate dropped from a high of 2.5% in 1985 to approximately 1.75% in 2010, the total number of citizens was estimated to be over 80 million people by 2010.

Population growth was concentrated among the poorer, rural, and Muslim segments of society.[10] The economic growth over the period did not allow for integration of this entire new nation. Indeed, the population had now doubled since Sadat had taken power.

The immigrant population had now dropped to represent only 0.22% of the national population, ranking it 188th out of 195 countries. Diversity seemed to have been replaced by a dominant Arab and Sunni Muslim community.[11] Incidents of ethnic conflicts began to be reported even against native Egyptian Copts. Latest government estimates accounted for as low as 3% Christians in the country.

Revolutionary Problems

Gamal Mubarak's Candidacy: Gamal Mubarak, an investment banker by experience and the younger of two Mubarak sons, rose to prominence during the first decade of the 21st century. Amid rumors that Mubarak was grooming him to assume power, Gamal quickly ascended the ranks of the ruling National Democratic Party (NDP) to become the head of its influential policies committee. The NDP's leadership positions were gradually filled by well-known business allies of the president's son. Commentators observed that the only institutional objection to Gamal's potential presidency stemmed from the military, who wanted to preserve the long held military tradition of fielding Egypt's presidents. Gamal's rise to fame also alienated the Egyptian public who grew disenchanted with the political system.

In 2005, in response to the unveiling of the "new" NDP, several protest organizations began to emerge. The Kifaya movement ("enough" in Arabic) was formed by a coalition of political activists calling for the lifting of emergency laws and vehemently opposed to Gamal's candidacy. Kifaya, though was continuously repressed and its leaders constantly jailed.

The 2010 Parliamentary Elections: The 2010, parliamentary elections were plagued by vast vote rigging in what seemed to be an attempt by Mubarak to solidify power before handing over to his younger son. Human rights groups condemned it as the most fraudulent poll in Egyptian history, as the ruling NDP captured 96% of the seats, up from 74% in 2005.[12] The election results spurred anger among the Egyptian public amid proclamations of free and fair elections by the NDP.

The Khaled Saeed Incident: The brutal killing of Khaled Saeed, a 28-year old well educated Alexandria resident, captured the soul of Egyptian public discontent with police brutality. Saeed was taken from the second floor of an internet cafe by two detectives. As an eye witness later described, "They dragged him to the adjacent building and banged his head against an iron door, the steps of the staircase and walls of the building... Two doctors happened to be there and tried in vain to revive him but (the police) continued beating him... They continued to beat him even when he was dead". This description given by the café owner was confirmed by the Egyptian Organization for Human Rights while the police and public forensic office maintained Khaled died as a result of suffocation from allegedly swallowing a packet of drugs he was attempting to hide from the detectives.[13] The public outcry in the aftermath resulted in 70,000 people joining the Facebook Group Kolena Khaled Saeed ("We are all Khaled Saeed" in Arabic). The group was the first to publicly call for protests on the 25th of January 2011 against the Mubarak rule.

Tunisian Revolution: In January 2011, the success of the Tunisian revolution in ousting the corrupt president Ben Ali stimulated Egyptian youth sentiment for protest and removed the fear barrier between the people and the regime.

The 2011 Egyptian Revolution

The 2011 revolution began on January 25th in a grass-root organized peaceful protest of tens of thousands of Egyptian civilians to stand against President Hosni Mubarak. As the waves of protesters and numbers increased, authorities extended their efforts to shut down both Internet and mobile phone services. As the military presence appeared in the streets *"The March of the Millions"* gathered in Tahrir Square for a peaceful protest requesting the immediate resignation the president. Under immense local and international pressure, Mubarak's resignation was announced on 11th of February 2011, 18 days into the revolution.

Role of the Military in the Egyptian Revolution

As the police was ordered to leave the streets, the army appeared in tanks across the country. Civilians, who viewed this as a victory over the police force, cheered the army's arrival. Over the next couple of weeks, the army maintained its position as a protector of the people and a bystander to the revolution. Its interference was limited to separating few clashes between anti-Mubarak and pro-Mubarak protesters, the latter often being assumed to be police forces and mercenary thugs.

On February 11th, as the Mubarak resignation was made official, the Supreme Council of Egyptian Armed Forces took power. The Council abruptly dissolved the parliament and suspended the constitution. It pledged to hold democratic elections, not to field any presidential candidate from the council, and that it would remain committed to all international treaties — most importantly to the 1979 peace treaty with Israel.

Travel bans started being imposed by the prosecutor general on past government officials and business leaders close to Mubarak. However, the legal process for judging these was inherently slow and unclear, as the Egyptian court system was known for often taking decades to issue a final verdict. At the same time, reports of civilians being detained by the army started to be released. Human Rights Watch declared that by September 2010 over 12,000 civilians were arrested and brought before military tribunals without proper access to legal advice.

Amendments to the Constitution and the Roadmap to Democracy

In March, Egyptian voters approved a referendum on constitutional changes that were set forth by the Supreme Council. Mubarak had initially proposed these amendments in his efforts for last-gasp reforms before he resigned. The established political forces, mainly the Muslim brotherhood and the remnant elements of the National Democratic Party, were the main supporters of this referendum. Its primary objective was to set a steady path for legislative and presidential elections through changes in the fielding of presidential candidates, the limits on presidential tenure, the conduct of elections, the court rulings on vote rigging, the appointment of presidents, and the terms of the emergency law.

Contention around Amendments

The referendum was well accepted by the Egyptian population with a 77% approval from voters. The turnout of 41% among the 45 million eligible voters did demonstrate the enthusiasm around this new democratic process. Nonetheless, many argue that the close to 60% absentee ratio was an early sign of division in the country.[14]

Indeed, many opposition leaders brought the attention to certain surprising amendments; such as the new eligibility criteria that restricted certain well prominent expatriates from entering the political scene. Some activist and regional analysts asserted that these amendments were the first act of alliance between the Military Council and the Muslim brotherhood, the only established opposition group.

Interim Constitution and Legislation

In April 2011 and less than two weeks after the result of the referendum, the Military Council presented a completely revised interim constitutional charter. The declaration included a total of 62 amended articles, which reached above and beyond the referendum's six article scope. The first point of critic was that it did not retract the 56-year old socialist article that reserved 50% of the seats in parliament to representatives of workers and farmers.

In addition to the above, the SCAF had been working on two new articles that would be considered "un-amendable" and fueled further resentment towards the military led government. Specifically, these articles aimed to (i) ensure that no army official, even retired, could be trialed in any court other than a military court martial and (ii) that the military budget be a line item in the government expenses that could not be enquired upon.

As a result of this new controversy, activists reclaimed Tahrir Square and voices of disapproval filled the streets of the country. The *25th January Revolution Youth Coalition* issued a statement days after the declaration that's said "we decided to stop protesting at Tahrir Square in order to give the government a chance to achieve the objectives of the 25 January Revolution, bring stability back and rebuild the country [. . .] while we were rebuilding our country, it took us by surprise that some are doing their best to steal the revolution [. . .] We will not allow the vestiges of the toppled regime — state security, Mubarak's NDP, thugs and corrupt business tycoons — to steal our revolution".[15] The Army's popular support appeared to have dwindled significantly, as many were starting to view them as the enemy of the revolution and democracy.

Interim Governments

In the nine months since the start of the revolution, the country changed prime ministers and cabinets an astonishing three times. This constant dissolution of and re-instatement process is reminiscent of the Mubarak day's where the blame for social complaints would always be passed on to heads and members of governments.

In this similar light, there has been no change to the Supreme Council's leadership, albeit with many protests, civilian uprisings and bloodshed.

Beyond the Revolution

The Economic Shock and Socio-economic Context: The country had previously faced shortages in bread, one of the main staples of Egyptian diet, due to shortages in wheat, a commodity heavily subsidized by the government. The revolution only deepened this issue further. A Gallup poll showed that by August 2011 over 40% of Egyptian found it "very difficult to get by on their income" (up from 22% in October 2010). Comparatively, the percentage of citizens "living comfortably" stayed relatively steady at 5%.[16]

Tourism: The first sector to bear the economic pains was tourism. Unfortunately, with close to 14 million visitors a year this sector was also one of the most significant for the Egyptian economy. It was estimated to represent 11% of the GDP and employ over two million Egyptians both directly and indirectly. The revolution hit the industry in a drastic way. While there were no attacks on tourists or reports of abuse on foreigners, the instability directed foreigners to other markets.[17]

Local and Foreign Investment: As the revolution unfolded, all investment activity came to a halt across the country. Local individuals and corporations were pre-occupied with ensuring their livelihood on a day-by-day basis, as businesses were affected both on a revenue perspective, as consumption dropped, and on the production side, as labor strikes and absenteeism increased across all industries. Foreigners did not wish to take any currency risk or proceed with any fixed assets investment given the uncertainty of policies going forward. In an effort to ensure that savings did not flee the country, the Central Bank of Egypt put in place restrictions on the repatriation of capital for individuals by capping it to one hundred thousand dollars per person. While no restrictions on corporations were implemented, the process for transfer of capital was made more extensive and lengthy to ensure the due purpose of such transfers.

Deep Inequalities: According to the World Bank in 2009, Egypt was ranked as the 90th most unequal nation globally with a Gini Coefficient of 0.344.[18] This appears to be a positive sign, as it ranked better than Tunisia or the US, but it was not descriptive of the local realities. Indeed, with over 30% illiteracy and unemployment close to 20%, the countrymen face great challenges. The lack of institutions providing healthcare support or social welfare left most citizens to their own demise. With close to 40% of the population under the poverty line of $2 a day, the nation faced incredible challenges to meet the needs of an exploding young generation. 30% of the population was under 14 years of age. In addition the inequalities stretched between genders, as women received lower education and wages than their males' counterparts. While they were given equal rights as men by law, the traditional Islamic and rural culture often pushed women to wear the veil in public (70% of population) and often get married at a young age (15% of girls between 15–19). Ultimately, as the population grew from 30 million people to over 80 million under the Mubarak regime, it appears that those who have been most left behind are the youth, the women, and the poor.[19]

Debt Issuance: In 2011, Egypt's domestic debt sales increased by over 25% over a single fiscal year. To fill the economic gap, the Ministry of Finance decided to rely on the use of short-term bonds. While most of the bonds are 1 to 5 year maturities, they have come at increasing yields. The current debt service already represents 25% of the country's total expenditures and much concern remains on the future ability to meet payments, as its one year borrowing rates have reached a high of 16% in the fourth quarter of 2011. Nevertheless, in a surprise move in June 2011 the government turned down a $3 billion loan from the International Monetary Fund, after it revised the government budget deficit down from 11% to 8.4%. Since then, the Ministry of Finance has already at least once annulled the issuance of notes due to the high interest rates demanded by the market. International governments have expressed their commitment to support Egypt financially when necessary. Due to political indecisiveness and popular pressure, there appeared to be little progress in these funding sources that may have been made available.[20]

Currency: Foreign direct investment, tourism, and the Suez Canal represent the three largest sources of foreign capital for the Egyptian economy. With the two first ones in dramatic decline, the country's capital account balances was put under tremendous pressure since the revolution. Indeed, estimates point at a 50% drop in the Central Bank of Egypt's foreign currency reserves over the last fiscal year. This dramatic drop has led most analysts to expect a significant devaluation of the currency in the near future. While this move would make its exports and tourism more attractive it would negatively impact the countries' ability to purchase its most important necessary imports such as wheat and maize and place more inflationary pressure on Egypt's vulnerable middle and lower classes. Ultimately, the interim army-led government seems to have preferred to stand still on both the currency and the debt fronts and delegate this responsibility to the newly elected government but time may well be running out.[21]

Preparing for the New Political Stage

While in most recorded revolutions, special tribunals, truth reports, and supervisory committees are put in place, the SCAF and interim governments in Egypt have put no efforts into forming such institutions. Many international institutions such as Human Rights Watch have redoubled their research efforts across the country. Nevertheless, there has been no evidence of these findings being included in the formal decision making process.

The trial of political figures such as Mubarak, his two sons, the interior minister, and six senior police officers, has been combined into one major trial. Mubarak and his co-defendants, if found guilty, could face the death penalty. The theatrics around this prominent trial has covered local news for months. The crucial testimony of Field Marshal Tantawi, still head of the SCAF, on whether orders were given to shoot and kill protesters was deemed incomplete and inconclusive.

On the business front, all claims are to be brought forward to the standard Egyptian judicial system. With hundreds of claims of corruption erupting, there have been no efforts to consolidate, coordinate, or prioritize judgments. This led to a tremendous amount of personal retributions and attacks. Many large businesses were put on halt for months due to extraordinary claims. Most of the claims relate to inappropriate issuance of licenses or land grants by the ex-government. Evidence has been difficult to gather making judgment lengthy and ineffective. Many of the largest business leaders decided to flee the country and find refuge in London or Dubai, where they avoid prosecutions and ensure their liberty won't be questioned by rising claims.

Control of Parliament

In accordance with the election process outlined by the SCAF, parliamentary elections would be held across Egypt from November 2011 onwards. The election would take place in three rounds to include all districts and governorates. The results would put a new parliament in place that then would be able to re-draft the constitution and oversee the upcoming presidential elections. While dozens of independent parties were created in the months following the revolution, only a few were expected to have a significant share of the votes in the elections. To avoid having an exhaustive list of candidates the process drafted by the SCAF's amendments attributed two third of the seats to party list members and one third to independent candidates.

The Muslim Brotherhood: The Brotherhood was undoubtedly the strongest party in Egypt after the NDP, as it was the only significant organization allowed to co-exist under the Mubarak regime. Founded in 1928, it has over a million members. It was one of the first parties to oppose the British rule of Egypt in 1936. Although it started as a religious awareness and social impact organization, it rose through the political scene across many decades and now operates under the political name of the Freedom and Justice Party. The organization's officially stated goal is to instill the Qur'an and Sunnah as the "sole reference point for ordering the life of the Muslim family, individual, community, and state" although in reality its considered as extremely moderate among the spectrum of Islamic movements. Mubarak tactically positioned this organization as the only alternative to his party for decades. He used the argument that if he was not in power then Egypt would become a Muslim state, an option clearly not acceptable for the interests of the international community and Egypt's affluent society. In 2005's parliamentary election, brotherhood candidates, who ran as independents because of the illegality of their political party at the time, won 20% of the votes.[22] Through decades of deteriorating economics under the NDP, the brotherhood rooted itself in Egyptian society by providing support services at local mosques, education to rural children, and medication to the ill across the country. It gained much appeal across the base of the pyramid and dictated the way of life for millions of Egyptians. During the start of the revolution, the Brotherhood did not officially support the protests and was active in asking citizens to avoid violence and obey curfews. It furthered its political involvement after the resignation of Mubarak, as it was the best organized political force on the ground, and was widely considered to be implicitly cooperating with the military council. The party has allegedly received hundreds of millions of dollars in monetary support from Gulf nations such as Qatar and Saudi Arabia. While it asserted that it would not field any candidates for the presidential elections, few of the existing front-runners are known to be ex-brotherhood members. The party is expected to become the biggest block in the new parliament, securing around 40% of total parliamentary seats.

The Salafist Movement: Salafism is associated with the literal and strict interpretation of Islamic theology. They were widely considered as the more extreme Islamic party, as they introduced hard-line fatwa's and sought a stringent religious government. Their proposed rules would ban interest rates, exclude non-Muslims from executive positions, segregate sexes in the workplace, outlaw alcohol, and restrict any display of public affection. The party has refused any coalition, even with the Muslim brotherhood, which they deem to be sell-outs of traditional Islam. The rise of this party has raised many concerns among Egypt's moderate Muslim and Christian community.

Liberal Coalitions: Given the rise of many independent liberal parties post-revolution and the parliamentary procedure outlined by the constitutional amendments, a consolidation effort took place amongst liberals that resulted into two main liberal coalitions vying for parliamentary seats.

Al Kotla Al Masreya (The Egyptian Masses) Coalition: The Free Egyptian party founded by Naguib Sawiris has led this coalition of several liberal parties. Funded by Sawiris, a Christian businessman who had amassed tremendous wealth under the Mubarak regime, the party insists on the principles of state secularity and civic society. Many intellectuals and prominent figures in Egypt support the coalitions' agenda. Nevertheless, the movement came under grave pressure due to its founder's poor political skills and inadvertent attacks against the Muslim religion. In addition, there has been credibility issues linked to his family's unclear ties with Mubarak and tremendous rise of wealth under the regime's auspices while younger brother was judged guilty for corrupt practices in post-revolution trials. Naguib Sawiris has since stepped down as the nominal party leader but remains the main financial backer.

Sawra Mostamera (The Revolution Continues) Coalition: This coalition was created by the amalgamation of youth and activist parties present in Tahrir square. It is a left leaning and secular alliance that was formed by two socialist, two liberal, and two Islamic parties. This coalition took place after much conflict amongst smaller parties and a lack of consistency in the demands of independent groups. Its efforts have been to reconcile the perspective of several entities and present a clear agenda going forward. Its main objective is to achieve all the popular demands of the youth during the revolution.

Overall the liberal parties, albeit with their coalitions, have remained very fragmented and unorganized. The lack of strong liberal leadership and the numerous voices in its ranks have dramatically weakened the chances for a significant liberal representation in parliament.

Old Regime Remnants: Mubarak's regime was part of the National Democratic Party, founded in 1978 by Anwar El Sadat. It has been an authoritarian centrist party. It remained the sole relevant party in existence under the Old regime by banning all opposition on the pretext of national security and absolving any political activists within its ranks. This allowed the NDP to have full control over the parliament, ministries, and even the judicial system. After protesters demolished its headquarters during the revolution, the party was dissolved in April 2011 by a judicial court order and all its assets were handed over to the new government. Many of the party members and leaders have since joined other parties or created their own political movements.

Presidential Elections

The first fully democratic presidential election in Egypt's history is scheduled to take place in July 2012. Most candidates running for the 2012 election have not formally allied themselves with any of the political parties currently in the running for parliamentary seats.

Many prominent Egyptian figures have already declared their candidacy; including Mohamed El Baradei, the Nobel peace prize laureate and ex-director general of the International Atomic Energy Agency, and Amr Moussa, ex-secretary general of the Arab league.

Several candidates closely related to the Muslim Brotherhood have come forward since the revolution but fear of vote-splitting among these candidates has led to much speculation on their respective future. Others are expected to present themselves for elections but have not yet confirmed their candidacy. These include Ayman Nour, a presidential candidate in the 2005 whose arrest on charges of forgery had spurred much controversy.

The Future of Egypt's Politics and Policies?

It was clear that Egypt's economic and social situation had deteriorated greatly and that there was little time left for any hopes of a turnaround. While diverse economic models had been attempted throughout recent history, their recurrent failures put into question certain fundamental aspects of the nation's pillars.

Were demographic and social changes the cause or consequence of the economic failures? What policies would turn this situation around? How could the new government work at improving productivity across the nation? The balancing act between economic development, government policy, and society's needs, appeared more relevant than ever.

Exhibit 1.   Egypt Map

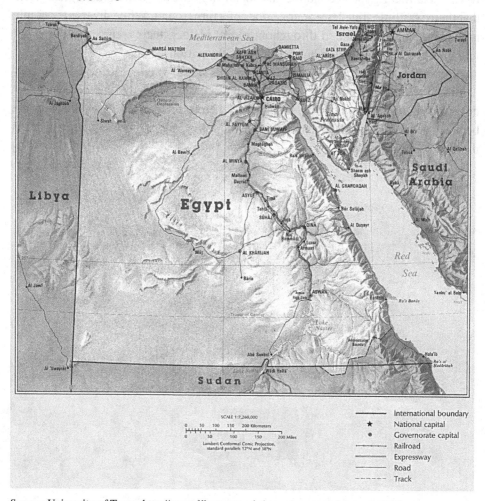

Source: University of Texas, http://www.lib.utexas.edu/maps/, accessed August 2012.

Exhibit 2. National Accounts of Egypt (1980–2011)

	1980	1982	1984	1986	1988	1990	1992	1994	1996	1998	2000
GDP (EGP billion)	15.5	22.5	31.7	44.1	61.6	96.1	139.1	175.0	229.4	287.4	340.1
GDP (% real change)	n/a	9.9	6.1	2.6	5.3	5.7	4.4	3.9	4.5	3.3	5.1
Real GDP ($ billion at 2005 prices)	31.3	35.7	40.7	44.5	48.1	53.3	56.3	60.2	65.6	70.5	77.7
GDP per head ($)	497.4	533.8	514.3	450.9	489.0	615.9	693.7	813.3	1,036.1	1,254.7	1,395.4
Structure of GDP (% of GDP)											
Consumption	71.3	64.5	65.3	64.2	70.7	71.7	72.6	74.6	76.9	76.7	75.9
Government Spending	16.5	16.0	15.6	14.6	14.0	11.3	10.4	10.3	10.4	11.3	11.2
Investment	26.3	27.4	28.1	28.9	32.7	27.0	19.1	16.6	16.0	21.3	18.9
Exports	27.9	26.3	20.2	13.7	17.4	20.1	28.4	22.6	20.8	16.2	16.2
Imports	41.4	37.9	32.7	22.3	35.2	32.8	30.9	28.6	26.6	25.7	22.8
Gross national savings rate (%)	26.0	21.5	21.9	21.7	29.3	29.3	24.9	16.6	16.3	18.6	18.7
Current-account balance (% of GDP)	−2.0	−7.4	−7.8	−7.7	−3.9	0.5	6.7	0.1	−0.3	−2.9	−0.8
Labor productivity growth (%)	n/a	n/a	n/a	n/a	n/a	n/a	n/a	n/a	3.1	0.0	1.3
Total factor productivity growth (%)	n/a	n/a	n/a	n/a	n/a	n/a	−0.9	5.3	2.8	0.3	2.0
Average real wage index (EGP, 2005 = 100)	n/a	n/a	n/a	n/a	n/a	n/a	31.9	40.8	49.3	56.3	75.4
Oil produc tion (thousand barrels a day)	n/a	n/a	n/a	820.0	890.0	920.0	930.0	920.0	920.0	880.0	812.5
Oil reserves (million barrels)	2,900.0	3,325.0	3,200.0	3,600.0	4,300.0	4,400.0	4,400.0	4,200.0	3,800.0	3,800.0	3,600.0
Exchange rate (EGP per 1$, period average)	0.7	0.9	1.3	1.9	2.3	2.7	3.3	3.4	3.4	3.4	3.5
Consumer prices (% change)	n/a	14.9	16.9	23.4	17.8	16.8	13.5	8.1	7.3	4.0	2.7
Lending interest rate (% on loans up to one year)	13.3	15.0	15.0	15.0	17.0	19.0	20.3	16.5	15.6	13.0	13.2
Population (in millions)	44.4	46.8	49.3	52.1	55.0	57.8	60.3	62.7	65.1	67.6	70.2
Labor Force (in millions)	n/a	n/a	n/a	n/a	n/a	14.3	15.8	16.8	16.9	17.6	18.9
Recorded Unemployment (%)	n/a	n/a	n/a	n/a	n/a	8.6	9.0	11.1	9.6	8.2	9.0

(Continued)

Exhibit 2.   (Continued)

	2001	2002	2003	2004	2005	2006	2007	2008	2009	2010	2011
GDP (EGP billion)	358.7	378.9	417.5	485.3	538.5	617.7	744.8	895.6	1,038.6	1,206.6	1,371.8
GDP (% real change)	3.5	3.2	3.2	4.1	4.5	6.8	7.1	7.2	4.7	5.1	1.8
Real GDP ($ billion at 2005 prices)	287.9	297.0	306.5	319.1	333.3	356.1	381.4	408.7	427.8	449.8	457.8
GDP per head ($)	1,264.1	1,155.2	962.9	1,034.3	1,207.9	1,372.5	1,651.2	2,021.8	2,256.7	2,538.7	2,680.0
Structure of GDP (% of GDP)											
Consumption	75.3	73.8	73.0	71.7	71.6	70.6	72.4	72.4	76.2	74.9	74.1
Government Spending	11.3	12.6	12.7	12.8	12.7	12.3	11.3	10.9	11.4	11.4	11.4
Investment	17.7	17.8	16.3	16.4	17.9	18.7	20.9	22.3	19.3	17.9	14.8
Exports	17.5	18.3	21.8	28.2	30.3	30.0	30.3	33.0	25.0	35.4	33.7
Imports	22.3	22.7	24.4	29.6	32.6	31.6	34.8	38.6	31.9	31.3	28.9
Gross national savings rate (%)	18.5	19.3	22.1	21.1	20.2	21.1	21.0	21.5	17.6	15.6	12.6
Current-account balance (% of GDP)	0.3	1.0	5.2	4.1	2.2	2.4	0.1	-0.8	-1.7	-2.3	-2.3
Labor productivity growth (%)	1.1	-0.9	2.0	0.8	1.2	1.1	0.7	3.3	2.4	1.6	-1.6
Total factor productivity growth (%)	1.2	-0.2	2.1	1.4	1.5	1.8	0.9	2.5	2.6	1.6	-2.5
Average real wage index (EGP, 2005 = 100)	79.7	84.4	89.4	94.6	100.0	105.8	113.7	127.4	146.5	164.1	178.8
Oil production (thousand barrels a day)	757.5	752.5	750.0	712.5	707.5	672.5	637.5	642.5	750.0	700.0	690.0
Oil reserves (million barrels)	3,700.0	3,500.0	3,500.0	3,600.0	3,700.0	3,800.0	4,100.0	4,200.0	4,400.0	4,500.0	4,400.0
Exchange rate (EGP per 1$, period average)	4.0	4.5	5.8	6.2	5.8	5.7	5.6	5.4	5.5	5.6	5.9
Consumer prices (% change)	2.3	2.7	4.5	11.3	4.9	7.6	9.5	18.3	11.8	11.1	10.2
Lending interest rate (% on loans up to one year)	13.3	13.8	13.5	13.4	13.1	12.6	12.5	12.3	12.0	11.0	12.0
Population (in millions)	71.5	72.9	74.3	75.7	77.2	78.6	80.1	81.5	83.0	84.5	86.1
Labor Force (in millions)	19.3	19.9	20.4	20.9	21.8	22.9	23.9	24.7	25.4	26.2	27.7
Recorded Unemployment (%)	9.2	10.2	11.0	10.3	11.2	10.6	8.9	8.7	9.4	9.0	12.2

Source: Compiled using data from *International Financial Statistics*, International Monetary fund; *EIU country data*, Economist Intelligence Unit.

Note: "EGP" stands for Egyptian Pounds. $ are U.S. Dollars. "N/A" indicates that no data is available. All numbers are rounded; some numbers are estimates.

Exhibit 3. Egypt Balance of Payments (1981–2011)

(in $ Billions)	1980	1982	1984	1986	1988	1990	1992	1994	1996	1998	2000
Current Account	(0.44)	(1.85)	(1.99)	(1.81)	(1.05)	0.18	2.81	0.03	(0.19)	(2.44)	(0.82)
Goods net	(3.0)	(3.7)	(6.2)	(4.5)	(6.6)	(6.4)	(5.2)	(6.0)	(8.4)	(12.4)	(10.5)
Exports	3.9	4.0	3.9	2.6	2.8	3.9	3.7	4.0	4.8	4.4	7.1
Imports	(6.8)	(7.7)	(10.1)	(7.2)	(9.4)	(10.3)	(8.9)	(10.0)	(13.2)	(16.8)	(17.6)
Services net	0.0	0.1	(0.1)	0.3	1.3	2.2	2.8	2.4	4.2	3.7	4.5
Credit	2.4	2.8	3.0	3.4	4.4	6.0	7.7	8.1	9.3	8.1	9.8
Debit	(2.3)	(2.7)	(3.1)	(3.0)	(3.1)	(3.8)	(4.9)	(5.6)	(5.1)	(4.4)	(5.3)
Income net	(0.3)	(0.7)	(0.6)	(0.7)	(0.2)	(1.0)	(1.9)	(0.8)	0.3	1.1	1.0
Credit	0.3	0.4	0.5	0.4	0.6	0.9	0.9	1.3	1.9	2.1	1.9
Debit	(0.6)	(1.1)	(1.1)	(1.1)	(0.8)	(1.9)	(2.8)	(2.1)	(1.6)	(0.9)	(0.8)
Current Transfers net	2.8	2.5	4.9	3.1	4.4	5.4	7.1	4.3	3.7	5.0	4.2
Credit	2.8	2.5	4.9	3.1	4.4	5.4	7.1	4.6	3.9	5.2	4.2
Debit	0.0	0.0	0.0	0.0	0.0	(0.0)	0.0	(0.3)	(0.2)	(0.1)	(0.1)
Capital and Financial Account											
Capital Accounts Net	0.0	0.0	0.0	0.0	0.0	0.0	0.0	0.0	0.0	0.0	0.0
Financial Account	N/A	1.5	1.9	2.0	1.3	0.3	1.9	0.4	1.5	2.6	(1.1)
Direct Investments net	0.5	0.3	0.7	1.2	1.2	0.7	0.5	1.2	0.6	1.0	1.2
Abroad	0.0	0.0	0.0	0.0	0.0	0.0	0.0	0.0	0.0	0.0	0.0
Domestic	0.5	0.3	0.7	1.2	1.2	0.7	0.5	1.3	0.6	1.1	1.2
Portfolio Investment Net	(0.0)	0.0	0.0	0.0	0.0	0.0	0.0	0.0	0.5	(0.6)	0.3
Other Investments net	N/A	1.2	1.1	0.8	0.1	(0.4)	1.5	(0.8)	0.3	2.1	(2.6)
Net errors and omissions	0.1	0.1	0.0	(0.2)	(0.4)	0.6	0.7	0.3	(0.1)	(0.7)	0.6
Change in Reserve Assets	N/A	0.2	0.1	(0.1)	0.1	(1.1)	(5.4)	(0.7)	(1.2)	0.6	1.3

(Continued)

Exhibit 3.   *(Continued)*

(in $ Billions)	2001	2002	2003	2004	2005	2006	2007	2008	2009	2010	2011
Current Account	0.25	0.85	3.72	3.24	2.05	2.56	0.05	(1.30)	(3.19)	(4.92)	(5.22)
Goods net	(8.5)	(7.5)	(6.2)	(9.3)	(11.3)	(12.7)	(20.8)	(26.8)	(22.5)	(27.0)	(25.6)
Exports	7.2	7.3	9.0	12.3	16.1	20.5	24.5	29.8	23.1	25.0	27.6
Imports	(15.8)	(14.7)	(15.2)	(21.6)	(27.4)	(33.3)	(45.3)	(56.6)	(45.6)	(52.0)	(53.2)
Services net	3.9	4.5	6.5	8.3	7.5	8.7	11.2	14.3	13.2	15.5	11.9
Credit	9.0	9.3	11.1	13.6	14.6	16.1	19.9	24.9	21.5	23.8	18.8
Debit	(5.1)	(4.8)	(4.6)	(5.3)	(7.1)	(7.4)	(8.7)	(10.6)	(8.3)	(8.3)	(6.9)
Income net	0.7	(0.2)	(0.2)	(0.3)	0.1	0.8	1.5	1.4	(1.9)	(5.8)	(6.0)
Credit	1.5	0.7	0.6	0.6	1.4	2.6	3.3	3.1	1.0	0.5	0.3
Debit	(0.8)	(0.9)	(0.7)	(0.9)	(1.4)	(1.7)	(1.8)	(1.7)	(2.9)	(6.4)	(6.4)
Current Transfers net	4.1	4.0	3.6	4.6	5.7	5.8	8.2	9.8	8.0	12.5	14.5
Credit	4.2	4.0	3.7	4.6	5.8	5.9	8.4	10.1	8.3	12.9	15.0
Debit	(0.1)	(0.0)	(0.1)	(0.0)	(0.1)	(0.2)	(0.2)	(0.3)	(0.3)	(0.4)	(0.5)
Capital and Financial Account											
Capital Accounts Net	0.0	0.0	0.0	0.0	0.0	(0.0)	(0.0)	0.0	(0.0)	(0.0)	(0.0)
Financial Account	(0.4)	(3.0)	(4.9)	(2.8)	1.1	3.2	3.9	10.0	5.3	7.2	5.6
Direct Investments net	0.5	0.6	0.2	0.9	5.2	9.7	10.2	5.7	5.6	4.0	(0.8)
Abroad	(0.0)	(0.0)	(0.0)	(0.2)	(0.1)	(0.1)	(0.7)	(1.9)	(0.6)	(1.2)	(0.7)
Domestic	0.5	0.6	0.2	1.1	5.3	9.9	10.9	7.6	6.1	5.2	(0.1)
Portfolio Investment Net	(0.6)	0.3	(0.0)	(0.7)	(0.0)	0.3	2.2	(0.7)	(4.2)	(7.7)	(0.5)
Other Investments net	(0.3)	(3.8)	(5.1)	(3.0)	(4.0)	(6.8)	(8.5)	5.1	3.9	10.8	7.0
Net errors and omissions	(1.1)	1.9	1.6	0.0	(2.4)	0.6	0.3	(2.9)	0.4	(2.1)	1.5
Change in Reserve Assets	1.3	0.2	(0.4)	(0.4)	(0.8)	(6.4)	(4.2)	(5.8)	(2.5)	(0.1)	(1.9)

Source: Compiled by casewriters from the EUI Country Data and International Financial Statistics.

Note: "Other Investments" includes exceptional financing. Parentheses are used to indicate negative numbers.

Exhibit 4. Egyptian Government Finances

	2002	2003	2004	2005	2006	2007	2008	2009	2010	2011
Budget balance (% of GDP)	−8.7	−7.8	−9.7	−9.6	−8.2	−7.3	−6.8	−6.6	−8.1	−10.0
Budget revenue (% of GDP)	21.4	22.3	25.5	20.6	24.5	24.2	24.7	27.2	22.2	19.3
Budget expenditure (% of GDP)	30.2	30.0	31.6	30.0	33.6	29.8	31.5	33.8	30.3	29.3
Debt interest payments (% of GDP)	5.4	5.7	5.7	5.5	5.6	6.4	5.6	5.1	6.0	6.2
Primary balance (% of GDP)	−3.3	−2.0	−4.1	−4.1	−2.5	−0.9	−1.2	−1.6	−2.1	−3.8
Public Debt (% of GDP)	123.1	138.3	129.6	133.2	116.5	102.5	86.2	83.5	81.5	84.3

Source: Compiled using data from *International Financial Statistics*, International Monetary Fund; *EIU Country Data*, Economist Intelligence Unit.

Exhibit 5. Comparative Macro Statistics for Select Countries in the Middle East

Tunisia	
Real GDP Growth	3.7%
CPIA Transparency (1-6)	n/a
Unemployment (%)	13.0%
Current Account Balance (% of GDP)	-4.8%
Regime in Power for >20 yrs	✓
Youth (15-29) Percentage of Population >40%	✓

Egypt	
Real GDP Growth	5.1%
CPIA Transparency (1-6)	3.1
Unemployment (%)	9.0%
Current Account Balance (% of GDP)	-2.3%
Regime in Power for >20 yrs	✓
Youth (15-29) Percentage of Population >40%	✓

Syria	
Real GDP Growth	3.2%
CPIA Transparency (1-6)	2.5
Unemployment (%)	8.3%
Current Account Balance (% of GDP)	-0.7%
Regime in Power for >20 yrs	✓
Youth (15-29) Percentage of Population >40%	✓

Libya	
Real GDP Growth	3.3%
CPIA Transparency (1-6)	n/a
Unemployment (%)	n/a
Current Account Balance (% of GDP)	20.5%
Regime in Power for >20 yrs	✓
Youth (15-29) Percentage of Population >40%	✗

Saudi Arabia	
Real GDP Growth	4.1%
CPIA Transparency (1-6)	4.6
Unemployment (%)	10.5%
Current Account Balance (% of GDP)	14.9%
Regime in Power for >20 yrs	✓
Youth (15-29) Percentage of Population >40%	✓

Jordan	
Real GDP Growth	3.1%
CPIA Transparency (1-6)	n/a
Unemployment (%)	12.5%
Current Account Balance (% of GDP)	-4.8%
Regime in Power for >20 yrs	✓
Youth (15-29) Percentage of Population >40%	✓

Source: Economist Intelligence Unit (EIU) World Bank database, 2010, accessed February 2012.

Exhibit 6.   Egypt Demographics

	Broad Age Group (%)			
Year	0–14	15–64	65+	Total
1950	39.7	57.4	3.0	100.0
1955	40.9	56.1	3.0	100.0
1960	42.5	54.3	3.3	100.0
1965	43.5	52.3	4.1	100.0
1970	41.4	54.3	4.3	100.0
1975	40.9	54.9	4.2	100.0
1980	41.4	54.7	4.0	100.0
1985	41.8	54.4	3.8	100.0
1990	41.1	55.1	3.9	100.0
1995	38.8	57.1	4.2	100.0
2000	35.9	59.6	4.5	100.0
2005	33.6	61.7	4.8	100.0
2010	32.5	62.5	5.0	100.0
2015	31.4	63.0	5.5	100.0
2020	29.7	63.9	6.4	100.0
2025	27.6	64.9	7.4	100.0
2030	25.8	65.8	8.4	100.0
2035	24.4	66.6	9.0	100.0
2040	23.3	66.8	9.9	100.0
2045	22.1	66.5	11.4	100.0
2050	20.9	65.8	13.3	100.0

Source: Alyaa Awad and Ayman Zohry, "The End of Egypt Population Growth in the 21st Century: Challenges and Aspirations." The 35th Annual Conference on Population and Development Issues, http://www.zohry.com/pubs/alyaa.pdf, 2005. Last accessed on November 2011.

Exhibit 7.   Egypt's Past Presidents

President Mohamed Naguib (1953–1954)   **President Gamal Abdel Nasser (1954–1970)**

President Anwar El-Sadat (1970–1981)   **President Hosny Mubarak (1981–2011)**

Source: http://commons.wikimedia.org/wiki/Main_Page, accessed August 2012.

Exhibit 8. Post-Revolution Living Standard in Egypt

Living on Present Household Income
Among Egyptian adults

■ % Living comfortably   ■ % Getting by   ■ % Finding it difficult

□ % Finding it very difficult

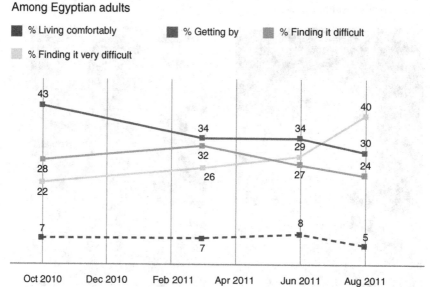

Have there been times in the last 12 months when you did not have enough money to buy food that you or your family needed?
Among Egyptian adults

■ Yes

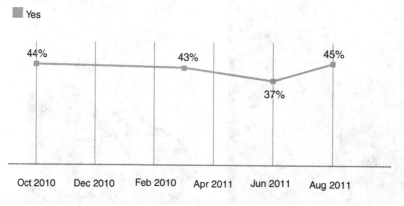

GALLUP

Source: Gallup poll, "More Egyptians finding it difficult to make ends meet," October 2011, http://www.gallup.com/poll/150356/Egyptians-Finding-Difficult-Ends-Meet.aspx?utm_source=add+this&utm_medium=addthis.com&utm_campaign=sharing#.Tq76ZySqcwY.facebook, accessed August 2012.

Exhibit 9. Historical Wheat Prices (1999–2011)

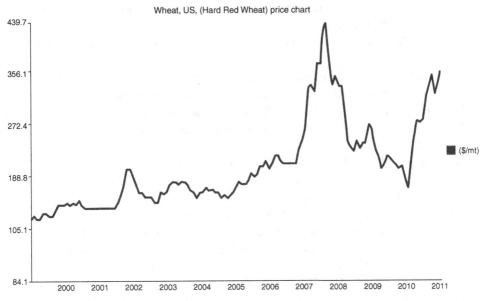

Source: Bloomberg.

Exhibit 10. Monthly Spending of Typical Egyptian Household (2010)

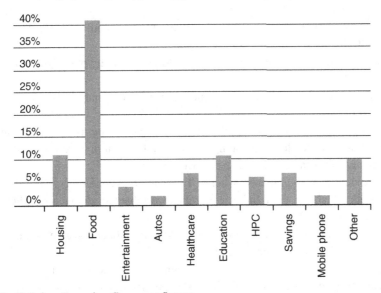

Source: Credit Suisse Emerging Consumer Survey.

Endnotes

[1] Dr. Assem Al-Desoky, "Major Landowners in Egypt: 1914–1952" (in Arabic, Dar Al-Shorouk, Cairo, 2007), quoted in Egypt on the Brink by Tarek Osman, Yale University Press, 2010, p. 45.

[2] M.A. Abu-Zeid and F. Z. El-Shibini (1997), Egypt's High Aswan Dam, *Water Resources Development*, Vol. 13, No. 2, pp. 209–217.

[3] Ibrahim G. Aoude, from national bourgeois development to Infitah: Egypt 1952–1992. Arab Studies Quarterly via Military and Government Collection database, 1994.

[4] World Bank Database, http://data.worldbank.org/, Accessed August 2012.

[5] Giles Keppel, *Muslim Extremism in Egypt: The Prophet and Pharaoh*, (California: University of California Press, 2003).

[6] Giles Keppel, *Muslim Extremism in Egypt: The Prophet and Pharaoh*.

[7] Marvin Weinbaum (1986), *Dependent Development and US economic aid to Egypt*, (Cambridge University Press, 1986).

[8] Egyptian Ministry of Finance, Public Expenditure figures for 2010–2011.

[9] Andrew Ross, Egypt's military, an economic giant, now in charge. http://articles.sfgate.com/2011-02-13/business/28532476_1_egyptian-economy-egypt-s-ge-sharm.

[10] Karima Korayem, *The Rural-Urban Income Gap in Egypt and Biased Agricultural Pricing Policy*, (California: University of California Press, 1981).

[11] NationMaster, "Immigrants as percentage of state population (most recent) by country", http://www.nationmaster.com/graph/imm_imm_pop_imm_as_per_of_sta_pop-immigrant-population-immigrants-percentage-state.

[12] "Egyptian Elections: Opposition Alleges Fraud," November 29, 2010, Associated Press, http://www.guardian.co.uk/world/2010/nov/29/egyptian-opposition-alleges-election-fraud, Accessed August 2012.

[13] Paul Schemm, "Egypt cafe owner describes police beating death", The San Diego Union-Tribune, 2011.

[14] Maggie Michael, "Constitutional Amendments Approved in Egypt Referendum," *Toronto Star*, March 11, 2001.

[15] Gamal Essam ElDin, "Egypt's Constitution: A controversial declaration" ElAhram Egypt, 2011.

[16] Gallup, Egyptian Revolution poll. http://www.gallup.com/poll/150356/Egyptians-Finding-Difficult-EndsMeet.aspx?utm_source=add+this&utm_medium=addthis.com&utm_campaign=sharing#.Tq76ZySqcwY.facebook.

[17] Mounir Abdel-Nour, Egyptian Minister of Tourism, press conference, May 2011.

[18] World Bank Database, Gini Index, http://data.worldbank.org/indicator/SI.POV.GINI/, Accessed November 2011.

[19] CIA World Factbook, https://www.cia.gov/library/publications/the-world-factbook/geos/eg.html, Accessed November 2011.

[20] EIU Egypt Country Report: Finance. http://country.eiu.com.ezp-prod1.hul.harvard.edu/FileHandler.ashx?issue_id=48710789&mode=pdf, Accessed August 2012.

21 Bank Andi, "The Egypt Economic Report," http://www.menafn.com/updates/research_center/Egypt/Economic/audi180411.pdf, April 2011.

22 Ashraf Swelam "Egypt's 2010 Parlimentary Elections: The Landslide" at http://www.yale.edu/worldfellows/fellows/documents/OccassionalPaper2-Egypt2010ParliamentaryElectionsTheLandslide.pdf, Accessed August 2012.

Peru: Family Groups and Competitiveness

Diego Comin, Gabriel Grados, Jiro Hiraoka and Silvia Luque

Country Background

Geography

Peru is the third largest country in South America in size (see **Exhibit 1**). The Peruvian population, estimated at 30 million, is a multiethnic mix of Amerindians, Europeans, Africans, and Asians.

The Andes divide the country into three main regions. The arid coastal region produces crops, such as sugar and cotton, under irrigation and is the most populous and richest region in per capita terms. The jungle comprises both the tropical rainforest and the eastern mountain slopes. The highlands are made up of the areas in the Andes above 2,000 masl.[a] In some of the highlands' valleys, farmers owning relatively small plots prosper supplying food for consumption to the cities or for exports. In some other areas, however, Indians practice subsistence farming.[1]

History

Peru is the birthplace of the Inca Empire. From their base in Cusco, the Incas extended over a vast region from northern Ecuador to central Chile. Andean societies were based on agriculture, camelid husbandry and fishing.[2] These societies had no notion of market or money so organization relied on reciprocity and redistribution.

---

[a]masl: meters above sea level.

Exhibit 1. Map of Peru

Source: Courtesy of the University of Texas Libraries, the University of Texas at Austin.

In search of Inca wealth, the Spanish Crown conquered Peru in the 16th century and established the Viceroyalty of Peru. Individuals favored by the Spanish viceroys were given "encomiendas". The latter were extensions of land that entitled the owner to collect tribute from a group of Indians who inhabited that land in exchange for guaranteeing their spiritual welfare. Indians were, in principle, allowed to keep the land they cultivated and use the produce to pay this tribute. However, idle land belonged to the Crown, which either granted or sold it to individuals. This allowed the Crown to take over land as Indians were relocated or as their numbers dwindled due to disease. The result was the creation of relatively large landholdings, called "haciendas", similar to plantations.

Peru declared independence from Spain in 1821, but it was in 1824 that the Spanish capitulated. By that time, Lima had become one of the most distinguished and aristocratic colonial cities in the Americas.

The military has been prominent in Peruvian history ever since independence. Coups have repeatedly interrupted civilian constitutional government. Even in the 20th century, the military took control during the coups of 1914, 1930, 1948, 1962 and 1968. The military played a crucial role in Peru's border disputes with Bolivia, Chile and Ecuador, whose boundaries were left unclear at independence. The biggest of these disputes was the War of the Pacific (1879–1883) between Peru, Bolivia and Chile.

The most recent period of military rule (1968–1979) began when General Velasco Alvarado overthrew elected President Belaunde Terry and took power with a left-wing nationalist agenda. Velasco's government resulted in an extensive land reform program and extensive nationalizations. Government spending and foreign borrowing significantly increased and the regime ended with a coup in 1975, when General Francisco Morales Bermudez became president. In 1979, Morales Bermudez called for a Constitutional Assembly and in May 1980 elections were held with Belaunde Terry as victor.

The 1980's were a decade of economic and social instability. The fall in international commodity prices, a debt crisis, a particularly severe El Niño[b] and political violence took their toll on the economy.[3] The economic collapse was reflected in worsening living conditions and provided a breeding ground for sociopolitical discontent. Guerrilla violence flourished, with Sendero Luminoso (Shining Path), a Maoist group, and Movimiento Revolucionario Tupac Amaru (MRTA), a pro-Cuban group.[4] The terrorists were financed in part from alliances with drug dealers, who had established strongholds in the Amazon.

In the 1985 general election Alan Garcia Perez, from the APRA[c] political party, took office. His unorthodox economic policies initially generated high GDP growth rates, but eventually led to hyperinflation and increased poverty. In 1987 a move to nationalize the banking system rallied the opposition. Mr. Garcia's economic policies in the late 1980s were a disaster, and by 1990 annualized inflation reached levels close to 10,000%.[5]

---

[b]A global weather phenomenon that disrupts fisheries and agriculture.
[c]"Alianza Popular Revolucionaria Americana" or Popular American Revolutionary Alliance.

The government of Alberto Fujimori (1990–2000) led a major crackdown on terrorism, ended hyperinflation, and liberalized the economy. However, discontent rose over his government's abuses of power and the government collapsed over a corruption scandal.

The two subsequent governments, led by Alejandro Toledo (2001–2006) and Alan Garcia (2006–2011), were successful in consolidating macroeconomic stability. Toledo's administration (2001–2006) was largely able to maintain a broadly orthodox economic policy direction, helping the government to keep a falling trend in the deficit. Peru's GDP grew at an average real rate of more than 4.7% per year during 2000–2008.

Ollanta Humala, a retired army commander, was elected president in June 2011 with a mandate to increase social spending and improve public services in order to reduce still high levels of poverty and inequality. A portion of the population was afraid of new political measures that could effectively increase government power in many industries, yet after two years the government had not changed the economic system. Humala maintained a pragmatic and broadly centrist policy stance and supported the private sector.

Economic Structure of Peru

Economic policy in the early 1990s focused on foreign direct investment led growth. The government encouraged private investment. The principal stimulus was the privatization program, which included sales of state companies in telecommunications, banking, tourism, diversified, ports, airports and infrastructure. The country embarked on a series of reforms that included fiscal consolidation, trade openness, exchange rate flexibility, financial liberalization, higher reliance on market signals and prudent monetary policy. Investment-led economic growth was strong.[6]

In terms of GDP growth, the Peruvian economy has outperformed virtually all other Latin American economies since 2001. After growing by an average of 5.8% between 2000 and 2011, GDP increased in 6.4% in 2012 (see **Exhibit 2**). This strong economic performance increased Peru's income per capita by more than 50% between 2000 and 2011, after almost 30 years of stagnation between 1960 and 1990.[7]

In 2012, public debt as a share of GDP was 19.8%, including local government debt. The main rating agencies, Standard & Poor's, Fitch, and Moody's, upgraded Peruvian sovereign debt to investment grade level. Exports increased six times in nominal terms between 1999 and 2011, growing from 14.8% of GDP to 28.7%.

Exhibit 2. GDP Breakdown Evolution (1991–2011)

Growth per year (%)	1991	1995	2000	2001	2002	2003	2004	2005	2006	2007	2008	2009	2010	2011
I. Internal Demand	3.4	11.9	2.3	−0.4	4.1	3.7	3.8	5.8	10.3	11.8	12.3	−2.8	13.1	7.2
a. Private Consumption	3.4	9.7	3.7	1.5	4.9	3.4	3.6	4.6	6.4	8.3	8.7	2.4	6.0	6.4
b. Public Consumption	2.0	8.5	3.1	−0.8	0.0	4.0	4.6	8.5	7.6	4.5	2.1	16.5	10.0	4.8
c. Internal investment	4.2	20.3	−2.7	−7.1	2.9	4.7	4.3	9.2	26.5	25.8	25.8	−20.6	36.3	10.0
i. Private	−0.2	27.3	−1.7	−4.7	0.2	6.3	8.1	12.0	20.1	23.3	25.9	−15.1	22.1	11.7
ii. Public	8.5	7.2	−15.8	−22.4	−4.1	3.9	6.1	13.8	20.7	18.9	33.6	21.2	27.3	−17.8
II. Exports[a]	5.8	5.5	8.0	6.8	7.5	6.2	15.2	15.2	0.8	6.9	8.2	−3.2	1.3	8.8
III. Imports[a]	17.2	27.1	3.8	2.9	2.3	4.2	9.6	10.9	13.1	21.4	20.1	−18.6	24.0	9.8
IV. GDP	2.1	8.6	3.0	0.2	5.0	4.0	5.0	6.8	7.7	8.9	9.8	0.9	8.8	6.9

Source: Banco Central de Reserva (BCR).

[a]Non-financial goods and services.

The economy emerged largely intact from the global recession, supported by strong fundamentals and a proactive macroeconomic response.

Peru's Central Bank maintains an inflation targeting regime in a credible and efficient manner. As a result, private sector expectations are anchored.[8] The private sector was the main engine of growth, increasing gross investment.

Growth has been reflected in higher employment, higher consumption capacity and better infrastructure. Large retail outlets are currently enacting aggressive, nationwide expansion strategies to meet growing demand.[9] However, there are still several weaknesses in Peru's business environment. The three main ones are sub par institutions, a rigid labor market and a low skilled workforce.

Inequality: The strong growth decreased the national poverty rate from 48.5% in 2004 to 27.8% in 2011 (see **Exhibit 3**). However, inequality has remained high with a Gini coefficient of 49% (2009). When compared with other countries in the

Exhibit 3. Evolution of Poverty Rates (%)

Year	Poverty
1991	54.0
1994	47.0
1995	45.3
1996	44.1
1997	42.7
1998	42.4
1999	47.5
2000	48.4
2001	54.8
2002	54.3
2003	52.0
2004	48.6
2005	48.7
2006	44.5
2007	39.3
2008	36.2
2009	34.8
2010	31.3
2011[a]	29.0
2012[a]	27.8

Source: Instituto Nacional de Estadistica e Informatica (INEI).
[a]2011 and 2012 are projected figures.

region, Peru ranks 4th behind Argentina, Uruguay and Mexico in 2010. Although there has been a decrease since the 56% level of 2001–2002, the improvement is not as dramatic when compared to 1990s' data in the high 40s, low 50s. When compared to the USA' Gini coefficient, often quoted to be between 45–49%, there does not seem to be much room for improvement, yet given Peru's history of social unrest, Peru's benchmarks should be European countries in the low 40s, high 30s. Poverty is more acute in the highlands and the scarcely populated Amazon region. In 2011,

Exhibit 4. Peru Main Macroeconomic Indicators

	2008	2009	2010	2011	2012	2013(f)	2014(f)
GDP							
Nominal GDP (US$ billion)	126.9	127	153.9	176.7	199.5	225.2	247.8
Nominal GDP (Ns billion)	371	382	435	487	526	573	625
Real GDP growth (%)	9.8	0.9	8.8	6.9	6.3	6.2	5.9
Expenditure on GDP (% real change)							
Private Consumption	8.7	2.4	6	6.4	5.8	5.9	5.2
Government Consumption	2.1	16.5	10	4.8	10.6	6.4	5.6
Gross Fixed Investment	27.1	−9.2	23.2	5.1	14.9	11.3	9
Exports Goods & Services	8.2	−3.2	1.3	8.8	4.8	5.3	6.6
Imports Good & Services	20.1	−18.6	24	9.8	10.4	10.4	9.2
Origin of GDP (% real change)							
Agriculture	7.2	2.3	4.3	3.8	5.2	3.6	4.5
Industry	10.2	−2.7	11.1	4.2	6	6.1	4.2
Services	10	2.3	8.4	11.8	6.5	6.5	6.7
Population and income							
Population (m)	29.2	29.6	30	30.4	30.8	31.2	31.6
GDP/capita (US$ at PPP)	8,457	8,487	9,231	9,946	10,615	11,323	12,054
Unemployment (av; %)	8.1	8.9	6.6	7.9	7.7	7.7	7.6
Fiscal indicators (% of GDP)							
Public-sector balance	2.4	−1.8	−0.4	2	2.1	1.1	0.8
Public-sector debt interest payments	1.6	1.3	1.2	1	1	1	0.9
Net public debt	22.9	25	21.9	19.9	16.6	14.5	12.8
Prices and financial indicators							
FX Ns: US$ (end-period)	3.14	2.89	2.81	2.7	2.55	2.53	2.52
CPI (av; % change)	5.8	2.9	1.5	3.4	3.7	2.4	2.8
PPI (av; % change)	8.9	−1.8	1.8	6.3	1.8	1.7	3.3
M1 (% change)	9.7	4.9	21.2	12.6	21.8	8.9	9
M2 (% change)	22.9	2.7	21.7	9.7	13.7	15.1	9.7

(Continued)

Exhibit 4.   (*Continued*)

	2008	2009	2010	2011	2012	2013(f)	2014(f)
Current account (US$ m)							
Trade balance	2,569	5,950	6,750	9,302	4,527	4,949	5,538
Goods: exports fob	31,018	26,962	35,565	46,269	45,639	49,461	52,948
Goods: imports fob	−28,449	−21,010	−28,815	−36,968	−41,113	−44,513	−47,410
Services balance	−2,056	−1,176	−2,345	−2,133	−2,258	−2,701	−3,003
Income balance	−8,774	−7,483	−10,053	−13,710	−12,701	−14,676	−16,654
Current transfers balance	2,942	2,887	3,027	3,199	3,296	3,948	4,344
Current-account balance	−5,286	−723	−3,782	−3,341	−7,137	−8,480	−9,776
External debt (US$ m)							
Debt stock	34,720	37,337	41,816	44,872	46,330	46,901	47,140
Debt service paid	5,263	4,365	6,789	3,310	6,098	4,181	4,054
Principal repayments	3,265	2,221	4,060	1,395	5,269	3,357	3,219
International reserves (US$ m)							
Total International Reserves	31,254	33,230	44,213	48,929	65,102	68,099	70,364

Source: Economist Intelligence Unit.

while the poverty rate was only 18.0% in urban areas, it stood at 56.1% in rural areas.

Yet consumer spending — fueled by easily approved bank loans and credit cards — is lifting more people out of poverty as the lower middle class expands. The government has ambitious goals to eradicate extreme poverty. In 2012, Humala announced plans to boost spending on social issues in order to reduce poverty to less than 15% by 2016. The government's program aims to provide equal access to basic services, employment and social security, reduce extreme poverty, reduce social conflicts, reduce environmental damage, and focus on social inclusion.

Principal industries: Mining lies at the heart of Peru's economic boom. It accounts for a large portion of exports and around 30% of total tax revenues. Peru is the world's largest producer of silver, the third largest producer of copper and zinc and the sixth largest producer of gold. The real value of mining output rose by 6.8% in 2012 and strong gains are expected in the medium term.[10]

The agricultural sector employs 7.5% of the work force. Most farming is for subsistence but the sector is also an important earner of foreign exchange. Peru is the world's sixth largest producer of coffee and exports more than 90% of its production. Other than coffee, farm exports include asparagus, table grapes, mangoes, avocados, prepared artichokes, paprika and evaporated milk.[11]

Corruption

Peru has high levels of corruption. According to the 2012 Corruption Perception Index,[d] Peru ranks 83 out of 176 counties, with a score of 38 (score of 0 means that the country is perceived as highly corrupt). While Peru's score and ranking is similar to the ones of Brazil (score: 43), Colombia (score: 36), Argentina (score: 35), Mexico (score: 34), Bolivia (score: 34) and Ecuador (score: 32), it is significantly higher than the score and rankings of Chile (score: 72), USA (score: 73).

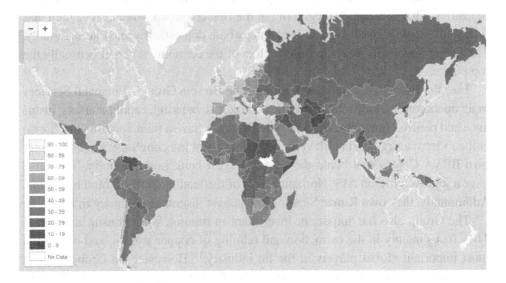

Family Groups

Grupo Brescia

The Brescia Group's founder was Mr. Fortunato Brescia Tassano, an Italian immigrant who arrived to the port of Callao, Peru in 1889. Since then, the Group has become one of (if not) the largest, most diversified and powerful business group in the country, with investments ranging from explosives to financial services.

The Group's origins were in real estate. After saving money from working at a small Italian shop in Callao, Mr. Fortunato Brescia decided to purchase a piece of agricultural land nearby Lima in order to supply Italian shops with products. Mr. Fortunato Brescia worked hard for two decades, he decided to expand

---

[d]The Corruption Perceptions Index ranks countries and territories based on how corrupted their public sector is perceived to be. A country or territory's score indicates the perceived level of public sector corruption on a scale of 0–100, where 0 means that a country is perceived as highly corrupt and 100 means it is perceived as very clean. A country's rank indicates its position relative to the other countries and territories included in the index. The 2012 index includes 176 countries and territories. http://cpi.transparency.org/cpi2012/results/.

his business and acquire more land. That is how in 1913, he purchased "Fundo Limatambo", which was four times larger than his original land and then continued acquiring land for the next several years. As the city of Lima grew in the 1930s, Mr. Brescia's agricultural land, which were located in the peripheries of the city, multiplied its value significantly due to its urbanization potential.[12]

The Group's investments in other industries started after Mr. Fortunato passed away in 1952 and his sons, Pedro and Mario Brescia Cafferata took over the helm of the company. During the 1960s, they decided to invest in the fishery and mining industries. That was just the beginning of the Brescia group, which, since then, has followed a very successful expansive strategy both domestically and internationally. The Group now owns assets in most sectors of the economy where it is usually the top player.

Like the Romero and Interbank groups, the Brescia Group's Financial Services main operations include retail banking, commercial banking, capital markets, insurance and pension fund management. The Brescia's have a joint venture with Banco Bilbao Vizcaya Argentaria (BBVA), the Spanish banking conglomerate, and jointly own BBVA Continental bank, the second largest bank in the country. They also have a joint venture on AFP Horizonte, one of the leading pension fund managers. Additionally, they own Rimac Seguros, the largest insurance company in Peru.

The Group also has important investment in mining, with Minsur and Raura. They focus mainly in the extraction and refining of copper and tin, and one of the most important global players in the tin industry.[13] However, the Group's assets don't only lie in these two sectors (see **Exhibit 5**), they are greatly diversified across other industries such as real estate (one of the largest real estate owners in Lima), hospitality (Libertador is one of the most hotel local chains), fishing (TASA is the largest fish meal producer in the world), health, paint and explosives. In the past few years, the group has begun an internationalization strategy with the $374 million acquisition of Taboca[14] (a Brazilian tin mine) and the $555 million acquisition of Melon[15] (a cement producer in Chile).

Brescia family members have always closely run the portfolio of companies in the Group. However, during the past decade, the tightly managed family group made a strategic decision to professionalize its operations and created a corporate center, which is run by non-family professionals. This corporate center has allowed them to exploit synergies across its portfolio of companies and better define their strategic direction. The Brescia Group has always been characterized of working extensively without creating any buzz, almost secretively one could argue (they don't even have a web page describing their holdings). But that has changed in the past decade, the Brescia Group has been one of the most active players in the Peruvian economy, investing hefty sums to develop projects or acquire competitors and has been a regular in the newspaper headlines. The Group has been recently renamed as "Breca Group", although it will take time for this name to settle on everyone's minds.

Exhibit 5. Family Groups' Companies and Sectors

Industry	Grupo Interbank	Grupo Romero	Grupo Brescia
Banking	Interbank	BCP	BBVA Continental
Insurance	Interseguro	Pacifico	Rimac
Pension Funds	AFP Interactiva (project)	Prima AFP	AFP Horizonte
Hospitality	Casa Andina		Intursa (Libertador)
Retail[a]	Supermercados Peruanos, Inkafarma, Real Plaza, Oeschle, Promart, Cineplanet, Bembos, China Wok, Popeye's, Papa Johns, Dunkin Donuts, Don Belisario[b]	MX Gestion Inmobiliaria (Multimercados Zonales)	Cubica Gestora Inmobiliaria (Mall Centers and Strip Malls)
Real Estate	Urbi	Centenario	Cubica
Health		Pacifico	Clinica Internacional
Education	Innova Schools		
CPG		Alicorp/Industrias del Aceite	
Manufacturing	Peruplast	Universal Textil/ Industrial Textil	EXSA (explosives), CPPQ (paint)
Logistics		Ransa	
Ports & maritime services		Terminal Internacional del Sur/Consorcio Naviero Peruano/ Tramarsa	
Ethanol		Caña Brava	
Agriculture/ Fishing		Palmas del Espino/ Pesquera Centinela	TASA, Hoja Redonda, BVO
Mining			Minsur, Raura, Taboca (Brazil)
Gas Station		Primax	
Cement			Melon (Chile)

Source: Case authors.

[a]Includes Shopping Centers.

[b]Brand names of supermarkets, pharmacies, shopping centers, department stores, home improvement stores, movie theaters, restaurants.

Grupo Interbank

Grupo Interbank is one of Peru's largest business groups, present in the financial services, retail, real estate, manufacturing, hospitality and education sectors. Interbank was incorporated in Lima in 1897 and formerly conducted business under the names Banco Internacional del Peru S.A. and Interbank. In 1944, the

International Petroleum Company acquired a controlling equity interest in Interbank and remained in control until 1967, when it entered into a joint venture with Chemical Bank New York Trust & Co. In 1970, Interbank was transferred to the Peruvian government as part of the then military government's banking reform. In August 1994, as part of the government's privatization efforts, 91% of Interbank's capital stock was acquired by Corporacion Interbank, which was owned by a group of investors led by Carlos Rodriguez–Pastor Mendoza, father of the Group's current chairman.[16]

Grupo Interbank's growth started in 1998, year in which the Group founded a Private Equity firm (Nexus Group) to identify, analyze and incubate new investments projects for the Group. Since 1998, the Group has expanded into six economic sectors and 15 business segments (see **Exhibit 5**).

Given the recent growth and relevance of this group, its importance is better understood by assessing its current business segments. At its core lies its financial services operations that include retail banking, commercial banking, capital markets and insurance.

Interbank is a full service bank providing to retail and commercial customers. After the acquisition by Intercorp in 1994, Interbank began conducting business under the name "Interbank" as part of a re-branding effort. Interbank has transformed itself into one of Peru's leading consumer finance providers and one of the country's most innovative banks, focusing mainly on retail banking and its convenient deposit gathering and distribution channels. In April 2001, Interbank acquired Banco Latino S.A.'s (at that time Peru's fifth largest bank) assets and liabilities, and in September 2002, purchased Aval Card Peru S.A.'s credit card portfolio. Over the four years ended in 2011, Interbank was one of the fastest growing banks in Peru, with net income growing at a compound annual growth rate of 25.9%.[17]

Interseguro was formed in 1998 as a joint venture between Intercorp and Bankers Trust. As a leading insurance company, Interseguro is active in the annuity and personal life insurance businesses. During 2008 Interseguro entered into the general insurance segment with success, concentrating on credit and debit card protection. Since its inception, the company has registered a compounded annual asset growth rate of 45.5%, higher than the 15.4% industry average. In the specific segment of annuities, Interseguro's main focus, the company remains a historic leader with a 25.3% market share of all annuities sold since 1996.[18]

Grupo Interbank's retail operations have leading market positions in the following business segments: supermarkets, pharmacies, shopping centers, movie theaters, department stores, home improvement stores and fast food chains. Through a combination of acquisitions and aggressive organic growth that capitalize on the major transformation of the Peruvian consumer markets, the Group has established a leading integrated platform with No. 1 or No. 2 market positions across several of the business segments[19]:

- The supermarket chain is the second largest in Peru, based on revenues, and operates four formats that together target multiple socioeconomic categories of the Peruvian population.[20]
- The pharmacy chain is the largest in Peru, based on revenues, and operates the most recognized pharmacy brand in the country.[21]
- Through the Real Plaza shopping center brand, Grupo Interbank operates the largest shopping center chain in Peru, based on gross leasable area ("GLA"). Between 2001 and 2011, Grupo Interbank developed 13 shopping centers throughout Peru, reaching over 252,000 square meters of GLA in 2011.[22]
- The movie theater chain is the largest in Peru, based on revenues and number of screens. It has more than 50% of the total movie theater screens of Peru.

In 1998, Grupo Interbank founded Urbi Propiedades, a Real Estate company that manages and develops commercial and residential projects in Peru. Urbi Propiedades develops and owns real estate properties that contribute to the Group's retail businesses through a large portfolio of premium locations and sites for future expansion.

Founded in 2003, Casa Andina has quickly become the most important hotel group in Peru, in terms of annual income and quantity of hotels, rooms and destinations covered. Currently, Casa Andina boasts a portfolio of 20 hotels.[23]

Grupo Interbank owns K–12 schools and two universities in Peru. Innova Schools is a school chain that offers high-quality preschool, primary, and secondary education with modern infrastructure at affordable prices to the country's emerging middle class.[24] Innova Schools was acquired in 2010. As of June 2012, the schools are present in ten Lima districts and reach 5,200 students. In 2012, the groups acquired controlling stakes in two Peruvian universities, UTP and UTCH.

In 2007, Grupo Interbank acquired Peruplast, the largest flexible packaging converter in Peru, in a joint venture with the Luksic Group, a Chilean economic group.

Grupo Romero

Grupo Romero is one of the best known and most traditional family groups in Peru. Its origins can be traced back to 1886 when Calixto Romero established an export business focused on Panama Hats in Catacaos, a small town north of Lima.[25] Although the business grew slowly at first, after 1891 the business benefited from rapid growth in hat demand and a cheap labor force. Thanks to his initial successful business, Mr. Romero entered cotton production and cotton production financing by 1908. The financing of cotton plantations and eventual default of many of these, let Romero appropriate the lands of former cotton producers. Cotton remained the family's main business until 1951, when they had to diversify as a result of increasing international competition and growing complexity of the cotton market. By 1970, the family group had created a new bank (Banco Continental)[e] and increased its non-controlling stake in Banco de Credito (BCP).

The turbulent times that began with General Velasco's coup in 1968 both benefited and damaged the group. It lost 50% of its assets as the result of nationalizations, yet it had already expanded beyond cotton. The group became the main recipient of development aid as its productive activities were concentrated outside of Lima; in the rural areas that the government wanted to develop. The most important victory, however, was the control of BCP as the result of the forced reduction of foreign ownership and the Romero's increasing power in the BCP board. BCP quickly became the family's flagship company and today the bank controls 35% of loans and 37% of deposits.[f] Politics did not settle after Velasco and when Alan Garcia came to power in 1985, the group was able to survive a new wave of nationalizations with political and business acumen. Later, in the 1990s when Alberto Fujimori opened Peru's economy to the world, the group faced increased competition, yet it had already established its influence in the financial, insurance, textile, agricultural and logistics industries. The second flagship company, Alicorp, was developed in the late 90s as the result of the acquisition and consolidation of foreigners' assets helped by cheap valuations as the result of the Mexican and Asian crisis which promoted the exit of multinationals from the Peruvian economy.

Today the Romero group operates in 13 different industries, owns at least 60 companies in Peru and 25 abroad and has annual revenues of US$4.5 billion,[g] of which BCP represents 39% and Alicorp 36%.[26, 27] Although the group's international experience is not recent, since 2000 it accelerated its international expansion using a two pronged approach. On the consumer industry, with Alicorp it has acquired consumer companies in Argentina, Bolivia, Canada, Chile, China, Colombia, Ecuador, Guatemala, Haiti, Honduras, Nicaragua and the U.S. and it has top five market shares in all the segments of the Latin American markets where it operates. International growth continues as Alicorp entered the Brazilian market with the recent US$97 million acquisition of Santa Amalia in February 2013.[28] On the financial services industry, BCP in 2012 acquired two boutique investment banks in Colombia and Chile with the aim of developing a new regional investment bank initially in the Andean region and in Latin America later on. BCP already operated as a commercial bank or representative office in the US, Panama and Bolivia since the late 1990s.

---

[e]Not related to Grupo BBVA Banco Continental, 50% owned the Brescia family.
[f]As of December 2012 (http://www.sbs.gob.pe — Accessed on January 2013).
[g]Fiscal year 2011.

Assessment of Competitiveness in the Retail and Financial Industries

In order to understand the effects, if any, that the family groups had and have in the Peruvian economy, the retail and financial industries offer the best case studies since these industries exhibit the highest importance and market share by family group owned companies. Given the large proportion of revenues that family groups derive from retail and financial operations, these industries can reflect the effect of large family owned conglomerates in competitiveness.

The Shopping Center (Retail) Sector

Importance of malls as an indicator of development

Historically, retail sales in Peru had been done in small mom and pop stores or street vendors (commonly referred to as traditional retail). Until the 1990s, few retail chains (or modern retail) existed and the number of malls in the country could be counted in one hand. However, the country's economic development during the latter half of the 1990s and the beginning of the new century, attracted local and foreign investors to the retail industry, as a growing middle class had increasing spending needs and patterns. This trend exploded in the second half of the 2000s, when the industry caught the attention of the large economic groups, which decided to heavily invest in expanding the retail sector through the construction of new malls.

Peru has seen a shift from buying from informal street vendors to buying from local and international formal companies, from buying in the street to a clean and closed environment with air conditioned, from haggling to one price, from doubting the precedence of the product to brands and guarantee. Modern retail has helped in the formalization of jobs and to decrease tax evasion by increasing formal commerce. Most importantly shopping malls have become a sign of prestige and prosperity for any town or city. Peruvian marketing expert Rolando Arellano mentioned: "A few years ago, the biggest symbol of prestige for a province, after having electric lighting and a road, was to have a National Bank agency. Later it was a university. Now, the new symbol of progress is a supermarket, or even better, a shopping mall. It is very important to consider the immense contribution to the perception of well-being to the provinces that a shopping mall generates". Likewise, the major of Huacho, a small town outside of Lima declared: "Plaza del Sol Huacho (from Grupo Romero) will significantly improve the quality of life of the population, because they will have a modern and safe shopping mall, which has international standards".[29] Regarding jobs, the President of the Chamber of Commerce of Piura said: "With the opening of the new shopping malls in Piura, the price of the surrounding land will appreciate and new job positions will be generated".[30]

Growth and competitiveness

The number of outlets has increased dramatically in Peru in the past decade. From a mere seven malls in 2000 concentrated in Lima (only one outside of the capital), the sector exploded to 55 malls by 2012, distributed all around Peru. From these 55 malls, 34 where located in Lima and 21 in provinces, and the trend if for a majority of new openings to be outside of Lima (see **Exhibit 6**). Likewise, sales through malls also experienced dramatic growth, in 2000 sales were $1.76 billion[31] and by 2012 they had reached $5.2 billion (see **Exhibit 7**). This growth trend had an important impact on the Peruvian's buying behavior, and by 2011, sales through retail malls represented 48% of all modern retail sales and 14% of the commerce component of the GDP.

This rapid expansion in shopping malls was led by the Peruvian family groups, especially by the Grupo Interbank and Grupo Romero which have been the pioneers on investing in provinces, in a time when other local and international groups were still hesitant to invest outside of Lima. The major of Juliaca, a poor town located at 3,824 meters of altitude in the Andes, explains the opportunity that these two pioneer groups saw first: "The inauguration of the Real Plaza Juliaca (of Grupo Interbank) demonstrates the interest of commercial operators for cities that are still unexploited in terms of modern retail".[32]

But even with this spectacular growth, Peru still is far behind other Latin American countries. As seen in **Exhibit 8**, in 2011, the Latin American average was 2.5 malls per 1 million inhabitants. Peru was below this average and only had 1.5 malls per 1 million inhabitants. Multiple mall projects have already been

Exhibit 6. Evolution: Number of Malls in Lima and the Rest of Peru

	2000	2001	2002	2003	2004	2005	2006	2007	2008	2009	2010	2011	2012
Lima	6	8	10	10	11	14	15	15	18	21	24	27	34
Provinces	1	1	2	2	3	3	4	6	10	10	12	17	21
Total	7	9	12	12	14	17	19	21	28	31	36	44	55

Source: Peruvian Shopping Center Association, Report Shopping Centers as a key for development.

Exhibit 7. Evolution: Sales in Malls

	2008	2009	2010	2011	2012
Sales (million USD)	2,290	2,519	3,189	4,427	5,211
Growth		43%	10%	27%	39%	18%

Source: Peruvian Shopping Center Association, Report on Data, keys and investment opportunities in a growing industry, 2012.

Exhibit 8. Mall Development in the Region (2011)

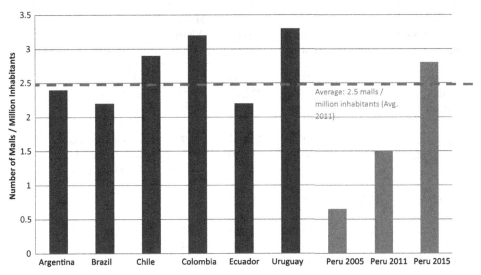

Source: Peruvian Shopping Center Association, Report Shopping Centers and inclusion.

announced and several are under construction, and the Peruvian economy is expected to continue its strong growth trajectory in the upcoming years, strengthening the middle class. For these reasons, experts estimate that Peru will surpass the Latin American average by 2015, and reach 2.8 malls per million inhabitants (considering that the average stays at 2.5). It is important to notice that until 2005, this figure was a mere 0.6 malls per million inhabitants. This year marked the entry of two large family groups (Interbank and Brescia) into the sector and they have become key players in expanding the industry and will continue to do so, having already announced multiple openings for 2013.

Presence of Family Groups

The large economic groups have been very active participants in the Mall sector and they have been responsible for fueling the growth (see **Exhibit 9**).

Grupo Romero: Through its MZ Gestion Inmobiliaria subsidiary, it has been the pioneer in this sector, starting operations in 1999 with its Minka mall, a large shopping complex catered towards the lower and middle income population. Minka still remain one of the biggest shopping centers in Peru, it started with only 150 stores in 50,000 squared meters and has grown to more than 1,000 stores in almost 115,000 squared meters. Additionally, Grupo Romero operated four other malls under its "Plaza del Sol" and "Plaza de la Luna" brands, all located outside of Lima. This is particularly important because the Grupo Romero were the first ones to invest

Exhibit 9.   Sector Breakdown by Players

Family/Business group	Country	Year of entry	Area for Lease	Market Share (%)	Brands	Number of Malls
Interbank	Peru	2005	262,000	17%	Real Plaza	11
Falabella	Chile	1995	222,450	15%	Open Plaza	8
Mall Plaza	Chile	2008	174,950	12%	Mall Aventura Plaza	3
Ibarcena	Peru	1998	146,000	10%	Boulevard de Asia	1
Romero (MZ)	Peru	2001	117,560	8%	Minka, Plaza del Sol, Plaza de la Luna	5
Altas Cumbres (Chile)	Chile	1997	111,000	7%	Jockey	1
Wong	Peru	2009	90,000	6%	Plaza Norte	1
Wiese	Peru	2002	82,880	6%	Megaplaza	2
Brescia (Cubica)	Peru	2005	73,371	5%	Molina Plaza, La Rambla	2
PUCP	Peru	1976	71,220	5%	Plaza San Miguel	1
Parque Arauco	Chile	2006	56,000	4%	Larcomar	1
Cencosud	Chile	2005	53,700	4%	Plaza Lima Sur	1
Ekimed (El Quinde)	Peru	2006	27,000	2%	El Quinde	2
Graña y Montero	Peru	2011	12,250	1%	Parque Agustino	1
Total			1,500,381			

Source: Peruvian Shopping Center Association, Report on Data, keys and investment opportunities in a growing industry, 2012.

outside of Lima and build modern shopping malls in cities that had traditionally been sidestepped by modern retail corporations. They hold an 8% market share on square meters for selling space.

Grupo Interbank: They are the largest players (in terms of selling space) and the fastest growing ones in this sector. They began investing in malls in 2005, but have aggressively done so. They currently own 11 different malls under their "Real Plaza" brand, and have a 17% market share in terms of square meters for selling space.

Grupo Brescia: Paradoxically enough, the Grupo Brescia has one of (if not) the largest real estate portfolios in urban cities in Peru. It was not until 2005 that they decided to enter the Malls sector and they have done so shyly. Until 2012, they only had 2 Malls with a 5% market share on square meters for selling space, but they have already announced the opening of six new malls (two full-fledged and four strip malls) for 2013.[33, 34]

The Financial System

Beginning with Fujimori's pro-market government in the 1990's, the potential growth of the Peruvian financial system increasingly attracted foreign investors. Although not many foreign institutions entered the local market until the 2000s, two important exceptions were Banco Santander from Spain[35] and Bancosur, new entity with Chilean and Spanish investors.[36] By 1999, Romero, Brescia and Rodriguez Pastor controlled 46% of loans and 55% of deposits. The insurance system demonstrated similar dynamics and by 1999, 61% of total premiums came from four insurers, including Romero (Pacifico) with 29% and Brescia (Rimac) with 19%.[37]

During the first half of the 2000s, investors were still cautious to enter the Peruvian financial system even if growth had been constant in the recent past. This translated into an increasing market share for local players, even if international banks understood Peru's potential.[38] International players were wary to expand given the frail political stability given the 2006 controversial elections.[39] After Alan Garcia demonstrated better economic judgment in his 2nd term,[h] international banks and insurers began to enter Peru in 2006 (see **Exhibit 10**). Immediately the increase in market share of the family-owned local banks stagnated, and even decreased in the case of insurance companies (see **Exhibit 11**).

By June 2012, the penetration of the financial system reached 31.4% in terms of deposits over GDP and 29.8% in terms of credits; an increase over the 2001 levels of 25.0% and 22.5%,[40] respectively. Although penetration had increased, Peru still lags behind the best Latin American performers; Chile, for instance, had an average penetration of 70%.[41] Although economists have explored the positive link between financial inclusion and competitiveness and growth,[42] there is no conclusive study on the role of Peruvian family groups spearheading the growth of the financial system.

Competitiveness and the Financial and Insurance System Metrics

Although there is no direct measure of competitiveness with respect to family group influence, the World Economic Forum Competitiveness Report provides an adequate starting point to compare the evolution of the financial system competitiveness (see **Exhibit 12**). Although Peru's index did not show the biggest improvement (13.4% over the period), Peru's ranking increased to 3rd from 5th, only behind Chile and the US.

In Peru, both the number of banks and insurers increased to reach late 1990s levels, but most important was the replacement of local banks with new international

---

[h]Alan Garcia had previously ruled between 1985 and 1990 with negative economic consequences.

Exhibit 10.   Number of Banks and Insurers in the Peruvian System

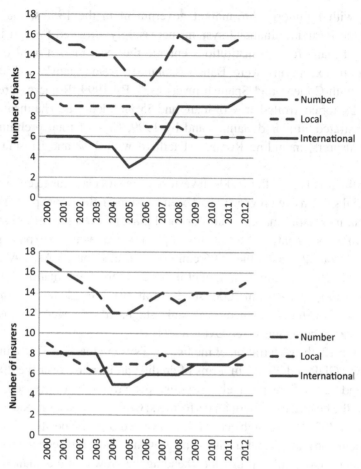

Source: Superintendencia de Banca y Seguros (SBS).

institutions that entered beginning in 2005. Yet the concentration of deposits and credits by the major family groups increased over the same period from 60% in deposits and 50% in credits in 2001 to 71% and 69% in 2012, respectively. In comparison, the top three banks in other similar Latin American countries did not reach the same level of concentration (see **Exhibit 13**). Family groups' insurer's market share increased initially from 56% in 2001 and ended the period at 66%.

The increased presence of international banks coupled with a growing economy translated to a moderate decrease in active and passive interest rates (see **Exhibit 14**). However, the spread remained roughly constant over the ten year period between 2002 and 2012. Return on equity in the banking sector increased through the period (see **Exhibit 15**) up to 2008, when the effects of the financial crisis reached Peru.

Exhibit 11. Market Share of Family Group-Owned Banks and Insurers

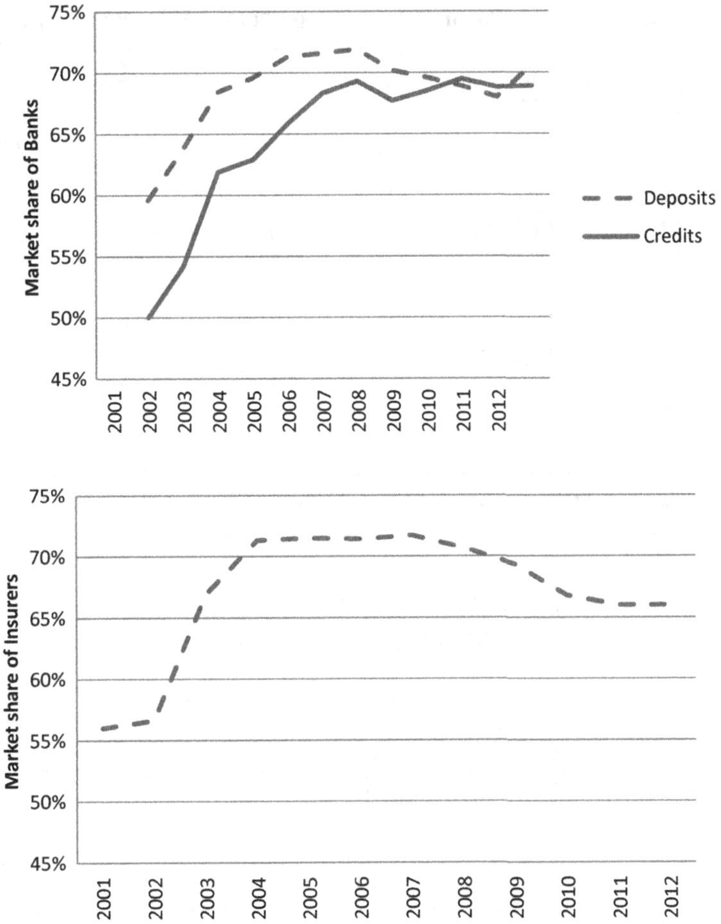

Source: Superintendencia de Banca y Seguros (SBS).

Yet the increase demonstrates that even with increasing competition, banks were able to obtain improving results.

Although irregular, the insurance system perceived a similar upward trend in ROE that went from being negative in 2001 to positive 16% by the end of 2012 (see **Exhibit 16**). The insurers' technical result[i] over premiums during the 10-year period decreased slightly, yet was highly volatile throughout (see **Exhibit 17**). Even with the entrance of more international insurance companies attracted by a low insurance penetration,[43] the system remained volatile and subject to the financial crisis.

---

[i]Technical result in insurance refers to the results generated by the underwriting of insurance contracts, including financial revenues and capital gains.

Exhibit 12.   WEF Competitiveness Report — Financial Market Development[a]

Global Rank 2012	Country	2006–2007	2012–2013	% change
16	United States	5.84	5.07	−13%
28	Chile	4.82	4.73	−2%
45	Peru	3.93	4.46	13%
46	Brazil	3.99	4.45	11%
61	Mexico	3.65	4.15	14%
67	Colombia	4.01	4.10	2%
83	Paraguay	3.22	3.89	21%
90	Uruguay	3.30	3.81	15%
96	Dominican Republic	3.35	3.74	12%
110	Ecuador	3.22	3.58	11%
126	Bolivia	3.17	3.33	5%
131	Argentina	3.25	3.18	−2%
133	Venezuela	3.48	3.11	−11%

Source: The Global Competitiveness Report 2012–2013 — World Economic Forum.
[a]Scale of 1 to 7 (best).

Exhibit 13.   Market Share (%) — Top 3 Banks Per Country 2012

	Deposits	Credits
Brazil	60%	51%
Mexico	53%	53%
Colombia	47%	49%
Chile	46%	50%
Argentina	31%	29%

Source: Banco Central do Brasil, Comision Nacional Bancaria y de Valores de México, Superintendencia Financiera de Colombia, Superintendencia de Bancos e Instituciones Financieras Chile, Banco Central de la República Argentina.

Presence of Family Groups

Brescia group: Banco BBVA Continental's market share increased from 15% to 23% in credits and from 21% to 23% in deposits. The most relevant development over the period was the acquisition of four microfinance institutions (MFIs) between 2008 and 2010 under the BBVA Microfinance Foundation.[44] Although the Brescia family does not own the Foundation, the MFIs rely on the Banco Continental's products and hence generate business for the family as well.

Exhibit 14. Evolution of Active and Passive Interest Rates

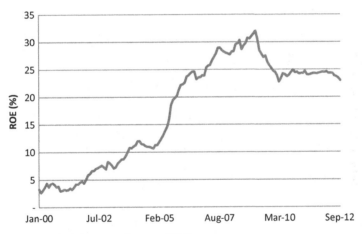

Source: Superintendencia de Banca y Seguros (SBS).

Exhibit 15. ROE — Banking Sector

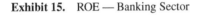

Source: Superintendencia de Banca y Seguros (SBS).

Romero group: Over the last 10-year period, the group's flagship company, Banco de Credito, increased its market share from 27% to 35% in credits and from 31% to 37% in deposits. Traditionally not a player in the microfinance space, Banco de Credito acquired Edyficar[45] in 2009 to tap into the microfinance market growth and react to the expansion of other players into this industry, namely the BBVA Microfinance Foundation.

Grupo Interbank: Interbank's market share increased from 7% to 11% in credits and from 7% to 10% in deposits. Although Interbank entered the microfinance space

Exhibit 16.   ROE — Insurance Sector

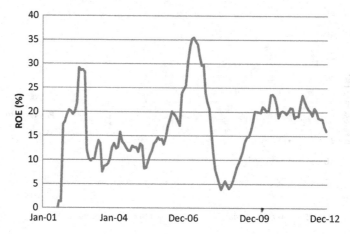

Source: Superintendencia de Banca y Seguros (SBS).

Exhibit 17.   Technical Result Over Premiums

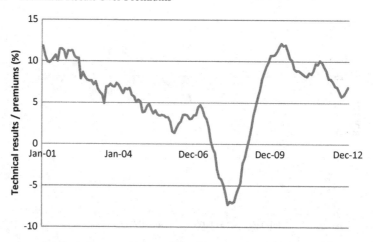

Source: Superintendencia de Banca y Seguros (SBS).

in 2009 through direct lending, in 2012 it acquired an undisclosed amount of the microfinance loan portfolio from its competitor Caja Nuestra Gente, owned by the BBVA Microfinance foundation.

Endnotes

[1] Diego Comin, *"Inkaterra,"* *HBS No. 9-713-022* (Boston: Harvard Business School Publishing, 2012), p. 2.

[2] http://en.wikipedia.org/wiki/Peru, accessed April 2013.

3 The Economist Intelligence Unit. "Peru Country Profile 2008", p. 5.

4 *Ibid.*

5 *Ibid.*

6 The World Bank, http://www.worldbank.org/en/country/peru/overview, accessed on April 2013.

7 *Ibid.*

8 *Ibid.*

9 "Peru, Quick view", http://news.zurichna.com/article/7fbe23fb547cddcfd38833a0bc 187ab4/peru-quick-view-formal-employment-continues-to-rise, accessed April 2103.

10 Euromonitor International. "Peru Country Profile", p. 3.

11 *Ibid.*

12 Enrique Vásquez Huamán, *Estrategias del Poder: Grupos Económicos en el Perú* (Lima, Peru: Universidad del Pacífico – Centro de Investigación, 2000).

13 http://www.minsur.com.pe/quienessomos.htm, Accessed on March 2013.

14 "Minsur completes Taboca acquisition," *MetalsPlace.com*, November 17, 2008, http:// metalsplace.com/news/articles/23744/minsur-completes-taboca-acquisition/, accessed March 2013.

15 "El grupo Brescia concretó la compra de activos de Lafarge Chile," *Gestion.pe*, http://gestion.pe/noticia/334482/grupo-brescia-concreto-compra-activos-lafarge-chile, accessed March 2013.

16 Intercorp Financial Services. http://www.ifs.com.pe/?centro=content&paqid=8& banner=history, accessed April 2013.

17 *Ibid.*

18 *Ibid.*

19 In Retail Peru Corp. http://www.inretail.pe/1/modulos/JER/JER_Interna.aspx?ARE= 1&PFL=1&JER=94, Accessed on January 2013.

20 *Ibid.*

21 *Ibid.*

22 *Ibid.*

23 Casa Andina. http://www.casa-andina.com/aboutcasaandina/?lang=en, Accessed on January 2013.

24 Inter-American Development Bank. http://www.iadb.org/en/news/news-releases/2012-07-03/colegios-peruanos-to-expand-quality-of-education,10051.html, Accessed on January 2013.

25 Enrique Vásquez Huamán, *Estrategias del Poder: Grupos Económicos en el Perú* (Lima, Perú: Universidad del Pacífico — Centro de Investigación, 2000).

26 Alicorp, "Nosotros," http://www.alicorp.com.pe/espanol/nosotros.html, accessed December 2012.

27 Superintendencia de Banca y Seguros y AFP, http://www.sbs.gob.pe/, accessed Janaury 2013.

28 "Peruana Alicorp ingresa a Brasil," *Diario Correo*, February 8, 2013, http://diariocorreo. pe/ultimas/noticias/3373405/edicion+lima/peruana-alicorp-ingresa-a-brasil, accessed March 2013.

29 *Ibid.*

30 *Ibid.*

31 "El impacto de los centros comerciales en la economía," *LaRepublica.pe*, December 17, 2011, http://www.larepublica.pe/columnistas/analisis/el-impacto-de-los-centros-comerciales-en-la-economia-17-12-2011, accessed February 2013.

32 Peruvian Shopping Center Association, The Industry of Shopping Centers in Peru, September 2011.

33 V. Takeshi Chacón Pichón, "Cúbica construye strip centers en La Victoria y Cercado de Lima," *Gestion.pe*, February 24, 2012, http://gestion.pe/noticia/1378695/cubica-construye-strip-centers-victoria-cercado-lima, accessed February 2013.

34 "Se abrirán 14 'malls' en el interior del país el próximo año," *ElComercio.pe*, November 10, 2012, http://elcomercio.pe/economia/1494568/noticia-se-abriran-14malls-interior-pais-proximo-ano, accessed March 2013.

35 "Banco Santander de Espana compra banco peruano," *Reuters — Noticias Latinoamericanas*, August 25, 1995, via Factiva, accessed October 2012.

36 "Grupo Chileno-Espanol compra Banco del Sur de Peru," *Reuters — Noticias Latinoamericanas*, January 26, 1996, via Factiva, accessed October 2012.

37 Superintendencia de Banca, Seguros y AFP. 1999 Annual Report on the Insurance System. Lima, 2000.

38 Carlos Astuquipan, "Extraordinario Crecimiento," *Business Peru*, December 3, 2007, via Factiva, accessed February 2013.

39 "Un escenario complicado para Humala," *El Comercio*, April 11, 2006, via Factiva, accessed March 2013.

40 Superintendencia de Banca, Seguros y AFP. 2012 Annual Report on the Banking System. Lima, 2013.

41 Melvin Escudero, "Día de la Banca y Finanzas 2011 — Parte 1," *El Comercio*, December 13, 2011, via Factiva, accessed March 2013.

42 *Ibid.*

43 Luis Davelouis, "Sector asegurador en Perú es uno de los más potentes de América Latina," *Noticias Financieras*, March 2, 2009, via Factiva, accessed March 2013.

44 BBVA Microfinance Foundation, "Caja Nuestra Gente, the best microfinance institution in Latin America and the Caribbean," http://www.mfbbva.org/english/press-room/historic-news/archive/2011//select_category/2/article/85/132.html?no_cache=1&tx_tt news%5Bfech%5D=2011&cHash=ec0b803cf0, accessed April 2013.

45 "Banco de Credito del Peru to acquire Financiera EDYFICAR," CARE press release, September 7, 2009, on CARE website, http://www.care.org/newsroom/articles/2009/09/edyficar-2009-09-07.asp, accessed April 2013.

Spain: Can the House Resist the Storm?

Diego Comin*

They say this is not a crisis, just a deceleration. Deceleration? Let me know where the pedal is and you'll see how I accelerate it.

— Paco Fernandez, taxi driver from Madrid

On March 10, 2011, Moody's downgraded Spain's government bonds ratings by one notch from Aa1 to Aa2 with a negative outlook on the Aa2 rating. The main triggers for the downgrade were:

(1) Moody's expectation that the eventual cost of bank restructuring would be €40 to €50 billion euros, versus the government estimate of €20 billion, leading to a further increase in the ratio of public debt to GDP.
(2) Moody's continued concerns over the ability of the Spanish government to achieve the required sustainable structural improvement in public sector finances, given the limits of central government control over the regional governments' finances, as well as the expectation of only moderate economic growth in the short to medium term.[1]

Despite the downgrade, Moody's continued to believe that "Spain's debt sustainability was not under threat and its baseline assumptions did not anticipate a need for the Spanish government to ask for the European Financial Stability Facility liquidity

*Reprinted with permission of Harvard Business School Publishing.
Spain: Can the House Resist the Storm 709-021.
This case was prepared by Professor Diego with the assistance of the European Research Center.

support."[2] The European Financial Stability Facility was a Eurozone mechanism to provide loans to member countries under stress or to buy their bonds.[3] However, Moody's added, "Spain's substantial funding requirements . . . made the country susceptible to further episodes of funding stress."

At stake was much more than the stability of the Spanish economy. Its weight in the EU made Spain's stress the most significant threat to the euro since its inception in 1999. What had brought Spain to this situation? What would it take it to end the Spanish slump? And would the euro survive its first real test?

Spain's Profile

In 2008 Spain was a developed country with the eighth-largest economy in the world.[4] Its population was 46 million and its per capita income, based on purchasing power parity (the price of a basket of goods and services that the currency buys), was estimated in 2007 at United States. $33,600, ahead of G7 countries such as Italy at $30,900, France at $32,600, or Japan at $33,500.[5]

The economy was structured as follows: 5% of GDP came from agriculture, 29% from industry and 67% from services. The tourist industry, the second-largest in the world, represented 10.7% of GDP, while construction (in 2006) represented 11% of GDP and nearly 13% of employment.[6]

Most Spanish trade — 61% of imports and 72% of exports — was with the rest of the European Union (EU).[7] The main exports were machinery, motor vehicles, foodstuffs and other consumer goods. Spain imported 77% of the energy it used; energy represented 14% of imports.

Since 1978, Spain had been a democracy, governed by a parliamentary system under a constitutional monarchy. The constitution sought to address the cultural diversity of the different regions of Spain through the *Estado de las Autonomías* ("State of Autonomous Communities"). As a result, Spain was one of the most decentralized countries in Europe, along with Switzerland, Germany, and Belgium.[8] All Autonomous Communities had their own elected parliaments, governments, public administrations, budgets and revenue sources. Health and education systems, among other things, were managed regionally. In addition, the Basque Country and Navarra preserved some historical fiscal privileges. A fully fledged autonomous police corps replaced some state police functions.[9]

Education in Spain was free and compulsory from the ages of 6–16. The Spanish health system combined both public and private healthcare and provided universal coverage. The Gini coefficient of income inequality was 34.7%, a level similar to Ireland and Australia, slightly higher than France (32.7%) but lower than Italy (36%), the United Kingdom (36%) or the United States (40.7%).

The Past: 1960–2000

The Dictatorship

After the end of the Spanish Civil War in 1939, Francisco Franco's dictatorial regime governed Spain. Ostracized by the United States and a democratic Western Europe and hobbled by interventionist policies, Spain's economy stagnated in the early years of his rule. As Cold War pressures grew in the 1950s, the West gained new interest in an alliance with Spain, considering its anti-communist credentials and location on the Iberian peninsula of great strategic value.

In the late 1950s, Spain changed gears and entered a new phase characterized by market liberalization, openness to international markets, buoyancy of the tourist sector and access to modern technologies through licenses, trade and foreign direct investment (FDI).[10] For a decade, Spain experienced intense GDP growth, averaging 7% per year. This catch-up process mimicked the post-war experience of most Western European countries, though with a delay of more than a decade.

The Transition

The aftermath of Franco's death in 1975 was a period of economic and political instability. Spain suffered a slowdown coinciding with the oil shocks that lasted into the early 1980s. Unemployment rose and social unrest added a new element of instability to a delicate political transition the country was undergoing. Franco's successor as head of state, King Juan Carlos I, took the first steps to ensure adoption of democracy. A new democratic government was elected and put in charge of drafting a constitution. In October 1977, the government, opposition parties, business associations and the main labor union, Comisiones Obreras, agreed on an economic package, the Moncloa Pacts,that delineated a new framework for labor relations and wage increases. This framework was designed to contain inflation and give legitimacy to government policies, preventing economic deterioration and buying time during the interim until the October 1978 referendum on the new constitution.[11]

Despite the emergence of democracy, domestic terrorism by Basque separatists was at its height. In 1981, in a climate of growing tension, military leaders led by Antonio Tejero, a Lieutenant-Colonel, stormed the Spanish Parliament in an attempt to overthrow the government. Support for the democratic government only strengthened when King Juan Carlos publicly denounced the coup attempt and urged citizens to support the elected parliament. Afterwards the fledgling democracy consolidated and a socialist government presided over by Felipe Gonzalez began the difficult process of modernizing the Spanish economy.

European Integration

In 1986, Spain joined the European Community (EC), the predecessor to the EU, gaining access to European markets and structural and cohesion funds distributed by the EC. These developments drove Spanish growth over the next six or seven years. Some countries used EC funds to strengthen their information technology sectors, while others used it to increase salaries of civil servants. In Spain the funds were primarily used to build public infrastructure. Free access to European markets drove exports from 13% to 17% of GDP.

The 1992 Maastricht treaty established the roadmap for adopting a single currency, the euro, on January 1, 1999. With the common currency, individual countries would lose two of the tools used more frequently when facing a recession: competitive devaluations and expansionary monetary policies. On the other hand, the euro would facilitate the flow of capital within the EU and the control of inflation. To adopt the euro, the Maastricht treaty required countries to adopt stringent monetary and fiscal policies. One of the priorities of the first conservative government, under Jose Maria Aznar (1996–2000), was to meet the Maastricht requirements. Led by Finance Minister Rodrigo Rato, Spain entered the euro together with 10 other countries. This process of monetary and fiscal convergence led to a reduction in the long-term interest rates.

The Spanish Labor Market

Despite economic expansion, unemployment remained high during Spain's early years of EC membership, from 1986 and 1992. Several institutional factors shaped the labor market.

Wage Bargaining

Employment conditions and wages of nearly all Spanish private-sector workers were determined by a collective bargaining system established by the 1980 Estatuto de los Trabajadores (Workers' Statute) that made moderating wage increases difficult.[12] Only around 10% or 15% of workers were covered by agreements negotiated at the firm level, commonly in the case of larger companies.[13] The bulk of workers, approximately 50%were covered by agreements that applied to all firms within a given sector across a province and around 25% were covered by sectoral agreements of national scope.[14] Regional and national agreements applied to all firms in the relevant sector and geographical region, even if they had not participated in the bargaining. In practice, it was quite difficult for a given firm to modify these broader agreements.[15]

Workers often saw little to lose by insisting on raises since, when management and labor reached an impasse in negotiations, existing agreements were automatically extended until a new agreement was signed. Over 60% of workers ended up being covered by agreements lasting more than a year and 30% by agreements lasting for more than two years.[16]

In the United States, Canada and the United Kingdom bargaining occurs at the firm level, while in Nordic countries and Austria bargaining occurs at the national level. A consensus agreed that under both of these bargaining models there was more wage restraint than under the Spanish model.[17]

Labor Contracts and Firing Costs

Together with France, Greece and Portugal, Spain had among the most stringent regulations in Europe limiting firms' ability to dismiss workers and requiring large severance payments.[18] Firms that laid off workers under long-term contracts were required to provide severance payments equaling 20 days of salary per year of job tenure (up to a maximum of one year of wages) if the dismissal was deemed "fair" and 45 days (up to a maximum of 42 months wages) if it was deemed "unfair."[19] A 1984 reform introduced short-term contracts (for 3, 6, or 12 months) with low severance costs at termination (12 days of wages per year of tenure). Short-term contracts could be renewed only for periods of up to three years. At this point, the firm had to decide whether to offer the worker a permanent contract or dismiss him or her.[20] This reform was inspired by French flexible labor contracts. However, the difference in dismissal costs between indefinite and fixed-term contracts was larger in Spain than in France.[21] By the mid-1990s, temporary workers represented 35% of employment (versus 12% in the then 15 EU member states and 13% in France). Spain thus had a *dual labor market* where permanent workers were very costly to dismiss and would rarely lose their jobs, while temporary workers would move from job to job as their contracts expired. The system had some clear adverse effects on firms' dismissal strategies and workers' incentives.[22]

Unemployment Benefits and Minimum Wage

Spain's generous unemployment benefits were often said to explain its high unemployment rate, as they gave unemployed workers had less incentive to search for a new job. Unemployed residents were entitled to approximately 65% of the national average earnings and the duration of the benefits was among the longest in the Organization for Economic Co-operation and Development (OECD), a group of mainly advanced nations. Those who had worked during six years before becoming unemployed could receive benefits for up to two years. However, the minimum wage was not particularly high relative to the average wage. Between 1990 and 2008, the ratio of the minimum wage to the average wage in Spain was roughly the same as the median in the OECD.

Reforms and Evolution

In 1993 Spain fell into recession along with the rest of Europe and unemployment skyrocketed to 24% in 1994 (see **Exhibit 1b**). That year, Gonzalez made it more feasible for firms to hire workers on part-time contracts, introduced private employment agencies and made some attempts to decentralize collective bargaining, but without much success. Unemployment responded only modestly to these reforms and the Aznar government initiated further reforms in 1997 and 1998. This second wave of reforms reduced firing costs and tried to introduce more flexibility in part-time contracts.

The prospects of the common currency reduced the costs of credit, propelling the Spanish economy from 1995 to 2000 at an average growth rate of 4% (see **Exhibit 1c**). Unemployment started a slow, steady decline. Still, unemployment remained the highest in the EU at 14% by 2000.

The Expansion: 2000–2007

Immigration Boom

Starting in 2000, Spain began to experience a massive inflow of immigrants. By 2007, its population had increased by almost 5 million people, or about 12%. About 80 percent of this increase was due to the arrival of new immigrants (**Exhibits 2a** and **2b**). In 2000, immigrants represented only 2.4% of Spain's population, but by 2007, they represented 10% of the population.[23]

Spanish immigrants came mostly from Latin America (36%), Africa (19%) and Eastern Europe (18%).[24] Different factors triggered the sudden increase in immigrant inflows. Latin American countries such as Argentina, Colombia, Peru, Ecuador and Bolivia were suffering severe recessions. Sub-Saharan Africans took advantage of improvements in the ships used to illegally reach the Canary Islands ("cayucos"), allowing illegal migration networks to reach further south along the West African coast.[25] Restrictions on leaving Eastern European countries began to ease and beginning in 2002, immigrants from Romania could work in Spain without special work permits.[26]

Since most immigrants were working age between 16 and 64, the inflow of immigrants coincided with an increase in the Spanish labor force from 18 million in 2000 to 22.2 million in 2007.[27] On average, immigrants had the same educational attainment as the local population.[28] But they tended to find jobs disproportionately in personal services, tourism and construction (see **Exhibit 2c**).

Despite the increase in labor supply, the unemployment rate continued to decline from almost 14% in 2000 to 8.25% in 2007 (see **Exhibit 1b**). Over this period real wages remained virtually unchanged (see **Exhibit 1a**), though there was significant variation across sectors (see **Exhibit 2c**).

As the number of workers increased, so did the potential to produce more goods and services in the Spanish economy. The continuous expansion of employment over the period 2000 to 2007 led to persistent growth in GDP. To accommodate the increased number of workers, businesses needed more capital. Real fixed investment grew by 44% between 2000– and 2007 (see **Exhibit 1d**).[29]

The Housing Boom and its Consequences

A generation of northern European retirees, on top of the influx of foreign workers, added further to population growth.[30] They all needed places to live. In addition, the number of divorces exploded in Spain over this same period.[31] As couples split, they sought new living accommodations. The supply of houses was relatively fixed in the short run, so heavy demand drove housing prices up. In 2000, prices increased by 7.7% — a significantly higher rate than the 4.5% average between 1995 and 1999. It was just the beginning of an unprecedented boom in housing markets (see **Exhibits 3a–d**).

The total value of the Spanish stock market represented only 86% of GDP, as compared with 130% in the United States.[32] In Spain, housing accounted for a majority of national wealth, so rising house prices led to a dramatic increase in wealth.[33] As individuals perceived their growing wealth, they began consuming more and the resulting demand fostered further economic growth.[34] Car sales increased, as did spending on many other consumer durables, staples and luxuries.

As Spain was enjoying this prosperity in the early 2000s, other European countries were experiencing economic recession. The collapse of the dot-com bubble, coupled with 9/11, stalled growth in Germany and France. This asymmetry in economic cycles also meant that Spain offered attractive investment opportunities. The housing sector in Spain was booming, while investment in most of Europe recovered slowly. Spanish construction companies and banks relished the opportunity to access the European savings at low interest rates (see **Exhibit 5a**) and invest in sunny Spain.

Without a domestic currency to appreciate, without a monetary policy tailored to the Spanish economic situation and with a high degree of capital-market integration, it was very difficult to prevent the Spanish economy from overheating.[35] Spanish households did not reduce their consumption much to finance housing investment. Private debt increased dramatically and was soon reflected in Spain's current account. From 2000– to 2007, Spain's current account deficit grew by about

Exhibit 1a.   Spain Economic Indicators

	1990	1995	2000	2001	2002	2003	2004	2005	2006	2007	2008	2009	2010*
Real GDP Growth (%)	3.8	2.8	5.1	3.7	2.7	3.1	3.3	3.6	3.9	3.7	0.9	−3.6	−0.1
Labor Productivity Growth (%)	1.2	0.3	−0.5	−0.5	−0.3	−0.9	−0.6	−1.9	−0.1	0.5	1.3	3.7	3.5
Consumer Price Index Growth (%)	6.7	4.7	3.4	3.6	3.5	3.0	3.0	3.4	3.5	2.8	4.1	−0.3	0.8
Nominal Wage Growth (%)	8.8	6.8	2.1	3.7	4.0	4.6	3.8	3.1	5.7	4.6	5.1	3.6	1.3
Unit Labor Costs Growth (in US$) (%)	28.5	13.7	−10.5	0.3	9.0	23.7	12.8	3.8	4.6	13.6	12.0	−3.7	0.9
Gross National Savings rate (%)	22.1	21.6	22.3	22.4	23.4	23.9	23.0	22.1	22.0	21.1	19.6	21.6	21.5
% GDP													
Current Account/GDP	−4.53	−0.34	−3.98	−3.95	−3.23	−3.49	−5.25	−7.37	−8.93	−10.09	−9.6	−5	−4.5
Public Debt/GDP	42.64	63.30	59.26	55.50	52.55	48.74	46.18	43.03	39.67	36.17	39.7	55.1	67.1
Fiscal Surplus (+) or Fiscal Deficit (−)/GDP	−4.14	−6.48	−1.00	−0.66	−0.48	−0.23	−0.35	0.97	1.79	1.90	−4.1	−11.4	−11.7
Units as shown													
Unemployment (% total)	16.23	22.90	13.88	10.53	11.48	11.50	10.95	9.18	8.50	8.28	11.33	18.20	19.80
Stock of Foreign Reserves and Gold (bn US$)	56.01	38.71	35.61	34.24	40.30	26.81	19.76	17.23	19.34	19.05	20.24	na	na
Exchange Rate (Euros: US$ (av))	0.79	0.76	1.08	1.12	1.06	0.88	0.80	0.80	0.80	0.73	0.68	0.72	0.70

Sources: Compiled by the author using data from the Economist Intelligence Unit, *EIU Data Services*, accessed February 18, 2010.

Note: *Estimates.

Exhibit 1b. Unemployment Rates

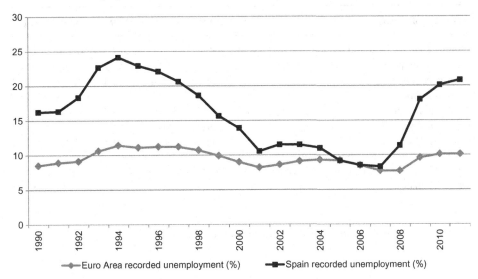

Source: The Economist Intelligence Unit, accessed September 7, 2011.

Note: Data for 2011 are projections.

Exhibit 1c. Spain Real GDP Growth (annual, %)

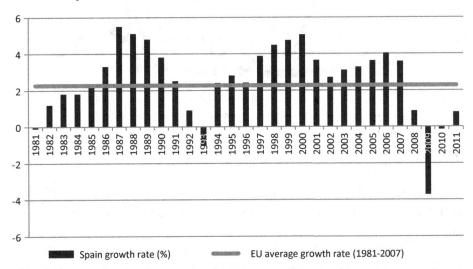

Source: Economist Intelligence Unit, accessed September 8, 2011.

Exhibit 1d.   Spain GDP and Composition

In Billions of Euros	2000	2007	2008	2009	2010*
Nominal GDP (in thousand million Euros) % GDP	630.7	1,052.7	1,088.5	1,036.6	1,048.5
Private consumption	59.7	57.4	57.2	56.9	56.3
Government consumption	17.2	18.4	19.4	21.3	21.5
Gross fixed investment	25.8	30.7	28.8	26.5	25.9
Change in inventories	0.5	0.3	0.4	0.0	0.0
Exports of G&S	29.0	26.9	26.5	22.9	25.2
Imports of G&S	32.2	33.7	32.4	27.6	29.0

Source: Compiled by the author using data from *EIU Data Services*, accessed February 18, 2010.
Note: *Estimates.

Exhibit 2a.   Population and Labor Force in Spain and the EU

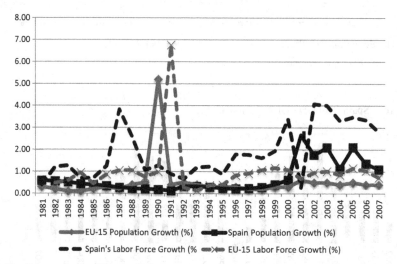

Source: The Economist Intelligence Unit.

seven-fold from $23.2–$145.3 billion dollars, representing 10% of GDP (see **Exhibit 4**). It was not long before Spain's net external debt had exploded to over $1 trillion.

Despite this growing imbalance, expectations of future appreciation in housing prices led many households to invest in more houses. Given the thinness of the stock market, Spaniards saw a house as a vehicle to save for retirement.

In this situation, it became even more profitable for construction companies to build additional houses. The expansion in the supply of houses was staggering. During several of the years in the period 2000–2007, more new houses were built in Spain than in Britain, France, Italy and Germany combined, even though

Exhibit 2b. Foreign-Born Residents in the Spanish Population (in millions)

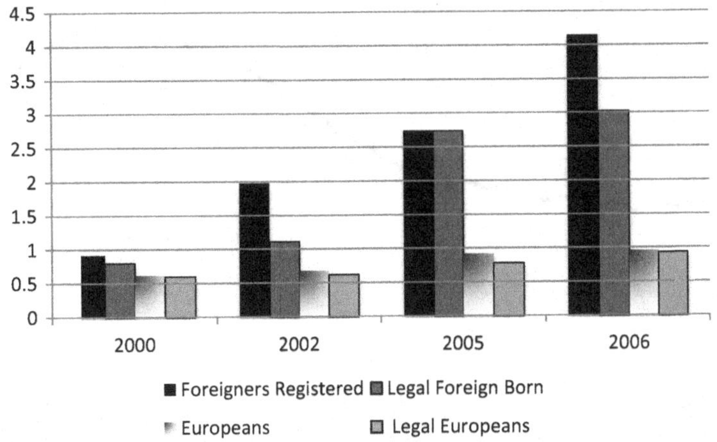

■ Foreigners Registered ■ Legal Foreign Born
▮ Europeans ▢ Legal Europeans

Source: Dolado, "Immigration: Economic and Political Effects" 2008.

Exhibit 2c. Employment Structure and Salary Growth in Spanish industries, 2000 through 2006

	Salary Level in 2006 (Euros)	Average Annual Salary Growth, 2000–2006	Number of Workers in 2006 (Thousands)	Change in Share of Total Employment (2000–2006)
All Industries:	19,364	3.3	16,814	0
Mining	24,331	3.4	66	−0.1
Manufacturing	21,728	3.7	3,107	−4.7
Electric, gas, and water	35,164	4.3	119	−0.1
Construction	17,919	3.9	2,543	1.8
Wholesale, retail, and repair	16,761	3.3	2,984	−0.5
Hotels and restaurants	12,761	3.4	1,403	1.3
Transport, storage, and communication	21,965	2.3	1,158	−0.2
Finance	38,806	3.7	473	−0.5
Business services	18,225	5.1	1,857	2.2
Education	18,694	3.6	1,109	0
Health, veterinary, and social services	22,488	3.3	1,181	0.6
Social, community, and household services	16,041	2.5	815	0.2

Source: Compiled from Gabinete Ténico Confederal de Comisiones Obreras, "Los salarios en España," Table 1, p. 13, September 2007.

Note: Full-time workers only. Agricultural and public-administration employees were excluded for lack of comparable data.

Exhibit 3a.   Spanish Housing Prices in Euros per Square Meter

Source: Calculated from Spain's Ministry of Development (Ministerio de Fomento), adjusted with GDP deflator from Economist Intelligence Unit, CountryData, both accessed September 8, 2011.

Exhibit 3b.   Average House Price/Average Annual Income

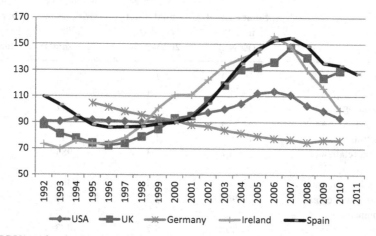

Sources: BBVA and author's calculations.

Spain had a smaller population than any of these countries. In 2006, over 600,000 new homes were constructed (see **Exhibit 3c**).[36] In Andalucia alone (a region with approximately 8 million people), more houses were built than in the whole United Kingdom. The thriving residential-construction sector grew to encompass 12% of the Spanish economy. In the United States, by comparison, the figure was about 5%, despite similar housing-market conditions.

Notwithstanding the increase in housing supply, prices continued to skyrocket, at an average annual rate of 12.1% from 2000 through 2007, 130% over the eight year

Exhibit 3c. Building Permits Index (2000 = 100)

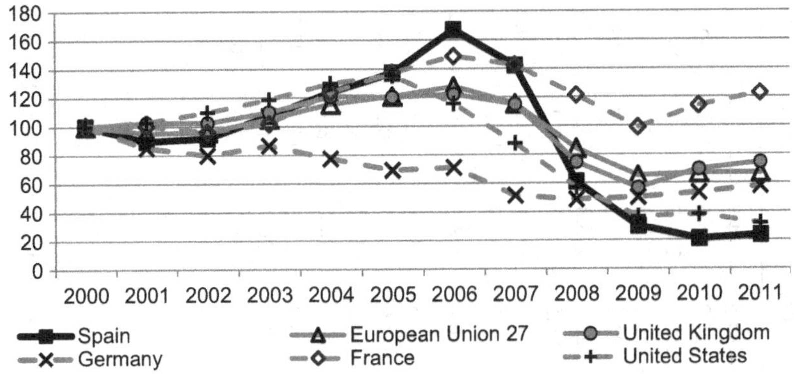

Sources: Adapted from Eurostat, Building Permits — quarterly data — index (NACE Rev. 2), for European nations, and U.S. Census Bureau, New Privately Owned Housing Units Authorized (unadjusted data), July 2010, for United States. Both accessed September 9, 2011.

Note: Building permits reported for residential buildings through 2001 quarter 1 (annual average over quarters).

Exhibit 3d. Mortgage Financing Conditions

	Interest Rate (%)	Term of Mortgage (Years)	Monthly Payment	Monthly Payment in Real Terms (Base 2006)	Price of Housing (100 m² apt.)
1990	14.0	10	877	1,552	56,500
2000	5.8	22	590	712	88,023
2007	5.19	28	1,159	1,128	205,084

Source: BBVA.
Note: Monthly Payments and Price of Housing Quoted in Euros.

period. By 2007, it was not uncommon to find apartments for sale in some Spanish cities such as Barcelona or Madrid at prices comparable to those in Manhattan.

Local and regional government finances benefitted from the increase in both housing prices and sales. A significant share of government revenues came from taxes on house sales amounting to approximately 8% of the price. These taxes helped regional governments balance their budgets, especially as the central government transferred to them the responsibility to provide for health care and education.

The Banking System and Mortgage Market

The Spanish banking sector consisted of commercial banks and *cajas* (savings and loans). *Cajas* were ultimately controlled by local governments and invested a significant share of their profits in social projects. Both types of financial institutions

Exhibit 4.   Spain's Balance of Payments

	2000	2001	2002	2003	2004	2005	2006	2007	2008	2009	2010
CURRENT ACCOUNT	-23.2	-24.1	-22.2	-30.9	-54.9	-83.4	-110.9	-144.5	-154.5	-75.3	-64.3
Trade Balance	-37.1	-34.5	-34.6	-45.2	-66.7	-85.2	-104.6	-125.2	-126.6	-59.0	-62.3
Export	115.8	117.5	127.2	158.0	185.2	196.6	220.7	264.1	284.7	228.7	253.0
Imports	-152.9	-152.0	-161.8	-203.2	-251.9	-281.8	-325.3	-389.3	-411.3	-287.7	-315.3
Net Services	19.3	20.5	21.5	26.4	26.9	27.5	28.1	31.7	38.2	35.7	36.5
Service: Credit	52.5	55.7	60.2	74.3	86.1	94.7	106.7	128.1	143.8	123.1	123.6
Service: Debit	-33.2	-35.2	-38.7	-48.0	-59.2	-67.1	-78.6	-96.5	-105.6	-87.4	-87.1
Net Income	-6.8	-11.3	-11.7	-11.7	-15.0	-21.3	-26.2	-41.4	-52.1	-41.1	-29.0
Net Transfers	1.5	1.3	2.5	-0.4	0.0	-4.5	-8.1	-9.6	-14.0	-10.9	-9.5
CAPITAL ACCOUNT	4.8	4.8	7.2	9.3	10.4	10.1	7.9	6.4	8.2	5.9	8.4
FINANCIAL ACCOUNT	15.3	18.2	17.8	4.4	37.0	73.9	107.9	138.6	149.8	81.8	60.3
Net Direct Investment	-18.6	-4.7	6.3	-3.2	-36.7	-17.3	-72.3	-72.9	3.9	-0.2	4.1
Inward Direct Investment	38.8	28.2	40.0	25.6	24.8	24.6	31.2	66.7	77.9	8.6	24.7
Outward Direct Investment	-57.4	-32.9	-33.7	-28.8	-61.5	-41.9	-103.5	-139.5	-74.0	-8.8	-20.6
Net Portfolio Flows	-1.2	-17.0	5.0	-46.1	102.0	53.4	232.4	118.2	4.3	73.7	47.7
Inward Portfolio	58.1	28.0	34.1	44.8	141.7	172.7	243.9	124.1	-26.9	71.7	-43.5
Outward Portfolio	-59.3	-45.0	-29.1	-90.8	-39.7	-119.4	-11.5	-5.9	31.2	2.0	91.2
Net Other	35.0	39.9	6.4	53.6	-28.4	37.9	-52.2	93.3	141.6	8.3	8.5
ERRORS AND OMISSIONS	0.2	-0.3	0.9	1.8	1.0	-2.5	-4.3	-0.2	-2.8	-6.4	-3.2
CHANGE IN RESERVES	2.9	1.3	-3.7	15.5	6.4	1.9	-0.6	-0.2	-0.7	-6.0	-1.1
STOCK OF RESERVES	35.6	34.2	40.3	26.8	19.8	17.2	19.3	19.1	20.2	28.2	31.9

Source: Balance of payments derived from IMF, Balance of Payments Statistics (BOP), total reserves derived from IMF, International Financial Statistics (IFS), accessed September 12, 2011.

Note: Billions of U.S. dollars.

Exhibit 5a. Benchmark Spanish Interest Rates

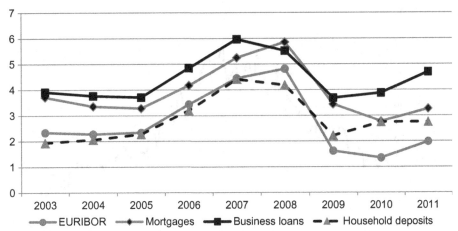

Source: Bank of Spain, Statistics Bulletin, July–August 2011.

Notes: Rates for EURIBOR and mortgages are yearly averages; rates for business loans and deposits are for December, except that they are for July in 2011. EURIBOR rates are 12-month; mortgage rates are for more than three years; business loans are up to one million euros. All rates are averages for all typical financial institutions.

Exhibit 5b. Loan Default Rates

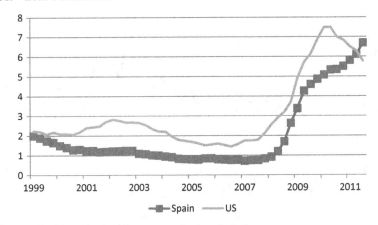

Source: Bank of Spain and Federal Reserve, author's calculations.

Note: Loans that are faulty for 90 days over total loans.

underwent a wave of consolidations during the 1990s and early 2000s in order to remain competitive in the face of globalization and the creation of the euro area. As a result of this process, Spain was left with two giant banks, BSCH (Banco Santander) and BBVA (Banco Bilbao Vizcaya Argentaria), a few smaller banks and 45 *cajas*.

Exhibit 5c.   New Mortgages Issued in Spain (billions of Euros)

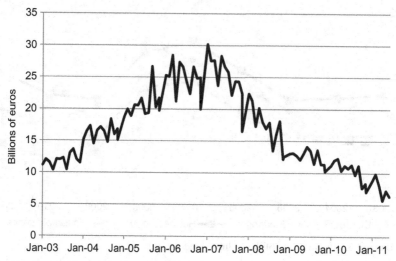

Source: Spanish Fuente: Monthly Statistics Bulletin. INE.

Exhibit 5d.   Spanish Financial Institutions' Quarterly Profits at Annual Rate (billions of Euros)

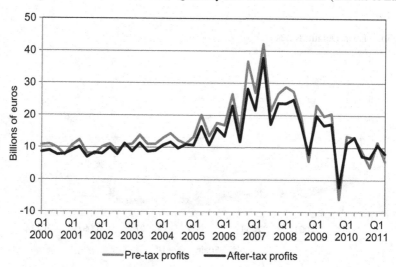

Source: Banco de Espana, Boletin Estadistico, chapter 4, tables 36.13 and 36.16.

Cajas held approximately 57% of deposits and 50% of the assets in the Spanish banking system.[37]

Mortgages in Spain typically required a 20% down payment. Borrowers who could not provide the 20% could still obtain the mortgage by having guarantors (*avalistas*) co-sign mortgages. In case the principal signer of the mortgage failed to

Exhibit 5e. Cost to Income Ratio (%) of Foreign Banks Acquired by BBVA

Bank	Country	2000	2002	2010	Year of Acquisition
Bancomer	Mexico	70.1	54.1	35.8	2000
B.Continental	Peru	53.2	49.8	30.6	1995
B.Ganadero	Colombia	87.4	81.9	41.3	1996
B.BHIF	Chile	61.2	59.8	48.9	1998
B.Provincial	Venezuela	70.6	50.1	48.0	1997
B.Francés	Argentina	61.7	58.3	55.4	1996

Source: BBVA.

Note: Cost to Income ratio is defined as general expenditures plus depreciation over gross margin. For 2000 and 2002, the denominator is ordinary margin, though results would be similar if gross margin was used as in 2010.

Exhibit 5f. Balance Sheet Items of the Spanish Banking System

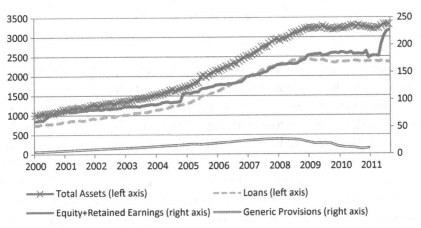

Source: Boletin Estadistico Bank of Spain.

Note: In billions euros. Equity is common equity plus the endowment of savings banks. Retained earnings also include current profits. Generic provisions includes the dynamic provisions instituted by the bank of Spain in 2000.

pay back the loan, the *avalistas* would be liable for it. Spanish law did not allow borrowers to walk away from their houses if they defaulted. Mortgages were backed not only by the home, but also by all other assets the borrowers and co-signers had at their disposal, including their income.[38] As a result, the default rate had been historically low even in recessionary periods (see **Exhibit 5b**). The most popular mortgages over the 2000–2007 period were 30-year with a variable interest determined by the euro interbank rate plus a fixed spread.[39] The lending rate remained relatively stable, averaging 5.86% from 2000 to 2007 (see **Exhibit 5a**).

Exhibit 5g.   Tangible Equity over Total Assets in U.S. Banking System

Source: Goldman Sachs.

The Spanish mortgage market differed significantly from other markets such as the United States in important dimensions.[40] In the 1990s, U.S. banks and other financial institutions began lending to borrowers whose income levels, down payments, credit history or employment status did not qualify them for "prime" mortgages. The Federal Reserve has estimated that the share of subprime mortgages to total mortgages grew from 5% ($35 billion) in 1994 to 20% ($600 billion) in 2006.[41] This expansion of subprime loans was due in part to relaxation of procedures for granting them. Many of the subprime loans required less documentation than traditionally demanded. In addition, many borrowers were offered mortgages with low initial interest rates that increased significantly and automatically after two years. They were willing to take these loans in the expectation that as housing prices rose in the future and they would be able to refinance on favorable new terms.[42]

American mortgage lenders financed subprime mortgages through a burgeoning secondary mortgage market. Investment banks bundled together mortgages from primary lenders and sold them to third parties as mortgage-backed securities (MBS). Legal entities called special purpose vehicles (SPV) would then buy these MBS and issue yet other financial instruments with different priorities on cash flows — the safer ones with higher priority paying lower returns and vice versa.[43] Rating agencies such as Standard & Poor's, Moody's and Fitch rated the MBS as well as the instruments issued by the SPVs using statistical models based on past performance. Given past trends in housing markets, many of the securities issued by SPVs obtained high ratings. U.S. regulators allowed sponsoring banks to keep them off their balance sheets, arguing that the value of many of these liabilities was contingent on events whose probability was difficult to estimate.[44]

Spanish financial institutions rarely used SPVs. The International Financial Reporting Standards (IFRS) established that SPVs be consolidated in the balance sheet if:

1. the originator held a majority of the risks of the SPV;
2. the originator's profits depended substantially on the SPV;
3. the nature of the business of the SPV was very similar to the originator's; or
4. the originator de facto controlled the SPV.

In the words of Jesus Saurina, Director of Financial stability at the Bank of Spain,

> "We forced financial institutions to apply the IFRS which obliged them to consolidate off-balance sheet vehicles that are basically parallel banks." The effect was to eliminate financial institutions' incentives to use SPVs. According to Jose Maria Roldan Alegre, general director of regulation of the Bank of Spain, "This showed that the growth of SIVs [elsewhere] was triggered by the arbitration of the capital requirements and credit provisions."

The Bank of Spain, introduced a system of so-called dynamic provisioning in 2000, at the beginning of the housing boom. The system forced banks to build up reserves against future hypothetical losses.[45] Credit provisions sums to cover losses that banks had to set aside when they issued credit, were now estimated based on the bank's portfolio of investments and the risks associated with those types of investment in the past. At the same time, the average level of credit provisions was increased.

The Bank of Spain's rationale for this reform was straightforward. The risk from a loan appeared the moment it was granted, rather than when a borrower defaulted. Defaults are counter-cyclical, so to mitigate their risk, the new system forced banks, during boom times, to set aside a provision for each new loan. The additional cost of lending was intended to limit growth in lending, as well as forcing banks to build a cushion against future losses. During downturns, banks could draw from the general provisions to cover bad loans, lessening their need to cut back lending or raise new capital. But this system also had drawbacks. As Juan Arena, former president of Bankinter, noted, it "took a toll on profits during the 2000–2007 period." For example, had the statistical provisions been required for all [of the year] 2000, instead of only the second half, profits before tax of all credit institutions would have only grown by 0.5% instead of their actual growth of 12%. According to Arena, another drawback of the new provisioning system was that it induced banks and *cajas* to take on more risk within each type of product since the provisions were based on historical means across financial institutions rather than on the specific risks of each institution."[46]

The New Conquistadors

The extraordinary growth of the Spanish economy was reflected in the emergence of a few champions whose success spread far beyond the nation's borders. In 2006, *Business Week* included three Spanish firms, Zara, Bankinter and ACS, among the 100 most innovative companies in the world.[47] Santander was the biggest bank in continental Europe; Telefónica became the third-biggest telecommunications company in the world; and Spanish construction groups such as ACS, Ferrovial and Sacyr Vallehermoso comprised five of the top seven such groups in Europe.

The comparative advantage of each of these champions had a different origin. Banks developed information systems that enabled them to economize on the costs of targeting multiple products to a given customer. (See **Exhibit 5e**.) Construction companies became world class by developing an expertise in building the massive infrastructure projects financed with EC funds after 1986. Florentino Perez, president of ACS (and chairman of the Real Madrid soccer club), highlighted the importance of a more intangible factor: the directors of these companies had known each other for a long time. "We studied together in the university and have been cooperating since then," he said. "If we have a better chance to get a project to build and manage a highway in Canada by making a joint bid with Acciona, we are very happy to go hand-in hand with them. If the next day we find it profitable to make a joint bid with Ferrovial, we will do it."[48]

The Spanish conquistadors obtained their first international experiences in Latin America during the 1990s searching for both new profitable business and geographical diversification in their revenues. Telefónica, along with banks and utilities, snapped up assets all across Latin America during a wave of privatizations. But with privatizations drying up and the rise of more left-leaning governments in Latin America in the early 2000s, Spanish champions searched for new markets.

In 2004, Santander pulled off Europe's second-largest cross-border banking deal with its $18 billion purchase of U.K.-based Abbey National. Spanish banking rival BBVA already was the largest bank in Texas. Telefónica bought the U.K. mobile-operator O2 for $30 billion, a former state-owned phone company based in the Czech Republic and a 10% stake in China Netcom. Construction companies tried to smooth their very cyclical profits by diversifying into less cyclical sectors. ACS acquired stakes in two of the largest Spanish electric utilities; Ferrovial became a leading private airport operator; Sacyr Vallehermoso diversified into infrastructure concessions; Acciona invested in renewable energies.

A Productivity Mystery

> *Productivity is very important, but people do not find it sexy.*
> — David Vegara, Spanish Secretary of Economy

Spanish productivity growth over the 1995–2007 period was dismal. Total factor productivity (TFP) growth, a measure of productivity growth net of the effect of capital accumulation, was negative every year between 1999 and 2006 and only slightly positive in 2007. Between 1995 and 2005 Spain underperformed the EU and the United States in virtually all sectors in terms of both labor productivity and TFP growth (see **Exhibit 6a**). The only exception was banking between 2000 and 2005. The evolution of productivity affected the competitiveness of the Spanish economy. Between 1999 and 2007, Spain had become 14% less competitive relative to its trading partners, while the EU as a whole had experienced a decline in its competitiveness of only 2%.[49]

The dismal productivity performance was even more puzzling given the growth rate of the economy and the educational gains of the Spanish workforce. Between 1995 and 2005, the proportion of the adult population that held an upper secondary-school degree rose from 17% to 28% and the proportion with a post-secondary degree rose from 12% to 20%.

Traditionally, it had not been easy to start a new business in Spain. According to the World Bank "Doing Business" report, Spain ranked 140 in the world in terms of costs of starting a new business.[50] It took 10 procedures and 47 days to start a new business. However, other than through a few new regulations from the regional governments that affected electricity and telecommunications, the regulatory burden had not increased in the last 15 years.[51]

Labor market institutions might have affected productivity growth. Over the period 1991–2005, Spanish companies that had higher shares of temporary workers and a worse record in making temporary workers permanent also had lower growth rates in TFP.[52]

Spanish companies were failing in upgrading their workers' skills and in incorporating frontier technologies. The share of workers receiving any form of on the job training was significantly lower in Spain that in Europe (24.5% versus 42%). The gap was particularly large for companies with fewer than 250 employees. Information technologies, such as computers or the internet, had much less penetration in Spain than in countries at similar income levels (See **Exhibit 6c**).

Another puzzling observation was that, unlike most advanced economies, labor productivity did not tend to increase when the Spanish economy was booming. (See **Exhibit 6b**.) According to J. Miguel Guerrero, president of the Industry Commission in the Spanish Confederation of Businessmen, "During booms, there is no pressure

Exhibit 6a.   Average Annual rates of Growth (%) of Gross Value Added per Hour Worked (LP) and Total Factor Productivity (TFP)

	Spain			EU-15*			US		
	LP			LP			LP		
	1970–1995	1995–2000	2000–2005	1970–1995	1995–2000	2000–2005	1970–1995	1995–2000	2000–2005
Total Industries	2.9	0.1	0.6	2.7	1.6	1.1	0.8	2.1	2.4
Electrical machinery and communication	5.6	3	2.3	5	8.3	5.7	4.3	10.4	9.7
Manufacturing, excluding electrical	3.7	−0.4	1.3	3.3	2.1	2.3	1.2	1.6	4.1
Other goods producing industries	5.3	0	0.2	3.7	1.5	1.4	0.5	−0.1	−0.2
Distribution services	2.1	0.9	0.4	2.5	2.2	1.3	1.7	4.8	3.2
Finance and business services	−0.6	0.1	2.3	0.9	0.4	0.4	−0.1	2	3.1
Personal and social services	1.1	−0.7	−1.1	0.3	0.3	−0.9	0.6	1.4	1
Non-market services	−0.4	0.6	0.4	1.3	1	0.3	0.1	0.8	0.8

	Spain			EU-15*		US		
	TFP			TFP		TFP		
	1980–1995	1995–2000	2000–2005	1980–1995	1995–2004	1980–1995	1995–2000	2000–2005
Market Economy	0.6	−0.8	−0.8	0.7	0.3	0.7	1.1	1.7
Electrical machinery and communication	2.2	−1.6	−1.2	2.9	4.7	3.8	6.9	7.1
Manufacturing, excluding electrical	1.3	−0.9	−0.3	1.7	0.6	0.9	0	2.4
Other goods producing industries	2.9	0.1	−1.5	0.2	0.5	1.2	−0.1	−1
Distribution services	0.1	−0.9	−1.5	1.4	0.4	1.8	3.4	2
Finance and business services	−2.3	−0.4	1.8	−0.7	−1.3	−2.3	−1.3	1.2
Personal and social services	−1.8	−2.1	−2.1	−1.1	−0.9	0.6	0.8	0.5

Source: Dolado *et al.* manuscript; EUKLEMS — November 2007.
Note: *Excluding Greece, Ireland, Luxembourg, Portugal and Sweden.

Exhibit 6b. Correlation between Real GDP Growth, Labor Productivity (LP) Growth and Total Factor Productivity (TFP) Growth from 1996–2007

	Corr(GDP, LP)	Corr(GDP, TFP)
France	0.50	0.74
Germany	0.52	0.85
Hungary	0.64	0.61
Italy	0.84	0.90
Slovenia	0.25	0.74
Spain	0.07	0.48
United Kingdom	0.89	0.89
United States	0.71	0.75

Sources: Economist Intelligence Unit and author's calculations.

Exhibit 6c. Computers per Capita

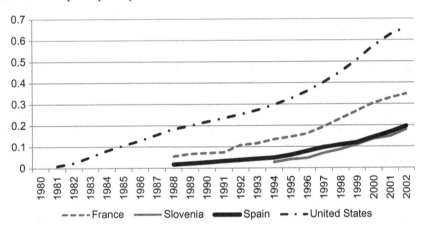

Source: CHAT Database.

to increase productivity."[53] The incentives of the average occupied worker might change with the cycle affecting the cyclicality of measured productivity growth.

David Vegara acknowledged that it was a mystery to the government why Spain's productivity growth had been so disappointing: "We have increased R&D subsidies and public spending on R&D, but it takes a while for these investments to show up."[54]

A Sliding Economy

Spain faced a general election on March 9, 2008. President Zapatero campaigned on the strength of the economy over the last four years. Mariano Rajoy, leader of the

Exhibit 7. Unemployed Individuals by Activity (thousands)

	2007QIV	2008QIV	2009QIV	2010QIV	2011QII
Total	1927.6	3207.9	4326.5	4696.6	4833.7
Agriculture, fishing, forestry	120.3	155.3	192.9	209	244.6
Extractive Industries	1.3	3.6	2.8	3.6	4
Manufacturing	132.3	282.7	313.4	213.6	225.7
Electric, gas, and water utilities	3.3	6.1	11.2	14.6	11.4
Construction	217.7	576.6	614.6	439.1	429.5
Retail trade, auto and appliance repair	183	276.9	333.8	300.7	322.1
Accommodation and catering	137.7	230.9	282.2	296.2	249
Transport and communications	57.6	85.7	122.4	117.8	127.6
Financial intermediation	10.9	22.7	27.5	23.4	17.3
Real estate, rental activities, and business services	101.6	170.9	216.3	201	194.1
Public Administration and defense	57.6	78.5	105.2	144.3	154.4
Education	31.8	37.8	52.9	53.7	58.1
Healthcare and social services	57.5	70.2	91.3	97.2	96.9
Arts, enterntainment, recreation	59.7	93.1	78.1	86.2	104.1
Domestic service	54	78.7	104.8	89.9	108
Unemployed for more than one year	515.8	789.1	1477.2	2049.2	2076.6
Unemployed seeking first job	185.6	249.3	299.8	356.8	410.1

Source: Government of Spain, Instituto Nacional de Estadistica (www.ine.es), Economically Active Population Survey, Table 4.25, "Unemployed by sex and branch of activity."

Note: Only persons unemployed for less than 12 months are classified by branch of activity.

main opposition party, campaigned on the claim that a recession was coming. The government denied this possibility and accused the opposition party of scare tactics. Zapatero's strategy paid off as his socialist party obtained a clear win, though it fell seven seats short of an absolute majority in parliament.

Unfortunately, recession was a very real possibility. In January 2008, the unemployment rate in Spain was in line with the EU average at 8.6%. By the end of 2008, Spain's unemployment rate had soared to 13.9% surpassing all other European countries.

The Collapse of the Construction Sector

> Revenues from construction could only go in one direction: down. That was the bad news. The good news is that we knew it. That is why we invested in other business.
> — Enrique Fuentes, Director of Market Analysis at Ferrovial

Already by late 2007, there was a widespread belief that housing prices were exorbitant and did not reflect the intrinsic value of houses.[55] This belief had been undermining demand and sales. To make matters worse, each year during the boom, construction companies had built more houses than needed. By the end of 2008, there might have been as many as one million new unsold houses on the market and probably a comparable number of unoccupied second-hand houses. Construction came to a halt (see **Exhibit 3c**). In August 2008, Martinsa–Fadesa, the largest residential builder in Spain, went bankrupt. Given the weight of the sector in the economy, the construction freeze threatened to stall Spain's aspirations for future growth. Housing prices started to decline, though at a slower pace than in the United States (see **Exhibit 3a**). By then, household debt had reached 80% of GDP (versus 60% in the euro area) while (non-financial) corporate debt was 200% of GDP. Growth expectations became more pessimistic, unemployment soared and consumption weakened (see **Exhibits 1a–d**).[56]

International Financial Crisis

After a 10-year run-up, U.S. housing prices started to fall in 2007 and the interest rates on subprime mortgages started to increase. As a result, many owners fell "under water."[57] The default rate skyrocketed, while the value of MBS plunged. Major U.S. financial institutions faced solvency problems (see **Exhibit 9**). The complexity of financial instruments based on MBS, distrust of the credit ratings of these assets and fears that they would face liquidity shortages in the future made banks reluctant to lend each other. A liquidity crisis brought financial markets to a halt. The strength of foreign financial companies that had bought American MBS was badly damaged, spreading the liquidity crisis internationally. Many governments responded immediately by injecting massive amounts of liquidity into their banks and some went as far to nationalize them (see **Exhibit 9**).

Spanish Financial Stability?

While banks around the world were struggling, the international financial press noticed the strength of Spanish banks.[58] Banco Santander used its liquidity to buy two British Banks, Alliance & Leicester and Bradford and Bingley. The new conglomerate formed by these two plus BSCH-affiliated Bank Abbey had 24 million depositors in the United Kingdom and was the second-largest U.K. mortgage lender. BSCH had also bought the remaining 75% of Sovereign Bancorp, a U.S. bank, for $1.9 billion. However, the Bank of Spain's governor, Miguel Angel Fernandez Ordonez, considered "a process of restructuring the Spanish financial sector, either through mergers or other instruments, absolutely unavoidable."[59] The IMF agreed and advised Spanish savings banks to improve their balance sheet after Fitch downgraded CajaSur, Caja Castilla La Mancha, Caixa Sabadell and Caixa Penedes and Standard and Poor's downgraded Bancaja. On March 29, 2009, the Bank of Spain rescued Caja Castilla-La Mancha. The central bank injected fresh liquidity to plug a €3 billion financing hole, provided €9 billion in loan guarantees and replaced the board of directors with a group of central bank administrators.

Credit had been slowing down since the end of 2006 (see **Exhibit 5c**). While over the 2000–2007 period lending grew at an annual rate of almost 15%, with peaks of 30%, during the first two quarters of 2008, it only grew at an annual rate of 10%. Car dealers and some other entrepreneurs argued that the slowdown in credit was caused by banks cutting down lending. A manager at one of Spain's larger car dealerships explained, "This crisis has a financial origin and 75% of the cars we sell need financing."[60] Juan Asua, member of the executive committee of BBVA, disagreed, saying, "We'd like to lend more, but people do not want to borrow. Our customer spread [the difference between the yield on loans and the interest on deposits] has not increased." A survey among the 10 largest banks showed that banks had restricted the supply of loans, though they had not changed their criteria. Essentially, conditions had changed and fewer business and individuals qualified for loans. Demand had also declined dramatically. The main reason that Spaniards delayed purchasing a house was not restrictions of credit but fear of becoming unemployed.[61]

Default rates increased fourfold since 2007, reaching 3% of outstanding mortgages and 5% of outstanding loans by September 2009 (see **Exhibit 5b**).[62] Despite that, Spanish banks were making profits (see **Exhibit 5d**). In 2008, the profits of all major Spanish banks grew. During the first half of 2009, profits before taxes reached €16.27 billion, a 17% decline from the same period in 2008.[63] Yet, the return on equity was still 12.2%, the highest in the EU. The solvency of Spanish banks was in line with EU average, with tier 1 capital of 9% risk adjusted assets, above the minimum requirement of 4%. Spanish banks' leverage was significantly lower than the EU average (18 versus 27).[64] A final source of concern was whether the Spanish banking system could assimilate massive defaults that construction companies and real estate developers might suffer if the sector's weakness persisted. The stock of credit provisions had topped €50 billion by the end of 2008, 70% of the size of "doubtful" loans (versus 50% in the EU). Approximately 50% of the credit provisions resulted from the dynamic provisions initiated in 2000.

Initial Policy Response

The government finally recognized the gravity of the situation in September 2008. It initially blamed the United States and its subprime mortgages. Building on the low stock of public debt, only 36% of GDP, it implemented an expansionary fiscal policy. It gave a €400 rebate to each income tax payer and a €2,500 lump sum per infant born. It opened a credit line of €3 billion to help property developers restructure their debts. Finally, it provided tax incentives to get real estate investment companies to list on the stock exchange with the aim of attracting more liquidity.

Some government officials thought that the crisis could be over soon if financial markets regained confidence.[65] Compelled by the deceleration of private credit and following the example of other EU countries and the United States, in October 2008, the government increased deposit insurance from €20,000 per bank account to €100,000 and created a €30 billion fund (expandable to €50 billion in 2009) to purchase healthy long-term securities from Spanish banks and thus provide them with liquidity to meet short term obligations. In June 2009, the government created the Fund for Orderly Bank Restructuring (FROB), with a potential size of €99 billion euros to manage the restructuring processes of credit institutions and assist them in increasing their capital.

The government was especially concerned about the effects of the recession on those at the bottom of the income distribution. To minimize them, the government extended unemployment benefits until February 15, 2010 and financed a two-year postponement of up to 50% of mortgage payments for newly unemployed workers.

Changing Course

Despite the expansionary fiscal policy, GDP declined at an annualized rate of 1.2% in the last quarter of 2008 and by 3.6% in 2009. Unemployment escalated to 20% at the beginning of 2010; 1.3 million households had no employed members.[66] Furthermore, Spain was the only major economy in the EU expected to experience negative GDP growth in 2010 and resume growth only in 2011. With the decline in government revenues and the increase in expenses from its new social obligations, the government lost fiscal capacity to maneuver. In 2009, the budget deficit topped 11.4% (see **Exhibits 8a** and **b**).

This new fiscal reality forced the government to change gears. It increased the VAT from 16% to 18%, and announced a tax hike on interest payments from bank accounts and deposits, on electricity bills, and on railway tickets, effective on January 1, 2010. The government also planned to bring down the budget deficit to 3% of GDP by 2013 by cutting current expenditures and investment in infrastructure by €50 billion over the next three years. On May 2010, it announced a 5% reduction of the 2010 civil servants' salaries and the freezing of the 2011 civil servant salaries and pensions. Despite the tightening of fiscal policy, the government announced a second six-month extension of unemployment benefits to take effect on February 15, 2010.

The labor market was hampering the recovery. Despite the decline in GDP and the historically low inflation rate, Spanish wages increased by 3% in 2009.

Exhibit 8a.   Fiscal Position Cross-County Comparison

Country/ Region	Budget Balance (% of GDP)						Public Debt (% of GDP)					
	2006	2007	2008	2009	2010	2011[1]	2006	2007	2008	2009	2010	2011[1]
Australia	1.3	1.4	−0.2	−4.9	−3.4	−2.6	15.5	14.5	16.5	22.6	28.8	30.3
Austria	−1.7	−1.0	−1.0	−4.2	−4.6	−3.6	62.1	60.8	64.1	69.8	72.3	72.1
Belgium	0.1	−0.4	−1.3	−6.0	−4.2	−3.8	91.7	88.1	93.3	100.5	100.7	99.7
Canada	1.5	1.3	−0.2	−5.6	−5.6	−4.0	70.3	66.5	71.1	83.3	84.0	83.6
China	−0.7	0.6	−0.4	−2.3	−1.6	−1.8	20.8	17.1	15.2	16.5	16.2	16.3
Finland	3.9	5.2	4.2	−2.9	−2.8	−1.7	39.6	35.2	34.1	43.8	48.4	49.0
France	−2.3	−2.7	−3.3	−7.5	−7.0	−5.8	63.9	64.2	68.3	79.0	82.4	85.8
Germany	−1.6	0.3	0.1	−3.0	−4.3	−1.0	67.5	64.8	66.4	73.5	83.4	80.6
Hungary	−9.4	−5.1	−3.7	−4.5	−4.2	1.2	65.7	66.1	72.3	78.4	80.2	76.1
Iceland	6.3	5.4	−13.5	−10.0	−7.8	−6.1	30.8	28.0	68.6	114.9	126.3	130.1
Ireland	2.9	0.1	−7.3	−14.2	−32.0	−10.1	24.7	24.9	44.4	65.3	94.9	109.2
Italy	−3.3	−1.5	−2.7	−5.4	−4.6	−4.0	106.4	103.5	106.1	115.9	119.1	120.3
Japan	−1.6	−2.4	−2.2	−8.7	−8.1	−8.3	172.1	167.0	174.1	194.1	199.7	208.6
Netherlands	0.5	0.2	0.5	−5.5	−5.3	−4.2	47.4	45.3	58.2	60.8	62.7	65.4
Norway	19.5	18.8	20.4	12.1	11.9	13.1	59.4	57.4	55.0	49.1	49.7	48.4
Poland	−2.4	−1.4	−1.9	−1.8	−3.2	−2.6	47.3	44.6	46.7	49.3	52.8	54.3
Portugal	−4.1	−3.2	−3.6	−10.1	−9.8	−6.7	63.9	68.3	71.6	83.0	93.3	103.5
Spain	2.0	1.9	−4.2	−11.1	−9.3	−6.5	39.6	36.1	39.9	53.3	60.1	67.9
Sweden	2.2	3.6	2.2	−0.9	−0.3	0.2	45.0	40.3	38.8	42.7	39.7	36.6
Switzerland	1.7	2.1	0.6	2.0	0.7	0.8	47.0	43.3	40.8	39.0	38.4	36.8
United Kingdom	−2.7	−2.8	−5.0	−11.3	−10.2	−8.8	43.4	44.4	52.6	68.2	76.0	79.4
United States	−2.2	−2.9	−6.3	−11.3	−10.6	−10.1	41.7	42.6	48.2	59.8	67.3	74.8
Euro Area	−1.4	−0.7	−2.0	−6.3	−6.0	−4.0	68.5	66.3	70.1	79.7	85.7	87.8

Source: Economist Intelligence Unit, Country Data, accessed Nov. 17, 2011. Except U.S. data from OECD Economic Outlook, May 25, 2011, appendix tables 27 and 33. (EIU excludes federal government debt owed to Social Security).

Note: 2011 data are estimates or projections.

A survey had found that 7 out of 10 Spaniards were against reducing the firing costs. The government drafted a labor market reform, approved in September 2010, that included a new contract for workers under 45 years reducing severance payments from 45 to 33 days per year worked. In case the firm had loses, expected loses, or experienced a persistent decline in revenues, the severance payment was further lowered to 20 days per year worked. Conversely, severance payments on temporary contracts were increased from 8 to 12 days per year worked starting in 2015. The reform subsidized hiring women or workers over 45 under indefinite contracts. It also contemplated more penalties for unemployed workers who missed training courses and for absent workers.

Exhibit 8b. Government Budget

	(Billion Euros)		% of GDP				
	2008		2009	2010	2011	2012	2013
Revenues	402.7	37	34.6	35.7	36.7	37.5	38.3
Taxes	229.8	21.1	18.2	19.5	20.3	20.9	21.6
Of which:							
Direct Taxes	117.5	10.8	9.5	10	10.3	10.6	11
Indirect taxes	107.6	9.9	8.3	9.1	9.5	9.8	10.1
Social security contributions		13.1	13.5	13.6	13.7	13.7	13.7
Other revenues		2.7	2.9	2.7	2.8	2.8	3
Expenses	446.9	41.1	46.1	45.5	44.2	42.8	41.3
Salaries and intermediate goods	177.5	16.3	18	18.1	17.3	16.2	15.1
Social Transfers	163.6	15	17.4	18.3	18.3	17.9	17.5
Interest payments	17.2	1.6	1.9	2.2	2.6	2.9	3.1
Subsidies	11.7	1.1	1.1	0.7	0.6	0.6	0.6
Gross fixed Capital Formation	41.6	3.8	4.8	4.1	3.4	3.1	2.9
Other expenses	35.3	3.2	2.9	2.2	2.1	2	2.1
Primary Balance	−27	−2.5	−9.6	−7.7	−4.9	−2.3	0.1
Budget balance	−44.3	−4.1	−11.4	−9.8	−7.5	−5.3	−3
Of Which:							
Central Administration	−30.5	−2.8	−9.5	−6.2	−2.5	−3.8	−1.9
regional Adminsitration	−17	−1.6	−2.2	−3.2	−4.2	−1.5	−1.1
Local governments	−5.2	−0.5	−0.5	−0.7	−1	−0.3	−0.2
Social security administration	8.5	0.8	0.8	0.2	0.2	0.2	0.2
Government Debt		39.7	55.2	65.9	71.9	74.3	74.1

Source: Ministerio de Economica y Hacienda.
Note: 2009–2013 are forecasts. 2010–2013 figures include the plan to reduce budget deficits.

However, the labor market reform did not include any significant reform of the collective bargaining process. Instead, the government just asked unions and business associations to reach an agreement. Wages increases planned for the next three years were as follows: 1% in 2010, between 1% and 2% in 2011 and between 1.5% and 2.5% in 2012. Firms facing financial stress could postpone these salary increases.

On July 2010 a new law for savings banks was approved. It allowed savings banks to adopt four organizational options, including spinning off banking operations to a commercial bank. This would allow savings banks to increase their capital. On the summer of 2010, the Bank of Spain also tightened the provisioning rules by (1) forcing financial institutions to cover the depreciation in the value of the collateral within a year, (2) imposing realistic haircuts on the value of real estate collateral

Exhibit 8c.   Long-term Government Bond Yields: Spain and Selected Eurozone Countries

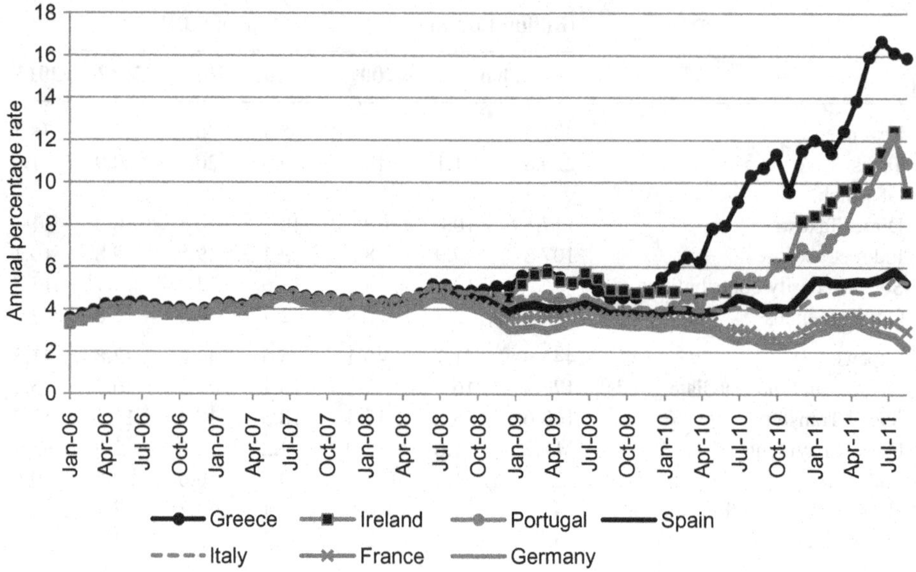

Source: Eurostat, accessed October 20, 2011.

and (3) providing incentives for financial institutions to take foreclosed assets off their balance sheets.[67]

Contagion and the EU?

As the crisis progressed, the fiscal balance of most European nations worsened. Markets considered necessary fiscal adjustment least likely to take place in Greece and to a lesser extent in Portugal and Ireland. Towards the end of 2009, interest rate spread between these countries' government bonds and German Bunds started to escalate.[68] The cost of borrowing for the Spanish government also rose. Country spreads declined temporarily with the bailout plan for Greece and the creation of the European Financial Stability Facility (EFSF) in May 2010. This facility, a SPV financed by members of the Eurozone, could provide loans to Eurozone countries, recapitalize banks, or buy sovereign debt. However, new concerns arose about Greece's ability to meet the conditions attached to its Eurozone loan and about the spread of the debt crisis to Portugal, Ireland, Spain and Italy. These concerns brought back high interest-rate differentials between Spain and Germany, sometimes reaching 400 basis points. On March 10, 2011, Moody's downgrade of Spanish government bonds coincided with an acceleration of some structural reforms intended to ensure the future stability of the economy.

Exhibit 9. Chronology of Significant Events in International Financial Markets between September 7, 2008 and October 27, 2008

7 September	
15 September	Lehman Brothers and Merrill Lynch do not resist the impact of the subprime crisis. Lehman Brothers goes bankrupt and Bank of America acquires Merrill Lynch.
17 September	The US Federal Reserve rescues American International Group (AIG), the largest US insurance and one of the largest in the world.
16–18 September	The financial turmoil affects several money market funds.
17 September	Lloyds TSB buys HBOS, the largest mortgage lender in the UK.
19 September	The US Treasury and the Federal Reserve Bank propose a rescue plan for the finance sector that includes the purchase of illiquid assets that drag down financial institutions.
21 September	Goldman Sachs and Morgan Stanley, the remaining investment banks, become commercial banks.
25 September	Washington Mutual, the largest US savings bank goes bankrupt and is acquired by JP Morgan.
28 September	The governments of Belgium, Netherlands and Luxembourg acquire part of Fortis, a stressed banking, insurance, and investment management company which was the world's 20th largest by revenue.
29 September	Wachovia goes bankrupt and is eventually acquired by Wells Fargo.
	The UK government nationalizes Bradford and Bingley's £50 billion mortgages and loans and Banco Santander acquires its £20 billion savings business.
	Hypo Real Estate obtains a credit line from the government and a consortium of German banks.
	The government of Iceland acquires 75% of Glitnir, one of the three major commercial banks in Iceland.
30 September	The Irish government for two years all the bank deposits, MBSs and bank debt. Belgium, France and Luxemburg rescue Dexia, a Belgium-French financial institution.
2 October	A version of the Paulson plan that increases the deposit insurance limit to $250,000 is approved by the US Congress.
	Greece guarantees 100% of the bank deposits
3 October	The Dutch government nationalizes the Dutch part of Fortis
4–5 October	The rescue plan for Hypo Real Estate fails and the government is forced to redesign it.
6 October	BNP Paribas buys Fortis Belgium and Luxembourg while the governments of Belgium and Luxembourg keep blocking minorities.
	The German and Danish governments guarantee 100% of the bank deposits.
7 October	Iceland nationalizes Landsbanki, the second-largest bank.
	EU27 finance ministers agree to increase the deposit insurance to at least €50,000.
	The Spanish government increases the deposit insurance to €100,000 and creates a temporary fund to acquire assets and increase liquidity.

(Continued)

Exhibit 9.   (*Continued*)

8 October	Coordinated action by the central banks of the main developed economies to reduce by 50bp their interest rates.
	The UK Treasury announces a rescue plan for the British banking sector that involves the provision of liquidity in exchange for equity through preferential shares.
	Banque Populaire and Caisee d'Epargne announce their contacts for a merge.
9 October	Belgium, France and Luxemburg announce a new plan to rescue Dexia.
	The Icelandic Financial Supervisory Authority took control of Kaupthing, the largest bank in Iceland.
12–13 October	The Euro area chiefs of state and govern agree on a common strategy to give confidence to the markets and reestablish the well-functioning of financial markets.
14 October	The US Treasury announces that it will provide capital to financial institutions and will guarantee the new debt issued by them
15 October	The European Commission increases to €100,000 the deposit insurance. The European Central Bank announces that it will provide all liquidity demanded by financial institutions without limit and at a constant interest rate.
16 October	The Swiss government injects capital to UBS, the world's largest manager of private wealth assets and the second-largest bank in Europe.
18–19 October	The Dutch government injects capital to ING
21 October	German bank Bayern LB requests help from the German government.
27 October	The Belgium government injects capital to KBC, one of the largest Belgium banks.

Source: Compiled by the author using data from "Informe trimestral de la economia Espanola," Bank of Spain, October 2008.

Reforms

Financial sector: Tier 1 capital had risen from 7.6% of risk adjusted assets at the end of 2007 to 9.5% on December 2010. By August 2011, the number of savings banks had been reduced from 47 to 15, the number of branches of banks and savings banks had declined by 10% and the number of employees had fallen by 8%. Over 90% of cajas' assets had been transferred to commercial banks and corporate governance had improved. Since January 2008, the banking sector had faced losses from impaired assets of €91 billion (€52 billion for the savings banks and €39 billion for the banks). To cover these losses, €53 billion euros had come from provisions that lowered reported profits, €16 billion from the provisions in place since 2000 and €22 billion from the FROB.

On February 2011, the government approved a decree to strengthen the financial sector requiring minimum tier I capital levels of 8% of risk adjusted assets. Financial institutions heavily dependent on wholesale funding, or with less than 20% of their equity owned by third parties, had a capital requirement of 10%. Institutions that did not meet these standards were advised in early March 2011. Those banks that did not find viable to access the markets to increase their capital had to resort to the FROB. In exchange for the loans, FROB acquired ordinary shares that it would sell within five years.

The Spanish banking system had limited exposure to sovereign debt from Greece, Ireland, Portugal and Italy which amounted to 0.4% of its assets. The sovereign debt of Spain represented 6.9% of the banking system assets. Spanish banks and cajas were exposed to 176,000 million of troublesome loans to real estate companies. The provisions for these loans amounted to 33% of their value.

Fiscal adjustment: The government cut spending with the goal of bringing the deficit of the general government (including regional and local governments as well as social security) from 11.1% of GDP in 2009 to 3% by 2013. In 2010, the deficit of the central government was 5% of GDP, lower than its 5.9% commitment, while regional governments ended the year with a 3.4% of GDP deficit, higher than their combined commitments of 3.1%. Local governments met their planned deficit of 0.6% of GDP and social security ended with a deficit of 0.2% of GDP, compared with its planned 0.2% of GDP surplus. During the first eight months of 2011, the deficit of the general government was reduced to €30.8 billion, approximately 2.8% of GDP. The planned year-end deficit was 6% of GDP.

The government did not allow regional governments to issue debt unless they had met their fiscal objectives in the previous year. On July 2011, the constitution was modified to incorporate a clause forbidding central and regional governments from running deficits above limits established by the EU. The new article allowed for exceptions in extraordinary circumstances such as natural disasters or economic recession.

A pension reform was approved on July 21, 2011. It enacted a gradual increase in the retirement age from 65 to 67 years, tightened eligibility conditions for early retirement and made partial retirement more costly. The new pensions would be computed as a function of contributions over the last 25 years of work (versus the last 15 years) and a minimum of 37 years of contribution would be necessary to receive the full pension.

In the fall, the government also planned to privatize the operation of major airports and 30% of the national lottery, as well as to auction spectrum for telephone services. The expected revenues from these measures were between €12 and €15 billion.

Collective bargaining: The failure of negotiations between the business organization and unions forced the government to approve a decree in June 2011 reforming collective bargaining mechanisms. The new process limited the automatic renewal of agreements to a maximum of 14 months and gave preeminence to negotiations at the firm level over those at the provincial level. The new law also allowed firms to opt out of an agreement if it weakened their competitive position.

Looking Forward

On May 15, 2011, thousands of citizens demonstrated all over Spain to protest against the government cuts, corruption, unemployment, lack of "real democracy," and the banks. Demon-strators demanded that public authorities respect basic rights such as "housing, employment, culture, health, education, political participation, free personal development and the right to consume the goods necessary for a healthy and happy life."[69] This movement, known as the "indignados" (the angry), had global repercussions and was echoed in other countries such as the United Kingdom, Israel and the United States. The opposition center-right Popular Party won local and regional elections of May 22 by an unprecedented margin.

In July 2011, 95% of the Spanish financial sector (versus an average of 60% in the EU) underwent a series of stress tests. The headline in the *Financial Times* on July 17 read: "Spain and Italy top results in stress tests." Only five Spanish institutions failed: Banco Pastor and four smaller cajas. The Bank of Spain considered that none of these institutions needed a capital injection because had stress tests included in their tier 1 capital the dynamic provisions Spanish financial institutions had accumulated over the last decade, none of them would have failed.

Despite that good news, economic uncertainty was enormous. The fear that the Greek sovereign debt crisis would spread to Spain seemed more real by the day as the EU was hesitant to make decisive steps towards supporting ailing countries. Would the EU emerge stronger from this crisis or would the first real test of the euro be also its last? Tourism was taking off with 8.6% more revenues from January to August 2011 than in the same period the previous year. However, would it suffice to lift an economy that had relied in what now seemed to be an obsolete productive model? Would the reforms improve the dismal productivity path of the Spanish economy? Would the unemployment rate drop back to acceptable levels?

Endnotes

[1] http://www.moodys.com/credit-ratings/Spain-credit-rating-600013487.

[2] http://www.moodys.com/credit-ratings/Spain-credit-rating-600013487.

[3] The European Financial Stability Facility (EFSF) was agreed to by the 16 countries that shared the euro on May 9, 2010. Its objective was to preserve financial stability of Europe's monetary union by providing temporary financial assistance to euro area member states in difficulty. For this objective, the EFSF could, with the support of the

German Debt Management Office (DMO), issue bonds or other debt instruments on the market to raise funds needed to provide loans to countries in financial difficulty. Bond issues would be backed by guarantees given by euro area member states of up to €440 billion on a pro rata basis, in accordance with their share in the paid-up capital of the European Central Bank (ECB).

4   This estimate is based on nominal GDP at 2007 exchange rates. Source: Economist Intelligence Unit.

5   Central Intelligence Agency, *The World Factbook.*

6   On tourism: The Global Guru, "Global Guru 'Analysis,'" http://www.theglobalguru. com/article.php?id=60&offer=guru001, accessed August 13, 2008. Also Bank of Spain, "Economic Report," accessed August 13, 2008. On construction: "A Sharp Construction Sector Retrenchment Would Hit Ireland and Spain Hard," Standard & Poor's, October 19, 2007.

7   "Pocket World in Figures," *The Economist*, 2008 Edition.

8   "Catalonians vote for more autonomy," CNN (June 18, 2006), accessed August 13, 2008. "Swiss Experience with Decentralized Government," The World Bank, accessed October 20, 2008.

9   "Economic Survey: Spain 2005," Organisation for Economic Co-Operation and Development, accessed October 20, 2008.

10   John Hooper, *The Spaniards: A Portrait of the New Spain* (Middlesex, England: Viking, 1986).

11   Barry R. Weingast, "Constructing Self-Enforcing Democracy in Spain," in Irwin L. Morris, Joe A. Oppenheimer and Karol Edward Soltan, eds., *Politics from Autarchy to Democracy: Rational Choice in Political Science* (Palo Alto, CA: Stanford University Press) April 2004.

12   Garcia-Perea, P. I. Garcia and A. Urtasun (1999). "La Estructura de la negociación Colectiva: Aspectos Normativos," Internal Document, Servicio de Estudios del banco de Espana.

13   This share was 15% in 1990 and declined to 10% by 2001.

14   These agreements were more common among medium-sized companies.

15   The labor relations system covered most workers employed by larger unions and firms that belonged to business associations, while temporary and some non-union workers were scarcely represented. Nobody represented the unemployed.

16   Mario Izquierdo, Ester Moral, and Alberto Urtasun (2003). "El Sistema de negociación Colectiva en espana: Un Analisis con datos Individuales de Convenios." Documento ocasional n. 0302. Bank of Spain.

17   On the consensus that both firm-level and national-level systems tended to support wage constraint, see John Calmors (1993), "Centralisation of Wage Bargaining and Macroeconomic Performance: A Survey." *OECD Economic Studies* No. 21; and Driffill, John (2006), "The Centralization of Wage Bargaining Revisited: What Have We Learnt?" *Journal of Common Market Studies*, Vol. 44, No. 4, pp. 731–756. Izquierdo *et al.*, "El sistema," find that wage increases in Spanish companies tended to be larger when they were bargained at the province level than at either the firm or the national level.

[18] Bentolila, S. and J.J. Dolado (1994). "Labour Flexibility and Wages: Lessons from Spain." *Economic Policy*, Vol. 18, pp. 53–99.

[19] There were two types of "fair" reasons for dismissal: Those attributed to a worker who was considered incompetent or negligent, and objective economic or technological reasons not be attributed to the worker. However, the scope of the second reason was very limited, and the burden of proof for establishing a fair dismissal had to be assumed by the firm.

[20] If a firm laid off a temporary worker, it had to wait for a year before rehiring him.

[21] "Two-Tier Labor Market in the Great Recession: France vs. Spain" S. Bentolila, P. Cahuc, J. Dolado, and T. Le Barbanchon, http://www.eco.uc3m.es/temp/franceand spain270410.pdf.

[22] O. Blanchard and A. Landier (2001) "The Perverse Effect of Partial Labor Market Reform: Fixed Duration Contracts in France" *NBER working paper 8219*; J. J. Dolado and R. Stucchi (2008) "Do Temporary Contracts Affect TFP? Evidence from Spanish Manufacturing Firms." *IZA working paper 3832*.

[23] Never before in its history had Spain received such an intense flow of immigrants. The United States had not experienced a comparable flow of immigrants as a share of its population over a comparable period since Irish migration of the 1850s.

[24] Eastern European countries began to gain access to the EU. These Europeans began to move to Spain to seek new opportunities in a country relatively close to their homes.

[25] Its southern European location made Spain a convenient destination for African immigrant. Still, the journey was long and dangerous. In 2006, the Pro-Human Rights Association of Andalucia documented the death of 1167 African immigrants trying to Spain, and it estimated that the total number of deaths could be as high as 7000. See http://www.apdha.org/media/fronterasur2006.pdf, accessed September 2011.
The first recorded "cayuco" (a type of ship) sailed from Mauritania to the Canary Islands in 1994 with two immigrants. On September 30, 2008, the largest "cayuco" so far (baptized a "super cayuco"), 30 meters long and carrying 230 immigrants from all over western Africa, sailed from Senegal to the island of Tenerife in only three or four days. The previous record was set on July 29, 2007, when 180 immigrants also reached Tenerife.

[26] Ana Bleahu (2004) "Romanian Migration to Spain: Motivation, networks and Strategies." *Policy Documentation Center*, mimeo.

[27] On immigrants' age: Juan J. Dolado, "Immigracion: Efectos Economicos y Politicas Eficaces. Sesion 1," Catedra "La Caixa": *Economia y Sociedad, Madrid*, January 21–23, 2008.

[28] C. Fernández, and C. Ortega (2008). "Labor market assimilation of immigrants in Spain: employment at the expense of bad job-matches?" Spanish Economic Review, Vol. 10, pp. 83–107.

[29] A study by the research department of one of the two largest Spanish banks, BBVA, attributed half of the growth in the Spanish economy during the 2000–2007 period to immigration.

[30] Ana Rubio Gonzalez, "La demanda y la oferta inmobiliaria en Espana," April 2008, p. 14.

[31] In 2006 the number of divorces was 141,000. This represented a 51% increase with respect to 2005 and a 277% with respect to 2001.

[32] Data for 2003, http://www.dubaided.gov.ae/statistics2006/wcy/Statistics/3.3.12.pdf.

[33] Of course, this effect was not symmetric across the population. It only had a positive effect on the wealth of those who had some residential investment. The rest saw how their relative real wealth declined as a significant lifetime aspiration (i.e. to buy a house) became much less affordable. Thus, the housing boom led to an increase in wealth inequality. Interestingly, whether one owns a house is highly correlated with age.

[34] Eva Sierminska and Yelena Takhtamanova (2007), "Disentangling the Wealth effect: Some International Evidence," *FRBSF Economic Letter, Number 2007–02.*

[35] The spread in Spanish interest rates due to country risk fell dramatically in the second half of the 1990s as it became clear that Spain could make it into the euro. See Ana Rubio Gonzalez, "La demanda y la oferta inmobiliaria," pp. 24 and 28.

[36] "After Years of Heavy Borrowing, Spain is Poised for a Slump" *Wall Street Journal,* October 9, 2008.

[37] Author's calculations based on data from BBVA and the Bank of Spain.

[38] In practice, in case of default, banks garnish any portion of the worker's take-home pay that is above the minimum wage.

[39] The Euro Interbank Offered Rate (or Euribor) is a daily reference rate based on the average interest rates at which banks offer to lend unsecured funds to other banks in the euro interbank market.

[40] The review of the U.S. financial markets borrows heavily from Julio Rotemberg, *"Subprime Meltdown: American Housing and Global Financial Turmoil," HBS No. 708-042* (Boston: Harvard Business School Publishing, January 2008); and Paul Healy, Krishna Palepu, and Georgios Serafeim, *"Sub-Prime Crisis and Fair Value Accounting," HBS No. 109-031* (Boston: Harvard Business School Publishing, October 2008).

[41] Ben Bernanke, "Fostering Sustainable Homeownership," Federal Reserve Board, March 14, 2008.

[42] See Rotemberg, "Subprime Meltdown," and Eric Rosengren, "Subprime Mortgage Problems: Research, Opportunities and Policy Considerations," December 2007.

[43] In the United States, SPVs were also known as special purpose entities (SPE). Two of the financial instruments issued by SPVs were collateralized mortgage obligations (CMOs) and collateralized debt obligations (CDOs).

[44] Specifically, they were "contingent liabilities," liabilities that might or might not be incurred depending on the outcome of a future event such as a court case. These liabilities were recorded in a company's accounts and shown in the balance sheet when both probable and reasonably estimable. A footnote to the balance sheet described the nature and extent of contingent liabilities. The likelihood of loss was described as probable, reasonably possible, or remote. The ability to estimate a loss was described as known, reasonably estimable, or not reasonably estimable. For example, structured investment vehicles (SIVs) pioneered by Citibank could be kept off bank balance sheets. Some SIVs relied on commercial paper with high ratings, just as CMOs and CDOs relied on mortgages or other debts. To obtain a high rating, the sponsoring bank provided a smaller line of credit and relied instead on outside investors who took an equity position in the SIVs.

[45] "La Reforma del Sistema de Provisiones de Insolvencia," Raimundo Poveda, Madrid, January 18, 2000; and "Spain's Bank Capital Reserves Offer a Model to Policy Makers," *Wall Street Journal*, November 10, 2008.

[46] http://bde.eu/provesta/impactoe.htm accessed January 30, 2010.

[47] Global Guru, "'Global Guru 'Analysis.'"

[48] Interview with Florentino Perez, Madrid July 2, 2008.

[49] ECB Harmonized competitiveness index. http://www.ecb.int/stats/exchange/hci/html/hci_ulct_2007-10.en.html. Accessed February 24, 2010.

[50] The higher the rank the higher the cost.

[51] Author's interviews with Enrique Fuentes and Juan Jose Toribio, July 2, 2008.

[52] Dolado, J. and R. Stucchi (2008), "Do temporary Contracts Affect Total factor Productivity?: Evidence from Spanish Manufacturing Firms," mimeo Universidad Carlos III.

[53] Author's interview on July 2, 2008. Indeed, the data support Guerrero's claim. Over the last 30 years, Spain's productivity had been counter-cyclical. That is, it has been growing faster in recessions than in booms. This puzzling pattern contrasts starkly with other advanced countries, where productivity is very pro-cyclical (see **Exhibit 6d**).

[54] Zvi Griliches, *Journal of Economic Perspectives*, 1987, shows however that the return to public R&D investments are much lower than the return of private R&D.

[55] See Standard & Poor's, "A Sharp Construction Sector Retrenchment."

[56] "After Years of Heavy Borrowing, Spain is Poised for a Slump," *Wall Street Journal*, October 9, 2008. Three major car makers announced layoffs or temporary cuts in their workforce in Spanish plants as early as September 2008.

[57] That is, the value of their houses became lower than the value of the mortgage.

[58] "Time for Central Bankers to take Spanish lessons," *Financial Times*, September 30 2008. "La invasion de los bancos espanoles en EEUU vista por Forbes." *El Pais*, August 6, 2009.

[59] "El retorno de la fusion de cajas: La crises recupera el debate con sus imperativos economicos," *El Pais*, October 17, 2008.

[60] *Wall Street Journal*, "After Years of Heavy Borrowing." See also "La falta de credito ahoga a las empresas," *El Pais*, October 19, 2008.

[61] "El paro, y no la falta de credito, primer factor para aplazar la compra de una casa" *El Mundo*, December 30, 2009.

[62] "Tasa de dudosidad Hipotecaria: Tercer Trimester 2009." Asociacion Hipotecaria Espanola. Madrid, January 2010.

[63] These are the profits for all Spanish credit institutions over the period mentioned.

[64] The leverage ratio is the ratio of total assets to own assets.

[65] On October 24th 2008, the minister of labor predicted that "the crisis should be over in two months, once the markets regain the confidence."

[66] The number of households with at least one active member was 12.9 million.

[67] Haircuts ranged from 20% for a borrower's principal dwelling to 50% for developable land parcels and building plots. At foreclosure, provisions were set aside of 10% of the loan value or the appraised value, whichever was lower. These provisions rose to 20% and 30% after loans had remained for 12 and 24 months on the asset side of the balance sheet.

[68] Bunds are the government bonds of Germany.

[69] "La manifestación de 'indignados' reúne a varios miles de personas en toda España" El Pais 05/15/2011, http://www.elpais.com/articulo/espana/manifestacion/indignados/ reune/varios/miles/personas/toda/Espana/elpepuesp/20110515elpepunac_12/Tes, accessed September 29, 2011.

III
Technology and Innovation

Introduction

Technology is a way to produce something. This is a very broad definition which includes most activities that lead to value creation by corporations. A new product that is developed is a technology if it provides the consumer better health, higher caloric intake or enhanced welfare. A new service is also a technology if it reduces the anxiety of the consumers over the risk they face, if they give them the pleasure of enjoying a vacation or a smoother way to process a payment. Of course technology is also something that makes companies more productive because they can use more advance machines and software or because they can organize more efficiently their productive processes.

Given its centrality to productivity and competitiveness, the central question is "why do (most) companies not develop or have access to the best possible technologies?" One possible answer is that the institutional rules that shape the environment in which companies operate do not make it possible/profitable. This is the type of answer studied in the previous module.

An alternative (or complementary) answer is that the problem is in the capacity of companies to implement and develop the technologies that would make them more productive. In this alternative view, companies lack an essential factor to implement technologies, technological knowledge. Knowledge is not something companies can buy in the market. And therefore, they have to stick with the inefficient technologies they can implement and operate. The cases discussed in this module provide examples of companies and activities where this narrative is relevant.

Once one accepts that the scarcity of knowledge is critical and that the market cannot provide this missing factor, a natural question is "what role should the government play?" Traditionally, we have tended to think that innovation is something that governments should leave to private companies. However, in reality, many of the most significant innovations have the government' stamp on them. This is the case of GPS, the internet, computers, and many of the pharmaceutical advances of the last century.

This observation raises at least a couple of important questions. First, should the government be directly involved in the development of technologies (in addition to its more wide-spread role as a financier of R&D)? Second, what role should it play when it comes to facilitating the diffusion of technologies? That is, when technologies have been already invented but despite that companies do not have the ability to implement them in their production processes?[a]

It is important to emphasize that, the cases in the module also enable participants to discuss the consequences for a company's strategy of the frictions that impede a

---

[a] See, e.g. Comin, 2014 Malaysia, Beyond 2020.

proper allocation of knowledge in society. For example, the ABB case discusses the risk of imitation of ABB technologies in China; ABB, CoET and Malaysia discuss the commercialization of technologies; Inkaterra emphasizes the possibility of using foreign knowledge to implement a domestically crafted innovation.

The cases in the module are designed and sequenced to explore the contrast and similarities between rich and emerging economies when it comes to technology. To this end, the first five cases focus on emerging economies, while the last four are centered in two rich countries (Germany and the U.S.). From a sectoral perspective, the cases broadly cover all sectors in the economy (e.g. services, agriculture, and manufacturing). Finally, when writing the cases, me and my co-authors have tried to provide a historical perspective that allows the reader to assess the relative importance for current developments of contemporaneous factors versus others that are inherited from the past.

Synopses and Assignment Questions

Inkaterra

The case presents the unique business model of Inkaterra, a leading eco-tourism organization in Peru, and the different strategies the company can pursue to grow. Through the experience of Inkaterra the case studies two general issues. First, it discusses the potential barriers that exist for the development of the tourism sector. Second, it presents the debate of whether governments may want to use tourism as an engine of growth, and if so, what is the best strategy to preserve the environment.

AQ:

1. What is Inkaterra's business model?
2. How should Inkaterra Grow?
3. What would it take for eco-tourism to take off in Peru?

ABB: "In China, for China"

ABB, a power and automation Swiss engineering company had to decide if they wanted to be even more integrated into the Chinese economy, ABB's biggest market, or if they should instead increase their presence in other emerging markets such as India and Brazil.

AQ:

1. Evaluate ABB's strategy in China. How well have they managed their technologies?

2. Were they right to agree to transfer high voltage direct current technology?
3. Is their mid-market strategy a good idea? If it succeeds, what will Winmation mean for ABB?

Low carbon, Indigenous Innovations in China

For the past seven years or so, the Chinese government has been powering ahead with industrial policies to promote low-carbon energy technologies-wind, solar, electric batteries and vehicles, nuclear power, and even carbon capture and sequestration. In 2009, the government focused broadly on "indigenous innovation," a policy to adopt and then develop technology in dozens of high-tech sectors. As with the earlier focus on renewables, explicit governmental policies and subsidies discriminate against foreign products and foreign companies invested in China. The net effects of these initiatives leave low-carbon energy industries in the United States in the dust.

AQ:

1. Why/How/where is China moving up the value chain?
2. Why is China pursuing indigenous innovations specifically in renewable energies?
3. Is it just China or can other countries do it too?
4. What should the US do with technologies to produce renewable energies?

CoET: Innovation in Africa

Dr. Jamidu Katima, the Principal of the College of Engineering and Technology (CoET) of the University of Dar es Salaam, knew that operating in Tanzania had its challenges. CoET's mission as a technology center that innovated to solve local problems could be a great way to contribute to the country's growth while training Tanzania's top talent. Yet, very few of its technologies developed at CoET had made it to market, and for those that had, the diffusion rate had been quite low.

AQ:

1. How should CoET be organized?
2. Do African firms adopt new technologies? Why?
3. What should be technological priority of African governments?

Malaysia: Standing on a Single Leaf

The case discusses the development of palm oil in Malaysia. This experience provides important insights about when and how government intervention can be successful in developing new sectors in the economy.

AQ:

1. Was the development of the palm oil sector in Malaysia the result of market forces or of government intervention?
2. Is the plantation sector a good sector to specialize?
3. When/how can economic activity shift to a new sector?

Fraunhofer: Innovation in Germany

Fraunhofer: Five Significant Innovations

Fraunhofer is one of the largest applied research organizations in the world. With 17,000 employees and a 1.6 billion euros budget, Fraunhofer has 60 institutes in Germany that cover most fields of science. The case examines the consequences that Fraunhofer has for the competitiveness of the German economy. It also explores whether the organization of R&D is affected by the size distribution of firms as well as by institutions in labor and financial markets.

AQ:

1. Is Fraunhofer an effective organization?
2. Are German companies competitive?
3. What role should the government play in innovation?

The Great Moderation, Dead or Alive?

The Great Moderation is a significant decline in the volatility of fluctuations in most macroeconomic variables that the United States and other developed and developing economies have experienced at least since the mid-1980s. This case describes the basic facts, presents contending explanations and explores the consequences of the Great Moderation for the likely amplitude of future business cycles.

AQ:

1. Which of the different potential drivers of the Great Moderation you consider most relevant?
2. How does the moderation affect companies? Is it good for business?
3. Is the Moderation Age gone or will it come back?

The US Current Account Deficit

Investors and policymakers throughout the world were confronted with the risk of painful economic consequences arising from the large US current account deficit. In

2007, the US current account deficit was $731 billion, equivalent to 5.3% of GDP. The implications of the deficit were debated with intensity. At one extreme, it was argued that large deficits would eventually resolve themselves smoothly, even if they persisted for many more years. Former Federal Reserve Chairman Alan Greenspan was among those expecting a "benign resolution to the US current account imbalance." Other analysts, such as economists at the World Bank, believed the large deficits raised the risk of a sharp and disorderly fall of the dollar and that necessary macroeconomic adjustment that could be painful, for the United States as well as for the rest of the world. The Financial Times asked: "How long will foreigners be prepared to make such generous 'gifts' to the US?" In this environment, Berkshire Hathaway, run by legendary investor Warren Buffett, postulated that current account imbalances would lead to "some chaotic markets in which currency adjustments play a part" and announced to shareholders a plan to increase investment in overseas companies to protect against this risk. It remained to be seen what the short and long-term implications of the current account deficit would ultimately yield.

AQ:

1. What drives the US CA deficit?
2. Should US companies be concerned about it? What about consumers?
3. Should the government strengthen US competitiveness? How? Should it create its own Fraunhofer?

Inkaterra

Diego Comin*, Rohan Gopaldas* and Diego Rehder*

On February 11, 2011, while Peruvians were getting ready to celebrate the centennial of Hiram Bingham's discovery of Machu Picchu, the President of Yale University Richard C. Levin announced the return of 5,000 archeological pieces from Machu Picchu. The objects, which included ceramic, stones, silver statues and human bones, had been taken from the iconic pre-Colombian site in 1916 and held "on loan" since. Once in Peru, the articles would be displayed in a new museum located in a former Inca palace. The museum would operate under the joint direction of Yale University and San Antonio Abad University in Cuzco.

The long impasse that began in 1916 saw a turning point in November 2001 at a dinner arranged by architect Travis Price at the residence of Greek Ambassador in the U.S. Alexander Philon. The dinner was attended by the Ambassador and his wife (Helena Philon), Terry Garcia, vice-president of the National Geographic Society, Bart Lewis, associate editor of National Geographic Traveller, Joe Koechlin, Founder of Inkaterra, and his wife Denise Koechlin. The theme to be discussed was the loot of universal treasures, including Machu Picchu's.

*Reprinted with permission of Harvard Business School Publishing.
This case was prepared by Professor Diego Comin and independent researchers Rohan Gopaldas and Diego Rehder
Inkaterra 713-022

Many steps were taken after the dinner involving numerous people both in Peru and in the U.S. Some actions fostered the goodwill between the parties. But others were eminently legal such as the high level commission designated by Congress for the recovery of patrimony, of which Joe Koechlin was one of six members, and the filing of a lawsuit by the Republic of Peru against Yale University in December 2008.

On July 2011, the Peruvian government invited the main actors in the return of the artifacts to the celebration of the centennial of the discovery of Machu Picchu. Joe Koechlin could stare the familiar, yet incomparable site, with a renewed sense of satisfaction. His country had emerged victorious from a long battle. Amidst those feelings, Joe could not help but wonder whether that moment would mark the beginning of a new era for tourism in Peru, and what role Inkaterra would play in that future.

Peru

Geography

Peru is the third largest country in South America, with an area of 1.28 million square kilometers (see **Exhibit 1**). The Peruvian population, estimated to be 30 million, is a multiethnic mix of Amerindians, Europeans, Africans, and Asians. The principle language is Spanish, although a significant number of Peruvians speak Quechua or other native languages. This mixture of cultural traditions has resulted in a wide diversity of expressions in fields such as art, cuisine, literature and music.[1]

Raw natural resources are abundant in Peru. Peru is the largest producer of gold in Latin America and a major producer of silver, tin, copper, lead and zinc. Much of the mining potential remains untapped due to geographical constraints, poor infrastructure and limited foreign investment.

The Andes run the length of the country, dividing it into three main regions and 25 provinces. The arid coastal region has the capacity to produce bountiful cash crops such as sugar and cotton under irrigation, and it is both the most populous and the richest region (per capita). The selva (jungle) is comprised of both the tropical rain forest (which once exported rubber) and the eastern mountain slopes where coca is grown. Lastly, the sierra (mountains) is made up of the area in the Andes above 2,000 meters. In some of the sierra's valleys, for example around Huancayo, farmers who own relatively small plots prosper by supplying foodstuffs for consumption in the cities. Wool for export is produced in other valleys. In some parts of the sierra, however, Quechua-speaking Indians practice subsistence farming, often under communal ownership, and find survival difficult.

Exhibit 1. Map of Peru

Source: Courtesy of the University of Texas Libraries, the University of Texas at Austin.

In Peru there exist 84 of the 104 world's ecological zones, and the country ranks among the first in the world in biodiversity. Peru ranks first in the world in its diversity in observable birds, with 1,835 species, second in primates, with 34 species, third in mammals with 508 species, fifth in reptiles, with 421 species, and fifth in amphibians, with 538 species.[2]

Historical Overview

Peruvian territory was home to Caral (Norte Chico) civilization, one of the oldest in the world, and to the Inca Empire, the largest state in Pre-Columbian America. Before Pizzaro's arrival in 1532, the Inca Empire covered a third of South America and had an estimated population of between 9 and 16 million. Under the Incas, all land was controlled by the state, though it was cultivated communally. The Incas also had a tax called the *mita*, which required individuals to work for a specified time for the state, in mines or public work projects, for example.

Individuals favored by Pizarro, and by the viceroys that succeeded him, were given *encomiendas*. This entitled them to collect tribute from a group of Indians in exchange for guaranteeing their spiritual welfare. Indians were, in principle, allowed to keep the land they cultivated and use the produce to pay this tribute. However, idle land belonged to the Crown, which either granted or sold it to individuals. This allowed the Crown to take over land as Indians were relocated or as their numbers dwindled due to disease. The result was the creation of relatively large landholdings, called *haciendas*. In addition, the Spanish used a variant of the *mita* system to force Indians to devote some of their time to work in mines. This forced labor allowed Peru to be the main American exporter of silver by 1600.

Peru obtained its independence from Spain in 1821. While constitutions from then on specified that power belonged to elected representatives, control often went to those that staged military uprisings. Even in the 20th century, the military took control during the coups of 1914, 1930, 1948, 1962 and 1968. Some of these coups, such as the 1948 Odria coup, favored liberalization, while others, particularly the 1968 Junta of Velasco, massively increased the role of the state in the economy. After independence, Indians remained at the bottom of the income distribution, which spurred recurrent revolts. These revolts were met with a mixture of bloody repression and legislation protecting Indian rights. However, many Indians were not given the right to vote until July 1980, the first election in which individuals who were not literate in Spanish were allowed to vote.

Growth and Inequality

Much of the economic development of Peru has been described as "export-led." This referred to the fact that, on several occasions, increases in the exports of commodities (sometimes due to increases in international demand, sometimes due to discoveries of new geological reservoirs) have been associated with bursts of growth in income and GDP. The first boom of this type may have been the guano boom of the 1840s. A more recent example was the production of fishmeal, which took off in the 1950s in part as a result of technological innovation. This expansion allowed total exports

Exhibit 2.   Country Profile

Capital City:	Lima
Language:	Spanish
Area:	1285000 sq. KM
Population (2011):	27.9 millions
GDP per capita (2011) current $:	$3990
GDP per capita (2011) PPP:	$6,624
Employment in agriculture (% total employment, 2007):	9.30%
Extractive industries (% in GDP, 2006):	15%
Unemployment rate (2011)	8.8%
Poverty rate (2010):	31.3%
Urban population with access to sanitation services:	85%
GINI coefficient: (2010)	48.14%
Literacy rate (2007):	89.6%
Life expectancy at birth (2008):	73
Number of documents required to export:	7
Number of documents required to import:	8
Easy of doing business (ranking, 2009):	56
Highest marginal tax rate (corporate/individual, 2008):	30% / 30%
Firms using banks to finance investment (2007):	30.90%
Terrestrial protected areas (% surface area):	13.8%
Marine protected areas (% surface area, 2010)	2.84%
Number of Unesco World Heritage sites (2010):	11
Forest area (% land area):	53.6%
Cereal yield (Ranking of Kg per Sq. Km):	47/177
Rural population (% total, 2008):	28.60%
Mammal species threatened:	53
Container port traffic (TEU: 20 foot equivalent units, 2008):	45/57
Registered carrier departures (Ranking, 2008):	39/105
Electricity production per capita (Ranking 2007):	95/134
Information and communication technology expenditure(% GDP, 2008):	3.4%
Paved roads (% of total, 2006):	13.9%

Source: World Bank, World Development Indicators, accessed September 2010. Prepared by the author.

to rise by a remarkable 21% per year from 1959 to 1962 and GDP to grow by 9% annually during that period.

While export booms centered on specific industries, Peru's exports became more diversified over time. One notable feature of most Peruvian export industries, however, was that they involved high concentrations of ownership. In some of these industries, a few large producers predominated from the beginning. In others, such as silver mining and fishmeal production, a large number of small producers competed initially but the industry consolidated over time. The resulting concentration of wealth was particularly dramatic at the beginning of the 20th century, when it was said that just 30 or 40 families owned most of the Peruvian assets used for exports.

This concentrated wealth and power was, at first, almost exclusively in the hands of whites. Over time, however, *mestizos* — a group that included both those of mixed European and Indian heritage, and the educated, white collar and urban Indians — were able to move into the middle and upper classes. Inequality, however, remained high with a Gini coefficient of 48% (2009). In 1980, the country started to suffer the terror of Maoist group *Sendero Luminoso* (Shining Path). The capture of Shining Path leaders led to its eventual demise. This coincided with a period of fast economic growth, with real GDP growing at a rate of 7.1% (5.5% in per capita terms) between 2005 and 2011. As a result, by 2011, per capita income reached $6,069 ($10,600, PPP adjusted).

Tourism and the Environment

With 11 UNESCO world heritage sites that represent an unparalleled cultural, environmental, and bio-diverse touristic offer, Peru has the potential to become one of the most visited countries in the world. However, the number of visitors did not seem to reflect all the country has to offer. In 2011, 2.2 million tourists visited Peru, generating revenues of $2.7 billion, which represented 3.7% of GDP.[3] By way of comparison, Argentina received 5.25 million international visitors, Colombia 2.2 million, Chile 2.8 million and Mexico 22.3 million.[4]

A study by a group of HBS MBAs on the reasons for the low number of tourists in Peru identified a series of factors that constrained both the demand and the supply of touristic services.[5] On the demand side, the study identified "the lack of a cohesive external marketing statement" of Peru's touristic attractions and the low degree of domestic tourism as significant constraints on the growth of the sector. The study identified a number of impediments that prevented the supply of competitive touristic services, which could be classified in three categories: lack of infrastructure, barriers to entry for new business ventures, and low involvement of local people (see **Exhibit 3**).

One type of tourism that has attracted increasing attention is eco-tourism. Eco-tourism can be defined as, "responsible travel to natural areas that conserves the environment and improves the well-being of local people."[1] This definition yields two metrics to evaluate the success of eco-tourism: the preservation of local flora and fauna and the increase in the income and well-being of the local citizens. Some early movers, such as Costa Rica, seem to have attained both of these goals (**Exhibit 4**).

Eco-tourism is also penetrating Africa. One of the world pioneering luxury adventure and conservation organizations &Beyond, (formerly Conservation,

Exhibit 3. Supply-Side Constraints for Tourism

Lack of Infrastructure

Hotels	Premium segment overpriced to other destinations
	Limited mid-range options for the budget traveler
Roads	Paved roads constitute only 12% of the total road network
	$45 billion current deficit on infrastructure spending
Transportation	Lack of direct international flights to Cusco
	Virtual monopoly on air traffic by LAN
	Limited rail networks
	Unsafe mass transit options (75% of mass transit vehicles over 20 years old)

Barriers to Entry

Licenses	Long process: locals cited up to 2–3 years for business licenses
Access to Credit	High interest rates: small business cost of debt at ~20–30% versus. Inkaterra cost of debt at ~6.5%
	Need for collateral: 130% collateralization required in most cases; unlimited liability
Taxes	High tax rates: 18% sales tax to make up for low direct tax-to-GDP ratio (~60% informal economy)

Low Involvement of Local Population

	Low specialized education and service training to meet foreign tourist demands
	Local people often relegated to menial professions, high value-add jobs retained by people from Lima

---

Source: Peru IXP 2010 presentation on "Can Tourism be the Engine of Growth in Peru?" Prepared by Authors.

Corporation Africa, or CCAfrica) is deeply rooted in this continent. CCAfrica started its operations in 1990 and currently runs 33 hotels and camps in five African countries (Tanzania, South Africa, Kenya, Botswana and Namibia). &Beyond has two distinctive features. First, they operate some of the most luxurious eco-resorts in the world, with prices that are typically in the $1,000 USD per person, per night range during high season. Second, &Beyond is recognized for the training and knowledge of its travel professionals and guides. Indeed, it has set the standards for lodge guides worldwide, and many hotel chains send their guides for training to &Beyond programs.

In 2005, &Beyond entered into a joint venture (JV) partnership with Taj Hotels Resorts & Palaces.[6] India, a country with over 400 national parks and countless wildlife, was a natural place for &Beyond to start its international expansion. With the JV, Taj could benefit from &Beyond's expertise in lodge-building and eco-tours, and more generally in its vast ecological knowledge. &Beyond, in turn, would have a chance to expand into India on the back of a luxury hotel operator. &Beyond would also benefit from Taj's local expertise in India and its political connections and would avoid having to navigate potentially treacherous waters alone.

Exhibit 4.   Timeline of Development of Eco-Tourism in Costa Rica

---

Success Indicators:

- 1970s: Balance of Payments Crisis → Government prioritizes tourism and other value-added industries.
- 1970s: Creation of 14 parks under national parks umbrella, with many funds coming from NGOs and World Bank.
- 1972: Monteverde Cloud Forest Preserve founded, funded through personal investment, land donation, and ongoing monetary donations by environmental NGOs like the WWF. Preserve maintained by Tropical Science Center, Costa Rican NGO dedicated to environmental study.
- 1986: Monteverde Conservation League formed to protect more land and conducts fundraiser under MCFP name. Garners support from individual donors and NGOs, ultimately raising funds to purchase ~6,500 hectares of land.
- 1994: Minister of Environment raises park entrance fees tenfold, preserving the environment through reduced park attendance but still resulting in net revenue increase.
- 1997: CR pioneers voluntary (albeit loosely-enforced) Certification of Sustainable Tourism for hotels and businesses.
- Ongoing: Private reserve ownership ensures that earnings are reinvested.
- Ongoing: Most/all hotels in Monteverde region are all of 3 star or less, which ensures that the operations are smaller-scale and more likely to be locally-owned, and sparks visitors to patronize local versus foreign-operated businesses.
- Ongoing: Locally-oriented attractions (Monteverde cheese factory tours, Butterfly Garden, and Hummingbird Gallery) are supplemented by adventure sports (Original Canopy Tour, zipline tours), resulting in holistic vacation offering.

Success Indicators:

- 1969 to 1982: Tourism growth averaged ~9%. 1986 to 1994: Tourism growth averaged ~14%.
- 2006: Tourism comprised 19.9% of exports.
- 1975: ICT recognized that the flora and fauna of Costa Rica were the main attraction for tourists vs. beaches.
- 1994: ICT survey indicates that, among visitors, 60% visited a national park and 26.3% visited a wildlife refuge.

Source: "Deconstructing Sustainable Tourism in Practice: A Comparative Case Study from Costa Rica and Egypt." Alefia A. Merchant, 2008. Produced by Peru IXP 2010.

Currently, the partnership has four lodges across India, co-branded under the Taj/ &Beyond name.

When confronting eco-tourism, governments must, to some degree, decide which of two models they adopt. The two models can be characterized as high volume, low cost versus low volume, high cost. In places like Kenya or Namibia, budget safaris offer affordable accommodation in low-impact camps. These countries tend to receive a relatively large number of visitors, which can impact local communities by leading to significant job creation and income growth for the local population. When following this strategy, countries hope that the scale the eco-tourism industry

Exhibit 5a. Distribution of Hotels and Rooms in the Sociedad Hoteles de Peru

Hotel Category	Number of Hotels	Number of Rooms
5 stars	37	4232
4 stars	18	1189
3 stars	27	1757

Source: Sociedad Hoteles del Peru
Authors calculations

Exhibit 5b. Ecologdes in the Madre de Dios Region

Hotel	Number of Rooms	Type of Rooms	Category
Inkaterra Reserva Amazonica	35	cabanas	5
Hacienda Concepcion	15	doubles/suites	4
Ecoamazonia Lodge	50	doubles	2
Sandoval Lake Lodge	25	doubles	3
Corto Maltes	25	doubles	2.5
	2	king	3
Tambo Jungle Lodge	12	doubles/triples	1.5
Posada Amazonas (Rainforest Expeditions)	30	doubles/triples	3
Refugio Amazonas (Rainforest Expeditions)	32	doubles/triples	3
Tambopata Research Center (Rainforest Expeditions)	18	doubles/triples	2
Inotawa	14	doubles/triples	2.5
	4	bungalow	3
Explorer's Inn	30	doubles/triples	2
Cayman Lodge Amazonie	28	individual/doubles/triples	1.5
Tambopata Ecolodge	18	suite	3.5
	30	superior	3
Wasai	16	doubles/triples	2
Sachavacayoc Lodge	2	for 15 people each	1.5
Albergue Tambo Tres Chimbadas	1	for 22 people	1
Estancia Bello Horizonte	13	doubles	2.5
Pariamanu Lodge	—		
Albergue Makisapa Amazon Adventures	—		
Pariamanu Lodge	—		
Albergue Valencia Lake Peru Ecologico	—		
Albergue Danny's Mirador	—		

Source: Authors collection. Number of Stars assessed subjectively by Authors.

Exhibit 6.   Inkaterra Hotels

Hotel	Number of Rooms	Date Opened	Capital Invested (million USD)	Number of Employees
Machu Picchu Pueblo Hotel	85	January 1, 1999	20	175
La Casona Cusco	11	April 29, 2008	2.67	25
Reserva Amazonica	35	December 12, 1995	2.5	105
El Mapi	48	August 1, 2008	4.9	55
Hacienda Concepcion	15	Jan-12	0.75	

Source: Inkaterra.com
(Lima — Cusco — Peru)

may achieve may put the country on the map and attract a particular type of eco-friendly tourist. On the other hand, the potential risk is that the scale ends up affecting the natural environments.

Across the border from Kenya's Masai Mara reserve, we find Tanzania's Serengeti's natural park. Both parks cover the Serengeti, 90% of its land falling in Tanzania and the remaining 10% in Kenya. However, Masai Mara receives 10 times more visitors than the Serengeti natural Park. For many decades, Tanzania has followed the low volume, high cost strategy.[7] With high park fees, low competition among hotels, and high-priced hotel rooms, Tanzania has developed a reputation as an expensive destination. The small number of tourists has remained local communities unaffected by tourism. Despite this, there are serious concerns about the preservation of natural environments in Tanzania. The infrastructure in the natural parks is inadequate and cannot handle the volume of visitors, despite low numbers. Recently, the public became very concerned about the plans to build a highway across the Serengeti to facilitate the transportation of minerals from Lake Tanganyika to the ports in the Indian Ocean.

Local populations can harm the environment in a variety of ways: Poachers threaten the subsistence of endangered species, inadequate sewage and illegal mining pollute rivers and mountains, and the expansion of agriculture depletes forest area. According to some, including Luisella Garmendia (Manager of Inkaterra La Casona Cusco Hotel), these local attitudes are due to lack of information; she asserts that "people lack information about tourism and about how to preserve the environment. Some people in the Sacred Valley are burning the land to increase their yields. This practice pollutes and may lead to fires." A different perspective was that these attitudes were individually rational responses to market forces. In response to high prices for gold and food, local inhabitants in Peru and elsewhere shift towards agriculture and illegal mining despite their negative externalities. Laws and regulations have proved ineffective in deterring locals from these activities. In Peru, for example, there are laws that ban both deforestation of protected areas and illegal mining. Yet, when officials tried to enforce regulations, illegal miners rioted and set fire to the land registry in Puerto Maldonado.

The difficulty of enforcing environmental regulations in weak-institution countries forces any successful environmental policy to rely on the market. In particular, local populations need to find alternative economic activities to those that damage the environment, which can often prove difficult in poorer areas. However, by providing a means of living which requires the preservation of the environment, a thriving eco-tourism sector may align the economic incentives of the local population with the broader goal of preserving ecological wealth. Peru's natural wealth concedes an unbound potential for eco-tourism. Yet, in 2010, the market was almost untapped. One exception was Inkaterra.

Inkaterra

Background

Founded in 1975, Inkaterra is a Peruvian sustainable tourism institution and eco-pioneer. A hotel developer and operator, Inkaterra is a provider of responsible travel services and one of Peru's leaders in conservation. Its mission is to conserve Peru's natural and cultural heritage, to protect its resources and endangered environment, and to sustain and enrich the country's rural communities.[8] Inkaterra is devoted and committed to the following:[9]

- Rescuing Peruvian resources with respect and support for the country's diversity and culture.
- Providing for the conservation and scientific research achieved through self-supported sustainable tourism respecting authentic cultural, social, and environmental values.
- Providing unique and proud Peruvian professionals a means to build a career .
- Enhancing Peruvian assets and converting them into world class products and services.
- Creating memories for visitors, through travel experiences, that will educate them.

Inkaterra cares for and has the stewardship over 17,000 hectares (40,800 acres) of rainforest in the Amazon basin in southeast Peru and property of 10 hectares (12 acres) of cloud forest in the urban area of the Machu Picchu Historical Sanctuary. Inkaterra received over 100,000 visitors in 2011 among its hotels and restaurants, has over 500 employees, and, in its 36 years, has served more than 900,000 travelers. There are 85 bungalows at Inkaterra Machu Picchu Pueblo Hotel, 35 cabins at the Inkaterra Reserva Amazónica lodge, 11 suites in the boutique hotel Inkaterra

La Casona in Cusco, and 48 rooms in the MaPi hotel in Aguas Calientes, the village of Machu Picchu.

Initial Vision and Journey

Joe Koechlin's involvement with the jungle started through the most unusual circumstances. In 1971, he approached renowned film director Werner Herzog to coproduce "Aguirre, the Wrath of God." According to Joe, "the initial plan was to produce a 16mm movie for the German TV, but the project escalated into a full-blown movie." The movie was filmed in Machu Picchu and off Iquitos, in the middle of the jungle, under very extreme conditions. Joe did not want to lose the group of people that had achieved such a feat. The question in his mind was how to employ them.

At the time, the main tourist destination in Peru was Cuzco, followed by Iquitos (northeast). Both locations were poorly accessible by transportation; a full day was lost making connections between airports in order to reach the final destination. This inconvenience spurred Joe's vision of creating a touristic circuit that would combine Cuzco, the gateway to Machu Picchu, and a new destination in the jungle near Cuzco. That was the genesis of the "Cusco Amazonico Lodge" in the Madre de Dios region.

Built in 1975, before the term "eco-tourism" was coined, this eco-lodge used local materials and staff, started without much in the way of investment, and was born of the idea of building a very rustic and simple place.

The next step was to settle at Machu Picchu. Joe was able to acquire land in the Machu Picchu district from the Peruvian government and private farmers. However, it would take 13 years to obtain all the permits to start developing the lodge in Aguas Calientes (Machu Picchu).

In the 1970's, protected areas such Manu; (Madre de Dios) were meant to be isolated from tourists. However, Joe saw the inherent appeal of the area to international and domestic tourists. He thought it was possible to conserve these areas while showing them to tourists. Indeed, he thought that without tourism, it might be impossible to preserve them as deforestation and agriculture supposed important threats for the preservation of their ecosystems.

This conviction led Joe to what would be a 30-year-long legal journey towards developing a legal framework for private concessions in naturally protected areas. In 1979, the ministry of agriculture issued a unique resolution that granted the use of 10,000 hectares in the Madre de Dios jungle to the "Lodge Cusco Amazonico", the first name of Inkaterra, for the creation of a touristic ecological reserve. The duration of the concession was 10 years, after which point, an appeal for its renewal could be filed. In 1989, Inkaterra asked for the concession's renewal, which was denied. Inkaterra repeatedly requested the extension of the concession. Meanwhile, part of the land previously under concession was invaded by local farmers who intended to cut down the trees in the area and cultivate the land.

In 1991, Alberto Fujimori issues a decree to foster private investment. Promoted by Joe Koechlin, the decree contains an attached article that allows the state to grant land to the private sector to develop eco-touristic activities. However, the article was not approved and this effort was ultimately fruitless. In 2000, the 1975 Law of Forests was updated, and the new draft introduced the notion of concessions to develop eco-touristic activities. Joe Koechlin participated in the commission that, together with INRENA (National Institute for Natural Resources,) drafted the concept of private reserves combined with ecologic, touristic, and research goals. In 2001, the new Law of Forests was approved, and in 2004, the concessions were granted.

Conservation

Inkaterra's approach to conservation is integral, innovative, and continuously evolving.

Research: According to Joe Koechlin, "when we started to think about how to preserve the jungle in Madre de Dios, we felt the need to first conduct an inventory of the ecological wealth of our ecosystems. Without knowing the species that lived in them, it was not possible to preserve them."

Producing such an inventory was a titanic task, impossible to accomplish without some external help. Joe Koechlin reached out to some of the most relevant ecologist and academic institutions. Since 1986, the Missouri Botanical Garden has contributed in the identification of the flora of the rainforest in Machu Picchu and in the Reserva Amazonica. The American Orchid Society validated the studies on the endemic orchids at the Machu Picchu Pueblo Hotel and announced that it holds the world's largest collection of native orchid species in their natural habitat. Harvard University Professor E.O. Wilson studied the ants in Inkaterra Reserva Amazonica and, in 1995, announced that it held the largest number of ant species (365) for a given place in the world.

The general effort in inventorying species had important by-products, some of them quite unexpected. Twenty-one new species were discovered: 12 orchids, one liana, one butterfly, two bromeliads and five amphibians, including the *Dendropsophus koechlini* (Koechlin's treefrog). The Inkaterra's NGO, Inkaterra Association (ITA), sponsored the visits of many scientists who came to conduct field research on its reserves.[10] This research has been published in scientific journals and books edited by academic presses. Inkaterra's resident biologists co-authored several books including *Cusco Amazónico: The Lives of Amphibians and Reptiles in an Amazonian Rainforest* (published by Cornell University Press, 2005); *Flórula de la Reserva Ecológica Inkaterra* (published by the Missouri Botanical Garden and Inkaterra Asociación, 2006); and *Orquídeas en Inkaterra Machu Picchu Pueblo Hotel* (published by Inkaterra, 2007). The National Geographic Society supports education on the natural and cultural wealth of the Tambopata rainforest at Hacienda Concepcion.

The production of such a vast amount of ecological knowledge is a distinct asset on which Inkaterra capitalized in various ways. Inkaterra's research has provided guests with educational instruments such as identifications and check-list plates for birds, orchids, and butterflies; educational CD recording of bird songs; an interactive DVD on rain forest and cloud forest birds, and large high quality prints. Inkaterra has invented a new method of preserving fresh orchids in acrylic cases, which allowed visitors to see blooming orchids out of season.

But surely, the most effective way to diffuse the knowledge created by this research is through tours guided by local "interpreters". The interpreters are trained guides who are domain experts in the habitats surrounding each hotel. The training programs were improved with the assistance of the Africa-based safari company, &Beyond (formerly known as CC Africa). Most of the interpreters are locals and thus have grown up in the region and are deeply concerned about the community. The role of the interpreter is to educate the guests on the entirety of the ecosystem they encounter during their stay. The interpreter leads treks into the rainforest, fishing trips, bird-watching trips to an elevated canopy, walk way and excursions to butterfly houses. The use of local interpreters, together with the fact that Inkaterra is involved in the collection of much of the transmitted knowledge, makes the Inkaterra experience very authentic.

Inkaterra's model has also attracted the attention of international organizations. The United Nation Global Environment Facility (GEF) via the International Finance Corporation (part of the World Bank Group) granted a loan to Inkaterra to develop the Inkaterra Canopy Walkway — a system of suspension bridges 344 meters long in the treetops — , a canopy tree house, and a bridge over a palm swamp, called Anaconda walk.

The environment: Resulting from a keen focus on conservation, Inkaterra directly has helped in capturing carbon emissions by 3,315,000 mt. This measurement was initiated in 1989 (before the Kyoto protocol) by the University of Leeds and Institute for Earth and Biosphere professor-specialists Dr. Oliver Philips and Dr. Timothy R. Baker at the Inkaterra Reserva Amazonica, the first site in Peru where carbon fixes were measured. Inkaterra has become a truly carbon-neutral organization, and every guest at Inkaterra has a 100% carbon neutral hotel stay. In addition, Inkaterra actively educates their clients and guests in the merits of carbon neutrality. Moreover, guests are given the opportunity to offset their carbon emissions of their flights through Sustainable Travel International's (STI) on line Carbon Calculator. Furthermore, Inkaterra indirectly fixes more than 12,600 ton/CO_2/ha/year through its support of a variety of external conservation programs. All Inkaterra hotels use clean technology and eco-friendly practices.[11] Inkaterra demonstrates its credentials through specific natural resource management programs, including:

- A rescue center for Andean or Spectacled Bears (endangered), butterfly breeding, and hummingbirds.
- The complete restoration of five hectares (12 acres) of native forest at the Inkaterra Machu Picchu Pueblo Hotel, where Inkaterra has registered 205 species of birds (18 of them hummingbirds), 111 species of butterflies, 372 native orchid species, ferns, bromeliads, medicinal plants, organic vegetables and a restored organic traditional tea plantation.
- Field monitoring by resident biologists permanently employed by Inkaterra.
- Full lodging to researchers and for students who come to practice, provided by Casa ITA (field station) and compensated by the visitors' work and knowledge.

Revenue generated by tourism is destined to the ITA and invested in conservation, particularly to assist in the protection of endangered flora and fauna species and to keep natural resources as the foundation of sustainable ecotourism in Peru.

Local populations: In addition to preserving the environment, Inkaterra's notion of conservation also includes the people that inhabit the land, starting with Inkaterra's employees. The majority of the employees at each location live within the confines of the property. As a result, they need to live in an environment that provides them the best possible quality of life. Joe makes sure that the employee housing are large, permanent residences that make the employees feel satisfied and proud of their association with Inkaterra.

After purchasing the land in Aguas Calientes (Machu Picchu), Joe donated part of the land to build the train station, the local hospital, housing, soccer field and a public school. Inkaterra has invested in programs to improve the health of local populations as well as to train these populations in the cultivation of higher value added crops and other rural activities such as beekeeping, fish farming, and the raising of wild animals.

Inkaterra also works to preserve authentic cultural and natural values, empowering local communities by giving them the capacity to act as professionals in eco-tourism. One example of Inkaterra's efforts to preserve local culture is the production of CDs of Peruvian music: *Café Inkaterra* (platinum recording of the year); *Serenata Inkaterra and Fiesta Inkaterra* (both nominated for a Latin American Grammy), weaving traditional Peruvian music in with modern musical trends.[12]

The Hotels

After opening what initially was a rustic lodge, the Inkaterra Reserva Amazonica near Puerto Maldonado, Joe decided to change his direction, from rustic to luxurious.

Exhibit 7.   Inkaterra Financials

Machu Picchu Pueblo Hotel

Revenues	Ejecutado: Dec-09 US$	%	Ejecutado: Dec-10 US$	%	Ejecutado: Dec-11 US$	%
Rooms	3,794,073	50%	3,355,967	52%	4,318,021	65%
Food	1,032,369	14%	862,116	13%	1,385,679	21%
Beverage	170,104	2%	162,018	2%	273,034	4%
Gift Shop	269,107	4%	199,831	3%	268,252	4%
Ecotourism	402,163	5%	341,367	5%	121,226	2%
Spa	128,883	2%	110,075	2%	132,604	2%
Telecommunications	631	0%	2,675	0%	4,888	0%
Tour Operations	42,931	1%	0	0%	0	0%
VILLAS URUBAMBA	384	0%	0	0%	0	0%
CASONA CUSCO	640,045	8%	629,810	10%	0	0%
Others	1,091,034	14%	838,226	13%	161,976	2%
Total Revenues	7,571,724	100%	6,502,086	100%	6,665,679	100%

Costs	US$	%	US$	%	US$	%
Rooms	466,026	12%	315,166	9%	465,541	11%
Food	675,885	65%	600,478	70%	958,958	69%
Beverage	103,893	61%	103,825	64%	139,346	51%
Gift Shop	233,265	87%	172,734	86%	228,926	85%
Ecotourism	91,386	23%	79,830	23%	109,044	90%
Spa	41,366	32%	34,637	31%	42,780	32%
Telecommunications	0	0%	0	0%	0	0%
Tour Operations	5,175	12%	780	0%	20,719	0%
VILLAS URUBAMBA	0	0%	0	0%	0	0%
CASONA CUSCO	87,650	14%	305,437	48%	0	0%
Others	390,973	36%	321,031	38%	366,857	226%
Total costs	2,095,620	28%	1,933,918	30%	2,332,171	35%

GROSS INCOME	5,476,104	72%	4,568,168	70%	4,333,508	65%

Undistributed Expenses	US$	%	US$	%	US$	%
Senior Managment	534,762	7%	559,303	9%	634,451	10%
Administrative and general	1,044,787	14%	1,058,295	16%	1,261,878	19%
Service	212,849	3%	196,745	3%	185,459	3%
Finance	307,430	4%	337,730	5%	375,209	6%
Sales and Marketing	864,561	11%	920,106	14%	777,234	12%
Property operations and Maintenance	516,158	7%	347,438	5%	161,129	2%
Utility Cost	92,165	1%	64,859	1%	118,370	2%
Total Undistributed expenes	3,572,711	47%	3,484,475	54%	3,513,730	53%

OPERATIONS MARGIN	1,903,393	25%	1,083,692	17%	819,778	12%

Rent, Property taxes and insurance						
Rent, Property taxes and insurance	143,160		108,328		81,211	
Property Taxes	0		34,606		28,482	
Insurances	57,305		57,650		63,148	
EBITDA	1,702,928	22%	883,109	14%	646,937	10%

(Continued)

Exhibit 7. (*Continued*)

Reserva Amazónica

	Ejecutado : Dec-09		Ejecutado : Dec-10		Ejecutado : Dec-11	
Revenues	US$	%	US$	%	US$	%
Rooms	1,085,556	48%	1,180,839	49%	1,458,023	53%
Food	417,889	19%	451,589	19%	511,368	19%
Beverage	169,495	8%	181,915	7%	161,251	6%
Gift Shop	76,832	3%	66,302	3%	74,786	3%
Ecotourism	229,216	10%	266,258	11%	306,173	11%
Spa	33,324	1%	37,890	2%	47,126	2%
Telecommunications	216	0%	1,276	0%	1,490	0%
Tour Operations	496	0%	55	0%	0	0%
Canopy	207,318	9%	216,963	9%	174,430	6%
Others	22,198	1%	29,461	1%	19,482	1%
Total Revenues	**2,242,539**	**100%**	**2,432,547**	**100%**	**2,754,128**	**100%**

Costs	US$	%	US$	%	US$	%
Rooms	243,958	22%	223,510	19%	253,422	17%
Food	345,358	83%	302,108	67%	345,930	68%
Beverage	41,389	24%	43,891	24%	49,669	31%
Gift Shop	55,139	72%	37,419	56%	42,199	56%
Ecotourism	170,604	74%	195,074	73%	232,610	76%
Spa	9,988	30%	9,485	25%	14,462	31%
Telecommunications	0	0%	0	0%	0	0%
Tour Operations	0	0%	0	0%	0	0%
Canopy	186,034	90%	132,917	61%	148,392	85%
Others	53,335	240%	232,359	789%	268,111	1376%
Total Costs	**1,105,805**	**49%**	**1,176,763**	**48%**	**1,354,794**	**49%**

GROSS INCOME	**1,136,734**	**51%**	**1,255,784**	**52%**	**1,399,334**	**51%**

Undistributed Expenses	US$	%	US$	%	US$	%
Senior Managment	38,630	2%	48,531	2%	58,074	2%
Administrative and general	203,286	9%	211,758	9%	303,867	11%
Service	27,372	1%	10,246	0%	10,577	0%
Finance	25,696	1%	50,502	2%	64,207	2%
Sales and Marketing	22,713	1%	21,958	1%	22,501	1%
Property operations and Maintenance	195,918	9%	197,375	8%	202,935	7%
Utility Cost	14,081	1%	5,885	0%	4,586	0%
Total Undistributed expenes	**527,696**	**24%**	**546,254**	**22%**	**666,747**	**24%**

OPERATIONS MARGIN	**609,038**	**27%**	**709,530**	**29%**	**732,587**	**27%**

Rent, Property taxes and insurance						
Rent, Property taxes and insurance	16,100		0		1,301	
Property Taxes	0		7,501		4,502	
Insurances	0		326		1,271	
EBITDA	**592,938**	**26%**	**701,703**	**29%**	**725,513**	**26%**

(*Continued*)

Exhibit 7. *(Continued)*

La Casona

Revenues	Ejecutado : US$	Nov-10 %		Ejecutado : US$	Dec-11 %
Rooms	522,097	83%		687,641	79%
Food	83,487	13%		121,938	14%
Beverage	7,914	1%		20,195	2%
Gift Shop	2,411	0%		11,958	1%
Ecotourism	60	0%		4,239	0%
Spa	6,635	1%		12,814	1%
Telecommunications	402	0%		904	0%
Tour Operadorating	511	0%		543	0%
Others	6,293	1%		13,347	2%
Total Revenues	629,810	100%		873,580	100%

Costs	US$	%		US$	%
Rooms	98,700	19%		97,239	14%
Food	79,708	95%		79,743	65%
Beverage	4,021	51%		6,110	30%
Gift Shop	873	36%		2,552	21%
Ecotourism	0	0%		0	0%
Spa	9,822	148%		10,109	79%
Telecommunications	0	0%		0	0%
Tour Operadorating	54	10%		248	46%
Others	3,130	50%		2,137	16%
Total costs	196,307	31%		198,138	23%

GROSS INCOME	433,503	69%		675,443	77%

Undistributed Expenses	US$	%		US$	%
Senior Managment	14	0%		4	0%
Administrative and general	40,333	6%		24,509	3%
Service	9,388	1%		0	0%
Finance	231	0%		-328	0%
Sales and Marketing	54	0%		443	0%
Property operations and Maintenance	42,564	7%		56,070	6%
Utility Cost	15,454	2%		14,537	2%
Total Undistributed expenes	108,038	17%		95,235	11%

OPERATIONS MARGIN	325,465	52%		580,208	66%

Rent. Property taxes and insurance					
Rent, Property taxes and insuranc	0			18,207	
Property Taxes	1,092			1,426	
Insurances	0			0	
EBITDA	324,373	52%		560,575	64%

(Continued)

Exhibit 7.   (*Continued*)

EL MAPI

Revenues	Ejecutado : Dec-09 US$	%	Ejecutado : Dec-10 US$	%	Ejecutado : Dec-11 US$	%
Rooms	676,308	82%	735,210	65%	1,150,585	53%
Food	137,005	17%	186,409	16%	723,914	33%
Beverage	7,346	1%	35,307	3%	119,910	6%
Gift Shop	0	0%	38,346	3%	157,399	7%
Ecotourism	210	0%	1,248	0%	6,745	0%
Spa	0	0%	0	0%	0	0%
Telecommunications	369	0%	970	0%	2,044	0%
Tour Operadorating	0	0%	0	0%	0	0%
Others	7,258	1%	134,625	12%	9,516	0%
Total Revenues	828,496	100%	1,132,116	100%	2,170,113	100%

Costs	US$	%	US$	%	US$	%
Rooms	100,710	15%	98,597	13%	152,489	13%
Food	125,396	92%	182,284	98%	596,927	82%
Beverage	3,806	52%	25,449	72%	63,020	53%
Gift Shop	0	0%	23,766	0%	107,182	0%
Ecotourism	0	0%	891	0%	4,177	0%
Spa	0	0%	0	0%	0	0%
Telecommunications	0	0%	0	0%	0	0%
Tour Operadorating	0	0%	0	0%	0	0%
Others	3,019	42%	74,230	0%	75,110	0%
Total costs	232,931	28%	405,216	36%	998,904	46%

GROSS INCOME	595,565	72%	726,899	64%	1,171,209	54%

Undistributed Expenses	US$	%	US$	%	US$	%
Senior Managment	6,030	1%	12,729	1%	24,710	1%
Administrative and general	50,188	6%	72,462	6%	113,389	5%
Service	20	0%	0	0%	139	0%
Finance	1,759	0%	5,885	1%	11,509	1%
Sales and Marketing	84	0%	2,319	0%	10,736	0%
Property operations and Maintenance	91,323	11%	109,275	10%	153,625	7%
Utility Cost	10,006	1%	17,673	2%	34,741	2%
Total Undistributed expenes	159,409	19%	220,345	19%	348,850	16%

OPERATIONS MARGIN	436,157	53%	506,555	45%	822,358	38%

Rent, Property taxes and insuran	US$	%	US$	%	US$	%
Rent, Property taxes and insuran	0		0		1,292	
Property Taxes	0		3,549		4,408	
Insurances	0		0		0	
EBITDA	436,157	53%	503,006	44%	816,659	38%

Source: Inkaterra

Exhibit 8a.   Guest Experience

"As the Inkaterra is a very good example for eco ecotourism, they have their own tea plantation, earn their own coffee and something else. The area has a park which can be visited by guided tours where you can see the great nature of Perú. It's a simple to go up to the Machu Picchu by bus. The accommodation includes a fire place and is very comfortable. The food is excellent. An Andean Sauna can be used (by extra payment), which was a great experience as well. Strongly recommendable."

"We said "let's splurge a little" OMG . . . this place is absolutely beautiful. The grounds and trails around the hotel were amazing. It's like the amazon was squeezed into a small mountains oasis. We especially loved the food, a 10 star meal served at breakfast, lunch and dinner. The little quinoa pancakes were superb yum!. The restaurant packed us boxed lunches fit for the Inca King himself".

"There was so much delicious food we had to share. The wait staff in the restaurant were great, they were efficient and very friendly. We were very well taken care of. The rooms were big, cozy and warm. The bathrooms were immaculate, TOP NOTCH! TONS! And tons of hot water, washing the sweat of the day away. We can't wait until we go back, this stay is a MUST!"

"Lovely hotel situated near base of Machu Picchu that is well designed to accommodate nature lovers, especially birders. Although I didn't try their spa, this is a great place to relax and indulge after climbing the "big stairs" of MP. I found this a perfect retreat to simply sit and watch all the bird life going on around the lodge. A must see/ stay place to visit. Enjoy!"

Source: TripAdvisor.com

Luxury was necessary to attract a more upscale clientele, trendsetters who would speak positively about Inkaterra to their acquaintances (**Exhibit 8a**). This word-of-mouth advertising would reduce the need for spending in traditional advertising channels, allowing for those funds to be used instead for research and conservation efforts.

To this end, special attention needed to be paid to the architectural and design elements of the hotels. Joe and Denise Guislain Koechlin, head in all architectural and design ventures, believe that the design has to be authentic in order to give guests a sense of time and place. For example, in the rainforest property near Puerto Maldonado, the lodges are built with wood and palm-thatched roofs to reflect the homes the locals reside in. The materials used in the construction are indigenous. Despite this apparent simplicity, the lodges and common areas are elegant, stylish, and comfortable. To produce all the unique elements that create the sense of authenticity, Inkaterra has three local carpentry shops solely dedicated to production for the Inkaterra hotels.

Given the geographic, environmental, historical and architectural differences between the different hotels, Inkaterra decided to treat each different location as a cluster. Each hotel handled its issues quite independently through a separate manager. Some of the managers had been in Inkaterra for a long time before reaching this position, while others came from other companies. The independence of each

Exhibit 8b. Recognitions

Travel + Leasure magazine, August 2011: # 41 Hotel worldwide (Inkaterra Machu Picchu Pueblo Hotel).

Travel + Leasure, September 2011: # 1 Family oriented hotel in South America (Inkaterra Machu Pichu Pueblo Hotel).

Conde Nast Traveller (UK), January 2011: Amongst 3 best hotel in the Americas, for Ambiance + Decoration (Inkaterra La Casona — Cusco).

RELAIS + CHATEAUX: their only one hotel in Perú (Inkaterra La Casona)

Latin America Traveler Association (LATA) UK, Best Amazon Lodge in South America.

World Travel and Tourism Council (WTTC) winner of the Conservation Award (2012).

National Geographic Adventure, June 2005, World-Class Lodges + Escapes (Inkaterra Reserva Amazonica).

Trip Advisor excellence for El MaPi (2011) Inkaterra La Casona, Inkaterra Reserva Amazonica and for Inkaterra Machu Picchu (2011).

National Geographic TRAVELER, Best Practices Award for Sustainable Travel 2002 (Inkaterra Machu Picchu Pueblo Hotel).

Travel & Leisure Global Vision Award for Conservation (2011).

Certified by Control Union (2012) first Worldwide for tourism, verified by Rainforest Alliance (2011).

World Travel and Tourism Council ( ) Winner of the Conservation Award 2012.

Source: Inkaterra.com

hotel pushed managers to find local solutions to local problems and strengthened the link between the hotel and the local community. For example, Denise Koechlin introduced dishes and drinks that extensively used local ingredients supplied by local farmers into the menu.

Guests appreciate the authentic luxury that has become one of the defining elements of Inkaterra hotels. This appreciation has also been evident by the numerous international awards the hotels have received from tourist organizations and the media (See **Exhibit 8b**).

In 2011, Inkaterra opened a new line of business in the four star range. Denoted as "by Inkaterra", the two new properties, El MaPi (in Aguas Calientes) and Hacienda Concepcion (close to Puerto Maldonado), represent Inkaterra's efforts both to tap into an underserved market segment and to prove that Inkaterra's principles could be extended beyond the upscale segment.

Growth Options

After more than 36 years of business, Inkaterra is still a relatively small hotel company with only five operational resorts. Thus, growth is a key focus for Joe. The question is in what way to grow.

One option is to capitalize on Inkaterra's reputation as a leader in the luxury eco-tourism segment and to expand in this segment by building more eco-resorts in other locations. So far, Inkaterra has constructed luxurious eco-lodges in the Amazon jungle, in the rainforest in Machu Pichu, and in Cuzco's historical center. These locations have allowed Inkaterra to cater to a number of cultural and ecological niches (birds, flowers, insects, and colonial and Inca architecture/history). The diversity of the geographic and ecological environments ensured the availability of new ecosystems in which increase Inkaterra's offerings.

Another option is to begin international expansion. Joe Koechlin has been offered the possibility to open Inkaterra's eco-resorts in Chile, Ecuador and Brazil. All of these options afforded Inkaterra an opportunity to explore new geographies and natural habitats. Inkaterra could capitalize on its expertise to build authentic eco-resorts and guided tours and at some point develop research that would allow the organization to provide authentic immersion experiences.

Oddly enough, the international expansion could also help Inkaterra cope with future competition in Peru. For years, the hotel landscape in India was dominated by the two indigenous hotel brands, Taj and Oberoi. However, over the recent years, a multitude of international brands entered the Indian market. This forced Taj and Oberoi to invest significantly in building brand awareness among the international guests who were visiting India. Taj and Oberoi achieved this by expanding within their major source markets, namely the US and Europe. Nikko Hotels in Japan experienced a similar phenomenon and attempted a similar response without the same degree of success. As a result, its brand power both within Japan and international is not strong.

One international growth opportunity was a joint-venture with &Beyond. The ecological wealth of Peru made it a clear target for CCAfrica when the company decided to move outside of the African continent. From &Beyond's point of view, a JV is an easier way to enter the Peruvian market than to build from scratch, given Inkaterra's familiarity with the local ecological wealth and the regulatory framework. Furthermore, the lack of land in Machu Picchu Pueblo, made the joint operation of Inkaterra's lodge the only viable possibility for &Beyond to get access to Machu Pichu. With a JV, Inkaterra would gain access to &Beyond's database of guests, which would allow it to market its lodges to a much larger clientele. The asymmetry in the sizes of the companies was one potential danger. Inkaterra would become the minor partner JV, and this might affect its control over the guest experience and its ability to continue producing cutting edge research. It was not clear that the JV would increase Inkaterra's value as a business entity. Even though &Beyond's revenues are greater than Inkaterra, Inkaterra maintains an EBITDA margin of 30%, while &Beyond's manager had mentioned that its margin was 11%. At the end, Joe discarded the possibility of a JV with &Beyond.

A different growth strategy was to focus on the mid-tier and academic markets rather than on the luxury market. These segments are newer for Inkaterra but not unknown. El MaPi and Hacienda Concepción have allowed Inkaterra to enter in the underserved mid-tier market with the brand "By Inkaterra." Casa ITA Field Station was conceived as a vehicle to attract students and researchers that would deepen Inkaterra's understanding of its own ecosystems. This ecological knowledge was critical to the preservation of the environment as well as to the services provided by Inkaterra to its customers.

As important as the direct impact of Inkaterra's strategy on its balance sheet was the response by other current and potential suppliers of eco-tourism services. Despite its ecological wealth, Peru was not an eco-touristic destination in the global market. This is in part due to the scarcity of eco-lodges not only in the luxury segment but also across the board (See **Exhibit 5b**). Limited supply reduced the options for potential guests and the pressure on the markups charged per room. As a result, tourists perceived Peru as an expensive destination, hence the importance in Joe's mind that other local eco-lodges replicated the Inkaterra's model.

Decision

With the rains having subsided and tourists returning to Machu Picchu in full force, Jose boarded the Peru Rail train, which would take him through the Sacred Valley en route to Cusco. Jose's mind was racing, perhaps faster than the train, as he considered all the opportunity in front of Inkaterra. Should Inkaterra venture into other niches? Should it continue to expand only within Peru or was it ready to venture to countries such as Brazil and Ecuador? Should it continue solo or merge forces with international companies? Should it remain focus in the luxury market or go down to other untapped segments where chances of replication by locals are higher? And, finally, what role should research play in the organization? Should Inkaterra be primarily a knowledge creator and preserving company or a hotel business? Would the current model be still valid for the new evolution of Inkaterra? And how could Joe and Inkaterra help Peru eventually reach its full touristic potential?

Endnotes

[1] http://www.britannica.com/EBchecked/topic/453147/Peru. Accessed on July 17, 2012.

[2] http://www.projectperu.org.uk/peru.htm. Accessed on July 17, 2012.

[3] http://www.observatorioturisticodelperu.com/mapas/partbcom.pdf. Accessed on July 17, 2012.

[4] http://data.worldbank.org/indicator/ST.INT.ARVL. accessed July 17, 2012.

[5] "Can Tourism Be the engine of Growth in peru?" F. Gu, S/ Khan. K. Kipp, C. Leprai, W. Masterson, Peru IXP, January, 2010.

[6] The Taj / &Beyond partnership consists of three parties who each hold an equal stake in the JV. Aside from Taj and &Beyond a financial sponsor is the third party.

[7] Diego Comin (2012), "An exploration of Luxury Hotels in Tanzania" *NBER wp. 17902*.

[8] http://inkaterra-hotels-peru.com/nature.html. Accessed on July 17, 2012.

[9] http://www.inkaterra.com/en/about-us/commitment. Accessed on July 17, 2012.

[10] San Marcos National University supports scientific research on the flora and fauna of the Peruvian Amazon Cloud forest and Rainforest. http://www.inkaterra.com/en/about-us/acknowledgenments. Accessed on July 17, 2012.

[11] http://www.inkaterra.com/en/carbon-neutral/inkaterra-role. Accessed on July 17, 2012.

[12] http://www.inkaterra.com/en/nature/programs/cap-I. Accessed on July 17, 2012.

ABB: "In China, For China"

J. Gunnar Trumbull*, Elena Corsi* and Elisa Farri*

We never considered China a mere manufacturing opportunity. We strongly believed in its fast-growing systemic demand for our products.

— Joe Hogan, ABB's CEO

China is nurturing our future competitors. We can only understand them if we are fighting in this market."

— Claudio Facchin, President and Chairman, ABB China

It was June 2010 and Joe Hogan, the CEO of ABB, a power and automation engineering company based in Zurich, Switzerland, contemplated how to respond to a recent wave of criticism of China's economic policies. Key competitors, including GE and Siemens, had been publicly critical of their recent treatment in China. Jeffrey Immelt, Chairman and CEO of GE, had caught the world's attention when he warned, "I am not sure that in the end they want any of us to win, or any of us to be successful."[1]

For ABB, the impression of China could not have been more different. Over the past decade, ABB's revenues from China had grown from $500 million to

---

*Reprinted with permission of Harvard Business School Publishing.

This case was prepared by Professor J. Gunnar Trumbull, Senior Researcher Elena Corsi and Research Assistant Elisa Farri.

ABB: "In China, For China" 711-044

$4.3 billion, representing 13% of global sales and the largest and fastest growing market for its most technically advanced products. In high speed rail and high voltage transmission technologies, China was leading world demand. With a large installed R&D capacity and 15,300 employees in 60 facilities across the country, China had been a major reason for ABB's recent strong financial performance.

One reason had been ABB's historic focus on China not as an export platform, but as a market. ABB called this strategy "In China, for China." This strategy included making major investments in the Chinese market. Over the past six years, ABB had invested an average of $100 million per year in new R&D and production capacity. ABB also brought their best technologies to China and worked closely with Chinese partners to develop new innovations that were suited to the local market. New gas-insulated substation switchgear installed in Jingmen represented the kind of evolutionary step in power generation that had emerged from its China R&D efforts.

Inevitably, operating in China raised challenges. For a technology-based company like ABB, China's weak enforcement regime for intellectual property rights (IPR) posed challenges. Recent reforms had strengthened China's IPR protections, but many foreign operators still perceived enforcement as weak. For foreigner companies that sold to government buyers, a new "Buy China" policy announced in 2009 also raised concerns that they might be increasingly discriminated against in public procurement contracts. Joerg Wuttke, Chairman of the European Union Chamber of Commerce in China, warned, "It's the first time foreigners have been singled out."[2] Some analysts believed that this retrenchment sentiment could eventually force some foreign companies to pull out of the Chinese economic arena.

The financial crisis triggered by the U.S. subprime mortgage meltdown had also had an effect on the Chinese economy. As foreign companies reacted to the crisis in their domestic markets, they reduced foreign direct investment (FDI) in emerging countries. Declining internal demand from industrial customers affected China's total production, as well as contributing to a 16% fall in exports in 2009. Yet the news was not all bad. In November 2008, the Chinese government had launched a stimulus package of about $600 billion to restore economic growth, and ABB could hope to benefit from some of the public procurement projects on which these new funds would be spent.

While other foreign firms worried about low returns from their China investments, the challenge that faced ABB and Hogan was in some sense the opposite. The very success of ABB's China operations and the high returns they had generated, raised strategic questions. Could they continue to grow in the internal Chinese market as domestic Chinese competitors developed competing products? More importantly, how would they compete with domestic Chinese competitors once they broke into the global market?

Company Background

Headquartered in Zurich, ABB supplied power and automation technologies to utilities and industrial customers. Its products and services were primarily designed to improve power grid reliability, increase industrial productivity and enhance energy efficiency. ABB's broad-based offerings ranged from equipment for electrical power generation and transmission, to high-speed trains, environmental control systems, automation and robotics.

In 2009, ABB had operations in over 100 countries and employed 116,000 people. Total revenues amounted to $31.8 billion, 10% less than the previous year. Asia accounted for 27% of total 2009 revenues, compared with 42% generated in Europe, 19% in the Americas and 12% in the Middle East and Africa.[3]

History

ABB was established in 1988 through one of the first transnational European mergers between the Swedish Asea AB and the Swiss Brown Boveri AG. Each partner retained 50% ownership of the newly formed company.[4] Hogan commented, "The way ABB was created proved extremely bold at that time. Cross-border mergers were rare in Europe in the late 1990s. Yet, neither Asea nor Brown Boveri hesitated to push their national boundaries further."

ABB's predecessor companies were among the European engineering firms that drove the second industrial revolution in the nineteenth century. Asea had played a leading role in the power generation and distribution businesses since its founding in 1883. It introduced electricity into Swedish homes and developed the first Swedish railway network. Brown Boveri, for its part, had supplied a wide range of electrical engineering products, including high-quality transportation equipment, throughout Europe, since 1891.

In its first two years of operation, ABB engaged in a large-scale program to expand in the power transmission and distribution businesses. The company grew very fast and acquired 55 companies in the U.S. and Western Europe.

Following the removal of the Iron Curtain in 1989, ABB gradually entered Central and Eastern Europe. Furthermore, during the first half of the 1990s, it invested aggressively in Asia through joint ventures (JVs) and acquisitions. In 1997, financial turmoil, which started in Thailand, hit the Asian economies hard. Production tumbled and skepticism rose among foreign companies. Yet, ABB kept investing in Asia as new buying opportunities arose. An $866 million expansion plan created 10,000 new jobs and almost tripled ABB's revenues in Asia, which rose from $3 billion in 1988 to over $8 billion in 1997.[5] ABB's expansion in emerging markets continued during the 2000s with more than 160 acquisitions. (See **Exhibit 1** for ABB's timeline.)

Exhibit 1.   ABB's Timeline

1988	Creation of ABB through the merger of ASEA and BBC. In the year prior to its merger with BBC, Asea has revenues of Skr 46 billion, earnings of Skr 2.6 billion and 71,000 employees; BBC has revenues of Skr 58 billion, earnings of Skr 900 million and 97,000 employees.
1989	ABB acquires some 40 companies in its first year, including the power transmission and power distribution businesses of Westinghouse Electric Corporation.
1990	ABB commences a large-scale program of expansion in central and eastern Europe following the removal of the Iron Curtain in 1989.
1993	ABB continues to focus its growth strategy on Europe, Asia and the Americas through a number of strategic investments, joint ventures and acquisitions.
1998	ABB acquires Elsag Bailey Process Automation, the largest acquisition in its history, to become the market leader in the global automation market.
1999	ABB divests its nuclear power, power generation and rail businesses in order to focus on developing its market strengths in alternative energy.
2000	ABB continues to consolidate its position in small-scale alternative energy solutions and completes several acquisitions of key software companies to complement its growing dominance in industrial IT.
2001	Specific customer divisions are formed, ABB lists on the New York Stock Exchange. Ranks number one in sustainability for third year in a row.
2002	ABB sells the majority of its Financial Services division and puts its Oil, Gas and Petrochemicals division and Building Systems business area up for sale. ABB streamlines its divisional structure to focus on two core areas of business: Power Technologies and Automation Technologies.
2003	ABB's two core divisions post improved quarterly results. Divestment program of non-core businesses continues. Group successfully launches three-part capital strengthening program.
2004	ABB sells part of its Oil, Gas and Petrochemicals division: appoints a new CEO, Fred Kindle and CFO, Michel Demaré, and announces it will build the world's longest underwater HVSC power link, connecting Norway and the Netherlands.
2005	ABB appoints Ulrich Spieshoffer as head of Corporate development and member of the Group's executive committee and Peter Terwiesch as the group's chief technology officer.
2006	A Plan of Reorganization to settle claims against ABB Lummus Global Inc. is finalized, drawing a line under the company's asbestos liabilities. ABB celebrates the inauguration of HVDC power link, connecting Estonia and Finland.
2007	ABB appoints Peter Leupp as head of ABB's Power Systems Division and Diane de Saint Victor as General Council.
2008	Sale of oil and gas business Lummus Global completes focus on power and automation. ABB set new financial targets to 2011 and signs contract for highly efficient transmission technology in China for the world's longest power link. ABB announces appointment of Joseph Hogan as new CEO.

Source: Company's documents.

ABB's Organizational Structure

In the late 1990s, ABB supplied a broad portfolio of products and services to different industries, such as rail, oil and gas, power generation and financial services. To eliminate inefficiencies and streamline its divisional structure, the company's top management decided to tightly focus ABB's portfolio on two core business areas: power and automation. As a consequence, ABB exited the power generation business in 1999 and sold its financial services branch to GE capital in 2003. "Worldwide market convergence in demand patterns for power and automation products has increased the attractiveness of ABB's portfolio and proved to be the right strategy," commented Hogan. "Power and automation will take us forward." (See **Exhibit 2** for data on ABB's revenues and EBIT margin development, 1988–2009.)

Following the internal re-organization of ABB, five new divisions were formed: Power Products, Power Systems, Automation Products, Process Automation and Robotics. Power Products and Power Systems served the power market.[a] The Power Products division was ABB's largest contributor of revenues, accounting for 32%

Exhibit 2. ABB's Revenues and EBIT Margin Development from 1988 to 2009

Revenue and EBIT margin development, 1988–2009

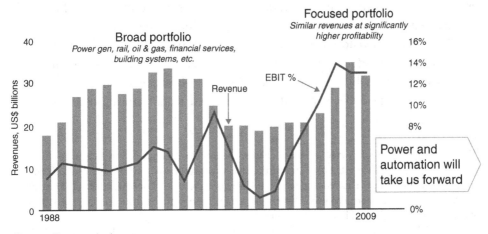

Source: Company's documents.

---

[a]The power market included two sectors. The first sector was the transmission system (or "electricity grid"), which delivered electricity from power generation facilities to local distribution networks over high-voltage power lines. The second sector, namely the distribution system, served electric power to residential, commercial and industrial customers. Power distribution systems comprised distribution substations, transformers and power lines, both overhead and underground. As customers' demand for reliable, high-quality electricity and efficient (or "smarter") grid [Not sure if "grid" should be singular or plural.] increased, electricity networks also incorporated sophisticated control devices to monitor operations and prevent damage from failures or stresses.

of total sales in 2009. It manufactured high and medium voltage products, as well as power and distribution transformers.[b] Key technologies included switchgears and apparatuses, circuit breakers for various current and voltage levels, sensors and products to automate and control electrical and other utility networks. The Power Systems division, on the other hand, contributed to 19% of total sales in 2009. It delivered systems in four areas: grid systems, network management, power generation and substations. Main technologies included substations, high-voltage power converters, cables for underground and sub-sea power transmission and systems to automate and control power plants and other utility networks.

In the automation market, ABB had enjoyed remarkable market shares since 1998, when it acquired the Netherlands-based Elsag Bailey, one of the leading market players in high-margin process-control automation.[c] The Automation Products division accounted for 25% of total sales in 2009. It operated in the building automation segment.[d] Its offerings covered a wide range of products and services for power distribution, protection and control and energy conversion. Key applications included switchboards, breakers, switches, generators and power electronics systems.

The Process Automation division contributed 21% of total sales in 2009. It offered products, systems and services for the automation and optimization of industrial processes, such as process control systems, plant electrification systems, information management systems and industry-specific application knowledge.

The Robotics division, whose headquarters had been moved to China in 2006, developed robot products, systems and services for the factory automation industries such as automobile, food and beverages and fabricated metals. Accounting for 3% of sales in 2009, it provided standardized manufacturing cells for many

---

[b]Transformers played a key role in power distribution systems. As power was generated in power plants at low voltage, it needed to be transformed in order to be transmitted efficiently over long-distances at high-voltage. This reduced losses and increased the amount of power that could be carried per line. Transformers were also used to decrease voltage for power distribution to end users, such as residential, commercial and industrial consumers.

[c]The automation market was comprised of three segments: process, factory and building automation. Process automation referred to control systems, plant electrification and other process applications applied in processes guaranteeing continuous production, like in the power industry. Factory automation included discrete operations that manufactured individual items for automotive and general industry areas. Product lines for this market included robots and modular manufacturing solutions, as well as low voltage products for control and power applications. Building automation offered a wide range of low-voltage products for control of climate, lighting and security for optimal management of the energy cost of buildings to the building industry.

[d]Generally, companies active in the building automation segment provided building automation systems (BAS), which were designed to monitor and control the mechanical and lighting systems in a building or in a factory.

applications, including machine tending, welding, cutting, painting, finishing and packing. In 2009, Robotics orders declined as a steep drop in demand from the global manufacturing sector continued into the fourth quarter.

An Overview of the Chinese Market

China opened its market in 1978 when Communist Party leader Deng Xiaoping adopted a series of policies to promote foreign trade and economic investment. Under the capitalist-inclined leadership of Deng, China underwent a gradual transition from a traditional planned to a modern market economy.

In December 2001, China joined the World Trade Organization (WTO). Its admission entailed a package of trade-promoting and investment-related reforms, including a strong crackdown on IPR violations. In the meantime, the Chinese government encouraged foreign direct investments (FDI) inland through the promotion of infrastructure development. Major projects included: expressways, bridges and highways to link once-stranded inland cities to coastal ports. Investments in power plants and airports further lifted the domestic economy. This increase of FDI inflows had a strong impact on China's economic growth. According to OECD estimates, total FDI reached a peak of $82.7 billion in 2007, equal to 3% of China's GDP. (See **Exhibit 3** for FDI-utilized inflows into China from 1984 to 2008.)

One of the main systemic reforms to further open the Chinese market included the deregulation of the electricity sector. In 2002, the State Electricity Regulatory Commission (SERC) was established to oversee the overall functioning of the industry, break up monopolies, increase efficiency and build a price mechanism that was fully compliant with the market economy.

Early Bird to the Chinese Market

The delivery of a steam boiler in 1907 was the first instance of cooperation between Asea, one of the two founding companies of ABB and China. Hogan commented:

> To fully understand our Chinese strategy, we have to go back to the beginning of the nineteenth century. At that time, Asea was an early entrant into the Chinese market. Our parent company made a very discrete choice when it preferred to expand in China rather than in more mature markets. With hindsight, Asea correctly foresaw the importance of taking ABB out of Europe [and into] a more promising environment.

In 1974, ABB was formally established in Hong Kong. The choice of this territory provided a valid springboard for doing future business with the Chinese mainland. Up until 1978, the Chinese market was very difficult to access because of its

Exhibit 3.   FDI Utilized Inflows into China from 1984 to 2008, in US$ billion

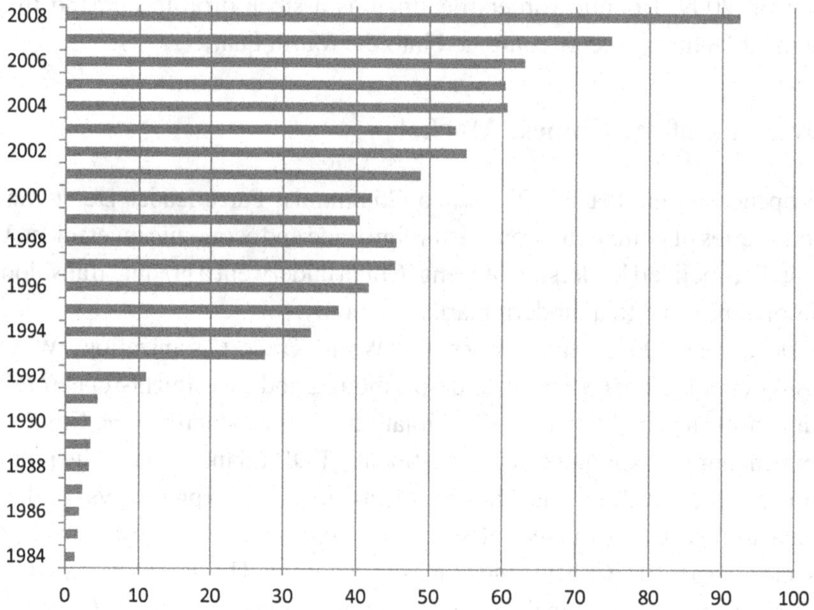

Source: Compiled by case writers, Ministry of Commerce of the People's Republic of China, accessed February 2010.

centrally planned economy. Thus, interaction between ABB and China was limited to exporting products and services to the Chinese market. In 1979, ABB opened its first permanent office in Beijing.

Production in China officially started in 1992 when ABB set up the first joint venture (JV) worth $10 million in Xiamen, named ABB Switchgear, producing medium voltage primary switchgears and circuit breakers. Peter Leupp, ABB Country Manager in China from 2001 to 2006 and now the Head of the Power Systems division and member of the ABB Executive Committee, explained:

> The key to our success in China is not only attributable to our decision to go there as an early entrant. It has a lot to do with our strategy of integrating ABB into the local market. While many international companies were transferring obsolete technologies, ABB entered China with its latest high-tech offering. We were committed to setting up a strong, local manufacturing footprint and even doing R&D in china. Moreover, we were also keen to localize and build management skills and transfer knowledge.

Market segment selection was one of the key considerations. In the mid-1990s, the Chinese market was served by domestic companies, joint ventures and international players, depending on product quality requirements. Leupp continued, "Based on this segmentation and the nature of our technology offering, we positioned ABB towards the high-end segment, which meant serving only a part of the total market but ensuring profitability, as barriers to entry were higher."

In 1994, ABB moved its China headquarters to Beijing. One year thereafter, the Chinese government officially authorized the setting up of wholly-owned foreign enterprises (WOFE) and ABB established its China holding company. In contrast to the JV, WOFE played an important role in protecting ABB's technology, as it reduced the risk of losing control over the company's know-how. Yet, this entry approach was very costly in terms of market penetration. Gary Steel, Executive Vice President, Head of Human Resources, commented, "This new entity is fully controlled by ABB. Thus, it leaves us enough scope for operational improvements. For example, in supply chain management, we are free to choose our own suppliers. But, in a JV we have to go through a double approval process. Finding agreements with our partners is time-consuming."

In 1997, the Chinese economy successfully weathered the Asian financial downturn. ABB's order volume benefited from China's policy response to the crisis, which aimed to promote the development of key industries such as energy. In 1998, ABB entered the power plants building business and set up its largest JV in Chongqing with a total investment of $73 million. The main purpose was to provide Southwest China with efficient, reliable and energy saving power transformers. (See **Exhibit 4** for the evolution of ABB's revenues in China from 1998 to 2005.)

Exhibit 4. Evolution of ABB's Revenues in China from 1998 to 2005

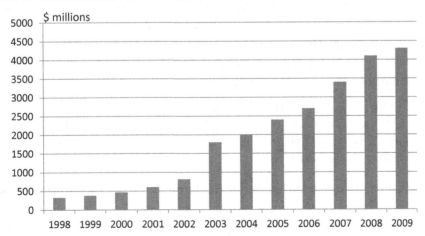

Source: Company's documents.

Crisis at ABB

In 2001, ABB's global business results were gloomy as the company encountered a major liquidity crisis triggered by the asbestos litigation against its U.S. subsidiary Combustion Engineering. Because of high asbestos-related costs, ABB cut 12,000 employees, equal to 8% of the total workforce and posted a record loss of about $700 million in revenues. Steel recalled, "We faced the most critical moment in our history in 2001. Balance sheets were sick and our relationships with banks were bad. We were not eligible to ask for more loans and we did not have enough money to repay our debts. Providentially, Credit Suisse and other banks saved ABB from bankruptcy at the end of 2002."

ABB's strong recovery started in 2004 and was mainly due to the company's new growth strategy. Steel continued:

> In 2003 I joined ABB as Head of HR. The patient was still bleeding. The CEO asked me to strategize our new way forward. I worked closely with Peter Voser, Head of Finance and Bain&Co, a U.S.-based consultancy. First, we needed to cut costs. Then, we focused on defining a strategy to expand in high-growth markets. We selected North America, India and China. Together with the CEO, we decided to go after the China strategy as it looked the best opportunity for ABB.

On a visit to China in March 2004, Leupp and the Executive Committee signed off on ABB's China strategy for the next five years. Leupp recalled, "It was good from a timing perspective. The market potential was promising with China's ambitious plans to build up its power infrastructure and push on industrial development. At the same time, the Chinese government was committed to global integration and taking concrete steps in that direction." As the government became more willing to embrace the principles of capitalism, ABB strongly reinforced their investment in China to establish a full range of business activities, including R&D, manufacturing and sales and service. It also enhanced its management team and distribution network in the Chinese territory. Hogan commented,

> "ABB had a strong fit in China because of its incredible overall infrastructure, such as high-way system, power system and huge industrial investments. For ABB, China was the place to go. We did not have a choice; neither did our competitors."

The China strategy led to huge growth in terms of revenues and workforce. Steel said, "The cooperation with local partners has played a key role in driving ABB's success in China. We went east with very high quality and the Chinese rewarded our long-term loyalty to them. Having a local presence helped us in terms of brand recognition and hiring highly-skilled people." In November 2003, ABB was rated as one of the ten best employers in China in the Employee Opinion Survey conducted jointly by Watson Wyatt Worldwide, Fortune China and Sohu.[6]

In 2005, ABB set up five new factories in China: two wholly-owned companies in Shanghai and three joint ventures in the provinces of Xian, Jiangjin and Datong. Moreover, it opened a new Corporate Research Center in Beijing with a branch in Shanghai, where researchers worked in close contact with local universities. As an integral part of the ABB global research network, the Center focused on power transmission and distribution, manufacturing and robotics. Hogan said, "ABB's strong commitment to R&D has helped us to keep our competitive edge in three key areas in China: Energy efficiency, grid reliability and industrial productivity."

To further reinforce local research and development as well as manufacturing capabilities, ABB relocated the headquarters of its robotics division to Shanghai in early 2006. Hogan commented, "Robotics was in bad shape in terms of costs and global presence. We decided to move it to China for three main reasons. First, we wanted to lower costs. Second, China looked a promising and booming market for our products. Last, we did not limit ourselves to moving the manufacturing there, but also the R&D unit. With hindsight, it has been one of our best experiments." A year later, ABB introduced its latest type of robot into local manufacturing firms in China.

Celebrating ABB's Centennial in China

In 2007, ABB celebrated its 100-year partnership with China. Total revenues amounted to $3.4 billion and orders rose to $4.1 billion, turning China into ABB's number one market.

ABB launched the Global Footprint Program in 2008. The aim was to enhance its commitment by transferring more resources to emerging markets and to establish common values in all branches of the organization. Main aspects of the program included business expansion, strong R&D investment, and local talent development. Steel commented:

> With a long-term commitment, ABB has steadily invested to expedite its localization process. ABB has also put a great emphasis on nurturing local talent. All employees, regardless of technical or managerial functions, go through a series of customized training programs. One of our success factors is the strong motivation of our workforce. ABB's average employee turnover rate is of 5%, compared to 12% in the industry.

In 2008, ABB had one holding company, 26 companies, an extensive sales and service network across 60 cities and 38 branch offices in China. (See **Exhibit 5** for

Exhibit 5.   Map of ABB's Presence in China

Source: Company's documents.

the map of ABB's presence in China.) With more than 12,000 employees, 99% of them Chinese, ABB manufactured 90% of its products locally.

One of the company's major challenges in China was increasing competition. Out of the top eight market players, only ABB and the German Siemens were not domestic companies. However, ABB was the second biggest power transmission and distribution manufacturer in China in terms of 2008 revenues, second only to the Chinese Xian Electric. Brice Koch, Country Manager of China from 2007 to 2009, commented:

> The high-end sector has become increasingly competitive in the last two years. The Chinese government has started to pay much more attention to high-tech products supplied by Chinese companies. Foreign companies are being more and more challenged by national champion companies. ABB has then additionally moved more to the growing mid-market segment, where the demand for mid-tech products was increasing. This was also a good way to defend the high-end market.

Apart from competition, Koch had to face another challenge: the global crisis. ABB weathered the storm with a strong order backlog, cost focus, emerging markets and portfolio scope. Hogan commented, "We did not slow down dramatically in China. In the transformer business, ABB lost 1.6% of total orders in 2009. We had been aggressive on cost cuts. The biggest savings came from sourcing, the rest from global footprint changes, productivity gains and general and administrative expense cuts."

The Chinese government reacted to the global financial crisis supporting exports, loosening its monetary policy and launching a huge stimulus program. China's expansionary policies promoted technical innovation and energy savings. It also targeted infrastructure investment as a priority to improve China's competitiveness.

According to some analysts, China's recent loss of confidence in the market growth might have been the prelude to the re-emergence of protectionism. Koch said:

> Going back to protectionism is a sensitive issue. More and more conservative politicians have started to look favorably at protecting the Chinese economy after the crisis, like in almost all the countries I know of. Yet, the "Buy China" policy is not clear to us. It could either imply buying what is produced in China or buying only from domestic companies. In the first case scenario, ABB will gain a lot from it.

Despite the ongoing debate on China's return to protectionism, Hogan knew that he had to consider three other aspects before making a final decision: technology transfer, IPR protection and government relations.

Managing Joint Ventures

ABB's early successes in China had initially focused on the high end markets. These included high speed rail technologies, power transmission and processing and manufacturing robotics and control software. For many of these products, ABB was not allowed to sell directly to customers. This meant that they required a joint venture and Chinese regulators told them which partners to form JVs with. ABB could refuse proposed partners when they were not a good fit. The very first partner proposed by the Ministry of Resources (MOR) had not been right and ABB had pushed for another partner. For all of its JV agreements, ABB sought 49% or 50% with management control.

Local joint venture partnerships helped ABB to overcome entry barriers in the Chinese market and drove its future growth strategy. Traditionally, in a JV agreement foreign companies shared ownership with local, private, or public interests. Both parties agreed to share capital and other resources in a common endeavor to undertake economic activity together, either in the form of one specific project or a continuing business relationship. Hogan commented, "We first needed reliable partners. Even if the Chinese government often interfered in the partner selection process, we generally favored local companies with high-quality products. We did not want to compromise the quality of our products or corruption. Only win–win joint ventures guarantee success in China. The establishment of very good partnerships has been one of our strengths."

JV partners shared the overall costs and risks of the new enterprise. They also brought influence with local governments, as well as local market knowledge and contacts with potential customers and domestic suppliers. In exchange, their local partners gained access to ABB technologies. Brice Koch, Country Manager of China from 2007 to 2009, commented, "For example, we need to share profits, but this is at the base of sustainable partnerships, which we fully support. Also, shared ownership arrangements could sometimes require extensive negotiations to define a common strategy of conduct."

JV deals gave ABB access to government buyers, but they came with their own headaches. Erich Koefer, Director of M&A for ABB China, explained:

> We found out early that our JV partners would find a way to commercialize the technology we brought. They might start a separate company to compete directly against us. The contracts we signed did not provide protection. Often our JV partners would sign without looking at them. To protect ourselves, we favored JVs with partners who had political connections and sales channels, but not direct experience in our product area. That limited their ability to compete against us.

At the extreme, ABB would fight legally to retain IP, but they did everything they could to avoid this solution. Another problem was caused by differences in business standards with their JV partners. Koefer recalls, "In one case our partner told us that we could accept an accounting treatment which was against GAAP and ABB guidelines. The accounting treatment had significant tax implications but the tax authorities accepted it. We decided that we had to comply with the GAAP and ABB rules and pay more taxes. Our JV partner wanted to be compensated for the lost revenue."

Research and Development

Part of the new landscape of operating in China was domestic R&D. While some international firms had made early moves to open R&D facilities in China, including IBM and Bell in the early 1990s, the surge came in 2005, when the Chinese government pushed for foreign firms to bring some of their R&D into China. By 2010, 500 foreign firms had set up R&D departments. Their labs focused primarily on adapting and developing products for the Chinese domestic market. The challenges were significant. Local R&D costs were very low and Chinese competitors were investing heavily to compete in the same markets. Tobias Becker, head of process automation for North Asia and China, explained, "For what Chinese R&D personnel earn in a month, our people in Europe work for 90 minutes. Effectively, they get more than 100 times the R&D manpower at work." This lower cost structure meant companies could approach R&D differently. Becker explained, "In a high-cost R&D environment, you cannot fail. In China, failure is less important. Chinese firms conduct R&D races, presenting two teams with the same challenge. ABB is trying to copy this strategy." There was also a risk that research employees could take technologies out of the company. Turnover among research employees was from 5 to 6% in 2009, down from 11 to 12% in 2008.

Technology Transfer: High Voltage Direct Current

> *We don't know what created what: the boom in the market, or putting technology on the table. But what do you do with technology if you cannot sell it?*
>
> — Rajendra Iyer, General Manager for HVDC

> *It is difficult to protect the high end, but ABB is trying to do it. Certainly this segment is not growing as fast as the mid-segment.*
>
> — Eric Koefer, Head of M&A, ABB China

In electrical transmission, energy loss increased with distance and decreased with voltage. ABB was one of only a handful of world-class power engineering firms (with Siemens and Areva) that had pioneered low-loss electrical transmission using direct current transmitted at very high voltages. A combination of geographical luck and public policy made China the perfect market for high voltage direct current (HVDC) transmission. Energy production was in the center and west of the country; energy consumption was focused on the eastern seaboard. That geographic fact, combined with sustained high growth rates, meant that China in 2010 represented 60% of the global HVDC market.

HVDC was also ideally suited to managing the variable loads from renewable energy sources. China's Three Gorges Dam project was, at 22 gigawatts (GW) of output, the largest hydroelectric generator in the world. To carry that electricity 1,500 miles to its target market, Shanghai, the Chinese government announced three separate contracts in 1999, 2002 and 2004. In addition, four other dams were planned in the same area. Two were about to come online in 2010 and would add an additional 20 GW of hydroelectric power. This new capacity would also be transmitted via HVDC. Wind power was another source of contracts for HVDC. In 2009, China had added 13 GW of wind turbines, most in western China. By 2020, China was planning to have 150 GW of power, more than the global installed base in 2010. Because of its distance from centers of energy demand, most of this new capacity would be transmitted to market via HVDC. In 2010, HVDC contracts in China were a $4 billion per year market, followed by India and Brazil.

The first Chinese offer for an HVDC transmission contract came in 1999, for a 600 kilovolt (kv) line that was the first phase of the project to take Three Gorges electricity to its target market in the Shanghai region. The offer was from State Grid, one of two major state utilities operators in China (with China Southern). Both Siemens and ABB bid on the contact and ABB won. The contract included a provision for a transfer of technology (ToT). ABB would receive a lucrative contract and in exchange would hand over related technology to Chinese companies. ToT provisions were not new to large technology contracts and ABB was willing to enter into them. Normally, the contracting utility sent some officials to Sweden to see the technology, but rarely was a serious effort made to master it. The Sweden–Chongqing Technology Transfer Agreement, signed in April 1999, proved to be very different.

For HVDC transmission, incoming alternating current (AC) had to be rectified to direct current (DC), stepped up to high voltage, transmitted and then stepped down again and reconverted to AC. The key technologies were at the points of conversion and involved four discrete steps: AC switches and filters, converter transformers (step up), converter valves (rectifier) and DC switches. At the heart of the HVDC conversion process were sophisticated solid state switches called thyristor valves. Previous HVDC contracts signed by ABB had treated the conversion technologies as a turnkey technology. State Grid negotiated to break them apart, with the underlying technology for each component transferred to a different company. By agreement, ABB held back core thyristor technology. It was quickly agreed at ABB that they would approach their ToT obligations in good faith. Hundreds of Chinese engineers spent days at ABB's Stockholm research labs working with ABB engineers to understand how the HVDC technologies worked. Although each Chinese company only received a single technology component, those that participated in subsequent ToT contracts with Siemens were able to piece together two or more component technologies.

All of the companies that received technologies in the 1999 ToT became successful competitors to ABB. In their 1999 contract, Siemens was the prime contractor and captured 80% of the contract value. By the third Three Gorges HVDC contract in 2004, ABB was a component supplier and its share of the deal was capped (informally) at 20%. In 2002, a high level decision determined that ABB would no longer enter ToT contracts.

In 2008, China put out a bid for contracts on two new transmission lines that would use new and more sophisticated 800 kv HVDC technology. The bid proposal included a ToT arrangement. When ABB declined, but undertook the entire design responsibility and settled with the back seat (the front seat was taken by the local suppliers). Ultimately, ABB won one contract for the Xianjiaba–Shanghai line (the other contract for the Yunan–Guandong line went to Siemens). ABB was able to capture 50% of the contract value. Said Iyer, "We didn't give them the 800 kw technology. Should we give everything and hope that they will open up on the contracting side?"

By 2010, HVDC in China was a $4 billion-per-year market, but only 20% of that value was available for foreign firms. Even for 800 kv projects, only 30% of the total project value was available for foreign firms, with the rest made up by domestic firms that had received technologies from ABB and Siemens. These firms were now starting to compete globally. For example, Siemens and the Chinese firm XD were bidding jointly on an HVDC project in India. Meanwhile, China's state energy companies were also moving to integrate vertically, absorbing some of the companies that had received ABB technologies. They were also internationalizing. State Grid had already acquired the Philippines electrical grid, invested 8 billion in transmission lines in Malaysia and were in the process of buying electrical grids in Brazil.

Moving Mid-Market

China is like New York. If you can sell it here, you can sell it anywhere.
— Becker

The second prong of ABB's China strategy was to move into mid-market technologies that were likely to be competitive in the domestic Chinese market and potentially in developing countries outside. Many of ABB's competitors were making the same move. The American General Electric called their approach "good-enough" design, intended to serve the "good-enough" market. One of the GE "good-enough" success stories was the CT scanner that they had developed for China while ABB's current CEO, Jim Hogan, had been heading GE's medical devices division. The device was portable and targeted at China's roughly 70,000 rural hospitals.[e] The device came with a generator to ensure energy supply and it produced slices by having patients stand on progressively higher blocks. Siemens was also pursuing the Chinese mid-market with a program called SMART, which stood for simple, maintenance-free,

---

[e]Business China, March 18, 2010.

affordable, reliable and timely to market. ABB didn't have a name, but they did have a strategy.

Moving into the mid-market was not necessarily easy. Products could not simply be scaled down. Koefer explained, "We are a high end player. In terms of quality and price, that is not what local companies need... In the early stage, they had to buy from us. Now they are catching up — we are helping them to catch up. This market is still interesting for us, but we don't have the products to remain competitive." The solution was to develop new, mid-market products and to make them cost-competitive with local producers. Koefer explained, "For most products, the hardware cost is only 30%. The mid segment products are typically 30–50% cheaper than the high end ones." Qianjin Liu, head of ABB's Beijing research center, explained, "The idea was good quality but affordable price for this market. This is not a comfortable zone for multinational companies. We had noticed the challenge of cost reduction and were addressing it in a proactive way."

In 2006, ABB began looking for a Chinese engineering firm they could acquire that could become the platform for their push into the mid-market. After three years of surveying potential acquisitions, Koefer concluded that they were not going to find a company without the kind of liabilities that ABB would be unwilling to take on. Koefer explained, "In the lower-mid segment in China, the companies are a big mess. They have no employees on their official payroll. They are receiving special tax treatment. Acquiring them would cause too many problems."

Winmation

The alternative solution was for ABB to create its own domestic Chinese company that could go head-to-head with its Chinese counterparts. Doing so meant breaking from the ABB mold. ABB was a consensus-driven company, with complicated approval processes and specialized review bodies with veto rights. Koefer brought the idea of a truly domestic Chinese subsidiary to Hogan, expecting it to be challenged. Instead, Hogan advocated for it. As with any new project, it would still have to go through a formal approval review, but it was agreed that this could happen after the company was formed. The result was Winmation, a Chinese firm wholly owned by ABB with results consolidated into ABB's annual report.

In three critical areas, Winmation would have to comply with ABB standards that were considered non-negotiable: safety, accounting and compliance. Critics worried that they would not be able to find employees willing to work within ABB standards in this area, but so far they had had no problem hiring. Becker explained, "Set the rules and you can find the people who will work within them. Our employees can go home and tell their families that they will never end up behind bars and will never get hurt."

Exhibit 6. Share of ABB Revenues, 2009

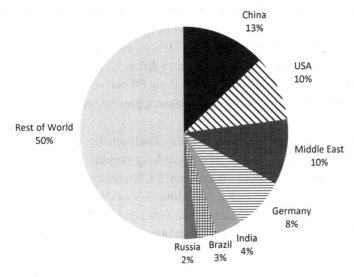

Source: Company data.

Outside of those areas, management could operate as they wished. It would not pay the ABB brand fee, nor use the ABB name. It would not use SAP, rather using a low-cost Chinese alternative called UFO, or Lotus Notes. Managerial decisions remained entirely within Winmation. Becker described his approach to decision-making at Winmation, "If I like a job candidate, he is probably the wrong person. If I like a design, our Chinese customer probably won't like it."

In August 2009, ABB founded Hangzho Winmation Automation Company to develop and produce distributed control systems (DCS) — software and hardware packages that controlled automated manufacturing lines. DCS were traditionally expensive, in part because they were customized and in part because of the need for reliability and stability over the long life of a factory. Winmation set out to change everything about the traditional business of manufacturing DCS. It was located in Hangzho, within five minutes of its four main domestic Chinese competitors. The first thing they did was change the way the product was made. Traditionally, DCS was designed using software libraries. Doing so required more upfront investments, but it made the code transparent, and because the software had to be supported for many years, it didn't matter if a particular software designer left the company. Winmation adopted a shorter term focus. Software designers used inline code, which was faster and cheaper to write. Becker explained, "In China, they love inline code. They don't care what happens beyond five years out."

Second, they changed their staffing policies. Becker explained, "We used to prioritize employees who spoke English, who were willing to travel. At Winmation, if you speak English and are willing to travel, we won't hire you. These employees would expect to be paid extra and we want employees who (focus) on the Chinese environment. Not even the general manager needs to speak English." Winmation also poached employees from its competitors. It was, as Becker described, "retaliation time." The incentive system was also entirely different. They reduced fringe benefits and maximized the face value of compensation. Of the base salary, 40% was floating salary, based on month-to-month performance, plus an annual performance bonus of up to 25%.

Another area of difference was in sales. Traditionally, high end products were sold by large teams of engineers who spent long periods with the potential client. Winmation borrowed the sales strategy of a Chinese competitor, SubCom. They operated with local cell networks, including 3–4 sales people and 4–5 engineers. "We hire local people, they communicate with headquarters, but they earn 40% of the typical salary. They depend on the center, but they enjoy autonomy and can be entrepreneurial. They don't speak English. We copied this." For many potential clients, the fact that Winmation did not look like a foreign company was an advantage. Their first order was from China's second-largest pharmaceutical company producing traditional medicines. This client explained that they would not have worked with ABB, which they saw as a brand with a premium reputation. ABB, they explained, was for companies like Sinopec or Petro China.

China and the Future of ABB

As Hogan contemplated ABB's future in China, it was easy to see it as a continuation of their past success. While other international companies struggled to make profits in the Chinese markets, ABB China had been a core profit center for the past 15 years. The Chinese market entailed clear challenges, but there were at least three compelling reasons to stay. ABB's historic strength was its world-class engineering capability. China was among the most dynamic markets in the world for the high end technologies in which they excelled, including power transmission, high-speed rail and robotics. Even if they were losing technology to domestic rivals in China, a stream of new product innovation would allow them to stay ahead of their competitors. These new technologies were not worth much if there was no market in which to sell them. In a sense, they were creating the market for new technologies at the same time that they were creating the technologies.

China had also become an R&D platform for new mid-market technologies that would be profitable in the domestic Chinese market and potentially might be exported to middle-income countries abroad. The challenge was to gain access to government contracts on an equal basis with domestic producers when they were

Exhibit 7. China's Power Grid Investment, 2005–2010

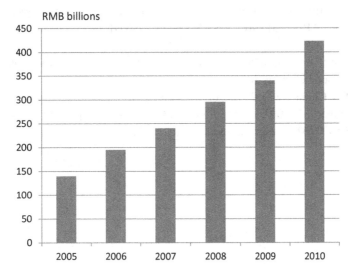

RMB billions

Source: Company data.

not working with a technological advantage. The recent move to "buy China" was a clear threat to the mid-market segments they hoped to succeed in.

Finally, China had also become an R&D platform for organizational innovation. Winmation was a learning platform for ABB. If it succeeded, the Winmation brand might spread to other products, including instrumentation, measurement products and motors. It was also a blueprint for how to compete in other product segments in China. Some elements might be borrowed for ABB operations in other countries. Success would bring challenging questions for the way in which ABB approached its global business. For a company that had traditionally deployed centralized labor and organizational practices, Winmation represented a major break. Its ultimate goal, however, was to ensure that ABB would not be taken by surprise if Chinese domestic mid-market companies broke out of their domestic market and began competing against ABB globally.

For all the challenges that came with operating in China, which were numerous, the logic of staying in the market was stronger than ever.

Endnotes

[1] Guy Dinmore and Geoff Dyer, "Immelt hits out at China and Obama," Financial Times, July 1, 2010, http://www.ft.com/intl/cms/s/0/ed654fac-8518-11df-adfa-00144feabdc0.html#axzz2FcQtTqFr, accessed December 20, 2012

[2] Joe McDonald, "Beijing: Buy China Policy Alarms Trade Partners," Associated Press, February 16, 2010, accessed via Factiva in March 2011.

[3] ABB 2009 Annual Report.

[4] For more information about the merger of Asea and Brown Boveri, please see Hugo Uyterhoeven, "ABB Germany," HBS No. 9-397-096 (Boston: Harvard Business School Publishing, 1997).

[5] ABB, "A Brief History of ABB, 1988–1991," ABB website, at www.abb.com/global/abbzh, accessed February, 2010.

[6] ABB, "ABB China Ranked One of the Top in Best Employers Survey, "ABB website, November 17, 2003, at http://www.abb.com/cawp/seitp202/6D65B43AF3FB71F 648256DE10007AE01.aspx, accessed March, 2011.

Low-Carbon, Indigenous Innovation
in China

Richard H. K. Vietor*

In September 2011, Goldwind installed three wind turbines (4.5 megawatts) in Minnesota. These were the first Chinese wind turbines installed in the United States. In that same year, U.S. imports of Chinese solar cells and modules doubled, reaching $2.6 billion — about 42% of the market and more than 30 times U.S. solar exports to China.[1] These imports were but the cutting-edge of China's massive drive to develop low-carbon energy sources in China. Over the next eight years, as China's wind, solar, electric-vehicle, "clean-coal" and nuclear industries expanded, its high-value added exports and investments in the world's low-carbon energy sector would also expand.

As early as 1997, this drive into low-carbon energy was increasingly seen as a central thrust of China's industrial policy. First came experimentation by power utilities, relying on technology licensing from the West. In 2004, the government inaugurated a concession project for wind farms that required 70% local content. Next came a series of renewable energy laws, creating subsidies and incentives for Chinese firms.

In 2006, Hu Jintao and Wen Jiabao began speaking of renewables as China's new pillar industries — to be built with indigenous technology. The 11th five-year

*Reprinted with permission of Harvard Business School Publishing.
This case was prepared by Professor Richard H. K. Vietor.
Low-Carbon, Indigenous Innovation in China 712-061
Copyright © 2005–2014 by the President and Fellows of Harvard College; all rights reserved.

plan (2006–2010) laid out ambitious targets for building renewables. And in 2007, the National Development and Reform Commission elaborated a more detailed plan for renewable development, "enhancing original innovation through co-innovation and re-innovation based on the assimilation of imported technologies."[2] To many in the West, this evinced a direct threat to intellectual property rights (IPR).

The drive toward "indigenous innovation" — or *zizhu chuangxin* — became formalized in November 2009, when the Chinese government released Circular 618: "Circular on Carrying Out the Work on Accreditation of National Indigenous Innovation Products." This announcement focused on six high-tech fields, including new energy, which would receive preferential treatment in government procurement, requiring Chinese ownership of the intellectual property.[3]

China's 12th five-year plan, released in March 2011, set nearly unbelievable targets for carbon intensity and renewable energy and was a roadmap for helping China become an "international leader" in a handful of low-carbon sources of energy.

With U.S. energy policy a shambles, with the few incentives for renewables about to expire and with intense congressional criticism of its solar subsidies, the Obama administration was growing deeply worried about China's energy policies. After he won the election in 2012, President Obama had to find some way to help save America's energy competitiveness.

Energy Demand, Carbon Growth and Renewables

With more than 1.3 billion people and an economy growing faster than 8% annually for more than 30 years, China needed a lot of energy. China's electric generation was powered mostly by coal and hydropower. Coal production, currently at about 3.7 billion tons (with 100 million tons imported) annually, was scheduled to rise toward 4.1 billion by 2015. This was almost four times the amount produced in the U.S. Power generation had grown at an accelerating pace — 7.5% annually in the 1980s to 12.2% annually in the 2000s.[4] (See **Exhibit 1** for China's net electricity generation.) China also burned natural gas, mostly imported and about 8.6 million barrels per day of petroleum (more than half of which was imported). As a consequence, carbon dioxide emissions from China reached 7.7 billion tons in 2011 — 30% more than in the United States, the second-largest emitter.[5] (See **Exhibit 2** for a comparison of the emissions in the two countries.)

Since the early 1990s, Western countries, concerned with the prospect of climate change, had pressed China (and the U.S.) to do something about carbon emissions. Given its immense thirst for energy and the many externalities associated with coal combustion, China had begun trying to improve its energy efficiency in the 1990s. In its 11th five-year plan (2006–2010), the government set an explicit target of reducing

Exhibit 1.   China Net Electricity Generation

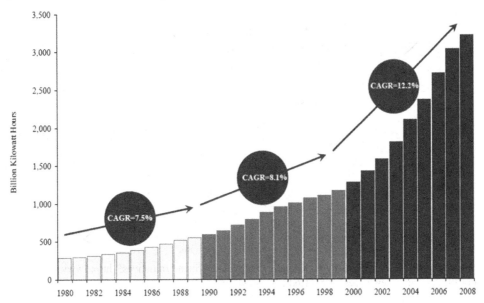

Source: National Foreign Trade Council, *China's Promotion of the Renewable Electric Power Equipment Industry*, p. 7.

Exhibit 2.   Carbon Emissions for China and the U.S.

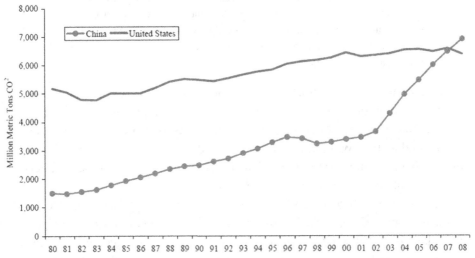

Source: National Foreign Trade Council, *China's Promotion of the Renewable Electric Power Equipment Industry*, p. 2.

Exhibit 3.   Energy Intensity Trends and Achievements in China

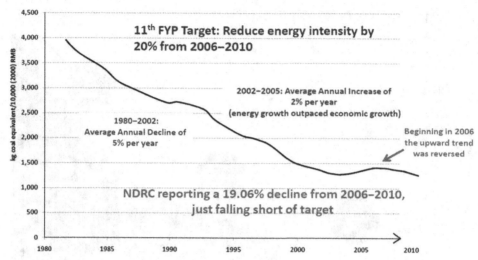

Source: World Resources Institute, "China's Energy and Climate Initiatives," http://www.chinafaqs. org/files/chinainfo/lewis_eesi_4-5-11.pdf, accessed June 6, 2012.

its energy intensity (energy/GDP) by 20%.[6] (See **Exhibit 3** for China's efforts to reduce energy intensity.) As the state council put it:

> China gives top priority to developing renewable energy. The exploration and utilization of renewable energy resources plays a significant role in increasing energy supply, improving the energy mix and helping environmental protection and is also a strategic choice of China to solve the contradiction between the energy supply and demand and achiev[ing] sustainable development.[7]

And because the plan set ambitious targets for renewable energy, it implied a reduction of its carbon intensity as well. The National Development and Reform Commission (NDRC) released new targets for renewables: hydropower at 190 gigawatts (GW), wind at 10 GW, biomass at 3.3 GW and solar at 0.3 GW.[8] In 2009, at the climate change conference in Copenhagen, the NDRC expanded these targets for 2020: wind at 200 GW, solar power at 30 GW.[9]

China's biggest formal step was the Renewable Energy Law, enacted by the National People's Congress, effective January 1, 2006. Renewables, for the purpose of the law, included wind, solar, hydropower, biomass and geothermal. The law basically required utilities to pay renewable energy developers the full cost for their electricity. A dedicated fund was established to support development of renewable technologies. Developers received an exemption from the value-added tax and wind-farm operators could claim carbon-reduction credits sold internationally through the Clean Development Mechanism.

Hardly taking a breath, the 12th five-year plan (2011–2015) extended the country's targets for the reduction of energy intensity another 16% and, by setting a target of 11.4% for non-fossil fuel energy, added a new target of 17% reduction in carbon intensity.[10] It was becoming quite clear that only a centralized, command-and-control economy could set, much less meet, such ambitious and detailed targets.

Nuclear Power

While not exactly "renewable," the generation of electricity by fission reaction is a well-established, low-carbon source of energy. After commercialization in North America during the 1960s and '70s, commercial nuclear reactors spread to Japan, Europe and Russia. China's first pressurized water reactor, producing 944 megawatts, began operating at Daya Bay (in Guangdong) in 1994. In 2011, China had 14 operating nuclear reactors (about 11,000 MW), 25 under construction, 38 planned and 86 under consideration.[11] (See **Exhibit 4** for a map of reactors in China.)

Exhibit 4.   Nuclear Power Reactors in China

Source: World Nuclear Association, "Nuclear Power in China," updated April 2012, http://www.world-nuclear.org/info/inf63.html.

Nuclear power in China is built and operated by government corporations —
primarily the China National Nuclear Corporation and the China Guangdong
Nuclear Power Group. Nuclear safety is regulated by the National Nuclear Safety
Administration (NNSA) and audited by safety review teams from the International
Atomic Energy Agency, the World Association of Nuclear Operators (WANO), or
the Chinese Nuclear Energy Authority. After the Fukushima accident in 2011, safety
checks of operating plants were performed immediately, construction reviews were
completed by October and new approvals were suspended pending review of lessons
learned.[12]

While conventional pressurized water reactors (PWRs) constitute existing
Chinese plants, a number of newer technologies dominate current construction and
future plans. China is already building the first two AP1000 (Westinghouse/Toshiba)
"third-generation" reactors and two Areva European Pressurized Reactors (EPRs).
An array of even newer technologies is being considered for planned projects, including small modular PWRs, high-temperature gas-cooled reactors (HTRs) and even
fast neutron reactors. The government plans to spend several hundred billion dollars
on nuclear development by 2020.

In its assessment of China's nuclear energy policy, the Center for Strategic and
International Studies concluded that four elements were key:

1. The emphasis on pressurized power reactors (PWRs) in the near future.
2. The indigenous assembly, fabrication and supply of nuclear fuels.
3. Maximizing domestic manufacturing of plants and equipment.
4. Become self-reliant on design and project management.[13]

It would not be unreasonable to expand these observations to cover all of China's
renewable energy policy.

Wind

In the early 1980s, regional governments pioneered the development of wind power
in rural areas to supply electricity for off-grid communities. By the mid- to late 80s,
Chinese utilities were acquiring larger turbines from Vestas for utility-scale power.
During the 9th five-year plan in the 1990s, the central government began encouraging
"a method of combining indigenous innovation and import-absorption innovation"
and provided subsidies for larger, 600 kilowatt (kW) turbines.[14] Under the plan, the
government initiated the "Ride the Wind Program," featuring joint ventures between
Chinese and foreign companies to develop wind farms in exchange for technology
transfers. Initially, 20% local content was expected, reaching 40% by 2002.

In 2004, the NDRC launched its Wind Power Concession Project. This program
required the government-owned grid operators to sign long-term power purchase

agreements with developers of wind farms of at least 100 megawatts (MWs) capacity. Local content, however, was central. In September 2004, developers bidding for concession projects were required to employ at least 70% local content. An order in July 2005 explicitly forswore foreign content in excess of 30%.[15] Notwithstanding one early concession win by Vestas, no foreign firms had won a single NDRC concession since. While several companies, including Suzlon and GE, have built plants in China, the concession projects go to Chinese manufacturers. As foreign firms were only allowed to bid for private, or regional wind farms (under 50 MW), their market share has dropped significantly (see **Exhibit 5** for a comparison).

Because renewable electricity is still more expensive than coal-fired power plants (ignoring externalities), subsidies and pricing policies have remained important. In mid-2008, the Ministry of Finance announced a Special Fund for [the] Wind Power Manufacturing Sector in China. This fund, which might have totaled "several hundred million dollars,"[16] was designated "to support state-owned and Chinese controlled stock companies conducting wind power equipment manufacturing (including turbine systems, gear boxes, generators, convertors, bearings and other major wind power components) within the territory of the People's Republic of China."[17] Under pressure from the World Trade Organization (WTO), the Chinese government terminated these subsidies in June 2011.

Exhibit 5.   Comparison of Newly Installed Capacity Market Share between Domestic and Foreign Companies in the Chinese Wind Power Market

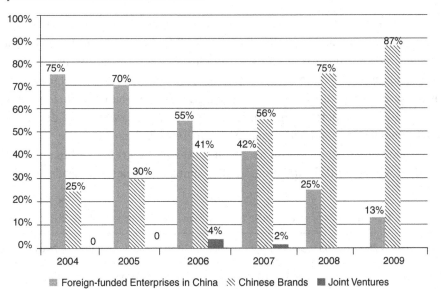

Source: Global Wind Energy Council, *China Wind Power Outlook 2010*, p. 37.

In August 2009, China shifted its wind-purchase policy from tendering (for concession projects) to a feed-in-tariff (which was already working well for biomass and solar). The NDRC set four different tariffs, according to the wind resources of different regions. These were initially set at 0.51 yuan/kW, 0.54, 0.58 and 0.61 ($0.075 to $0.09).[18] Given China's relatively low costs for turbine installation and operations, these rates were far closer to costs, perhaps even allowing for some profits.

Over the previous decade, the effects of all these policy initiatives had been remarkable. Foremost was the rapid expansion of wind capacity. The most recent estimate available, from the Global Wind Energy Council, showed China's wind capacity expanding at 60% annually! (See **Table A**.)

In fact, China actually caught and then surpassed the U.S, now the second-largest wind market, in 2010 (see **Exhibits 6a** and **6b** for comparisons of the Top 10 countries). Another aspect of this amazing growth, and the local-content requirements of the government, was that more than 100 Chinese companies got involved in manufacturing wind turbines and blades. While many of these were relatively small and produced smaller turbines of dubious quality, several firms had emerged as global leaders. In 2011, four Chinese manufacturers (Goldwind, Sinoval, United Power and MingYang) were among the world's Top 10 manufacturers, with a combined market share of 27%.[19] (See **Exhibit 7a** for lists of the Top 10 wind turbine manufacturers.) All four produced multi-megawatt machines and at least two had entered the market for offshore wind. Within the China market, Chinese firms were now dominant, with as much as 87% share. (See **Exhibit 7b** for Chinese companies' shares of the market.)

The biggest problems experienced during this wind-power boom had been quality, profitability and access to the electrical grid. In the U.S, wind-farm developers were generally hesitant to buy Chinese turbines, despite competitive prices, because of problems with quality. In China, where government claims that foreign equipment was not price-competitive, the EU complained about low-ball bids, low or negative profitability by the purchasing utilities (all government-owned) and disregard for quality, maintenance and performance over a 20- to 25-year life cycle.[20]

But the biggest shortcoming had been access to the grid. As China pushed the growth of wind-turbine installations at 60% annually, its electrical grids rapidly fell

Table A.   China's Cumulative Installed Wind-Power Capacity, 2001–2011

Year	2001	2002	2003	2004	2005	2006	2007	2008	2009	2010	2011
MW	404	470	568	765	1,272	2,559	5,871	12,024	25,828	44,733	62,364

Source: Global Wind Energy Council, *Global Wind Report: Annual Market Update 2010*, p. 35.

Exhibit 6a. Wind Cumulative Capacity

Exhibit 6b. Wind Installed Capacity

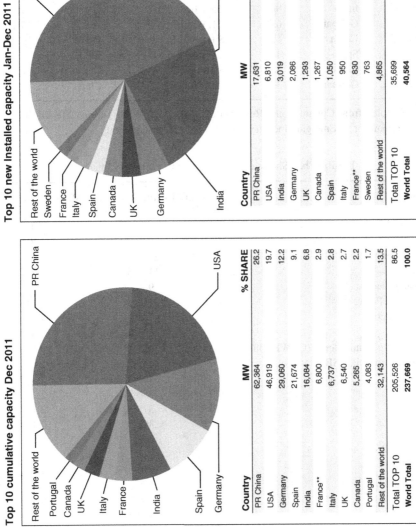

Top 10 cumulative capacity Dec 2011

Country	MW	% SHARE
PR China	62,364	26.2
USA	46,919	19.7
Germany	29,060	12.2
Spain	21,674	9.1
India	16,084	6.8
France**	6,800	2.9
Italy	6,737	2.8
UK	6,540	2.7
Canada	5,265	2.2
Portugal	4,083	1.7
Rest of the world	32,143	13.5
Total TOP 10	205,526	86.5
World Total	**237,669**	**100.0**

** Provisional Figure

Source: GWEC

Top 10 new Installed capacity Jan-Dec 2011

Country	MW	% SHARE
PR China	17,631	43
USA	6,810	17
India	3,019	7
Germany	2,086	5
UK	1,293	3.2
Canada	1,267	3.1
Spain	1,050	2.6
Italy	950	2.3
France**	830	2.0
Sweden	763	1.9
Rest of the world	4,865	12.0
Total TOP 10	35,699	88
World Total	**40,564**	**100.0**

** Provisional Figure

Source: GWEC

Source: Global Wind Energy Council, *Global Wind Report: Annual Market Update 2010*, p. 12.

Exhibit 7a.   Global Wind Turbine Manufacturers — Top 10 in Market Share, 2008–2011

2008			2011		
Manufacturer	**Country**	**Share %**	**Manufacturer**	**Country**	**Share %**
Vestas	Denmark	17.6	Vestas	Denmark	12.7
GE Wind	USA	16.7	Sinovel	China	9.0
Gamesa	Spain	10.8	Goldwind	China	8.7
Enercon	Germany	9.0	Gamesa	Spain	8.0
Suzlon	India	8.1	Enercon	Germany	7.8
Siemens	Germany	6.2	GE Wind	U.S.	7.7
Sinovel	China	4.5	Suzlon (&Repower)	India	7.6
Acciona	Spain	4.1	Guodian United Power	China	7.4
Goldwind	China	3.6	Siemens	Germany	6.3
Nordex	Germany	3.4	MingYang	China	3.6

Source: Adapted from Congressional Research Service, "U.S. Wind Turbine Manufacturing: Federal Support for an Emerging Industry"; and www.rechargenews.com.

Exhibit 7b.   Shares of Wind Turbine Capacity in China

Company	2011 Annual (MW)	Market Share %
Goldwind	3600	20.4
Sinovel	2939	16.7
United Power	2847	16.1
MingYang	1177.5	6.7
Dong Fang Electric	946	5.4
XEMC Wind Power	712.5	4
Shanghai Electric	708.1	4
Vestas	661.9	3.8
China Creative Wind Energy (CCWE, Huachuang)	625.5	3.5
China Southern Rail, CSR (Nanche)	451.2	2.6
GE	408.8	2.3
CSIC	396	2.2
Windy	375	2.1
Gamesa	361.6	2.1
Envision	348	2
Yinxing	221	1.3
SanYi	179.5	1
CET Xuji group	166	0.9
Suzlon	96.2	0.5
Others	410.4	2.4
Total	17630.9	

Source: Global Wind Energy Council, *China Wind Power Outlook 2011*.

behind in their ability to absorb variable-output power. Especially in places where wind power grew fastest, such as Inner Mongolia, inadequate grid capacity left hundreds of turbines inoperative. The State Electricity Regulatory Commission has estimated that 2.8 terawatt hours (TWh) of wind power went unused in the first half of 2010.[21] And the National Energy Bureau has banned wind construction in areas with over 20% of installed capacity lying idle.[22]

Solar

China's solar-power industry has also developed rapidly, but in a very different manner. In wind, the plan was to build a domestic industrial base, strengthen intellectual property and indigenous innovation and then move on to nurture world-class competitors. In the solar business, however, Chinese companies became manufacturers and exporters of polysilicon, wafers and solar cells, dominating about 60% of the global market by 2011.[23] But there was little use of solar power in China. (See **Exhibits 8a** and **8b** for comparisons of Chinese and global use.) Only recently did the government decide it needed to develop the domestic solar market in flat panels for electricity, in building-integrated thin film and in thermal solar.

The Chinese solar industry got started in the mid-1980s, with firms producing polysilicon and/or wafers for the semiconductor industry. Some of the firms at this upstream end of the value chain integrated into semiconductors and then began

Exhibit 8a.   Global and Chinese Solar PV Production Volume and Demand, MW, 2002–2011

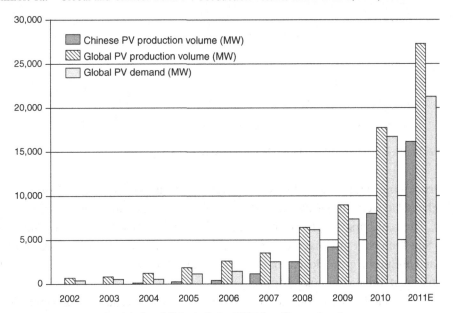

Source: China Greentech Initiative, "China's Solar PV Value Change," p. 6.

Exhibit 8b.   Global and Chinese Solar PV Producers

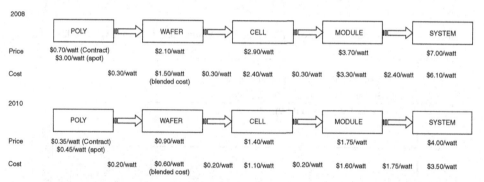

Source: China Greentech Initiative, "China's Solar PV Value Change," p. 12.

Note: System installers include companies that provide rooftop, building integrated and ground-mounted applications of solar power.

Figure A.   Solar Value Chain, Costs and Average Selling Price Assumptions

2008

	POLY		WAFER		CELL		MODULE		SYSTEM
Price	$0.70/watt (Contract) $3.00/watt (spot)		$2.10/watt		$2.90/watt		$3.70/watt		$7.00/watt
Cost		$0.30/watt	$1.50/watt (blended cost)	$0.30/watt	$2.40/watt	$0.30/watt	$3.30/watt	$2.40/watt	$6.10/watt

2010

	POLY		WAFER		CELL		MODULE		SYSTEM
Price	$0.35/watt (Contract) $0.45/watt (spot)		$0.90/watt		$1.40/watt		$1.75/watt		$4.00/watt
Cost		$0.20/watt	$0.60/watt (blended cost)	$0.20/watt	$1.10/watt	$0.20/watt	$1.60/watt	$1.75/watt	$3.50/watt

Source: Barclays Capital, *Solar Energy Handbook*, May 1, 2009, p. 76.

experimenting with solar cells. With government support, Ningbo, Kaifeng and Qinghuagdao were among the earliest firms to acquire the equipment to manufacture cells. The real burst of growth came after 2000 when Baoding Yingli Solar and then Sun Tech built manufacturing plants using indigenous technology.[24] As market demand in Europe grew, dozens of firms entered the business at some point or points in a five-part value chain (see **Figure A**).

Solar demand — first from Europe, which was trying to reduce carbon emissions and then from the U.S. (primarily California) — outstripped supply until about 2008, driving up the price of polysilicon from $35 to $500 per kilogram. But when demand collapsed with the financial crisis, a huge glut emerged, driving prices back down to $30 (**Exhibits 9a** and **9b** for polysilicon trends). At the other end of the value chain, prices for modules and systems were declining, with lower material costs, improved cell technology and scale economies. Costs per kilowatt hour (kWh) of

Exhibit 9a.   Polysilicon — Capacity, Supply and Demand

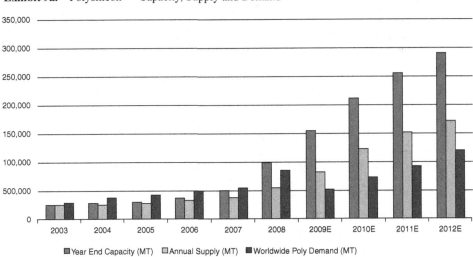

Source: Barclay's Capital Research, *Solar Energy Handbook*, May 2009, p. 86.

Exhibit 9b.   Polysilicon — Spot and Contract Pricing Trends

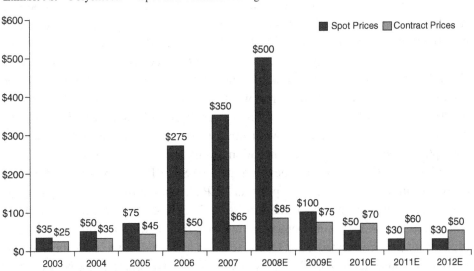

Source: Barclay's Capital Research, *Solar Energy Handbook*, May 2009, p. 86.

Exhibit 10.   Recent Prices of Chinese Crystalline Modules

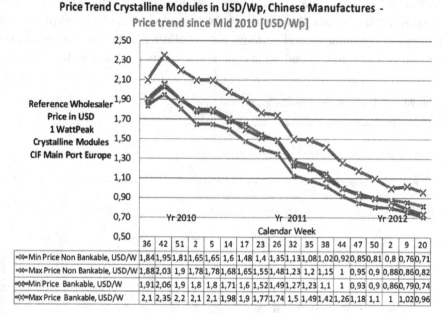

Price Trend Crystalline Modules in USD/Wp, Chinese Manufactures -
Price trend since Mid 2010 [USD/Wp]

	36	42	51	2	5	14	17	23	26	32	35	38	44	47	50	2	9	20
✕ Min Price Non Bankable, USD/W	1,84	1,95	1,81	1,65	1,65	1,6	1,48	1,4	1,35	1,13	1,08	1,02	0,92	0,85	0,81	0,8	0,76	0,71
✕ Max Price Non Bankable, USD/W	1,88	2,03	1,9	1,78	1,78	1,68	1,65	1,55	1,48	1,23	1,2	1,15	1	0,95	0,9	0,88	0,86	0,82
✕ Min Price Bankable, USD/W		1,91	2,06	1,9	1,8	1,8	1,71	1,6	1,52	1,49	1,27	1,23	1,1	1	0,93	0,9	0,86	0,79	0,74
✕ Max Price Bankable, USD/W		2,1	2,35	2,2	2,1	2,1	1,98	1,9	1,77	1,74	1,5	1,49	1,42	1,26	1,18	1,1	1	1,02	0,96

Source: Europe-Solar.de, "Price Trend PV Modules," http://www.europe-solar.de/catalog/index.php?
main_page=page_3, accessed June 6, 2012.

power generated had fallen from $0.35 to near $0.16, approaching "grid parity" of something like $0.10 to $0.12 (see **Exhibit 10** for prices of Chinese crystalline modules).[25]

Until the 11th five-year plan, government policy had not focused on solar power. As of 2005, only about 70 MW of solar photovoltaic (PV) power was installed, mostly in remote locations. But after the 11th plan identified wind and solar power as strategic, support grew rapidly. In 2007, the NDRC released its "Medium and Long Term Development Plan for Renewable Energy" in China, wherein it set targets for solar PV (as well as wind and other renewables) of 300 MW by 2010 and 20,000 MW by 2020. Fiscal policy, government procurement and subsidies would be used to incent this development. And like wind, the government would seek to "enhance the absorption, assimilation, and re-innovation of imported technologies."[26]

In 2009, the Chinese government initiated the Solar Roofs program, publishing rules for building-integrated PV projects (BIPV), with subsidies of 20 yuan/Wp (watt peak). Four months later, the Ministry of Science and Technology (MOST) announced the Golden Sun Demonstration Program, calling for 600 MW of PV capacity in grid-connected solar farms, to be constructed in the next three years. Subsidies would be 50% of the investment cost. By November, 314 projects had been approved.[27]

With this huge burst of policy support and the growing worldwide demand for solar panels, dozens of companies and a billion yuan flooded into China's PV industry. Polysilicon capacity jumped from 73,000 to 206,000 tons between 2008 and 2010. Global demand also rose, but only to 134,000 tons — thus, the glut. More than 1,000 Chinese firms got involved in the solar PV value chain (see **Exhibit 11**) and collectively now dominated world markets (see **Exhibits 12** and **13**).

Paths to vertical integration by Chinese firms have varied widely over different segments of the value chain. Relatively few firms have integrated backward into polysilicon manufacturing — a relatively specialized business. More have integrated forward, into cells, modules and systems. While the Top 5 firms in the module segment control 60% of production capacity, surprisingly little consolidation has yet taken place.[28]

Lithium-ion Batteries and Electric Vehicles

The Chinese government's interest in electric vehicles emerged, ironically, out of the fruits of its own successful pillar industries strategy. In 1996, the government of Deng Xiaoping identified five industries that it would aggressively pursue as industrial policy. One of these was automobiles. The government sought to build an automobile industry that would manufacture 20 million vehicles annually. By 2011, the country did produce 16.5 million, causing extraordinary traffic jams, raw material needs and severe air pollution.

As early as 2001, as part of the 10th five-year plan, the Ministry of Science and Technology moved to deal with these problems by initiating the 863 Electric-Drive

Exhibit 11.   PV Manufacturers in China along the Value Chain

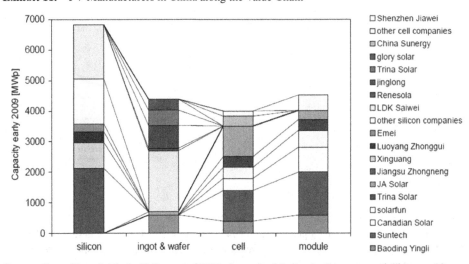

Source: Grau, Huo, & Neuhoff, *Survey of PV Industry and Policy in Germany and China*, p. 12.

Exhibit 12.   Direction of Wind Power Technology Transfers, 1988–2008

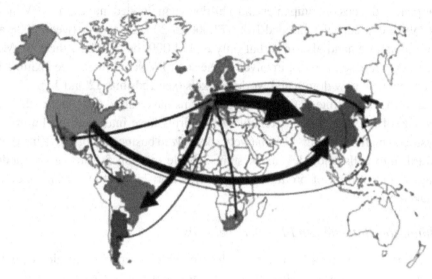

Source: World Bank and Development Research Center of the State Council of China, *China 2030: 2012*, p. 261.

Note: This figure illustrates the transfer of technologies from Annex I countries under the UNFCCC to non-Annex I countries, as measured by duplicate patent filings for wind power technologies in non-Annex I countries.

Exhibit 13.   Global Solar Business — Top-20 Companies' Sales and Geographic Distribution

Country	category	name	2011	2010	Growth
China	poly/wafer/energy	GCL Poly	$3,285,974	$2,375,489	38.33%
China	module	Suntech	$3,146,600	$2,901,931	8.43%
USA	energy/module	First Solar	$2,766,207	$2,563,515	7.91%
China	module/systems	Yingli Green Energy	$2,332,094	$1,893,937	23.13%
Norway	poly/wafer/module	REC	$2,320,338	$2,563,714	-9.49%
USA	energy/module	Sunpower	$2,312,494	$2,219,230	4.20%
China	poly/wafer/module	LDK Solar	$2,187,644	$2,509,347	-12.82%
China	module	Trina Solar	$2,047,902	$1,857,689	10.24%
China	module/systems	Canadian Solar	$1,898,923	$1,495,509	26.98%
Germany	poly/wafer/module	SolarWorld	$1,868,082	$2,200,150	-15.09%
China	cell/module	Ja Solar	$1,705,279	$1,781,936	-4.30%
Germany	energy/cells/modules	Q-Cells	$1,304,172	$1,712,960	-23.86%
China	wafer/cell/module	Jinko Solar	$1,173,351	$705,281	66.37%
Germany	projects/module	Conergy	$1,019,902	$1,345,835	-24.22%
China	module/OEM	Hanwha SolarOne	$1,019,477	$1,140,453	-10.61%
China	wafer/module	Renesola Solar	$985,279	$1,205,579	-18.27%
Taiwan	cell	Motech	$953,192	$1,321,204	-27.85%
Taiwan	cell	NeoSolarPower	$696,437	$703,102	-0.95%
Taiwan	cell	Gintech	$636,277	$982,516	-35.24%
Taiwan	wafer	Green Energy Tech	$612,169	$601,634	1.75%

LDK an estimate of revenue for 2011

Production and installed capacity in China

Geographical growth distribution 2011

Country	2011 totals	2010 totals	Average of Growth
China	$ 19,782,523	$ 17,867,151	12.75%
Germany	$ 4,192,156	$ 5,258,945	-21.06%
Norway	$ 2,320,338	$ 2,563,714	-9.49%
Taiwan	$ 2,898,075	$ 3,608,456	-15.57%
USA	$ 5,078,701	$ 4,782,745	6.05%
Grand Total	$ 34,271,793	$ 34,081,011	0.23%

Source: "Seeking Alpha; Solar Global View: Chinese Set to Lead in 2012 While New Markets Emerge," http://seeking alpha.com/article/475551-solar-global-view-chinese-set-to-lead-in-2012-while-new-markets-emerge; National Foreign Trade Council, *China's Promotion of the Renewable Electric Power Equipment Industry*, March 2010, p. 76.

Exhibit 14. Intermittency of U.S. Policy: Historic Impact of PTC Expiration on Annual Wind Installation

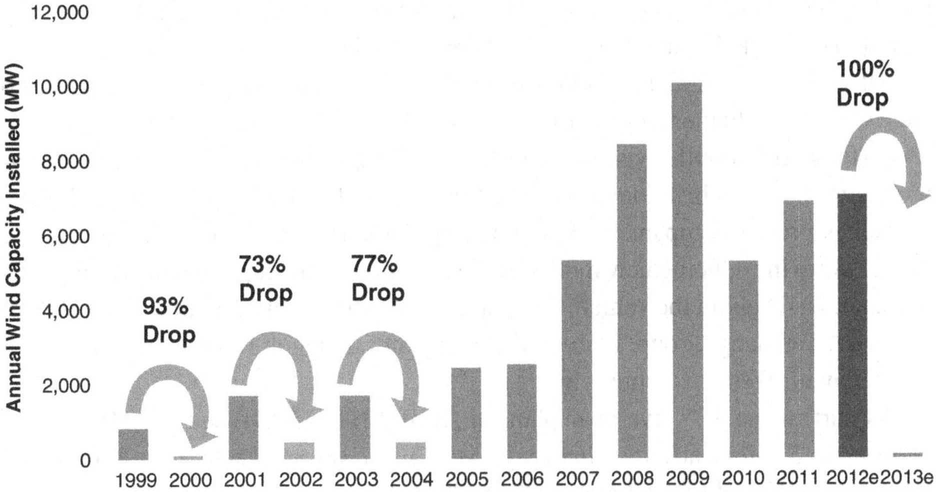

Source: American Wind Energy Association, "PTC Fact Sheet" (PDF file), downloaded from AWEA website, http://www.awea.org/_cs_upload/issues/federal_policy/7785_6.pdf, accessed June 5, 2012.

Fuel Cell Vehicle Project, with an initial investment of RMB800 million (just under $100 million).[29] The R&D mechanism was developed with three horizontal plans: for fuel-cell electric vehicles (FCEVs), hybrid electric vehicles (HEVs), and electric vehicles (EVs); and with three vertical plans: assembly, electric motors and dynamic batteries.[30] In 2006, as part of the 11th five-year plan, MOST would invest another RMB1.1 billion in an Energy-Saving and New Energy Vehicles Project.

Two years later, MOST joined with the Ministry of Finance, the NDRC and the Ministry of Industry and Information Technology to sponsor the 1,000 Vehicles, 10 Cities Demonstration Project. Over the next few years, these government agencies would invest about U.S.$2.5 billion to establish 10 pilot areas where 10,000 EVs would be deployed. This was eventually expanded to 20 cities. The government created different-sized subsidies for different vehicles. For light commercial vehicles or passenger vehicles, the subsidy (paid to the manufacturer) ranged from U.S.$7,300 (for an HEV) to U.S.$8,800 for an EV. For buses, the subsidies ranged from U.S.$7,300 to $73,000 (and even U.S.$88,000 for a fuel-cell vehicle).[31] This was indeed a serious effort to kick-start an electric vehicle industry.

To accommodate this many electric vehicles in nearly two dozen cities, a charging infrastructure was obviously needed. For the electric utilities, this was a huge opportunity, if charging could be done off-peak. It meant that grid companies could aggressively participate in the automobile industry. State Grid and Southern Grid drafted bold investment plans for thousands of charging stations. By the end of

2011, State Grid had completed 87 stations (with 7,000 charging posts) and had plans to build 2,300 more stations. Southern Grid partnered with Better Place on an EV demonstration project and had 14 charging stations in operation. Even the big oil companies had begun investing in charging stations.[32]

All of these investments and government largesse drew dozens of entrants into the EV business. In the truck-and-bus segment, BYD, ZAP, Liuzhou Wuling Motors, FAW (First Automobile Works), Lujo EV and Zonda Bus were the leading groups producing vehicles. In automobiles, state enterprises like FAW and DonFeng Motor, as well as private companies (Haima, Chery, Jiangnan, Brilliance, GM Buick and SAIC), were introducing new models of HEVs or EVs, but experiencing disappointing sales. And behind the vehicle companies stood the battery manufacturers (BYD, Zhejiang, Tienneng Group, Lishen, Wanxiang and Shuzhou Phylion), struggling to catch up with Western technology.[33]

As part of the 12th five-year plan, in April 2011, MOST and the Ministry of Industry and Information Technology (MIIT) introduced the Energy Saving and New Energy Vehicle Development Plan (2011–2020), which envisioned 5 million new energy vehicles (electric or fuel-cell) by 2020. Government's investment would be RMB100 billion — about U.S.$16 billion! The idea here was to push the various existing programs, all lagging behind, into high-speed commercial realization.[34]

"Clean Coal"

With 3.7 billion tons of coal produced annually and more planned by 2015, China had severe problems with both localized air pollution (e.g. particulates, sulfur dioxide and nitrogen oxides) and carbon emissions. Indeed, the government was intensely aware of this and in both the 11th and 12th plans, it undertook serious initiatives to reduce its carbon intensity and even to curb carbon emissions.

Burning anything, or even breathing for that matter, creates CO_2. Thus, "clean coal" is a bit of an oxymoron. The accumulation of CO_2 in the atmosphere traps infrared solar radiation, causing it to warm, gradually. China, like the U.S. and Europe, was now working to develop technologies that generate power more efficiently or actually capture the CO_2 and then sequester it. Super-efficient boilers and integrated gasification, combined cycle generation (IGCC) are a couple of the technologies — very expensive technologies — that reduce carbon emissions.

Another type of technology, which several large engineering companies like Siemens and Alstom developed, actually captured the CO_2 chemically, creating a liquid that could be injected in deep wells underground — carbon capture and sequestration (CCS). These technologies, to date, were energy inefficient (with an energy penalty of 15%–25%) and expensive.[35]

In its 11th plan, the Chinese government committed 2 billion yuan, both for R&D and for building a 250 MW IGCC demonstration plant. In the 12th plan, another 3 billion yuan was committed to IGCC demonstration and the beginning of a GreenGen project in Tianjin to demonstrate CCS.[36] But given that these technologies were experimental and a long way from commercially feasible, there was little likelihood that they would make a significant impact in the next decade.

Indigenous Innovation and Intellectual Property Rights

Indigenous innovation is the strategic sequel to Deng Xiaoping's "reform and opening policy." In February 2006, when the State Council unveiled its "medium and long-term development plan," it called for reliance on the guiding principle of *zizhiu chuangxin*, or *indigenous innovation*.[37] The Medium to Long-term Plan (MLP) blueprint targeted 11 key sectors that included energy, water and mineral resources, environment, agriculture, manufacturing, transportation, information and services, population and health, urbanization, public security and national defense.[38] Within these sectors were 68 priority areas, one of which was renewable energy:

> China will actively promote the development of renewable energy technologies and industries, building up a renewable energy technology innovation system. By 2010, China will basically have achieved the ability to produce domestically the main renewable energy equipment it uses. By 2020, local manufacturing capability based mainly on home-grown intellectual property right[s] (IPR) will be achieved.[39]

To accomplish these goals, the NDRC identified a half-dozen policies that the government could use: Favorable price policies, mandated market share policies, government investment, government concession programs "and other measures."[40] The same plan also identified a handful of megaprojects as vehicles for import substitution though co-innovation. Among these, for example, were advanced nuclear reactors.

In 2008, when the Ministry of Finance published its "administrative measures for government procurement on Initial Procurement and Ordering of Indigenous Innovation Products," it made clear the requirements of procurement by state-owned enterprises:

1. Shall be indigenous innovation products accredited by related government departments;
2. Shall comply with the needs of national economic development and represent the trend of advanced technological development;
3. Manufacturers and suppliers shall be Chinese enterprises and institutions licensed with the territory of China;
4. Shall be products which are first introduced to market, temporarily do not possess market competitiveness but enjoy great market potential and require special support of the government;

5. Shall enjoy great potential for mass production and high quality;
6. Shall comply with China's laws, regulations and policies.[41]

Apparently, the financial crisis and stimulus package ($586 billion) approved in October 2008 really provided significant funding for indigenous innovation. The Ministry of Science and Technology, NDRC and China's State Development Bank were the intermediaries providing subsidies and R&D for renewable energy.

All of this support crystallized with the publication of Circular 618: "Circular on Carrying Out the Work on Accreditation of National Indigenous Innovation Products," November 15, 2009. It made clear that an indigenous innovation product must entail intellectual property owned by a Chinese company with a commercial trademark registered within China. One month later, the Ministries of Technology, Trade and Finance catalogued 240 types of industrial equipment that the government wanted domestic companies to produce.[42]

By 2010, foreign companies were beginning to understand the emerging "China model" and the array of industrial policies and market access barriers designed to implement it. Companies like Siemens, BASF Google and GE started to complain. "I am not sure that in the end they want any of us to win," complained Jeff Immelt, chairman of GE, "or any of us to be successful."[43] Thereafter, the government backed off a bit, revising the most controversial provisions of Circular 618.

Intellectual property rights were on the other side of the indigenous innovation problem. Since the early 1980s, China had passed various laws to protect intellectual property — counterfeiting, patents, trademarks and copyrights. Enforcement, however, was often lax or nonexistent. Entry into the WTO further raised these standards, resulting in increased enforcement, but also worrying some Chinese leaders (see **Exhibit 12**). "Under the rules of the WTO," complained MOST Minister Xu Guanghua, "intellectual property rights, technical barriers to trade and anti-dumping have become a major barrier for most of China's companies to compete in the international arena."[44] (See **Exhibits 15** and **16**.)

In 2012, for example, American wind-equipment manufacturer AMSC brought a suit in China for $1.2 billion, alleging that Sinovel misappropriated the software that AMSC made to operate turbines.[45] Similar problems existed as well in lithium-ion batteries.

Renewable Policies in the United States

Unlike China, there was no energy policy in the U.S. — no Renewable Energy Law, no Ride the Wind program, no Medium- and Long-Term Development Plan for Renewable Energy, no 11th or 12th five-year plans and no Golden Sun Demonstration Program. There was no central government setting energy-efficiency targets or 15%

Exhibit 15.   Projected Annual Chinese Exports of Green Products and Services, 2030

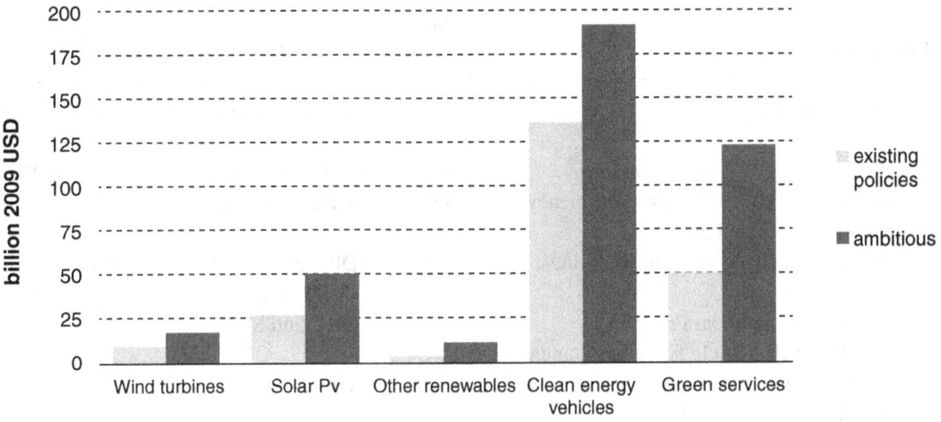

Source: World Bank and Development Research Center of the State Council of China, *China 2030: 2012*, p. 244.

Note: The ranges given above compare two scenarios defined by the IEA. The "existing policies" scenario is one in which the G20 countries follow through with their commitment to reduce fossil fuel subsidies, countries fulfill their Cancun Decision pledges to reduce greenhouse'1 gas emissions and other CO_2 mitigation policies are implemented (i.e. the "New Policies" scenario in the *IEA World Energy Outlook 2010*). The higher estimates correspond to the "ambitious" scenario in which countries take ambitious action to limit atmospheric concentrations of CO_2 from rising above 450 parts per million (i.e. the "450" scenario in the *IEA World Energy Outlook 2010*).

Exhibit 16.   Recent Key Energy Policies Supporting China's 20% Reduction Goal

Energy Policies	Date Effective	Responsible Agency
Fuel Consumption limits for Possenger Cars	2004	
Medium and Long-Term Plan for Energy Conservation	2005	National Development and Reform Commission (NDRC)
Renewable Energy Law	2005	
Government Procurement Program	2005	NDRC and Ministry of Finance (MOF)
Nationol Energy Efficient Design Standard for Public Buildings	2005	Ministry of Construction (MOC)
Eleventh Five-Year Plan	2006	NDRC
The State Council Decision on Strengthening Energy Conservation	2006	State Council
Reduced Export Tax Rebates for Many Low-Value-Added But High Energy-Consuming Products	2006	MOF
Top 1,000 Energy-Consuming Enterprise Program	2006	NDRC

(Continued)

Exhibit 16.   *(Continued)*

Energy Policies	Date Effective	Responsible Agency
"Green Purchasing" Program	2006	Ministry of Environment Protection (MEP) and MOF
Revision of Energy Conservation Law	2007	Nationol People's Congress and NDRC
Allocation of Funding on Energy Efficiency and Pollution Abatement	2007	MOF and NDRC
China Energy Technology Policy Outline	2007	NDRC and the Ministry of Science and Technology
Government Procurement Program	2007	NDRC and MOF
National Phase III Vehicle Emission Standards	2007	
Interim Administrative Method for Incentive Funds for Heating and Metering and Energy Efficiency Retrofit for Existing Residential Buildings in China's Northern Heating Area	2007	MOF
Law on Corporate Income Tax (preferential tax treatment for investment in energy-saving and environmentally friendly projects and equipment)	2008	NDRC
Allocation of Funding on Energy Efficiency and Pollution Abatement	2008	MOF and NDRC
Appliances Standards ond Labeling	Various Years	General Administration of Quality Supervision, Inspection, and Quarantine

Source: Levine, Zhou and Price, "The Greening of the Middle Kingdom: The Story of Energy Efficiency in China," *The Bridge*, Summer 2009, p. 52.

renewables targets for 2020. What the U.S. government did have was a president who supported renewable energy, a handful of tax credits and an array of state subsidies and renewable energy portfolios. Of course, vigorous capitalism and a healthy venture capitalism sector helped, but the market alone did not seem able to match the thrust of centralized Chinese ambition.

The U.S. Department of Energy (DOE) — the lead cabinet department in energy matters — was currently budgeted at about $27 billion, of which $2.3 billion was for renewable energy and another $5 billion for energy research (much of the rest of the DOE budget was for nuclear power, including fuels for nuclear weapons). In the area of research, the American Competes Act of 2009 created ARPA-e (Advanced Research Programs Administration-energy), modeled after the incredibly successful DARPA. ARPA-e was budgeted for about $500 million annually. The DOE also ran 20 national research laboratories, of which the most germane was the NREL (National Renewable Energy Laboratory) in Colorado.

Exhibit 17. U.S. receipts from China and Rest of World, Royalties and License Fees by Type of Intangible Asset, 2004–2008 ($ millions)

	Industrial Processes	Books, Records, and Tapes	Broadcasting and Recording of Live Events	Franchise Fees	Trademarks	General-Use Computer Software	Total
China							
2008	1,080	2	21	204	292	727	2,326
2007	831	3	20	156	231	605	1,846
2006	663	2	7	114	202	528	1,516
2005	159	5	1	21	28	71	285
2004	185	3	1	17	48	61	315
Rest of world							
2008	39,050	1,551	556	4,168	12,260	31,564	89,149
2007	35,960	1,497	538	3,739	11,534	28,621	81,889
2006	31,752	1,471	418	3,156	10,181	22,127	69,105
2005	6,321	684	241	672	1,422	6,184	15,524
2004	5,472	652	200	585	1,666	4,689	13,264

Source: U.S. Bureau of Economic Analysis, as cited in: U.S. International Trade Commission, *China: Intellectual Property Infringement, Indigenous Innovation Policies and Frameworks for Measuring the Effects on the U.S. Economy*, pp. 2–11.

The American Recovery and Reinvestment Act of 2009 (the "stimulus") earmarked $43 billion for clean energy, of which $36.7 billion was administered by the DOE. Of this, $4.5 billion was for smart grid applications, $4 billion for loan guarantees, $2.3 billion for manufacturing tax credits and $2.5 billion for R&D.[46] In addition to research, the Obama administration used these funds to support wind and solar facilities, electric batteries and electric vehicle plants. Also in 2009, Obama signed legislation to extend automobile fuel-efficiency standards to 35 miles per gallon and for the first time, applied standards to light and heavy-duty trucks.

Currently, the key policies of the federal government were a variety of tax measures: A production tax credit, an investment tax credit and the modified accelerated cost-recovery system (MACRS). The production tax credit that was first enacted in 1994 and most recently renewed for four years in 2008, provided about $.018 per kilowatt-hour of electricity generated by new renewable projects for 10 years. The history of the production tax credit (PTC) in the U.S. wind sector had created a stop-start industry; as it disappeared, the industry collapsed (see **Exhibit 14** for the impact of the PTC expiration). The investment tax credit (ITC), enacted in 2005, provided a 30% tax credit for solar power, fuel cells and small wind and 10% for geothermal. The stimulus allowed all PTC-eligible renewable sources to receive the ITC, in lieu of the PTC. The MACRS allowed renewable electricity assets to be depreciated rapidly.

Exhibit 18.   Counterfeit Manufacturing Operations in China

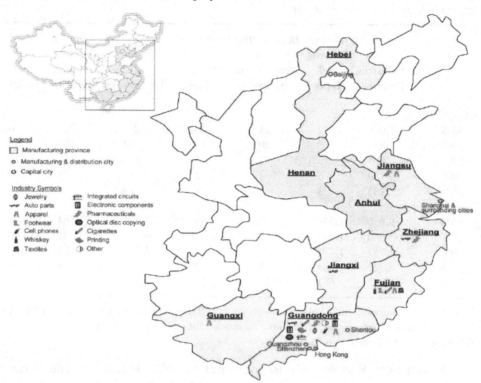

Source: U.S. International Trade Commission, *China: Intellectual Property Infringement, Indigenous Innovation Policies and Frameworks for Measuring the Effects on the U.S. Economy*, pp. 3–19.

Note: The above map represents areas reported to contain large-scale counterfeit manufacturing and markers by province for particular reported counterfeit industries.

Finally, the state governments in the U.S., impatient for action from Washington, enacted subsidy programs (such as California's $3 billion subsidy for rooftop solar panels), tax incentives and renewable energy portfolio standards. The latter, now covering about 38 states, required utilities to attain between 10% of their electricity from renewable energy (in several mid-western states) and 33% (in California) to a high of 50% (in Alaska), by 2020, 2025, or 2030. These standards really created the market for renewables throughout the United States.

China's Renewables in the Global Marketplace

The government of China, its renewables industries, its engineers and its workers labored incredibly hard during the past decade to replace carbon fuels and to build industries that were globally competitive. In wind, solar and electric vehicles, the country's manufacturers now led the U.S. and Europe in the global marketplace.

Exhibit 19.   Advanced-Technology Exports from the U.S. to China, 2000–2009

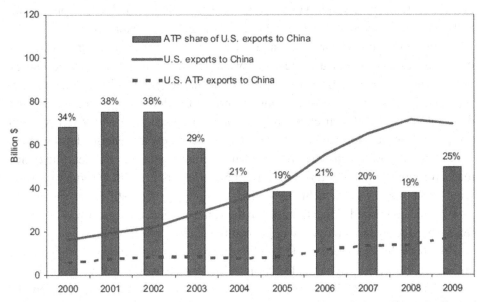

Source: World Trade Atlas, as cited in U.S. International Trade Commission, *China: Intellectual Property Infringement, Indigenous Innovation Policies and Frameworks for Measuring the Effects on the U.S. Economy*, pp. 2–8.

Exhibit 20.   Advanced-Technology Imports from China to the U.S. 2000–2009

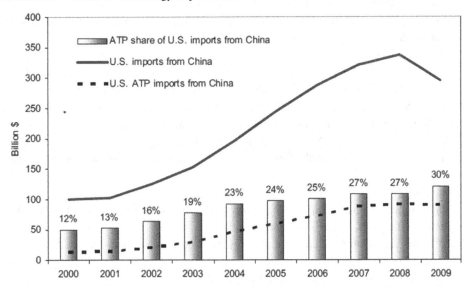

Source: World Trade Atlas, as cited in U.S. International Trade Commission, *China: Intellectual Property Infringement, Indigenous Innovation Policies and Frameworks for Measuring the Effects on the U.S. Economy*, pp. 2–9.

In nuclear power, China was catching up fast and certainly taking the lead in third-generation reactors. Even in supercritical coal-fired boilers and in carbon capture and generation, the country's engineers were struggling to catch up.

There were many reasons for China's incredible success at building these industries and businesses, but a critical one was the government's renewable energy policy. These policies aggressively acquired technology, subsidized procurement, subsidized research and development, set prices for domestic purchases, favored domestic content and restricted foreign content and used tariff and VAT taxes and even the Clean Development Mechanism to support renewable energy development.

China was now a major exporter of solar cells and modules, of towers and lattice masts for wind projects and of lithium-ion batteries. Its firms had begun exporting wind turbines and electric vehicles — the first signs of successful industrial policy. As Wen Jiabao pushed China to move up the value chain in exports, it was clear that renewable energy technologies would be at the leading edge.

So where did this leave the U.S. whose technology and markets for renewable energy led the world just half a decade ago? With no clear energy strategy and fragmented, half-hearted policies for renewables, could the U.S. even hope to keep up?

Endnotes

[1] U.S. International Trade Commission, "Crystalline Silicon Photovoltaic cells and Modules from China," Publication 4295, December 2011.

[2] Quoted in James McGregor, "China's Drive for 'Indigenous Innovation' A web of Industrial Policies," Global Intellectual Property Center, 2011, p. 4.

[3] Innovation Center Denmark — Shanghai, Report: China's Indigenous Innovation Program, p. 3; http://www.shanghai.um.dk/NR/rdonlyres/BCB7B066-3502-4447-96D4-C3E6F470E016/0/ChinasIndigenousInnovationProgramReport.pdf.

[4] Dewey & LeBoeuf LLP, for the National Foreign Trade Council, *China's Promotion of the Renewable Electric Power Equipment Industry*, March 2010, p. 7.

[5] Sarah Ladislaw and Jane Nakano, "China — Leader or Laggard on the Path to a Secure, Low-Carbon Energy Future?" Center for Strategic & International Studies, September 2011, p. 3.

[6] *Ibid.*, p. 11.

[7] State Council, *China's Energy Conditions and Policies*, December 26, 2007, cited in Dewey & Leboeuf, *China's Promotion*, p. 1.

[8] 11th Five Year Plan for Renewable Energy, Section 2(2), cited in Dewey & Leboeuf, *China's Promotion*, p. 33.

[9] "China to Postpone Issuance of New Energy Revitalization Plan," *SinoCast*, January 26, 2010.

[10] Joanna Lewis, "Energy and Climate Goals of China's 12th Five-Year Plan," Pew Center on Global Climate Change, March 2011, p. 1.

[11] World Nuclear Association, "Nuclear Power in China," pp. 16–19, http://www.world nuclear.org/info/inf63.html, downloaded April 5, 2012.

[12] *Ibid.*, p. 3.

[13] Ladislaw and Nakano, "China — Leader or Laggard," p. 23.

[14] "Interim Measures for Administering Capital Construction Project of New Energy," *Ji Jiao Neng* (May 1997), No. 955; cited in Dewey & Leboeuf, *China's Promotion*, p. 49.

[15] NDRC, "The Notice of Requirements for the Administration of Wind Power Construction," *Fa Gai Neng Yuan* (July 2005), No. 1205, Section 3; cited in Dewey & Leboeuf, *China's Promotion*, p. 53.

[16] Office of the United States Trade Representative, "China Ends Wind Power Equipment Subsidies Challenged by the United States in WTO Dispute," June 2011.

[17] China Ministry of Finance, "Announcement on Issuing the 'Management Regulations on Special Fund for Wind Power Manufacturing Sector in China,'" MOF Document [2008] No. 476, August 11, 2008, http://www.cresp.org.cn/uploadfiles/ 2/981/mof_476_eng.pdf.

[18] Yvonne Chan, "China sets feed-in tariff for wind power plants," *Business Green*, July 27, 2009, http://www.businessgreen.com/bg/news/1801182/china-sets-feed-tariff-wind-power-plants.

[19] North American Windpower, "Report Reveals Top 10 Wind Turbine Manufacturers for 2011," http://www.nawindpower.com/e107_plugins/content/content.php?content. 9581. The others included Vestas (1), Enercon (5), Suzlon (7), Siemens (9), and GE Wind (6).

[20] EU Chamber of Commerce in China, "European Business in China Position Paper 2009–2010" (2009), p. 113.

[21] "Weak grid connections stalling China's wind energy growth," Modern Power Systems, February 27, 2011, http://www.modernpowersystems.com/story.asp?section code=131&storyCode=2058965.

[22] "China bans wind farm construction in grid-poor areas," *Wind Power Monthly*, March 30, 2012.

[23] China Greentech Initiative, *China's Solar PV Value Chain*, Spring 2011, p. 6, http://www.china-greentech.com/sites/default/files/CGTI2011-RE-WS1-Solar-PV-Value-Chain.pdf.

[24] Susan Myers and LY Yuan, "China's Solar Energy Industry: Polisilicon 2007–2011," http://www.altenergymag.com/emagazine.php?issue_number=07.06.01&article =china.

[25] Richard Vietor, *Suntech Power, HBS No. 710-013* (Boston: Harvard Business School Publishing, 2009).

[26] State Council, "Guidelines for the Medium-and-Long-Term National Science and Technology Development Program (2006–2020)," Part VIII, p. 2, cited in Dewey and LeBoeuf, *China's Promotion*, p. 26.

[27] Dewey and LeBoeuf, *China's Promotion*, p. 77.

[28] China Greentech Initiative, "China's Solar PV Value Chain: Opportunities to Improve Profits," Spring 2011, pp. 10–11.

[29] United Nations, Department of Economic and Social Affairs, Commission on Sustainable Development, "Electric Vehicles in the Context of Sustainable Development in China," Background Paper No. 9 (CSD19/2011/BP9, p. 7.

[30] FinPro China, "Electric Vehicle Study in China," December 2010, p. 6, http://www.finpro.fi/documents/10304/c6b1eb43-6420-49a1-a749-9f2ed1118587.

[31] *Ibid.*, p. 9.

[32] China Greentech Initiative, "Electric Vehicle and Charging Infrastructure in China," Summer 2011, pp. 9–10.

[33] United Nations, "Electric Vehicles in the Context of Sustainable development," 5; FinPro, "Electric Vehicle Study in China," p. 4.

[34] China Greentech Initiative, "Electric Vehicle," pp. 4, 6.

[35] Richard Vietor, *"AEP: Carbon Capture and Storage," HBS N1-711-036* (Boston: Harvard Business School Publishing, 2010).

[36] China Greentech Initiative, *The China Greentech Report 2011*, pp. 62–64; and H. John Heinz Center for Science, Economics and the Environment, *Carbon Capture and Storage Development in China*, 2010, p. 25, http://www.heinzctr.org/Major_Reports_files/Carbon%20Capture%20and%20Storage%20Development%20in%20China.pdf.

[37] McGregor, "China's Drive for 'Indigenous Innovation,'" p. 13.

[38] *Ibid.*, p. 14.

[39] NDRC, "Medium and Long-Term Development Plan (2007)," p. 6.

[40] *Ibid.*

[41] Dewey & LeBoeuf, *China's Promotion*, p. 28.

[42] McGregor, "China's Drive for 'Indigenous Innovation,'" p. 20.

[43] Quoted in Daniel Drezner, "The Death of the China Lobby," *Foreign Policy*, July 23, 2010.

[44] Quoted in McGregor, "China's Drive for 'Indigenous Innovation,'" p. 26.

[45] Bijoy Koyitty, "AMSC seeks $1.2 billion from Sinovel in Contract Row," Reuters, November 9, 2011, http://uk.reuters.com/article/2011/11/09/us-amsc-idUKTRE7A83LB20111109.

[46] National Academy of Sciences, "The Power of Renewables: Opportunities and Challenges for China and the United States," p. 121.

CoET: Innovation in Africa

Diego Comin,* Diana Dimitrova* and Yukiko Tsukamoto*

"Innovation distinguishes between a leader and a follower"

— Steve Jobs

Introduction

Dr. Jamidu Katima, the Principal of the College of Engineering and Technology (CoET) of the University of Dar es Salaam, knew that operating in Tanzania had its challenges. Compared to neighboring countries such as South Africa and Kenya, Tanzania was lagging in a number of business friendliness indicators and the gap between its neighbors and itself seemed to be widening.

CoET's mission as a technology center that innovated to solve local problems could be a great way to contribute to the country's growth while training Tanzania's top talent. Yet, very few of its technologies developed at CoET had made it to market, and for those that had, the diffusion rate had been quite low.

Dr. Katima wasn't sure what was causing the poor performance but he knew that things had to change. Should the institute stop trying to commercialize its innovations? Did it have the right distribution channels? Should it seek a partnership with the government? The options were many but one thing was clear, a new strategic path was imminent and necessary.

*Reprinted with permission of Harvard Business School Publishing.

This case was prepared by Professor Diego Comin and Diana Dimitrova and Yukiko Tsukamoto (MBAs 2012).

CoET: Innovation In Africa 713-021.

Background of Tanzania

In the late 19th century, Germany ruled a vast area of Eastern Africa, including the current mainland region of Tanzania, known as Tanganyika at that time. The English took control of the area after World War II, and in 1961, Tanganyika peacefully gained independence. In 1964, Zanzibar was added to Tanganyika, forming present day Tanzania.

Around the 1950s, political parties emerged. One of them was the Tanganyika African National Union, led by England educated Julius Nyerere. He was one of the few native Tanzanians who had obtained higher education under German and English rule. In 1961, Julius Kambarage Nyerere was elected the first Tanzanian president. In 1964, Nyerere launched his Five-Year Plan for Economic and Social Development. The plan called for national income to grow at 6.7% per year through industrialization and increased productivity.[1] At the time, Tanzania was still a member of the East African Currency Board, which administrated East African shillings backed by the British pound. The currency was used across Kenya, Uganda, Zambia and South Yemen. However, failure to attract private investment led Tanzania to miss its growth targets.

Frustrated by the result, in 1968, president Nyerere presented the Arusha Deceleration, which directed Tanzania toward socialism. The declaration suggested that most 'means of production' such as land, minerals, water, oil and electricity, news, media, banking, communication, 'any big factory', etc. would be owned by the state. Soon after the declaration, a number of laws were passed to nationalize major institutions, and The Second Five-Year Plan was put in place to guide the economy. The plan aimed for 6.5% annual GDP growth via industrialization, while minimizing the trade deficit to 4% of GDP.[2] The Arusha Declaration was widely supported by Western nations, especially Nordic countries, which increased their donations to Tanzania. Per capita net official development assistance to Tanzania tripled between 1969 and 1975.

Again, both targets were missed. Deteriorating performance at state owned firms forced the government to run large fiscal deficits, which were financed by the Bank of Tanzania. Inflation resulted, and the Tanzanian shilling's real value on the black market deteriorated (at this time, the Tanzanian government still had a fixed exchange rate). In order to control prices, the government launched the National Price Commission (NPC) in 1973, which controlled 3,000 prices by the end of 1975. These controls artificially decreased prices of key products such as coffee and resulted in reduced accumulation of capital in the economy. Severe droughts from 1973 to 1975 also affected the economy, and the black market for foreign currency and goods flourished.

The relationship between the government and the International Monetary Fund (IMF) soured at the end of 1979, when the IMF suggested devaluing the Tanzania shillings. As a result, Nyerere furiously expelled the mission. The economy further declined, as Tanzania was cut off from IMF support. Tanzania survived this period on aid money from Nordic countries, recurring debt (total debt to % of GDP remained around 85%),[3] and at times bartering exports for imports. The relationship with the IMF remained poor until President Nyerere passed the presidency to his handpicked successor, Ali Hassan Mwinyi in 1985. Although his policies led Tanzania to be one of the poorest nations in the world, Nyerere is regarded as founding father of Tanzania and widely respected among Tanzanians to this day.

In 1986, Tanzania formally adopted reform policies that focused on the devaluation of the Tanzanian shilling, a tighter fiscal policy, liberalization of price (i.e. abolition of NPC in 1984), and trade. Reform also reopened access to World Bank loans and encouraged aid money to flow into the country. Net official development assistance jumped from 5% of the GDP in 1985 to 19% in 1987. External debt also drastically increased from 48% of the GDP in 1985 to 103% in 1987. As a result, the GDP per capita showed moderate constant growth at 3% average. Poverty rate decreased as the GDP per capita increased.[4]

Since 1986, Tanzania has almost consistently shown slow but relatively constant growth. In 2000, Tanzania reached its previous peak GDP per capita, which had been achieved in 1976. Tanzania also seemed to come out of the global financial crisis in a strong position by marking a 5.5% GDP growth in 2009 and 6.2% in 2010. Yet, the economy is still heavily dependent on agriculture, which constitutes 25% of GDP and 75% of the workforce.[5] The current account deficit is 9% of the GDP.[6] Tanzania is still heavily dependent on foreign aid, which still makes up 22.5% of the GDP (see **Exhibit 1** for detailed history and present day economic data).[7]

Business Environment and Competitiveness

As of 2012, Tanzania is ranked as the 14th largest economy in Africa, with a GDP per capita of US$550. However, in 2011, Tanzania ranked 120th out of 140 countries in the Global Competitiveness Report (GCR), whereas neighboring Kenya scored 102nd and South Africa, 50th. Although, Tanzania scored relatively high in the area of political stability, specifically in categories such as 'public trust of politicians' and 'relative evenhandedness in the government's dealings with the private sector', low-quality infrastructure such as roads, information technology, and electricity supply, a population with overall limited exposure to educational opportunities, and a lack of basic health of its labor force held the country back. (see **Exhibit 2** for country education data).

Exhibit 1. Economic Performance of Tanzania

	Unit	1970	1975	1980	1985	1990	1995	2000	2005	2010
Real 2005 GDP (constant 2005 USD)	($B)	$3.9	$4.5	$5.3	$6.1	$7.5	$8.1	$10.1	$14.1	$19.7
Real GDP growth rate (5 year growth rate)	%	na	116.3	116.3	116.3	121.7	109.3	123.5	140.6	139.4
Real GDP Per Capita (constant 2005 USD)	($)	$281.8	$280.3	$282.1	$283.4	$295.6	$273.8	$298.4	$374.4	$470.5
Real GDP per capita growth rate (5 year growth rate)	%	na	99.5	100.6	100.4	104.3	92.6	109.0	125.5	125.7
Real exchange rates (USD = 1)		568.0	478.6	449.7	1,089.1	1,777.5	1,109.3	905.4	1,128.9	1,012.2
Real exchange rate growth rate (5 year growth rate)	%	na	84.3	94.0	242.2	163.2	62.4	81.6	124.7	89.7
CPI indices		0.3	0.5	0.9	3.2	11.2	43.1	78.0	100.0	150.8
CPI indices growth rates (5 year growth rate)	%	na	190.9	182.4	373.1	344.8	384.2	181.0	128.3	150.8
Agriculture, value added (% of GDP)	%	na	na	na	na	46.0	47.1	33.5	31.8	28.1
Manufacturing, value added (% of GDP)	%	na	na	na	na	9.3	7.2	9.4	8.7	9.8
Current Account (based on 2010 USD)	($B)	na	na	na	na	($1.0)	($0.9)	($0.4)	($1.1)	($1.7)
Current Account as % of GDP	%	na	na	na	na	(13.1)	(11.2)	(4.2)	(7.8)	(8.6)
Net official development assistance and aid (constant 2005 US$)	($B)	$0.5	$1.5	$2.2	$1.9	$2.5	$1.6	$2.2	$2.4	$0.0
Life expectancy at birth	(years)	46.7	48.8	50.5	51.2	50.6	49.6	50.4	53.3	0.0
Poverty headcount ratio at $2 a day (PPP)	(% of population)	na	na	na	na	91.31*	na	95.25*	87.87*	na
Population, total	(M)	13.6	16.0	18.7	21.8	25.5	29.9	34.0	38.8	44.8

Source: The World Bank, *World Development Indicators*, http://data.worldbank.org/country, Accessed on April 2012.
Note: *Poverty data is from 1992, 2000 and 2007.

Exhibit 2. Education in Tanzania

Education Levels	Tanzania	Kenya	Ghana	S. Africa
Primary School Completion Rate (%)	85	93	71	92
Progression to Secondary School (%)	58	N/A	87	88
Tertiary Enrollment (%)	1.48	2.75	5.84	15.41

Source: CCP Project Team, Emerging Market Group Ltd. *Tanzania National Competitiveness Assessment, 2009* http://www.ccp-tpsf.org/images/Downlink/CCP_National%20Compet%20Assess_30Sep09_pdf.pdf, Accessed June 2012.

Exhibit 3. Tanzania Business Friendliness

Business Sophistication-GCR Rank	TZ	Kenya
Local Supplier Quality	123	66
Local Supplier Quantity	116	34
Value Chain Breadth	118	69
Control of International Distribution	120	56
Extent of Marketing	115	71
Production Process Sophistication	124	101

Obtaining a License	TZ	Kenya	S. Africa	Singapore
Cost of licenses (% income per cap)	2087	46	28	21
Days to obtain a license	308	100	174	38

Source: CCP Project Team, Emerging Market Group Ltd. *Tanzania National Competitiveness Assessment, 2009* http://www.ccp-tpsf.org/images/Downlink/CCP_National%20Compet%20Assess_30Sep09_pdf.pdf, Accessed June 2012.

Tanzania is known for an unfriendly business environment compared to Kenya, lagging behind in local supplier quality and quantity, breadth of value chain, production, and process sophistication.[8] Also, Tanzania's cost of licensing is approximately 50 times higher and time to obtain a permit is around three times longer than that of Kenya (see **Exhibit 3** for business friendliness rankings).

Access to capital poses an additional challenge for Tanzanian corporations. Isolation from the global financial market kept Tanzania intact from the recent financial crisis in 2008, and, as a result, the country's banking sector grew significantly. In 2008, the deposit level grew by 30%, reaching 32% of the GDP. However, equity markets are still in their infancy. In 1997, Tanzania established the Dar es Salaam Stock Exchange, aiming to diversify the sources of capital. However, the market remains extremely small. In 2007, 10 years after its establishment, the stock exchange only lists seven local companies.[9] As a result, companies in Tanzania remain small and fragmented. Close to 80% of Tanzania's formal industries are small or medium enterprises, which each employ between 5 and 99 people.[10]

Research and development (R&D) expenditure is another area of weakness for Tanzania. Tanzania only spends 0.43% of GDP on R&D, whereas United States spends 2.66%, Germany 2.52%, and Japan 3.4% of their respective GDP's.[11] Tanzania's spending is also lower than neighboring nations. Kenya marked 0.44% and South Africa 0.99%. In particular, R&D expenditure in agriculture is much lower than in other countries in the region such as South Africa (over 2% of agricultural production) or Kenya (over 1% of agricultural production).[12] More worryingly, Tanzania's competitiveness in R&D spending has been declining. In 2009, Tanzania's ranking according to 'Company spending on R&D' in the GCR dropped from 58th to 114th, while Kenya scored 37th.

The first National Strategy for Growth and Reduction of Poverty, announced in 1995, recognized explicitly the role of technology in promoting the goal of sustainable broad-based growth (increasing technological innovation, upgrading existing technology, and using new technologies). In order to reach its goal, Tanzania established R&D institutions to develop local capacity for technological innovations and development.

CoET, its Mission, and Achievements to Date

The College of Engineering and Technology (CoET) is part of the University of Dar es Salaam. The Faculty of Engineering (FoE) was started at the University in 1973 with the help of the German government. The main goal of the FoE was to provide engineering education and training at the undergraduate level. The University and the FoE went through a number of transformations in the 1990s and expanded their educational offerings to meet demand for more specialized degrees and postgraduate education. In 2005, the College of Engineering and Technology (CoET) was formally established. CoET has three main pillars: the academic departments, the Technology Development and Transfer Center (TDTC), and the Bureau of Industrial Cooperation (BICO).[13] (**Exhibit 4**)

The six academic departments are Chemical and Mining Engineering (CME), Structural and Construction Engineering (SCE), Electrical and Computer Systems Engineering (ECSE), Mechanical and Industrial Engineering (MIE), Transportation and Geotechnical Engineering (TGE), and Water Resource Engineering (WRE). In 2009, CoET had 201 academic staff members (**Exhibit 5**) and a total of 284 postgraduate students. The largest program at the post-graduate level was Mechanical and Industrial Engineering, with 120 students enrolled (42% of the total). (See **Exhibit 6**.) At the undergraduate level, ECSE was most popular, with 511 students enrolled, representing 32% of total.[14] (**Exhibit 7**)

Exhibit 4. The Pillars of CoET

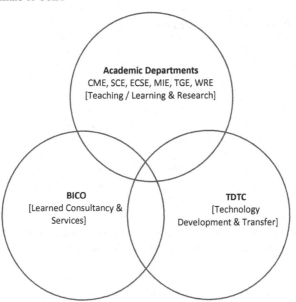

Source: CoET Information Brochure 2009–2010.

Exhibit 5. College Academic Staff by Rank as of December 2009

Rank	Total	%
Professors	9	4
Associate Professors	24	12
Senior Lecturers	39	19
Lecturers	22	11
Assistant Lecturers	39	19
Tutorial Assistants	68	34
Total	**201**	**100**

Source: CoET Information Brochure 2009–2010.

The second pillar, the Technology Development and Transfer Center, coordinates and develops technology at the college. It produces prototypes and carries out manufacturing of innovations for sale. The TDTC has at its disposal all academic and technical staff of the six CoET academic departments. To date, CoET has developed 44 technologies that have been produced for the mass market.

The Bureau of Industrial Cooperation (BICO) is the consulting arm of the CoET, and it aims to provide engineering, knowledge-based consulting, and expert professional services to industry and organizations. It also offers professional development courses to practicing engineers.[15] BICO is a profit earning business unit

Exhibit 6.   Total Postgraduate Students Enrollment in 2008/2009

Program	PGD			Masters			PhD			Total		
	M	F	T	M	F	T	M	F	T	M	F	T
CME	0	0	0	14	0	14	0	4	4	14	4	18
ECSE	0	0	0	33	5	38	4	4	8	37	9	46
MIE	5	0	5	93	10	103	10	2	12	108	12	120
SCE	3	2	5	25	4	29	6	0	6	34	6	40
TGE	5	0	5	14	1	15	5	0	5	24	1	25
WRE	2	1	3	13	12	25	6	1	7	21	14	35
Total	**15**	**3**	**18**	**192**	**32**	**224**	**31**	**11**	**42**	**238**	**46**	**284**

Source: CoET Information Brochure 2009–2010.

Note: CME = Chemical and Mining Engineering, SCE = Structural and Construction Engineering, ECSE = Electrical and Computer Systems Engineering, MIE = Mechanical and Industrial Engineering, TGE = Transportation and Geotechnical Engineering, and WRE = Water Resource Engineering.

Exhibit 7.   Undergraduate Students' Enrolment for 2008/2009 Academic Year

Program	1st Year			2nd Year			3rd year			4th Year			Total		
	M	F	T	M	F	T	M	F	T	M	F	T	M	F	T
CME	73	17	90	66	28	94	76	35	111	68	36	104	283	116	399
ECSE	116	18	134	112	32	144	99	34	133	80	20	100	407	104	511
MIE	28	16	44	20	16	36	52	23	75	47	15	62	147	70	217
SCE	48	1	49	43	6	49	40	8	48	37	4	41	168	19	187
TGE	36	4	40	15	5	20	40	5	45	38	7	45	129	21	150
WRE	26	3	29	25	12	37	30	8	38	29	7	36	110	30	140
Total	**327**	**59**	**386**	**281**	**99**	**380**	**337**	**113**	**450**	**299**	**89**	**388**	**1244**	**360**	**1604**

Source: CoET Information Brochure 2009–2010.

Note: CME = Chemical and Mining Engineering, SCE = Structural and Construction Engineering, ECSE = Electrical and Computer Systems Engineering, MIE = Mechanical and Industrial Engineering, TGE = Transportation and Geotechnical Engineering, and WRE = Water Resource Engineering.

(See **Exhibit 8** for financials). The consulting work is performed by faculty members for clients that include government agencies, utility and water companies, private firms, and individuals. Typical consulting engagements include infrastructure development such as water and sanitation design, mechanical design of bridges and roads, and environmental assessment. BICO does not perform any R&D; rather, it provides expert advice based on research and prototypes completed by the other two areas of CoET. A consulting team can be composed of any of the 120 academic and 135 technical staff at CoET. BICO is typically hired either through word

Exhibit 8. BICO Gross Income from Core Business in USD

Year	Consultancy	Service	PDP*	Others	Total (USD.)
1991/92	88,900	74,700	31,000	—	**194,600**
1992/93	195,000	73,200	27,350	—	**295,550**
1993/94	206,600	74,750	12,250	—	**293,600**
1994/95	201,700	97,980	14,750	—	**314,430**
1995/96	355,950	109,980	8,074	—	**474,004**
1996/97	418,054	230,975	19,771	—	**668,800**
1997/98	439,792	239,901	65,964	—	**745,657**
1998/99	413,676	213,028	61,460	—	**688,165**
1999/00	293,129	256,314	75,834	19,265	**644,542**
2000/01	297,106	242,236	83,995	22,854	**646,192**
2001/02	368,872	179,715	151,756	58,049	**758,392**
2002/03	540,198	199,031	85,952	87,264	**912,444**
2003/04	325,947	241,764	215,863	71,178	**854,751**
2004/05	440,189	270,394	295,372	105,728	**1,111,683**
2005/06	443,347	258,376	87,614	89,325	**878,661**
2006/07	742,577	270,370	121,745	62,558	**1,197,249**
2007/08	1,311,524	352,557	301,898	103,434	**2,069,413**
2008/09	1,488,597	481,646	132,606	99,547	**2,202,396**
2009/10	1,232,695	432,648	43,664	149,739	**1,858,746**
2010/11	1,386,542	410,909	80,351	142,037	**2,019,839**

Source: COET Annual reports.
Note: *Professional Development Programmes.

of mouth recommendations or through proactively responding to advertisements in newspapers. Consulting projects are priced based on a cost plus 20% mark-up model.

The CoET Innovation Process and its Challenges

The origin of the innovation developed at CoET was diverse. Some innovations resulted from the interest of donors that conditioned their funding to the conduit of research in a particular field. An example is the Tanzania Cotton Board, which donated equipment and financial support to the development of the Textile Engineering department at COET.[16] The origin of other innovations came from alumni graduates who brought industry problems to the TDTC. The TDTC involved expert faculty in designing a solution that it could later manufacture and sell. Finally, a third type of innovations originated from targeted research by faculty in their fields of interest. For example, faculty have innovated water drainage systems tailored to the Tanzanian environment. Most innovations at COET resulted from the donation-funded research performed by the academic departments. The latter two routes rarely resulted in innovation activity. COET would typically hold the rights to patent innovations.

Once the designs were completed, they were forwarded to the TDTC. The TDTC completed and tested the prototypes in the field and gathered feedback. Once this process was complete, the product was ready for commercialization. Informal estimates by COET suggested that only about 1% of the design ideas would reach the commercialization stage.[17]

On average, the TDTC produces three to four prototypes a year, and it takes approximately three to four years to bring a prototype to market. Commercialization is carried out via exhibitions where products are advertised with the help of marketing brochures. A manager at the TDTC noted, "exhibitions are not very effective, we see lots of interest, but few orders result. One of our major challenges is that a copycat product is out the day after the exhibition".[18] (A full list of products and number of units sold available in **Exhibit 9**)

The TDTC manufactures units in-house as ordered. The college had tried to outsource production, but external manufacturers did not have the capital to carry out the projects. This is partly due to the fact that manufacturing companies have a difficult time obtaining credit in Tanzania; the financing system prefers trade credit because the duration of the loans is shorter. The college has similarly had difficulty in securing manufacturing loans resulting in long delivery times. Commercial banks are the only source of funding for these types of projects and frequently charge upward of 20% interest. As a result, production costs resemble one-off manufacturing costs rather than mass production unit costs. The pricing of units is based on the fully loaded fabrication costs plus a notional amount to allow for manufacturing of other prototypes. No explicit mark-up is placed on products.[19]

Copycats are a major issue, particularly because their use of cheaper materials allow their prices to be lower.[20] The two main reasons CoET retains a client is quality and customization. When neither of those factors matter, CoET tends to lose the job on the back of price. Additionally, since local copycat companies' main focus is the reproduction of prototypes, they tend to be more nimble and market-oriented. Cheaper competition doesn't just come from local copycats; customers also have the option to import the same innovations from China.[21]

CoET presently does not have a presence in the retail space. Tanzania does however have retail stores that are suitable to carry CoET's innovations.[22]

What Lies Ahead for CoET?

As time went on and CoET's progress stagnated, questions arose. Given the low rate of commercialization, should CoET even be focusing on mass-market innovations? Would the market be better served if CoET were to focus its resources exclusively

Exhibit 9. Technologies Developed by the College of Engineering & Technology

Equipment	Drive	Units Sold	Customers (region/country)
Construction and Low Cost Housing			
Cement-sand brick making machines	Manual	175	Dar es Salaam, Pwani, Mwanza, Shinyanga, Dodoma, Mbeya, Mtwara, Mara, Lindi, Kigali (Rwanda)
Vibrated block making machine	Electric	45	Dar es Salaam, Arusha, Iringa, Dodoma, Kilimanjaro
Interlocking and non-interlocking soil brick presses	Manual	289	Country-wide, Kenya, Rwanda
Vibrating pavement-block making	Electric	42	Dar es Salaam, Pwani, Iringa, Mtwara, Mara, Mwanza, Kilimanjaro, Mbeya, Morogoro, Dodoma
Stone crusher	Diesel Engine	1	Morogoro
Road compactor	Diesel Engine	0	
Concrete Mixer	Electric	1	Dar es Salaam
Sand Sieving Machine	Diesel Engine	—	
Culverts moulds	Manual	2	Morogoro
Small Scale Mining and Mineral Processing			
Amalgam Retort for Gold Recovery	Electric	7	Arusha, Dar es Salaam, Mwanza, Morogoro
Ball mill	Electric	1	Mbeya
Winch	Manual	1	Mbeya
Shaking Table	Manual	10	Arusha, Dar es Salaam
Denver Jig	Electric	2	Morogoro, Tanga
Food Processing			
Grain mill and huller	Electric	56	Dar es Salaam, Mwanza, Kagera, Mozambique, Malawi, Mbeya, Dodoma, Ruvuma, Shinyanga, Pwani
Animal feed mill and mixer	Electric	15	Dar es Salaam, Arusha, Zanzibar, Pwani, Iringa, Mozambique
Salt grinder	Electric	1	Pwani
Salt Iodator	Manual	1	Pwani
Palm oil processing equipment	Electric	7	Dar es Salaam, Pwani, Manyara, Morogoro, Kagera, Kigoma
Sunflower oil processing equipment	Electric	0	
Rice sheller	Electric	0	

(*Continued*)

Exhibit 9.   *(Continued)*

Equipment	Drive	Units Sold	Customers (region/country)
Fruit juice blender	Electric	6	Dar es Salaam, Morogoro
Peanut butter making machine	Electric	4	Morogoro, Tabora
Small scale sugar processing plant	Electric/ Manual	8	Arusha, Ruvuma, Kilimanjaro, Mara, Morogoro
Soya Milling Machine	Electric	1	Morogoro
Maize sheller	Electric	0	
Sieve-less maize milling machine	Electric	0	
Pulper	Electric	0	
Spice Grinder	Electric	0	
Chicken defeathering machine	Electric	0	
Energy			
Energy Saving Wood Stoves and Ovens		17	Dar es Salaam, Mbeya, Iringa
Solar tunnel dryer		0	
Integral solar water heater		0	
Centrifugal water pump	Solar	0	
Solar dryers		2	Pwani, Morogoro
Ethanol distillation column	Electric/ biofuel	5	Dodoma, Kilimanjaro, Morogoro
Ethanol fermenter	Electric/ biofuel	0	
Soap making			
Soap boiling kettle	Electric	8	Dar es Salaam, Zanzibar, Arusha, Zimbabwe
Soap extruder	Electric	8	Mbeya, Zanzibar, Dar es Salaam, Arusha, Kigoma, Zimbabwe
Soap stamping and cutting machine	Manual	6	Mbeya, Zanzibar, Dar es Salaam, Arusha, Kigoma, Zimbabwe
Seaweed grinder	Electric	2	Zanzibar
Soap grating machine	Electric	2	Zanzibar, Arusha
Health			
Medical Waste Incinerator	Electric	2	Dar es Salaam, Mwanza
Non-Burn medical waste Treatment	Electric	0	

Source: COET Annual reports.

on education? Yet, would the education component suffer if the practical design element were removed?

If the commercial front were a path worth pursuing, is realignment of the resources needed? Does the innovation process make sense? Should the college be more market-oriented? How would it carry out that shift and where would the funding come from?

Could distribution be the main issue? Are the exhibitions enough? Does a retail approach warrant exploration?

To tackle the copycat challenge or lower manufacturing costs, does a public-private partnership with the government make sense? Could the government provide assistance to help CoET increase its commercialization rate?

As CoET was drafting its future, answers to these pertinent questions were imminent.

Endnotes

[1] Edwards, Sebastian. *Is Tanzania A Success Story? A long Term Analysis.* Cambridge: National Bureau of Economic Research, 2012, p. 13.

[2] *Ibid*, p. 18.

[3] *Ibid*, p. 62.

[4] *Ibid*, pp. 62, 63.

[5] Data is 2006 figure. The World Bank, *World Development Indicators*, http://data.worldbank.org/country, Accessed on April 2012.

[6] Data is 2009 figure. The World Bank, *World Development Indicators*, http://data.worldbank.org/country, Accessed on April 2012.

[7] Data is 2009 figure. The World Bank, *World Development Indicators*, http://data.worldbank.org/country, Accessed on April 2012.

[8] CCP Project Team, Emerging Market Group Ltd. *Tanzania National Competitiveness Assessment, 2009* http://www.ccp-tpsf.org/images/Downlink/CCP_National%20Compet%20Assess_30Sep09_pdf.pdf

[9] Dar Es Salam Stock Exchange, *DSE Journal Issue Number 35.* 2008 http://www.dse.co.tz/upload/15.pdf

[10] Bekefi, Tamara. *Tanzania: Lessons in Building Linkages for Competitive and Responsible Entrepreneurship*, United Nations Industrial Development Organization and Harvard University, John F Kennedy School of Government, 2006 http://www.unido.org/fileadmin/import/69451_CSRI_09.pdf

[11] The World Bank, *World Development Indicators*, http://data.worldbank.org/country, Accessed on April 2012.

[12] Beintema, Nienke and Stads, Gert-Jan. *African Agricultural R&D in the New Millennium*. International Food Policy Research Institute and Agricultural Science and Technology Indicators. Washington, DC and Rome, Italy. 2011 http://www.ifpri.org/sites/default/files/publications/pr24.pdf

[13] College of Engineering and Technology, University of Dar es Salaam Information Brochure 2009/2010.

[14] *Ibid.*

[15] *Ibid.*

[16] *Ibid.*

[17] *Ibid.*

[18] Dr. A.K. Temu, interviewed by author, Cambridge, MA, April 5, 2012.

[19] Dr. A.K. Temu, interviewed by author, Cambridge, MA, April 5, 2012.

[20] J.H.Y. Katima, interviewed by author, Cambridge, MA, March 1, 2012.

[21] *Ibid.*

[22] *Ibid.*

Malaysia: Standing on a Single Leaf

Diego Comin, Maurice Kuykendoll* and Monne Williams*

[Palm Oil] has the scent of violets, the taste of olive oil and a colour which tinges food like saffron but is more attractive.

— Ca'da Mosto, 15th Century Portuguese Explorer

Tan Sri Bernard Dompok, Minister of plantation industries and commodities, sat in his office and reflected on the success of the Malaysian palm oil industry. From a minor producer of 100,000 tonnes 50 years earlier, Malaysia had become one of the world's largest palm oil producers accounting for 39% of the world's production and 44% of the world's exports (see **Exhibits 1** and **2**).[1] The industry occupied 14% of the country's total land area, more than half the land utilized for agriculture and employed as many as 1.5 million people either directly or indirectly.[2] Palm oil and related products are the fourth largest contributors to GDP and are credited with leading Malaysia into middle-income status on a GDP per capita basis. However, there are some challenges approaching for this strong and stable industry in Malaysia.

A report released in 2011 by Wetlands International claimed that, between 2005 and 2010, almost one-third of Malaysia's swamp forests were cleared for palm oil production, primarily in the state of Sarawak on Borneo Island. In addition, pressure is currently growing for palm oil producers to lessen the impact of palm oil plantations on the environment, as retailers around the world announce plans to

*Reprinted with permission of Harvard Business School Publishing.

This case was prepared by Professor Diego Comin and Maurice Kuykendoll and Monne Williams Malaysia: Standing on a Single Leaf 713-007.

Exhibit 1.   Global Palm Oil Importers and Exporters

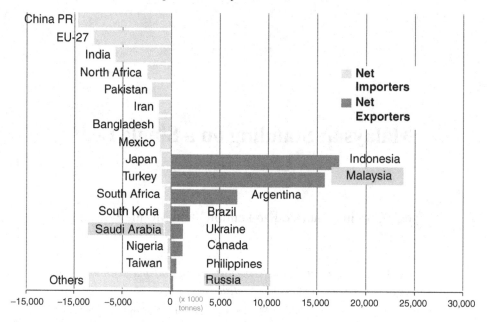

Source: Kuala Lumpur Kepong Berhad company documents.

Exhibit 2.   Importance of Palm Oil to External Trade, 2008

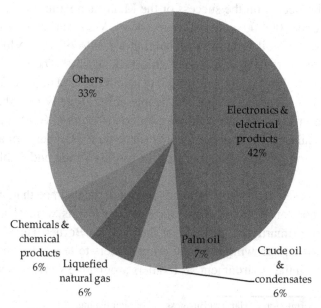

Source: Sime Darby, "Palm Oil Industry in Malaysia: Skills and Knowledge for Sustained Development in Africa" (PDF file), downloaded from World Bank website, http://siteresources.worldbank.org/EDUCATION/Resources/278200-1121703274255/1439264-1242337549970/Malaysian_Palm_Oil_Industry.pdf, accessed February 2012.

Exhibit 3.   Global Palm Oil Production by Country, 2010/2011

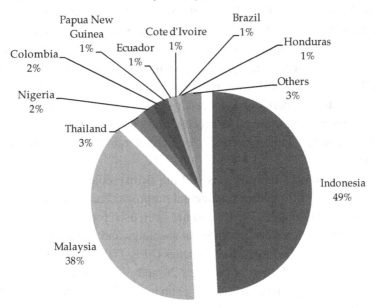

Source: Kuala Lumpur Kepong Berhad company documents.

limit their purchasing to palm oil that meets the standards outlined by the Round Table on Sustainable Palm Oil (ROPO).[3]

Other countries have taken note of Malaysia's success in the industry and are making significant investments in growing this industry. Recently, Indonesia surpassed Malaysia as the world's largest producer of palm oil, as its government offers incentives to companies and small farmers that invest in the industry (see **Exhibit 3**). Outside of Asia, Guatemala increased the land allocated to palm oil plantations by 146% between 2005 and 2010.[4,5]

As part of Prime Minister Najib's Vision 2020 to make Malaysia a high-income country, the leaders of the government have undertaken a number of initiatives aimed at growing the economy. Should palm oil continue to be an industry of focus for the government? If so, how should Malaysia compete in the changing global oils and fats market? Are there lessons from Malaysia's experience in the palm oil industry that may be applicable to other industries, sectors, or products in order to allow the country to grow? What role should the government of Malaysia play in this industry or in others?

Origins of Palm Oil in Malaysia

Britain's demand for rubber fueled the country to seek rubber sources outside of Brazil, where the majority of supply came from naturally occurring trees. An

Englishman, Sir Henry Wickham, took thousands of rubber seedlings from Brazil to the Kew Gardens in London.[6] The seedlings were studied and cultivated in London and later taken to present day Malaysia and other British colonies for commercial plantations. The British also imported immigrant labor to grow rubber plantations in Malaysia, as the British thought that immigrant labor, mostly Indian and Chinese, would be better at cultivating rubber than native workers. Early experimental attempts to create commercial rubber estates in India led the British to believe that importing labor could improve the process and profits in Malaysia in the 1870s. Malaysia became the largest producer of natural rubber around the turn of the 20th century.

In the 1800s, while Malaysia was still the British colony of Malaya, oil palm trees were introduced for purely ornamental purposes. The oil palm tree originated in West Africa and Equatorial Africa and has been used for millennia as a source of food and energy.[7] The tree is grown from seedlings and takes roughly 30 months to start bearing fruit called fresh fruit bunches (FFBs) (see **Exhibits 4a** and **b**). The economic life of a single tree is between 20 and 30 years, making it one of the longest producing crops in the world. Oil palm has a relatively tight band of climate conditions around the equator in which the species can grow and even more specific criteria in order to obtain the ideal yield from the crop (see **Exhibit 5**). Malaysia is geographically suited for oil palm production.

As the British Industrial Revolution forged on, palm oil became highly sought after by British traders, causing more commercial oil palm planting and harvesting to take hold outside of the plant's native West Africa. In 1917, French rubber

Exhibit 4a.   Oil Palm Tree

Source: Malaysian Palm Oil Council, "The Oil Palm Tree," http://www.mpoc.org.my/The_Oil_Palm_Tree.aspx, accessed April 2012.

Exhibit 4b. Oil Palm Tree Kernel

Source: Malaysian Palm Oil Council, "Palm Images," http://www.mpoc.org.my/imageofthemonth. aspx?ddlID=657f08e6-5526-446e-977e-b3ff442ff7b3&catID=443754e8-d761-426b-b92a-90fb0ffc 1e63&Page=5, accessed April 2012.

Exhibit 5. Global Oil Palm Cultivation Areas

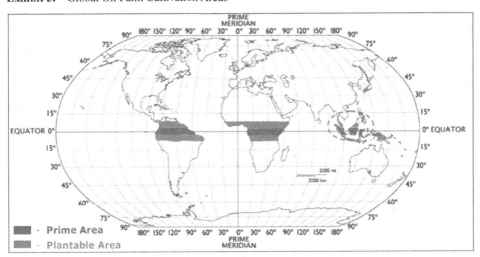

Source: Sime Darby, "Palm Oil Industry in Malaysia: Skills and Knowledge for Sustained Development in Africa" (PDF file), downloaded from World Bank website, http://siteresources.worldbank. org/EDUCATION/Resources/278200-1121703274255/1439264-1242337549970/Malaysian_Palm_ Oil_Industry.pdf, accessed February 2012.

and coffee planter Henri Fauconnier predicted that oil palm would become the next cash crop and commercially planted the crop at the Tennamaran Estate in Selangor, Malaysia. This made Fauconnier the first documented commercial planter of Malaysian oil palm. As the Industrial Revolution fueled growth, demand for palm oil as an industrial lubricant for steam engines and other machinery continued to grow. Malaysia had a labor force that was trained in plantation work. Access to plantation managers, as well as labor knowledgeable in planting and harvesting, was important to the initial success of the commercial plantings by the British. Malaysia continued to be heavily involved in the rubber industry during this time period, but there were still significant parcels of land that could be cultivated for palm oil, making the oil palm tree an attractive crop for plantation owners. British conglomerates operating in Malaya were encouraged by the growth in palm oil demand and started to convert existing rubber plantations and new land into oil palm plantations. Two of the most prominent conglomerates involved in oil palm were Sime Darby Estate and Guthrie Plantation Group.[8] By 1925, 3,350 hectares of oil palm had been planted, and by the mid 1940's that number had grown to 20,000 hectares.[9]

By 1957, Malaysia's economy was mainly dependent on tin and rubber. These two commodities accounted for more than 50% of GDP at the time and the government was focused on exporting these two products as the primary engine of growth. However, the introduction of the cheaper synthetic rubber negatively affected the development of Malaysian rubber. Natural rubber prices fell, as the cheaper synthetic rubber became more prevalent. In response, the government introduced the Agricultural Diversification Program to reduce the country's reliance on rubber and tin.[10] The British also looked for more staple crops that could grow in their colonies. The growing global demand for palm oil, coupled with rubber's declining prices, encouraged British plantation owners and other agricultural workers to switch from rubber to palm oil as the next big cash crop (see **Exhibits 6**).

Poverty continued to be a challenge for Malaysia. This stress on society culminated in bloody race riots in 1969, which were mainly driven by the income inequality

Exhibit 6.   Agricultural Land-use Changes over Time, 1990–2008

Year	Palm Oil (million ha)	Rubber (million ha)	Cocoa (million ha)	Coconut (million ha)	Total (million ha)
1990	2.029	1.836	0.393	0.314	4.572
2000	3.377	1.431	0.076	0.159	5.043
2002	3.670	1.348	0.051	0.155	5.224
2004	3.880	1.282	0.044	0.147	5.353
2005	4.051	1.250	0.033	0.144	5.478
2006	4.165	1.225	0.033	0.142	5.565
2007	4.305	1.248	0.028	0.117	5.698
2008	4.480	1.247	0.021	0.115	5.863

Source: Adapted from Malaysian Palm Oil Board and American Palm Oil Council, "Palm oil development and performance in Malaysia" (PDF file), downloaded from APOC website," http://www.americanpalmoil.com/pdf/USITCpre-PublicHearing-V2.pdf, accessed March 2012.

between the rural population (mainly ethnic Malays) and the urban dwellers (mainly ethnic Chinese). Rural poverty in 1970 was at a high of 59%, with incidences of poverty in the paddy subsector (88%), fishermen (73%), rubber smallholders (65%) and coconut smallholders (53%).[11] The racial riot prompted the government to formulate the New Economic Policy, (NEP) (1970–1990) with the objective of "achieving national integration and unity through reducing and eradicating of poverty and restructuring the Malaysian society to correct economic imbalances and eliminate the identification of race with economic function."[12] Agricultural development was emphasized as a way to provide employment and income earning opportunities to the rural poor. The government then introduced land settlement schemes for planting oil palm.

The Golden Crop: Malaysia Invests in Palm Oil

Federal Land Development Authority (FELDA)

FELDA, now over 50 years old, was started in order to group, organize and train poor, rural farmers and to develop them into cooperatives. The initiative gave each farmer 10, 12, or 14 acres of plantable land and another acre on which to build a home. The land granted was forested land that was surveyed by the government for agricultural use. The farmers selected for the program were primarily poor and landless applicants and also tended to be married, physically fit males, aged 21–50. FELDA had a model of land development that was highly centralized. Farmers accepted into the plan were only given subsistence payment until the first crop harvest. After that, credit facilities and other support services were provided through cooperatives.[13] The program was funded with a loan from the World Bank and was aimed at alleviating poverty.

Today, the FELDA group has become Felda Holdings Bhd (Felda Holdings), one of Malaysia's largest and most diversified agro-based enterprises. It runs the commercial businesses related to FELDA, as well as the 880,000-hectare plantation land bank associated with it. It has 19,000 employees, with an additional labor force of over 45,000 workers at 300 estates, 70 palm oil mills, seven refineries, four kernel-crushing plants, 13 rubber factories, numerous manufacturing plants, and several logistic and bulking installations spread throughout Malaysia and several locations overseas. It also has more than 50 active subsidiaries, associated companies and joint venture companies. One such subsidiary is Felda Palm Industries Sdn Bhd (FPI), a private limited company, formerly known as Felda Mills Corporation. Felda Mills was initially established in July 1975, as an agency under FELDA. FPI is principally engaged in the purchasing and processing of Fresh Fruit Bunches (FFB) from Felda schemes, estates owned by the Felda Group and external suppliers. The company is

72% owned by FELDA Holdings, with the remaining portion owned by Koperasi Permodalan Felda (KPF). KPF was established on July 1, 1980, to prosper the local farming community through ownership of Felda Holdings equities. Membership is exclusive to Felda settlers, Felda Group Staff, their wives and adult children, as well as members of the Settler Co-operative and Staff Co-operative. As of the end of December 2007, KPF has RM 1.17 billion in share capital, with a total of 186,268 members.[14]

Government Coordination

The government played an important role in galvanizing resources to stimulate global demand for palm oil. Many international players, including U.S. soybean producers, criticized palm oil early on as unfit for human consumption. This greatly impacted the demand for the palm oil that Malaysia was producing. The government mounted an effort to challenge these views directly by launching the Malaysian Palm Oil Council (MPOC) to market the benefits of palm oil, its unique properties and stimulate its global demand. The MPOC was joined in the fight by the Malaysia Palm Oil Association (MPOA), a trade group of palm producers that advocates on behalf of the industry.

Malaysian Palm Oil Association (MPOA): The Malaysian Palm Oil Association (MPOA) was created in the late 1990s to act as an umbrella organization for the several trade organizations that had developed after Malaysia entered the commercial palm oil sector. The Malaysian government supported a rationalization of the organization that represented the palm oil industry. All of the predecessors of the MPOA attempted the same function: Coordinating the needs and interests of all parts of the palm oil industry in order to enable outcomes that were best for the entire industry. In addition, the MPOA helped the industry gather information across various parts of the country from different sized players and all segments of the value chain in order to best explain and prioritize the greatest threats and opportunities that the industry faced.[15]

Malaysian Palm Oil Board (MPOB): The Malaysian Palm Oil Board (MPOB) is the official government agency created to promote and further develop the national palm oil industry. The organization was officially incorporated in 2000 by merging the functions of two of its key predecessors, Palm Oil Research Institute of Malaysia (PORIM) and the Palm Oil Registration and Licensing Authority (PORLA). PORLA's general function was to ensure the orderly development and quality of the palm oil industry. PORLA issued licenses to those involved in the production, transportation, storage, exports, and sale of palm oil and its products.[16] All trade contracts were to be registered with PORLA and traders were required to declare the quality of the palm oil to be exported and ensure that the exported palm oil met the quality specifications as declared in the contract. The task of improving productivity, value-added, quality, and all other aspects of the industry's output performance was PORIM's main function. PORIM managed all aspects of R&D in palm oil in order to enhance the performance of the industry. In promoting exports, PORIM was also engaged in providing technical support and information on palm oil to increase consumer knowledge on palm oil and palm oil products through the Technical Advisory Services (TAS), whose activities are aimed at increasing the utilization of palm oil.[17]

The agency was funded by a tax imposed on every tonne of palm oil produced. It was charged with implementing policies that encouraged the wellbeing of the national industry. It developed new market opportunities for Malaysian palm oil, coordinated industry-wide training, regulated activities and standards and, most notably, conducted and promoted R&D efforts for the industry. The MPOB is regarded as the premier palm oil R&D body within the country. Many research initiatives are dedicated to improving yields, such as the MPOB initiative, which is focused on breeding "dwarf" oil palm trees. The "dwarf" variation is equal or better in yield than its standard oil palm counterpart but also requires much less effort and time to harvest the FFBs. The overall effect is the ability to harvest more FFBs in less time, thus improving plantation productivity and worker safety.[18,19] Another key function for MPOB involves finding new uses for palm oil to increase demand for the oil, both absolutely and relative to other edible oils (see **Exhibit 7**). One recent example focused on palm oil as a key ingredient in the creation of cheese analogs that were to be used in food processing.[20] The MPOB also allocates resources to ensure that research findings are circulated throughout the industry and media to increase awareness and utilization of its research. Members of the MPOB are appointed by the Minister of Plantation Industries and Commodities and there is representation from both government and industry.[21]

Malaysian Palm Oil Council (MPOC): Palm oil historically suffered from a negative reputation as lower quality edible oil and was even sometimes referred to as "poor man's oil."[22] The Malaysian Palm Oil Council (MPOC) was established to promote the market expansion of palm oil. The MPOC aims to both improve the international image of palm oil and products containing palm oil and educate consumers on the advantages of palm oil relative to alternatives. More recently, MPOC has directed much of its effort to communicating the environmental sustainability of Malaysian Palm Oil plantation methods. MPOC acts as the coordinating national body for marketing, sales and education. MPOC also leads efforts to ensure that international trade standards are upheld in order to prevent other countries or edible oil organizations from unjustly claiming more negative palm oil attributes than have been substantiated. For example, in 2011, western NGOs, particularly in Australia,

Exhibit 7.   Palm Oil Percentage in Global Oils and Fats Production, 1980–2010

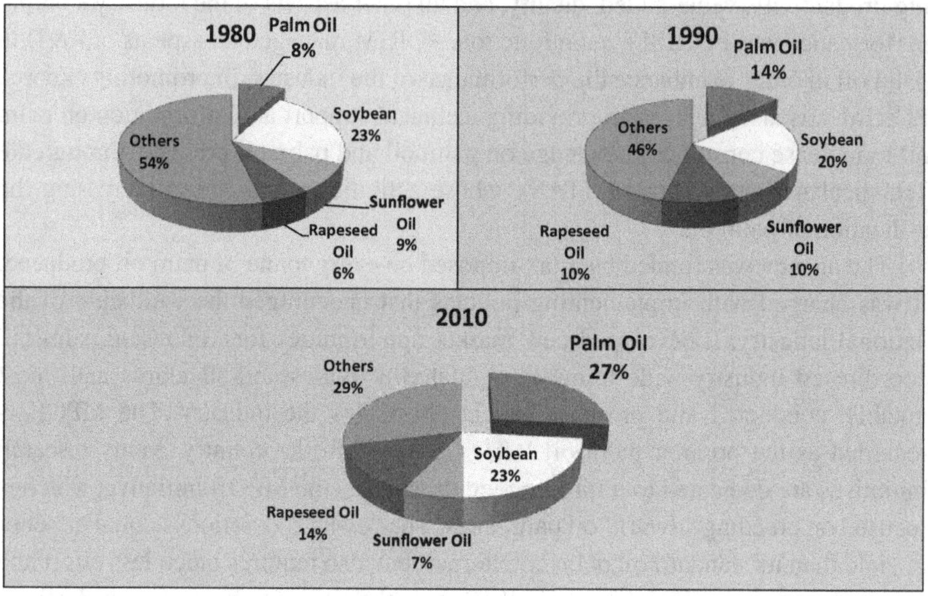

Source: Kuala Lumpur Kepong Berhad company documents.

lobbied for legislation that required palm oil to be more clearly identified in product ingredients. The NGOs had long criticized Malaysian palm oil producers for deforestation and other unsubstantiated complaints. MPOC utilized its CEO Blog and other resources to respond to this accusation and propose that the legislation should not be enacted.[23] MPOC aggregates and provides much of the information available about the international palm oil market through its website and publications.[24]

A Cluster Booming?

After the drop in rubber prices and early successes in palm oil, Malaysian companies and the government moved quickly to become the first country to pursue commercialization of palm oil on a large scale. The Malaysian government borrowed lessons from rubber commercial planting, such as utilizing foreign labor expertise and often taking advantage of cheaper wages. Another key lesson from the rubber industry included studying and when possible creating partnerships with, countries with longer, more successful palm oil production histories. Specifically, Malaysia's Department of Agriculture created an exchange program with West African economies and four private plantations to form the Oil Palm Genetics Laboratory in order to create better oil palm breeding. Malaysian governmental entities supported industry players, as they invested in expertize and technology to prevent

Exhibit 8. Malaysian Palm Oil Production

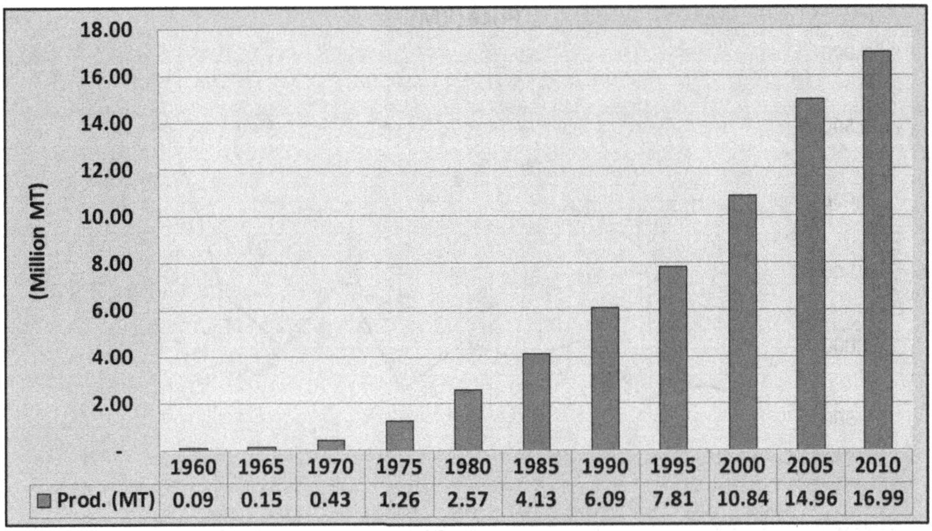

	1960	1965	1970	1975	1980	1985	1990	1995	2000	2005	2010
Prod. (MT)	0.09	0.15	0.43	1.26	2.57	4.13	6.09	7.81	10.84	14.96	16.99

Y-axis: (Million MT), scale from - to 18.00 in increments of 2.00

Source: Kuala Lumpur Kepong Berhad company documents.

other countries from being able to quickly emulate their methods. As palm oil's significance in the Malaysian economy grew, more attention was dedicated to making Malaysian palm oil as competitive as possible. In fact, the R&D applications and plantation management fueled a 10-fold increase in crude palm oil production from 1975 to 2009 (see **Exhibits 8** and **9**).[25]

This was the foundation of the subsequent R&D efforts that propelled the expansion of the Malaysian palm oil industry. In addition, as more scientists were needed to continue Malaysia's industry improvements, the country invested in recruiting and training scientists and other professionals to fuel further growth in the industry.[26] These steps led to the founding of University Pertanian Malaysia (UPM), which was designed to train engineers and business people for the agricultural sector.[27] UPM and a plethora of other research bodies allowed Malaysia to create a vehicle by which to recruit and train professionals to develop knowledge in oil palm breeding and oleochemical improvement.

Palm Oil Exchange

The first formal securities business organization in Malaysia was the Singapore Stockbrokers' Association, established in 1930. It was re-registered as the Malayan Stockbrokers' Association in 1937. The Malayan Stock Exchange was established in 1960 and the public trading of its shares commenced. In 1964, the Stock Exchange of Malaysia was established. With the secession of Singapore from Malaysia in

Exhibit 9.   Malaysian Palm Oil Prices, 1960–2010

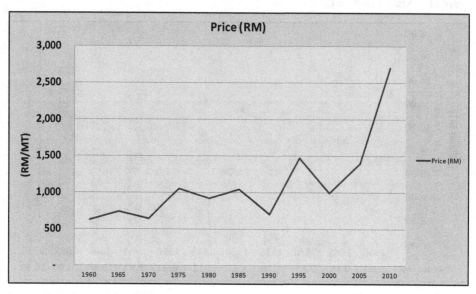

Source: Kuala Lumpur Kepong Berhad company documents.

1965, the Stock Exchange of Malaysia became known as the Stock Exchange of Malaysia and Singapore. In 1973, currency interchangeability between Malaysia and Singapore ceased and the Stock Exchange of Malaysia and Singapore was divided into the Kuala Lumpur Stock Exchange Berhad and the Stock Exchange of Singapore.[28]

Now, Bursa Malaysia Berhad, following a demutualization exercise, owns 75% of Bursa Malaysia Derivatives Berhad (BMD), formerly known as Malaysia Derivatives Exchange Berhad (MDEX). BMD provides, operates and maintains a futures and options exchange. BMD operates the most liquid crude palm oil futures (FCPO) contract in the world.[29]

Private Sector

In the 1960s, the government initiated nationalizations of the major oil palm companies after the race riots and communism challenges of the decade. The majority of private companies in Malaysian palm oil started as British multinationals and became Malaysian during this period; this trend was often referred to as Malaysianization. These companies' origins as multinationals, though, were an important source of knowledge in how to move up the value chain and continued to be a source for talent.

To incentivize private companies to move downstream in palm production, the government levied a 33% export duty on crude palm oil, while having no duty on refined oil. This was matched with government programs that gave tax credits and subsidies to build local refineries. This combination incented large global players to invest within Malaysia. Indonesia, however, proved a formidable competitor, as the country's firms were able to produce and refine palm for lower costs than Malaysia. This forced Malaysia to reevaluate the duty.[30]

Government Linked Investment Companies (GLICs) and Government Linked Companies (GLCs)

GLCs are companies that have a primary commercial objective and in which the Malaysian Government has a direct controlling stake. This controlling stake could refer to the Government's ability to appoint board members, hire or fire senior management, make major business decisions related to contract awards, strategy, restructuring and financing, acquisitions and divestments for GLCs either directly or through government-linked investment companies (GLICs). GLICs are companies that allocate some or all of their funds to GLC investments defined by the influence of the federal government in appointing or approving members of management or the board of directors, as well as in providing funds for operations and/or guaranteeing capital. Currently, there are seven GLICs: MKD, Kumpulan Wang Simpanan Pekerja (EPF), Khazanah Nasional Bhd, Permodalan Nasional Bhd (PNB), Lembaga Tabung Haji (LTH), Kumpulan Wang Persaraan (KWAP) and Lembaga Tabung Angkatan Tentera (LTAT).[31]

The influence of GLICs and GLCs can be found throughout the Malaysian economy and palm oil is not an exception. Of the 3.67 million hectares of oil palm planted in Malaysia in 2002, 60% were under private ownership. The largest among these companies, were the publicly listed Kumpulan Guthrie Berhad, Golden Hope Plantations Berhad, Kuala Lumpur Kepong Berhad and IOI Corporation Berhad. However, most plantation companies in the industry are not entirely privately run. Permodalan Nasional Berhad (PNB), a GLIC, owns equity in Golden Hope, Kumpulan Guthrie, and Sime Darby Berhad, making PNB a major shareholder in a number of large plantation players. In the public sector, the key player is the Federal Land Development Authority (FELDA), a government agency responsible for managing government land schemes and commercial development of plantations (see **Exhibit 10**).[32]

The Way Forward

Looking towards the future, Tan Sri Dompok considered the direction in which Malaysia should go. Today, Malaysia is still one of the world's largest exporters of palm oil and the growth of emerging markets is expected to continue to drive demand for palm oil. However, the industry faces challenges to continued growth within Malaysia.

Exhibit 10.   Palm Oil Plantation Ownership, 2008

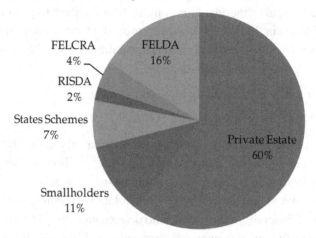

Source: Malaysian Palm Oil Board and American Palm Oil Council, "Palm oil development and performance in Malaysia" (PDF file), downloaded from APOC website, http://www.americanpalmoil. com/pdf/USITCpre-PublicHearing-V2.pdf, accessed March 2012.

Environmental Issues and Capacity

Conservation groups continue to challenge Malaysia on its environmental practices. Specifically they challenge the country's record of the conservation of forests and endangered wildlife. Malaysia has responded with a series of steps aimed at reframing the discussion about palm plantations. The MPOA has released RSPO guidelines for sustainable palm oil production, and the country is moving to have all production certified by the end of this decade. The MPOC has also unveiled a new marketing spin emphasizing that Malaysian palm trees reduce CO_2 emissions that offset all of the carbon dioxide produced in the country, not just by this industry. It is branding Malaysia as a net importer of CO_2 emissions globally. Finally, industry supporters point to the progress Malaysia has made in banning tree burning to clear plantations, recycling plantation waste to use it as organic fertilizers, use of animals to naturally control pests instead of pesticides and making products from virtually all parts of the palm tree and FFBs.

Malaysia is a small country that has committed to land conservation levels, which it is quickly approaching. In the last several years, Malaysian companies have begun outsourcing the plantation process to other countries in Africa, Asia, and the Caribbean that have more land mass. A recent deal between Sime Darby and the government of Liberia is indicative of the moves that are being made to acquire land for planting more oil palm plantations. The deal was for a 63-year concession for 220,000 hectares of land in exchange to building infrastructure and supporting local poverty alleviation efforts based on the FELDA model.[33]

Moving up the Value Chain

To double GDP per capita in the next few years, Malaysia will need to continue to produce higher value-added services. Oleochemicals provides an example of how it can be done. In the 1970s, most oleochemicals were produced from tallow and coconut oil. In 1980, Malaysia built its first plant and over the next three decades became the world's biggest producer accounting for 17% of global output, or two million tonnes per year (see **Exhibit 11**). Oleochemicals have a variety of uses including cosmetics, personal care products, candles, printing inks, crayons and many industrial products.[34]

Exhibit 11. Diagram of Palm Oil Processing Plant

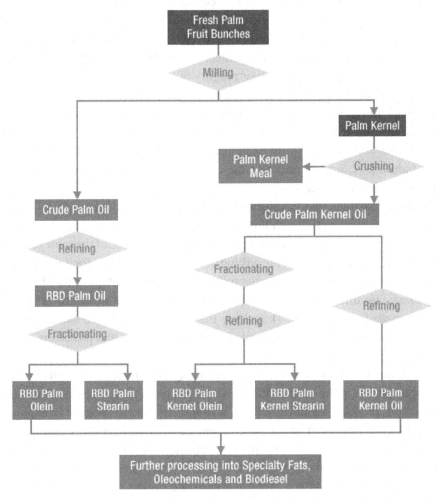

Source: Wilmar International Limited "Palm and lauric oils and related products," http://www.wilmar-international.com/business_merchandising-processing.htm, accessed May 2012.

Even with its success to date in producing many varieties of products, currently only about 25% of the complete value chain accrues to Malaysia. The country would like to move the value chain capture to 50% over the next 10 years by looking to the next set of core products, including transport, specialty fat production and petroleum. The leaders admit that moving further up the value chain will be a challenge because of the need to acquire new knowledge but expect to apply the lessons learned from other successful palm oil applications.[35]

Concentration Risk

Another challenge faced by the country is the concentration of economic activity tied to palm oil. Among middle-income countries, Malaysia is more diversified than some others that rely on single commodity exports to drive growth. Few will disagree, though, that much of the growth over last few decades in the country is tied to this single crop. Palm oil contributed 14% to the GDP in 2003, according to a United Nations report, representing roughly 50% of the value of all exports and covering most of the agricultural land. One official described it as "standing on a single leaf." In the past, swings in commodity prices have adversely affected the economy and social stability to the detriment of the country. First was the drop in rubber prices and even palm oil experienced price volatility in the nascent years of the industry. A drop in prices in the coming years could prove disastrous for Malaysia's growth prospects.

Private companies and government agencies are still looking at two ways in which the country can deal with this challenge. The first is diversifying outputs as opposed to inputs. Palm oil is the most profitable crop and one of the most profitable industries in the country, so few are willing to depart from it solely for diversification. However, they consider the products produced from the plant quite variable. Many think prices are unlikely to drop to previous lows because of the diversification products made from palm oil. They argue that a floor is set by the market for palm oil because of its connection to petroleum production such that producers will use palm oil for refining if prices fell.

The second is to look for other industries in which to invest to fuel future growth. What was it about palm oil that made its success possible in Malaysia? Are there other sectors, products, or industries that have similar characteristics to be exploited? What was most important about government policies and actions to promote the success of palm oil and how can these be replicated for a different sector? Is the private sector ready to move from palm oil as a main driver of growth to support nascent industries? These and other questions are on the minds of Malaysians as they prepare for Vision 2020. Can Malaysia do it again?

Endnotes

1   Malaysian Palm Oil Council, "Malaysian Palm Oil Industry," http://www.mpoc.org.my/ Malaysian_Palm_Oil_Industry.aspx, accessed March 2012.

2   Malaysian Palm Oil Council, *Malaysian Palm Oil: A Success Story* (Selangor: Malaysian Palm Oil Council, 2009), p. 8.

3   Tom Young, "Malaysian Palm Oil Destroying Forests, Report Warns," The Guardian: Business Green, February 2, 2011, http://www.guardian.co.uk/environment/2011/feb/ 02/malaysian-palm-oil-forests, accessed March 2012.

4   Felicity Lawrence, "Global Food Crisis: Palm Rush Proves Costly for Guatemala's Small Farmers," The Guardian, May 31, 2011, http://www.guardian.co.uk/global-development/poverty-matters/2011/may/31/global-food-crisis-palm-oil-guatemala, accessed March 2012.

5   Laurence Caramel, "Is Palm Oil a Kernel of Development for Countries Like Liberia," The Guardian, March 8, 2011, http://www.guardian.co.uk/environment/2011/mar/08/ africa-asia-palm-oil-caramel, accessed March 2012.

6   Kew Royal Botanical Gardens, "Rubber," http://www.kew.org/plants/rubber.html, accessed March 2012.

7   Malaysian Palm Oil Council, *Malaysian Palm Oil: A Success Story* (Selangor: Malaysian Palm Oil Council, 2009), p. 8.

8   Malaysian Palm Oil Council, "Malaysian Palm Oil Industry," http://www.mpoc.org.my/ Malaysian_Palm_Oil_Industry.aspx, accessed March 2012.

9   Malaysian Palm Oil Council, *Malaysian Palm Oil: A Success Story* (Selangor: Malaysian Palm Oil Council, 2009), p. 8.

10   Malaysian Palm Oil Council, "The Oil Palm Tree," http://www.mpoc.org.my/ The_Oil_Palm_Tree.aspx, accessed February 2012.

11   Arif Sime and Tengku Mohd Ariff Tengku Ahmad, "The Case Study on Malaysian Palm Oil" April 3–5, 2001, Regional Workshop on Commodity Export Diversification and Poverty Reduction in South and South-east Asia; United Nations Conference on Trade and Development, available on UNCTAD website, http://r0.unctad.org/infocomm/ Diver-sification/bangkok/palmoil.pdf, accessed March 2012.

12   *Ibid.*

13   *Ibid.*

14   FELDA, "Koperasi Permodalan Felda," http://www.feldaholdings.com/content.php? lang=EN&h=173, accessed March 2012.

15   Malaysian Palm Oil Association, "Introduction to MPOA," http://www.mpoa.org. my/v2/index.php? option=com_content&view=article&id=19&Itemid=27, accessed March 2012.

16   Arif Sime and Tengku Mohd Ariff Tengku Ahmad, "The Case Study on Malaysian Palm Oil" April 3–5, 2001, Regional Workshop on Commodity Export Diversification and Poverty Reduction in South and South-east Asia; United Nations Conference on Trade and Development, available on UNCTAD website, http://r0.unctad.org/infocomm/ Diver-sification/bangkok/palmoil.pdf, accessed March 2012.

[17] Arif Sime and Tengku Mohd Ariff Tengku Ahmad, "The Case Study on Malaysian Palm Oil" April 3–5, 2001, Regional Workshop on Commodity Export Diversification and Poverty Reduction in South and South-east Asia; United Nations Conference on Trade and Development, available on UNCTAD website, http://r0.unctad.org/infocomm/ Diversification/bangkok/palmoil.pdf, accessed March 2012.

[18] Malaysian Palm Oil Board, "Crop & Production Management Unit," http://www.mpob.gov.my/component/content/article/485-achievements, accessed April 2012.

[19] Malaysian Palm Oil Councils, "Palm Images" http://www.mpoc.org.my/imageofthemonth.aspx?ddlID= 657f08e6-5526-446e-977e-b3ff442ff7b3&catID=443754e8-d761-426b-b92a-90fb0ffc1e63&Page=3, accessed April 2012.

[20] Malaysian Palm Oil Board, "Achievements," http://www.mpob.gov.my/en/technologies-for-commercialization/achievements, accessed April 2012.

[21] Malaysian Palm Oil Board, "About Us," http://www.mpob.gov.my/en/about-us/about, accessed April 2012.

[22] Tan Sri Lee Oi Hian, "Possible case study on Palm Oil promotions," e-mail message to Diego Comin, January 19, 2012.

[23] Dr Yusof Basiron, "A Scam Behind the Australian Palm Oil Labelling Bill?", CEO's blog, Malaysian Palm Oil Council, August 19, 2011, http://www.ceopalmoil.com/ 2011/08/the-scam-behind-the-australian-palm-oil-labelling-bill/, accessed April 2012.

[24] Malaysian Palm Oil Council, "Corporate Profile," http://www.mpoc.org.my/Corporate_Profile.aspx, accessed April 2012.

[25] National Economic Advisory Council, "NEM2: Palm Oil Industry" (PDF file), downloaded from NEAC website, http://www.neac.gov.my/files/Palm_Oil_Industry.pdf, accessed April 2012.

[26] Sime Darby, "Palm Oil Industry in Malaysia: Skills and Knowledge for Sustained Development in Africa," downloaded from World Bank website, http://siteresources.worldbank.org/EDUCATION/Resources/278200-1121703274255/1439264-12423375 49970/Malaysian_Palm_Oil_Industry.pdf, accessed February 2012.

[27] National Economic Advisory Council, "NEM2: Palm Oil Industry" (PDF file), downloaded from NEAC website, http://www.neac.gov.my/files/Palm_Oil_Industry.pdf, accessed April 2012.

[28] Bursa Malaysia, "History," http://www.bursamalaysia.com/website/bm/about_us/the_organisation/history.html, accessed April 2012.

[29] *Ibid.*

[30] National Economic Advisory Council, "NEM2: Palm Oil Industry" (PDF file), downloaded from NEAC website, http://www.neac.gov.my/files/Palm_Oil_Industry.pdf, accessed April 2012.

[31] Khazanah Nasional, "Frequently Asked Questions," http://www.khazanah.com.my/faq.htm, accessed April 2012.

[32] Darryl Ong, Bala Ramasamy and Matthew Yeung, "Firm Size, Ownership and Performance in the Malaysian Palm Oil Industry," Asian Academy of Management Journal of Accounting and Finance Vol. 1, 2005, http://web.usm.my/journal/aamjaf/vol%201/ 1-5.pdf, accessed March 2012.

[33] Sime Darby, "Sime Darby Plantation in Liberia," http://www.bursamalaysia.com/website/bm/about_us/the_organisation/history.html, accessed April 2012.

[34] Malaysian Palm Oil Council, *Malaysian Palm Oil: A Success Story* (Selangor: Malaysian Palm Oil Council, 2009), p. 8.

[35] Tan Sri Mohd Isa Bin Hj Abdul Samad, interview by author, via telephone, March 8, 2012.

Fraunhofer: Innovation in Germany

Diego Comin*, Gunnar Trumbull* and Kerry Yang*

Innovation and economic growth are two sides of the same coin, which are to serve as the foundation of an internationally competitive [. . .] Germany in [the] future.

[T]op scientists work in collaborative teams today and render top technological performances. [. . .] More and more large research institutes develop the leading innovations that determine our future.

— Angela Merkel, German Chancellor[1]

In 2010, for the second time in history, a research organization was awarded the EARTO Innovation Prize for research with a high potential for future impact on the economy and society. The awarded research was conducted by a team of scientists at the Fraunhofer Institute for Solar Energy Systems (ISE) in Freiburg, Germany. Dr. Andreas Bett and his colleagues had developed concentrator solar cells that, by superimposing three different solar cells sensitive to different solar spectra, yielded almost double the efficiency levels of conventional silicon-based cells. Working in partnership with Azur Space Solar Power, Europe's leading manufacturer of solar cells for use in space, Fraunhofer ISE expected to have the new technology on the market in 2011.

*Reprinted with permission of Harvard Business School Publishing.

Fraunhofer: Innovation in Germany. 711-022.

This case was prepared by Professors Diego Comin and Gunnar Trumbull and independent researcher Kerry Yang (Harvard University, 2011).

Fraunhofer, the institute behind the discovery, had just celebrated its 60th birthday. Founded in 1949 as an applied counterpart to Germany's more famous basic research labs, the Max-Planck Institutes, Fraunhofer had over the years developed a solid reputation in Germany for technological innovation.[2] In 2010 it had a budget of 1.6 billion euro, representing 2.5% of total research and development (R&D) expenditures in Germany and making it one of the largest research organizations in Europe.

As the world exited the global financial crisis, some observers wondered whether Fraunhofer could cope with the new challenges that global competition posed. The most poignant of these was China, which in 2009 surpassed Germany as the world's top exporter. Others saw in these challenges the best rationale for the existence of organizations such as Fraunhofer, which increased the competitiveness of domestic firms by improving their technology.

Yet the very premise of the institution raised questions. In an increasingly market-focused world, did a non-profit organization with 60% of its budget covered by public funds still have a role to play? And with public funds increasingly constrained, was it the most efficient way for a government to foster innovation?

Late Industrialization

Germany emerged in its modern form in 1871, riding a wave of nationalist fervor following victories against Austria–Hungary and France. Under the leadership of King Wilhelm I and his chancellor, Otto von Bismarck, the new state undertook an ambitious plan of economic development.

By European standards, Germany came late to industrialization (see **Exhibit 1**). The new German state pursued it through a three-part program. The first part of the program was import substitution. The Tariff Law of 1879, along with the follow-on general tariff of 1902, raised import duties on grains and steel products to roughly 50%.[3] These tariffs were backed by an alliance of interests forged by Bismarck between landed Eastern "Junkers" (of which Bismarck was one), who were threatened by cheap wheat imports from Russia and America, and western industrialists, who were threatened by imports of new manufactured goods from England. The resulting "marriage of iron and rye" created a protected domestic environment in which German industrial firms were able to consolidate and flourish.[4] By the turn of the century, tariff revenues were increasingly being channeled into steel-intensive naval construction.

The second part of Germany's late industrialization strategy was what economic historian Rudolf Hilferding described as "finance capital." Under finance capital, industry, organized as trusts or cartels, was consolidated with large banks through dense cross-share holdings.[5] These bank-affiliated cartels were seen as a means to

Exhibit 1.   Long Run Log GDP Per Capita (thousands 1,900 dollars)

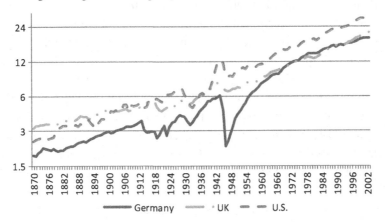

Source: Adapted from A. Maddison, http://www.ggdc.net/MADDISON/oriindex.htm, accessed December 2010.

protect producers from ruinous price competition, and were supported by economic nationalist intellectuals like Friedrich List, whose critique of Adam Smith resonated deeply among German industrialists.[6] Cartels were also embraced by organized labor, which saw them as limiting the impact of business cycles, and by political liberals, who saw them as a counterforce to centralized state power.[7]

The third leg of Germany's industrialization strategy was worker pacification. Beginning in 1863, in the context of growing concern about worker mobilization, Bismarck pursued an anti-socialist campaign waged through a combination of carrots and sticks. The main stick was an outright ban on labor party participation in electoral politics. Through the end of World War I, Germany's large socialist party was entirely excluded from the Reichstag. The carrot was a new sickness insurance fund that provided workers with universal medical care, followed later by an accident fund and old age insurance. Bismarck explained in 1871: "The only means of stopping the Socialist movement in its present state of confusion is to put into effect those Socialist demands which seem justified and which can be realized within the framework of the present order of state and society."[8]

Education and Research

Even before the consolidation of modern Germany, its constituent states were becoming leaders in fundamental research. In 1820, Justus von Liebig, a professor of chemistry at the University of Giessen in Hesse, pioneered the idea of a professor-run research laboratory with graduate students working below him on projects. Competition among the German states drove political support for high levels of funding for university research labs. In the 1870s, German firms pioneered the first corporate in-house laboratories.[9] Now university-trained researchers could not move easily from academics into a familiar lab setting within industry. In the newly emerging field of pharmaceuticals, the results were nothing short of stunning. Between 1880 and 1930, Bayer and Hoechst alone developed 44 new chemical entities, more than the entire output of the U.S. and U.K. combined.[10]

Equally important was Germany's embrace of engineering training. At the core of German school system was training by technical institutes, of which Kaiser Wilhelm in particular became a strong advocate. By 1900, Prussia and Saxony alone already boasted over 300 technical institutes.[11] Their goal was "to secure for science a foothold in the workshop."[12] Over time, Germany's technical institutes would come to rival the country's vaunted Universities. As one foreign contemporary observer noted: "The whole German people are being educated scientifically in the arts of industrial production."[13] Between 1900 and 1910, Germany trained 30,000 engineers, compared to 21,000 in the United States.[14]

Innovation and War

The interwar period was trying for German producers. Until 1925, Germany was required under the terms of the Treaty of Versailles to keep tariffs low. Producers responded by consolidating in order to reduce costs. The largest steel producers formed Vereinigten Stahlwerke (VSt); chemicals producers formed IG Farben. By 1925, cartels controlled 100% of coal production and 80% of steel production.[15] By the late 1920s, almost all large industrial producers had also created their own in-house research labs.[16]

The Kaiser Wilhelm Institutes (KWG, later renamed the Max-Planck Institutes) were founded in 1911 to bring together state and private sector funds to support basic research that would ultimately benefit industry. These were elite institutions that lured the best talent with high salaries, expensive research equipment, and no teaching responsibilities.[17] During WWI, these institutes developed chemical weapons used in trench warfare and the technique of fixing nitrogen in order to produce artificial fertilizers. So critical had they been to the German military during the war that the Treaty of Versailles imposed stringent restrictions on the kinds of research they could undertake following the war (although some of this research continued in secret).

The collapse of the Weimar Republic proved devastating for German science. First, hyperinflation in the late 1920s wiped out the endowments of the KWG and other public research institutes. Second, the rise to power of the National Socialist (Nazi) party in 1933 led to an exodus of scientists. In the fields of math and physics, fully 20% of German university and KWG researchers were dismissed because they were Jewish.[18] At the University of Goettingen alone, where the fledgling field of quantum mechanics was being born, two thirds of all math and physics faculty lost their posts. An estimated 2,600 scientists left Germany in 1933, including 25% of all physicists.[19] Most ended up abroad, with an estimated 70% of emigrating researchers settling in the United States and Britain.

In 1936, Germany began focusing on an autarkic industrial strategy that would allow the country to continue functioning during a wartime blockade. New KWG institutes were opened, and funding was reinforced. In 1937, a new Reich Research Council (RFR) was created to coordinate academic research for the war effort. From these research efforts emerged an impressive array of new technologies, including radar, the high-speed jet-propelled Messerschmitt 262 and joy-stick controlled flying bombs. Industry also mobilized to produce synthetic replacements for blockaded imports of leather, rubber, and mineral oil.[20] Alongside these impressive innovations came horrendous crimes. Researchers in psychiatry, psychopharmacology and medicine conducted monstrous experiments at Nazi concentration camps. As many as 20,000 prisoners at the Mittelbau-Dora concentration camp as estimated to have died while working as slave labor for rocket engineer Wernher von Braun to develop the V-2 rocket.[a]

The technical knowledge that had developed in Germany did not go un-noticed. With the end of World War II, the U.S.-led Project Paperclip identified thousands of skilled German researchers and brought them to work in the United States. Advocates described the program as "intellectual reparations."[b] The Soviet occupation also lured and then, on October 20, 1946, forcibly deported the remaining German scientists and engineers operating in their zone. Producers like the Zeiss and Schott optical works were entirely dismantled and relocated.[21]

The Economic Miracle

With the end of World War II, the Allies placed a ban on horizontal cooperation of the sort that had especially emerged in the interwar period. Large firms were broken apart, and both VSt and IG Farben were dissolved.[22] Liberalization of the economy in 1948, under the director of the bizonal economic administration, Ludwig Erhard, set a solidly anti-planning trajectory for Germany. The idea of the reforms was based on a distinctly German view of capitalism, called ordoliberalism that emphasized the importance of competition and price signals, but also advocated a regulatory framework to ensure that real competition occurred and that weaker parties were not taken advantage of.[23] An important piece of this protection for labor was the

---

[a]Michael J. Neufeld, "Wernher von Braun, the SS, and Concentration Camp Labor: Questions of Moral, Political and Criminal Responsibility," *German Studies Review* 25/1 (2002), p. 57.
[b]John Gimbel, "Project Paperclip: German Scientists, American Policy, and the Cold War," *Diplomatic History* 14/3 (2007), p. 349.

institution of codetermination, formally legislated in 1951, that granted workers representation on the board of directors. Industry accepted this move in part because the allied powers had already installed labor representatives on the boards of directors of firms operating in the Ruhr.[24] For industry, the earlier focus on breaking up large firms was abandoned, and the 1957 cartel law granted a wide range of exceptions for manufacturer cartels, so long as they were considered to be in the public interest.[25] This system of active competition within framing institutions came to be called the social market economy. Together with direct foreign aid under the European Recovery Program (the "Marshall Plan"), these reforms set the trajectory for dramatic growth. By 1960, Germany's *Wirtschaftswunder*, or 'economic miracle', had allowed it to grow so that its GDP exceeded that of the U.K.

Postwar Market Institutions

Four distinctive features of the German economic system had their roots in the immediate postwar period: labor representation, worker training, a dynamic small and medium size sector, and a central role for banks.

First was the structure of its labor markets. From the early 1950s, German workers enjoyed strong representation in their companies. That representation took three forms. First, sectoral unions negotiated wage agreements with sectoral industry associations that were binding on all association members. Non-members typically also mirrored negotiated wage scales. Second, worker representatives participated in works councils (*Betriebsräte*) that consulted with management about issues of workplace safety, worker training, and other topics relating to the quality of the workplace environment. Third, workers in many firms were represented on the advisory board. For smaller firms, they enjoyed one-third representation. For larger firms, representation was at parity, although the chairman could step in to break ties. This system of work representation, called Mitbestimmung, gave workers input into decisions about company strategy and operations.

A second distinctive feature was Germany's extensive system of vocational training (see **Exhibit 2a**). Germany established an elaborate apprenticeship system based on a "dual-training" arrangement, in which employers and the state jointly paid for technical education for future employees. Students who participated in the programs received technical certificates that were overseen by the German Chamber of Industry and Commerce (DIHT).[26] Most apprenticeships were arranged in collaboration with Germany's network of technical high schools (*Fachhochschule*). The 1969 Vocational Training Act formalized the dual system, which by the 1990s was providing certificates in 378 formally defined occupations, most through three-year training programs.[27] Approximately two-thirds of Germans aged under 22 were enrolled in vocational training.

Exhibit 2a. Apprentices in Germany by Qualification Area

	1960	1965	1970	1975	1980	1985	1990
Total	1,279	1,338	1,269	1,329	1,715	1,831	1,477
Industry and commerce	743	752	725	634	787	875	756
Crafts	447	468	420	505	702	688	487
Other	89	118	124	190	226	268	234

Source: Adapted from J.R. Shackleton, Training for Employment in Western Europe and the UnitedStates (Brookfield, Vt.: Edward Elgar, 1995), p. 123, accessed December 2010.

Exhibit 2b. Sizes of Firms by Country

	% of firms with less than 10 employees	Employment share in firms with:	
		<10 employees	>250 employees
Austria	86.7	25.5	31.7
Belgium	92.1	29	33.3
Denmark	86.8	19.6	34.5
Finland	85.4	21.9	41
France	92.2	23.3	39.2
Germany	83	19.6	39.8
Ireland	84.2	23.1	32.3
Italy	94.5	47.1	18.5
Netherlands	88.1	28.9	31.9
Portugal	92.4	39.8	19.2
Spain	92.2	38.6	20.9
Sweden	90.9	20.4	38.2
U.K.	86.4	17.8	46.2
U.S.	74.0	11.0	49.1[a]

Source: U.S. Census Bureau, Stenkula (2006) accessed December 2010. Mikael Stenkula (2006) The European size Distribution of Firms and Employment, IFN wp# 683, 2006.

Note: [a] 500 employees or more.

A third critical feature of the German economic system was the large number of relatively small companies in the manufacturing sector (see **Exhibit 2b**). These *Mittelstand* companies targeted typically high-end niche markets, and were frequently family owned or controlled. Examples included well-known firms like Porsche and Haribou, and relatively unknown specialty firms that produced bearings, knives and manufacturing equipment. Mittelstand firms relied heavily on local technical schools to help train their workforce. Many were too small to have their own research labs, and those that did frequently collaborated on joint research projects organized through a cooperative research association (the Arbeitsgemeinschaft industrieller Forschungsvereinigungen).[28]

The final distinctive feature of the German economy was the central role of banks in financing industry investment. In the so-called *Hausbank* system, individual firms retained close ties with partner banks that provided financing while also consulting on potential investments. Especially for smaller *Mittelstand* firms, the *Hausbank* provided a buffer against economic cycles, since they were often willing to invest in new processes during economic downturns. The banks, for their part, had direct influence over firms through networks of direct ownership and indirect proxy voting rights granted to them by depositors. One third of German banks, including state savings banks, were state-owned.[29]

State-Funded Research

With the end of World War II, the two core institutions of German research were retained. The RFR became the German Research Councils (DFG). The KWG was renamed the Max Planck Institute (MPI). Under pressure from Allied occupiers, the new MPI shifted to fundamental research funded exclusively through government grants. In order to fill the gap left by this shift toward fundamental research, the new Fraunhofer Institute, founded in 1949 through a joint effort of industry and universities, moved to fill the applied research space that the MPI had abandoned. Together, the DFG, MPI and Fraunhofer Institute constituted the core of Germany's publicly funded research apparatus.

The Fading Miracle

Between 1945 and 1973, the German economy combined high growth, high employment, and social stability. At the peak of the German miracle, between 1950 and 1960s, real GDP grew at 8.2% per year. From 1960 to 1973, GDP growth averaged a respectable 4.4%. The first oil shock, in 1973, signaled an end to rapid growth. Between 1973 and 1990, economic growth averaged 2.1%. Unemployment rose from 1% in 1974 to over 9% in 1983.[c] The fiscal and social stresses of German reunification in 1989/90 kept economic annual economic growth below 2%. From 1982, policymakers within the governing Christian Democratic Union (CDU) began advocating a program of economic liberalization — including tax reductions and deregulation — that would restart Germany's growth engine.

Importing American Innovation

The success in the United States of biotechnology startups in the late 1980s and software startups in the 1990s, offered a stark contrast to the seemingly slow, backward

---

[c]Herbert Giersch, Karl-Heinz Paque and Holger Schmieding, *The Fading Miracle: Four Decades of Market Economy in Germany* (Cambridge: Cambridge University Press, 1992), pp. 4, 10.

German economy. In 1989, for example, Germany had 17 small firms working in biotechnology, compared to 388 in the United States.[30] The apparent backwardness of Germany's emerging high-tech sectors created pressure to import American entrepreneurial institutions into Germany. The Munich-based IFO Institute argued: "If there is an 'innovation crisis' in Germany, then that [crisis] is due . . . to a high degree of inertia in shifting capital investments, human resources, and existing ingenuity talents from traditional to new high-tech areas promising higher growth rates in the future."[31] Critics pointed in particular to the dearth of venture capital, to illiquid markets in corporate control that made it hard for early investors to exit, and to a lack of incentives to encourage skilled scientists to commercialize new technologies.[32]

Beginning in 1989, two German public finance institutions — the Kreditanstalt für Wiederaufbau (KfW) and the Technologiebeteiligungsgesellschaft (Tbg) — started providing matching funds up to DM 1 million for equity investments in start-up firms. Critically, the German Research Ministry agreed to absorb 90% of any private investor's losses.[33] By 1997, these government-funded programs held shares in 398 startups, representing 64% of all seed financing in Europe.

In 1995, a federal "BioRegio" program launched a series of competitions for federal research funds that were explicitly intended to foster innovation clusters. A similar InnoRegio competition was open to all sectors but limited to the five new eastern states. These programs led to the creation of 17 technology start-up offices across Germany, with the goal of encouraging professors to launch new startups in the biotechnology area. Supported programs included technology parks, start-up funds, and consultants hired "to persuade university professors of their students to commercialize their research findings and help them develop viable business plans."[34]

In 1996, the federal government set aside 200 million DM per year to support so-called "public venture capital," in which the government became a "silent partner" in new VC startups. In 1999, 45% of those funds went to internet-related start-ups, and 27% to biotechnology startups.[35] To provide an exit strategy for the newly created firms, authorities in 1997 created a new technology stock exchange, the Neuer Markt, modeled on the U.S. Nasdaq. In particular, the requirement that any firm show 7 years of profit before being listed on the stock exchange was abolished. At its peak, in 2000, the market listed 300 companies. In 1998, restrictions on companies buying and selling their own shares were loosened in order to make way for stock-option compensation plans.[36] Capital gains tax on divested corporate share holdings were also reduced to zero, allowing for easy divestiture.[37] Between 1995 and 1998, the number of new biotechnology startups per year grew from 75 to 300.[38]

Yet the results of these efforts were largely disappointing. In the biotechnology sector, most innovations were in manufacturing platform technologies, not in new therapeutic drugs. Software startups tended to be focused on the enterprise software segment in which the German firm SAP had become a world leader. The financial crisis that followed in the wake of the dot.com boom also threw the new system of equity capital into disarray. With no new initial public offerings (IPOs) in the pipeline, the Neuer Markt collapsed in 2003.[39] By the late 2000s, the performance of Germany's software and biotechnology sectors was largely perceived as mediocre.[40]

Sources of New Success

While German policymakers were experimenting with American-style technology policies, other parts of the German economy were experiencing surprising export success. All advanced industrialized economies had observed a decline in the share of manufacturing beginning in the 1970s, but Germany's manufacturing decline had been less pronounced. In 2008, manufacturing still represented 22% of German GDP, compared to 10% in the United States (see **Exhibits 3a–c**). Much of this was thanks to strong export performance. Exports represented 36% of German GDP in 1980, and peaked at 58% of GDP in 2008. (See **Exhibits 3d–3f.**) Machinery, transport equipment and chemicals represented over 61% of exports in 2009. Export success over the 2000s drove large trade and current account surpluses (6.7% and 5% of GDP in 2010, respectively).

Small and Medium Enterprises (SME)

An important determinant of German success was the prevalence of small and medium enterprises.[41] In 2003, the so-called *Mittelstand* accounted for 70.2% of

Exhibit 3a.   GDP and components of GDP

	1991	**2000**	**2008**	**2009**	**2010**[a]	**2011**[b]
Nominal GDP (€ bn)	1,534.6	2,062.5	2,481.2	2,397.1	2,484.1	2,533.6
Expenditure approach						
Private consumption (%)	57.3	58.9	57.0	58.9	57.4	57.5
Government consumption (%)	19.1	19.0	18.1	19.7	19.7	19.6
Gross fixed investment (%)	23.2	21.5	19.0	17.6	18.0	18.2
Stockbuilding (%)	0.7	0.3	−0.5	−1.1	−0.4	−0.5
Exports (%)	25.8	33.4	47.5	40.8	50.2	54.6
Imports (%)	26.2	33.0	41.0	35.9	44.8	49.4
Production approach						
Agriculture (%)	1.4	1.3	0.9	0.8	0.8	0.8
Industry (%)	36.7	30.3	29.8	26.6	27.9	27.8
Services (%)	61.9	68.5	69.3	72.6	71.3	71.4

Source: World Development Indicators, World Bank, accessed December 2010.

Notes: [a]estimates;
[b]forecasts.

Exhibit 3b. Productivity and Unit Labor Costs

	1980–1985	1985–1990	1990–1995	1995–2000	2000–2005	2005–2010
Real GDP Growth	1.16	1.62	2.07	2.49	2.70	3.38
Labor productivity Growth	2.00	1.68	−0.92	1.28	0.84	−0.10
TFP Growth	0.77	1.04	−1.36	0.82	0.44	−0.22
Average real Wage Growth (in LCU)	0.91	3.31	−0.90	0.91	−0.07	0.22

	1991	1995	2000	2005	2010
Unit labor costs Index (US$)	93.7	106.1	74.3	100.0	108.2
Labor costs per hour (US$)	21.6	29.9	22.7	33.4	38.1

Source: Economist Intelligence Unit, accessed December 29, 2010.

Exhibit 3c. Share of Manufacturing in GDP, 2008

	Manufacturing as Share of GDP
World	16.7
Australia	10.5
Austria	20.4
Belgium	15.4
China	32.9
Denmark	14.3
France	11.9
Germany	22.7
Japan	19.9
Korea, Rep.	27.9
Netherlands	13.7
Singapore	19.4
Spain	14.5
Sweden	18.4
Switzerland	20.1
United Kingdom	11.6
United States	13.1

Source: World Development Indicators, World Bank, accessed December 2010.

private employment, 41.2% of sales and 49% of value added.[42] These impressive numbers hid underlying cross-sector variation. The *Mittelstand* represented over 80% of sales in construction, hotels and restaurants and other services, but less than 10% in motor vehicles, petroleum refining, air transport and telecommunications 10%.

Exhibit 3d.   Exports as Share of GDP

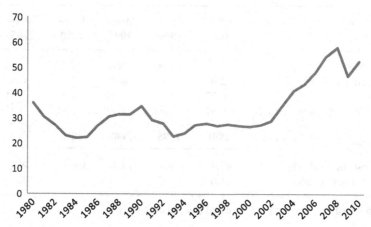

Source: World Development Indicators, World Bank, accessed December 2010.

Exhibit 3e.   Main Trade Partners and Products

Export		Import	
Main international markets			
France	10.2	Netherlands	12.7
U.S.	6.7	France	8.3
Netherlands	6.7	Belgium	7.2
U.K.	6.6	China	6.9
Exports[a]		**Imports**	
Main goods traded			
Machinery & transport equipment	45.7	Machinery & transport equipment	34.6
Chemicals & related products, n.e.s.	15.4	Chemicals & related products, n.e.s.	12.8
Food, drinks and tobacco	5.5	Mineral fuels, lubricants, & related materials	11.3
Mineral fuels, lubricants, & related materials	2.2	Food, drinks and tobacco	7.6

Source: World Development Indicators, World Bank, accessed December 2010.
Note: [a]Estimates.

The significance of the German *Mittelstand* went beyond their raw scale in employment and output. *Mittelstand* firms were the cornerstone of the German vocational training system, representing 81.9% of all student apprenticeships. *Mittelstand* firms also contributed directly to Germany's export success, representing 21% of German exports.[43] Over half of all companies with between 5 and 10 million euros in revenue exported their products.

Exhibit 3f. Balance of Payments (euro billions)

	1996	1998	2000	2002	2003	2004	2005	2006	2007	2008	2009
Current Account[a]	**-8.4**	**-6**	**-23**	**47.9**	**-97.3**	**95.9**	**102**	**151**	**188**	**171**	**119**
Balance on Goods	98.5	64.9	55.9	133	130	156.1	158	159	195	179	136
Balance on Services	-53.1	-34.1	-44.3	-35.5	-34.3	-29.4	-28.9	-14	-13.3	-12.8	-9.4
Net Income	1.7	-6.5	-1.2	-14.7	-15.9	13.1	20.8	46.1	50.6	44.7	33.8
Current Transfers	-51.3	-27.3	-27	-28.1	-28.3	-27.9	-28.5	-27.1	-31.6	-33.1	-32
Capital Transfers	**0**	**0.7**	**15.3**	**-0.2**	**0.3**	**0.4**	**-1.2**	**-0.2**	**0.1**	**-0.2**	**-0.2**
Financial Account[b]	**23.2**	**16.4**	**10**	**-42.8**	**89.4**	**-120**	**-122**	**-74.4**	**-221**	**-201**	**-141**
Net Direct Investment	-68	-57.9	138	37.6	20.4	-19.3	-15.8	-55.9	-62.8	-75.2	-19.5
Net Portfolio Investment	96	4.5	-164	63.8	70.9	14.4	-23.9	-12.3	143	35	-90.8
Net Financial Derivatives	-8.8	-6.9	-3.8	-0.9	-1.9	-7.2	-7.2	-6.2	-85.2	-25.4	20.4
Net Other Investment	4	76.7	39.7	-143	-137.9	-107.4	-74.6	-104	213	-131.1	51.1
Errors and Omissions	**-13.4**	**-7.4**	**-8.1**	**-7.2**	**7.5**	**22.6**	**17.6**	**24.3**	**34.3**	**32**	**18.9**
Change in Reserve Assets	**1.9**	**-3.6**	**5.8**	**2.1**	**0.4**	**1.5**	**2.2**	**2.9**	**-1**	**-2**	**3.2**

Source: Deutsche Bundesbank.

Notes: [a]Includes supplementary trade items.
[b]Excludes balance of capital transfers.

The competitiveness of German manufacturing depended on its technological advantage, and the *Mittelstand* contributed significantly to the advancement of technology in Germany through their R&D investments. One study showed that smaller firms invested a larger share of their revenues and devoted a larger share of their workforce to R&D than larger firms (see **Exhibit 4a**).[44] Their engagement in innovation activities was substantial: 46.3% of *Mittelstand* firms innovated in-house accounting for 9% of total R&D expenditures in Germany; 61% were involved in some innovation activity, and over 51% had introduced organizational and/or marketing innovations. Many *Mittelstand* firms also resorted to contract research to update their technology. One third of Fraunhofer's revenues from research contracts came from *Mittelstand* firms. Two thirds of all *Mittelstand* firms reported offering products that had been "significantly improved" within the past two years, and these products accounted for 11% of total sales (see **Exhibit 4b**).

Policymakers across the advanced industrialized economies have also frequently looked to SMEs as a source of manufacturing job growth.[45] In Germany, *Mittelstand* firms with a strong science base consistently produced strong jobs growth.[46]

Labor

Germany's elaborate institutions of worker representation had created a labor market that was characterized by low conflict, high wage compression, and high skill formation. Compared to other European countries, Germany's trade unions rarely engaged in work stoppages. But it also had other consequences that supported Germany's innovation-intensive export sectors. Most important was Germany's system of patterned wage bargaining, in which metal sector wage negotiations set

Exhibit 4a. R&D Efforts by Size of Firm and Employment

	Private R&D-expenditures Over Sales by Employment Size	Share of R&D-personnel in Overall Employment by Firm Size
<20	13.9	21.8
20–49	6.6	11.0
50–99	4.9	8.0
100–249	3.6	5.6
250–499	2.9	4.8
500–999	3.5	6.5
1,000–1,999	4.5	6.8
2,000–4,999	2.2	6.6
5,000–9,999	3.4	6.8
>10,000	5.9	8.1

Source: Adapted from Gunterberg, B. and G. Kayser, "SMEs in Germany: Facts and Figures" IfM Bonn 2004, accessed December 2010.

Note: Data corresponding to 2001.

Exhibit 4b. Innovation in SMEs across Countries

	Germany	France	Denmark	Netherlands	U.K.	Sweden	Spain
% SMEs innovating in-house	46.30	28.30	40.80	27.30	na	41.80	8.00
% SMEs with innovation activities	61.00	na	45.50	34.50	37.50	43.30	5.00
% SMEs that have new products or income from new products:	66.50	59.60	53.80	65.70	73.40	65.60	32.70
Share of SMEs' turnover from new or significantly improved products and services	11.00	7.00	6.00	9.00	14.00	11.00	53.80
% SMEs introduced organisational and/or marketing innovation	51.21	na	34.26	18.02	na	na	24.60

Source: Adapted from European SMEs Under Pressure. Annual Report on EU Small and medium-Sized enterprises 2009. European Commission.

the pattern of wage rates across all sectors of the economy. The large proportion of labor contracts covered by negotiated wages made it possible for unions to impose broad-based wage restraint in order to control inflation or to increase export competitiveness. For example, between 2001 and 2005, real wages in Germany declined by 4% even as productivity grew (see **Exhibit 5a**). The cost reduction allowed German producers to enjoy export growth during a period of strong euro appreciation.

Coordinated wage bargaining had two other consequences. First, unions negotiated wage scales that generated a high degree of wage compression across seniority and skill levels. Income inequality in Germany was unusually low. With a Gini coefficient of 0.27 in 2009, Germany ranked 125 out of 134 countries in terms of inequality (even including the 16 million new citizens assimilated during German reunification, and whose incomes still averaged 40% lower than incomes in the west).[47] Second, because coordinated wage bargaining imposed the same wage scale on competing firms, the poaching of skilled workers was uncommon in Germany (see **Exhibit 5b**). With firms not having to worry about losing skilled workers, and workers not expecting to move frequently between firms, both sides tended to invest heavily in firm-specific skills.

Research and Development

Formally, the activity we call research and development (R&D) comprises three distinct activities: basic research, applied research, and experimental development (see **Exhibits 6a–e**).

Exhibit 5a.   Wage and Productivity Growth, Germany and the U.K., 1993–2007.

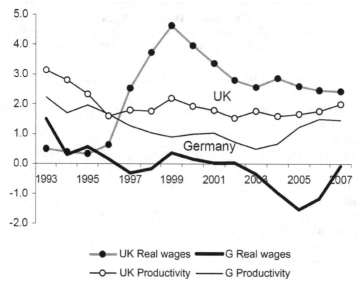

Source: Wendy Carlin and David Soskice, "German Economic Performance: Disentangling the Role of Supply-side Reforms, Macroeconomic Policy and Coordinated Economy Institutions," June 2008, http://eprints.ucl.ac.uk/16061/1/16061.pdf, accessed December 2010.

Exhibit 5b.   Tenure of Job with Current Employer, 1991 (average number of years)

	Men	Women	All
Finland	9.4	8.5	9.9
France	10.6	9.6	10.1
Germany	12.1	8.0	10.4
Japan	12.5	7.3	10.9
Netherlands	8.6	4.3	7.0
Spain	10.6	8.2	9.8
U.K.	9.2	6.3	7.9
U.S.	7.5	5.9	6.7

Source: Adapted from J.R. Shackleton, Training for Employment in Western Europe and the U.S. (Brookfield, Vt.: Edward Elgar, 1995), p. 160.

(i) Basic research consists of original investigations undertaken in order to increase scientific knowledge by forming hypotheses or theories. It is conducted with no consideration for specific goals or applications.

(ii) Applied research consists of original investigations that utilize knowledge discovered through basic research to confirm the feasibility of commercialization

Exhibit 6a.   Non-Defense R&D Expenditures as a Share of GDP

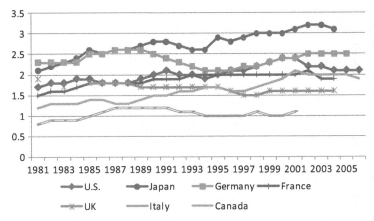

Source: National Science Foundation, accessed December 2010.

Exhibit 6b.   Composition of R&D Expenditures

	Share of Basic Research in Total R&D Expenditures[a]	R&D Expenditures in Services Over Total R&D Expenditures
Japan	14.4	10.0
U.S.	19.1	38.0
Germany	21.2	8.5
France	24.1	13.0
U.K.		20.0

Source: Eurostat, accessed December 2010.
Note: [a]2003.

for a specific purpose. It includes the search for new applications for scientific knowledge that has already been commercialized.

(iii) Experimental development is the use of scientific knowledge to produce new or substantially improved materials, devices, products, processes or services.[48]

R&D involves a number of externalities that make it economically "special." The origin of these externalities can be traced to three properties of R&D: non-rivalry, difficult excludability, and low replication costs. The knowledge created as a result of R&D is non-rival in the sense that its use by an economic agent, typically, does not preclude others from using it. It is often difficult to exclude agents from benefiting from the outputs of others' R&D efforts. This is the case for two reasons. First, much of the R&D output is intangible. That is, it is not embodied in a good. (Think, for example, about all the knowledge created in experiments and through trial and error when trying to develop a new product or process or about most basic

Exhibit 6c.   International R&D Expenditures for Selected Countries, by Funding and Performing Sectors: Selected years, 2004–2006

			Source of R&D funds				Performers
	All sources	Industry	Government	Higher Education	Private Nonprofit	Abroad	(% Distribution)
Japan (2004) (¥ bn)	15,782,743	11,807,293	2,852,667	962,235	109,716	50,833	100
Industry	11,867,276	11,658,708	148,798	1,249	9,667	48,854	75
Government	1,497,546	12,853	1,481,095	1,203	2,333	64	10
Higher education	2,119,125	58,639	1,081,542	959,343	19,128	473	13
Private nonprofit	298,796	77,093	141,232	440	78,588	1,442	2
Percent distribution, sources	100.0	74.8	18.1	6.1	0.7	0.3	na
Germany (2004) (€ MM)	55,215	36,866	16,771	0	215	1,363	100
Industry	38,611	35,449	2,251	na	23	888	70
Government	7,514	219	6,917	na	192	186	14
Higher education	9,089	1,198	7,603	na	na	289	17
Private nonprofit	na	na	na	na	na	na	na
Percent distribution, sources	100.0	66.8	30.4	0.0	0.4	2.5	na
United Kingdom (2004) (£ MM)	20,331	8,991	6,659	215	960	3,507	100
Industry	12,816	8,484	1,334	na	5	2,993	63
Government	2,089	195	1,726	11	89	69	10
Higher education	4,759	243	3,169	198	761	388	23
Private nonprofit	667	69	430	6	105	57	3
Percent distribution, sources	100.0	44.2	32.8	1.1	4.7	17.2	na
U.S. (2006) (US$ MM)	340,429	223,371	97,274	9,297	10,488	na	100
Industry	242,129	219,569	22,560	na	na	na	71
Government	37,388	0	37,388	na	na	na	11
Higher education	46,642	2,452	31,605	9,297	3,288	na	14
Private nonprofit	14,271	1,350	5,721	na	7,200	na	4
Percent distribution, sources	100.0	65.6	28.6	2.7	3.1	na	na

Source: National Science Foundation, accessed December 2010.

Exhibit 6d. Productivity of R&D, 2000

	Number of Triadic Patents per million Inhabitant	Number of Triadic Patents per 100 million euros of R&D Expenditure
European Union (27 countries)	26.5	7.5
Germany	68.7	11.2
Spain	3.5	2.4
France	33.8	6.6
Italy	10.7	4.9
Netherlands	62.3	13.0
Sweden	67.2	na
United Kingdom	26.2	5.3
South Africa	0.8	na
United States	48.0	4.7
Japan	111.4	9.2
Taiwan	1.8	na
Korea (Republic of) (South)	15.3	5.4
Singapore	16.8	na

Source: Adapted from various datasets on Eurostat, accessed December 2010.

Note: Triadic patents are innovations patented in the U.S., the EU and Japan. Because of the higher patenting costs, these innovations are considered more significant that non-triadic patents.

research.) As a result, it is hard to patent. Second, even for tangible outputs of the R&D process, replicating (i.e. copying, imitating) the output is frequently less expensive than inventing it for the first time. This is the case because the fixed costs of invention or development are significantly larger than the fixed costs of imitation and (much) larger than the variable costs of producing the good. As a result of these low replication costs, patent protection is necessary for innovators to appropriate the market value of their tangible R&D outputs.

Nevertheless, patents also present challenges. They expire after a fixed number of years. They create monopolies in which producers sell R&D outputs at high markups that result in an undersupply of the R&D outputs. When patenting a new product or process, innovators must reveal technical information about the invention. Other researchers may use this information to develop better versions of the innovation that render obsolete the original one.[49] To prevent this from happening, many inventors do not patent their inventions. For this and other reasons, knowledge created through R&D activities may diffuse more slowly than what would be socially desirable, reducing the effectiveness of future R&D investments in the economy.

The possibility of being taken over by competitors is a significant concern for inventors. This may affect decisions about how much to invest in R&D as well as

Exhibit 6e.   Composition of Manufacturing R&D

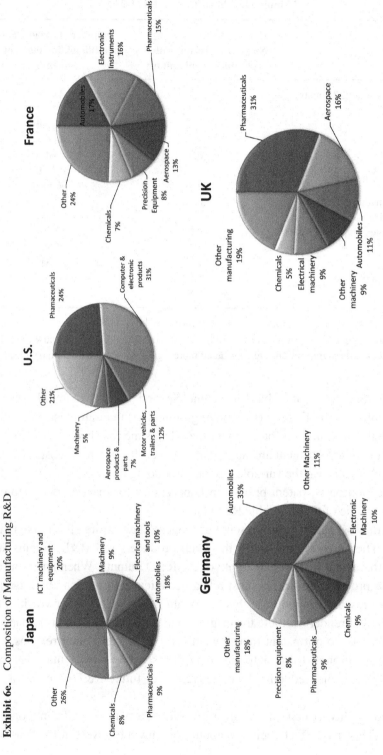

Source: Japan: Statistics Bureau. "Report on the Survey of R&D." Other countries: OECD, "R&D Statistics."

what type of R&D projects to engage in. Firms under take-over threat may prioritize less risky projects with smaller gestation lags even though other projects, if successful, would yield higher private (and social) returns. They may find applied R&D less attractive than experimental development of products and processes that take place later in the innovation cycle. These effects may be accentuated by a lack of foresight, a lack of funds, or difficulties accessing the financial markets.

Often, R&D activities yield findings that are relevant to develop new products and processes in other areas of science. Absorbing and applying correctly this knowledge requires multidisciplinary research teams that are rare in private research organizations that tend to have a narrow focus. As a result a significant portion of the knowledge created is lost.

The presence of significant positive externalities and monopolies suggest that there is, in principle, a tendency for an overall underinvestment in R&D. This inefficiency, in principle, provides a rationale for the government to step in and improve the market allocation of resources to R&D activities. Most often, governments try to mitigate the underinvestment in R&D with subsidies, grants and tax-breaks for spending on R&D. However, it is unlikely that reducing the private cost of conducting R&D suffices to correct the natural bias of private research organizations towards short term projects, their aversion for risky projects, and the relatively narrow scope of research organizations. Correcting these inefficiencies might require direct involvement of public institutions in the performance of R&D activities.

Fraunhofer

Structure

Fraunhofer was composed of 60 institutes with approximately 300 workers each. Institutes were scattered all over Germany and operated as independent partners of the Fraunhofer headquarters. The central administration identified broad areas of research with the greatest innovation potential. These areas received special funding and marketing efforts.[50] However, the headquarters did not mandate research plans or goals to its laboratories; rather, the directors of respective laboratories determined their own paths of research.

Research institutes specialized in one or two fields covering most areas of natural science and engineering. Institutes were classified into seven Groups: microelectronics, materials and components, production, surface technology and photonics, life sciences, information technology, and defense. Each Group consisted of between 5 and 12 institutes. While they did not have official controlling functions, the Fraunhofer Groups provided an informal platform for these related institutes to communicate market demands and share industry contacts. Institutes were encouraged to initiate joint marketing projects within groups and plan major investments together.

Each Fraunhofer institute partnered with at least one of Germany's 70 research universities. The director of the institute often was a senior professor at the partner university. According to Andre Sharon, Director of the Center for Manufacturing Innovation, a Fraunhofer Institute associated with Boston University, "this double affiliation eliminated any barrier between the university and the institute." Collaborations were beneficial for all parties.[51] University students could perform assistantships and develop their dissertations at the institute. The university was able to add practical science applications to curricula, as well as gain access to costly equipment. Meanwhile, Fraunhofer was able to recruit many junior scientists and interns while gaining access to basic research.[52]

Another way to obtain access to basic science was by attracting pure scientists from the Max-Planck Institute. Fraunhofer offered five-year contracts to Max-Planck scientists who had ideas about how to apply their basic research. The contract came with five million euros that they could use to fund the team they needed to conduct their project. (By comparison, grants offered by the U.S. National Science Foundation to promote technology start-ups were capped at $150,000. More funds were made available at later stages.)

Bridging the R&D Gap

Getting new technologies from Research to Development involved two kinds of challenges that Fraunhofer hoped to overcome. The first is a funding gap. Basic research is financed by public funds that often go to universities. Development (i.e. once you have a prototype that works) is financed by venture capital, investors or industry. But the bridging function, applied R&D, is often considered too applied for public funds and too risky for private capital to jump in.

The second element that creates a barrier between research and development is a knowledge gap. In Andre Sharon's view: "Basic researchers are typically not best suited or motivated to develop the research into functional technologies." On the other hand, most companies do not have the capabilities to transform basic research into well-developed products and services. Cross-country differences in these capabilities could explain the large cross-country differences in the distribution of R&D expenditures across sectors (see **Exhibits 6b** and **e**).

According to Sharon, Fraunhofer filled both the financing and knowledge gaps: "Fraunhofer acts at an early stage of the innovation process where most venture capitalists prefer to wait for products and processes that have been successfully developed and tested. Fraunhofer has the scientific knowledge and expertise to assume the risk." That in-house scientific and technical knowledge also allowed Fraunhofer to absorb and accumulate further knowledge that emanated from its own and other R&D efforts. This ability was known as absorptive capacity, and it was key for the success of R&D organizations.[53] A factor that surely enhanced Fraunhofer's absorptive capacity was its dense coverage of virtually all areas of science, which enabled its scientists to interpret experimental findings and their consequences beyond a narrow field.

Sources of Revenue

Research contracts: Fraunhofer maintained close ties with industry (see **Exhibits 7a–c**). Both large and small companies regularly contacted Fraunhofer when they faced technological challenges. Fraunhofer responded by assembling a team of scientists and engineers, often from several institutes, to work on the project. Project durations were usually less than two years. A stock of knowledge from previous research put Fraunhofer in a unique position to provide technological

Exhibit 7a. Fraunhofer Budget, 2009

Income	
Revenue from base funding	
Federal government	552.5
Länder governments	68.9
Revenue from own activities	
R&D activities	
Federal government	
Project funding	257.9
Contracts	10.9
Länder governments	
Project funding	133.1
Contracts	4.1
Business, industry & trade organizations	427.8
Research funding organizations & others	106.7
Increase in work in progress	3.5
Other internally constructed and capitalized assets	8.0
Other operating income	74.5
Income from non-current marketable securities and non-current loans	0.2
Other interest	2.8
Total base funding and revenue from own activities	1650.8
Changes in special reserve	
License-fee revenue reserve	43.8
Grants relating to fixed assets	−126.2
Grants used to finance current assets	−33.6
Total income available to cover expenditures	1534.8

(Continued)

Exhibit 7a.   *(Continued)*

Outflows

Cost of materials	243.6
Personnel expenses	736.5
Amortization of intangible assets and depreciation of property, plant & equipment	235.0
Other operating expenses	220.8
Amortization of financial assets & current marketable securities	0.1
Total expenditures	1436.0
Net income on ordinary activities	98.9
Extraordinary expenses (allocation to foundation capital)	−98.4
Net income for the year	0.4
Retained earnings	0.4

Source: Thum, Martin. Fraunhofer Annual Report 2009 | With Renewed Energy. Publication. München, Germany: Fraunhofer-Gesellschaft, 2009. pp. 66–67, accessed February 2011.

Exhibit 7b.   Composition of Research Contracts (in thousand euros)

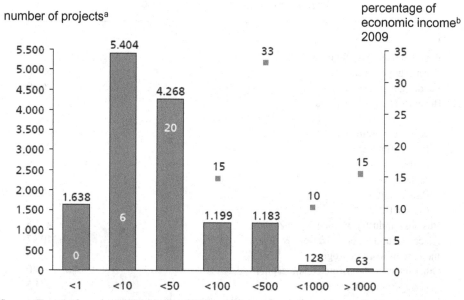

Source: Fraunhofer, accessed December 2010.

Notes: [a]Bars; projects with economic income in 2009 (period under consideration 2007–2013).
[b] Squares; license income included.

solutions reasonably fast. The broad scientific span of Fraunhofer's institutes made them capable of tackling virtually any problem, even one's requiring highly multi-disciplinary solutions. In the words of one Fraunhofer senior executive, "Fraunhofer is full of solutions in search of problems."

Exhibit 7c.   Share of Fraunhofer R&D by Activity

Industry	% of Fraunhofer R&D
Broadcasting & Entertainment	19.3
Electronics	11.3
Automobiles & Parts	9.2
Support Services	6.9
Semiconductor	5.9
Consumer, Personal, Household Goods	5.5
Retail	4.9
Chemicals & Basic Materials	4.5
Computer & Software	3.8
Metals & Mining	3.8
Aerospace & Defense	3.3
Financial Services	3.0
Construction & Materials	2.8
Telecommunications	2.1
Utilities	1.8
Pharmaceuticals and Biotech Utilities	1.8
Medical Equipment	1.7
Forestry & Paper	1.6
General Industrials	1.6
Public Services	1.1
Oil & Gas	1.0
Food Producers & Farming	0.8
Transport & Logistics	0.7
Travel & Leisure	0.6
Waste & Disposal Services	0.3
Insurance	0.3
Clothing & Accessories	0.1

Source: Fraunhofer, accessed December 2010.

The terms of the relationship between Fraunhofer and a corporation were governed by a contract that specified prices and intellectual property rights. The price Fraunhofer charged was proportional to the costs of developing a project. It did not include the historical cost incurred by Fraunhofer to develop the knowledge used in the project, and was independent of the success of the final product. A small markup, typically 15%, was charged over the development cost. Fraunhofer engaged in between 6,000 and 8,000 industry projects per year. The size of these projects varied significantly, ranging from less than 1,000 euros to several million euros (see **Exhibit 7b**).[54] Revenues from research contracts represented approximately 35% of Fraunhofer's budget.

Spin offs: Some technologies developed by Fraunhofer scientists became the basis for new companies. Spin offs had a failure rate of less than 10%. This was considerably lower than the failure rate of startups in the U.S. and elsewhere. Although the estimates vary considerably, the failure rate faced by startups in the U.S. in the early 2000s was 90%. If a spin off did not work, scientists had the option of returning to Fraunhofer during the first two years after they had left. Given this implicit insurance, the volume of new technologies developed at Fraunhofer, and the odds of success, it was surprising that only between 30 and 40 spin offs appeared every year.

Spin offs were encouraged by Fraunhofer, which saw them as an effective channel to transfer technology developed in its labs. They were also a source of revenue. Often, spin off companies leased other Fraunhofer technologies and engaged in research contracts with Fraunhofer. In about half of all spin offs, Fraunhofer kept a share of the new companies, though this was never higher than 25%.

Financing for spin offs came mostly (90%) from venture capital. The remaining 10% was evenly split between business angels and bank loans. The most common exit strategy was through trade sale. For example, in 2005, Yahoo paid $160 million for a spin off started in 1999 based on software for digital audio files and downloads. In 2007, Dolby bought Coding Technologies, a spin off founded in 2000 to commercialize audio compression technology, for $260 million. From these deals Fraunhofer earned $688,000 and $11.7 million, respectively.

With most spin offs, Fraunhofer's initial ownership stakes became highly diluted in subsequent rounds of venture capital. With an average of 40 spin offs per year, revenues from sales were just 21 million euros in 2008. Spin offs were managed by a division called Fraunhofer Venture. Fraunhofer Venture did not calculate rates of return on its portfolio of projects.

Questioned about the potential revenues that could be generated from a more active commercialization of Fraunhofer's IP via spin offs, a senior executive observed that their scientific staff tended to "maximize their personal satisfaction via research more than their revenues. That is one limitation of the system." There was also a political concern. Some feared that increased revenues from private sources would be offset by a reduction in the sources of public financing that had proved so sable over the past decades. The executive explained: "Politicians and bureaucrats are averse to change."

Public funds: The remaining 65% of Fraunhofer's budget came from public sources. Approximately 25% of Fraunhofer's funding was obtained through national and international research grants. The remaining 40% of its budget was basic funding that came from the German government. Two-thirds of that basic funding (representing 27% of all revenue) was allocated to individual institutes according to a formula that induced institute directors to attract revenues from the EU and from the industry (see **Exhibit 7d**). A further 10% of basic funding was assigned competitively following a

Exhibit 7d. Fraunhofer Rule to Allocate Institutional Funding to an Institute

1. Fixed Amount:	0.6 Million euros
2. Unconditional Variable:	12% of the Institute planned budget
3. Percentage of industry revenues from previous year:	10% of industry revenues if share of previous year budget was between 0 and 25%
	40% of industry revenues for revenues that exceeded 25% until 55%
	10% of industry revenues for revenues that exceeded 55% of previous year budget
4. Percentage of revenues from the European Union:	15% of revenues from EU the previous year

Source: Author's Calculations.

round of proposals that sought to open new research fields. These high-risk research projects were an opportunity to foster cooperation among institutes, and many of the successful proposals were collaborative. Another 10% of the basic funding was spent to purchase new equipment. Finally, the remaining 15% of basic funding was used by the Executive Board to finance various significant investments, such as the infrastructure of new institutes, relocation of institutes, special strategic projects, etc.

This funding scheme had been set up by Alexander Imbusch, a former Fraunhofer director, in the 1970s, and its implementation coincided with the beginning of Fraunhofer's expansion in terms of its resources, output and reputation. Within this common framework, institute directors pursued very different financing strategies that depended on their priorities. Generally speaking, public funds were used to finance longer-term projects (3–10 years), while private funds went to shorter-term projects (1–2 years). The flexibility of the scheme allowed Fraunhofer to pursue projects that the private sector, often pressed for short-term payoffs, would not have pursued.

People

As a publicly funded research organization, Fraunhofer' internal business processes and administration were bound by the same rules that governed all public-service organizations. This meant Fraunhofer employees received lower salaries than workers with similar qualifications in the private sector.[55] Despite that, Fraunhofer was voted one of the most attractive employers for recent undergraduates in 2007 due to the engaging, challenging, and autonomous style of the work. Fraunhofer also covered the patenting fees of workers that wanted to patent their discoveries. These amounted to 8,000 euros for a German patent and up to 20,000 euros for a Europe-wide patent. In exchange, the royalties and licensing fees were split between the institute and the inventor on a 70/30 basis.

Exhibit 8.   Fraunhofer Innovations

When	Invention	Description	Institute
1951	Video Recorder	Device for magnetic recording of picture and sound signals	HHI
1978	Liquid Crystal Displays		IAF
1990	Lithium-ion battery for Electric Car	An attempt at fueling lithium-ion run electric cars	
1994	MP3 Compression Algorithm	Used new method of audio compression to store audio files more efficiently	
1998	Liquid Wood Plastic Material	Had the potential to save fossil fuel and natural resources	ICT
2000	High performance coatings for short wavelengths in optical coating	Extended wavelength range research from 157 nm to 1 nm.	IOF
2001	Microoptical sensor for online characterization of textile fibers	For use in modern textile industry to meet specific demands for geometrical extension of the detector housing, measurement speed, and operation temperature and humidity	IOF
2002	Modulated RGB-laser source for digital photo finishing	To overcome the problem of laser-scanning systems that offer excellent picture quality but require a large amount of space	IOF
2003	Diamond turning of micro-optical structures	Used in the manufacture of plastic optics.	IOF
2004	Ultra-thin vision system based on artificial compound eyes	Developed a technical compound eye that is of minimum thickness	IOF
2005	EUV Multilayer Optics	Enhanced optical resolution to structure and observe smaller details	IOF
2006	Near infrared camera	The whole camera optical system was set up in a vacuum and cooled with liquid nitrogen	IOF
	Tracker for Online Pirated Audio Files	Could help curb the sharp rise in online music piracy	IPSI
	OLED and LCD	Combination of Olds and LCDs were used to transform laminated glass into display panels	APR
2007	Microoptics for LED light sources	Allowed for efficient light sources illuminating rectangular or circular spots with high homogenous luminance	IOF
	E-Puzzler	Computerized conveyer belt that runs shards of shredded and torn paper through a digital scanner to display original document	IDMT
2008	2kW incoherent beam combining of four narrow-linewidth photonic crystal fiber amplifiers'	Using the technique of beam combination, power scaling reached higher levels	IOF
	Laser Beams to Weld Batteries	Used for a new generation of automobiles	IWS

(Continued)

Exhibit 8. *(Continued)*

When	Invention	Description	Institute
2009	Nanostructured SIS Solar Cells	Improved upon the electrical properties of mass production processes of solar cells	IOF
	Smart Tableware	Made of a wax-like substances, these tablewares would be able to keep contents at an ideal temperature	
	Smart Metering	Technology allowed one to use mobile phone to regulate energy consumption of appliances	ESE
	Optimized Microsystems	Made it possible to develop both micropumps and highly efficient particle filters for living microorganisms	IBMT
	Artificial Tissue as Alternative to Animal Experiments	New method to produce models of living human tissue with a functioning system of blood vessels to be used as more ethical and reliable alternative to animal experiments in pharmaceutical research	IGB
	Mobile Blood Diagnosis	Particularly relevant in developing countries, this provides rapid means of identifying suitable donors and contaminated samples	IBMT
	Injecting Noise to Save Energy	Used injection of artificial noisy to suppress interference caused by switching operations in DSL connections, could potentially reduce electricity bills	ESK
	Telemedicine Software	Based on an easily adapted molecular structure, this software package would facilitate the flow of medical care for patients	ISST
	Talking Blood Products	Wireless networks used to label blood products in order to monitor temperature and blood type while not interfering with other medical devices in a hospital	IIS
	Satnav for Mountain Rescue Teams	A new geo-location system capable of pinpointing a victim's location to the nearest cm in the case of an avalanche	IML
	Secure Windowpanes	Windowpanes were made with a special coating that detect motion	IAP
	Coordinated Swarm of Micro-Helicopters	Software that enabled a single operator to control a swarm of micro-helicopters to distribute aid more efficiently in rescue missions	IITB
	Inspection Robot for Wind Turbines	A robot trained to perform inspections in extreme conditions of wind turbine operations	IFF
	New Car Horn	Cars would be equipped with horns that sound in emergency situations even when parked.	INT

(Continued)

Exhibit 8.   *(Continued)*

When	Invention	Description	Institute
	Explosive Brand-Name Protection	Technique for nano structuring of steel surfaces onto name brand products to prevent counterfeit copies	ICT
	Lightweight Seat Post for Bicycles	A flexible seat post that is 30% lighter and more comfortable	ICT
	Wireless Sensors for Aircraft	Sensors that generated their own power supply and sent their data to a receiver to monitor the outer skin of the fuselage	IPM
	Steel-Cutting Technique for Car Manufacturers	Based on electromagnetic pulse technology, this technique worked faster than other laser methods and was more efficient	IWU
	Escort for Traveling Artworks	An environmental sensor that would permanently monitor the microclimate inside crates used to transport valuable artworks.	ISC
	Multimedia Assistance for Drivers	A central display featuring 3D vision would be adapted automatically to the driver's viewing position	HHI
	Universal Diesel Filter	A high-precipitation ceramic diesel particle filter that would reduce wastage in diesel engine cars	IKTS
	Method of Harvesting Water	A method to convert vapor in the air of arid climates into liquid water using solar energy; yet to be demonstrated in entirety	IGB
	Ultra-efficient Gem Cutting	An automated gem cutting process that would be 10 times more precise while increasing yield of the stones by 30%	ITWM
	Adaptable Photo bioreactor	An adaptable photo bioreactor that extracted CO_2 and converted it to useful products such as vitamins and biomass	IGB
	Environment-Friendly Metal-Cutting Process	Method for cutting sheet metal with a laser beam that softened the surface before cutting, creating less noise and improving quality	IPT
	Rubber from Dandelion Milk	A targeted genetic modification of the dandelion plant that would allow the milk to be processed into a form of natural rubber	IME
	Power Plan Concept	Won the 2009 German Climate Protection Prize for coming up with a way to combine different characteristics of green installations with a pump storage system	IWES
	Power Cells from the Printer	Batteries that could be manufactured on a printer and could be integrated into products such as check cards and printed brochures	ENAS

(Continued)

Exhibit 8. (*Continued*)

When	Invention	Description	Institute
	Simulation Program for Solar Cells	Enabled efficient calculation of optimum layout of solar energy cells	ISE
	Biogas Plant: Energy from Waste	A plant that used only organic agricultural waste as feedstock	IKTS
2010	High efficiency concentrator solar cells and modules	Concentrator solar cells would allow more sunlight to be converted into electricity'	ISE
	Eye Tracker	A device for cars that triggered an alarm when drivers were about to fall asleep	
	OLED Manufacturing Process	New process for manufacturing organic light-emitting diodes that could significantly reduce production expenses	ILT
	Interactive Dress for Electronic Textiles	Was able to translate movements of the body into visual patterns of light	IZM

Source: Fraunhofer, accessed December 2010.

There was a high turnover of staff within Fraunhofer, with about one-third of all employees working on short-term contracts at any time. New employees were offered a contract of up to five years, after which they had to apply for an unlimited-duration contract. This flexibility allowed Fraunhofer to alter the size of its staff in response to fluctuations in market demand and economic conditions.

The Fraunhofer human resources policy aimed to prepare qualified scientists for the German innovation system, and not just for the purposes of Fraunhofer. Every year approximately 400 Fraunhofer employees moved into jobs in industry.[56] Fraunhofer scientists were sought after for the skills and knowledge they gained while at Fraunhofer. Often, the route to employment began with participation in a contract research project. Industry professionals also had the opportunity to learn skills from Fraunhofer employees at the Fraunhofer Academy, which provided seminars and courses in collaboration with major universities.[57]

International Expansion

Fraunhofer began its international expansion in 1994 in the United States by establishing contacts at top American universities. Initially its U.S. institutes struggled, partly because Fraunhofer was not yet known there, and partly because American firms were not used to dealing with research organizations such as Fraunhofer. The U.S. market had a vacuum in applied research, with virtually no private applied R&D companies. Two exceptions were Tiaxx and Battelle, which covered much fewer areas of science than Fraunhofer and relied heavily on contracts with the U.S. Department of Defense.

Fraunhofer's success grew as relationships between the Fraunhofer headquarters in Germany and the institutes in the U.S. transformed from parent–child relations to partnerships, and the American institutes grew more independent. There were seven small Fraunhofer operations in the U.S. as of 2009, and Fraunhofer hoped to receive funding from the American government for these institutes, much in the way German institutes received funding from the German state.

As time passed, Fraunhofer expanded its horizons beyond the U.S. By 2010 Fraunhofer ran a liaison office in Brussels, created in 2000, and had established representative offices in China, Japan, South Korea, Indonesia and Dubai. It also opened research subsidiaries in Austria (2008), Portugal (2008), Italy (2009) and Chile (2010). In 2010, 21.4% of direct contract research revenue with industry came from companies outside Germany.

The Future of German Innovation

As the world slowly emerged from the global financial crisis, Germany's economy was rising to new heights. By December 2010, German unemployment had fallen to 7%; GDP growth in 2010 was projected to come in at 3.6%; and the Ifo Institute's business climate index gave Germany its highest grade since reunification in May 1990. German Chancellor Angela Merkel, who held an engineering PhD from the Central Institute for Physical Chemistry in Berlin, observed these developments with obvious satisfaction. One of the developments she was proudest of was the reputation of the products made in Germany: "We are not going to be punished because the good products made in Germany are exported everywhere."[58]

Yet, the R&D that formed the foundation of the country's prosperity had continuously to be renewed, and doing so required a combination of incentives, institutions, and actors adapted to the risks inherent in the innovative process. Amid success, sober Germans wondered how long institutions forged in the 1940s and 1950s would continue to provide a recipe for success in the increasingly competitive world of global capitalism.

Endnotes

[1] EBN24, European Business Network, http://www.ebn24.biz/index.php?id=32685& L=1, accessed January 2011.

[2] Fraunhofer was named for the Munich researcher, inventor, and businessman, Joseph von Fraunhofer (1787–1826) who discovered the dark absorption lines known as Fraunhofer lines in the Sun's spectrum. He invented several optical instruments such as the spectroscope, a new method for processing lens and produced both optical glass and instruments such as microscopes and achromatic telescope objectives. In 2009, Fraunhofer scientists applied for 522 new patents.

3   Kevin H. O'Rourke and Jeffrey G. Williamson, *Globalization and History: The Evolution of a Nineteenth Century Atlantic Economy* (Cambridge: MIT Press, 1999) p. 95.

4   Alexander Gerschenkron, *Bread and Democracy in Germany* (Berkeley: University of California Press, 1943); Cheryl Schonhardt-Bailey, "Parties and Interests in the 'Marriage of Iron and Rye'," *British Journal of Political Science*, 28/2 (1998), p. 295.

5   Rudolf Hilferding, *Das Finanzkapital* (Vienna: 1910).

6   Jeff Fear, Organizing Control: August Thyssen and the construction of German Corporate Control (Cambridge: Harvard University Press, 2005), p. 236.

7   Rudolph Hilferding, *Das Finanzkapital* (1910).

8   Cited in: David M. Cutler and Richard Johnson, "The Birth and Growth of the Social Insurance State: Explaining Old Age and Medical Insurance Across Countries," *Public Choice* 120/1–2 (2004), p. 92.

9   Mark Lehrer, "Knowledge Spillovers and Organizational Heterogeneity: An Historical Overview of German Technology Sectors," in Jordi Suriñach, Rosina Moreno, Esther Vayá, eds., *Knowledge Externalities, Innovation Clusters and Regional Development* (Northampton, Mass.: Edward Elgar, 2007), pp. 46–47.

10 Basil Achilladelis and Nicholas Antonakis, "The dynamics of technological innovation: the case of the pharmaceutical industry," *Research Policy* 30/4 (2001), p. 555.

11 *Journal of the Franklin Institute* (February 1899), p. 170.

12 Arthur Henry Chamberlain, *The Condition and Tendencies of Technical Education in Germany* (Syracuse, New York: C. W. Bardeen, 1908), p. 87.

13 *Ibid.*

14 Fear 2005, p. 191.

15 Fear 2005, p. 242.

16 Walter E. Grunden, Yutaka Kawamura, Eduard Kolchinsky, Helmut Maier and Masakatsu Yamazaki, "Laying the Foundation for Wartime Research: A Comparative Overview of Science Mobilization in National Socialist Germany, Japan, and the Soviet Union," *Osiris* 20/2 (2005), p. 86.

17 Grunden *et al.* 2005, p. 83.

18 Jean Medawar and David Pyke, Hitler's Gift: The True Story of the Scientists Expelled by the Nazi Regime (New York: Arcade, 2000), p. 10.

19 *Ibid.*, p. 29.

20 Walter E. Grunden, Yutaka Kawamura, Eduard Kolchinsky, Helmut Maier and Masakatsu Yamazaki, "Laying the Foundation for Wartime Research: A Comparative Overview of Science Mobilization in National Socialist Germany, Japan, and the Soviet Union," *Osiris* 20/2 (2005), p. 82.

21 Henry Ashby Turner, *German Big Business and the Rise of Hitler* (New York: Oxford University Press, 1985), p. 212.

22 S. Jonathan Wiesen, West German Industry and the Challenge of the Nazi Past, 1945–1955 (Chapel Hill: UNC Press, 2001), p. 56.

23 Herbert Giersch, Karl-Heinz Paqué and Holger Schmieding, *The Fading Miracle: Four Decades of Market Economy in Germany* (Cambridge: Cambridge University Press, 1992), p. 31.

[24] Giersch *et al.* 1992, p. 85.

[25] Giersch *et al.* 1992, p. 85.

[26] Pepper Culpepper, *Creating Cooperation: How States Develop Human Capital in Europe* (Ithaca: Cornell University Press, 2003), p. 98.

[27] J.R. Shackleton, *Training for Employment in Western Europe and the United States* (Brookfield, Vt.: Edward Elgar, 1995), pp. 120–123.

[28] Horst Siebert, *The German Economy: Beyond the Social Market* (Princeton: Princeton University Press, 2005), p. 127.

[29] Horst Siebert, *The German Economy: Beyond the Social Market* (Princeton: Princeton University Press, 2005), p. 219.

[30] Karen Adelberger, "Semi-Sovereign Leadership? The State's Role in German Biotechnology and Venture Capital Growth," *German Politics* 9/1 (2000), p. 108.

[31] Kristof F. Buchtemann and Kurt Vogler-Ludwig, Das deutsche Ausbildungsmodell unter Anpassungszwang: Thesen zur Humankapitalbildung in Deutschland (Munich: Ifo Institut, 1997).

[32] Rodney Loeppky, "History, Technology, and the Capitalist State: The Comparative Political Economy of Biotechnology and Genomics," *Review of International Political Economy* 12/2 (2005), p. 277.

[33] Adelberger, p. 114.

[34] Steven Casper, "Institutional Adaptiveness, Technology Policy, and the Diffusion of New Business Models: The Case of German Biotechnology," *Organization Studies* 21/5 (2000), pp. 887–914.

[35] Steven Casper, "The German Economy and the 'Silicon Valley Model': Convergence, Divergence, or Something Else," in Bruce Kogut, ed., *The Global Internet Economy* (Cambridge: MIT, 2004), p. 245.

[36] Casper, 893.

[37] Loeppky 2005, p. 278.

[38] Karen Adelberger, "Semi-Sovereign Leadership? The State's Role in German Biotechnology and Venture Capital Growth," *German Politics* 9/1 (2000), p. 107.

[39] Richard Deeg, "The Comeback of *Modell Deutschland*? The New German Political Economy in the EU," *German Politics* 14/3 (2005).

[40] Mark Lehrer, "Knowledge Spillovers and Organizational Heterogeneity: An Historical Overview of German Technology Sectors," in Jordi Suriñach, Rosina Moreno, Esther Vayá, eds., *Knowledge Externalities, Innovation Clusters and Regional Development* (Northampton, Mass.: Edward Elgar, 2007), p. 44.

[41] Mittelstand can be translated as small or medium sized companies (SMEs). The definition of SMEs varies. In this case we adopt a common definition which is companies with less than 250 employees.

[42] Brigitte Gunterberg and Gunter Kayser, "SMEs in Germany: Facts and Figures" Ifn-Materialien Nr. 161.

[43] Statistic for 2002. Gunterberg and Kayser, *ibid.*

[44] Gunterberg and Kayser, ibid. Broader international evidence suggests that SMEs have a higher propensity to patent than large companies. Scherer, Frederic M., 1983, The

Propensity to Patent, International Journal of Industrial Organization, 1, 107–128. Bound, John, Clint Cummins, Zvi Griliches, Bronwyn H. Hall, and Adam Jaffe, 1984, Who Does R&D and Who Patents?, in Z. Griliches (ed.), R&D, Patents, and Productivity, Chicago, IL: University of Chicago Press, 21–54.

[45] In the U.S. Davis, S. J. Haltiwanger and S. Schuh (1997) "Job Creation and Destruction" MIT Press. Cambridge, MA. In Sweden, Heshmati, A. (2001) On the Growth of Micro and Small Firms: Evidence from Sweden, Small Business Economics, 17(3), November, 213–228. In Finland, Hohti, S. (2000) Job Flows and Job Quality by Establishment Size in the Finnish Manufacturing Sector, 1980–1994, Small Business Economics, 15(4), December, 265–281. In the Netherlands, Broesma, L. and P. Gautier (1997) Job Creation and Job Destruction by Small Firms: An Empirical Investigation for the Dutch Manufacturing Sector, Small Business Economics, 9, 211–224. In Norway, Klette, T. and A. Mathiassen (1996) Job Creation, Job Destruction and Plant Turnover in Norwegian Manufacturing, Annales d'Economie et de Statistique, 41/42, 97–125.

[46] Fritsch, M. (1993) The Role of Small Firms in West Germany, in Z.J. Acs and David B. Audretsch (eds.), Small Firms and Entrepreneurship: An East-West Perspective, Cambridge: Cambridge University Press, pp. 38–54. Wagner, Joachim (1995) "Firm Size and Job Creation in Germany", Small Business Economics, 7(6), 469–474; Weigand, J. and D. Audretsch (1999), Does Science Make a Difference? Investment, Finance and Corporate Governance in German Industries, Institute for Development Strategies Discussion Paper 99–1, Indiana University.

[47] Gerd Hardach "Economic Integration of East Germany" in *Europe since 1945: An Encyclopedia,* Bernard A. Cook, Ed. vol. 1. Taylor and Francis p. 496.

[48] The line that separates applied research from development is fine and how a particular activity is classified depends on how far from bringing to the market the resulting product or process is.

[49] When Fraunhofer introduced the MP3 for of audio compression in the 1990s, MP3 players and files became so popular for music consumption that CD sales in the U.S. alone dropped nearly one-third between 1996 and 2008. "Music Sales Decline for Seventh Time in Eight Years." *Wall Street Journal.* January 2, 2009. Web. 25 Feb. 2010.

[50] Behlau, Lothar. Strategic Management of a Contract Research Organization — The Fraunhofer Model — Munich: Fraunhofer-Gesellschaft, 2009. p. 10.

[51] Behlau, Lothar. Strategic Management of a Contract Research Organization — The Fraunhofer Model — Munich: Fraunhofer-Gesellschaft, 2009. p. 15.

[52] Fraunhofer was also able to offer opportunities to its employees for further scientific qualifications by either teaching classes or earning a further degree.

[53] Cohen, W. and D. Levinthal (1990), "Absoptive Capacity: A New Perspective on Learning and Innovation", *Administrative Science Quarterly*, Vol. 35(1) pp. 128–152.

[54] Most of these smaller payments corresponded to measurements and recalibrations from ongoing projects.

[55] Savage, Charles M. Fifth generation management co-creating through virtual enterprising, dynamic teaming, and knowledge networking. Boston: Butterworth-Heinemann, 1996. Print.

[56] Behlau, *ibid.* p. 12.
[57] Behlau, Lothar. Strategic Management of a Contract Research Organization — The Fraunhofer Model —. (Munich: Fraunhofer-Gesellschaft, 2009). p. 13.
[58] "Merkel, reelegida con mas del 90% como presidenta del CDU." El Pais. November 15, 2010, accessed January 2011.

Fraunhofer: Five Significant Innovations

Diego Comin*, Gunnar Trumbull* and Kerry Yang*

Salus-Haus: An Innovative Way of Sorting Tea

Tea had always been a large part of German culture, and Germans consumed around 17,000 metric tons of tea per annum. Salus-Haus was a leading tea manufacturing company headquartered in Bruckmühl, Germany that processed and sold a range of premium teas. The word "salus" means health, well-being and flourishing. The company viewed tea as more than just a drink, but also an established part of German culture that bestowed a wide variety of health benefits. In producing the tea, they placed an emphasis on respecting nature and on supporting the rural communities around the production sites. In 2010, the company had 455 employees and 100 million euro annual turnover. Salus-Haus produced over 500 tea varieties, as well as a wide range of tonics, elixirs, juices, cosmetics, herbal tablets and coated capsules that were available in pharmacies and health food stores across Germany and in over 50 foreign countries.[1]

*Reprinted with permission of Harvard Business School Publishing.

This case was prepared by Professors Diego Comin and Gunnar Trumbull and independent researcher Kerry Yang.

Fraunhofer: Five Significant Innovations 711-058.

Founded in 1916 in Munich, Salus first produced therapeutic teas aimed at warding off illnesses and disease. The early products were developed by the company's founder, Dr. Otto Greithner, who discovered that problems of digestion could aggravate many other disorders. His "Salus Treatment" was the first of many therapeutic teas he developed, and it sold in pharmacies alongside healing oils and tablets. In 1960, Salus expanded by acquiring Floradix Medicinal Products Factory in Wiesbaden. By 1968, the company had grown so large that its headquarters needed to be moved outside of Munich in order to accommodate a larger workforce and more production space. When it moved its headquarters to Bruckmühl (pop. 16,000), they had just over 100 workers.

As it grew, Salus married technical sophistication with an environmental focus. In 1976, Salus responded to growing consumer demand for trial samples by developing an automated packaging machine that produced up to 40,000 samples daily. In 1978, the company was awarded a gold medal for skillful architectural design that helped the factory blend into the rural environment. By 1985, Salus had expanded its product line to include a wide range of natural oils, creams, tablets, and other body-care products. In 1991, acquired its main competitor in the health food market, Schoenenberger in Magstadt, making Salus one of Germany's market leaders in health food manufacturing. Another expansion of premises occurred in 1999, with the construction of one of the most modern laboratories in Germany, as well as a new extraction plant. In 2005, another new warehouse was completed.[2]

In 2003, Salus sought out research organizations to help with a problem. In the tea-making process, between harvesting, drying, storing and transporting the herbs and tea plants, foreign objects such as pebbles, parts of other plants and parts of the tea plants themselves were inevitably mingled into the actual product. During production, these foreign objects had to be removed. Until recently, the tea had been sorted manually in a process that was costly, wasteful and imprecise. Manual sorting resulted in 10% of the good tea product being thrown out. As new competition emerged from abroad, it became increasingly untenable to maintain manual sorting at its German plant. Either sorting had to be moved to lower-wage workers abroad, or the process had to be automated in Bruckmühl.

With the help of a consultant, Salus-Haus contacted the Fraunhofer Institute for Information and Data Processing IITB, which had experience in sorting different types of bulk solids. Fraunhofer IITB had already developed an automated sorting system for a tobacco company, using a process that involved a conveyer belt, a camera, high-speed image analysis and selective rejection system that employed automated air jets. Fraunhofer IITB proposed a variation on this system that would be catered to tea. After considering other contract research institutions with comparable pricing, Salus opted to work with Fraunhofer.[3] Fraunhofer IITB helped Salus conduct preliminary tests on a small purpose-built system, develop a pilot system, advertise the product through Fraunhofer publications, and finally turn the pilot system into a commercial system by presenting it to potential customers through IITB's demonstration center.[4] In June of 2005, a prototype developed by Fraunhofer in response to Salus' sorting problem began operating successfully.

The solution was an automatic sorting method called Food Control. Modified from the system that sorted tobacco, it was an advanced opto-electronic sorter that removed all foreign matter from a diversity of dried foods with extremely high reliability. The system included a vibrator that distributed the dried product evenly onto a conveyer belt with laminar airflow that carried the product at nearly 3 meters per second. A high-resolution color line-scan camera took continuous images of the dried foods as they moved by on the belt. Those images were then analyzed by a dedicated image interpreter that classified particles into eight categories based on color and surface properties. Finally, a high-speed valve block with 256 nozzles ejected any foreign particles that were detected from the stream of product.[5] The new system allowed 100 kg of raw material to be automatically sorted every hour.[6] Salus-Haus engineers implemented and maintained the new automatic sorting system.

For Fraunhofer, the Salus-Haus project was an evolution of technologies they had already developed for other customers. In fact, most of the components were borrowed directly from elements of existing Fraunhofer innovations. The Salus-Haus system would in turn become the basis for subsequent manufacturing solutions. To bring together the necessary technologies in this promising new field, Fraunhofer in 2009 merged IITB with a newly acquired lab specializing in optro-electronics to form a new Institute of Optronics, System Technologies and Image Exploitation (IOSB). IOSB brought together knowledge on automated exploitation and fusion of images from diverse networked optical sensors, including infrared, laser, radar and video.[7] Among the many follow-on projects Fraunhofer IOSB was working on were innovative sensors for more efficient manufacturing and production plants and intelligent sensors for damage inspection in sewerage systems.[8]

For Salus-Haus, the Fraunhofer technology made them the first producer to use a fully automated opto-mechanical system to sort tea. Implementing the system improved efficiency and productivity across the board. Loss of good materials was reduced to 1%. Production costs were significantly reduced and sorting speed was dramatically higher compared to conventional types of sorting. This new system allowed Salus to create a better product than its competitors, while keeping the sorting function in Germany. The entire project took about two years from the initial proposal to implementation in the factory. Much of the actual development work done in Fraunhofer labs with support from nearly 250 Fraunhofer employees.[9]

At a cost of around 150,000 euros for Fraunhofer's services, Salus was able to retain production of teas and other health products in Bruckmühl. All of the employees formerly employed in sorting were moved into other positions. Fraunhofer retained intellectual property over the new system and was experimenting with applying it to a wider range of products, including herbs, fungus, fruits and cereals.[10] With more research, the system showed promise for application to other industries, including sorting diamonds.[11]

The contract partnership between Salus-Haus and Fraunhofer did not end at the successful implementation of the new sorting system. Two years after the first sorting system was up and running, Salus purchased another sorting system from Fraunhofer. Up to the point this case was written, representatives from Fraunhofer IOSB still met with Salus periodically to discuss potential improvements or updates they could implement. These meetings sought to optimize the productivity of the existing system with software updates and hardware modifications. Fraunhofer IOSB also benefited from the partnership, as Salus granted the institute permissions to advertise the success of this system to other companies.[12] Ultimately, with this partnership, Salus was able to tackle a costly problem with an innovative technology, improve its efficiency and market position as a result and continue to work with the technology to improve it further.

A Diagram of the Automatic Sorting Process

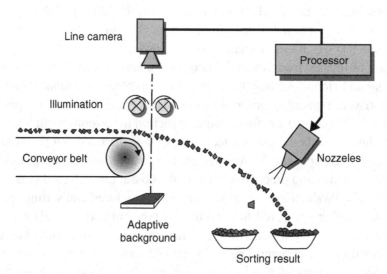

Source: Vieth, Dr. Kai-Uwe. *Automatic Sorting of Bulk Material*. Karlsruhe: Fraunhofer Institute of Optronics, System Technologies and Image Exploitation IOSB. p. 2.

Source: Vieth, Kai-Uwe. *FoodControl: For a Better Food Quality*. Karlsruhe: Fraunhofer Institute of Optronics, 2005.

PhenoStor: A More Secure Data Storage System

How can private information be better protected from hackers and other intruders? This was the question Bayer Innovations GmbH sought to answer with the help of Fraunhofer. Historically, sensitive personal information had been stored on magnetic strips on credit, debit, or health information cards. These cards had low capacity and were relatively easy to copy or manipulate. Bayer Innovation GmbH (BIG) developed an idea for a card-based data storage system that had significantly higher storage capacity and was more difficult to copy or manipulate. The core technology was holography, in which information was written and read with the aid of light.[13] The finished product, christened PhenoStor, would hold 10,000 times more data than the conventional magnetic strip and could only be read using a special reading device. The world's first system based on holographic data storage, PhenoStor would look like an ordinary credit card with an orange, glossy metal coating instead of the familiar dark magnetic strip and it had the potential to revolutionize the future of security technology. Instead of using the usual ones and zeros to store data, an interference pattern was burned into a light-sensitive polymer, creating an image that could only be converted back into the original data using the same reference beam that was used to encode the data. Hackers stood no chance against this special encryption technique. Even better, PhenoStor did all of this at a price comparable to that of the conventional card.[14] How did Bayer Innovations GmbH develop, execute and market such a technology?

BIG was a fully-owned subsidiary of Bayer AG, a large chemical and pharmaceutical company founded in Barmen, Germany. Bayer was known for its aspirin, but it was also the inventor of the first antibiotic (prontosil) and of heroin (for colds) and polyurethane. In the wake of World War II, Bayer grew into a global enterprise that eventually specialized in the fields of health care, nutrition and high-tech materials.[15] The mission of BIG was to identify and develop new areas of growth to match Bayer's overall concept, "science for a better life." The group focused on forward-looking technologies that would be relevant for future markets, with the goal of developing products that could eventually be committed to commercial integration with appropriate Bayer subgroups. BIG often teamed up with external partners such as universities, research institutes and other companies to find the best combination of competencies to develop new products.[16] The PhenoStor technology would draw both on Bayer's hardware and on its materials expertize.[17] In order to move from idea to market-ready product, BIG looked at several potential partners before finally settling on Fraunhofer.

In a first stage, BIG worked with the Fraunhofer Institute for Physical Measurement Techniques (IPM). This particular branch of Fraunhofer specialized in developing optical sensors and imaging systems, as well as systems based on thin film technology.[18] Among its repertoire of products were technical solutions for process monitoring, for railroad measurement and for micro identification. Working with BIG, Fraunhofer helped refine the holographic read/write technology and create a working prototype. A first prototype developed in-house by they Bayer team had been clunky and, in the words of one developer, "a bit like a shoe box."[19] Scientists at Fraunhofer IPM were able to miniaturize the optical components, while keeping the price down by using components that were already available on the market.[20] Combining secure encryption, a high archiving capacity and flexible storage materials, the new storage cards offered an attractive alternative to magnetic stripe cards. Fraunhofer IPM also developed a prototype reader for the Phenostor storage cards.[21]

In a second stage, Bayer worked with the Fraunhofer Institute for Applied Polymer Research (IAP) and the Fraunhofer Institute for Interfacial Engineering and Biotechnology (IGB) to develop synthetic polymers for the storage film that were both efficient and environmentally sustainable. Fraunhofer IAP specialized in developing efficient sustainable materials. Its expertise lay in a range analytic methods used to execute process monitoring, materials testing and routine analysis. IAP labs were staffed by a team of highly skilled specialists who worked with cutting-edge equipment.[22] Fraunhofer IGB developed biotechnological processes and products for environment, health and industrial technology. Their repertoire of products included tissue engineering for drug development and environmental consultancy for companies across multiple sectors. IGB provided a wide range of contract R&D services, ranging from basic research to the design, engineering and testing of industrial plants.[23] Working together, the two Fraunhofer institutes refined the design and assessed the feasibility of the new memory cards.[24]

Next, Bayer teamed up with the Fraunhofer Institute for Secure Information Technology (SIT) and the Fraunhofer Institute for Computer Graphics Research (IGD). Fraunhofer SIT was a leader in IT security and employed over 100 specialists who worked together to offer multi-technology services across a variety of industries. Its expertise included the latest security technologies, ranging from encryption technology to business continuity plans. Fraunhofer SIT operated in three locations across Germany, each with their own competencies.[25] Fraunhofer IGD was the world's leading institute for applied research in visual computing, a broad area that included computer graphics and virtual reality. Founded in 1992, IGD had by 2010 grown to include 13 R&D departments in four locations, including one in Singapore.[26] Working with BIG, these two Fraunhofer institutes ran detailed studies on standardization and certification processes for identity cards.[27] Fraunhofer SIT studied how the technology could be applied for personal and government identification documents. It emphasized the importance of two unique characteristics of the PhenoStor system that were particularly of interest to government agencies concerned with increases in identity theft: A high level of overall protection against unwanted copying, access, or manipulation; and improvements in storage capacity and data transfer efficiency.[28]

The PhenoStor data storage system turned out to be a great success. Developed within 24 months by 40 Bayer employees, it was rated the best security product of 2006 in the access control category by Germany's renowned security magazine "Detektor."[29] The new system broke ground in the areas of counterfeit protection, data protection and data security. When Bayer challenged physicists at Munster University to try to hack into the system, the academics were unable to overcome the increased security of the system.[30] Bayer Innovation went on to develop a range of PhenoStor products, including writing and reading equipment that combined holographic smart card technology with biometric detection and software.[31] Although Bayer had approached PhenoStor as a means to secure medical data, such as prescriptions, it was also a platform technology that had the potential to expand into a wide range of applications.[32]

The PhenoStor®card: The Data are Stored in the Orange Strip

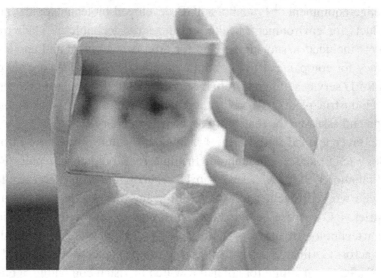

Source: "Keeping a Keen Eye on Security." *The Bayer Scientific Magazine*. Bayer AG, November 23, 2010. Web. December 28, 2010. <http://www.research.bayer.com/edition_17/Data_security_with_holograms.aspx>. Accessed on December 2010.

Card reader

Source: *PHENOSTOR — Access the Future*. PhenoStor. Web. December 28, 2010. http://www.phenostor.de/ english/pages/applications.htm. Accessed on December 2010.

The versatile field for PhenoStor applications:

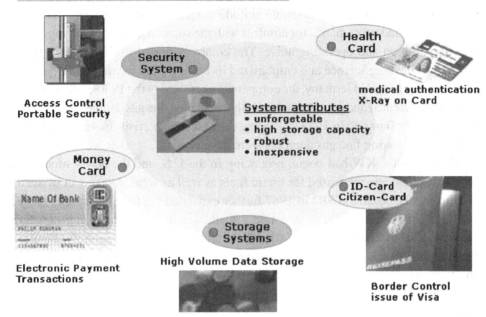

Security System

Access Control Portable Security

Health Card

medical authentication
X-Ray on Card

System attributes
• unforgetable
• high storage capacity
• robust
• inexpensive

Money Card

Name Of Bank

Electronic Payment Transactions

Storage Systems

High Volume Data Storage

ID-Card Citizen-Card

Border Control issue of Visa

Source: *PHENOSTOR — Access the Future*. PhenoStor. Web. December 28, 2010. http://www.phenostor.de/ english/pages/applications.htm. Accessed on December 2010.

Kutzner–Weber: An Advancement in Home Heating

Flue gas systems were used all over Germany to heat houses in winter. Flue gas systems relied on ducts to remove waste gasses and smoke created by gas or oil-fired flame heaters. Turbulent air currents generated by the blower and the burning flame produce a low frequency vibration and the resulting resonance could then be heard as a deep hum coming from the exhaust vent or mouth of the chimney.[33] Flu gas hum disturbed the peace of many German neighborhoods and the disputes between neighbors could make it all the way to court.

Traditionally, the hum had been dampened using a bulky porous flue gas silencer. For houses that did not have the space required for a porous flue gas silencer, installation could be expensive or impossible. German producers of flue gas dampers were trying instead to develop a smaller, active system for damping the low frequency sounds emitted by the flue gas system. Yet any active damping system would have sensitive components that would need to be protected from high temperatures and condensation emitted from the heating devices.[34] It would also have to be inexpensive enough to be affordable by German families.

Kutzner–Weber (KW) was a major German player in the flue gas engineering business. It adopted a responsible attitude toward the natural environment that balanced the modern demands for comfort with the societal goals of reducing atmospheric pollution and operating noise. The company prided itself on being at the forefront of heating science and emphasized its cutting-edge technologies.[35] Headquartered in Maisach, Germany, the company was created in the 1930s, when Werner Diermayer invented and patented a thermally controlled flue gas damper marketed as the Diermayer Damper. In 1973, following the first energy crisis, more applications of the energy-saving flue gas dampers were developed.

By the 1980s, KW had begun producing in the U.S. and the newly motorized Diermayer dampers were used for liquid fuels as well as solid. A takeover of Servo Instruments Deutschland SID in 1987 further expanded the flue gas damper range. The German company sold its first flue gas silencer in 1988, becoming a leading provider of silencers in 1999. In 2001, KW teamed up with the Fraunhofer Institute for Building Physics (IBP) in Stuttgart to try to tackle the technical problems of an efficient silencer.[36] This license partnership between KW and Fraunhofer IBP initiated work on the development of integrated solutions for the boiler and flue gas industry.[37]

Fraunhofer (IBP) work in R&D, testing, demonstration and consulting in all fields of building physics. Areas it studied included energy conservation, indoor climate, emissions of building materials and preservation of buildings and historical monuments. The institute also developed new building materials, components and systems. Critically for KW, IBP also specialized in noise control and the optimization of sound. Fraunhofer IBP conducted research in partnership with a range of private companies — civil engineering, mechanical and plant engineering and architecture — as well as with public planning and licensing authorities and building-research commissioners.[38] IBP was also a member of the Fraunhofer Building Innovation Alliance, a consortium of various Fraunhofer institutes that collectively had the expertise to offer consulting services to construction companies at every stage of the construction cycle. During Alliance projects, Fraunhofer IBP took responsibility for heating, ventilation and solar systems as well as the total energy balance in the building construction process.[39,40]

After learning about a prototype that Fraunhofer IBP had developed for an improved flue gas silencer, KW approached them with the idea of working on a commercial system based on an exclusive licensing partnership. The system would provide KW with the support to develop products rapidly and then market them, as well as a new line of products into the future.[41]

The first product of the joint venture was to be called AKTIV PLUS (AKTIV+). The idea was to use a loudspeaker, microphone and amplifier to create a noise-cancelling acoustic barrier that would prevent noise from escaping the burner. The benefits of this system lay in its compactness: It was only half a meter in length, compared to the conventional silencer, which was around three meters long. Its small size meant AKTIV+ could be installed virtually anywhere and it promised to operate virtually maintenance free. It was also entirely sealed off from the corrosive exhaust gas and worked equally well in high or lowpressure environments. A special heat-resistant film protecting the system allowed it to operate in temperatures up to 200° Celsius.[42] The AKTIV+ system was effective in absorbing sound in frequencies ranging from 125 to 2,000 Hz.

A second product to come out of the partnership was a filter for low-frequency noise, in the 63–80 Hz range. A specially-designed computer program calculated the optimal performance of the silencers from the temperature and flow rate of the system it was silencing. These low-frequency silencers, developed in collaboration with Fraunhofer IBP, could be applied to combined heat and power plants whose unpleasant humming sounds once disrupted the surrounding environment.[43] The robust design of these low-frequency silencers made them durable and particularly long lasting.

Various other silencers were also developed over time, including passive silencers made of mineral fiber porous sound absorbers, which were ideal for medium to high frequencies in regular combustion heating appliances. Different types of mineral fibers were acoustically tested in the Fraunhofer IBP labs to find the optimum mineral fiber for the technology.[44] Other patent-protected technologies produced from the partnership included slot absorbers (ideal for complicated spaces within boilers), chimney top silencers and passive silencers for larger plants.[45]

The partnership between Fraunhofer IBP and KW also allowed KW to offer its customers throughout Germany, Austria, Hungary and Switzerland a service for measuring noise levels. All noise-measurement partners with which KW worked were required to attend training by Fraunhofer IBP.[46]

Each of the silencing systems developed in the collaboration between KW and Fraunhofer IBP were patent protected. Since the start of partnership, KW's share of sales generated with flue gas silencers increased from 6% to 23%. In addition, the company was able to enter new markets with its latest products, increasing its market share in its specific segment of home heating systems from 5% to 20%. Up to the point this case was written, the partnership between KW and Fraunhofer IBP continued to keep up to date with the latest scientific findings, periodically adding new product families. In addition, KW was able to maintain its unique selling point of improving the natural environments of communities and neighborhoods across Europe could enjoy quieter winters.[47]

AKTIV + Low-Frequency Silencers

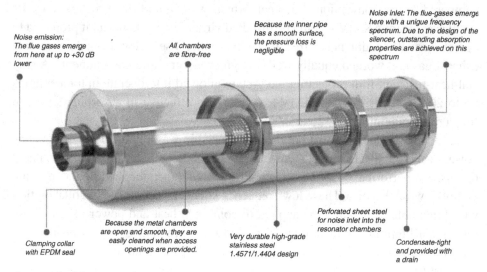

Noise emission:
The flue gases emerge
from here at up to +30 dB
lower

All chambers
are fibre-free

Because the inner pipe
has a smooth surface,
the pressure loss is
negligible

Noise inlet: The flue-gases emerge
here with a unigue frequency
spectrum. Due to the design of the
silencer, outstanding absorption
properties are achieved on this
spectrum

Clamping collar
with EPDM seal

Because the metal chambers
are open and smooth, they are
easily cleaned when access
openings are provided.

Very durable high-grade
stainless steel
1.4571/1.4404 design

Perforated sheet steel
for noise inlet into the
resonator chambers

Condensate-tight
and provided with
a drain

Source: *The Silencer Product Range*. Maisach, Germany: Kutzner + Weber. p. 9.

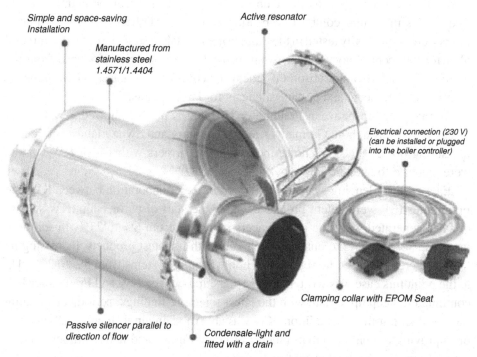

Simple and space-saving
Installation

Manufactured from
stainless steel
1.4571/1.4404

Active resonator

Electrical connection (230 V)
(can be installed or plugged
into the boiler controller)

Passive silencer parallel to
direction of flow

Condensale-light and
fitted with a drain

Clamping collar with EPOM Seat

Source: *The Silencer Product Range*. Maisach, Germany: Kutzner + Weber. p. 11.

Three alternatives with flue gas damper control for solid fuels:

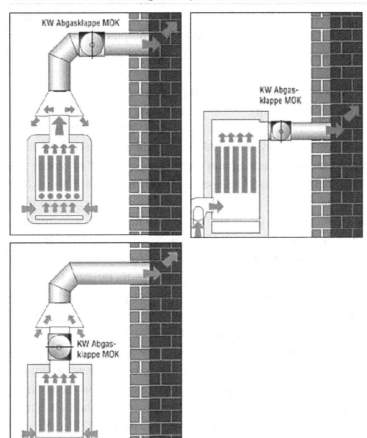

Source: "Kutzner Weber: Diermayer Dampers, Motorised." Kutzner Weber: Home. Web. 5 Jan 2011. <http://www.kutzner-weber.de/gb/products/flue-gas-dampers/diermayer-dampers-motorised.html>.

LED: Lighting for the New Century

It was prevalent in the car headlights and street lamps illuminating highways across the world. It lit up office buildings and personal flat-screen TVs. It brightened up bill-boards and brought color to artistic architectural displays. The light-emitting diode, more commonly known as the LED, forever changed the way society interacted with light. LED technology had been steadily improving for over 30 years and its low power allowed it to be particularly conducive to solar power, making it a friend of the environmentally conscious.[48] In addition, it required little maintenance, was more reliable than conventional counterparts and did not burn or emit dangerous gases.[49]

In technical terms, LED was the first visible-spectrum semiconductor laser.[50] It was used to read CD and DVD disks, to illuminate alarm clocks, traffic lights and billboards, and to transmit signals to electronic equipment from remote controls. It was also used increasingly as backlighting for multicolored displays. Because of its longevity and efficiency, the LED was a potential green alternative to conventional lighting. It was considered the future of professional and industrial lighting, replacing fluorescent lighting.[51]

The LED was invented in 1929 by a little-known Russian scientist, Oleg Vladimirovich Losev. Losev observed that a light was emitted when current was passed through zinc oxide and silicon carbide crystal rectifier diodes used in radio receivers. He quickly realized the potential for this invention to relay telegraphic and telephone communications at unprecedented speeds. Because of the siege in his city, Leningrad, Losev was never able to publish his findings.[52] Instead, American Nick Holonyak Jr. would be credited with discovery of the LED in 1962.

Around the 1980s, Fraunhofer began investing significant into refining LED technology. An initial problem with the LED was its brightness. Although it was able to produce small amounts of light, it did not produce sufficient light output to take the place of fluorescent bulbs. This changed in 2007, when the Fraunhofer Institute for Applied Optics and Precision Engineering (IOF) teamed up with scientists from OSRAM Opto Semiconductors to create a thin-film LED that was at once affordable, energy efficient, and bright enough to rival fluorescent light. Fraunhofer IOF specialized in optical systems technology, focusing on the control of light.[53] Fraunhofer IOF researchers discovered a two-part lens through which the LED could shine its brightest. By 2008, these new models of LED were being used in car headlamps.[54]

Another problem with the LED was that high brightness LEDs for general lighting or backlighting of displays overheated easily. At the Fraunhofer Institute for Reliability and Microintegration (IZM), researchers developed technologies that were resistant to high temperatures in order to address this problem. Fraunhofer IZM also specialized in system integration and the packaging of electronic products. Using this knowledge, Fraunhofer IZM worked to improve the assembly process for LED chips in order to optimize package design and production speed. The new assembly allowed Fraunhofer IZM to assemble LED displays with outstanding color accuracy, even at large dimensions.[55]

Fraunhofer IZM also worked with an Israeli company called Oree to develop improved backlight units for flat screen televisions. With LED, LCD screens had better color accuracy and were greater energy efficient. Whereas the fluorescent-style backlighting on traditional LCD televisions altered over time, the LED did not show any evidence of color degradation.

As usage of the LED grew, there was greater demand to improve the product. Fraunhofer IZM contracted with chip and module manufacturers in the early 2000s in Germany, around Europe and in the U.S. to address these issues.[56] These contracts focused mainly on optimization via process transfer and ranged from 3,000 euro to 100,000 euro. Fraunhofer IZM also worked on some larger, publicly funded projects, with investments ranging from 600,000 euro to 800,000 euro.[57]

One particular Fraunhofer IZM project was an application of the LED for general lighting. The idea was to create a 6×6 cm flat panel that was thin, cheap and energy-efficient, to be used for office lighting. The panel would have a high coloring index and it would be brighter and softer than conventional lighting, with the goal of improving the productivity of people in the office. The Fraunhofer Institute for Applied Solid State Physics (IAF) was also involved in this project. Fraunhofer IAF institute developed and produced micro- and optoelectronic circuits and systems for mobile communications networks and optical data transfer.[58] The two institutes collaborated with OSRAM, the University of Ulm and several other small companies on the project. Both Fraunhofer institutes involved in the project had their own budget, but coordinated their technology to ensure that the scientists at Fraunhofer IZM would be able to assemble the LED die that the Fraunhofer IAF scientists developed.[59]

Another problem with LED technology was the difficulty of combining various colors to make pure white light. Fraunhofer IAF tackled this problem successfully by developing a single-chip LED that produced white light by combining the chip's natural blue light with a layer of fluorescent yellow light. Now that LEDs could produce white light in a much simpler way, they became a more efficient and versatile choice.[60]

LED was brought to industry with the help of the Fraunhofer Institute for Solar Energy Systems (ISE), which was committed to developing ways to supply energy in an efficient and environmentally sound way. As part of this commitment, the institute offered services to businesses to analyze their energy and lighting situations. Not only did the institute offer to provide information on lighting systems and LED technology, it provided the service of calculating the optimal system layout for energy-efficient lighting. It would then develop the optimal lighting system in its laboratories and, once implemented at the client site, check back periodically to measure any changes or developments in the system.[61]

By the early 2000s, LED had become a serious competitor for halogen and standard incandescent light bulbs. LED bulbs were able to illuminate more with less power, making it conducive to solar powered systems that operated with a limited energy supply. LED bulbs were used for outdoor lighting, path lighting and orientation lighting. Its ability to reflect a wide spectrum of colors made it an increasingly popular option for decorative and accent lighting.[62] Fraunhofer IZM consulted with the company that maintained Berlin's street lamps, Braun Schaltgeräte und Service and convinced them to refit the city with LEDs.[63]

LEDs were also increasingly used as the backlight for multicolored digital screens. Samsung Electronics, the world's largest LCD television maker by volume in the early 2000s, reported rapidly growing sales of LED-backlit LCD screens in 2009. These sales were expected to grow fourfold in 2010 alone. LED TVs were thinner, had brighter displays that were visible from more angles and had more brilliant color than conventional LCD televisions, which were lit by cold cathode fluorescent lamps. Samsung planned to introduce its first three-dimensional LED TV in 2010.[64] The Fraunhofer Institute for Applied Polymer Research (IAP) also worked to develop organic light-emitting diodes, or OLEDs, which were adopted for screens on cell phones and mp3 players.[65] In 2010, the LED was used to backlight the screen of the revolutionary iPad, which Apple claimed was its "most advanced technology."[66] By the 2010s, the LED market was expected to exceed U.S. $15 billion.[67]

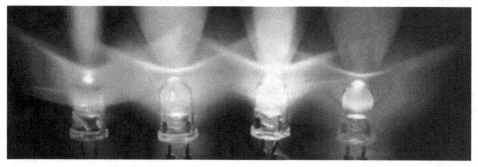

Source: Harlfinger, Julia. *MP3, LEDs Und Co: Innovationen Made by Fraunhofer*. Rep. München: Fraunhofer Gesellschaft. p. 20.

Mp3: A Revolution in Music Consumption

By the mid-2000s, the mp3 audio format had become one of the most widely used technologies on the Internet. With its high level of compression without apparent loss in sound quality, the mp3 shaped a new wave of audio technology use that drove CDs, tapes and other conventional forms of music consumption into obscurity. The use of iPods and other popular mp3 players replaced CD players and Walkmans for music consumers, while many popular music artists skipped directly to publishing their music online in the form of mp3s rather than producing CDs. The mp3 also altered the academic landscape, allowing professors to post recordings of lectures online and universities to move to distance-learning formats accessible over the internet.

The MPEG-1/MPEG-2 Layer 3, more commonly known as the mp3, was a perceptual audio coding algorithm that compressed audio files with a "lossy" technique.[68] In other words, the mp3 was a technology used to store digital audio by compressing the size of a sound file with minimal or no reduction to the audio quality.[69] While a raw audio file on a CD would consume around 10 megabytes (MB) of space, the same audio material would only take up 1 MB of space in an mp3 file. The mp3 was designed to analyze patterns in the audio stream and compare them to models of human hearing. Many components in music were inaudible to the human ear and the mp3 would discard large amounts of this information, leaving only the data necessary to maintain intelligible signal.[70] The resultant audio file could be as small as around one-tenth of the original audio data, while maintaining a similar level of quality.[71] The mp3-file was unique in that it was specially created to be compatible with all current and future digital audio players, and all old hardware and software devices could play mp3-files made with the most recent software.[72]

The technological capabilities that later led to the development of the mp3 format began at Fraunhofer in the 1970s when researchers were searching for a way to transmit music over a digital phone line. The first milestone was reached in 1979, when the first digital signal processer capable of audio compression was created. In the early 1980s, Karlheinz Brandenburg, a doctoral graduate from Germany's University of Erlangen-Nuremberg, began working with scientists at the Fraunhofer Institute for Integrated Circuits (IIS) on developing a way to compress audio files while maintaining the quality of the original sound data. Established in 1985, Fraunhofer IIS specialized in contract research and development for industry and public authorities. Researchers at IIS specialized in developing microelectronic systems and devices as well as wireless communication systems and technologies for satellite navigation and industrial automation.[73]

Brandenburg first developed the OCF (Optimum Coding in the Frequency Domain) algorithm in 1989. A core group of around 10–15 people, including Fraunhofer researchers and affiliated students at the University of Erlangen-Nuremberg who were working on thesis research, helped with the development of the technology.[74] With the help of private partners AT&T and Thomson, along with contributions from Hannover University, the OCF codec evolved into the powerful new algorithm called ASPEC (Adaptive Spectral Perceptual Entropy Coding).[75] At the time, Fraunhofer scientists were competing with many other groups of researchers around Germany and abroad looking to find similar solutions to audio compression. The Motion Picture Experts Group (MPEG) of ISO, the body that set the standards for audio compression, received 14 proposals for audio coding at the time.[76]

After several formal tests, MPEG suggested a family of three layers of audio coding schemes based on ASPEC and another algorithm developed by Philips, an international electronics company that specialized in lighting, healthcare and consumer lifestyle and other companies.[77] Layer 3, developed by Fraunhofer, was the most complex of the three.

The technology was given its official name of "mp3" in 1995.[78] It was initially implemented solely for professional broadcast equipment. Fraunhofer produced and sold studio equipment that was used to transmit music successfully via Integrated Services Digital Network (ISDN) between broadcasting studios.[79] To help boost the popularity of Layer 3 over the other layers in the family, Fraunhofer built a prototype of a portable music player based on the mp3. The Fraunhofer marketing team ensured that engineers had booths at trade shows that demonstrated the capabilities of the mp3. Fraunhofer began selling mp3 software over the Internet just as PCs became fast enough to encode and decode mp3 files efficiently and computer memory became much more affordable.[80]

Catastrophe struck when a student in Australia hacked the online software and distributed it for free on the Internet. With a business model based on selling the software online, Fraunhofer's success with the mp3 was jeopardized. However, as the free software helped the popularity of the mp3 explode, Fraunhofer was eventually able to reap the rewards of the software.[81] By 1997, Microsoft introduced a version of Windows Media Player that supported mp3 files. The first portable mp3 devices were introduced in 1998, and since then the usage of mp3 players and files has continued to increase.[82]

After the mp3 format was developed, medium-sized companies in Germany began utilizing the new technology by creating products with mp3 capabilities. In 1993, the German public transportation system began using mp3 files for passenger information announcements using a newly developed technology from Meister Electronic GmbH in Cologne.[83] By 1994, the German company Intermetall/Micronas created the first mp3 decoder chip that could be used in mobile mp3 players. As of 2009, the mp3 secured over 10,000 jobs and provided over 300 million euros in annual tax revenues for Germany.[84] Fraunhofer held a number of patents for mp3 coding and decoding, so companies had to obtain a license from Fraunhofer in order to use the mp3 algorithm.[85]

The mp3 gave way to the creation of many peer-to-peer (P2P) networks primarily for sharing music. These networks were different from typical client-server models, in which information was centralized at one server. P2P networks allowed users to directly access files in every other computer on each network. Napster, created by two college students in 1999, was one of the first widely used P2P networks. However, Napster was not purely a P2P network; all of the shared files were indexed on a centralized server. This led to Napster's downfall in 2001, when parties in the record industry could easily target Napster for the sharing of tens of millions of copyrighted music files without permissions. Despite the short life of Napster, sharing music files in mp3 format via the Internet continued.[86] In 1999, Fraunhofer teamed up with the Recording Industry Association to develop an industry-wide copyright strategy called the Secure Digital Music Initiative in an effort to prevent the spread of pirating.[87]

By 2009, the mp3 had revolutionized the way people play, share and listen to music. Artists were able to publish their own music without the aid of industry professionals and listeners were now able to store large volumes of music on their computers and sort through the files very quickly.[88] The Internet allowed music consumers to record, transfer and listen to mp3 files by the hundreds of thousands daily.[89] Because of the mp3, iPods and other mp3 devices replaced CD players as the primary ways in which people consumed music. The mp3 provided a cheap, convenient way to record, share and listen to music to anyone with a computer. According to Fraunhofer IIS, the mp3 became the "de facto standard for digital music."[90]

Until the standardization of the mp3 format, the money used to develop this audio coding system came from the government. Once the mp3 was standardized and there was room for further developments, money began coming in from industry.[91] Royalty payments from mp3 patents generated tens of millions of euros for Fraunhofer alone and hundreds of millions of computers and devices with mp3 capability were used worldwide.[92] By the late 2000s, Fraunhofer was reporting yearly revenues of more than 50 million euros from mp3 licensing income. As Fraunhofer put it, the mp3 created a "worldwide cultural phenomenon."[93]

In 1997, Fraunhofer pushed the limits of audio compression by releasing Advanced Audio Coding (MPEG-2 AAC), an advanced spinoff of the mp3 that allowed for up to 48 simultaneous channels of surround sound. This was a marked improvement from the usual two channels that were previously used for stereo surround sound. Fraunhofer developed the MPEG-2 AAC in conjunction with AT&T Corp, Dolby and Sony Corp.[94] The new technology allowed even more compression and better sound quality than the mp3. After the success of the mp3, Fraunhofer began expanding upon audio coding technology in other directions, including video coding (at the Fraunhofer Heinrich Hertz Institute) and 3D audio (Fraunhofer IIS).[95]

Endnotes

[1] "Environmental Engagement." *Environmentalism*. Salus Export. Web. 22 Dec. 2010. <http://www.salus-haus.com/4/0/content.html>.

[2] "History." *The Salus Story*. Salus Export. Web. 22 Dec. 2010. <http://www.salus-haus.com/42/3/content.html>.

[3] Salus had previously worked with Fraunhofer on a much smaller scale, but this was the first time they collaborated on such a big project. Thomas Günther. Project Manager at Salus. Phone call, 30 December 2010.

4 Kemlein-Schiller, Hark. *Succeeding with Fraunhofer: Cooperating for the Future* (Munchen: Fraunhofer Gesellschaft, 2008), p. 12.

5 Vieth, Kai-Uwe. *FoodControl: For a Better Food Quality* (Karlsruhe: Fraunhofer Institute of Optronics, 2005).

6 Greither, Otto. *General Environmental Declaration 2006–2009*. Rep. Bruchmuhl: Salus-Haus, 2009. p. 5.

7 *About*. Fraunhofer IOSB. Web. December 22, 2010. <http://www.iosb.fraunhofer.de/servlet/ is/6974/>.

8 *MRD — Products and Services*. Fraunhofer IOSB. Web. December 22, 2010. <http://www.iosb.fraunhofer.de/ servlet/is/4811/>.

9 *Ibid.*

10 Kemlein-Schiller, Hark. *Succeeding with Fraunhofer: Cooperating for the Future*. Munchen: Fraunhofer Gesellschaft, 2008. Page 12.

11 Thomas Günther. Project Manager at Salus. Phone call, December 30, 2010.

12 Thomas Günther. Project Manager at Salus. Phone call, December 30, 2010.

13 Kemlein-Schiller, Hark. *Succeeding with Fraunhofer: Cooperating for the Future* (Munchen: Fraunhofer Gesellschaft, 2008). p. 5.

14 Keeping a keen eye on security. *Encryption*. Page 88. http://www.research.bayer.com/edition_17/Data_security_with_holograms.aspx

15 Schäfer, Jörg. *Annual Report 2009*. Rep. Leverkusen, Germany: Bayer, 2009. p.e 3.

16 "The Bayer Innovation GmbH." *Bayer Innovation — Homepage*. Bayer, March 24, 2010. Web. December 23, 2010. <http://www.bayer-innovation.com/en/homepage.aspx>.

17 Keeping a keen eye on security, p. 89.

18 "Fraunhofer IPM Welcome." *Fraunhofer IPM Willkommen*. Nov. 2010. Web. December 24, 2010. <http://www.ipm.fraunhofer.de/fhg/ipm_en/index.jsp>.

19 www.research.bayer.com/edition_17/17_encryption.pdfx.

20 Keeping a keen eye on security, p. 89.

21 "Fraunhofer IPM ID-Cards." *Fraunhofer IPM Willkommen*. Nov. 2010. Web. 24 Dec. 2010. <http://www.ipm.fraunhofer.de/fhg/ipm_en/solutions_services/security/faelschungssicherheit/id_karten/index.jsp>.

22 "Pioneers in Polymers." *Fraunhofer IAP*. 2010. Web 24 Dec. 2010. <http://www.pioneers-in-polymers.com/>.

23 http://bayern-innovativ.de/1fff7e5c-3b80-1a68-55fc-e523b03ec2ad?Edition=en&PP=d9041d41-dbbb-2f3a-b232-082697213771

24 Succeeding with Fraunhofer, p. 5.

25 "The Institute – Fraunhofer Institute for Secure Information Technology." *Fraunhofer-SIT — Fraunhofer-Institut Für Sichere Informationstechnologie*. 2010. Web. 26 Dec. 2010. <http://www.sit.fraunhofer.de/en/das_institut/>.

26 "Institut." *Fraunhofer IGD*. 2010. Web. 26 Dec. 2010. <http://www.igd.fraunhofer.de/en/Institut>.

27 Succeeding with Fraunhofer, p. 5.

28 Henniger, Olaf, Dirk Scheuermann, and Ulrich Waldmann. *Usability of Holographic Data Storage Technology for Biometric Data in Governmental ID Documents*. Rep. Darmstadt, Germany: Fraunhofer Institute for Secure Information Technology SIT, 2006. Page iii.

29 Succeeding with Fraunhofer, p. 5.

30 *Encryption*, p. 90.

31 New, By Using. "Bosch, Axis and Bayer Innovation — over All Winners of Detektor International Award 2006 | News | AR Media International AB." *Hem | AR Media International AB*. Armedia, November 09, 2006. Web. December 26, 2010. <http://www.armedia.se/en/news_armedianews_print.asp?nid=65>.

32 "Holographic Data Storage Medium Offers Ultimate Security for Passes." *Press Release Distribution Services — WebWire*. WebWire, October 10, 2006. Web. December 27, 2010. <http://www.webwire.com/ViewPressRel.asp? aId=21841>.

33 Zimmermann, Stefan. "Fraunhofer-Gesellschaft — Research News: Muffling Noisy Central Heating Systems." *Muffling Noisy Central Heating Systems*. Feb. 2002. Web. December 30, 2010. <http://www.fraunhofer.de/archiv/presseinfos/pflege.zv.fhg.de/english/press/pi/pi2002/md02_t5.html>.

34 Kemlein-Schiller, Hark. *Succeeding with Fraunhofer: Cooperating for the Future* (Munchen: Fraunhofer Gesellschaft, 2008), p. 9.

35 *The Silencer Product Range*. Maisach, Germany: Kutzner + Weber. p. 3.

36 "Kutzner Weber: Service." *Kutzner Weber*. Web. December 30, 2010. <http://www.kutzner-weber.de/gb/service.html>.

37 "Kutzner Weber: History." *Kutzner Weber*. Web. December 30, 2010. <http://www.kutzner-weber.de/gb/company/history.html>.

38 "About." *Fraunhofer Institute for Building Physics*. Web. December 31, 2010. <http://www.hoki.ibp.fhg.de/>.

39 "Fraunhofer Building Innovation Alliance — Fraunhofer-Gesellschaft." *Fraunhofer-Gesellschaft*. Web. December 31, 2010. <http://www.fraunhofer.de/en/institutes-research-establishments/groups-alliances/building-innovation.jsp>.

40 "IBP – Fraunhofer Building Innovation Alliance." *Fraunhofer-Allianz BAU*. Web. December 31, 2010. <http://www.bau.fraunhofer.de/en/details/IBP/>.

41 Succeeding with Fraunhofer, p. 9.

42 "Fraunhofer-Gesellschaft — Research News: Muffling Noisy Central Heating Systems." *Startseite — Fraunhofer-Gesellschaft*. Web. December 31, 2010. <http://www.fraunhofer.de/archiv/presseinfos/pflege.zv.fhg.de/english/press/pi/pi2002/md02_t5.html>.

43 *The Silencer Product Range*. Maisach, Germany: Kutzner + Weber. p. 8.

44 *Ibid* 12.

45 *Ibid* 15.

46 "Kutzner Weber: Service." *Kutzner Weber: Home*. Web. December 31, 2010. <http://www.kutzner-weber.de/gb/service.html>.

[47] Succeeding with Fraunhofer, p. 9.

[48] "LED Lighting Technology — Fraunhofer ISE." *Willkommen Beim Fraunhofer-Institut Für Solare Energiesysteme ISE — Fraunhofer ISE.* October 21, 2010. Web. January 17. 2011. <http://www.ise.fraunhofer.de/areas-of-business-and-market-areas/applied-optics-and-functional-surfaces/lighting-technology/testing-and-qualifying-lighting-systems/led-lighting-technology>.

[49] Harlfinger, Julia. *MP3, LEDs Und Co: Innovationen Made by Fraunhofer.* Rep. München: Fraunhofer Gesellschaft. p. 18.

[50] Ivan, Moreno, and Sun Ching-Cherng (2008), "Modeling the radiation pattern of LEDs." *Optics Express*, Vol. 16, Issue 3, pp. 1808–1819.

[51] "Winners' Circle: Nick Holonyak, Jr." *Lemelson-MIT Program.* Web. January 28, 2010. <http://web.mit.edu/invent/a-winners/a-holonyak.html>.

[52] "The life and times of the LED — a 100-year history." *Nature Publishing Group* 1 (2007): pp. 189–192.

[53] "Welcome to Fraunhofer Institute for Applied Optics and Precision Engineering." *Fraunhofer IOF.* Oct 2010. Web. 31 Dec. 2010. <http://www.iof.fraunhofer.de/index_e. html>.

[54] Bräuer, Andreas. "Light from crystals." *Research News 1 Topic 7.* Fraunhofer-Gesellschaft, Apr. 2008. Web. January 27, 2010. <http://www.fraunhofer.de/archiv/pi-en-2004-2008/EN/press/pi/2008/01/ResearchNews01 2007Topic7.html>.

[55] "Fraunhofer IZM LED light sources." *Fraunhofer IZM Assembly and Packaging Technologies for Microsystems.* Fraunhofer-Gesellschaft, Apr. 2009. Web. January 27, 2010. <http://www.izm.fraunhofer.de/EN/fue_ergebnisse/system_integration/archiv_2006/LEDLichtquellen.jsp>.

[56] "Fraunhofer IZM Giant flat screens: Color accuracy and energy efficiency thanks to Fraunhofer's LED technology." *Fraunhofer IZM Assembly and Packaging Technologies for Microsystems.* Fraunhofer-Gesellschaft, May 2008. Web. January 27, 2010. <http://www.izm.fraunhofer.de/EN/news_events/news/RiesigeFlachbildschirme farbechtundenergieeffizientdankFraunhoferLEDTechnologie.jsp>.

[57] Jordan, Rafael. Leader of Optical Projects, Fraunhofer IZM. Phone call, January 17, 2011.

[58] "Science for Systems — Fraunhofer Institute for Applied Solid State Physics." *Science for Systems — Fraunhofer-Institut Für Angewandte Festkörperphysik.* Web. 17 Jan. 2011. <http://www.iaf.fraunhofer.de/en/ index.jsp>.

[59] Jordan.

[60] Harlfinger, Julia. *MP3, LEDs Und Co: Innovationen Made by Fraunhofer.* Rep. München: Fraunhofer Gesellschaft. p. 18.

[61] "What we can do for you." *Fraunhofer ISE.* Fraunhofer-Gesellschaft, May 28, 2008. Web. January 27, 2010. <http://www.ise.fraunhofer.de/areas-of-business-and-market-areas/applied-optics-and-functional-surfaces/lighting-technology/testing-and-qualifying-lighting-systems/led-lighting-technology/what-we-can-do-for-you/what-we-can-do-for-you>.

[62] "LED Lighting Technology." *Fraunhofer ISE*. Fraunhofer-Gesellschaft, August 28, 2008. Web. Januray 27, 2010. <http://www.ise.fraunhofer.de/areas-of-business-and-market-areas/ applied-optics-and-functional-surfaces/ lighting-technology/led-lighting-technology>.

[63] Jordan.

[64] Jung-ah, Lee. "Samsung Tops Its Goal For Sales of LED TVs." *New York Times*. January 4, 2010. Web. January 27, 2010.

[65] Harlfinger 23.

[66] "iPad." *Apple*. Web. January 27, 2010. <http://www.apple.com>.

[67] "The life and times of the LED — a 100-year history." *Nature Publishing Group* 1 (2007): pp. 189–192.

[68] "MP3: MPEG Audio Layer III." *Fraunhofer IIS*. Sept. 2007. Web. 27 Dec. 2009. <http://web.archive.org/web/20080124200925/http://www.iis.fraunhofer.de/EN/bf/amm/projects/mp3/index.jsp>.

[69] "Mp3licensing.com — About mp3." *Mp3licensing.com — Home*. 2009. Web. December 26, 2009. <http://www.mp3licensing.com/mp3/index.html>.

[70] "Fraunhofer IIS mp3 Working principle." *How Does Perceptual Audio Coding Work?* Dec. 2009. Web. December 26, 2009. <http://www.iis.fraunhofer.de/EN/bf/amm/products/mp3/mp3workprinc.jsp>.

[71] Hacker, Scot. *MP3 The Definitive Guide*. North Mankato: O'Reilly Media, Inc., 2000. Print. p. 2.

[72] "Mp3licensing.com — About mp3." *Mp3licensing.com — Home*. 2009. Web. December 26, 2009. <http://www.mp3licensing.com/mp3/index.html>.

[73] "About us." *Fraunhofer Institute for Integrated Circuits IIS*. 2010. Web. 31 Dec. 2010. <http://www.iis.fraunhofer.de/en/profil/>.

[74] Brandenburg, Karlheinz. Phone Call. January 11, 2011.

[75] Rose, Matthias. Head of Marketing Communications. Phone Call. 26 January 2011.

[76] Rose.

[77] "Philips — Businesses." *Home — Royal Philips*. October 19, 2010. Web. January 13, 2011. <http://www.usa.philips.com/about/company/businesses/index.page>.

[78] The History of MP3 — The Fraunhofer IIS.mp3. Fraunhofer IIS, 2007. MP3.

[79] The History of MP3 — The Fraunhofer IIS.mp3. Fraunhofer IIS, 2007. MP3.

[80] Rose, Matthias. Head of Marketing Communications. Fraunhofer Institute for Integrated Circuits IIS. Email Correspondence.

[81] Rose.

[82] Ewing, Jack. "How MP3 Was Born." *Business Week* (2007). Print.

[83] "Fraunhofer IIS MP3 — Eine deutsche Erfolgsgeschichte." *1993 — MP3 Announcements at Public Transport Stops*. July 2009. Web. December 26, 2009. <http://www.iis.fraunhofer.de/EN/bf/amm/products/mp3/mp3history/ erfolgsgeschichte.jsp>.

[84] The History of MP3 — The Fraunhofer IIS.mp3. Fraunhofer IIS, 2007. MP3.

[85] Katz, David J. *Embedded media processing*. Boston: Elsevier/Newnes, 2005. Print. p. 183.

[86] Katz, Mark. *Capturing sound: How technology has changed music* (University of California, 2004). Print, pp. 161–162.

[87] Schmid p. 2.

[88] Hacker 1.

[89] Hacker, Scot. *MP3 The Definitive Guide*. North Mankato: O'Reilly Media, Inc., 2000. Print. Abstract.

[90] The History of MP3 — The Fraunhofer IIS.mp3. Fraunhofer IIS, 2007. MP3.

[91] Brandenburg.

[92] Ewing.

[93] The History of MP3 — The Fraunhofer IIS.mp3. Fraunhofer IIS, 2007. MP3.

[94] Schmid, John. "German Creators of MP3 March to Different Tune - NYTimes.com." *The New York Times — Breaking News, World News & Multimedia*. November 05, 2001. Web. January 05, 2011. <http://www.nytimes.com/2001/11/ 05/business/worldbusiness/05iht-itmp3_ed3_.html>.

[95] Brandenburg.

The Great Moderation, Dead or Alive?

Diego Comin*

On February 20, 2004, Ben Bernanke, Chairman of the Federal Reserve, reflected on a trend that by then had attracted the attention of much of the macroeconomics profession: "One of the most striking features of the economic landscape over the past 20 years or so has been a substantial decline in macroeconomic volatility."[1] This stability was very significant and pervasive across both developed and developing countries. The variability of quarterly growth real output (as measured by its standard deviation) [in the U.S.] had declined by half since the mid-1980s, while the variability of quarterly inflation has declined by about two thirds.[2] Several writers on the topic have dubbed this decline in aggregate volatility "the Great Moderation."

According to Bernanke, "reduced macroeconomic volatility has numerous benefits. Lower volatility of inflation improves market functioning, makes economic planning easier, and reduces the resources devoted to hedging inflation risks. Lower volatility of output tends to imply more stable employment and a reduction in the extent of economic uncertainty confronting households and firms. The reduction in the volatility of output is also closely associated with the fact that recessions have become less frequent and less severe."

Or at least that is what had occurred until the so-called "Great Recession" that hit the U.S. and many other countries around the end of 2007 or the beginning of 2008. During the following 18 months of recession, U.S. GDP contracted by 4.1%.

*Reprinted with permission of Harvard Business School Publishing.
The Great Moderation, Dead or Alive 709-023.
This case was prepared by Professor Diego Comin.

This was the longest recession and the largest GDP contraction in the U.S. since the Great Depression.

The 2007–2009 recession gave ammunition to old critics of the Great Moderation while also fueling new critiques of the theory. Some went even further and questioned the possibility of a persistent decline in aggregate volatility. The arguments differed in their specifics but all implied that in periods of economic stability, agents took actions that planted the seeds for future instability.[3]

To settle this debate it was necessary to explore some questions: What caused the Great Moderation? Did the Moderation end with the Great Recession? What lessons could these 60 years of business-cycle history teach us about the amplitude of business-cycle fluctuations in the coming 60 years?

The Macroeconomic Facts

Exhibit 1 displays the annual growth rate of GDP in the U.S. between 1930 and 2010. It is clear that over the last 25 years fluctuations in GDP growth have become more muted. Researchers have debated whether the moderation is best characterized by a secular trend or by a few discrete changes in aggregate volatility. Regardless of this debate, it is clear that since around 1984 it has been harder to observe large deviations from the average growth rate.

To formalize this intuition, we measure the volatility of the economy at year "t" by computing the standard deviation of "T" consecutive annual growth rates of GDP

Exhibit 1.   Annual Growth of Real GDP in the U.S.

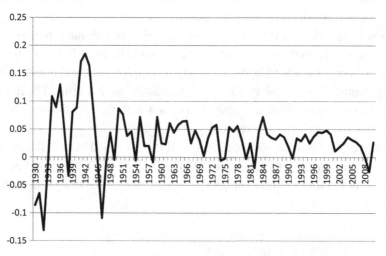

Source: Compiled by author using data from Bureau of Economic Analysis (BEA), www.bea.gov, accessed January 2011.

Exhibit 2a. Volatility of Real GDP in the U.S.

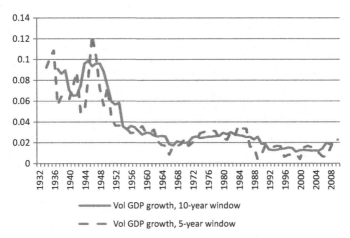

—————— Vol GDP growth, 10-year window

– – – Vol GDP growth, 5-year window

Source: Compiled by author using data from www.bea.gov, accessed January 2011.

Note: Ten-year centered rolling windows of standard deviations of growth rates.

centered around year "*t*". By rolling this window, we can measure the evolution of volatility.[4] In **Exhibit 2a** we consider two horizons (T) over which to compute GDP growth volatility: ten and five years. The exhibit illustrates a downward trend in aggregate volatility. The U.S. economy was more volatile before than after World War II. It was also more volatile shortly after the war than later on, and it was more volatile before 1984 than after 1984.[5] The evolution of GDP volatility in **Exhibit 2a** and of other variables used in the note are robust to the length of the windows used to compute volatility. For brevity, I shall report only volatility measures using 10-year windows.

The higher stability of the economy has affected other variables in addition to GDP. **Exhibits 2b–g** plot the evolution of the volatility of growth in hours worked, consumption, investment, labor productivity, total factor productivity (TFP) and the stock market.[6] While most of these variables have experienced stabilization by roughly the same magnitude, the stock market has not stabilized significantly. If anything, it has become more volatile over the last few decades. This observation raises questions about the practice, widespread in the press and accepted by some academics, of predicting the magnitude of upcoming macroeconomic events by looking at the magnitude of stock market fluctuations.

The Great Moderation is not only a U.S. phenomenon. It has been observed in a majority of countries, both developed and developing. **Exhibit 3** plots the volatility in GDP growth during the period 1961–1983 against volatility during the period 1984–2007. If a country is below the 45° line in the graph, it has experienced a decline in volatility; if it is above the line, it has experienced an increase in volatility.

Exhibit 2b.   Volatility of Annual Hours Worked

Source: Compiled by author using data from Bureau of Labor Statistics (BLS), http://bls.gov, accessed January 2011.

Note: Hours worked in the business sector.

Reported as 10-year centered rolling windows of standard deviations of annual growth rates.

The great majority of countries — 63 out of the 88 countries with sufficiently long time series for GDP — have experienced a decline in volatility. **Exhibit 3** also makes it clear that the decline in aggregate volatility has occurred in both developing and developed economies.

The Microeconomic Facts

If the US economy has become more stable, does this mean that individual firms have on average become more stable too? One of the most striking facts about the evolution of volatility in the U.S. is that while the aggregate economy has become more stable, on average, the profits, sales and employment of individual publicly-traded companies have become more volatile (see **Exhibits 4** and **5**).[7-9]

This divergence is possible because the performance of individual firms is mostly driven by factors other than aggregate conditions (i.e. firm-specific factors). An example can illustrate this idea. More competition between firms is likely to lead to higher firm volatility because they face a greater probability of more extreme outcomes such as capturing a new market or losing their own market share. But, to a large extent, one firm's gains are another firm's losses. So, the effect of the higher competition on the volatility of aggregate production is small.[10] Firm specific-factors may therefore increase firm volatility without affecting aggregate volatility.

Exhibit 2c. Volatility of Real Consumption

Source: Compiled by author using data from www.bea.gov, accessed January 2011.

Note: Consumption defined as nondurables and services.

Reported as 10-year centered rolling windows of standard deviations of annual growth rates.

Exhibit 2d. Volatility of Investment

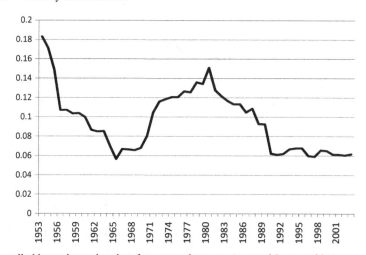

Source: Compiled by author using data from www.bea.gov, accessed January 2011.

Note: Gross Private Fixed Investment reported. Reported as 10-year centered rolling windows of standard deviations of annual growth rates.

Smaller, non-publicly traded companies, instead, seem to have experienced a decline rather than an increase in volatility (see **Exhibit 5**). However, though tempting, it would be wrong to conclude from this fact that the volatility of small companies has driven the decline in aggregate volatility. Firm-specific factors are even

Exhibit 2e.   Volatility of Labor Productivity

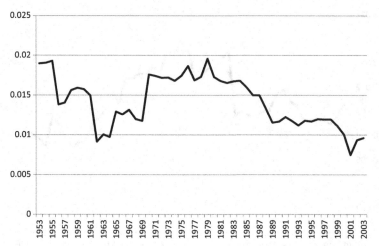

Source: Compiled by author using data from www.bea.gov, accessed January 2011.

Note: Defined as non-farm private business productivity. Reported as 10-year centered rolling windows of standard deviations of annual growth rates.

Exhibit 2f.   Volatility of TFP

Source: Compiled by author using data from www.bea.gov, accessed January 2011.

Note: 10-year centered rolling windows of standard deviations of growth rates.

more important to explaining the performance of small than big companies. Since aggregate measures of performance such as GDP are not affected by these factors, trends in the variability of firm-specific factors that drive the volatility of small and large companies are all but irrelevant for aggregate volatility measures.[11]

Exhibit 2g. Volatility of Stock Returns

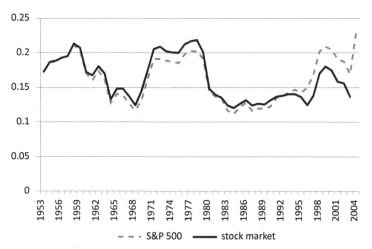

Source: Compiled by author using data from Center for Research in Security Prices (CRSP), www.crsp.gov, accessed January 2011.

Note: 10-year centered rolling windows of standard deviation of growth rates. Return measures include distributions. Stock market includes NYSE/AMEX/NASDAQ.

Exhibit 3. Standard Deviation of Growth Rates of Output over Period

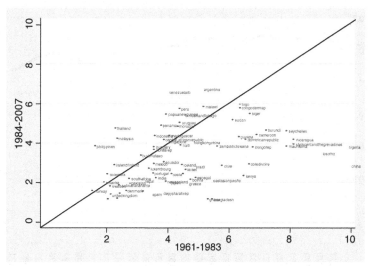

Source: Compiled by author using data from CHAT dataset.[31]

Aggregate volatility is driven by factors that affect the performance of multiple firms simultaneously — those that affect the co-movement in their performance. If the performance of firms becomes less correlated (i.e. more independent), then

Exhibit 4.   Turnover of Industry Leaders

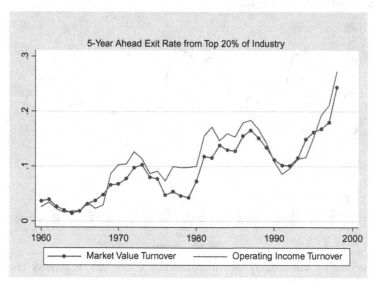

Source: Compiled by author using data from COMPUSTAT and Comin and Philippon (2006).

Note: Probability of dropping from the top 20% (publicly traded companies) in the 2-digit sector based on market value of profits over the next five years.

Exhibit 5.   Evolution of Firm Volatility by Type of Firm

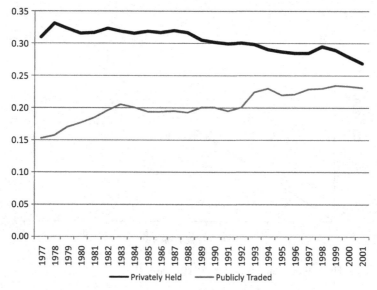

Source: Compiled by author using data from Longitudinal Business Data Base and Davis *et al.*, 2007.

Note: Measures based on centered 10-year rolling windows of employment growth at the firm level aggregated using the employment share.

Exhibit 6. Volatility of Wage Growth for Heads of Households

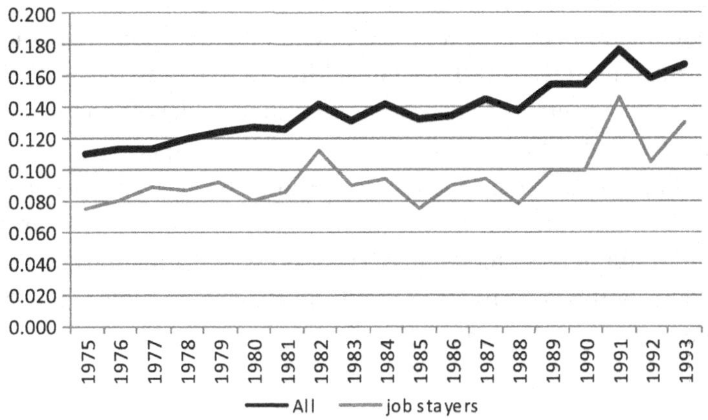

Source: Compiled by author using data from PSID and Comin, Groshen, and Rabin, 2009.

Note: Ten-year centered rolling windows of standard deviations of growth rates. Job stayers defined as workers that did not change jobs over the 10 years.

GDP will be more stable. In sum, the Great Moderation results from the decline in the co-movement of firms' performance.

Though firm-level volatility does not help in accounting for the evolution of aggregate volatility, it may still be important. In particular, it could explain why most people have not perceived the Great Moderation in their daily lives. An interesting puzzle is that, while aggregate volatility has declined, the volatility of the earnings of the average U.S. worker has increased since the 1970s (see **Exhibit 6**). One possible solution to this puzzle could be related to changes in the variability of large-firm performance. As the fortunes of large companies have become more volatile, compensation schemes that condition wages on firm performance have translated into higher earnings volatility. Further, since around 1980 large companies have increasingly conditioned workers' compensation on firm performance.[12] Both of these channels may account for a significant fraction of the increased variability of wages experienced by the average U.S. worker during the last three decades or so.

Some Rationalizations of the Great Moderation

Economic fluctuations are the result of shocks that hit the economy and, in turn, have ripple effects on GDP. For example, an increase in oil prices may reduce the incentives of firms to invest in new capital, and reduced investment will lead to a decline in GDP. To explain the Great Moderation we must follow one of two avenues. Either the shocks that hit the economy are less volatile or the mechanisms that propagate shocks throughout the economy amplify them less.

Understanding what caused the Great Moderation may be far more important that explaining a historical curiosity. If the Great Moderation is just the result of transitory factors such as the absence of volatile external shocks like oil crises comparable to those of the 1970s, then it might not be reasonable to expect its persistence in the near future. If instead the Great Moderation resulted from structural changes that are likely to persist in the future, it would be reasonable to expect that future exogenous impulses will result in more moderated business cycle fluctuations. In that scenario, large recessions will be less likely, though still may be possible if the disturbances that hit the economy are large enough.

Lower Variance in Shocks

The 1970s and early 1980s was a convulsive period from a macroeconomic point of view. The oil shocks and surges in other commodity prices were accompanied by some of the worst recessions since the Great Depression. Some of these shocks were clearly exogenous — caused by non-economic factors such as the 1973 Arab–Israeli War and the ensuing oil crisis.[13] These shocks could have taken place in the 1960s or the 1990s, but instead they took place in the 1970s and early 1980s. Thus, part of the higher instability we observe during this period is due to bad luck. Similarly, part of the higher stability experienced afterwards is due to the lack of large negative shocks such as the oil crises.

Some commentators have adhered to the good luck hypothesis. Robert Reich nicely summarizes this view and its implications: "No one knows for sure what caused the Great Moderation. Some had credited increased sophistication of financial markets and the wisdom of the Federal Reserve Board. Hindsight suggests it was more luck than anything else. Well, folks, it turns out the great moderation was something of a fluke."[14]

One challenge for the Good Luck hypothesis is identifying the disturbances that made the pre-1980s period volatile. Natural candidates to focus on are oil and commodity prices. However, the share of commodities and energy in GDP is relatively small. Hence, though commodity prices may be very volatile, their effect on GDP fluctuations is much more modest. Further, since around 2000, commodity prices have been highly volatile and yet output volatility has remained very low (see **Exhibit 7**). Thus, it is hard to argue that the main driver of the Great Moderation is a decline in the volatility of commodity price shocks. Of course, other shocks might have become more muted across the Great Moderation. However, without a precise identification of the nature and magnitude of the shocks before and during the moderation it is difficult to prove the role of the good luck hypothesis.

Exhibit 7. Commodity Price Volatility

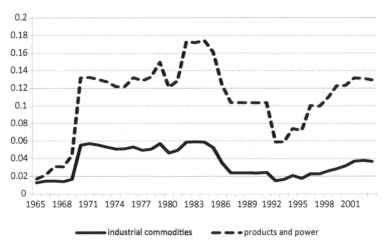

Source: Compiled by author using data from www.bea.gov, accessed January 2011.

Note: 10-year centered rolling windows of standard deviations of growth of commodity prices.

Reduced Amplification

Authors have looked in different places for factors that may have reduced the amplification of exogenous disturbances in the economy. The proposed explanations include changes in sectoral composition, globalization, inventory management, monetary and fiscal policy, demographics and the speed of technology diffusion.

Change in the Sectoral Composition of the Economy: Not all economic sectors are equally volatile. Some, like manufacturing, are more cyclical than others, like services. The share of manufacturing in the economy has declined secularly (27% in 1950, 23% in 1970 and 12% in 2007), while the share of services has increased. Can this shift in the composition of the U.S. economy toward less cyclical services explain the Great Moderation?

Several authors have explored this question and have concluded that the answer is "no". **Exhibit 8a** displays the evolution of the volatility of services. Manufacturing is significantly more volatile than services. But it is also true that both manufacturing and services have become more stable since the early 1980s. Another way of exploring this question points to the same answer. **Exhibit 8b** plots the actual volatility of GDP versus the evolution of a measure of volatility that fixes the shares of services and goods producing sectors at their 1950 level. If the shift in composition were an important driver of the Great Moderation, the second measure of volatility, with fixed shares, should be much flatter than the former. However, both measures evolve quite similarly. Hence, the changing weights of services and goods producing sectors did not contribute much to the Great Moderation.

Exhibit 8a.   Volatility of Value Added in Goods Producing and Services Producing Sector

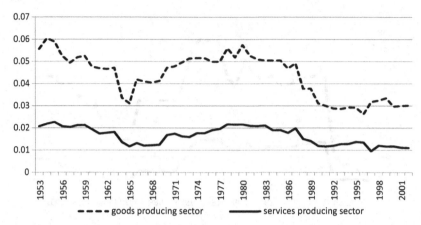

Source: Compiled by author using data from www.bea.gov, accessed January 2011.

Note: Goods Producing sector consists of agriculture, forestry, fishing, and hunting; mining; construction; and manufacturing. Services Producing sector consists of utilities; wholesale trade; retail trade; transportation and warehousing; information; finance and insurance; real estate and rental and leasing; professional, scientific and technical services; management of companies and enterprises; administrative and waste management services; educational services; health care and social assistance; arts, entertainment, and recreation; accommodation and food services; and other services, except government.

Exhibit 8b.   Effect of Sectorial Compositional Change on Aggregate Volatility

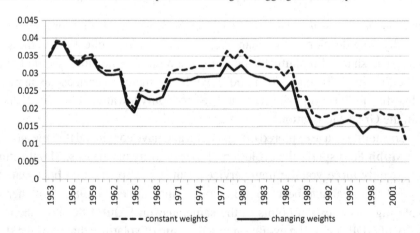

Source: Compiled by author using data from www.bea.gov, accessed January 2011.

Note: Changing weights measures the volatility of GDP. Constant weights measure the volatility of GDP at 1952 shares, holding constant the shares of goods producing and services producing sectors at 1952 levels.

Globalization: The great moderation coincides with the last wave of the globalization movement. The increasing share of goods and services produced overseas allows countries to smooth country-specific shocks and, in this way, experience lower volatility in production. For example, if a hurricane destroys the tomato crop at home, the tomato soup industry can import tomatoes from overseas and reduce the impact of the hurricane.

One shortcoming of globalization explanations is that they do not account for the declining volatility of productivity growth. Productivity growth could just as easily experience large fluctuations in a globalized economy as in a national economy. But **Exhibits 2e** and **f** show that the reduced volatility of productivity growth since 1984 has been as significant as the reduced volatility of output growth. In addition, it is quite natural to think that both are related. After all, productivity is just output per worker. Further, **Exhibit 8a** shows that the decline in aggregate volatility has not been limited to manufacturing goods, which are traded. It has also been driven by services, which are typically not traded.

Inventory Management: The 1970s saw the introduction of new inventory management techniques like the just-in-time method. This method allowed firms to have better control over the stock of inputs and avoid disruptions in production due to bottlenecks. According to Margaret McConnell and Gabriel Perez-Quiros, ironing out these bottlenecks resulted in a smoother firm-level output.[15]

Nevertheless, the view that better inventory management leads to lower output volatility has not been uncontroversial. In an imaginary anticipation of how the world would look like in 2009, Niall Ferguson, from Harvard, wrote: "the more the world came to resemble an intricate, multi-nodal network operating at maximum efficiency — with minimal inventories and just-in-time delivery — the more vulnerable it became to a massive systemic crash."[16]

Another difficulty of this explanation is that it predicts that firms that adopt just-in-time methods will experience larger declines in volatility than firms that do not. However, modern inventory control methods were predominantly adopted by larger companies which, as noted, experienced increases rather than reductions in volatility. Ultimately, to explain the Great Moderation, we need to explain why firm-level fluctuations have become less correlated, not why they have become more or less volatile. The inventory management hypothesis does not answer this question.

Policy: One natural avenue to explain changes in macro volatility is by identifying changes in macroeconomic policy, that is, in fiscal and monetary policy.

Most textbooks describe monetary policy as the actions taken by central banks to affect the money supply, which, in turn, is one of the variables that determine prevailing interest rates in the economy.[17] In the real world, however, many central banks set a target for a reference interest rate and affect the money supply through actions to achieve that target.[18] Naturally, the interest targets set by central banks depend on economic conditions. Two of the variables that best describe economic conditions are output and inflation.

Research by John Taylor and others has shown that "placing a positive weight on both the price level and real output in the interest-rate rule is preferable in most countries" as a way to achieve output and price level stability. "One policy rule that captures the spirit" of this approach is the following:[19]

Federal Funds Rate

$$= \text{Inflation} + 2\% + 0.5 \times (\text{Inflation} - 2\%) - 0.5 \times (\text{Output Gap}) \quad (1)$$

Here, the "Federal Funds Rate" is the interest rate targeted by the Federal Reserve, "Inflation" is the percentage rate of increase of the GDP deflator over the four previous quarters, and the "Output Gap" is (the inverse of) the percent deviation of real GDP from an exponential trend.[20,21]

According to Taylor, "policy rule (1) has the feature that the federal funds rate rises if inflation increases above a target of 2 percent or if real GDP rises above trend GDP. If both the inflation rate and real GDP are on target, then the federal funds rate would equal 4%, or 2% in real terms."[22] Beyond arguing for the normative desirability of what has been known as the Taylor rule, Taylor was the first to see its value as a description of what central banks were doing in practice: "What is perhaps surprising is that this rule fits the actual policy performance during the last few years remarkably well." (See **Exhibit 9a**.) "In this sense the Fed policy has been conducted as if the Fed had been following a policy rule much like the one called for by recent research on policy rules."[23]

Exhibit 9a.   Federal funds Rate and Interest Rate According to Taylor Rule

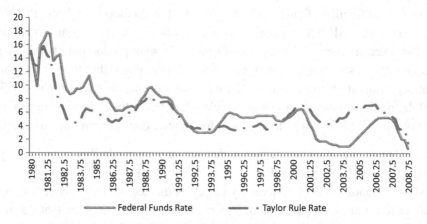

Source: Compiled by author using data from St. Louis Federal Reserve Bank, http://research.stlouisfed.org/fred2/series/FEDFUNDS?cid = 118; www.bea.gov, both accessed January 2011.

Exhibit 9b. Inflation

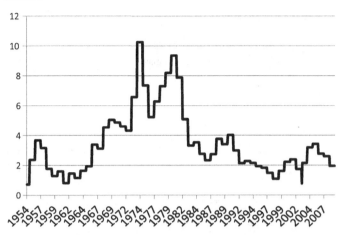

Source: Compiled by author using data from www.bea.gov, accessed January 2011.

Note: Inflation calculated as percentage change in GDP deflator over the calendar year.

A feature of the Taylor rule worth noting is that, according to it, the Fed responds to inflation more than one-to-one. This is a theoretical condition for the stability of inflation.[24] The Fed has not always followed the Taylor principle when conducting monetary policy. According to Richard Clarida, Jordi Gali, and Mark Gertler, only after Paul Volcker's appointment as Fed chairman in 1979 has interest rate policy been so sensitive to changes in inflation.[25] This more pro-active policy has contributed to the stabilization of the economy, these authors argue, because rather than letting inflation reach unacceptable levels and then having to clamp down hard, the Fed has maintained inflation within a narrower range (see **Exhibit 9b**). As a result, the Fed has accommodated more shocks to the U.S. economy, lowering the interest rate more when inflation slowed and raising it more when they accelerated. Naturally, this policy may have led to shocks having smaller effects on GDP volatility.

Some authors disagree with this argument and have claimed that the monetary policy practices adopted by many central banks of developed nations may in fact have been de-stabilizing.[26] According to Richard Clarida: "The focus on price stability, combined with the fact that many central banks had limited or no supervisory role meant, according to this view, that they ignored or failed to incorporate into their rate setting decisions the very real, systemic threats arising from credit and asset price bubbles that had been building during the Great Moderation. By confining monetary policy to only setting a path for short term interest rates, many countries were unable to prevent both booms and busts in real economic activity and inflation resulting from excesses in financial markets."[27] The evolution of U.S. bank liabilities over the last 30 years is clearly consistent with this view (see **Exhibit 9c**).

Exhibit 9c.   The Great Leveraging

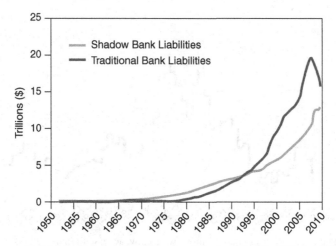

Source: Pozsar, z., T. Adrian. A. Ashcraft, H. Boesky, "Shadow Banking," Federal Reserve Bank of New York, Staff Report no. 458, July 2010.

Exhibit 9d.   Government Expenditures as a share of GDP

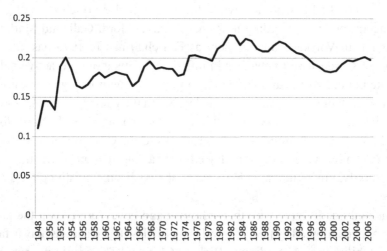

Source: Compiled by author using data from the *Economic Report of the President*, 2008; www.bea.gov, accessed January 2011.

More generally, the overall scope of macroeconomic policy — not just monetary policy but fiscal and even industrial policy — may help stabilize economic downturns. Over the postwar period, automatic stabilizers such as unemployment insurance and Social Security have been put in place. These are international in scope, even in developing countries to some extent. How significant could the effect of fiscal policy be on the moderation of the economy? **Exhibit 9d** plots the evolution of the share of government expenditure in U.S. GDP. It is true that the importance of the government in the economy has increased, but the magnitude of the increase has been quite modest. In the 1950s the share of government spending in GDP was around 18% while in the 2000s it was around 20%.

It could still be the case that the government has more actively conducted expansive fiscal policies in recessions. To measure the counter-cyclicality of fiscal policy we can compute the correlation between GDP growth and the government deficit as a share of GDP. Between 1947 and 1983 this correlation was 3.3%, while after 1984 it increased to 12.7%. This increment goes in the wrong direction to explain the Great Moderation. A counter-cyclical fiscal policy should mean that the deficit rises when GDP falls: the correlation should be negative. That is, the government was conducting less counter-cyclical fiscal policy over the more recent period than early on.

Demographics: A different form of compositional change is in demographics. Over the post-war period, the population of developed economies has become older (see **Exhibit 10**). According to Nir Jaimovich and Henry Siu, this may have implications for the Great Moderation. When a shock hits the economy and lowers real wages, younger workers tend to curtail their labor supply more than older workers. Therefore, as the share of younger workers in the population diminishes, the response of aggregate labor supply to shocks also diminishes. The result is a reduction in aggregate fluctuations.[28] One virtue of this argument is that these demographic changes have occurred across a majority of countries which have experienced the

Exhibit 10. Labor Force Structure

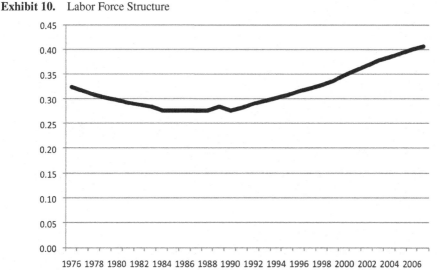

Source: Compiled by author using data from www.bls.gov, accessed January 2011.

Great Moderation. Therefore this explanation has the potential to account for the international dimension of the trend.

Faster Technology Diffusion: One of the most significant changes experienced by the U.S. and many other economies over the last 200 years is that the speed of the diffusion of new technologies has accelerated dramatically. It took 46 years for 25% of U.S. households to have access to electricity. It only took 16 years for 25% of U.S. households to have a computer and seven years for them to have access to the internet (see **Exhibits 11a** and **b**).

According to Diego Comin and Ana Maria Santacreu, this dramatic reduction in adoption lags has had important consequences for the amplification of the shocks that cause the business cycle. First, because there are fewer technologies waiting to be adopted at a given point in time, it leads to smaller fluctuations in the demand for resources necessary to adopting the existing technologies such as capital and labor. Smaller fluctuations in the factors of production stabilize output. Second, a recent study shows that it also leads to smaller fluctuations in the price of investment, hence reducing the volatility of investment.[29]

Since the acceleration in the diffusion of technologies has been documented in virtually all countries, this hypothesis has the potential to explain the international dimension of the Great Moderation.

Exhibit 11a.   The Spread of Products into Households

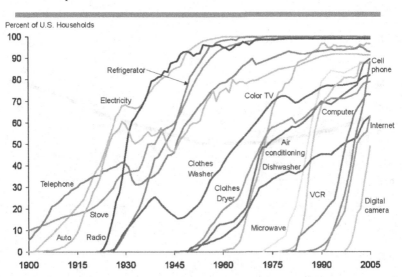

Source: W. Michael Cox and Richard Alm, Federal Reserve Bank of Dallas, 1996 Annual Report, "The Economy at Light Speed." Data updates provided by W. Michael Cox.

Exhibit 11b. Spread of Products to One-Fourth of the Population

Product	Year Invented	Years to Spread
Electricity	1873	46
Telephone	1876	35
Automobile	1886	55
Airplane	1903	64
Radio	1906	22
Television	1926	26
VCR	1952	34
Microwave Oven	1953	30
Personal Computer	1975	16
Cellular Phone	1983	13
Internet	1991	7
DVD Player	1996	6

Source: W. Michael Cox and Richard Alm, Federal Reserve Bank of Dallas, 1996 Annual Report, "The Economy at Light Speed." Data updates provided by W. Michael Cox.

Is It Over?

After the global financial crisis, the question in everybody's mind was whether the economy would restore the Great Moderation regime or initiate a new macroeconomic era characterized by more frequent and deeper recessions. Of course, the debate was far from settled.

One view was summarized by Richard Clarida: "Now and for the foreseeable future, we are in a world in which average outcomes – for growth, inflation, corporate and sovereign defaults, and the investment returns driven by these outcomes — will matter less and less for investors and policymakers. This is because we are in a [...] world in which the distribution of outcomes is flatter and the tails are fatter. As such, the mean of the distribution becomes an observation that is very rarely realized, creating at least three fundamental consequences for investment strategy. [...] Investors had 25 years to get comfortable with the Great Moderation. The sooner they recognize those days are over, the better."

Others believed that the global financial crisis had just been a bad recession. Recessions are times were aggregate volatility increases (see **Exhibit 12**).[30] Therefore, it was natural to observe an increase in aggregate volatility measures during the financial crisis, and to expect a higher volatility for a few years thereafter (see **Exhibit 2a**). After such a period, volatility could be expected to come back to levels similar to those observed in the 1984–2007 period because there had been no

Exhibit 12.   Cyclicality of GDP Volatility

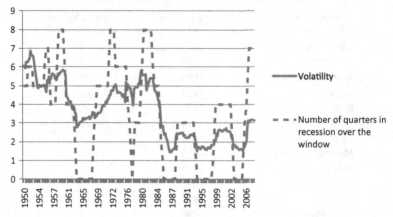

Sources: Author's calculation.

Volatility computed using a 5-year rolling window on quarterly GDP growth.

Cyclicality measured by the number of quarters in the 5-year window that the NBER dates as in a recession.

Correlation between the two series: 0.75. Significant at the one percent level.

significant change in the amplification mechanisms of the economy. An observation that supported this hypothesis was that, during the financial crisis, aggregate volatility had not reached the levels observed during most of the pre-1984 period, despite the Great Recession being the longest and deepest recession since the Second World War.

What would it be: Great stability or volatility? What could we expect in the future?

Endnotes

[1]   It was first noted in 2000 by McConnell and Perez-Quiros (2002), "Output Fluctuations in the United States: What has Changed Since the Early 1980's," *American Economic Review*, Vol. 90(5), pp. 1464–1476.

[2]   Blanchard, Olivier, and John Simon (2001). "The Long and Large Decline in U.S. Output Volatility," *Brookings Papers on Economic Activity*, Vol. 1, pp. 135–164.

[3]   Richard   Clarida: http://www.pimco.com/Pages/WhatHas%E2%80%93andHasNot%E2%80%93BeenLearnedAboutMonetaryPolicyinaLowInflationEnvironmentAReview ofthe2000s.aspx, accessed: January 10, 2011. Niall Ferguson: http://www.niallferguson.com/site/FERG/Templates/ArticleItem.aspx?pageid=198, accessed January 10, 2011.

[4]   Formally, let $g_x(t)$ be the growth rate of variable x between periods $t - 1$ and t; let $\overline{g_{x(t)}}$ be the average of the growth rates in the T period window centered at t. Then the centered

volatility of a T-period rolling window is given by:

$$\sigma(g_x(t)) = \sqrt{\frac{\sum_{\tau=t-\frac{T}{2}}^{t+\frac{T}{2}-1}(g_x(\tau) - \overline{g_{x(t)}})^2}{T}}$$

[5] McConnell and Perez Quiros, *ibid.* and Stock and Watson (2002) estimate that there is a trend break in volatility in the first quarter of 1984. Stock and Watson, "Has the Business Cycle Changed and Why?" NBER Working Paper 9127.

[6] TFP is usually measured as the residual in output growth once we account for changes in the factors of production (typically, labor and capital).

[7] Specifically, these measures are computed by using the volatility measure described above to each company and then averaging firm volatility (for example weighting by employment share or sales share) across all publicly traded companies in a given year.

[8] That is also the case for financial measures of performance such as the rate of return. See Diego Comin (2000), "An Uncertainty-driven Theory of the Productivity Slowdown" Harvard University dissertation.

[9] This trend is not driven by compositional change. That is by a change in the nature of the representative publicly-traded firm. An extensive set of checks to make sure this is not the case have been conducted in two recent articles: Comin and Mulani (2006), "Diverging Trends in Macro and Micro Volatility" review of Economics and Statistics, and Comin and Philippon (2006), "The Rise in Firm-Level Volatility: Causes and Consequences," NBER Macroeconomics Annual 20.

[10] Comin and Philippon (2006), *ibid*, show that one of the most important drivers of the increased volatility of publicly-traded companies is the faster turnover in market positions which in turn results from increased competition faced by these companies.

[11] See Davis, Garmin, Haltiwanger, and Miranda (2007), "Volatility and Dispersion in Business Growth Rates: Publicly Traded versus Privately Held Firms," NBER, Macroeconomics Annual, 21.

[12] See Comin, Groshen, and Rabin (2009), "Turbulent Firms, Turbulent Wages?" *Journal of Monetary Economics* (January). It turns out that the relationship between firm volatility and age volatility is much weaker for small companies which are the ones that have experience a decline rather than an increase in firm volatility.

[13] The oil shocks were the result of complex political interactions between oil producing countries. From a political standpoint, they took place in the 1970s for a reason. However, for most economies, the shocks were exogenous developments.

[14] http://robertreich.blogspot.com/2008/07/end-of-great-moderation-bailouts-of.html, accessed January 11, 2011.

[15] See McConell and Perez-Quiros (2000), *op. cit.*

[16] Niall Ferguson, "An Imaginary Retrospective of 2009" January 15, 2009. http://www.niallferguson.com/site/FERG/Templates/ArticleItem.aspx?pageid=198, accessed January 11, 2011.

[17] Money supply or money is the stock of assets used for transactions. There are different ways to measure the stock of money. The most commonly used are M1 (currency in

circulation plus demand deposits) and the monetary base (currency in circulation plus bank reserves).

[18] There are different actions central banks can take to alter the money supply. The most common are purchases and sales of government bonds in its balance sheet. These are known as open market operations. Open market operations affect currency in circulation and therefore money supply.

[19] Taylor, J. (1993), "Discretion versus. Policy rules in Practice." Carnegie-Rochester Conference Series on Public Policy Vol. 39 pp. 195–214.

[20] That is, in recessions the output gap is positive and in booms it is negative.

[21] Though this is the way Taylor calculated the output gap, there is a number of ways to approximate the deviation of output from potential output. One is Okun's law who, in 1962, claimed that for every one percent increase in the unemployment rate, GDP will be an additional two percent lower than potential GDP. Another approach is to use a Hodrick-Prescott (or some other) filter to separate the cyclical component of GDP from its trend component which could be interpreted as potential GDP.

[22] Taylor, J. *ibid*.

[23] Taylor, J. *ibid*.

[24] Intuitively, if the Fed responds to inflation pressures by less than one-to-one, real interest rates will decline causing an increase overheating of the economy and further inflationary pressures.

[25] Clarida, Gali, and Gertler (2000), "Monetary Policy Rules and Macroeconomic Stability: Evidence and Some Theory," *Quarterly Journal of Economics*, Vol. 115, No. 1.

[26] These include, for example, Benjamin Friedman from Harvard. Friedman, B. "Why the Federal Reserve Should Not Adopt Inflation Targeting," International Finance 7:1, 2004: pp. 129–136.

[27] Speech Delivered to the Boston Federal Reserve Bank Conference, October 15, 2010. http://www.pimco.com/Pages/WhatHas%E2%80%93andHasNot%E2%80%93Been LearnedAboutMonetaryPolicyinaLowInflationEnvironmentAReviewofthe2000s.aspx, accessed January 11, 2011.

[28] See Jaimovich, N. and H. Siu (2007), "The Young, the Old and the Restless: Demographics and Business Cycle Volatility" The American Economic Review, forthcoming.

[29] See Comin, D. and A. M. Santacreu (2011), "Technology Diffusion and Aggregate Volatility," mimeo. Intuitively, the price of new capital is inversely related to the efficiency with which new capital is produced in the economy. This is, in turn, positively related to the stock of adopted technologies. The reduction in the volatility of the flow of adopted technologies leads to smaller fluctuations in the price of new capital over the medium term. In the present of costs of adjustment to the flow of investment, the current price of installed capital is related to the future price of new capital. This study concludes that the reduction in adoption lags is responsible for a decline in the volatility of output growth of 30%. That is 60% of the observed decline in output growth volatility.

[30] See, for example, Todd Clark "Is the Great Moderation Over? An Empirical Analysis" http://www.kansascityfed.org/PUBLICAT/ECONREV/pdf/09q4Clark.pdf Accessed January 11, 2011; Olivier Coibion and Yuriy Gorodnichenko, "Does the Great

Recession really mean the end of the Great Moderation?" http://www.voxeu.org/index. php?q=node/4496, accessed January 11, 2011.

[31] The cross-country historical adoption technology (CHAT) dataset has been developed by Comin, Hobijn and Rovito (2006) "Five Facts You Need to Know about Technology Diffusion" NBER Working Paper #12886, and is an elaboration of the data set introduced by Comin and Hobijn (2004), "Cross-country Technology Adoption: Making the Theories Face the Facts," *Journal of Monetary Economics*, Vol. 51, pp. 39–83.

The U.S. Current Account Deficit

Laura Alfaro* and Rafael Di Tella*

In 2014, worldwide fears were raised by ongoing political battles over U.S. government budgets and the Federal Reserve Bank's winding down of long-term bond purchases, even as Europe remained in practical recession after its sovereign debt crises and Chinese and some other developing-country economies seemed precarious. Having avoided a total economic collapse during the financial crisis of 2008–2009, investors and policy-makers were confronted with slow recovery and the lingering effects of the crisis.

As analysts revised the growth prospects for the world economy, the role of the U.S. current account deficit had receded into the background. In fact, the current-account deficit had declined from an average of almost 5% of GDP from 2000 through 2007 to only 2.5% of GDP in 2013 (see **Exhibit 4b**). Much of the reason for that moderation was presumably not long-term: The slow U.S. growth had reduced imports. The financial counterpart of the U.S. current account deficits was the continuing capital inflow from abroad, as foreigners financed Americans' spending in excess of their income. As these inflows accumulated, the gap between U.S. holdings of foreign assets and foreign holdings of U.S. assets (known as the NIIP and net international invetsment position) was sinking to an unprecedented nadir.

*Reprinted with permission of Harvard Business School Publishing
The U.S. Current Account Deficit, 9-706-2002
This Case was prepared by Professors Laura Alfaro and Rafael Di Tella and Research Associates Ingrid Vogel, Renee Kim and Matthew Johnson. It was revised by Research Associate Jonathan Schlefer under the supervision of Professor Richard Vietor.

Still balanced in 1985, the NIIP had reached more than $4.5 trillion deficit in 2013. (See **Exhibit 8**).

Most U.S. policymakers had long downplayed the risks implied by the large current account deficit and net international investment position. They insisted that the deficit and NIIP simply reflected the attractiveness of the U.S. economy as a destination for global investment. For example, the 2006 *Economic Report of the President* focused on the current account's counterpart, namely foreign investment in the United States. A 24-page chapter of the report entitled "The U.S. Capital Account Surplus" noted: "What factors encourage large and persistent U.S. foreign capital inflows? Several factors, which reflect U.S. economic strengths, encourage these inflows. In particular, a high rate of U.S. growth encourages foreign capital to be 'pushed' toward the United States."[1] However, when the United States someday resumed healthy growth, its current-account deficit could well rise back to 5% of GDP. Since the mid-1970s, among the world's industrial countries, only smaller economies, such as Australia, New Zealand, Spain and Ireland had experienced current account deficits exceeding 5% of GDP.[2] For the latter, the markets had become deeply concerned about their prospects.

Many analysts agreed that the current account could continue to be funded at higher levels, focusing in particular on the "insatiable appetite" of Asian central banks — most notably China — to invest in U.S. assets as a means of keeping the dollar strong and supporting U.S. spending on Asian exports.[3] Even in 2013, with much of the world economy stagnating and export demand therefore weak, China's current account surplus was $189 billion (up from $134 billion in 2005), while its international reserves (the majority in U.S. dollar assets such as Treasuries) increased by about $500 billion that year. (See **Exhibits 9a and 10**).[4]

Other observers were less optimistic about the implications of the large U.S. current account deficit. They believed the United States was mortgaging its future in favor of consumption in the present and argued that delaying adjustment to end U.S. external imbalances would only increase the severity of the eventual inevitable adjustment.[5] Berkeley economist Maurice Obstfeld and Harvard economist Kenneth Rogoff remarked: "In our view, any sober policymaker or financial market analyst ought to regard the U.S. current account deficit as a sword of Damocles hanging over the global economy."[6] They forecasted further depreciation of the trade-weighted dollar, which fell by roughly 21% between January 2002 and July 2014.[7]

Furthermore, it was noted that high levels of external indebtedness made the U.S. financial system vulnerable to a loss of market confidence that could induce a "sudden stop" in capital inflows. Of course, unlike emerging economies more commonly associated with sudden stops, the U.S. could borrow in its own currency, meaning that it could pass the risk of future real depreciations on to its creditors.[8] Even so, former U.S. Treasury Secretary Robert Rubin warned that "the traditional immunity of advanced countries like America to third-world-style crises is not a birthright."[9]

Many global investors appeared to be in agreement with these concerns. Berkshire Hathaway, a holding company run by world famous investor Warren Buffett, increased the value of its foreign exchange contracts, consisting predominantly of short positions against the dollar, from $12 billion in 2003 to $21 billion in 2004. By the time of Berkshire's annual shareholder meeting in May 2006 — given the climb of the dollar in 2005 — such positions had cost the company around $500 million.[10] Even so, Buffett continued to emphasize the need to protect against further dollar declines. In May 2011, in view of inflationary pressures from massive U.S. budget deficits and monetary emissions, he continued to maintain, "There's no question the purchasing value of the dollar will decline."[11] But in view of troubles elsewhere, he thought that the purchasing value of many other currencies could also decline. (See **Exhibits 1–4** for basic U.S. macroeconomic data.) There were also questions about how global imbalances would influence the short and long-term future of the dollar as a world currency and the United States' role in trade and finance.

A Historical Perspective on U.S. External Balances

Global Gold Standard (1870–1914)

Only in the late 19th century when the United States was rapidly industrializing were the U.S. current account deficit and NIIP close to their early 21st century levels.[12] During this period, large current account imbalances were common among many nations, with long-term "development finance" capital tending to flow from already industrialized countries of Western Europe with current account surpluses to emerging economies that needed to fund major infrastructure projects.[13] For example, in the 19th century most British investment in the United States flowed into bonds issued by canal, turnpike, and railroad companies or state governments that used the revenues to build public works.[14]

The global gold standard, which fixed major currencies against one another — and which the United States joined in 1879 — encouraged these high levels of capital mobility. In 1879, global holdings of foreign assets were estimated at approximately 7% of world GDP. This rose quickly to close to 20% in 1900–1914 (see **Exhibit 5**).[15] Academics noted that the gold standard acted as a "seal of approval" for countries issuing sovereign debt.[16] Participating countries had much smaller spreads than non-participants over interest rates in London, where global capital markets were centered, with the British serving as "bankers to the world."[17]

U.S. adherence to the gold standard, however, generated opposition at home. Pegging the dollar to gold caused intermittent deflations, which increased the real

Exhibit 1a.   U.S. Balance of Payments, 1972–2013 (current billions US$)

	1972	1976	1980	1984	1988	1992	1996	2000	2001	2002	2003	2007	2008	2009	2010	2011	2012	2013
Current Account	**−6**	**4**	**2**	**−94**	**−121**	**−52**	**−125**	**−411**	**−395**	**−458**	**−521**	**−719**	**−687**	**−381**	**−444**	**−459**	**−461**	**−400**
Net Goods	−6	−9	−26	−112	−127	−97	−191	−447	−423	−476	−542	−823	−834	−510	−649	−741	−743	−702
Exports of Goods	49	115	224	220	320	440	612	785	731	697	730	1164	1307	1070	1290	1499	1561	1592
Imports of Goods	−56	−124	−250	−332	−447	−537	−803	−1232	−1154	−1173	−1272	−1986	−2141	−1580	−1939	−2240	−2304	−2294
Net Services	1	3	6	3	12	58	87	74	61	57	48	117	125	127	154	193	205	226
Exports of Services	18	28	48	71	111	177	239	287	271	277	288	485	527	505	559	623	650	682
Imports of Services	−17	−25	−41	−68	−99	−120	−153	−213	−210	−220	−239	−367	−402	−378	−405	−430	−445	−456
Net Income	8	16	30	35	19	24	22	19	30	25	43	101	146	124	178	221	203	200
Income receipts on U.S.-owned assets abroad	15	29	73	109	136	132	224	348	288	278	318	829	809	601	672	747	750	767
Income payments on foreign-owned assets in U.S.	−7	−13	−43	−74	−116	−105	−198	−322	−251	−245	−267	−718	−651	−469	−486	−518	−538	−558
Net Compensation of Employees	na	na	na	na	−1	−3	−4	−7	−7	−8	−8	−11	−12	−9	−8	−8	−8	−9
Net Unilateral Transfers[a]	−9	−6	−8	−20	−25	−37	−43	−57	−64	−64	−70	−114	−124	−121	−127	−132	−126	−124
Financial Account	**8**	**−13**	**−25**	**76**	**138**	**94**	**134**	**478**	**400**	**501**	**533**	**611**	**764**	**186**	**423**	**481**	**431**	**373**
Increase in U.S.-owned Assets Abroad, net (Financial outflow (−))	−14	−51	−87	−40	−107	−74	−413	−561	−383	−295	−325	−1,454	332	−129	−910	−475	−129	−586
U.S. Official Reserve Assets, net	0	−3	−8	−3	−4	4	7	0	−5	−4	2	0	−5	−52	−2	−16	−4	3
U.S. Government (nonofficial) Assets, net	−2	−4	−5	−5	3	−2	−1	−1	0	0	1	−22	−530	541	8	−104	85	3
U.S. Private Direct Investment, net	−8	−12	−19	−16	−23	−48	−92	−159	−142	−154	−150	−414	−329	−310	−301	−419	−333	−350
U.S. Private Foreign Securities, net	−1	−9	−4	−5	−8	−49	−149	−128	−91	−49	−147	−367	197	−227	−139	−145	−248	−445

(Continued)

Exhibit 1a. (*Continued*)

	1972	1976	1980	1984	1988	1992	1996	2000	2001	2002	2003	2007	2008	2009	2010	2011	2012	2013
U.S. Other Private Assets, net	−5	−24	−51	−11	−75	21	−178	−272	−144	−88	−31	−651	998	−81	−475	208	371	203
Increase in Foreign-Owned Assets in the U.S., net (financial inflow (+))	22	38	62	116	245	168	548	1,038	783	795	858	2,065	431	315	1,333	956	559	959
Foreign Official Assets, net	11	18	17	3	40	40	127	43	28	116	278	481	555	480	397	243	397	286
Direct investment	1	4	17	24	58	20	87	321	167	84	64	221	310	150	206	236	175	236
U.S. Treasury securities	0	3	3	23	20	37	147	−70	−14	100	91	67	163	−15	298	185	156	193
U.S. Securities excl U.S. Treasury Secs	5	1	5	13	26	30	103	460	394	283	221	605	−166	2	141	−54	197	58
U.S. currency	na	1	3	2	4	11	14	−3	24	19	11	−11	29	13	28	55	57	38
Other	6	10	18	50	97	30	70	288	184	192	194	701	−460	−315	262	290	−423	148
Financial derivatives, net	**na**	**na**	**na**	**na**	**na**	**na**	**na**	**na**	**na**	**na**	**na**	**6.2**	**−32.9**	**44.8**	**14.1**	**35.0**	**−7.1**	**−2.2**
Capital account transactions, net	**na**	**na**	**na**	**na**	**na**	**1**	**0**	**0**	**13**	**0**	**−2**	**0**	**6**	**0**	**0**	**−1**	**7**	**0**
Statistical discrepancy	**−2**	**9**	**23**	**19**	**−17**	**−44**	**−10**	**−67**	**−18**	**−42**	**−10**	**101**	**−50**	**150**	**7**	**−55**	**30**	**30**

Sources: Adapted from BEA, Table 1, "U.S. International Transactions," accessed Aug. 2014. The BEA has begun releasing a new series for international transactions, Table 1.1. The headline data, such as overall current account and financial account, for the two series remain the same, but subcategories differ.

Note: [a]Unilateral Transfers consist of U.S. government grants, private remittances, cross-border tax payments and other payments.

Exhibit 1b.   U.S. Current Account and Real Exchange Rate, 1950–2014

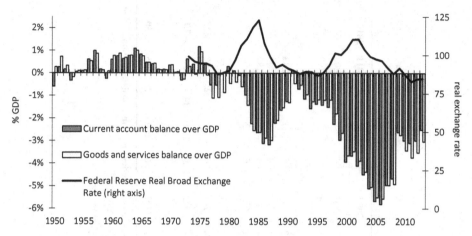

Sources: Created by case writers based on BEA Table 1.1.5 and 4.1 and Federal Reserve Price Adjusted Broad Dollar Index; accessed Aug. 2014.

Exhibit 1c.   U.S. Trade Balance by Sector, 1979–2014 (billions US$)

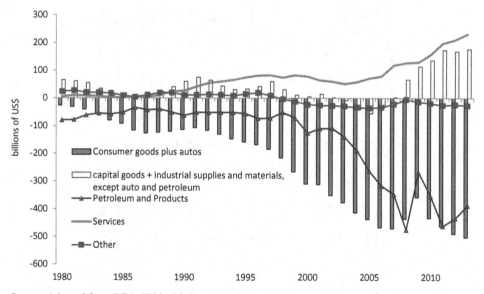

Source: Adapted from BEA, Table 4.2.5, accessed Aug. 2014.

value of loan repayments. Eastern bankers benefitted while Western and Southern farmers and other borrowers were harmed. A large faction of the Democratic Party, often called "populists," pressed for the United States to abandon gold in favor of a *de facto* silver standard. Although the movement was ultimately unsuccessful,

Exhibit 1d.   Imported Crude Oil Prices, 1980–2014 (US$)

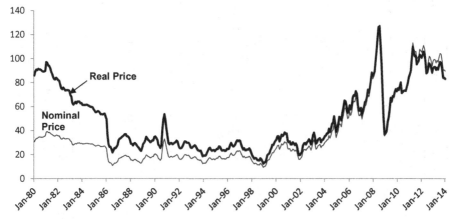

Sources: Energy Information Administration (EIA), refiner average imported crude oil acquisition cost historical series, Global Financial Data for prices, accessed Aug. 2014.

speculators put pressure on the dollar in anticipation of an eventual departure from the gold standard. Between 1891 and 1897, the U.S. Treasury was forced to deter continued speculative dollar sales and maintain the fixed exchange rate by increasing interest rates dramatically. This resulted in a harsh recession.[18]

The Interwar Period (1914–1939)

After the commencement of World War I in 1914, worldwide holdings of foreign assets fell dramatically. (They would only return to their prewar levels around 1980.) The gold standard fell apart, and monetary policy around the world became directed toward domestic goals, such as financing war efforts through issuing bonds and printing money.[19] Countries limited both international trade and investment through tariffs and capital controls.

After the war ended in 1918, there was interest in returning to the prewar gold standard that seemed to have offered stability and prosperity. Initial attempts failed in the face of inflation in Europe and high levels of European debt to the United States. Only in 1925 was a new gold standard finally initiated, under which countries held reserves in dollars, sterling, or gold, and the United States and United Kingdom agreed to exchange dollars or sterling, respectively, for gold on demand at fixed parities.[20]

Under the new gold standard, the United Kingdom made the political decision to set the value of sterling against the dollar at the prewar exchange rate. Since there had been inflation during the war, this rate implied that the pound was overvalued, which encouraged investors to sell pounds in exchange for gold. With the United Kingdom politically unable to raise interest rates to prevent such outflows of gold,

Exhibit 2. U.S. International Investment Position, 1980–2013 (billions current US$, percent where noted)

	1980	1984	1988	1992	1996	2000	2001	2002	2003	2007[a]	2008	2009	2010	2011	2012	2013
Net International Investment Position	360	167	-167	-411	-463	-1,337	-1,875	-2,045	-2,094	-1,796	-3,260	-2,275	-2,249	-3,670	-3,867	-4,565
U.S.-Owned Assets Abroad	930	1,205	1,830	2,332	4,032	6,239	6,309	6,649	7,638	18,400	19,465	18,559	20,555	21,594	21,555	21,914
as % category:																
U.S. Official Reserve Assets	18%	9%	8%	6%	4%	2%	2%	2%	2%	2%	2%	2%	2%	2%	3%	2%
U.S. Government (nonofficial) Assets	7%	7%	5%	4%	2%	1%	1%	1%	1%	1%	3%	0%	0%	1%	0%	0%
U.S. Private Direct Investment[b]	42%	29%	28%	28%	25%	25%	27%	28%	27%	19%	19%	22%	21%	21%	23%	24%
U.S. Private Foreign Bonds	5%	5%	6%	9%	12%	9%	9%	11%	11%	9%	6%	8%	8%	9%	10%	10%
U.S. Private Foreign Corporate Stocks	2%	2%	7%	13%	25%	30%	26%	21%	27%	29%	14%	22%	24%	21%	25%	29%
U.S. Private Other	26%	48%	47%	40%	32%	33%	35%	37%	31%	28%	24%	27%	26%	24%	22%	21%
Foreign-Owned Assets in the U.S.	569	1,038	1,997	2,743	4,496	7,576	8,184	8,694	9,732	20,196	22,725	20,834	22,804	25,263	25,422	26,479
as % category:																
Foreign Official Assets	32%	20%	16%	16%	18%	14%	14%	14%	16%	17%	17%	21%	22%	21%	22%	22%
Direct Investment[b]	22%	22%	20%	20%	17%	19%	19%	17%	16%	12%	11%	12%	12%	11%	12%	12%
U.S. Treasury Securities	3%	6%	5%	7%	10%	5%	5%	5%	5%	3%	4%	4%	5%	5%	6%	7%
U.S. Corporate and other Bonds (excluding Treasury)	2%	3%	10%	11%	12%	14%	16%	18%	18%	16%	12%	14%	13%	11%	12%	12%
U.S. Corporate Stocks	11%	9%	10%	11%	14%	21%	18%	14%	18%	14%	8%	12%	13%	13%	15%	19%
U.S. Currency	3%	3%	2%	3%	3%	3%	3%	3%	3%	1%	1%	2%	2%	2%	2%	2%
Other	27%	38%	37%	32%	26%	25%	26%	28%	24%	24%	20%	20%	19%	18%	17%	17%
Addendum: NIIP as % GDP	12.6%	4.1%	-3.2%	-6.3%	-5.7%	-13.0%	-17.7%	-18.6%	-18.2%	-12.4%	-22.1%	-15.8%	-15.0%	-23.6%	-23.9%	-27.2%

Sources: Compiled from BEA, Table 1. International Investment Position of the United States at the End of the Period, accessed Aug. 2014.

Notes: [a] A break in the series in 2005 reflected the introduction of U.S. Department of Treasury data on financial derivatives, which were included in "U.S. Private Other" category starting that year. Because of this change percentage figures do not add up.

[b] Direct investments were valued at current cost, under which NIIP turned negative in 1986. Under prior classifications of direct investments valued at market cost, NIIP turned negative in 1989.

Exhibit 3a.   Reserves of Selected Countries, billions of US$ except as noted

	2000	2002	2004	2006	2007	2008	2009	2010	2011	2012	2013
Level of foreign reserves (International Monetary Fund)											
Total reserves	1,936	2,408	3,748	5,253	6,704	7,346	8,165	9,265	10,206	10,952	11,686
Held in U.S. dollars	1,080	1,194	1,739	2,158	2,631	2,685	2,848	3,193	3,525	3,731	3,791
Held in euros/other currencies	438	602	916	1,158	1,488	1,525	1,742	1,970	2,128	2,354	2,434
Held in unknown currencies	418	612	1,093	1,938	2,585	3,136	3,575	4,101	4,553	4,866	5,461
Dollar reserves as % of total	56%	50%	46%	41%	39%	37%	35%	34%	35%	34%	32%
Level of foreign reserves held in U.S. dollars (Federal Reserve)											
Total foreign reserves held in dollars	na	1,162	1,909	2,795	3,475	3,932	4,306	4,745	5,115	5,476	5,815
Bank deposits and other liabilities	na	145	270	285	398	254	186	178	206	204	266
U.S. Treasuries	na	763	1,233	1,558	1,763	2,412	2,846	3,304	3,642	3,980	4,054
Other U.S. securities	na	254	405	952	1,314	1,267	1,274	1,262	1,267	1,292	1,494
Reserves held in U.S. dollars by:											
Asia	na	760	1,388	2,061	2,517	3,005	3,345	3,644	3,874	4,033	4,277
Europe	na	284	357	477	601	517	545	647	710	841	915
Other countries	na	118	163	257	361	408	416	455	532	603	623
Major holders both official and private of U.S. Treasuries (Treasury Department)											
Total, of which:	1,056	1,162	1,752	1,993	2,201	2,624	3,506	4,126	4,668	5,379	5,593
Asia (1), of which:	542	615	1,068	1,221	1,304	1,424	1,998	2,351	2,611	2,807	2,897
China (2)	66	97	196	378	480	550	940	1,115	1,315	1,160	1,279
Japan	320	362	675	615	621	638	721	817	885	1,120	1,135
Oil exporters (3)	47	53	57	112	135	163	210	209	244	268	258
Total foreign reserves and imputed purchases of foreign reserves held as U.S. Treasuries with maturities of a year or more (Treasury Department)											
Total reserves	na	561	912	1,213	1,452	1,684	2,054	2,617	3,103	3,489	3,648
Change in reserves	na	na	259	134	239	232	370	563	486	386	159
Estimated valuation changes	na	na	−46	−73	7	84	48	61	−14	94	−111
Imputed purchases of reserves	na	na	305	207	232	148	322	502	500	292	270

(Continued)

Exhibit 3a.   *(Continued)*

	2000	2002	2004	2006	2007	2008	2009	2010	2011	2012	2013
Total foreign reserves held in all currencies by:											
Asia	958	1,285	2,195	2,814	3,448	3,949	4,680	5,317	5,904	6,103	6,636
China (2)	169	295	619	1,073	1,534	1,953	2,426	2,876	3,213	3,341	3,849
Japan	362	470	845	895	973	1,031	1,049	1,096	1,296	1,268	1,267
U.S. current account balance	−411	−458	−634	−807	−719	−687	−381	−444	−459	−461	−400
U.S. financing need net of FDI	249	528	804	808	912	706	541	539	642	619	514

Sources: Level of foreign reserves (International Monetary Fund): IMF COFER database. Level of foreign reserves held in U.S. dollars (Federal Reserve): Federal Reserve, International Summary Statistics, Selected U.S. Liabilities to Foreign Official Institutions (3.15). Major holders of U.S. Treasuries (Treasury Department): U.S. Treasury, TIC (Treasury International Capital) database. Total foreign reserves held as long-term U.S. Treasuries (Treasury Department): U.S. Treasury, Foreign Portfolio Holdings of U.S. Securities as of June 30, 2014. Total foreign reserves of Asian countries and U.S. current account and FDI data: Economist Intelligence Unit, CountryData. All data for this exhibit accessed Aug. 2014.
Notes: 1. Asia includes China, Japan, Hong Kong, South Korea, Singapore, Taiwan and Thailand. 2. The figures for China's holdings of U.S. Treasuries from the Treasury Dept. are much lower than would be expected from the figures for China's total foreign-reserve holdings from the EIU. It appears that the Treasury Dept. figures are low because they do not fully include China's purchases of Treasuries from intermediaries. 3. Includes Ecuador, Venezuela, Indonesia, Bahrain, Iran, Iraq, Kuwait, Oman, Qatar, Saudi Arabia, the United Arab Emirates, Algeria, Gabon, Libya, Nigeria.

Exhibit 3b.   Countries with the Largest Total Foreign Reserve Holdings 2011–2013 (billion US$)

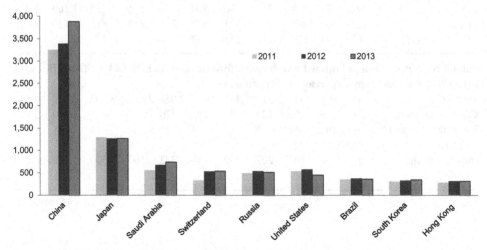

Source: World Development Indicators, accessed Aug. 2014.

Exhibit 4. Global Current Account Balances, 1995–2013 (billions US$)

	1995	2000	2005	2007	2008	2009	2010	2011	2012	2013
United States	−113.6	−416.3	−739.8	−713.4	−681.3	−381.6	−449.5	−457.7	−440.4	−379.3
Australia	−18.6	−15.6	−43.4	−63.6	−51.3	−46.0	−43.9	−41.5	−64.0	−44.2
Canada	−5.2	18.6	21.6	11.4	1.8	−40.0	−56.7	−49.0	−62.3	−58.9
Japan	111.4	119.6	166.1	212.1	159.9	146.6	204.0	119.3	60.4	34.3
Euro Area	n.a.	−35.7	50.3	46.4	−96.5	33.1	72.7	109.2	246.0	366.0
United Kingdom	−8.1	−42.9	−42.9	−62.5	−25.5	−31.4	−61.9	−36.0	−92.7	−84.6
Switzerland	20.9	30.1	52.4	38.8	11.0	53.7	81.0	59.0	60.9	62.5
Oil exporters[a]	1.7	86.1	208.0	258.8	340.3	73.5	191.3	423.4	445.1	352.0
China	1.6	20.5	132.4	353.2	420.6	243.3	237.8	136.1	193.1	188.7
Developing Asia, excluding China	−38.9	22.4	10.4	41.6	8.8	32.6	0.9	−38.7	−89.0	−43.5
Latin America and Caribbean	−38.0	−48.4	32.4	6.2	−39.5	−30.0	−62.1	−79.4	−107.1	−153.3
Russia	7.0	46.8	84.4	71.3	103.9	50.4	67.5	97.3	72.0	33.0
Emerging and developing Europe[b]	−17.0	−75.3	−142.9	−201.0	−258.4	−100.7	−151.8	−216.1	−152.9	−108.6
Rest of the world[c]	36.6	114.3	244.1	277.6	290.3	187.8	276.0	344.8	272.7	239.4

Source: World Economic Outlook Database, April 2014, accessed Aug. 2014.

Notes:[a] Oil exporters defined as: Algeria, Bahrain, Iran, Kuwait, Libya, Oman, Qatar, Saudi Arabia, Sudan, Syria (omitted in 2011–2013 for lack of data), UAE and Yemen.

[b]The "rest of the world" category includes a very large statistical discrepancy. (If individual countries' current accounts are added together, the sum indicates that "world" often runs a large current-account deficit or surplus with itself.) These data therefore should not be used with any confidence.

Exhibit 5. Worldwide Foreign Assets and Liabilities (current billion US$)

	1825	1855	1870	1900	1914	1930	1938	1945	1960	1971	1980	1985	1990	1995
Assets														
United Kingdom	0.5	0.7	4.9	12.1	19.5	18.2	22.9	14.2	26.4	—	551	857	1,760	2,490
France	0.1	—	2.5	5.2	8.6	3.5	3.9	—	—	—	268	428	736	1,100
Germany	—	—	—	4.8	6.7	1.1	0.7	—	1.2	—	257	342	1,100	1,670
Netherlands	0.3	0.2	0.3	1.1	1.2	2.3	4.8	3.7	27.6	—	99	178	418	712
Other Europe	—	—	—	—	—	—	4.6	—	—	—	503	715	1,777	2,855
United States	—	—	—	0.5	2.5	14.7	11.5	15.3	63.6	—	775	1,300	2,180	3,350
Canada	—	—	—	0.1	0.2	1.3	1.9	—	—	—	92	129	227	302
Japan	—	—	—	—	—	—	1.2	—	—	—	160	437	1,860	2,720
Other	—	—	—	—	—	—	6.0	2.0	5.9	—	94	123	214	337
Total	0.9	0.9	7.7	23.8	38.7	41.1	57.5	35.2	124.7	—	2,799	4,509	10,272	15,536
World GDP	—	—	111	128	221	491	491	722	1,942	4,733	11,118	12,455	21,141	25,110
Sample GDP	—	—	16	43	76	149	182	273	671	—	7,806	9,705	17,250	21,956
Assets/Sample GDP	—	—	48%	55%	51%	28%	32%	13%	19%	—	36%	46%	60%	71%
Assets/World GDP	—	—	7%	19%	18%	8%	12%	5%	6%	—	25%	36%	49%	62%

(*Continued*)

Exhibit 5.   (*Continued*)

Liabilities

	1825	1855	1870	1900	1914	1930	1938	1945	1960	1971	1980	1985	1990	1995
Europe	—	—	—	5.4	12.0	—	10.3	—	7.6	—	1,457	2,248	5,406	8,592
North America	—	—	—	2.6	11.1	—	13.7	—	12.5	—	684	1,412	2,830	4,681
Australia and NZ	—	—	—	1.6	2.0	—	4.5	—	2.2	—	71	118	216	318
Japan	—	—	—	0.1	1.0	—	0.6	—	0.3	—	147	307	1,530	1,970
Latin America	—	—	—	2.9	8.9	—	11.3	—	9.2	57	250	—	505	768
Asia (excl. Japan)	—	—	—	2.4	6.8	—	10.6	—	2.7	29	129	—	524	960
Africa	—	—	—	3.0	4.1	—	4.0	—	2.2	19	124	—	306	353
Developing Countries	—	—	—	6.0	13.0	—	25.9	—	14.1	107	506	—	1,338	2,086
All (includes others)	—	—	—	18.0	45.5	—	55.0	—	39.9	—	3,368	—	12,655	19,728

Sources: Adapted from Maurice Obstfeld and Alan M. Taylor, "Globalization and Capital Markets," National Bureau of Economic Research Working Paper 8846, March 2002, pp. 57 and Greenspan, 2004, footnote 7, p. 22, Table 2.

the Federal Reserve intervened, increasing U.S. money supply in order to decrease interest rates in the United States to levels comparable to levels in Great Britain.

Gold outflows from Great Britain halted, but excess credit in the United States was thought to have contributed to a major stock market boom. In 1928 and early 1929, the Federal Reserve raised interest rates to respond to the speculative bubble, but failed to prevent the stock market crash of October 1929. After lowering interest rates through 1930, the Federal Reserve was forced to raise interest rates in 1931 to defend its gold reserves after Great Britain withdrew the pound from the gold standard following massive gold and capital outflows.[21] It was argued that tighter monetary conditions in the United States contributed to waves of bank failures in 1931 and 1932.[22] The United States withdrew from the gold standard in 1933. With the withdrawal in 1936 of Switzerland, France and the Netherlands, this period of gold standard came to a definitive end.

The unified monetary system implied by the gold standard was blamed by some economists for spreading economic problems from the United States to Europe and precipitating the Great Depression of the 1930s. It was argued that governments were forced to protect their reserves of gold by keeping interest rates high and credit tight for too long, which had a devastating impact on credit, spending, and prices.

The Bretton Woods System of Fixed Exchange Rates (1950–1971)

In 1944, in the later stages of World War II, 44 countries met in Bretton Woods, New Hampshire, to establish a new global monetary regime. Under the Bretton Woods system of fixed exchange rates, the dollar was pegged to gold while other currencies were pegged to the dollar.[23] The U.S. government agreed to make dollars convertible upon demand by foreign central banks into gold at the agreed price of $35 per ounce. All other countries were required to maintain their pegs to the dollar through active foreign exchange intervention, but were allowed to alter their par values to correct any "fundamental disequilibrium" in their balance of payments. They were formally encouraged to make use of capital controls to maintain external balance in the face of potentially destabilizing "hot money" flows.[24] In 1945, the United States overtook Britain as the major international asset holder and became the new "banker to the world."[25]

In the initial years of the Bretton Woods arrangement, current account transactions had to be regulated. Strong European demand for U.S. products as European nations engaged in rebuilding efforts drove up U.S. current account surpluses (see **Exhibit 4b**) and caused a "dollar shortage." In order to control the use of scarce dollars, European policymakers chose to prevent open purchases and sales of foreign exchange. The United States officially encouraged European countries to build dollar exchange reserves by expanding European exports to the U.S. market while maintaining restrictions on U.S. imports. By the end of the 1950s, European nations had accumulated sufficient dollar reserves to defend their chosen par values and to allow currency trading associated with international trade in goods and services. Current account convertibility was thus restored for the major European currencies.

Beginning in 1958, U.S. monetary authorities as well as other analysts and policymakers worldwide became concerned about what were considered "balance-of-payments imbalances" in the United States. These imbalances — which focused on liquidity within the balance of payments rather than on modern definitions of current and financial accounts — emerged as current account surpluses became insufficient to fund U.S. long-term investments abroad.[26] External balance was maintained through foreign central bank accumulation of short–term liquid claims on the United States. As the stock of official dollar liabilities held by foreign monetary authorities mounted, the risk of a run on U.S. monetary gold reserves increased. By 1964, official liabilities exceeded the U.S. monetary gold stock.[27] A shared interest among countries in maintaining the system as well as U.S. pressure on monetary authorities to refrain from converting dollar holdings into gold helped prevent such a run. As such, in 1968 the system switched to a *de facto* dollar standard — although the threat of gold conversion was still present.[28]

The problems associated with the official settlements deficit were exacerbated by U.S. economic expansion. After 1965, the U.S. economy began to overheat and inflation began rising in the face of major increases in social spending and escalating military expenditure in support of the Vietnam War (see **Exhibit 3b**). As the dollar became overvalued against other currencies, foreign central banks were forced to defend their pegged rates by buying dollars. Buying dollars increased foreign domestic money supply, which led to inflation abroad.[29]

In 1971, the U.S. trade balance turned negative for the first time since 1893.[30] Facing low returns on dollar assets and worried about a possible future devaluation of the dollar against gold to restore competitiveness, private investors began to flee from the dollar and some countries began to request the exchange of dollars into gold.[31] When Britain also revealed its intent to convert to gold, flight from the dollar intensified. Reluctant to raise interest rates to defend the currency (particularly in an election year) and aware that support for the Bretton Woods system was failing — both internationally and domestically with growing protectionist pressures — President Richard Nixon suspended convertibility of the dollar into gold, thereby "closing the gold window." Nixon remarked:

> In recent weeks, [international money] speculators have been waging an all-out war on the American dollar. . . . I have directed the Secretary of the Treasury to . . . suspend temporarily the convertibility of the dollar into gold or other reserve assets. . . . Now this action will not win us any friends among the international money trader. But our primary concern is with the

American workers, and with fair competition around the world. . . . I am determined that the American dollar must never again be hostage in the hands of international speculators.[32]

Later in 1971 new par values were set for currencies, no longer backed by gold, but persistent speculation against the new values forced the system's collapse. In 1973, the world's currencies became independently floating. A worldwide recession followed as inflationary pressures took hold, exacerbated by the 1973 oil crisis.

Twin Deficits of the 1980s

After remaining close to balance through the rest of the 1970s — ranging from a surplus of 1.1% of GDP in 1975 to a deficit of 0.7% in 1977 — the U.S. current account dramatically changed course in the 1980s. After Ronald Reagan became president in 1981, taxes were cut in an effort to spur supply-driven growth of the sluggish U.S. economy, and at the same time defense spending was increased. The resulting expansionary fiscal policy encouraged domestic spending that supported GDP growth. In order to reduce inflation, the Federal Reserve kept interest rates high. High interest rates, in turn, attracted foreign investment, dramatically appreciating the value of the dollar. The appreciated dollar made U.S. exports more expensive for foreigners and imports cheaper for the United States, resulting in a widening trade deficit. In addition, economic growth rates of U.S. trading partners slowed relative to growth in the United States, implying that foreigners had less demand for U.S. exports while the United States had more demand for imports. These factors contributed to a widening of the current account balance, which passed from 0.1% of GDP in 1980 to a deficit of 3.3% in 1986. Over the same period, the government budget deficit increased from 2.8% to 4.8% of GDP. With changes in the same direction and of roughly the same magnitude, the current account and fiscal budget deficits became known as the "twin deficits."[33]

In order to address problems associated with the appreciated dollar, the United States, France, West Germany, Japan, and the United Kingdom (the G5 at the time) decided to intervene actively in currency markets to devalue the dollar against the yen and Deutsche Mark. They formalized this agreement in September 1985 with the Plaza Accord. The agreement proved successful, with the trade-weighted dollar falling 40% over two years.[34] (In fact, the program proved too successful: In February 1987, participants in the Plaza Accord plus Canada — the G6 at the time — signed the Louvre Accord outlining steps to halt continued decline of the dollar.)

The U.S. current account balance improved between 1987 and 1989, from a deficit of 3.4% to a deficit of 1.8% of GDP. GDP growth in the rest of the world increased relative to growth in the United States, which helped to shrink the current account deficit through trade channels as well as through increasing income on U.S. holdings of foreign assets relative to foreign holdings of U.S. assets. However, the effect was not large enough to shift the current account balance to a surplus. By 1986, as a result of the continual current account deficits, the U.S. NIIP (with assets and liabilities valued at market prices) turned negative, implying that the country had become a net debtor to the rest of the world.[35]

New Economy of the Late 1990s

By the late 1990s, the "twin deficits" appeared to have become separated. As the government budget deficit moved into surplus, the current account widened. In the second half of the 1990s, with the backdrop of the "new economy" defined by accelerated gains in productivity growth through effective use of information and communication technology,[36] the U.S. stock market and other U.S. equity returns experienced a boom. Business investment rose dramatically, particularly in information technologies, from 5.5% of GDP in 1992 to 8.6% in 2000. Low unemployment rates, growing wealth, and optimistic assessments of future income led to increased consumer spending and lower household savings rates, which dropped from 6.5% of GDP in 1992 to less than 1% in 2000. Rising stock prices drove up taxable income and government savings — which helped to move the federal budget from a deficit of 5% of GDP in 1992 to a surplus of 3% in 2000. But this was insufficient to close the widening gap between private investment and domestic private savings.[37]

At the same time, as outlined by Ben Bernanke, subsequent Federal Reserve Board chairman, there was evidence of a "global savings glut" driven by demographic factors. With slowly growing or declining workforces, many advanced economies outside the U.S. faced a dearth of domestic investment opportunities. The aging populations of these countries required high current savings to provide for impending sharp increases in the number of retirees relative to the number of workers.[38] Foreign investors, attracted by rapidly rising equity returns and productivity gains, chose to invest a portion of their excess savings in the United States. Foreign capital inflows became increasingly focused on private-sector investments, thereby helping to finance the innovation and productivity growth of the "new economy." The share of U.S. assets in foreign portfolios of the rest of the world increased to 35% in 1999; these assets were heavily weighted toward U.S. equities, which increased to 51% of foreign equity portfolios that same year (see **Exhibit 6**).[39] Overall, the U.S. NIIP fell from −$411 billion in 1992 to $2,045 billion in 2002, equivalent to a move from −6% to −19% of GDP (see **Exhibit 8**).[40]

With the creation of the euro in 1999, many analysts anticipated a decline in the ability of the United States to finance its large and growing current account deficit.

Exhibit 6a.   U.S. Federal Government Fiscal Accounts, 1980–2013 (% GDP, except as noted)

% GDP, except where noted	1980	1984	1988	1992	1996	2000	2001	2002	2007	2008	2009	2010	2011	2012	2013
Income (current billion dollars)	**517**	**666**	**909**	**1,091**	**1,453**	**2,025**	**1,991**	**1,853**	**2,568**	**2,524**	**2,105**	**2,163**	**2,303**	**2,450**	**2,775**
Income (% GDP)	18.5	16.9	17.6	17.0	18.2	19.9	18.8	17.0	17.9	17.1	14.6	14.6	15.0	15.2	16.7
Individual Income Tax	8.7	7.5	7.8	7.4	8.2	9.9	9.4	7.9	8.1	7.8	6.4	6.1	7.1	7.0	7.9
Corporation Income Tax	2.3	1.4	1.8	1.6	2.2	2.0	1.4	1.4	2.6	2.1	1.0	1.3	1.2	1.5	1.6
Social Security and Retirement Receipts	5.6	6.1	6.5	6.4	6.4	6.4	6.6	6.4	6.1	6.1	6.2	5.8	5.3	5.3	5.7
Other	1.8	1.8	1.5	1.6	1.4	1.6	1.4	1.3	1.1	1.2	1.1	1.4	1.4	1.4	1.4
Expenditure (current billion dollars)	**591**	**852**	**1,064**	**1,382**	**1,560**	**1,789**	**1,863**	**2,011**	**2,729**	**2,983**	**3,518**	**3,457**	**3,603**	**3,537**	**3,455**
Expenditure (% GDP)	21.1	21.5	20.6	21.5	19.6	17.6	17.6	18.5	19.0	20.2	24.4	23.4	23.4	22.0	20.8
Total Discretionary	9.9	9.6	9.0	8.3	6.7	6.1	6.1	6.7	7.3	7.7	8.6	9.1	8.8	8.0	7.2
National Defense (% GDP)	4.8	5.8	5.6	4.7	3.3	2.9	2.9	3.2	3.8	4.2	4.6	4.7	4.5	4.2	3.8
Nondefense	5.1	3.8	3.4	3.6	3.3	3.1	3.2	3.5	3.4	3.5	4.0	4.5	4.2	3.8	3.5
Total Mandatory	9.4	9.1	8.7	10.1	9.9	9.4	9.5	10.2	10.1	10.8	14.5	12.9	13.2	12.6	12.2
Medicare and Medicaid	1.7	2.1	2.3	3.1	3.6	3.3	3.5	3.7	4.4	4.5	5.2	5.4	5.4	5.0	5.1
Income and Social Security	5.8	5.8	5.3	6.2	5.9	5.3	5.4	5.8	5.5	5.9	7.1	7.7	7.3	7.0	6.9
Other Mandatory	1.9	1.3	1.1	0.9	0.4	0.8	0.6	0.7	0.3	0.4	2.2	-0.1	0.4	0.7	0.2
Net Interest	1.9	2.8	2.9	3.1	3.0	2.2	2.0	1.6	1.7	1.7	1.3	1.3	1.5	1.4	1.3
Surplus (+)/Deficit (−) (current $ bn)	**−74**	**−185**	**−155**	**−290**	**−107**	**236**	**128**	**−158**	**−161**	**−459**	**−1413**	**−1294**	**−1300**	**−1087**	**−680**
Surplus (+)/Deficit (−) (% GDP)	**−2.6**	**−4.7**	**−3.0**	**−4.5**	**−1.3**	**2.3**	**1.2**	**−1.5**	**−1.1**	**−3.1**	**−9.8**	**−8.8**	**−8.4**	**−6.8**	**−4.1**
Addendum: State and Local Government Surplus (+)/Deficit (−) (current $ bn)	5	21	17	−38	−13	10	−65	−121	−73	−165	−272	−237	−216	−233	−225

Sources: Congressional Budget Office, Bureau of Economic Analysis; accessed Aug. 2014.

Exhibit 6b.   U.S. Federal Fiscal Balance and Debt as % GDP, 1940–2013

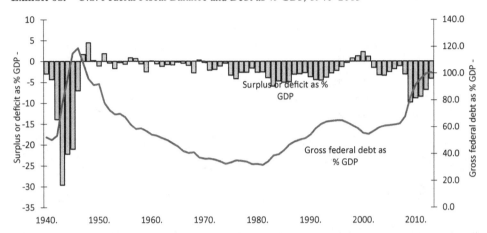

Source: Adapted from Economic Report of the President, 2014, Table B-79, and Table B-20, accessed Aug. 2014.

Nobel Laureate Robert Mundell, on the eve of euro creation, warned:

> It would be a mistake to ignore [the fact that] in the last 15 years U.S. current account deficits have turned the U.S. from the world's biggest creditor to its biggest debtor. . . . The low-saving high-debt problems will one day come home to roost. . . . There will come a time when the pileup of international indebtedness makes reliance on the dollar as the world's only main currency untenable.[41]

However, contrary to predictions, the dollar strengthened for several years (see **Exhibit 7**), and the current account deficit continued to widen.

Escalating Current Account Deficits (2000–2005)

In 2000, the dot-com bubble burst, leading to a mild recession in the United States between 2001 and 2002. Furthermore, oil prices increased the value of U.S. petroleum imports from $68 billion in 1999 to $104 billion in 2002 (see **Exhibit 4c** and **4d**). The government responded with a fiscal stimulus in the form of a tax cut, and the Federal Reserve responded with a monetary stimulus in the form of record-low interest rates. Rising government expenditures and falling tax receipts decreased the federal budget balance from a surplus of 2.4% in 2000 to a deficit of 3.4% in 2003.[42]

In spite of the worsening fiscal situation, the U.S. current account deficit continued to be funded, largely by official investment from foreign central banks. As $2.3 trillion of U.S. current account deficits accumulated from 2002 through 2005, the value of total foreign reserves held in dollars increased by $1.2 trillion,

Exhibit 7.   Share of U.S. Assets in Foreign Asset Portfolio of Rest of World, 1980–2003 (percent)

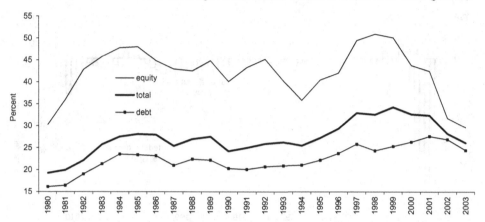

Sources: Adapted from Philip R. Lane and Gian Maria Milesi-Ferretti, "A Global Perspective on External Positions," prepared for the NBER conference G7 Current Account Imbalances: Sustainability and Adjustment, May 3, 2005, p. 34, Fig. 7.

Exhibit 8.   U.S. Exchange Rate Indices, January 1993–July 2013 (January 1997 = 100)

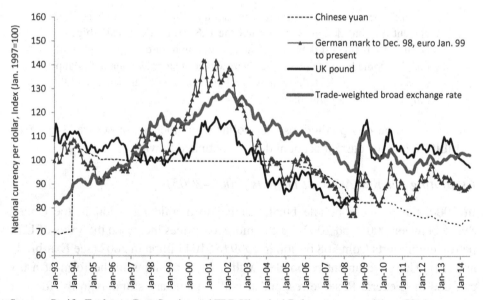

Sources: Pacific Exchange Rate Service and FRB Historical Releases, accessed Aug. 2014.

according to the Federal Reserve, while private and other non-official investment financed the rest.[43] (See **Exhibit 9a** for data from the U.S. Federal Reserve and the Treasury, as well as a comparison with data from the International Monetary Fund.) Foreign reserves held by Asian nations alone rose by $1.1 trillion. By buying reserves to prevent appreciation of their currencies against the dollar,

Exhibit 9. U.S. Net International Investment Position (NIIP) and Changes, 1998–2013 (billions US$)

	1998	2000	2002	2004	2005	2006	2007	2008	2009	2010	2011	2012	2013	(1998–2013)
NIIP	−858	−1,337	−2,045	−2,253	−1,932	−2,192	−1,796	−3,260	−2,275	−2,249	−3,670	−3,867	−4,565	
Change in NIIP	−72	−606	−170	−159	321	−260	396	−1,464	985	26	−1,421	−197	−698	−3,707
Current Account Deficit (−)	−215	−411	−458	−634	−745	−807	−719	−687	−381	−444	−459	−461	−400	−8,032
Valuation Change	143	−195	288	475	1,066	547	1,114	−778	1,366	470	−961	263	−298	

Source: BEA, Table 1, "International Investment Position of the United States at the End of the Period," accessed Aug. 2014.

Exhibit 10.   Currency Composition of Selected U.S. External Assets, 1994–2008 (billions US$ or percent)

	1994	1997	2001	2004	2005	2006	2007	2008
Long-term debt securities[a]	**304**	**547**	**502**	**993**	**1,028**	**1,294**	**1,607**	**1,261**
% U.S. dollar-denominated	48%	60%	66%	72%	76%	75%	73%	na
% German mark, French franc, Italian lira, Spanish peseta-denominated	19%	13%	na	na	na	na	na	na
% Euro-denominated	na	na	18%	15%	11%	10%	12%	na
% U.K. pound sterling-denominated	4%	5%	3%	3%	3%	3%	4%	na
% Yen-denominated	10%	6%	5%	4%	3%	3%	4%	na
% Canadian dollar-denominated	6%	8%	4%	3%	3%	3%	3%	na
% Other currency-denominated	13%	9%	3%	3%	4%	5%	5%	na
Short-term debt securities	na	na	**147**	**233**	**263**	**368**	**357**	**282**
% U.S. dollar-denominated	na	na	84%	84%	87%	92%	92%	na
FDI (at historical cost basis)[b]	**613**	**871**	**1,460**	**2,161**	**2,242**	**2,455**	**2,791**	**3,162**
% in Canada	12%	11%	10%	10%	10%	9%	9%	8%
% in Europe	48%	49%	53%	55%	54%	55%	56%	65%
% in Latin America/Caribbean	19%	21%	19%	16%	17%	17%	17%	20%
% in Africa and Middle East	2%	2%	2%	2%	2%	2%	2%	2%
% in Australia and New Zealand	4%	4%	2%	na[c]	4%	3%	3%	3%
% in Japan	6%	4%	4%	3%	4%	4%	4%	3%
% in rest of Asia	8%	9%	10%	14%	10%	10%	10%	11%
Portfolio equity	**567**	**1,208**	**1,613**	**2,560**	**3,318**	**4,329**	**5,248**	**2,748**
% in Europe	48%	61%	58%	53%	49%	51%	49%	50%
% in Asia	26%	18%	19%	22%	26%	24%	23%	24%
% in Canada/Latin America/Caribbean	21%	17%	20%	21%	22%	21%	24%	22%
% in Australia/New Zealand	4%	3%	2%	3%	2%	3%	3%	2%
% in other	1%	1%	1%	1%	1%	1%	1%	2%
(note: % of total foreign portfolio equity in ADRs)	na	21%	20%	15%	16%	17%	17%	0%
Total of Selected Assets	**1,484**	**2,626**	**3,722**	**5,947**	**6,851**	**8,446**	**10,003**	**7,453**
Total U.S. External Assets (at cost basis)[d]	**2,754**	**4,032**	**6,239**	**9,341**	**11,962**	**14,381**	**17,640**	**19,888**

Source: Calculated based on data in U.S. Treasury, U.S. Portfolio Holdings of Foreign Securities at end-year 2003, March 31, 2005 and subsequent years.

Notes: [a]Based on Appendix Table 18 Canada was based on text Table 8.

[b]Historical cost basis data for FDI differs from BEA IIP data.

[c]BEA reported that data for this year was suppressed to avoid disclosure of individual companies' data.

[d]Other remaining assets included, for example, claims reported by banks and non-banking concerns, mostly denominated in dollars. R-S and Gourinchas Rey both estimated that 55% of foreign U.S. assets were denominated in foreign currency.

Asian central banks maintained competitiveness of their countries' export sectors. The strategy was particularly important for China's economy. Exports to the United States accounted for 15% of China's 2006 GDP, up from 8% in 2000.

The strategy also supported low U.S. interest rates, which served to increase the value of a wide range of assets, particularly in the non-traded goods sector. This was particularly clear in residential real estate,[44] where dramatic increases in value raised the wealth of many U.S. residents, many of whom chose to borrow against their assets as well as let asset price appreciation substitute for savings.[45] Low interest rates also drove high levels of household debt. In 2003, for example, household credit card debt averaged $9,205, which represented a 25% increase with respect to the previous five years.[46]

In contrast to Asian central banks, European central banks did not intervene to prevent appreciation of the euro and the pound against the dollar. In nominal terms, after appreciating by 53% against the euro and 12% against the pound between summer 1995 and early 2002, the dollar depreciated 54% against the euro and 36% against the pound through December 2004.[47]

Depreciation of the U.S. dollar against European currencies helped offset some of the impact of accumulated current account deficits on the NIIP. While current account deficits between 2001 and 2012 totaled $7.1 trillion, the NIIP deteriorated by only $2.6 trillion over the same period (see **Exhibit 11a**).[48] The difference reflected changes in the valuation of the existing stock of U.S. assets and liabilities. Since a large portion of U.S.-owned assets abroad were located in Europe (see **Exhibit 12**), the fall in the value of the dollar against European currencies increased the dollar value of U.S. holdings of foreign assets.[49]

Regardless of valuation effects, U.S. liabilities to foreigners remained far in excess of U.S. claims on foreigners. Even so, the net investment income portion of the current account balance of the United States remained positive as the United States continued to receive more income from its investments abroad than foreigners received on their U.S. assets (see **Exhibit 4a**). In part, this was due to low U.S. interest rates. Harvard economists Ricardo Hausmann and Federico Sturzenegger had another more controversial explanation. They labeled the gap between official statistics indicating a negative U.S. NIIP and positive net income payments suggesting a positive NIIP "dark matter." They postulated that official data underestimated the true economic value of U.S. assets abroad by failing to capture important factors. These included "know-how" such as, for example, business ideas (rather than just plant, property, and equipment) that made U.S. foreign direct investment particularly productive, the provision of "liquidity services" in the form of foreign holdings of dollars in cash (on which the United States earned seignorage[50]) and the selling of "insurance" in that investors were willing to hold safer U.S. debt and equity at returns that were lower than those required to invest in the foreign countries where

516   L. Alfaro and R. D. Tella

Exhibit 11a. Employment and Annual Percentage Change in Employment by Industry, 2000–2014 (July of each year)

	2000	2014	2002	2004	2007	2008	2009	2010	2011	2012	2013	2014
	All Employees (Thousands)		Change in the Number of Employees (year-on-year percentage change)									
Total nonfarm	132,015	139,004	**−1.3**	**1.3**	**1.7**	**0.0**	**−5.3**	**−0.3**	**1.1**	**1.8**	**2.0**	**1.9**
Total private	111,148	117,082	−1.8	1.5	1.9	−0.4	−6.4	−0.4	1.9	2.3	2.4	2.2
Natural Resources and Mining	601	916	−5.4	4.0	6.8	7.2	−11.7	3.5	11.8	7.2	1.8	5.7
Construction	6,794	6,041	−2.3	3.6	1.7	−6.0	−17.1	−7.5	0.1	2.2	3.6	3.6
Manufacturing	17,325	12,160	−6.9	−0.5	−2.5	−2.8	−13.1	−1.4	1.6	1.6	0.2	1.5
Wood products	616	369	−3.4	3.2	−5.0	−9.5	−25.6	−2.7	−4.1	2.2	4.7	4.9
Nonmetallic mineral products	556	385	−5.1	3.9	0.6	−5.3	−17.6	−5.6	−1.2	−1.4	3.1	3.1
Primary metals	626	402	−10.1	−0.4	−3.8	−2.0	−20.9	3.2	7.6	3.5	−3.6	2.4
Fabricated metal products	1,761	1,456	−7.2	2.5	0.9	−1.7	−16.0	0.3	4.6	4.7	0.7	1.9
Machinery	1,466	1,129	−9.8	0.9	0.1	0.8	−16.1	−1.0	6.1	3.9	0.1	2.4
Computer and electronic products	1,832	1,058	−13.2	−0.8	−4.5	−1.9	−9.7	−1.9	−0.8	−1.2	−2.7	−0.9
Electrical equipment	596	373	−10.2	−2.4	−3.7	−1.0	−12.4	−2.4	1.7	0.7	0.7	0.0
Transportation equipment	2,061	1,573	−5.4	−0.8	−3.4	−4.5	−17.6	0.9	2.5	6.1	1.9	4.9
Furniture and related products	683	370	−4.6	1.0	−2.6	−6.9	−24.4	−5.5	0.1	−2.3	2.7	3.3
Miscellaneous durable goods	735	581	−3.7	−0.4	−2.4	−2.3	−6.5	−3.0	1.7	1.2	−0.6	0.2
Food manufacturing	1,559	1,470	−2.1	−1.0	1.4	−1.4	−0.5	−0.6	0.6	0.8	−0.5	0.3
Beverage and tobacco products	206	0	−1.5	−2.0	0.3	−2.0	−3.2	−3.5	5.2	*	*	*
Textile mills	380	117	−11.7	−7.7	−14.1	−11.1	−17.8	−2.4	2.0	−3.4	−0.8	0.1
Textile product mills	216	113	−5.9	−0.8	−7.1	−5.8	−15.6	−4.0	−1.9	−1.3	−3.0	0.3

(Continued)

Exhibit 11a. (*Continued*)

	All Employees (Thousands)		Change in the Number of Employees (year-on-year percentage change)									
	2000	2014	2002	2004	2007	2008	2009	2010	2011	2012	2013	2014
Apparel	497	132	−15.4	−7.3	−14.5	−8.6	−13.5	−6.8	−4.3	−1.5	−4.5	−6.3
Leather and allied products	70	0	−10.5	−3.9	−10.8	0.9	−13.2	−5.5	7.7	*	*	*
Paper and paper products	605	375	−4.9	−3.4	−2.2	−0.7	−11.5	−1.8	−1.4	−3.1	0.2	−1.2
Printing and related	809	441	−7.9	−2.5	−2.5	−4.0	−13.5	−5.6	−4.3	−1.0	−3.5	−1.5
Petroleum and coal products	123	114	−3.1	−2.4	−3.5	1.9	0.9	−1.1	−2.3	0.2	−1.0	2.5
Chemicals	977	803	−3.4	−1.9	−3.4	−0.4	−7.2	−1.8	0.8	−0.8	1.5	1.0
Plastics and rubber products	953	664	−4.7	−0.3	−4.8	−3.2	−15.5	2.1	1.3	1.8	1.6	1.0
Miscellaneous nondurable goods	*	238	*	*	*	*	*	*	*	*	3.5	3.4
Service-providing	107,295	119,887	−0.3	1.3	2.2	0.6	−3.7	0.2	1.1	1.8	2.1	1.8
Private service-providing	86,428	97,965	−0.8	1.7	2.5	0.4	−4.5	0.2	1.9	2.3	2.7	2.1
Government	20,867	21,922	1.6	−0.1	0.9	1.6	0.0	0.3	−2.4	−0.6	0.3	0.4

Sources: Compiled from Bureau of Labor Statistics, "The Employment Situation," news release, various years, Table B-1, "Employees on nonfarm payrolls by industry sector and selected industry detail," July data, seasonally adjusted, accessed Aug. 2014 and earlier years.

Note: *In 2012 headings and aggregation procedures for some nondurable manufacturing were modified. Categories were not included in years where there is an asterisk.

Exhibit 11b.   Industry Breakdown of U.S. GDP, 1976–2013 (as a % of GDP, except as noted)

	1975	1980	1985	1990	1995	2000	2005	2007	2008	2009	2010	2011	2012	2013
Total Private Industries	**84.9**	**86.3**	**86.2**	**86.1**	**86.6**	**87.1**	**86.8**	**86.8**	**86.4**	**85.7**	**85.7**	**86.1**	**86.5**	**87.0**
Agriculture and Mining:	**5.2**	**5.5**	**4.3**	**3.2**	**2.3**	**2.0**	**2.7**	**3.2**	**3.8**	**3.0**	**3.3**	**3.9**	**3.9**	**4.3**
Agriculture, forestry, fishing	3.1	2.2	1.8	1.6	1.2	1.0	1.0	1.0	1.1	1.0	1.1	1.3	1.2	1.6
Mining	2.1	3.3	2.5	1.5	1.0	1.1	1.7	2.2	2.7	2.0	2.2	2.6	2.6	2.7
Construction	**4.5**	**4.7**	**4.2**	**4.2**	**4.0**	**4.5**	**5.0**	**4.9**	**4.4**	**4.0**	**3.6**	**3.5**	**3.6**	**3.6**
Manufacturing:	**20.6**	**20.0**	**17.8**	**16.7**	**15.9**	**15.1**	**13.0**	**12.8**	**12.3**	**11.9**	**12.2**	**12.4**	**12.5**	**12.4**
Durable goods	12.2	12.2	10.9	9.6	9.1	9.0	7.3	7.1	6.7	6.0	6.4	6.5	6.6	6.5
Nondurable goods	8.4	7.9	6.9	7.1	6.8	6.1	5.7	5.7	5.5	5.9	5.8	5.9	6.0	5.9
Private services:	**54.6**	**56.0**	**59.8**	**62.0**	**64.4**	**65.4**	**66.1**	**65.9**	**65.9**	**66.8**	**66.6**	**66.3**	**66.6**	**66.7**
Utilities	2.4	2.2	2.7	2.5	2.4	1.8	1.5	1.6	1.6	1.8	1.8	1.8	1.7	1.7
Trade (Wholesale and Retail)	14.7	13.8	13.7	12.9	13.3	12.8	12.3	12.0	11.8	11.6	11.6	11.6	11.6	11.6
Transportation & warehousing	3.7	3.7	3.3	3.0	3.1	3.0	2.9	2.8	2.9	2.8	2.9	2.9	2.9	2.9
Information	3.7	3.9	4.2	4.1	4.2	4.6	4.9	4.9	4.9	4.9	4.8	4.8	4.8	4.8
Finance, insurance, and real estate[a]	15.2	16.0	17.5	18.1	19.0	19.4	20.2	19.9	19.1	19.9	19.7	19.4	19.5	19.6
Professional and business services	5.3	6.2	7.5	8.9	9.3	10.8	11.0	11.4	11.9	11.5	11.5	11.7	11.9	11.9
Education, health care, social assistance	4.5	4.8	5.3	6.5	7.1	6.6	7.3	7.4	7.8	8.4	8.3	8.3	8.2	8.3
Acconodation, food, entertainment[b]	2.8	3.0	3.1	3.4	3.4	3.8	3.7	3.7	3.6	3.6	3.6	3.6	3.7	3.7
Other services, except govt	2.4	2.5	2.5	2.7	2.7	2.7	2.4	2.3	2.3	2.3	2.2	2.2	2.2	2.1
Government	**15.1**	**13.7**	**13.8**	**13.9**	**13.4**	**12.9**	**13.2**	**13.2**	**13.6**	**14.3**	**14.3**	**13.9**	**13.5**	**13.0**
Addendum: GDP in current trillion $	**1.6**	**2.8**	**4.2**	**5.8**	**7.4**	**10.3**	**13.1**	**14.5**	**14.7**	**14.4**	**15.0**	**15.5**	**16.2**	**16.8**

Source: Adapted from Bureau of Economic Analysis, Gross-Domestic-Product-by-Industry Accounts, Value Added by Industry, released Apr. 25, 2014, accessed Aug. 2014.

Notes: [a]Includes rental and leasing.
[b]Includes recreation and arts.

Exhibit 11b.   Source of Changes in U.S. NIIP, 1990–2013 (billion US$)

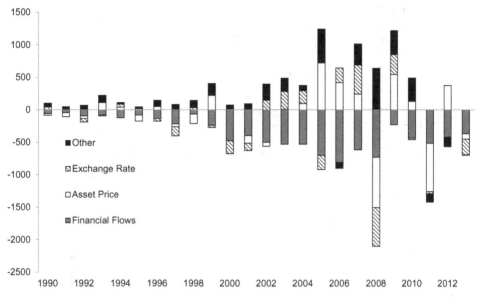

Source: BEA, Components of Changes in Foreign-Owned Assets in the U.S, accessed Aug. 2014.

U.S. residents invested.[51] Hausmann and Sturzenegger concluded that "once dark matter is taken into account, the world is not far from balance. The stock of dark matter has been growing quite steadily. If this persists, the picture does not look that bad."[52]

Soft or Hard Landing for the U.S. Economy?

The implications of the U.S. current account deficit were debated with intensity. At one extreme, it was argued that large deficits would eventually resolve themselves smoothly, even if they persisted for many more years. For example, in an August 2006 report, the U.S. Congressional Budget Office estimated that current account deficits would grow more slowly than GDP through 2008 before stabilizing in 2016, implying shrinking deficits in terms of GDP over time.[53] Other groups believed the large deficits would soon lead to a necessary macroeconomic adjustment that could be painful for the United States as well as the rest of the world. Focusing in particular on the U.S. current account deficit, former European Central Bank President Jean-Claude Trichet expressed concern over "global imbalances" exemplified by capital flowing, in aggregate, from the developing to the industrialized world.

A "Benign Resolution"

Some economists attributed "global imbalances" to potential growth differentials among various regions of the world and to differences in these regions' abilities to

Exhibit 12. U.S. Bilateral Trade Patterns: 1982–2013 (current billion dollars and percent of trade)

	1982	1986	1990	1994	1998	2000	2001	2002	2003	2007	2008	2009	2010	2011	2012	2013
Goods Exports, bn $	211	223	387	503	670	785	731	697	730	1,164	1,307	1,070	1,290	1,499	1,561	1,592
as % exports																
European Union	22%	23%	26%	21%	22%	21%	22%	21%	21%	21%	21%	21%	19%	18%	17%	17%
Canada	19%	25%	22%	23%	23%	23%	22%	23%	23%	21%	20%	19%	19%	19%	19%	19%
Latin America[b]	16%	14%	14%	18%	21%	22%	22%	21%	21%	21%	22%	22%	23%	25%	26%	26%
China	1%	1%	1%	2%	2%	2%	3%	3%	4%	6%	5%	7%	7%	7%	7%	8%
Japan	10%	12%	12%	10%	8%	8%	8%	7%	7%	5%	5%	5%	5%	4%	5%	4%
Other Asia[a]	17%	15%	17%	19%	17%	17%	16%	17%	17%	16%	15%	16%	17%	16%	16%	16%
Remainder	15%	10%	8%	7%	6%	7%	8%	7%	7%	9%	11%	10%	10%	10%	11%	11%
Goods Imports, bn $	248	368	498	669	917	1,232	1,154	1,173	1,272	1,986	2,141	1,580	1,939	2,240	2,304	2,294
as % imports																
European Union	17%	20%	20%	18%	19%	18%	19%	19%	19%	18%	17%	18%	17%	17%	17%	17%
Canada	20%	19%	19%	20%	19%	19%	19%	18%	18%	16%	16%	14%	15%	14%	14%	15%
Latin America[b]	16%	11%	13%	13%	16%	17%	17%	18%	17%	18%	18%	18%	19%	20%	20%	19%
China	1%	1%	3%	6%	8%	8%	9%	11%	12%	16%	16%	19%	19%	18%	19%	19%
Japan	15%	22%	18%	18%	13%	12%	11%	10%	9%	7%	7%	6%	6%	6%	6%	6%
Other Asia[a]	18%	18%	21%	20%	19%	17%	16%	16%	15%	13%	12%	13%	13%	13%	13%	13%
Remainder	13%	8%	7%	5%	5%	9%	9%	8%	9%	12%	14%	11%	12%	13%	11%	10%

Sources: Adapted from BEA International Transactions Accounts Data, Table 2a, U.S. Trade in Goods, accessed Aug. 2014.
Notes: [a]'Other Asia' redefined as Asia Pacific, excluding Japan and China, following BEA's reclassification of Asia in 1999.
[b]Includes rest of Western Hemisphere.

produce financial assets for global savers. They argued that imbalances could be maintained if these differences persisted.[54] Other studies focused on trade aspects, forecasting that faster economic growth outside of the United States would coincide with slower U.S. economic growth, leading to an improvement in the U.S. trade balance as foreign demand for U.S. products increased while U.S. demand for imports fell.[55] However, many economists argued that this analysis was too simplistic and failed to account for the fact that GDP growth in the United States increased U.S. imports more than foreign GDP growth increased U.S. exports.[56] The asymmetry was even more extreme for imports and exports of goods, but was reversed for imports and exports of services. The asymmetry implied that, assuming a constant exchange rate, the U.S. current account deficit could fail to improve even if the rest of the world grew at a faster rate.[57]

Meanwhile, in 2004 and 2005 Alan Greenspan, then chairman of the Federal Reserve, focused on financing the deficit. He noted that the ratio of global debt and equity claims to trade, as well as to GDP, had been rising for almost half a century, most rapidly since 1995. He argued that steady increases in financial intermediation (driven, for example, by global financial deregulation) facilitated the financing of continually widening current account deficits and surpluses around the world. At the same time, there appeared to be a trend toward reversal in the "home bias" phenomenon describing investors' tendency to put the majority of their wealth into assets from their own country rather than into foreign assets.[58] In 1993, 95% of domestic savings around the world flowed into domestic investments. By 2002, this value fell to 80%. In particular, global savings flowed into the United States with its favorable investment climate, strong investor protection framework, and expected real rates of return higher than in other countries.[59] Greenspan concluded: "Spreading globalization has fostered a degree of international flexibility that has raised the probability of a benign resolution to the U.S. current account imbalance."[60] Other members of the Federal Reserve Board of Governors were in agreement.[61]

Rather than playing down the risks of the current account deficit, then U.S. Treasury Assistant Secretary for International Affairs Randal Quarles referred to it as "our gift to the world."[62] He was supported by economists who agreed that the widening deficit provided "the engine for growth for the rest of the world"[63] by encouraging export-led economic expansion, particularly in Asia. A major issue, therefore, was the degree to which Asian central bank dollar purchases would continue. Many observers believed that Asian countries would choose to maintain their heavily managed exchange rates against the dollar since the benefits to Asian export sectors outweighed the costs of holding U.S. assets yielding low — or even negative if further dollar depreciation was expected — returns. In part, this was due to the major structural changes taking place in industrializing Asia. For example, it was noted that China relied on rapid export-led growth to absorb 200 million surplus agricultural workers into the modern industrial traded sector.[64]

In 2004, former U.S. Treasury Secretary Larry Summers (Harvard University President at the time) used the term "balance of financial terror" to refer to the situation in which the United States was relying on the costs to the rest of the world of not financing the U.S. current account deficit as assurance that financing would continue.[65] In particular, it was argued that China would continue to buy billions of U.S. dollars each month in order to avoid a dollar collapse that would undermine U.S. consumption and the global stability upon which China's economic miracle was based. It followed that the United States would avoid tough sanctions to punish China's undervalued currency because such action would trigger inflation, higher interest rates, and recession.[66] Other economists referred to the situation more mildly as "vendor finance" or "Bretton Woods II."[67]

A Change in Trajectory

There was no guarantee, however, that Asian central banks would continue to support the dollar.[68] In mid-March 2005, Yoon Jeung Hyun, South Korea's top banking regulator, hinted at a gradual move away from this system: "There is widespread recognition that the ongoing trade imbalance between Asia and the United States — that is, Asian savings financing U.S. consumption — cannot be sustained and could potentially pose a systemic risk to the global financial system." Just days before, Japanese Prime Minister Junichiro Koizumi said his country should consider diversifying its currency holdings.[69] And in mid-March, 2009, China's Premier Wen Jiabao admitted publicly that "we are a little bit worried…we hope the US honors its word." Hours later, President Barack Obama retorted, "There is no safer investment in the world than in the USA."[70]

Pressure on Asian countries to reduce purchases of U.S. dollar assets also came from the United States itself. Although foreign investment in U.S. Treasuries helped to keep U.S. interest rates low and U.S. consumption high, it also contributed to growing U.S. trade deficits, which intensified protectionist pressures. As such, the United States demanded that China allow its currency to become stronger against the dollar, even after the country loosened its exchange rate regime in mid-2005. U.S. imports from China were growing at a rapid pace, implying major shifts in U.S. employment (see **Exhibit 13a** and **13b**), especially as Chinese production moved up the value-added chain from textiles to furniture and auto parts[71] (See **Exhibit 14**). In 2004 and 2005, Congress introduced various bills that would levy extra tariffs on Chinese goods.[72] Six U.S. Senators wrote to then Vice President Dick Cheney that China's exchange rate policy "has become a destabilizing force in the world economy, has led to major international exchange rate and trade imbalances throughout the world."[73] In mid-May 2006, the U.S. Treasury warned China that it could be cited by the U.S. as a currency manipulator, a process that could lead

Exhibit 13a.   U.S. General Economic Indicators, 1970–2013 (units as indicated)

	1970	1975	1980	1985	1990	1995	2000	2001	2002	2003	2007	2008	2009	2010	2011	2012	2013
Per capita GDP (thousands 2009 dollars)	23.0	24.9	28.3	31.8	35.8	38.2	44.5	44.5	44.8	45.7	49.3	48.7	46.9	47.7	48.1	48.9	49.6
Nominal GDP (current trillions dollars)	1.1	1.7	2.9	4.3	6.0	7.7	10.3	10.6	11.0	11.5	14.5	14.7	14.4	15.0	15.5	16.2	16.8
Real GDP growth (% change on prior year)	0.2	−0.2	−0.2	4.2	1.9	2.7	4.1	1.0	1.8	2.8	1.8	−0.3	−2.8	2.5	1.6	2.3	2.2
Consumer prices (% change on prior year)	5.7	9.1	13.5	3.6	5.4	2.8	3.4	2.8	1.6	2.3	2.8	3.8	0.4	1.6	3.2	2.1	1.5
M2 (% change on prior year)	6.4	12.7	8.5	8.0	3.7	4.4	6.6	9.4	6.3	4.6	5.8	10.4	2.2	4.5	10.3	7.6	5.6
Real exchange rate (% change on prior year)	na	−1.2	1.5	4.1	−2.7	−2.7	3.8	5.8	0.1	6.0	−4.8	4.2	4.1	−4.7	−5.1	2.1	0.3
Federal surplus or deficit (% GDP)	0.3	−3.3	−2.6	−5.0	−3.7	−2.2	2.3	1.2	−1.5	3.3	−1.1	3.1	−9.8	−8.8	−8.4	−6.8	−4.1
Stockmarket Index (annual % change)	0.1	31.5	25.8	26.3	6.6	34.1	−10.1	−13.0	−23.4	26.4	3.5	−38.5	23.5	12.8	0.0	13.4	29.6
Unemployment (% civilian population)	5.0	8.5	7.2	7.2	5.6	5.6	4.0	4.7	5.8	6.0	4.6	5.8	9.3	9.6	9.0	8.1	7.4
Productivity (output/hr; index; 2009=100)	45	50	53	59	64	69	80	82	86	89	96	97	100	103	104	105	106
Compensation (per/hr, index; 2009=100)	13	19	29	39	50	58	74	77	79	82	96	99	100	102	104	107	109
Unit labor costs (index; 2009=100)	29	38	55	67	78	84	92	94	92	92	100	102	100	99	101	102	103

Sources: Bureau of Economic Analysis; Federal Reserve, Bureau of Labor Statistics, Congressional Budget Office, Global Financial Data, accessed Aug. 2014.

Exhibit 13b.   U.S. Interest Rates (annual average rate) and Consumer Price Inflation, 1962–2013 (percent)

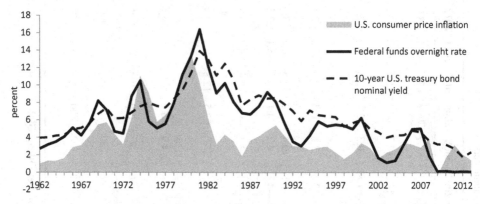

Source: Adapted from Federal Reserve Board, http://www.federalreserve.gov/releases/ h15/data.htm, and Bureau of Labor Statistics, accessed Aug. 2014.

to economic sanctions, if it did not move toward a more flexible exchange rate. To similar threats in 2005, China's Deputy Chief of the State Administration of Foreign Exchange Wei Benhua responded: "There is no timeframe for such a change as conditions are not ready yet," and noted that the United States should "put its own house in order before blaming others" for its trade deficit.[74] (The yuan appreciated 27% between January 2005 and January 2013).

Furthermore, it was thought that continued U.S. current account deficits could lead to the U.S. NIIP becoming unsustainable. In 2005, it was estimated that maintaining current account deficits at 5% of GDP would imply that the NIIP would eventually stabilize at −83% of GDP (or, alternatively, that stabilizing the U.S. NIIP at −25% of GDP would require the U.S. current account deficit to fall to 1.5% of GDP).[75] Among large industrial countries, the 2013 U.S. NIIP of 27% of GDP was already among the highest, although some commentators noted that some smaller industrial countries had accumulated positions higher than 50% of GDP without obvious adverse effects.

For example, Australia's NIIP stood at −59% of GDP and New Zealand's at −131% in 2003.[76] Most economists, however, doubted whether the United States, with a share of exports to GDP of only 10% versus 17% for Australia and 35% for New Zealand, could sustain an NIIP at equivalent levels.[77]

Analysts also noted that income payments associated with the growing stock of external financial obligations that had to be paid out of current production would become increasingly difficult for the United States to meet. They disregarded the "dark matter" argument that official statistics incorrectly valued U.S. assets abroad. For example, Goldman Sachs advisor Willem Buiter concluded that only possibly

Exhibit 14a. U.S. National Income Accounts: 1980–2013 (% of GDP except when noted)

% GDP, except where noted	1980	1984	1988	1992	1996	1998	2000	2001	2002	2003	2007	2008	2009	2010	2011	2012	2013
GDP (current trillion dollars)	**2.9**	**4.0**	**5.3**	**6.5**	**8.1**	**9.1**	**10.3**	**10.6**	**11.0**	**11.5**	**14.5**	**14.7**	**14.4**	**15.0**	**15.5**	**16.2**	**16.8**
Household Consumption:[a]	**61%**	**62%**	**64%**	**64%**	**65%**	**65%**	**66%**	**67%**	**67%**	**67%**	**67%**	**68%**	**68%**	**68%**	**69%**	**69%**	**68%**
Durable goods	8%	8%	9%	8%	8%	9%	9%	9%	9%	9%	8%	7%	7%	7%	7%	7%	7%
Nondurable goods	20%	18%	16%	16%	15%	15%	15%	15%	15%	15%	15%	15%	15%	15%	16%	16%	16%
Services	33%	36%	38%	41%	41%	42%	42%	43%	44%	44%	44%	45%	46%	46%	46%	45%	46%
Government Consumption:	**21%**	**20%**	**21%**	**21%**	**18%**	**18%**	**18%**	**18%**	**19%**	**19%**	**19%**	**20%**	**21%**	**21%**	**20%**	**20%**	**19%**
Federal Nondefense	3%	3%	2%	3%	2%	2%	2%	2%	3%	3%	3%	3%	3%	3%	3%	3%	3%
Federal defense	6%	7%	7%	6%	5%	4%	4%	4%	4%	5%	5%	5%	5%	6%	5%	5%	5%
State and local	11%	10%	11%	12%	11%	11%	12%	12%	12%	12%	12%	13%	13%	12%	12%	12%	11%
Gross Private Investment:	**19%**	**20%**	**18%**	**15%**	**18%**	**19%**	**20%**	**18%**	**18%**	**18%**	**18%**	**16%**	**13%**	**14%**	**14%**	**15%**	**16%**
Nonresidential	14%	14%	13%	11%	13%	14%	15%	14%	12%	12%	13%	13%	11%	11%	12%	12%	12%
Residential	5%	5%	5%	4%	4%	5%	5%	5%	5%	6%	5%	4%	3%	3%	2%	3%	3%
Change in inventories	0%	2%	0%	0%	0%	1%	1%	0%	0%	0%	0%	0%	−1%	0%	0%	0%	0%
Exports	**10%**	**7%**	**8%**	**10%**	**11%**	**10%**	**11%**	**10%**	**9%**	**9%**	**11%**	**13%**	**11%**	**12%**	**14%**	**14%**	**13%**
Imports	**10%**	**10%**	**11%**	**10%**	**12%**	**12%**	**14%**	**13%**	**13%**	**13%**	**16%**	**17%**	**14%**	**16%**	**17%**	**17%**	**17%**
Real GDP (bns 2005 $)	6.5	7.3	8.5	9.3	10.6	11.5	12.6	12.7	12.9	13.3	14.9	14.8	14.4	14.8	15.0	15.4	15.7

Source: Adapted from Bureau of Economic Analysis (BEA), Table 1.1.5 Gross Domestic Product, and Table 1.1.6 Real Gross Domestic Product, accessed August 2014.

Note: [a]Figures may not add up precisely due to rounding.

Exhibit 14b.   U.S. Investment and Savings, 1970–2013 (% GDP)

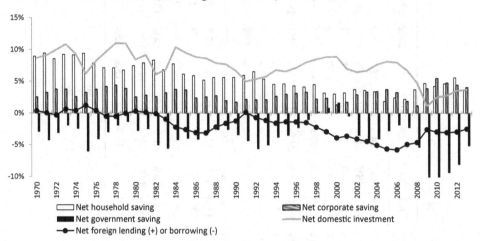

Net household saving   Net corporate saving
Net government saving   Net domestic investment
Net foreign lending (+) or borrowing (−)

Source: Adapted from BEA Table 5.1., saving and Investment and Table 1.1.5., Gross Domestic Product, accessed August 2014.

Notes: Net domestic investment refers to public and private investment and is net of depreciation. In 2013, gross private domestic investment was 15.8% of GDP, gross public domestic investment was 3.6%, and depreciation was 15.7% of GDP. Net domestic investment was 3.7% of GDP. There is a statistical discrepancy of −1.3% of GDP in the saving and investment data used for this chart.

up to $0.5 trillion — representing seignorage on dollar cash holdings abroad — of the $3 trillion of "dark matter" identified by Hausmann and Sturzenegger was valid. He concluded that the paradox of the net investment income portion of the current account balance remaining positive even as the U.S. NIIP widened would be resolved simply by net income payments becoming negative: "In short, Hausmann and Sturzenegger believe they have found dark matter. Instead they have, thus far, found mainly cold fusion."[78] As a matter of fact, in 2014, the U.S. Bureau of Economic Analysis was beginning to publish a new series reevaluating international investments that, far from crediting the existence of "dark matter," put the U.S. NIIP at an ever greater negative −32% of GDP.[79]

The problem of possible future U.S. difficulties meeting growing interest payments was compounded by the fact that capital inflows from abroad were not moving into the tradeables sector where extra export capacity generated could be used to service debt.[80] Economists Obstfeld and Rogoff noted: "As long as non-traded goods account for the lion's share of U.S. output, a sharp contraction in net imports — a significant closing of the U.S. current account — will lead to a large exchange rate adjustment under most plausible scenarios. That adjustment will be sharper the longer is the initial rope that global capital markets offer to the United States."[81] In 2004, they estimated a possible depreciation of the trade-weighted dollar of up to 40% or more.

Exhibit 15. Federal Budget Deficit (actual and projected): 1980–2024 (as a % of GDP)

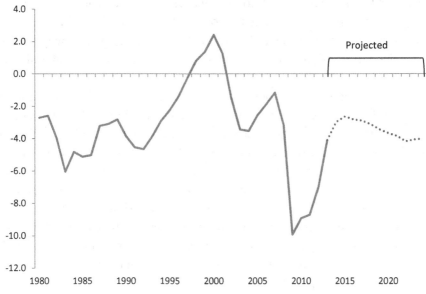

Sources: Adapted from Congressional Budget Office, "Budget and Economic Outlook," accessed Aug. 2014 and earlier years in the same series (some with different titles and table numbers). Accessed Aug. 2014.

Some economists pointed to valuation effects to argue that the further expected depreciation of the dollar would shrink the NIIP and, therefore, reduce future income payments abroad. More specifically, economists made a rough calculation that a further 10% depreciation of the dollar would represent a transfer of 5% of U.S. GDP from the rest of the world to the United States.[82] It was noted that the effect of a sufficiently large negative valuation effect could lead to a sudden stop in capital flows that would force the trade balance to move into surplus.[83]

Global "Hard Landing"

> *Unilateral exchange rate adjustments will run into very substantial competitive pressures against those who allow a unilateral exchange rate appreciation. And so exchange rate appreciation is likely to be more politically acceptable and more economically acceptable if it does not take place unilaterally but takes place in a coordinated fashion. This, too, is a remedy that doesn't work very well on its own, as exchange rate adjustment in Asia and an associated substantial reduction in foreign purchases of U.S. Treasury bills would put American interest rates and the American recovery at significant risk with, again, risks to the global economy.[84]*
>
> — Larry Summers, 2004

Another scenario also involved a "hard landing" for the United States and global economies.[85] Economists Nouriel Roubini and Brad Setser explained the risk: "The current account deficit will continue to grow on the back of higher and higher payments on U.S. foreign debt even if the trade deficit stabilizes. That is why sustained trade deficits will set off the kind of explosive debt dynamics that lead to financial crises."[86]

It was also noted that the widely projected inevitable large future dollar depreciation could lead to severe inflation and a rapid increase in U.S. long-term interest rates. A resulting sharp fall in the price of a range of assets, including equities and housing, could lead to a severe slowdown in the United States. The fall in U.S. imports associated with the U.S. slowdown and the depreciated dollar could lead to a global severe economic slowdown or even recession.[87] Some economists predicted that the impact would be much more severe in Europe and Japan than in the United States.[88] With initial signs of such a slowdown as the U.S. housing market showed signs of softening in September 2006, Morgan Stanley Chief Economist Stephen Roach noted the importance of countries reducing dependence on expansion of U.S. domestic demand to support their own growth:

> As the U.S. housing bubble bursts, the American consumer is likely to stumble. . . . With consumers elsewhere in the world unlikely to fill the void, growth in the world economy could well be at risk. This could come as quite a surprise to global investors, most of whom are banking on a continuation of the four-year boom in world economic growth. Financial markets have begun to discount such a possibility, but further adjustments could well lie ahead. . . . But in the end, there must be more to rebalancing the global economy than a drop in U.S. consumption. An export-dependent world economy has leaned too hard for too long on the American consumer as the sustenance of economic growth. As the housing bubble bursts, overextended U.S. consumers can't afford to carry that load any longer. Other countries must now learn to grow the old-fashioned way — drawing greater support from their home markets rather than free-riding on the United States.[89]

Furthermore, U.S. policy-makers were urged to reduce dependence on external financing.[90] For example, the IMF in its 2005 World Economic Outlook underscored the importance of reducing U.S. fiscal deficits as part of a cooperative approach also involving gradually allowing exchange rate flexibility in Asia and adopting structural economic reforms in Europe and Japan.[91] The report proceeded by chiding the United States for being insufficiently ambitious with its deficit reduction target, as well as for failing to meet that target. While chairman of the Federal Reserve, even Greenspan agreed that the federal budget, with open spending on homeland security and "the war on terror," needed to be brought closer to balance.[92] The *Economist* was blunter still in its complaints about U.S. fiscal profligacy:

> America's commitment to budget discipline is a sham...Anyone who thinks more tax cuts and fewer spending cuts add up to budget discipline lives in fiscal fantasyland.... The cowardice surrounding spending cuts makes the obsession with cutting taxes still further even harder to forgive. Despite healthy economic growth, federal revenues stand at 16% of GDP, the lowest in 50 years. Yet Mr. Bush and majorities in both houses of Congress want to make existing tax cuts permanent and push through new ones.... Proposing such tax cuts just as the baby-boom generation retires is fiscal delusion not fiscal discipline.[93]

In response to the severe recession that began in December 2007, the U.S. Congress passed a $787 billion stimulus package in February 2009 to prevent a collapse in economic activity. The stimulus package, the slump in tax revenues caused by the recession and the rising expenditures on healthcare and unemployment all contributed to deficit of nearly $1.5 trillion — just under 10% of GDP (**Exhibit 3a**). It dropped to about 7% of GDP in 2012, and then, after the "fiscal cliff" tax adjustments and higher growth, to an estimated 4% of GDP in 2013. The nonpartisan Congressional Budget Office projected that $7.8 trillion worth of U.S. government debt would accumulate over the coming decade.[94] The CBO estimated this would actually only represent an increase of 1% of GDP.

Beginning in 2011, a political struggle over budget policy grew increasingly intense. For the first time in history, several political leaders saw a requirement for Congress to raise the borrowing limit by August 2, 2011, as a "unique opportunity" to forge a "grand bargain" reducing future deficits.[95] The ensuing game of political chicken, about just what form that bargain would take, unnerved financial markets worldwide, as well as voters.[96] As tension mounted, on July 14, the rating agency Standard & Poor's put the United States on a negative watch, warning that it might well downgrade U.S. credit from AAA, the top grade, for the first time ever.

After several failed attempts, only on August 2 itself, when supposedly the U.S. government would have to stop paying its bills, did Congress and Obama cobble together a stop-gap measure. It called for budget cuts in two phases. The first phase, beginning in October when the next fiscal year started, was projected to reduce deficits by $900 billion over the next decade.[97] The next phase required creating a bipartisan committee to devise a plan to reduce deficits another $1.3 trillion over the next decade. Otherwise, cuts would automatically take effect, evenly from military and non-military spending — a policy that nearly everyone saw as too blunt but that did, in fact, take effect in 2013.

At least, the United States could continue borrowing. Across the Atlantic, investors worried about sovereign debt in Europe, or even a collapse of the euro. On August 3, 2011, yields on two-year Treasury notes fell to 0.26%, the lowest rate ever.[98] Yields on one-month bills actually fell below zero before settling at zero. On Friday, after the markets had closed, Standard & Poor's did downgrade U.S. sovereign debt to AA+. It noted that "the downgrade reflects our view that the effectiveness, stability, and predictability of American policymaking and political institutions have weakened at a time of ongoing fiscal and economic challenge."[99] Hours later, Beijing issued a sharp statement that Washington must "cure its addiction to debts" and "live within its means."[100]

Although China had shown some reluctance to buy U.S. Treasuries, its Treasury holdings actually increased between 2009 and 2013, although they fell a percentage of its total reserves.[101] As a spokesman for the State Council put it, "For policymakers in Beijing seeking alternative ways to invest the massive foreign exchange reserves and to reduce its rapid accumulation remain the crucial challenges."[102] Yet at least for the time being, demand for U.S. debt hardly weakened. The yield on 10-year U.S. bonds fell from 2.58% on Friday before Standard & Poor's announcement to 2.4% on the following Monday and was still 2.4% in August 2014.[103] It remained to be seen if the U.S. would continue to hold its place as the world's financial center.

Endnotes

[1] 2006 Economic Report of the President, p. 140, available at http://www.gpoaccess. gov/eop/index.html, accessed September 6, 2006.

[2] Full list: Australia, Austria, Denmark, Finland, Greece, Iceland, Ireland, Malta, New Zealand, Norway and Portugal, according to Sebastian Edwards, "Is the U.S. Current Account Deficit Sustainable? And if Not, How Costly is Adjustment Likely To Be?" prepared for presentation at the Spring 2005 meeting of the Brookings Panel on Economic Activity, March 16, 2005, p. 10.

[3] This view was most famous in Michael P. Dooley, David Folkerts-Landau, and Peter Garber, "An Essay on the Revived Bretton Woods System," National Bureau of Economic Research Working Paper 9971, September 2003 and Michael P. Dooley, David Folkerts-Landau, and Peter Garber, "The Revived Bretton Woods System: The Effects of Periphery Intervention and Reserve Management on Interest Rates and Exchange Rates in Center Countries," Bureau of Economic Research Working Paper 10332, March 2004.

[4] Changes in reserves often do not match the current account because of changes in the value of reserve assets that central banks hold.

[5] Economists Nouriel Roubini and Brad Setser noted: "The core contradiction in the current international monetary order is simple. The United States is currently financing itself by selling low-yielding dollar debt, which offers foreign investors little protection against a future fall in the dollar. Yet the United States' large trade deficit and rapidly rising external debt to GDP ratio imply that a large future fall in the dollar will be needed

to reduce the U.S. trade deficit to more sustainable levels. The longer foreign investors finance the United States on current terms — particularly investors from countries whose currencies have yet to fall at all against the dollar — the larger their likely capital losses on their dollar assets." Nouriel Roubini and Brad Setser, "Will the Bretton Woods 2 Regime Unravel Soon? The Risk of a Hard Landing in 2005–2006," written for the Symposium on the "Revived Bretton Woods System: A New Paradigm for Asian Development?" organized by the Federal Reserve Bank of San Francisco and U.C. Berkeley, San Francisco, February 4, 2005, p. 11.

6   Maurice Obstfeld and Kenneth Rogoff, "Global Current Account Imbalances and Exchange Rate Adjustments," May 17, 2005, available at elsa.berkeley.edu/~obstfeld/global_current.pdf, accessed September 19, 2006.

7   Calculated from Federal Reserve, "Foreign Exchange Rates: Nominal Broad Dollar Index," www.federalreserve.gov/releases/H10/Summary/indexb_m.html, accessed Aug. 2014.

8   Nouriel Roubini and Brad Setser, "The US as a Net Debtor: The Sustainability of the US External Imbalances," NYU, August 2004, revised: November 2004, available at http://www.stern.nyu.edu/ globalmacro/Roubini-Setser-US-External-Imbalances.pdf, accessed September 14, 2006, p. 45.

9   Roubini and Setser 2004, p. 44, citing Peter G. Peterson, "Presentation of the Book (Running on Empty: How the Democratic and Republican Parties are Bankrupting Our Future and What Americans Can Do about It)." Institute for International Economics, August 9, 2004, available at http://www.iie.com/publications/papers/peterson0804. pdf, accessed June 9, 2005.

10 Alistair Barr, "Deficits may hit dollar, fuel inflation: Buffett says Iscar deal is part of strategy to protect against a drop in buck," May 6, 2006 available at http://www. marketwatch.com, accessed September 14, 2006.

11 Carla Fried, "Where Warren Buffett Is (and Isn't) Putting His Money Now," CBS MoneyWatch, May 3, 2011. http://moneywatch.bnet.com/economic-news/blog/daily-money/where-warren-buffett-is-and-isnt-putting-his-money-now/2590/, accessed August 17, 2011.

12 In 1894, the U.S. NIIP was estimated to have reached a level close to the 2004 level of −22% of GDP. Around the same time, the current account deficit fluctuated around 4% of GDP. From Maurice Obstfeld and Kenneth Rogoff, "The Unsustainable U.S. Current Account Position Revisited," National Bureau of Economic Research Working Paper 10869, October 2004, pp. 5–6, referring to Maurice Obstfeld and Alan M. Taylor, Global Capital Markets: Integration, Crisis, and Growth (Cambridge: Cambridge University Press, 2004).

13 See Maurice Obstfeld and Alan M. Taylor, "Globalization and Capital Markets," National Bureau of Economic Research Working Paper 8846, March 2002, p. 57; and Greenspan 2004, footnote 7.

14 For an interesting discussion of the financing of railroad construction in the United States see Bradford DeLong, "Slouching Towards Utopia?: The Economic History of the Twentieth Century," available at http://www.j-bradford-delong.net/TCEH/Slouch_Gold8.html, accessed June 9, 2005.

[15] Obstfeld and Taylor 2002.

[16] Michael D. Bordo and Hugh Rockoff, "The Gold Standard as a "Good Housekeeping Seal of Approval," Journal of Economic History 56, June 1996, pp. 389–428.

[17] Obstfeld and Taylor 2002, p. 21.

[18] Obstfeld and Taylor 2002, p. 10.

[19] See, for example, Obstfeld and Taylor 2002, p. 5.

[20] For more on the gold standard, see Daniel Pope and Thomas K. McCraw, "The U.K. and the Gold Standard in 1925," HBS No. 383-081, revised April 24, 1998.

[21] Michael D. Bordo, "The Classical Gold Standard — Some Lessons for Today," Federal Reserve Bank of St. Louis Review 63, no. 5, May 1981, pp. 2–17.

[22] See for example Milton Friedman and Anna J. Schwartz, A Monetary History of the United States, 1867–1960 (Princeton: Princeton University Press, 1971).

[23] See also Louis T. Wells Jr., "The Bretton Woods System of Exchange Rates," HBS No. 797-093, March 25, 1997.

[24] For more on Bretton Woods, see Michael D. Bordo, "The Bretton Woods International Monetary System: An Historical Overview," National Bureau of Economic Research Working Paper 4033, March 1992; Michael D. Bordo and Barry Eichengreen (eds.), *A Retrospective on the Bretton Woods System: Lessons for International Monetary Reform* (Chicago: University of Chicago Press, 1993); Barry Eichengreen, "From Benign Neglect to Malignant Preoccupation: U.S. Balance-Of-Payments Policy in the 1960s," National Bureau of Economic Research Working Paper 7630, March 2000; and Barry Eichengreen, *Globalizing Capital: A History of the International Monetary System* (Princeton, NJ: Princeton University Press, 1996).

[25] Obstfeld and Taylor 2002, p. 25.

[26] For more on this, see Bordo 1992, p. 37; and Michael Dooley and Peter Garber, "Is It 1958 or 1968? Three Notes on the Longevity of the Revived Bretton Woods System," Paper prepared for Brookings Panel on Economic Activity, March 31–April 1, 2005, which addresses the difference between the then-definition of Balance of Payment deficit and current account and financial account deficits focused on today.

[27] Bordo 1992, p. 37.

[28] Michael D. Bordo, "Historical Perspective on Global Imbalances," NBER Working Paper 11383, May 2005, p. 13; and Bordo 1992, p. 48.

[29] As described in Eichengreen 2000, the United States did not follow a policy of "benign neglect" and did try to counteract associated problems with other measures. As he describes on p. 2: "The Kennedy, Johnson and Nixon Administrations resorted to a series of indirect policy initiatives — differential tax treatment of domestic and foreign investments, reductions in the value of the goods American tourists could bring into the country, tied foreign aid, and finally an across-the-board import surcharge — in an effort to remedy the balance of payments problem and free up monetary and fiscal policies for the pursuit of domestic objectives."

[30] See Bordo 1992, Eichengreen 2000, and Michael G. Rukstad, "Nixon's New Economic Policy: 1971," HBS No. 386-063, revised March 8, 2000. For more on U.S. balance of payments issues in the late 1960s, see also John W. Rosenblum, "Nixon's Economic Strategy-1969," HBS No. 378-258, revised March 8, 2000.

[31] Bordo 1992, p. 55 and Eichengreen 2000, p. 34 discuss countries wanting to convert.

[32] Richard Nixon, Presidential Message, August 15, 1971, as quoted in HBS No. 386-063.

[33] Catherine L. Mann, "Perspectives on the U.S. Current Account Deficit and Sustainability," Journal of Economic Perspectives Vol. 16, No. 3, summer 2002, p. 138.

[34] Obstfeld and Rogoff 2004, p. 5.

[35] Exactly when the NIIP turned negative depended on whether direct investments were valued at current cost or market values. Under direct investments at current costs, NIIP turned negative in 1986. Under market values, NIIP turned negative in 1989.

[36] See Mann 2002 for further citations of definition of new economy. See also, Huw Pill, "The U.S. in 2001: Macroeconomic Policy and the New Economy," HBS No. 701-113, revised February 25, 2002.

[37] Mann 2002 and Greenspan 2004.

[38] (At the time of publication of this article, Bernanke was a Federal Reserve Board Governor.) Ben S. Bernanke, "The Global Saving Glut and the U.S. Current Account Deficit," Remarks at the Sandridge Lecture, Virginia Association of Economics, Richmond, Virginia, March 10, 2005, available at http://www.federalreserve.gov/boarddocs/speeches/2005/200503102/default.htm, accessed June 9, 2005.

[39] Philip R. Lane and Gian Maria Milesi-Ferretti, "A Global Perspective on External Positions," prepared for the NBER conference G7 Current Account Imbalances: Sustainability and Adjustment, May 3, 2005, p. 12.

[40] Calculated from Bureau of Economic Analysis, International Investment Position data.

[41] Mundell 1998.

[42] Roubini and Setser 2004, p. 21, and Roubini and Setser 2005.

[43] Calculations of values of reserves are from Exhibit 9. Due to changes in the valuation of individual Treasuries and other dollar-denominated securities used as reserves, such as government and corporate bonds and stocks, the difference in the value of reserves differs somewhat from the purchases of reserves.

[44] Lawrence H. Summers, "The U.S. Current Account Deficit and the Global Economy," Per Jacobsson Lecture, October 3, 2004, p. 6.

[45] Roubini and Setser 2005.

[46] Roger Cohen, "China and the Politics of a U.S. Awash in Debt," International Herald Tribune, May 21, 2005.

[47] Calculations based on Federal Reserve data.

[48] These figures are calculated from the data in Exhibit 11a.

[49] See valuation discussion in Tille 2003, which noted: "while changes in foreign trade patterns are likely to emerge only over time, valuation changes have the advantage of taking effect immediately."

[50] The Federal Reserve Bank defined seignorage as: "The profit which results from the difference between the cost of making coins and currency and the exchange value of coin and currency in the market." (See www.minneapolisfed.org/glossary.cfm.) In essence, the coins and notes outstanding were like an interest-free loan from currency holders to the issuing central bank.

[51] Ricardo Hausmann and Federico Sturzenegger, "Dark Matter Makes the U.S. Deficit Disappear," Financial Times December 8, 2005, p. A15. See also overview in Barry

Eichengreen "Global Imbalances: The New Economy, the Dark Matter, the Savvy Investor, and the Standard Analysis," University of California, Berkeley March 2006.

[52] Ricardo Hausmann and Federico Sturzenegger, "Can Dark Matter Prevent a Big Bang?" presentation in Cambridge, March 1, 2006.

[53] Congress of the United States, Congressional Budget Office, "The Budget and Economic Outlook: An Update; Total Outlays and Revenues as a percentage of gross domestic product," August 2006, available at http://www.cbo.gov/ftpdocs/74xx/ doc7492/08-17-BudgetUpdate.pdf, accessed September 14, 2006.

[54] Ricardo J. Caballero, Emmanuel Farhi, and Pierre-Olivier Gourinchas, "An Equilibrium Model of 'Global Imbalances' and Low Interest Rates," February 8, 2006.

[55] Chairman of the Council of Economic Advisors, 2005 Economic Report of the President, p. 38, available at http://www.gpoaccess.gov/eop, accessed June 9, 2005.

[56] The long-run elasticity of U.S. imports with respect to U.S. GDP was 1.8, while the long-run elasticity of U.S. exports with respect to foreign GDP was 0.8, as calculated by Peter Hooper, Karen Johnson, and Jaime Marquez, in "Trade Elasticities for G-7 Countries," Federal Reserve Board of Governors, International Finance Discussion Papers 609, 1998.

[57] Mann 2002, p. 138. Phenomenon first noted, as cited in Greenspan 2004, footnote 2, in H. S. Houthakker, and S. P. Magee, "Income and Price Elasticities in World Trade," *Review of Economics and Statistics* 51, May 1969, pp. 111–125.

[58] See Mann 2002 for description of "home bias" and Remarks by Chairman Alan Greenspan at the European Banking Congress 2004, Frankfurt, Germany November 19, 2004 for discussion of decrease.

[59] Remarks by Vice Chairman Roger W. Ferguson, Jr. to the Economics Club of the University of North Carolina at Chapel Hill, Chapel Hill, North Carolina, April 20, 2005, "U.S. Current Account Deficit: Causes and Consequences," available at http://www.federal reserve.gov/boarddocs/Speeches/2005/20050420/default.htm, accessed October 3, 1996.

[60] Remarks by Chairman Alan Greenspan at the 21st Annual Monetary Conference, Cosponsored by the Cato Institute and The Economist, Washington, D.C., November 20, 2003. See also Greenspan 2004, in which Greenspan remarked: "Should globalization be allowed to proceed and thereby create an ever more flexible international financial system, history suggests that current imbalances will be defused with little disruption."

[61] See "Wise Men at Ease; the American Economy," The Economist, April 30, 2005.

[62] Comment made at Foreign Correspondents' Club of Japan March 10, 2005, quoted in various sources, including James Simms, "U.S. Treasury Quarles: Need More Global FX Flexibility," Dow Jones Newswires, March 11, 2005.

[63] Michael P. Dooley, David Folkerts-Landau, and Peter Garber, "An Essay on the Revived Bretton Woods System," National Bureau of Economic Research Working Paper 9971, September 2003, p. 5.

[64] Dooley and Garber 2005, see China: To Float or Not to Float (A), HBSP No. 706-021 for more on this.

65 Lawrence H. Summers, "The U.S. Current Account Deficit and the Global Economy," Per Jacobsson Lecture, October 3, 2004, p. 8.

66 See summary of Summers' argument in Frederick Kempe, "Thinking Global: U.S., China Stage an Economic Balancing Act; Growing Tensions Will Test Logic That Neither Wants To Declare a Trade War," The Wall Street Journal, March 28, 2006.

67 Summers 2004 for discussion of "balance of financial terror" and for reference to "vendor finance" and Dooley et al., 2003 and 2004 for discussion of "revived Bretton Woods."

68 See, for example, Lane and Milesi-Ferretti 2005, pp. 16–17.

69 Jag Dhaliwall and Daniel Moss, "S. Korean Regulator Says Asia Can't Keep Funding U.S. Spending," *Bloomberg*, March 15, 2005.

70 Quoted in China Daily, March 15, 2009.

71 Roubini and Setser 2005, pp. 14–15.

72 Summers 2004, p. 8. See also Elizabeth Becker, "Trade Deficit Narrows to a 6-Month Low," The New York Times, May 12, 2005.

73 Mervyn King, "The International Monetary System," Speech by Mervyn King, Governor of the Bank of England, at the "Advancing Enterprise 2005" conference, London, February 4, 2005, available at http://www.bis.org/review/r050217b.pdf, accessed June 9, 2005. (The open letter was from U.S. senators Schumer, Bunning, Durbin, Graham, Dodd and Bayh to Vice President Richard Cheney, January 22, 2004.)

74 "China Hits Back in War of Words: Officials Dismiss U.S. Criticism of Yuan Policy; Call Steps to Curb Textile Exports Unfair," May 18, 2005, http://money.cnn.com/2005/05/18/news/international/china.reut/, accessed June 9, 2005.

75 Truman 2004 (referred to it as "back-of-envelope" calculation).

76 Michael Mussa, "Exchange Rate Adjustments Needed to Reduce Global Payments Imbalance," in Bergsten, C.F. and J. Williamson (Editors): Dollar Adjustment: How Far? Against What? (Institute for International Economics: Washington D.C., November 2004.

77 Roubini and Setser 2004, pp. 25–26, footnote 38.

78 Willem Buiter, "Dark Matter or Cold Fusion?" Global Economics Paper No. 136, Goldman Sachs Global Economic Website, January 16, 2006, available at http://www.nber.org/~wbuiter/dark.pdf, September 26, 2006.

79 Bureau of Econoimc Analysis Table 1.1, "U.S. Net International Investment Position at the End of the Period," release date June 30, 2014, and Table 1.1.5. "Gross Domestic Product," release date July 30, 2014. Both accessed August 2014.

80 Summers 2004.

81 Obstfeld and Rogoff 2004.

82 See, for example, Pierre-Olivier Gourinchas and Hélène Rey "International Financial Adjustment," National Bureau of Economic Research Working Paper 11155, February 2005. They gave a "back-of-envelope" calculation that a 10% depreciation of the dollar represented a transfer of 5% of U.S. GDP from the rest of the world to the United States — compared with a trade deficit on goods and services of 4.4% of GDP in 2003 (p. 2). The paper modeled the problem in detail.

83 Lane and Milesi-Ferretti 2004.

[84] Summers 2004, p. 12. At the time, Summers was President of Harvard University.

[85] Term "hard landing" used, for example, in "Wise Men at Ease; The American Economy," The Economist, April 30, 2005.

[86] Roubini and Setser 2005.

[87] Roubini and Setser 2005, p. 5.

[88] Olivier Blanchard, Francesco Giavazzi, and Filipa Sa, "The U.S. Current Account and the Dollar," National Bureaus for Economic Research Working Paper 11137, January 26, 2005.

[89] Stephen Roach, "In Search of Big Spenders; American consumers spend nearly $ 9 trillion a year, or 20% more than Europeans. But the binge is now coming to an end," Newsweek International, September 11, 2006.

[90] Roubini and Setser 2005, p. 2.

[91] This strategy was first outlined in Communiqué of the International Monetary and Financial Committee (IMFC) of the Board of Governors of the International Monetary Fund October 2, 2004, available at http://www.imf.org/external/np/cm/2004/100204.htm, accessed June 9, 2005. See also IMF World Economic Outlook 2005, pp. 114–115 and 26–27. The report proceeded by chiding the United States for being insufficiently ambitious with the fiscal goal, for failing to include expenses associated with Iraq and Afghanistan, and because of the substantial risk that the objective will not be met.

[92] See, for example, Testimony of Chairman Alan Greenspan before the Committee on the Budget, U.S. House of Representatives, "Economic Outlook and Current Fiscal Issues," March 2, 2005.

[93] "Fiscal Fantasyland; America's budget," The Economist, April 9, 2005.

[94] Congressional Budget Offic "Updated Budget Projections: Fiscal Years 2013 to 2023," May 2003, Table 1.

[95] The agreement to use the legal requirement — or supposed legal requirment, since many lawyers, including former President Bill Clinton, argued that it was unconstitutional and in any event unenforcable as no one had legal "standing" to enforce it — was bipartisan, and used the terms in quotes: Jackie Calmes, "A 'Unique Opportunity,' Squandered," New York Times, July 26, 2011.

[96] On the U.S. Chamber of Commerce pressing Republicans whose campaigns it had heavily financed to raise the debt limit: Binyamin Appelbaum, "After Aiding Republicans, Business Groups Press them on Debt Ceiling," New York Times, July 27, 2011.

[97] Catherine Rampell, "In Need of Deficit Plan, Congress Opts for Several," New York Times, August 5, 2011, on the projected $900 billion reduction and the $1.3 trillion plan.

[98] Nelson D. Schwartz, "Nervous Investors Chase Low-Risk Assets," New York Times, August 4, 2011.

[99] Binyamin Appelbaum and Eric Dash, "S & P. Downgrades Debt Rating of U.S. for the First Time," New York Times, August 5, 2011.

[100] David Barboza "China Tells U.S. It Must 'Cure Its Addiction to Debt.'" New York Times, August 6, 2011.

[101] Calculated from Exibit 9a. These data are for all Chinese holdings of U.S. Treasuries, not just official reserves. No data for official reserves held in Treasuries are available.

[102] Chen Daofu, director of research at the State Councils Policy Research Center, quoted in Li Xiang and Li Xing, "China's Foreign Exchange Dilemma," China Daily, August 2, 2011.

[103] Global Financial data, U.S. 10-year Bond Constant Maturity Yield (series IGUSA10D), accessed August 15, 2011 and August 21, 2014.

Drivers of Competitiveness

By: **Diego Comin** *(Dartmouth College, USA)*

In this day and age, technology has become ever more prominent and omnipresent in our lives. As technological developments emerge and become more ubiquitous, it becomes vital to understand and analyse the impact of technology on society.

Drivers of Competitiveness focuses on technology and seeks to analyze its causes and consequences on productivity and competitiveness and to examine the dynamic relationships between the different factors in various contexts. Building on state of the art research, the book illustrates the global, institutional and technological factors that shape the performance of business and countries.

Unlike most existing books in the field, *Drivers of Competitiveness* is a self-contained case book and is ideal for classroom use. The cases in the book are brand new and are written in the context of the global financial crisis, providing a new perspective that sheds light on its effect on competitiveness and on the diversity of responses by companies and countries. The cases and the analytical framework that emerges from the book constitute an essential kit for current and future managers, policy-makers and observers of global dynamics.

Readership

Students in advanced undergraduate, graduate, and executive courses on international business; current and future managers, policy-makers and observers of global dynamics

Key Features

- Presents a new and original conceptual framework to explore the drivers of competitiveness and productivity
- Incorporates state of the art research on the drivers and consequences of technology
- Based on new case studies, all written in the context of the recent global recession, which provides a new perspective on the crisis and new managerial insights

Main Subject Classification:

(1) Business & Management: Innovation/Technology/Knowledge/Information Management
(2) Business & Management: General management
(3) Business & Management & Economics: International Trade
(4) Economics: Development economics
(5) Economics: Political Economy

Keywords: Productivity, competitiveness, business, technology

Diego Comin is a Professor of Economics at Dartmouth since 2014. He received his B.A. in Economics in 1995 from the University Pompeu Fabra, Barcelona, Spain and his PhD in Economics from Harvard University in 2000. Between 2000 and 2007, Comin was the Assistant Professor of Economics at New York University. Between 2007 and 2014, Comin served as the Associate Professor of Business Administration at the Harvard Business School (HBS) where he taught both MBA and executive programs. He has also designed and led immersion programs in Peru and Malaysia for which he received the Apgar Prize for Innovation in Teaching from the HBS Dean.

Comin is Research Fellow at the Center for Economic Policy Research and Faculty Research Fellow in the National Bureau of Economic Research's Economic Fluctuations and Growth Program. Comin is a fellow for the Institute of New Economic Thinking (INET) and his work has been supported by the Gates foundation, the National Science Foundation, the C.V. Star Foundation, and the Zentrum für Europäische Wirtschaftsforschung (ZEW). He is advising the Prime Minister of Malaysia on its development strategies and has consulted for the World Bank, IMF, Federal Reserve Bank of New York, Citibank, Danish Science Ministry, and the Economic and Social Research Institute (ESRI) of the government of Japan.

Comin works on macroeconomics broadly understood. Part of his research consists of studying the process of technological change and technology diffusion both across countries and over time. A second avenue of his work studies the sources and propagation mechanisms of fluctuations at high and medium term frequencies. A third line of research pursued by Comin has explored the evolution of firm dynamics and their implications for the evolution of the US economy. His work has been published in academic journals, including the American Economic Review, the American Economic Journal, the Journal of Monetary Economics, the Review of Economics and Statistics and the Journal of Economic Growth.

Comin has written the book *Malaysia Beyond 2020* where he presents a new approach to development policy that aims to create a knowledge-friendly eco-system where companies can move up in the value chain.

Epilogue

The global financial crisis did not make competitiveness relevant. It has always been. However, it made competitiveness an absolute priority for companies. In particular, it made clear that competitiveness does not only involve trying to capture your competitor's market but also learning to cope better with the challenges and opportunities brought by the global economy, business cycles, credit conditions and other aggregate determinants of a company's bottom line.

Seven years after the crisis, companies and countries must know that they need to think about the medium term, that they need to find ways to improve their productivity and that creating value is not an option but just the only way to stay ahead of the competition.

Indeed, what troubles me most of the post-recession recovery is not so much the fact that it is slow and is accompanied with low productivity growth — these are predictions of my models![a] What I find really worrisome is the fact that many leaders are adopting the same complacent attitude that brought the global economy to the brick of collapse. Often politicians and business leaders do not seem to have learnt that growth without productivity improvements is not sustainable. That booms in aggregate demand are often followed by bursts, and that a focus on developing the capabilities to improve the technological sophistication and quality of the products and services offered are the best possible protection against head winds. If that is not absolutely clear by now, this recession has taught us nothing.

---

[a] See Comin, and Gertler (2006) Medium Term Business Cycles *American Economic Review* Vol. 96, No. 3, Comin, Loayza, Pasha and Serven (2014) Medium Term Business Cycles in Developing Countries *American Economic Journal: Macroeconomics* Vol. 6, No. 4, and Comin and Gertler (2015) Endogenous R&D and Technology Adoption as Sources of Business Cycle Persistence *mimeo*.

My hope and conviction is that those that have read this book and discussed the cases contained in it have developed a deep understanding not only on the relevance of competitiveness but also on its drivers, and are now in the process of applying the principles contained in the book towards an action plan for their companies and countries.

Cambridge, May 2015

Index

Printed in the United States
By Bookmasters